REFERENCE

Women
in the
Middle Ages

Women in the Middle Ages

AN ENCYCLOPEDIA
Volume II: K–Z

Edited by

KATHARINA M. WILSON
and
NADIA MARGOLIS

GREENWOOD PRESS
Westport, Connecticut • London

Library of Congress Cataloging-in-Publication Data

Women in the Middle Ages : an encyclopedia / edited by Katharina M. Wilson and
Nadia Margolis.
    p. cm.
  Includes bibliographical references and index.
    ISBN 0-313-33016-6 (set : alk. paper)—ISBN 0-313-33017-4 (vol. 1 : alk. paper)—
  ISBN 0-313-33018-2 (vol. 2 : alk. paper)
    1. Women—History—Middle Ages, 500–1500—Encyclopedias.   I. Wilson, Katharina M.
  II. Margolis, Nadia, 1949–
HQ1143.W643   2004
305.4′09′0203—dc22   2004053042

British Library Cataloguing in Publication Data is available.

Library of Congress Catalog Card Number: 2004053042
ISBN: 0-313-33016-6 (set)
     0-313-33017-4 (vol. I)
     0-313-33018-2 (vol. II)

First published in 2004

Greenwood Press, 88 Post Road West, Westport, CT 06881
An imprint of Greenwood Publishing Group, Inc.
www.greenwood.com

Printed in the United States of America

The paper used in this book complies with the
Permanent Paper Standard issued by the National
Information Standards Organization (Z39.48-1984).

10 9 8 7 6 5 4 3 2 1

This volume is for
Chris

and in memory of
Peter

Contents

Alphabetical List of Entries

Guide to Related Topics

ABBESSES AND PRIORESSES
Agnes of Assisi, St.
Aldegund, St.
Caesaria, St.
Constance of Castile
Egburg
Gertrude of Nivelles, St.
Gualdrada de' Ravignani
Hazzecha of Krauftal
Heloise
Herrad of Hohenberg/Landsberg
Hild (Hilda), St.
Hildegard of Bingen, St.
Isabel de Villena
Petronilla of Chemillé
Radegund, St.
Theuthild
Umiltà of Faenza, St.

ARTISTS, CRAFTSWOMEN, AND SCRIBES
Artists, Medieval Women
Boccaccio, Women in, *Des Cleres et Nobles Femmes*
Dress, Courtly Women's
Dress, Religious Women's (Western, Christian)
Embroidery
Marcia in the Middle Ages
Scribes and Scriptoria

COMMUNITIES, GROUPS, AND CIRCLES (RELIGIOUS AND LAY)
Beguines
Berthgyth
Bizzoche
Boniface, St., Mission and Circle of
Bugga

Convents
Double Monasteries
Egburg
Eustochium, St.
Ivetta of Huy
Leoba
Mulieres sanctae
Nunneries, Merovingian
Pinzochere
Prous Boneta, Na
Unterlinden, Sisters of

CULTURES (ETHNIC, NATIONAL, AND RELIGIOUS)
Aztec Warrior Women
China, Women in
Desert Mothers
Fatimid Egypt, Women in
Jewish Women in the Middle Ages
Muscovy, Women in
Norse Women
Syrian-Christian Women

DEVIANTS AND MARGINALS
Lesbians in the Middle Ages
Prostitution
Slaves, Female
Transvestism
Witches

DOCTORS, HEALERS, AND CAREGIVERS
Concubines
Elisabeth of Hungary/Thuringia, St.
Fedele, Cassandra
Medea in the Middle Ages
Medicine and Medieval Women

WRITERS (LITERARY), POETS, TRANSLATORS, AND PATRONS

Adela of Blois
Alaisina Yselda
Alamanda
Almuc de Castelnou
Azalais d'Altier
Azalais de Porcairagues
Bietris de Roman
Boccaccio, Women in, *De Claris Mulieribus*
Boccaccio, Women in, *Des Cleres et Nobles Femmes*
Boccaccio, Women in, Works Other than *De Claris Mulieribus*
Carenza, Na
Castelloza, Na
Catalan Women Poets, Anonymous
Christine de Pizan
Clara d'Anduza
Comnena, Anna
Compiuta Donzella
Comtessa de Dia
Cornaro, Caterina
Eleanor of Aquitaine
Elisabeth of Nassau-Saarbrücken
Epistolary Authors, Women as
Ermengard of Narbonne
Eucheria
Eudocia
Filipa de Lencastre
Garsenda of Forcalquier
Gaudairenca
Gormonda de Montpellier
Guilielma des Rosers
H., Domna
Heloise
Hildegard of Bingen, St.
Hrotsvitha of Gandersheim
Iseut de Capio
Izumi Shikibu
Jóreiðr Hermundardóttir í Miðjumdal
Jórunn skáldmær
Katherine of Sutton
Leonor López de Córdoba
Li Qingzhao
Lombarda
Margareta von Schwangau
Maria de Ventadorn
Marie de Champagne
Marie de Compiègne
Marie de France
Mirabai
Murasaki Shikibu
Pinar, Florencia
Proba, Faltonia Betitia
Reyna de Mallorques, La
Rhetoric, Women and
Sei Shonagon
Skáldkonur (Old Norse-Icelandic Women Poets)
Steinunn Refsdóttir
Theodosia
Theosebeia
Tibors
Wallādah
Xue Tao
Ysabella, Domna

K

KATHARINA VON GEBWEILER/GEBERSCHWEIER (c.1260–c.1330). Katharina von Gebweiler, Guebweiler, or Geberschweier, a mystic and chronicler, spent her career at the Dominican convent at Unterlinden, in the city of Colmar, in Alsace, a province now in France. She entered the convent as a child in around 1260. While there she wrote her *Vitae Sororum (Lives of the Sisters)*, an account of the virtues, visions, and ecstasies of forty-four nuns who comprised the first two generations at Unterlinden, founded in 1232. Katharina includes herself in the catalogue of nuns and is listed as the ninety-second; an obituary lists her death as January 22 without including the year, but it is believed that she died at an old age because of details she provides in the prologue to her book.

The *Vitae Sororum*, which historians believe to have been written c.1310–1320, describes the mystical life at the convent of Unterlinden. In her work, Katharina distinguishes between that which she herself knew and saw firsthand as an eyewitness and that which she "heard from credible sisters, who have sworn to the truth, that which they heard from the sisters during their lifetime." Katharina testifies that the fervor, ardor, and strength of the convent had remained in God's grace up to and through her time.

The *Vitae Sororum* was written in Latin, but it soon became the model for many similar compositions written in the vernacular in southern Germany.

See also Sister-Books (*Schwesternbücher*); Unterlinden, Sisters of

BIBLIOGRAPHY

Primary Sources
Katharina von Gebweiler. [Latin Convent Chronicle of Unterlinden, excerpt] "Adelheid von Rhinefelden." In *Mystische Texte aus dem Mittelalter*, edited by Walter Muschg, ch. 2. Klosterberg and Basel, Switzerland: Schwabe, 1943. [Medieval German text only, Modern German notes].

Secondary Sources
"Katharina von Gebweiler." In *Deutsches Literaturlexikon*, edited by Wilhelm Kosch, vol. 8. Berne and Munich: Francke, 1984.
"Katharina von Gebweiler." In *Die Deutsche Literatur des Mittelalters: Verfasserlexikon*. Edited by Wolfgang Stammler. Berlin and Leipzig: de Gruyter, 1936.

EDITH BRIGITTE ARCHIBALD

KATHERINE GROUP. *See* **Hagiography (Female Saints)**

KATHERINE OF SUTTON (fl. 1363–1376). Katherine of Sutton, a Benedictine abbess of Barking Abbey and author of Latin liturgical dramatizations, has been dubbed the first English woman playwright, notably of Easter-related scenes, as in the *Depositio crucis* (Deposition from the Cross), the *Elevatio hostiae* (Elevation of the Host) ceremonies, and a *Visitatio Sepulchri* (Visit to the Sepulchre) pageant. Katherine's works constitute remarkable evidence of the emotional power of sacramental-symbolic ritual in medieval drama as a forerunner of modern drama.

The record of the rites and customary devotional practices of the nuns at Barking enable us to appreciate how Katherine's work was inspired rather than hindered by life at this convent. The *ordinale*, a manual for conducting the year's services at Barking, contains much that is typical of Benedictine religious houses of either sex in the later fourteenth century. Yet in a way at least somewhat analogous to Hrotsvitha's situation at Gandersheim four centuries earlier, Katherine created a dramatic form different from anything else at the time. The renditions of the *Depositio crucis* the *Elevatio hostiae*, and the *Visitatio sepulchri* attributed to her employ many of the familiar antiphons—sentences from Scripture usually recited before and after the Psalms and Canticles—and typical rubrics—ceremonial "stage directions" printed in service manuals—associated with these liturgical ceremonies. They also contain clear evidence of Katherine's intention to heighten the realism, immediacy, and dramatic power of these ceremonies. The *Depositio* involves the actual removal of the body of Christ, the *corpus*, from the cross and washing of the wounds represented on the corpus by two priests "*in specie Josephi et Nichodemi*" ("resembling Joseph and Nicodemus"). She assigned traditional antiphons for this ceremony to different voices with some care: a feature not necessarily unique in itself, except that her particular choices suggest a grasp of the ceremony's literary and dramatic potential quite unusual for its time, at least in the Latin liturgical forms, particularly in the above-mentioned corpus and especially the rubric *in specie*.

The *Elevatio* is even more impressive. It contains the typical *Tollite portas* (Lift up the Gates [for the Harrowing of Hell]) chant, but also a rather exceptional degree of what moderns would term audience involvement: all the nuns of the abbey are within the chapel, "*figurantes animas sanctorum Patrum ante adventum Christi*" ("representing the souls of the holy patriarchs before the coming of Christ"). Again, the word *figurantes* can be seen as an ordinary indication of the medieval sacramental perspective—which it no doubt is—but in this context it also suggests a vivid dramatic sensibility and sensitivity, certainly not as striking or extended, but also not totally different from the sensibility and sensitivity of Hrotsvitha. Katherine's *Visitatio sepulchri*, like many of its contemporaries, involves a clear sense of dialogue in the assignment of the antiphons and responses and a rather sophisticated overall staging. The extended dialogue between Mary Magdalene and the angels, then between her and the disciples, reflects a manifest attempt at dramatic elaboration. We should also not overlook another important innovation, perhaps paralleled in other rites associated with religious houses for women but not so clearly documented elsewhere: that the roles of Mary and Mary Magdalene were to be played by women, not men, the latter being the custom of the time. For that time and place, an aspect we have since long taken for granted arises as yet another milestone in dramatic verisimilitude.

In writing and (it is tempting to imagine) directing her dramatic liturgical ceremonies, Abbess Katherine was motivated by her desire to increase the involvement and to revitalize the responses of the faithful, who had evidently sunk into torpor and indifference, as the Ordinale tells us. In this desire, she evidences a sincere piety typical of her culture and perhaps of true devotion in any age. Katherine appears quite unique in the methods she devised and elaborated to fulfill that desire, because of which we concur with Nancy Cotton in calling her the first English woman playwright.

See also Bride of Christ/*Brautmystik*; Convents; Hildegard of Bingen, St.; Hrotsvitha of Gandersheim; Music, Women Composers and Musicians

BIBLIOGRAPHY

Primary Sources
Tolhurst, J. B. L. *The Ordinale and the Customary of the Benedictine Nuns of Barking Abbey.* 2 vols. London: Henry Bradshaw Society, 1927–1928.

Secondary Sources
Cotton, Nancy. "Katherine of Sutton: The First English Woman Playwright." *Educational Theater Journal* 30 (1978): 475–81.
———. *Women Playwrights in England, c. 1363–1750.* Lewisburg, Pa.: Bucknell University Press/ London and Toronto: Associated University Presses, 1980.
Young, Karl. *The Drama of the Medieval Church.* 2 vols. Oxford: Clarendon Press, 1933.

WILLIAM PROVOST

KEMPE, MARGERY (c.1373–c.1440). Author of the autobiographical *Book of Margery Kempe*, Kempe combined the life and work of a married woman with the vocation of a religious seeker and mystic. Solidly rooted in the upper burgher class of King's Lynn in East Anglia, she was the daughter of John Burnham, five times mayor and six times member of parliament; she married John Kempe (from another entrenched burgher family) and bore fourteen children. As evidence of the successful work of God in her conversion, Kempe described her fierce struggles against pride, avarice, and lust. She frankly reported her sins and failures, interpreting business losses and sexual shame as divine admonition against overworldliness.

During a severe mental illness following the birth of her first child, Kempe was visited by Jesus in the form of a beautiful and comforting young man; from that time on she pursued an extraordinary vocation involving tears, pilgrimage, and intimate conversation with Jesus, Mary, and God the Father. She struggled for years to remove herself from John Kempe's bed, from repeated childbearing, and from household responsibilities. At about forty years of age, she concluded a bargain with her husband, won the consent of the bishop, and set off on pilgrimage. Eventually she traveled as a pilgrim through much of England as well as Prussia, Spain, Italy, and the Holy Land, encountering spiritual and physical challenges and adventures. Margery Kempe's unconventional and conspicuous habits, including criticizing others' behavior and crying loudly in and out of church, annoyed neighbors, fellow pilgrims, and certain clerks. She was suspected of troublemaking and "hypocrisy"; more dangerously, she was several times accused of Lollardy (a movement reacting against the corrupt wealth of the Church in England that preached poverty) by civil and ecclesiastical authorities, although she managed to escape conviction. Seeking always to reassure herself that her spiritual encounters were not "demonic illusions" and that her spiritual practices accorded with the will of God and (if possible) of

Holy Church as well, she paid frequent visits to local clergy and sought out counselors of distinguished reputation, including Julian of Norwich.

Although Margery Kempe could not read or write, she heard reading in church and from her various confessors and advisors. She was well acquainted with the language of Scripture, the lives of the saints, and the writings of such notable contemporary women as St. Birgitta of Sweden and Marie d'Oignies, a noted *mulier sancta* (holy woman), whose stories interested and influenced her. In later life, when Kempe set out to recount God's grace in her own life, she dictated her book to two scribes. The first could not write English well and died before the task was finished, but the second, a priest, rewrote the existing material and finished the account. Scholars differ sharply about the role of the second scribe and the extent of his influence in shaping the material, but no one denies that this is essentially Margery's *Book*.

King's Lynn was a busy port, with a merchant class tied by family and business connections to the religious culture of Continental Europe. Lynn was a rich nursery for someone of Margery Kempe's interests and affections; most of the currents of contemporary spirituality found their way across the North Sea. Like so many of her contemporaries, Kempe loved preaching and heard as many sermons as possible. She certainly was exposed to Franciscan piety, with its emphasis on compassion and on imitation of the suffering Christ. In meditation she placed herself at Mary's side in the stable and at the Cross, participating in the Gospel stories as devout Christians were directed to do by spiritual authorities from Anselm through Bernard to the Franciscans and beyond. In England in 1410, the Carthusian Nicholas Love produced *The Myrrour of the Blessed Lyf of Jesu Christ*, a translation of parts of the thirteenth-century Pseudo-Bonaventure's *Meditations on the Life of Christ*; Love's *Myrrour* prescribed a homely, intimate, and affective piety with strong resemblances to Margery's devotional life. Her aspirations and some of her practices were unusual for a laywoman, especially for an English woman (more especially for a married woman), but they were not unique. Her desire for austerity of life, her passionate love of Jesus, and familiarity with the saints (especially Mary Magdalene) fell squarely within a well-established tradition of affective devotion, while her piety and practices resembled those of a significant cohort of Continental holy women.

Kempe's unusual status and vocation—neither nun nor housewife—brought her into contact with people of low and high status, including the archbishops of York and Canterbury. The encounters with high churchmen reported in the *Book* were characterized by a remarkably free and frank manner on her part, while the churchmen responded, in general, by respectful attention to the woman, her vocation, and her claims to direct communication with the divine. Margery Kempe roused strong feeling in both admirers and detractors who knew her in life, as later in those who know her through her *Book*. She has remained a controversial as well as fascinating figure.

The unique manuscript of *The Book of Margery Kempe*, discovered in 1934, was known long before that in the form of a "treatise" published in 1501 by the famous printer Wynkyn de Worde, consisting of extracts that may have been selected by Robert Springold, Kempe's confessor and parish priest (Holbrook 1987). This much-abridged version toned down Margery's religious enthusiasm and omitted much of her vivid representation of daily struggles, the kind of material that tends to arouse disapproval and anxiety in those with different expectations of mystics and their writings. The discovery of the complete manuscript in 1934 was hailed with joy, followed quickly by dismay provoked by its concrete detail and ecstatic tone. The owner of the manuscript, William Butler-Bowdon, published a modern English translation of the *Book*, and the American scholar Hope Emily Allen, with Sanford Meech, produced a critical edition for the Early English Text Society in 1940. Allen's notes connected Margery with several Continental women and their writings and revelations, an undertaking that continues; significant associations have been established between *The Book of Margery Kempe* and the works of Birgitta of Sweden, Marie d'Oignies, Elisabeth of Hungary, and Dorothea of Montau, among others.

Although the literary importance of this first autobiography in the English language was recognized immediately, its author/protagonist did not fit conventional and respected forms of mystical experience and discourse. Margery Kempe incurred the disapproval of scholars such as the great historian of English mystical and monastic traditions, David Knowles, who disliked the personal tone and religious "excess" of the *Book*, its homely details, and "self-centered" piety. Considering its unique position and wealth of resources for social and religious history, the *Book* attracted surprisingly little serious and extensive scholarly work for several decades.

Margery Kempe was rediscovered in the 1980s under the influence of feminism and of new trends in historical and religious studies—a new interest in the history of women and in popular (as opposed to elite and learned) religious belief and behavior. In recent decades, feminist literary critics as well as historians have entered the discussion, looking at questions of female authority and authorship, at the subversion of patriarchy through narrative strategies, and at expressions of spiritual experience in and through the body. Not only has the body itself acquired a history, but issues of embodiment, of "writing the body," pervade current discussion of women's religious as well as secular experience and expression. Analogous issues concerning the gendered meanings of the Incarnation have entered Christian historical theology. Margery Kempe and her *Book* not only survive, but thrive, on deconstruction. Once an embarrassment on the margins of Christian mysticism, *The Book of Margery Kempe* has become a central text at the intersections of religious and gender studies, feminist literary criticism, and social history.

See also Birgitta of Sweden, St.; Dorothea of Montau, St.; Elisabeth of Hungary/ Thuringia, St.; Julian of Norwich; *Mulieres Sanctae*

BIBLIOGRAPHY

Primary Sources

Kempe, Margery. *The Book of Margery Kempe*. Edited by Sanford B. Meech and Hope Emily Allen. Early English Text Society, o.s. 212. London: Humphrey Milford, 1940.

———. *The Book of Margery Kempe*. Edited by Barry A. Windeatt. Harmondsworth, U.K. and New York: Viking Penguin, 1985. New ed. Longman Annotated Texts. New York: Longman, 2000.

———. *The Book of Margery Kempe: A New Translation, Contexts, Criticism*. Translated and edited by Lynn Staley. Norton Critical Editions. New York: Norton, 2001.

Secondary Sources

Aers, David. "Rewriting the Middle Ages: Some Suggestions." *Journal of Medieval and Renaissance Studies* 18 (1988): 221–40.

Atkinson, Clarissa W. *Mystic and Pilgrim: The Book and the World of Margery Kempe*. Ithaca, N.Y.: Cornell University Press, 1983.

Bhattacharji, Santha. *God is an Earthquake: The Spirituality of Margery Kempe*. London: Darton, Longman & Todd, 1997.

Beckwith, Sarah. "A Very Material Mysticism: The Medieval Mysticism of Margery Kempe." In *Medieval Literature: Criticism, Ideology and History*, edited by David Aers, 195–215. New York: St. Martin's, 1986.

Dickman, Susan. "Margery Kempe and the Continental Tradition of the Pious Woman." In *The Medieval Mystical Tradition in England: Papers Read at Dartington Hall, July, 1984*, edited Marion Glasscoe, 150–68. Cambridge: D. S. Brewer, 1984.

Dinshaw, Carolyn. "Margery Kempe." In *The Cambridge Companion to Medieval Women's Writing*, edited by Carolyn Dinshaw and David Wallace, 222–39. Cambridge: Cambridge University Press, 2003.

Ellis, Deborah S. "Margery Kempe and King's Lynn." In *Margery Kempe: A Book of Essays*, edited by Sandra J. McEntire, 139–63. New York: Garland, 1992.

Goodman, Anthony. "The Piety of John Brunham's Daughter, of Lynn." In *Medieval Women*, edited by Derek Baker, 347–58. Studies in Church History, Subsidia, 1. Oxford: Basil Blackwell, 1978.

Hirsh, John C. "Author and Scribe in *The Book of Margery Kempe*." *Medium Ævum* 44 (1975): 145–50.

Holbrook, Sue Ellen. "Margery Kempe and Wynkyn de Worde." In *The Medieval Mystical Tradition in England*: 27–46. *See above under* Dickman.

Kieckhefer, Richard. *Unquiet Souls: Fourteenth-Century Saints and Their Religious Milieu*. Chicago: University of Chicago Press, 1984.

Lochrie, Karma. *Margery Kempe and Translations of the Flesh*. Philadelphia: University of Pennsylvania Press, 1991.

Partner, Nancy. "Reading the Book of Margery Kempe." *Exemplaria* 3 (1991): 29–66.

Staley, Lynn. *Margery Kempe's Dissenting Fictions*. University Park: Pennsylvania State University Press, 1994.

Szell, Timea K. "From Woe to Weal and Weal to Woe: Notes on the Structure of *The Book of Margery Kempe*." In *Margery Kempe: A Book of Essays*, 73–91. *See above under* Ellis.

Voaden, Rosalynn. *God's Words, Women's Voices: The Discernment of Spirits in the Writing of Late-Medieval Women*. Woodbridge. Suffolk, U.K. & Rochester, N.Y.: University of York Medieval Press/Boydell Press, 1999.

Weissman, Hope P. "Margery Kempe in Jerusalem: *Hysteria compassio* in the Late Middle Ages." *Acts of Interpretation: The Text in Its Contexts 700–1600. Essays on Medieval and Renaissance Literature in Honor of E. Talbot Donaldson*, edited by Mary J. Carruthers and Elizabeth D. Kirk, 201–17. Norman, Okla.: Pilgrim Books, 1982.

CLARISSA W. ATKINSON

KHARJA. From the Arabic for "exit," the *kharja* (plural *kharajāt*) is the final couplet in poems of the Arabic and Hebrew genre known as the *muwashshah* (spelling varies), prevalent in al-Andalus (Muslim Spain). Many *kharajāt* (English-speaking scholars also refer to *kharjas*), especially those identified as Romance or Mozarabic, manifest feminine or female features, in contrast to those mainly in literary Arabic following the more masculine tone of classical Arabic poetry. This article concentrates on the nonclassical Arabic *kharajāt*, which includes those in vernacular Andalusi Arabic, and especially those in Romance and Mozarabic (a hybrid dialect consisting of Romance and Arabic language elements).

The *muwashshahs* (*muwashshahāt*), whether panegyrics—songs of praise—dedicated to male notables or love poems addressed to beloved boys or girls, were composed by male poets for male audiences, but usually sung by women. The final couplet, the *kharja*, is always in the quotational mode, meaning that it is pronounced by a speaker other than the protagonist of the rest of the *muwashshah*. In most cases, though not in all, the *kharja* quotes the words of a young woman or girl. This practice was already noted by the Egyptian authority on the genre, Ibn Sanā' al-Mulk (c.1150–c.1211) in his treatise and anthology. The transition from a male to a female voice takes place in the penultimate lines of the *muwashshah* and is affected by three main modes: (1) by introducing a female figure—sometimes the beloved of the poem's dedicatee or connected to the male figures of the poem in another way—to sing the *kharja*, (2) by having a man sing the *kharja* but qualifying his singing as "feminine" ("I/he sang like a maiden"), and (3) by referring to an explicit generic term for women's song ("he/she sang a maiden's song"; Rosen-Moked 1985; 1991).

The *kharajāt* are characterized by their literal, nonfigurative, but nonetheless piquant style. Ibn Sanā al-Mulk mandates their effect within each poem to be comparable to "naphtha and cinders . . . the spice of the *muwashshah*; its salt and its sugar, its musk and amber." The provocative sting of these final verses reflects the intense female eroticism motivating them, in which frustrated young women sing their unrequited love, and less frequently, express their joy and ecstasy in consummated love. The woman in the *kharja* differs greatly from her counterpart in other types of Arabic and Hebrew love lyrics, and even from the female figure(s) in the main text of its own encompassing *muwashshah*. The *kharja* woman is not the lofty, frigid, silent lady who torments her lover with her indifference; she is passionate and effusive, sometimes even the initiator of an amorous encounter, as in these verses: "I'll give you much love but only if you'll bend/My anklets right down over to my earrings." More often, however, they are love's victims: "Oh Lord, how shall I bear a life with this deceiver/Who, even before he greets a girl, threatens to leave her." The *kharajāt* thus open a window to the hidden, anxious domain of women as they present scenes of young girls consulting female confidante figures, whether mothers, sisters, friends or fortune-tellers.

The gender aspect of the *kharja* is inextricable from its linguistic and cultural bearings. Therefore, like its message, the language of most *kharajāt*, except for those in *muwashshahs* written entirely in the male-centered classical Arabic tradition, differs from that of the main body of the *muwashshah*. Whereas the *muwashshah* obeys the orthodox grammar of classical Arabic or Hebrew, the *kharja* usually employs one of the popular or vernacular dialects of Al-Andalus: vernacular Arabic, Romance, or Mozarabic. This linguistic shift at the *muwashshah*'s conclusion was already observed by the oldest Andalusian authority, Ibn Bassam (d. 1147). It is not uncommon to find a *kharja* introduced within a given *muwashshah* by allusions to its "foreign" speech: an Arabic *muwashshah* will use the term *'ajamiah* to signal its Romance-language *kharja*, and a Hebrew *muwashshah* might herald its Arabic kharja using expressions like "she sang in the tongue of the Ishmaelites—or "in Aramaic" (a Hebrew dialect from ancient Syria), or "Edomite," for Romance *kharajāt* (Rosen-Moked 1985, 1991). This poetic-linguistic hybridization of *muwashshah* and its corresponding kharja occurred principally in combinations of classical Arabic/vernacular Arabic, Arabic/Romance, Hebrew/Arabic, and Hebrew/Romance. It reflects the sociolinguistic makeup of Al-Andalus intermingling Muslim, Jewish, and Christian peoples, possibly in interfaith marriages, with the *muwashshah* text mirroring the Muslim "hegemonic" or dominant, conquering culture, and the *kharja* representing the minority, or submissive, culture. Since sociohistorically, as James Monroe and David Swiatlo have shown, while classical Arabic *kharajāt* are predominantly male-voiced, Mozarabic ones are mostly female-voiced. The latter case reflects the extent to which Al-Andalus culture was pervaded by varied confrontations between Arab male conquerors and the enslaved Christian, Romance-speaking female natives. In a typical love poetry situation, we would find represented the sexual tensions between the dominating-male *muwashshaḥ* versus the alternatingly coquettish, mocking or lamenting female voice of the *kharja*.

The *muwashshaḥ*'s bilingualism derives an additional gendered aspect from the fact that learned or high culture was open to men but scarcely to women, who consequently drew from the folkloric oral tradition. The predominantly women's-voiced *kharajāt* and the terms introducing them ("maiden's song," "gazelle's song," "love song," "lover's lament," "song to a friend," etc.) have caused some scholars to trace them back hypothetically to lost genres of Peninsular women's oral tradition. The expressions announcing the *kharajāt* resemble genres of medieval woman's songs arising elsewhere in Europe from late Antiquity through the thirteenth centuries: the Latin *cantica puellarum* (maidens' songs) or *cantica amatoria* (love songs); the German *Frauenlieder* (women's songs), Anglo-Saxon *winileodas* (songs for a lover), French *chansons de femme* (women's songs), and Galician-Portuguese *cantigas de amigo* (songs to a friend) (Stern 1946) (1974; Spitzer 1952; Monroe 1977; Rubiera Mata). However, scholars are divided over the authenticity of the Mozarabic *kharajāt* as feminine creations—were they composed by living female poets rather than pseudo-feminine lyrics invented by male poets?—as much as over the question of their position in Peninsular, and more generally Romance, lyric evolution. Debates on these questions involve such scholars as Samuel Armistead, Alan Jones, and Keith Whinnom; while Mary Jane Kelly offers a feminist contestation of the *kharajāt* as women's poetry.

Because the *kharajāt* may constitute the earliest instances of any Romance poetry ever written, and also the earliest examples of any women's poetry, this double alleged antecedence explains the eager interest of literary critics, including recently a number of feminists, as well as that of Romance philologists, in this genre-within-a-genre. *Kharja* studies really flourished as an independent field in the wake of findings by S. M. Stern, a polyglot combining expertise in Hebrew, Arabic, and Romance languages, the first to recognize, in 1948, an initial group of twenty Mozarabic *kharajāt* in Hebrew *muwashshaḥs*, previously mistaken for the work of neglectful scribes writing Arabic texts in the Hebrew alphabet. Stern deciphered and identified them instead as relics of Mozarabic—a dialect, spoken by the offspring of Peninsular Christian converts to Islam, combining Romance vernacular with Arabic to make a sort of pidgin Old Spanish, of which the *kharajāt* are probably the earliest evidence. Since Stern, some 229 scholarly publications emerged as of 1977 (Hitchcock), with many more since then, dealing with the identification, editing, and interpretation of the *kharajāt* and, like the genre itself, reaffirmed more than reconciled the rift between Romance and Arabic studies. Most of the ongoing debate revolves around the original metrics of the *kharajāt* and *muwashshaḥāt*, since their meter does not readily appear to conform to the standard (Khalilian) classical Arabic system: were their meters originally quantitative, as in classical Arabic, or syllabic-stressed, as in Romance? Scholars of the Romance School (García Gómez, Monroe, Armistead), guided by the description given by founding critics Ibn Bassam and especially that by Ibn Sanā al-Mulk of *muwashshaḥ* composition ("having found the basis, [the poet] holds the tail [*kharja*] fast and puts the head [*muwashshaḥ*] on it"), asserting that the poet either found among old Romance sources the *kharja* (or its main components) according to which, thematically and formally, he then created the *muwashshaḥ* in which to enclose it. The

Romance theorists concluded that the *kharja*'s meter would likewise dictate the metrics of the entire poem, and that since the kharja, being in a Romance language, was syllabically stressed, so should the *muwashshaḥ* be. On the other hand, the Arabist theorists (including Jones, Ghazi, and Latham) advocate the primacy of the genre's Arabic roots via such approaches as paleography (Jones) and reproach pioneering anthologist-editor García Gómez (1952) for deliberately editing the *muwashshaḥ* and *kharja* texts to fit syllabic stress. A third view, exemplified by Corriente's studies of scansion, accommodates both theories and equates the classical-Arabic long-quantity syllable with the Romance stressed syllable. Taken beyond the question of scansion, this tertiary view, as represented most expansively by Menocal, in keeping with the current growing appreciation of multiculturalism, calls for recognition of the pluralism in these genres as indicative of Andalusian cultural diversity at that time, a nexus of Arabic and European lost after the Christian reconquest of Spain over the thirteenth through fifteenth centuries.

See also Chanson de Femme (Women's Song); *Frauenlied*; Jewish Women in the Middle Ages; *Muwashshaḥ*

BIBLIOGRAPHY

Primary Sources

García Gómez, Emilio, ed. *Las Jarchas romances de la serie arabe en su marco.* Madrid, 1965; 2nd ed. Barcelona: Seix Barral, 1975; 3rd ed. Madrid, 1990.

Ghāzī, Sayyid, ed. *Dīwān al-muwashshahāt al-Andalusiyah.* 2 vols. Alexandria: Munshaat al-Maarif, 1979. [Critical ed., counterbalancing above, in Arabic with facsimiles].

Ibn Sanā' al-Mulk. *Dār al-tirāz fī amal al-muwashshahāt talīf al-Sa'īd Abī al-Qāsim ibn Hibat Allah ibn Jafar ibn Sanā al-Mulk/Dār al-Tiraz, poétique du muwassah.* Edited by Jawdat al-Rikābī. 2nd ed. Damascus: Dār al-Fikr, 1977 [Critical ed. of Arabic text based on Cairo and Leiden mss., with facsimiles]; another ed. by Muhammad Z. 'Inani, Beirut: Dār-al-Thaquafa, 2001.

Rubiera Mata, María Jesús, ed. *Poesía femenina hispano-arabe.* Madrid: Castalia/Instituto de la Mujer, 1989. [Spanish translations and commentary].

Sola-Solé, Josep M., ed. *Corpus de poesía mozarabe (las hargas anadalusies).* Barcelona: Hispam, 1973.

———. *Los Jarchas romances y sus moaxajas.* Madrid: Taurus, 1990. [Revised version of above: transliterations of original text and Spanish translations of sixty-four known *kharajāt* and their corresponding *muwashshaḥs*].

Secondary Sources

Abu Haidar, J. "The Kharja of the Muassah in a New Light." *Journal of Arabic Literature* 9 (1978): 1–14.

Armistead, Samuel G. "Some Recent Developments in Kharja Scholarship." *La Corónica* 8 (1980): 199–203.

———. "Speed or Bacon? Further Meditations on Prof. Alan Jones' 'Sunbeams'." *La Corónica* 10 (1982): 148–55.

———, and James T. Monroe. "*Albas, Mammas,* and Code-Switching in the Kharjas: A Reply to Keith Whinnom." *La Corónica* 11(1983): 174–207.

———. "Beached Whales and Roaring Mice: Additional Remarks on Hispano-Arabic Strophic Poetry." *La Corónica* 13 (1985): 206–42.

Compton, Linda. *Andalusian Lyrical Poetry and Old Spanish Love Songs: The* Muwashshah *and its* Kharja. New York: New York University Press, 1976.

Corriente, Federico, and Angel Saenz-Badillos, eds. *Poesia estrofica : actas del Primer Congreso Internacional sobre Poesia Estrofica Arabe y Hebrea y sus paralelos romances (Madrid, diciembre de 1989).* Madrid: Institute de Cooperación con el Mundo Arabe, 1991.

Heger, Klaus. *Die bisher veröffentlichen Hargas und ihre Deutungen.* Tübingen: Max Niemeyer, 1960.

Hitchcock, Richard. *The Kharjas: A Critical Bibliography.* London: Grant & Cutler, 1977.

Jones, Alan. *Romance Kharjas in Andalusian Arabic Muwassah Poetry. A Paleographical Analysis.* London: Ithaca Press/Oxford University Oriental Studies, 1988.

———. "Sunbeams from Cucumbers? An Arabist's Assessment of the State of *Kharja* Studies." *La Corónica* 10 (1981): 38–53.

Kelly, Mary Jane. "Virgins Misconceived: Poetic Voices in Mozarabic Kharjas." *La Corónica* 19 (1990–1991): 1–23.

Latham, D. "The Prosody of an Andalusian Muwassah Re-examined." In *Arabian and Islamic Studies*, edited by Robin L. Bidwell and Gerald R. Smith, 86–99. London: Longman, 1983.

Menocal, María Rosa. *The Arabic Role in Medieval Literary History.* Philadelphia: University of Pennsylvania Press, 1987.

Monroe, James T. "Kharjas in Arabic and Romance: Popular Poetry in Muslim Spain?" In *Islam: Past Influence and Present Challenge*, edited by Alford Welch and Pierre Cachia, 168–87. Edinburgh: Edinburgh University Press, 1979.

———, and David Swiatlo. "Ninety-three Arabic Hargas in Hebrew Muwassahs: Their Hispano-Romance Prosody and Thematic Features." *Journal of the American Oriental Society* 97 (1977): 141–63.

Rosen, Tova. "The Muwashshah." In *The Literature of Al-Andalus*, edited by María Rosa Menocal, Raymond Scheindlin, and Michael Sells, 165–89. Cambridge and New York: Cambridge University Press, 2000.

———. *Unveiling Eve: Reading Gender in Medieval Hebrew Literature.* Jewish Culture and Contexts. Philadelphia: University of Pennsylvania Press, 2003.

Rosen-Moked, Tova. *Le-ezor shir: al shirat ha-ezor ha-Ivrit bi-yeme ha-benayim/The Hebrew Girdle Poem (Muwashshah) in the Middle Ages.* Haifa, Israel: University of Haifa, 1985.

———. "Towards Kharja: A Study of Penultimate Units in Arabic and Hebrew Muwashahāt." In Corriente et al., 279–88. *See above.*

Rubiera Mata, María Jesús. "Jarchas de Posible Origen Galaico-Portugues." *Actas do IV Congreso da Associação hispânica de literatura medieval* 4: 79–81.

Spitzer, Leo. "The Mozarabic Lyric and Theodor Frings' Theories." *Comparative Literature* 4 (1952): 1–22.

Stern, Samuel M. *Les Chansons mozarabes: les vers finaux (kharjas en espagnol dans les muwashshahs arabes et hébreux).* Palermo: Manfredi, 1953. Reprint Oxford: Bruno Cassirer, 1964.

———. *Hispano-Arabic Strophic Poetry.* Edited by Leonard P. Harvey. Oxford: Clarendon Press, 1974. [Includes reprints of his seminal articles and 1946 dissertation].

———. "Les Vers finaux en espagnol dans les muwassahs hispano-hébraïques." *Al-Andalus* 13 (1948): 299–346.

Whinnom, Keith. "The *Mamma* of the *Kharjas* or, Some Doubts Concerning Arabists and Romanists." *La Corónica* 9 (1981): 11–17.

Zwartjes, Otto. *The Andalusian xarjas: Poetry at the Crossroads of Two Systems?* Nijmegen, Netherlands: O. J. Zwartjes, 1995.

———. *Love Songs from al-Andalus: History, Structure, and Meaning of the Kharja.* Medieval Iberian Peninsula. Texts and studies, 11. Leiden and New York: Brill, 1997.

TOVA ROSEN

KOMNENE, ANNA. *See* **Comnena, Anna**

LADIES' TOURNAMENT. *See Frauenturnier*

"LADY H." *See* **H., Domna**

LADY OF THE LAKE. The Lady of the Lake, or, in French, La Dame du Lac, is a title that designates several female characters whose frequent namelessness, which makes it difficult to tell them apart, may betray their fairy or quasi-fairy nature. When the Lady is named, she can be Eviène, Niviane (or Niniane), Nyneve, Viviane, Nymue, or variations on any of those. Arthurian legend knows the Lady of the Lake as the fairy woman who gave Excalibur to Arthur and, sometimes, as the person who raised Lancelot.

In the Prose *Lancelot* (thirteenth century), Ninianne is one of the fairies who "knew the powers of words and stones and herbs, which allowed them to retain youth and beauty and enjoy whatever wealth they wished." In that work, too, she is the same as the Lady of the Lake who takes Lancelot from his mother and raises him. As a mentor, she is highly Christianized, emphasizing to Lancelot that "knighthood was established to defend the Holy Church."

In his *Morte Darthur* (c.1469), Malory gives the name Nymue to the "Chief Lady of the Lake." It is she who entombs Merlin.

See also Arthurian Women; Enchantresses, Fays (Fées), and Fairies; Morgan le Fay

BIBLIOGRAPHY

Primary Sources
[Grail Legends, French]. *Le Livre du Graal*, vol. 1. Critical ed. and trans. [Modern French] by Philippe Walter et al. 2 vols. Paris: Éditions de la Pléiade/Gallimard, 2001–2003.
Lancelot roman en prose du XIIIᵉ siècle. Edited by Alexandre Micha. 9 vols. Textes Littéraires Français, 247, 249, 262, 278, 283, 286, 288, 307, 315. Geneva: Droz, 1978–1983.
Lancelot-Grail: The Old French Arthurian Vulgate and Post-Vulgate in Translation, vol. 2: *Lancelot, Part I*. Translated by Samuel N. Rosenberg, 11, 59. General editor Norris J. Lacy. Garland Reference Library of the Humanities, 1826. New York: Garland, 1993.
Malory, Sir Thomas. *Morte Darthur*. Edited by John Matthews. London: Cassell, 2000.

Secondary Sources

Fenster, Thelma S., ed. *Arthurian Women: A Casebook*. Arthurian Characters and Themes, 3. New York: Garland, 1996. [Collection of critical essays on wide-ranging aspects, with introduction].

THELMA S. FENSTER

LANGMANN, ADELHAID (c.1316–1375). Adelhaid, or Adelheid, Langmann, a German Dominican nun who authored a book evoking her mystical visions, hailed from a family of Nuremberg nobility and councilors. Married to Gottfried Teufel at the age of thirteen and widowed at fourteen, she opposed her family's insistence on remarriage. Instead of remarrying, she followed what she believed was her calling to the Dominican cloister at Engelthal in 1330. Engelthal had been founded in 1240 and had, by the time Adelhaid entered, a tradition of intense mysticism. Adelhaid had to first overcome some difficult spiritual conflicts, which seem to have troubled her for many years. She then gave herself wholeheartedly to her visionary experiences, her intensified prayers, and a strict mortification and castigation of the flesh.

In her book *Offenbarungen* (*Revelations*), which a superior encouraged her to write, Langmann describes her way into mysticism and her experiences of union with God. The work is available in three different fifteenth-century manuscripts: one in Berlin (MGQ B66), in Munich (CGM99), and Vienna (H.W. Nr. 2). All three manuscripts descend from a revised copy probably based on Langmann's original manuscript, possibly an autobiography, as indicated by the superabundant usage of the first-person singular.

Adelhaid enunciates a type of religious edification and *Brautmystik* (mystical marriage) via the persona of a nun who demonstrates a childlike piety: an inward-looking and totally submissive devotion. The nun in the work also speaks of her doubts, temptations, sufferings, and even more intensely of her spiritual longings. In her visions, she unites with God and meets the Virgin Mary, among others. She also sees Jesus either in the form of a nobleman, or as a peaceful and powerful king; at other times she sees Him as a small child or adolescent. In one vision, Jesus marries her and writes his name in her heart, while in another He carries her out of the world to behold nine choirs of angels. Adelhaid's mystical-narrative fervor occasionally leads her to extremes. Her experiences assume an erotic quality as she portrays herself striving for heavenly confirmation and approbation. Her visions, however, reflect prevailing medieval piety and are common for many of the Dominican nuns at such convents as Töss, Diessenhoven, Unterlinden, and Engelthal, as recorded in each convent's *Schwesternbuch* (sisterbook), or chronicle. Together with her contemporaries, Christina Ebner (1277–1376) and Christine Stommeln (1242–1312), Adelhaid Langmann is considered a "practical" mystic who was influenced by the earlier mystics, Heinrich Suso (c.1295–1366), Johannes Tauler (d. 1361), Meister Eckhart (c.1260–c.1328), Mechthild of Magdeburg (c.1207–1282), and Hildegard of Bingen (1098–1179). In her turn she won the admiration of significant modern religious thinkers, even Jewish activist mystics such as Martin Buber (1878–1965), in his *Ekstatische Konfessionen* (*Ecstatic Confessions*) of 1909.

See also Bride of Christ/*Brautmystik*; Convents; Ebner, Christina; Gertrude the Great, of Helfta, St.; Hildegard of Bingen, St.; Mechthild of Magdeburg; Sister-Books/ *Schwesternbücher*

BIBLIOGRAPHY

Primary Sources

Martin Buber. *Ecstatic Confessions: The Heart of Mysticism.* Edited by Paul Mendes-Flohr. Translated by Esther Cameron. Syracuse, N.Y.: Syracuse University Press, 1996.

Langmann, Adelheid. *Die Offenbarungen der Adelheid Langmann, Klosterfrau zu Engelthal.* Edited by Philipp Strauch. Quellen und Forschungen zur Sprach- und Kulturgeschichte der germanischen Völker, 26. Strassburg (now Strasbourg): Trübner, 1878.

Secondary Sources

Garber, Rebecca L. *Feminine Figurae: Representations of Gender in Religious Texts by Medieval German Women Writers 1100–1375.* Studies in Medieval History and Culture, 10. New York: Routledge, 2003. [ch. 5].

"Langmann, Adelhaid." In *Deutsches Literatur-Lexikon,* edited by Wilhelm Kosch, vol. 9. Berne and Munich: Francke, 1984.

"Langmann, Adelhaid." In *Die deutsche Literatur des Mittelalters: Verfasserlexikon,* edited by Karl Langosch and Wolfgang Stammler, vol. 3. Berlin and New York: De Gruyter, 1977.

"Langmann, Adelhaid." In *Neue Deutsche Biographie,* vol. 13. Historische Kommission der Bayerischen Akademie der Wissenschaft. Berlin: Francke, 1982.

EDITH BRIGITTE ARCHIBALD

LAUDINE. In Chrétien de Troyes's *Yvain, ou le chevalier au lion* (*Ywain, or the Knight with the Lion,* c.1177) and in the Middle-High German romance it inspired, Hartmann von Aue's *Iwein* (c.1210?), the beautiful Laudine marries Ywain after he has killed her husband, defender of the magic fountain. Her confidante Lunete has persuaded Laudine that no man could better protect the fountain than the man who defeated her husband. Related to the French *Yvain* is a Middle-Welsh tale, *Owein,* or *Chwedyl iarlles y ffynnawn* (*Owain,* or the *Lady of the Fountain*), contained in the collection called the *Mabinogion* (thirteenth century?).

See also Arthurian Women; Lunete

BIBLIOGRAPHY

Primary Sources

Chrétien de Troyes. *Yvain, ou le Chevalier au lion.* Edited and translated (Modern French) by David F. Hult. Lettres gothiques. Paris: Livre de Poche, 1994. [Bilingual Old-French-Modern French ed.].

Hartmann von Aue. *Iwein.* Edited and translated by Patrick M. McConeghy. Garland Library of Medieval Literature, 19A. New York: Garland, 1984.

Owein, or *Chwedyl iarlles y ffynnawn.* Edited by R. L. Thomson. Medieval and Modern Welsh Series, 4. Dublin: Dublin Institute for Advanced Studies, 1968. [Middle-Welsh text only].

———. In *The Mabinogion,* translated with introduction by Jeffrey Gantz, 192–216. Harmondsworth, U.K. and New York: Penguin, 1976. Reprint 1981.

———. In *Mabinogion,* translated by Gwyn Jones and Thomas Jones. Introduction by Gwyn Jones. Preface by John Updike. Everyman's Library, 168. New York: Knopf/Random House, 2001.

Secondary Source

Fenster, Thelma S., ed. *Arthurian Women: A Casebook.* Arthurian Characters and Themes, 3. New York: Garland, 1996. [Collection of critical essays on wide-ranging aspects, with introduction].

THELMA S. FENSTER

LAURA (14th century). Like Beatrice, the other female figure of fourteenth-century Italian letters whose name was destined to achieve undisputed prominence in the European poetic tradition, Laura is inevitably identified with the poet who created her: as Beatrice is "Dante's Beatrice," so is Laura "Petrarch's Laura." The Beatrice of Dante's *Vita Nuova* (*New Life*, 1290) and the *Divina Commedia* (*Divine Comedy*, 1321) is Laura's principal vernacular antecedent, and she shares much with her literary sister: surpassing beauty, an early death, her poet's continuing devotion, and two poetic masterworks—the *Rime sparse* (*Scattered Rhymes*) or *Canzoniere* (*canzone* = type of lyric-poetic genre) and the *Trionfi* (*Triumphs*) in which her unique qualities are celebrated.

Even more than Beatrice, Laura is a creature of her creator. While Francesco Petrarca (Petrarch, 1304–1374) left ample documentation of his activities both as poet and as Europe's "first Renaissance man of letters," the historical identity of his Laura—indeed her historical existence—is uncertain, despite repeated attempts to confirm it; the most famous among these dates from the eighteenth century when the Abbé de Sade claimed her as his ancestor. Petrarch himself transcribes only the following, possibly fictitious, record, on the flyleaf of his cherished manuscript of the Classical Roman poet Virgil: he met Laura in the church of St. Clare in Avignon, France at the matins ceremony on April 6, 1327; she died and was buried in that same church exactly twenty-three years later. The portrait of the lady for which two of Petrarch's sonnets praise his compatriot, famed painter Simone Martini (d. 1344), is lost. In his Latin *Secretum* (*Secret*), staging a dialogue with his spiritual mentor, the "Doctor" of the Church, St. Augustine (354–430), Petrarch attributes to the latter the suggestion that he had sought the laurel crown and written of the laurel only because of its identification with the lady's name; in a letter to a friend, he protests the idea that she was a fiction invented to serve his poetic ambition. "If only that were true!" he exclaims, "if she had indeed been a fiction and not a madness!"

Petrarch's celebration of Laura is inseparable from his poetic ambition because her name is the feminine form of *lauro*, the laurel plant whose leaves crowned poets—among them, in a Roman ceremony in 1341, Petrarch himself—as well as emperors. The early first-century poet Ovid's tale (*Metamorphosis*, 1) of Apollo's pursuit of a nymph who was transformed into a laurel tree to escape the god's possession is the central mythological subtext of the *Rime sparse*, one in which amorous frustration is transformed into poetic immortality: as Apollo consecrated the laurel to the memory of the lost Daphne, so Petrarch aspires to render immortal the name of his own lady. That task, however, is fraught with anxiety. Fragmented into syllables in its first appearance in the collection, it suggests not only laud and reverence, but also that which, sacred to Apollo, may not be spoken. Other poems add other resonances to her name: it yields sensuous associations with the breeze, "l'aura," and with gold, "l'auro," and is brought into juxtaposition through phonic play with the goddess Aurora whose arrival at dawn makes the poet envisage "Laura ora."

The textual Laura is thus as elusive as her putative historical self. She is enlisted as Love's agent to affect the poet's *innamoramento*, and she is the object of his ceaseless pursuit. Her presence, however, is most often illusory, the presence of indelible memory traces or of images obsessively projected onto nature. Although Petrarch recorded their meeting in Avignon, Laura's setting is invariably the landscape of Valchiusa (the Vaucluse, southern France), her portrayal so intimately linked to its hills, woods, rocks, and waters that her forms readily blend or metamorphose into those of nature. The enchantment of

Petrarch and Laura introduced to the emperor at Avignon. By Vacslav Brozik. Courtesy of North Wind Picture Archives.

her song and of the sound of her words are repeatedly evoked, but her speech is recorded only once, and even then it is filtered through the mythic account of a poem in which she is made to preside at the poet's metamorphoses; her language is a silent language conveyed by her glances, gestures, sighs, or tears. While some of her attributes—golden hair scattered to the breeze or restrained by braids or gems, eyes flashing with laughter or with anger, a white hand bereft of its glove—became the clichés of Petrarchan imitators, her own physical depiction is fragmented. At its extreme, reified, it renders her as a composite of snow, of ice, of colors, of gems.

The roles attributed to Laura in the *Rime sparse* are also difficult to seize in their extraordinary variety. She has readily accessible vernacular prototypes in addition to Beatrice. Her inaccessibility makes of her not only the chaste, idealized madonna of the *dolce stil nuovo* ("sweet new style")—or *stilnovisti*—poets (late thirteenth century), but also the incarnation of the cold, haughty, sometimes willfully cruel lady of the Provençal lyric. She has also a number of mythological precursors in addition to the Ovidian Daphne. Dramatically, her beauty and her anger both evoke the threat of petrification represented by Medusa; or she plays vengeful Diana, too intimately glimpsed, to the poet's fearful Acteon. The female figure depicted sensuously bathing in the waters of the river Sorgue in one famous poem is said in another to surpass in her resolute chastity the Roman Lucrezia. She is the phoenix rising from its ashes, Eurydice destroyed in her youth. In two poems that reveal her integration into her poet's broader humanistic enterprise, she is likened to the virtuous Roman warrior Scipio Africanus (236–183 B.C.E.), the hero of Petrarch's unfinished Latin epic, *Africa*.

The textual Laura exists then, like Pygmalion's statue evoked in one poem, both as the object of the poet's desire and as his creation. Inaccessible in person, she provokes exaltation, but also a repressed anger that finds rare expression as a desire for vengeance; the range of the lover's conflicting readings and responses reveals itself as a threat to his stability, even to his sanity. Poetically, however, she is his creature, his idol—"my idol sculpted in green laurel"—and this status, about which he exults in some poems, is intermittently suggested in others as a threat to his salvation, the ambivalence of her portrayal contributing to the prevasive tension in the collection between desire and the anxiety of desire, between *cupiditas* (lust) and *caritas* (love).

In the *Rime sparse* that ambivalence is not resolved even with Laura's death. For the mourning poet she assumes the role of spiritual guide who, like Dante's Beatrice, offers consolation and indicates the way toward heaven. Yet even as he imagines her in Paradise, her appearances in dream or fantasy at his bedside are marked by sensuous elements, and she remains the object of his obsessive recollection in her familiar landscape. Her name is absent from the final poem of the collection, the great penitential canzone addressed not to her but to the Virgin; the poem records instead the "mortal beauty, deeds, and words" that have long burdened the poet's soul, and confesses that "Medusa and my own error" have long delayed his attention to his salvation.

The story of Petrarch's love for Laura is rewritten in the *Trionfi*, a work in which the model of the *Commedia* is both formally and thematically prominent. Now the phases of her story are revealed to the poet-narrator as representations of the successive triumphs of Love, Chastity, Death, Fame, Time, and Eternity. She herself is the protagonist of the second of these, and in this work the ambiguities characteristic of her presentation in the *Rime sparse* are definitively resolved. This Laura, unlike the Laura of the *Rime*, is loquacious; now she attests to their mutual love, explaining that her coldness had been adopted to promote the poet's good. Now more present and more consistently characterized than in the *Rime*, she becomes at the same time more abstract, a determined, militant figure contrasting strikingly to the Laura of the lyric collection as she leads a band of chaste ladies in an attack that leaves the god of love bound in chains.

The elusive Laura was to retain her fascination for generations of poets throughout Europe; meanwhile, the vogue of Petrarchism led to repeated efforts to disclose the woman behind the poems. Italian and French commentators in particular devoted substantial attention to the question. In a widely publicized example in 1533, the young French poet Maurice Scève found what was believed to be Laura's tomb in Avignon. He and numerous other Renaissance poets composed collections of amorous verse in the Petrarchan style on the model of the *Rime sparse*. Joachim Du Bellay, in his *L'Olive* (1549) and Pierre de Ronsard each announced his aspiration to make of his own lady a "new Laura." When Ronsard, who in his early *Amours* (1552–1553) produced the most successful of those collections, later attempted to distance himself from the Petrarchan shadow, it was by denouncing the Petrarchan "experience," commenting ironically on the implausibility of the protracted Platonic relationship recorded in the *Rime*. Following the Petrarchan experimentations of generations of poets throughout Europe, Byron in *Don Juan* (1819–1824) captured with equal irony the degree to which Laura had come to figure the relation between amorous frustration and poetry: "Think you, if Laura had been Petrarch's wife,/He would have written sonnets all his life?"

See also Beatrice; *Belle Dame Sans Merci*

BIBLIOGRAPHY

Primary Sources

[Several critical eds. of the above mentioned authors in their original languages are available].

Petrarca, Francesco. *Petrarch's Lyric Poems: The "Rime sparse" and Other Lyrics.* Translated and edited by Robert M. Durling. Cambridge, Mass.: Harvard University Press, 1976. [Excellent introduction and notes].

Secondary Sources

Bernardo, Aldo. *Petrarch, Laura, and the "Triumphs."* Albany: State University of New York Press, 1974.

Durling, Robert. "Petrarch's 'Giovene donna sotto un verde lauro'." *Modern Language Notes* 86 (1971): 1–20.

Estrin, Barbara L. *Laura: Uncovering Gender and Genre in Wyatt, Donne, and Marvell.* Durham, N.C.: Duke University Press, 1994.

Foster, Kenelm. *Petrarch, Poet and Humanist.* Edinburgh: University of Edinburgh Press, 1984.

Hainsworth, P. R. J. "The Myth of Daphne in the *Rerum vulgarium fragmenta.*" *Italian Studies* 34 (1979): 28–44.

Sturm-Maddox, Sara. *Petrarch's Metamorphoses: Text and Subtext in the* Rime sparse. Columbia, Mo.: University of Missouri Press, 1985.

———. *Petrarch's Laurels.* University Park: Pennsylvania State University Press, 1992.

Vickers, Nancy J. "The Body Re-Membered: Petrarchan Lyrics and the Strategies of Description." In *Mimesis: From Mirror to Method*, edited by John D. Lyons and Stephen G. Nichols, 100–109. Hanover, N.H.: University Press of New England, 1982.

SARA STURM-MADDOX

LAW, CANON, WOMEN IN. Canon law began as one of many different legal systems (Roman law, feudal law, the King's law, customary law, common law, etc.) existing at different times or simultaneously in different places throughout the Middle Ages. As its name indicates, medieval canon law governed the Church's members and their interrelationship, from the professional clergy down through the various monastic levels (monks, nuns, friars, etc.) in Europe and the East. But canon law also regulated many activities of the secular population or laity, particularly in significant phases of their lives requiring religious sanction: ceremonies of birth, marriage, burial, and also in matters of inheritance and donations. Canon law eventually evolved to override other, less cohesive legal codes, thus also affecting medieval women's lives by serving to establish norms for their position in both religious and secular societies.

The Sources and Their Evolving Traditions. The earliest legal heritage of the Christian communities consisted in the sacred Jewish Scriptures forming the Christian Old Testament. Old and New Testaments together, the canonical scriptures par excellence, are the essential basis of all further inner-ecclesiastical legal development, that is, "canon law" in a broad sense. This development would prove as variegated as its base in undergoing significant changes throughout history.

Originally, the term canon law derives from ecclesiastical "laws" enacted by councils or synods (assemblies of ecclesiastical authorities), in general called *kanones* (canons) in opposition to the *nomoi* (laws) of the Roman/Byzantine emperors, who, after having adopted Christianity (fourth century), also intended to regulate ecclesiastical affairs themselves. The decisions of some councils, beginning with that of Nicaea (325), another being the Council of Chalcedon (451), gained particular esteem and were thus considered binding for all Christians (the decisions, or canons, of these councils are thus labeled by the determining council's name—such as Nicaea, Chalcedon, etc.—in this article's parenthetic citations). However, even most of the so-called Ecumenical ("universal") councils remained in dispute among the rising number of different professions of Christian faith. In any case, many synods never attained more than local significance.

The great Eastern collections of received ecclesiastical law include both canons and imperial laws (in particular those "Novels," as they are referenced, of the famous Emperor Justinian [r. 527–565] dealing with ecclesiastical affairs) and therefore called *Nomokanones* (Greek: *nomos* = "a law"; *kanon* = "canon") or, Nomocanonical Collections. Highly influential among these was an anonymous collection, the *Nomokanon in 14 titles* (early seventh century), edited at various times between the ninth and eleventh centuries and commented on by the leading twelfth-century Byzantine scholars Aristenos, Zonaras, and Balsamon. The best-known medieval collection for Western canon law is the *Concordia Discordantium Canonum* (*Concord/Code of Discordant Canons*, twelfth century), a collection of about 4,000 conciliar decrees, patristic texts (writings of the early founders of the Church, called the Church Fathers), and papal pronouncements covering all areas of Church discipline, by Gratian (d. c.1160), who, for this achievement, is considered the father of canon law. Gratian's collection became known as his famous *Decretum*, or *Decretum Gratiani* (c.1140), and formed the basis of the *Corpus Iuris Canonici* (*Body of Canon Law*), which would serve as the official canonical collection of the Catholic Church until the beginning of the twentieth century (1917). The *Corpus Iuris Canonici* can be seen as the Western Church's counterpart to the *Corpus Iuris Civilis* (*Body of Civil Law*) for civil law, codified under Emperor Justinian, also influential into the early modern era. The major strengths of both codes lay in their unprecedented systematic and logical presentation of their respective codes making them at once authoritative while enabling further clarification when necessary by legal scholars.

However, for the Eastern Churches there has been no codified canon law in any strict sense to this day, except in the case of the Eastern Catholic Churches, for which the so-called *Code of Canons of the Oriental Churches* was enacted, and even then only recently (1990). An influential modern collection frequently used in the legal procedures of the Orthodox Eastern Churches is the so-called *Pedalion* (*Rudder*), composed in the tradition of the early Byzantine commentaries, by Nikodemos Hagiorites (St. Nicodemus of the Holy Mountain, c.1749–1809) and published in 1800. Nikodemos's *Pedalion* included the standard twelfth-century commentaries and a considerable number of Byzantine canonical answers. A more scholarly edition of this collection was then done by Georgios Rhallis and Michael Potlis (Athens 1852–1856). The Assyrian Church of the East and the Eastern Orthodox Churches (Armenian Apostolic, Syrian Orthodox, Coptic, and Ethiopic Orthodox) each have their own collections. In this article, we shall be referring to the *Synodicon of the West Syrian Tradition*, the medieval canonical "sourcebook" of the Syrian Orthodox Church.

The source material of the Eastern canonical collections and their Western supplements goes back to the first millennium. This material is not comprised exclusively of canons in the proper sense, although, beginning in the fourth century, council legislation did become particularly important for this phase of canonical development. Another legal genre typical of this formative period in Christianity is the so-called "Church Orders": anonymous or pseudonymous collections of materials dealing with canonical questions, including the liturgy (prescribed services of the Church). Examples of "Church Orders" include the *Didascalia Apostolorum* (*The Catholic Teaching of the Twelve Apostles*, third century), various recensions (critical revisions) of the so-called *Traditio Apostolica* (*Apostolic Tradition*) *of Hippolytus*, among which are the *Apostolic Constitutions* (fourth century), the so-called *Canons of Hippolytus* (fourth century), and the *Testamentum Domini* (*Testament of the Lord*, fifth century or later). These would all play a role in female ministries. In addition, the *Canonical Epistles* of prominent ecclesiastical authorities (not only by the increasingly influential Roman bishops, but also decrees issued by the Alexandrian hierarchs, for example) attempted to resolve certain questions. A subgroup of the latter consists in the so-called *Canonical Answers*, of which a famous example is the *Epistle to Bishop Augustine*, ascribed to Gregory the Great (d. 604), writing on behalf of the Church in canonical disputes arising during the Roman mission among the Anglo-Saxons. Such sources occasionally provide a clearer idea than council legislation, amid the often divergent opinions of medieval ecclesiastical authorities, on hotly debated issues like female purity and impurity.

The purity issue, because it involved such questions as whether or not a man may have sex with his wife during her menses, or if a menstruating woman should be allowed to attend church (see Synek 2000b), exemplifies the extent to which early ecclesiastical law covered a much broader spectrum than most Westerners would consider legally relevant nowadays. Canon law dictated other aspects of everyday life: including laywomen's dress codes, hairstyles, cosmetics, bathing, and diet. The first Church Orders and canonical collections therefore combined prescriptions for ecclesiastical ministries with marriage regulations and admonitions on family life, as in the correct behavior of husbands and wives toward each other and likewise between parents and children, between masters and slaves. Restrictions on sexual life play a considerable part in these areas.

At least within the first millennium, there is no strict division between law, morals, and customs in the normative substratum of Christianity, since this was lacking in the Jewish authority, the *Talmud*, and the Islamic one, the *Quran*. Although the following discussion will focus on this formative period up to 1000, rather than on the all-too-complex reception history of these doctrines in the second millennium, we shall attempt to note significant examples for gender issues, such as women's admission to the clergy and their role in liturgy. Despite these delimitations, we are wary of presenting an oversimplified image, because the wide range of local differences and changes over time cannot here be demonstrated in detail. We can only emphasize the continued existence of tensions and contradictions even in specific individual sources. To give an example: the *Didascalia Apostolorum*, created in Greek-speaking Syria in the third century, prohibits widows from teaching (ch. 15: ed. Vööbus, 2: 114–45). The *Didascalia* cites the behavior of Jesus, among other examples, as justification: Jesus had entrusted no woman with the task of teaching, although many female followers were available. In *Didascalia*, chapter 16, of course, the same female adherents of the Jesus movement, who first have to act as witnesses for the exclusion of women from teaching, are called to justify the necessity of employing deaconesses in female pastoral care and catechesis, as in preparing women for baptism (2: 156–58; see Synek 1993). Even more inconsistency must be expected between sources of unrelated origin. Thus, for instance, on the one hand, we find prescribed for female deacons: "A woman must not be ordained before the age of 40 and that after a careful inquiry. If after having received ordination and after having exercised her ministry for some time, she wants to marry, thereby scorning the grace of God, let her be excommunicated as well as him who has united herself to her" (Canon 15 of the Council of Chalcedon, 451; trans. in L'Huillier, 243); while on the other hand and at the same time (fourth to sixth centuries), a number of Gallic synods take the opposite stance arguing strongly against the ordination of female deacons (Gryson, 162–72).

Contradictions accumulate in more recent compilations, though a tendency toward unification is also noticeable in the process of compilation, excision, and emendation of the eventual canons (whether for doctrinal or other reasons) with uneven consequences for women. As an example, a number of manuscripts of Canon 19 Nicaea read "deacons" instead of "deaconesses," thus rendering women holding positions in ecclesiastical ministries (despite some dispute) during the first millennium increasingly invisible after 1000, not only in actual ecclesiastical life but also in Christianity's evolving self-image. Problems in textual dissemination of the canons were aggravated by interpreters who often missed the original sense of a prescription completely, causing serious departures from its original intent. As a result, the basic canonical textual heritage created during early Christianity that was generally regarded as normative and graven in stone as the canon law in force to this day by Eastern Church tradition, had, in fact, undergone appreciable alteration in its journey from its original church scriptorium. However, once cut off from its original context, an old prescription's importance could become reborn in a new context.

Another example of this process is the incorporation of Canon 15 Chalcedon into the *Decretum Gratiani*, the great canon law source for the West. Gratian's collection, compiled following scholastic (rigorously systematic) principles, has moved the aforementioned Chalcedon Canon 15 to its own chapter 23 (C. 27 q. 1), the section on marriage law. This precept is used to assert that those who take a vow of celibacy cannot marry. The initial topic of the council decision—the ordination of women with its conditions and legal consequences—is not directly disputed by Gratian (C. 15 q. 3 princ.), who states that women cannot be elevated to the priesthood, nor can they even attain the diaconate (become deaconesses). The question remains whether Gratian himself meant this in the sense of *ius divinum* ("unalterable" divine law) or exclusively in the sense of the factual *ius ecclesiasticum* (positive law of the Church). Gratian's commentators, who found themselves forced to explain the term "deaconess" (appearing also in ch. 38 C. 11 q. 1 and C. 27 q. 1 c. 30) arrived at different interpretations (Gillmann): while some regarded women's ordination possible at least for the past, like Roland Bandinelli, the future Pope Alexander III (d. 1182), and the anonymous *Summa Monacensis*, others postulated that women could not be ordained in a sacramental sense, like Rufinus and Huguccio (d. 1210), who also quoted opposite opinions. With Thomas Aquinas (d. 1274) the idea of absolute inordainability of women won the battle at least in the West (Müller). In the East, evidence of deaconesses faded during the second millennium, though, at least theoretically, bishops retained the power to ordain one.

Struggling for Equality: Marriage versus the Ascetic Life. This question of female ordination leads directly to the central problem of law in general and of canon law in particular insofar as the gender issue is concerned: the law's unequal treatment of men and women. One of the oldest Christian texts, the baptismal formula in the New Testament, Gal. 3.28—"in Christ there is neither Jew nor Greek, slave nor free, male nor females; for you are all one in Christ Jesus"—speaks of the transcending of gender "in Christ." But the equality option is not kept throughout all the New Testament texts. Both proemancipation texts (e.g., the Easter stories, which attest women as first witnesses of the Resurrection; passages that mention women in the service of the first Christian communities, as in, for example, the greeting list of Rom. 16 and 1 Cor. 7 with its ascetic prerogatives) and antiemancipation texts (such as, for example, the commandment to remain silent in the church in 1 Cor. 14. 34–35 and the prohibition of teaching in 1 Tim. 2. 11–12) were taken over into the biblical canon. The tendency to sanction a conservative image of women is especially evident in the *litterae pastorales* (pastoral letters: those addressed by a bishop to all members of his diocese and not just the clergy).

The subsequent legal development shows a corresponding ambivalence. "The legislators were men, therefore legislation is against women" (Gregory of Nazianzus, *Oratio* 37:6). The contradiction postulated by Gregory of Nazianzus (d. c.390) between (Roman) civil law, prone to using a double standard, and the "equality of the (Divine) Legislation" to be attained within the Church, inadequately describes the situation during the fourth and fifth centuries, when basic questions about Church order were being decided. After Constantine (d. 337) had legalized Christianity in the Roman Empire, there was rising influence of Roman law and custom within its Christian communities. This combined with and partially altered the Jewish heritage of the Church.

The Christian perception of marriage is rather significant in this development (see Arjava), for when the Church definitively accepted only monogamous marriages as was standard in Roman legal culture, it abandoned its Jewish heritage, since the Old Testament had sanctioned polygamy. In other questions, however, Jewish and Roman tradition coincided harmoniously, so that the Church of the Roman Empire saw no reason to relinquish the right of a *paterfamilias* (father, head of family) to decide his children's marriages. Noticeable Church modifications of Roman law tended to follow evolving social practice, for example, when marriage as a result of abduction (clearly prohibited in Roman civil law) was not absolutely rejected by all Church Fathers (see Beaucamp, 2: 357). Contradictions and tensions appearing in canonical regulations regarding marriage and family life often find their counterparts in the secular legal system and social norms, respectively, which were not always identical with the laws.

Sexual morality, and questions pertaining to it, constitutes one of the few domains in which the Church truly postulated a more comprehensive equality between men and women than that found in traditional Roman law (Synek 1999). The context of Gregory of Nazianzus's *Oratio* 37. 6, for instance, is the legal treatment of extramarital relations: Roman law (as did Antique legal ordinances in general) defined adultery as disrupting marriage to a married man. This means that a married man who has extramarital sex commits adultery only if his mistress is married. Conversely, a married woman who has extramarital relations commits adultery in any case. Adultery does not exist if a man has relations with a female slave or any free woman provided she is unmarried. According to Roman law, therefore, a man never transgresses against his own marriage. But the Church Fathers condemned male extramarital relations in the same way as those of women. In reality, however, this requirement of a higher sexual morality for men did not automatically improve women's legal position. The Church's fundamentally negative view of women regarding divorces might even be seen as a change for the worse compared with the much more liberal standards of classical Roman law. While the general ecclesiastical tendency was to disapprove of divorce, including divorce by mutual consent, and to punish subsequent remarriages, we can at the same time observe some willingness to grant privileges to the male. Hence, the only grounds for the dissolution of a marriage widely accepted by early Christian ecclesiastical authorities were a man's wife's adultery and his decision to commit himself to an ascetic life. In cases of divorce on grounds of the wife's adultery, a great number of late-antique sources such as the so-called *Canonical Letters* of Basil the Great (c.330–c.379) tolerate remarriage by the man while his first spouse is alive (see, for example, Forzieri Vannucchi). Yet women with adulterous husbands, as with battered women or those with husbands squandering the family estate, generally were not granted the same privilege. This tendency to restrict the grounds for divorce affected Roman/Byzantine law as well.

In the second millennium, when the Church was gaining full jurisdiction over marriage in the Latin West, the Roman Church, at least in principle, enforced the absolute prohibition of divorces (Brundage 1987). Unhappy couples might separate, but no second marriage could be concluded so long as both parties were alive. The only way to circumvent the Latin Church's rigorous policy was to obtain a formal annulment of the first marriage. This was possible for both men and women only on specific grounds deemed sufficient by ecclesiastical courts to nullify the marriage contract.

Byzantine ecclesiastical courts, which, in principle, had to apply canon law together with Roman civil law, at the same time adopted a comparatively liberal *praxis*, or established practical application (see Katerelos). In late Byzantine times, they began to grant divorces also on grounds unforeseen by civil law. In general, this development favored women. De facto divorces, even by mutual consent, returned in later Byzantium, although they could not be determined on the same grounds as they had been under the old legal system, which had permitted divorce by mutual consent only if the parties committed a celibate life thereafter.

This leads us to a Church ruling that gained particular importance with regard to gender equality: ecclesiastical authorities set all adults on an equal footing with respect to freedom in choosing a way of life; in other words, they allowed both women and men to decide freely about celibacy. The Augustan (named after Roman emperor Augustus Caesar, d. 14 C.E.) laws on marriage, in favoring marriage and the conception of children, also placed those without spouses and children at a disadvantage, especially in matters regarding inheritance. These laws were abolished in Late Antiquity. According to the Justinian Code (1: 3. 54, par. 5), parents may not prevent their children from either entering a monastery or from becoming a cleric, nor can they disinherit them on that account.

During the time before asceticism was "domesticated" by the cloistered life, opting for an ascetic lifestyle might have been the better choice for a woman, at least with regard to her autonomy. A Christian wife, as her Jewish or pagan sister, had further to accept her husband as her "head"—though ideally a head who should love his wife as Christ loved the Church (Ephesians 5. 21–33). Conversely, the vow of virginity or widowhood liberated woman from her subjugation to man, as Thomas Aquinas points out in his *Expositio super primam epistulam ad Corinthos* (*Commentary on 1 Corinthians*, ch. 11. 2). Christ Himself would be the only (male) head of professed virgins or those avowedly abstaining from remarriage after being widowed. The ascetic circles of early and medieval Christianity were well-known breeding grounds for misogyny, linked to contempt for sexuality. But it was also within the ascetic milieu that the egalitarian impetus of early Christianity exerted more impact than with the majority of those Christians leading "worldly" lives, married and with children. Even when hierarchic family structure again won out in monastic circles, the head of a convent was a woman and not a man. As a rule, early medieval nuns had the same status as monks, and abbesses enjoyed the same rights and obligations as their male counterparts, although the common usage to have an ordained priest as the male superior of a monastery brought on new areas of inequality. Progressive clericalization of monastic life beyond that point was more a feature of Western than of Eastern Christianity and did not take place before the second millennium (for Byzantine developments, see Konidaris). Remarkably enough, this Western progression culminated in an ecclesiastical law imposing strict cloister on all solemnly professed nuns of the Latin Church: *Periculoso*. Of course, the cloistered life was by no means invented by Pope Boniface VIII (d. 1303). Respective admonitions are as old as the beginnings of female monastic life, but in practice, a great diversity continued among female houses. Until the famous papal decree *Periculoso* was issued in 1298, unrestricted open communities had continued to exist side by side with houses of strictly confined sisters. "It seems that, as the number of priests among monks (and friars) increased, the traditional fear of 'pollution' by contact with women [...] grew as well. Increasingly dependent on priest-monks, the differences rather than the similarities between monks and nuns began to be most evident. These differences would in turn breed more distinctions—practical, theological, and legal" (Makowski, 15).

Female Ministries: Widows, Deaconesses, Abbesses. In contrast to such late-thirteenth-century developments, during the first millennium the equality option prevailed to a far greater extent in the monastic milieu though not among the upper clergy (Osborne). It happened, here, as elsewhere, that the legislators were men who, circumstances permitting, did not refer to "equality in Divine Legislation," but instead emphasized the "natural inequality" of men and women, citing "tradition" as a precedent, or found appropriate divine commandments in the Holy Scripture.

The canonical heritage reflects no doubt that, beginning with the enforcement of the monarchic episcopacy (system of Church rule by bishops), the ordination of women as bishops was utterly rejected by the so-called "Great Church" (Rome). Yet, this rejection did not affect the fact that, in an early phase—as revealed in *Epistle* 75 of Bishop Firmilian of Caesarea (d. 268)—women did still perform tasks already considered by the bishops as part of their own monopoly, at least in certain ecclesiastical communities. Though opinions on such activity in the communities from this early phase did not necessarily agree on this point, very soon, however, Church practices arrived at a far-reaching consensus, one excluding women from their previous functions. This exclusion became considered as most fundamental to the Christian cult, in which the offering of the Eucharist and administration of (at least regular) baptism became strictly male privileges.

This would not mean that women were totally excluded from ecclesiastical ministries and the ordained clergy. Some legal sources, especially the Syrian *Testamentum Domini*, do mention the function of ordained widows or female presbyters. According to the *Testamentum*, the ecclesiastically recognized widow performed liturgical tasks as well as catechetic functions, that is, supervising responsibilities and others relating specifically to prayer. Such widows helped with the baptism of women and in some way even seem to have participated in offering the Eucharist. This situation at least afforded them a place among the male clergy during the offering, in the sanctuary, in which laypersons of both sexes were not allowed. There is also evidence for deaconesses within the *Testamentum*, but here it is the widow who, being ordained, obviously has the more important position in community life. Restrictive dispositions, although not completely missing, are rather exceptional for that Church Order. In any case, the widow "should keep silent in church" (1 Cor. 14.34, quoted in *Testamentum Domini* 1.40; p. 96). However, other editions of the *Traditio Apostolica*, as well as the *Didascalia Apostolorum*, go much farther in their restrictive tendencies, enlisting widows "for prayer" only. The *Traditio Apostolica* argues strongly against the ordination of a widow, indicating that "she does not offer the oblation nor does she have any liturgical function" (*Traditio Apostolica*, p. 30). As we have seen previously, the *Didascalia* and the *Apostolic Constitutions* attack the teaching and baptismal functions of widows but ascribe some respective tasks to female deacons.

More positive evidence survives for deaconesses than for ordained widows. As mentioned previously, in certain regions of the Roman (Byzantine) Empire and among Syrian Christians living under Islamic rule, women were ordained deaconesses until the second millennium, as demonstrated in the comprehensive studies by Gryson and Eisen. Such studies show how biblical references, epigraphic evidence (Eisen, 154–192), and ordination rituals (see Theodorou 1954/1955), as well as the voices of Church Fathers and saints' lives, all attest that the ministry of deaconesses was widespread.

On this and related points, some of the most important canonical references given above in passing deserve review along with other key sources. For the Imperial Church of the Roman (Byzantine) Empire, one should consult the canons of the Ecumenical councils as well as imperial law: Canon 19 of Nicaea (held in 325), whose correct reading is disputed; Canon 15 of Chalcedon (451), and the Canons 14 and 40, Trullo (691–692); Justinian, *Novels* 3: 6.123–31. For various old Church Orders mentioned in connection with female ministries, as discussed by Sebastian Brock: the *Didascalia Apostolorum* (third century), the *Apostolic Constitutions* (fourth century), and the *Testamentum Domini* (fifth century or later). Among those canonical answers, which became part of the *Synodicon of the West Syrian Church*, we have the so-called *Chapters from the Orient* (early sixth century), *Johannan's Answers to Sargis* and *Ja'qob's Answers to Addai* (All in *Synodicon*, ed. Vööbus, 1: 157–68; 197–205; 235–44, resp.) refer also to deaconesses. For the Church of the East, see in particular Canon 9 of the Synod of George (held in 676).

Evidence for other Eastern regions is scarcer. Inscriptions are available for the Palestinian context, whereas for Egypt and Armenia the old sources are so far not conducive to a clear documentation on female deacons. Yet, there is clear evidence for Armenian deaconesses in the second millennium, in particular in modern times. As far as medieval Georgia is concerned, the codices contain formulas for ordaining a deaconess adopted from other churches that were probably if not certainly used in practice. There is even less proof that the Byzantine practice of ordaining deaconesses was ever adopted by the medieval Slavic world, only the ecclesiastical ministry of *proscurnici* (women whose task was to prepare the bread used for the Eucharistic offering) in the Russian Church might be a late vestige.

As for the West, various local synods repeatedly issued canons against the naming of deaconesses. The same negative attitude is attested by Ambrosiaster, the unknown author of a set of commentaries on St. Paul's Epistles (fourth century), falsely identified with St. Ambrose. Because Ambrosiaster's writings, offer precious glimpses of the Pre-Vulgate (just before St. Jerome's definitive Latin version of the Bible, the Vulgate, late fourth century) text of Paul, they contribute to our understanding of the early Latin Church. Ambrosiaster contains enough evidence for a positive reception of the deaconess, including ordination rituals (see Ysebaert). Links between the reception of the deaconess and the particular Western institution of the canoness are very probable (Ulrich).

Anne Jensen, among others, argues that the ministry of deaconess attained recognition only after the repression of widows, and therefore represents the "domesticated" form of an ecclesiastical office for women (Jensen, 141–64). There is good evidence for this argument. Nonetheless, the *Testamentum Domini*, which has ordained widows overseeing deaconesses and not the other way round, as the *Apostolic Constitutions* prefer, is a comparatively late Church Order (fifth century or even later), thus indicating that the ascription of particular duties to one or the other female office was not only a question of time, but also one of local developments.

In any case, the attempted domestication of women is quite apparent in various prohibitions, especially catechetic (instructing those preparing for baptism) and liturgical. Compared with male deacons, as a rule, women deacons were assigned fewer and more limited duties. Deaconesses also had to meet stricter requirements for ordination. Though not always followed in practice, the above-quoted Canon 15 of Chalcedon (reconfirmed at Trullo in 692) requested that "a woman must not be ordained before the age of 40," while the canonical minimum age for men was twenty-five. Celibacy requirements were also stricter for female than for male clerics: while Western councils favored celibacy for all higher clergy already in Late Antiquity, at least in the East, male deacons and presbyters could and did decide freely to continue marital relations as long as matrimony was concluded before ordination. From the fourth century onward, however, only women living in celibacy (widows who had not been married but one time and preferably virgins) were admitted for ordination. Justinian, not wanting to comingle family estates with church property, definitely prohibited episcopal ordination of married men, in particular of such men, who had children (Code of Justinian I: 3. 41 [42], plus others). Although this contradicted the pertinent *Apostolic Canons*, with the time the Byzantine Church (and with it also all the other Eastern Churches) adopted *Justinian's* decision in principle.

Some of the most drastic measures are associated with the infringement of the celibacy vow of a deaconess. While Canon 15 of Chalcedon recommends excommunication in such cases, Justinian's famous Novel 6. 6—referring to ancient pagan Sacral Law—stipulates dispossession and even threatens the death sentence for deaconesses found guilty of fornication. Intriguingly enough, the emperor has thus placed the Christian deaconess on equal footing with the Vestal Virgins (the old Roman cult of the hearth goddess Vesta, whose members were aristocratic maidens revered for their purity). By contrast, male clerics were only punished with deposition and degradation to lay status for the same offense. A later Novel refrains from capital punishment, but discrimination nevertheless persists: a deaconess living with a man, and thus suspected of having been "dishonored," shall be banished to a convent for the rest of her life. Furthermore, she will lose all her possessions, which are then divided between the convent and possible children or otherwise go to the church to which the woman had belonged. For male deacons, subdeacons, and priests guilty of fornication, the same Novel penalizes them only with deposition, dispossession, and return to the city in which they had served.

In the end, mechanisms were introduced for supervision and social control. The prohibition against a deaconess's cohabitation with a man was followed by the repression of "free" deaconesses in favor of those living in community with other religious women, under a common mother superior. It also appears in general that a deaconess's ministry became increasingly restricted to her fellow sisters. This shift took occured both in the East since around the time of the Council of Chalcedon (451) as well as in the West. Certain isolated cases differed: the Syrian Churches, where monasteries largely served as "pastoral centers," and the Armenian Church, where the medieval cloister deaconesses were (and still are) integrated into the community ministry. Finally, the old community office was to some extent conflated with the abbess's function.

Some confusion in terminology inevitably arose concerning these offices, as when certain medieval theologians and canonists, stumbling on the term "deaconess" while reading older sources, interpreted it as an equivalent of "abbess" (Gillmann, 242). This was, of course, an anachronism with regard to the ministry as understood by ancient sources. But as with all differences, some true constants can be singled out, for example, the case of the mother superior who, even though not an ordained deaconess, was still consecrated by the bishop. Both offices—deaconess and abbess—involved pastoral, catechetic, and liturgical functions. Late Antique canonical sources, however grudgingly, could grant abbesses markedly greater jurisdiction than deaconesses. Within Western medieval feudal structures, the abbess's jurisdiction might even extend to governing men, as with male members of double monasteries, clerics serving the female community, and villagers subject to the convent (Synek 2000a).

Women's Role in the Liturgy: Prayer, Discipline, and Purity. General statements prove unsatisfactory in describing women's specific liturgical tasks. We can say that, as a rule, gender hierarchy and a tendency toward gender separation had a considerable impact on women's place in the cults as it had on their position within the Christian community in general (Berger; Synek 2001). This explains why Late Antique Church Orders willingly assigned female officeholders intermediate functions (such as porters and ushers) between women and the male clergy, including some auxiliary services to the latter, as well as certain monitoring duties over other women.

The right to perform baptism furnished a major sacramental starting point for ecclesiastically approved female ministries. Eastern canonical texts regularly insist that, as a matter of decency, the male minister who baptizes an adult woman should be assisted by a deaconess (according to the *Testamentum Domini*, by an ordained widow). It was the task of the female minister to help a woman to undress and, after baptism, to redress, and, more important, to anoint her body. East Syrian sources even prescribe that the deaconess should perform the water rite so that the male minister could stay separated from the baptismal candidate behind a wall or curtain (Synek 1998). However, even the *East Syrian Baptismal Order* (in trans. Diettrich, 96ff.) reserved the pronouncement of the baptismal formula for the male cleric in charge. Canonical sources do not tell us whether this restriction against the deaconess was also to be upheld in the case of an emergency baptism. They do state that male deacons can perform emergency baptism alone.

The issue of baptism reveals some remarkable differences between Eastern and Western sacramental theology. Although the Eastern Churches defined baptism as an exclusively priestly prerogative, the Western Church supported the position of the African Church Father Tertullian (d. c.225), that, in principle, a layperson might also administer baptism.

But "laypersons" in this case meant laymen only, a concept generally presupposed in the aftermath of Tertullian, who had solemnly condemned the administration of baptism by women (Tertullian, *De Baptismo*, 17). The decree *Super quibus* of Urban II (d. 1099) is the first canonical source to entertain the possibility that baptism might be performed by a woman as well as by a man. But it is obvious that *Super quibus* did not want to put laywomen on an equal footing with laymen with regard to baptism, even in emergencies, for which a strict order of alternates was imposed, granting women last place.

The same question of precedence arose in regard to that most central of sacraments, the Holy Eucharist. There seems to have been a widely accepted consensus in the East that deaconesses could administer Holy Communion to women and small children under particular circumstances. The Syrian *Chapters from the Orient* (ch. 9), explicitly approved the practice that "where the superiors of the monastery are deaconesses" they "distribute the mysteries (= Holy Eucharist) to those who are under their authority." This permission, however, was granted only in the event that no male cleric (priest or deacon) was available, as prescribed in *Answers of Mar Johannan to Sargis* (no. 33) and the *Answers of Jaqob to Addai* (no. 41; all in *Synodicon*, ed. Vööbus, 1: 159, 203, 242, resp.).

Distributing the Eucharist is only one aspect of the crucial issue of women's access to the *sacra* (sacred things, places, rituals, including sacraments) and closely connected with permitting them into the altar area. As already mentioned, the *Testamentum Domini* expressly allows ordained widows in the sanctuary. But other sources, beginning with the *Canons of Laodicea* (fourth century), took the opposite stance; in addition, Canon 11 of Laodicea prohibited the institution of female presbyters (elders in the early Church, overseen by bishops). According to Canon 44, women in general could not enter the sanctuary. This decision was historically upheld, in Byzantium (Synek 2000b, 36–40) as well as in the West (Van der Meer, 112–22). The idea that women should be separated from the sacra as far as possible is also echoed in other medieval prohibitions, such as touching the altar clothes or the Eucharistic vessels.

There were, however, always women to whom special permits were granted for practical reasons. During the first Christian millennium in particular, the Syrian and the Byzantine deaconess was permitted access to the sanctuary. What she was allowed to do there or not remained a matter of dispute. The canonical answers incorporated into the *West Syrian Synodicon* give a good impression of how the issue was negotiated in detail. Despite certain cases addressed in the *Synodicon*, in principle, deaconesses were prohibited from entering the sanctuary if a priest were present in the monastery (*Synodicon*, Art. 33: ed. Vööbus, 1: 203). According to this source, she might nonetheless serve the priest by mixing wine and water with extra permission from the bishop (Art. 38). She is also permitted to place the incense (Art. 34) and to wash the sacred vessels (Art. 35).

The same collection gives further evidence that "normal" nuns were at least occasionally allowed to step in for the disabled deaconess (Arts. 38, 39). This gave way to the deaconess's fading from history over the second millennium, with many of her former duties routinely taken over by nuns. Their natural gender notwithstanding, religious women, according to medieval gender perceptions, did not count so much as "women" as "worldly" wives and mothers, which apparently enabled them to gain access to the sacra more easily than laywomen. This was even more so when the question of ritual purity came to the fore, since the same authors who viewed menstruation and childbirth as a source of ritual impurity (see below) also held that sexual abstinence be required of all married couples before communion and even more of clerics serving at the altar (Frassetto 1998). So in terms of ritual (im)purity, religious women were comparatively well regarded due to their asexual way of life. While the meaning of "total abstinence" for male clerics remained a subject of debate between Eastern and Western Church authorities, it was evident that a nun was allowed no sexual relations at all. But gender separation also seems to have worked in favor of monastic women, who, as a rule, were allowed a more active part in the liturgy in general than was accessible to laywomen in normal parish life. As usual, local differences must be taken into consideration in certain particular cases.

The same seems all the more true for the nonmonastic context. Although Syrian canon law definitely favors female choirs (Harvey) and some Greek and Latin Church Fathers at least had no principal objections against choirs of virgins, the Council of Auxerre (578) forbade these as well (Mansi, 9: 913). Some Fathers, like Cyril of Jerusalem (d. 386 or 387), extended the biblical commandments of keeping silence during the assembly of the Christian community and restraint from teaching (1 Cor. 14. 34–35 and 1 Tim. 2. 11–12) in a way, that even saying prayers aloud was considered inappropriate for a woman (Cyril, *Procatechesis*, 14).

While the prohibitions against preaching, singing, or even praying aloud are evidently linked to biblical heritage, the analogous link between the Old Testament menstruation taboo and prohibitions against entering the sanctuary and for serving at the altar is less obvious (Synek 2000b). For a relatively long time, the taboo itself was disputed. An illustrative example of this situation is the author of the *Testamentum Domini*, who, though aware of the theological weakness of the idea of ritual impurity due to menstruation, nonetheless gave in, stating that a bleeding woman may indeed enter a church, but must not approach the altar—"not because she would be impure, but as a question of honoring the altar" (ch. 1. 42: ed. Rahmani, 100). The author of the *Didascalia* more logically deemed abstinence from the sacra and ritual washing for the menstruating woman (also after sexual intercourse and male pollution) "foolish observances" (*Didascalia*, 26: ed. Vööbus, 2: 245). His position was reconfirmed by the *Apostolic Constitutions*. But more or less at the same time, Bishop Dionysius (the Great) of Alexandria (d. c.264) and his successor, Timothy (d. 385), took the opposite stance and categorically prohibited a woman to approach the sacra during her menses—an opinion that won out in the Byzantine canonical collections (see Can. 2 of Dionysius, which originally formed part of a longer canonical epistle and the *Canonical Answers of Timothy of Alexandria*, nos. 6 and 7). As a rule, therefore, Eastern canon law does not permit a menstruating woman (nor a woman who has given birth until being "purified" after a forty-day period) to partake in Holy Communion or to be baptized.

For the West, the decisive moment came when Gregory the Great spoke against a general Communion prohibition in his *Canonical Answers to Augustine* within the context of Roman missionary activities among the Anglo-Saxons (Bede, *Hist. Eccl.* 1: 27). According to Gregory, a menstruating woman wishing to receive Holy Communion should be allowed to do so, but one who would refrain out of respect is considered praiseworthy. However, other sources as manuals for confessors, in particular, indicate that such "restraint" was imposed also by Western ecclesiastical authorities at times, though not as generally as in the East (Lutterbach).

The whole discussion must be seen within the broader context of "institutionalization" and "sacralization," which were common features of Late Antique and Early Medieval

Christianity. In this multifold process, Christian re-reading of Old Testament purity requirements and cultic prescriptions favored women's exclusion from the sanctuary while menstruating and after childbirth. However, it did not necessarily lead to a full exclusion from ecclesiastical ministries or to a general exclusion from the sanctuary, as we have seen above. To what extent the menstrual taboo contributed to the disappearance of female ministers from the historical scene is an open question. In the fourteenth century, the Byzantine canonist Mathew Blastares (fl. 1335) took it as an argument, but that signifies little in regard to real historical development.

See also Celibacy; Convents; Double Monasteries; *Frauenfrage*; Law, Women in, Anglo-Saxon England; Marriage; *Mulieres Sanctae*; Norse Women; *Periculoso*; Prostitution; Rules for Canonesses, Nuns, and Recluses; Syrian-Christian Women; Teachers, Women as; Virginity; Widows

BIBLIOGRAPHY

Primary Sources

Ambrosiaster. *Corpus Scriptorum Ecclesiasticorum Latinorum*, vol. 81: 1–3. Edited by Heinrich J. Vogels, Vienna: Hoelder-Pichler-Tempsky, 1966–1969.

Apostolic Constitutions/Les constitutions apostoliques. Edition and French translation by Marcel Metzger. Sources Chrétiennes, vols. 329, 329, and 336. Paris: Éditions du Cerf, 1985–1987.

Bede, the Venerable. *Historia Ecclesiastica*. Edited and translated by Bertram Colgrave and R. A. B. Mynors. Oxford Medieval Texts. Oxford: Oxford University Press, 1969. Reprint with historical commentary by J. M. Wallace-Hadrill, 1988.

Blastares, Matthew. *Syntagma*. In *Patrologia Graeca*, edited J.-P. Migne, 140: 960–1400.

Botte, Bernard. *Liturgiewissenschaftliche Quellen und Forschungen*, vol. 39. Münster: Aschendorffsche Verlagsbuchhandlung, 5th ed. 1989.

The Canons of the Council in Trullo. The Council in Trullo Revisited. Edited by George Nedungatt and Michael Featherstone, 41–186. Kanonika, 6. Rome: Pontificio Istituto Orientale, 1995.

Cyril of Jerusalem. *Procatechesis*. In *Patrologia Graeca*, 33: 353–66.

Concilia Africae A. 345-A. 525. Edited by Charles Munier. *Corpus Christianorum, Series Latina* [=CCSL], 259 (recte: 149). Turnhout, Belgium: Brepols, 1974.

Concilia Galliae A. 314-A. 506. Edited by Charles Munier. CCSL, 148. Turnhout: Brepols, 1963.

Concilia Galliae A. 511-A.695. Edited by Charles de Clercq. CCSL, 149. Turnhout: Brepols, 1964.

Corpus Iuris Civilis. 3 vols. Edited by Theodor Mommsen et al. Dublin and Zürich: Weidmann, 1970–1973.

Corpus juris canonici. Edited by E. Richter. Revised by Emil Friedberg. 2 vols. Leipzig, Germany: Tauchnitz, 1879. Reprint Graz, Austria: Akademische Druck und Verlaganstalt, 1955.

The Didascalia Apostolorum in Syriac. Edition and translation by Arthur Vööbus. *Corpus Scriptorum Christianorum Orientalium* [= CSCO]. Scriptores Syri, 175, 176, 179, and 180. Louvain, 1979.

East Syrian Baptismal Order/Die nestorianische Taufliturgie. German translation by Gustav Diettrich. Giessen, Germany: Ricker, 1903.

Firmilian, *Letter to Cyprian*. In Sancti Cypriani Episcopi Epistularium. Edited By G. F. Diercks, 581–604. CCSL, 3C. Turnhout: Brepols, 1996.

Gregory of Nazianzus. *Oratio 37*. In *Patrologia Graeca*, 36: 270–308.

Pseudo-Hippolytus. *So-called Canons*. In *Patrologia Orientalis*, 31.

———. *The Canons of Hippolytus*. Grove Liturgical Study, 50. Edited by Paul F. Bradshaw. English translation by Carol Bebawi. Bramcote, Nottingham, U.K.: Grove Books, 1987.

Mansi, Johannes D. *Sacrorum Conciliorum nova et amplissima collectio*. Florence: Antonio Zatta, 1759–1798. Reprint 54 vols. in 59. Graz, Austria: Akademische Druck, 1960–1961.

Nikodemos Hagiorites. *Pedalion: ton Orthodoxon Ekklesias etoi hapantes hoi hieroi kai theioi kanones* [. . . .]. Athens: Papademetriou, 1957.

————. *The Rudder* (Pedalion) *of the Metaphorical Ship of the Holy Catholic and Apostolic Church of the Orthodox Christians, or, All the Sacred and Divine Canons.* Translated by Denver Cummings. Chicago: Orthodox Christian Educational Society, 1957.

Rhallis, Gregorios, and Michael Potlis, eds. *Syntagma ton theion kai hieron kanonon,* 6 vols. Athens: Typographia G. Charotphylakos, 1852–1859. Reprint Kassandra M. Grigoris, 1966.

The Synodicon in the West Syrian Tradition I–II. Edited and translated by Arthur Vööbus. CSCO, 367–68, 375–76. Scriptores Syri, 161–64. Louvain: CSCO, 1975–1976.

Tertullian. *De baptismo/Traité du baptême.* Edition and French translation by R. F. Refoulé and M. Drouzy. Sources Chretiénnes, vol. 35. Paris: Éditions du Cerf, 1952.

Testamentum Domini Nostri Jesu Christi. Edition and Latin translation by Ignatius E. Rahmani. Mainz, Germany: Franz Kirchheim, 1899.

Thomas Aquinas. *Sancti Thomae de Aquino Opera Omnia.* Rome: Leonine Commission; Paris: J. Vrin, 1882–. [Authoritative, ongoing ed.].

————. [*Summa Theologica,* 90–97]. *Treatise on Law.* Translated with introduction by Richard Regan. Indianapolis, Ind.: Hackett, 2000.

Traditio Apostolica/La Tradition apostolique de Saint Hippolyte. Essai de reconstruction by Bernard Botte. Liturgiewissenschaftliche Quellen und Forschungen, vol. 39. 5th ed. Münster: Aschendorffsche Verlagsbuchhandlung, 1989.

Secondary Sources

Arjava, Antti. *Women and Law in Late Antiquity.* Oxford: Clarendon Press: 1996.

Beaucamp, Joëlle. *Le Statut de la femme à Byzance, 4e–7e siècles.* 2 vols. Travaux et mémoires du Centre de recherche d'histoire et civilisation de Byzance, 5–6. Paris: De Boccard, 1990.

Berger, Teresa, and Albert Gerhards, eds. *Liturgie und Frauenfrage: Ein Beitrag zur Frauenforschung aus liturgiewissenschaftlicher Sicht.* Pietas liturgica, 7. St. Ottilien: EOS, 1990.

Brock, Sebastian P. "Deaconesses in the Syriac Tradition." In *Woman in Prism and Focus: Her Profile in Major World Religions and Christian Traditions,* edited by Prasanna Vazheeparampil, 205–18. Rome: Mar Thomas Yogam, 1996.

Brundage, James A. *Law, Sex and Society in Medieval Europe.* Chicago: University of Chicago Press, 1987.

————. *Medieval Canon Law.* The Medieval World. London and New York: Longman, 1995.

Eisen, Ute E. *Amtsträgerinnen im frühen Christentum. Epigraphische und literarische Studien.* Forschungen zur Kirchen- und Dogmengeschichte, 61. Göttingen, Germany: Vandenhoeck & Ruprecht, 1996.

Forzieri Vannucchi, Olga. "La risoluzione de matrimonio nel IV–V secolo. Legislazione e pensiero della Chiesa." *AMAT "La Colombaria"* 50 (1985): 65–172.

Frassetto, Michael. *Medieval Purity and Piety: Essays on Medieval Clerical Celibacy and Religious Reform.* Garland Medieval Casebooks, 19. New York: Garland, 1998.

Gillmann, Franz. "Weibliche Kleriker nach dem Urteil der Frühscholastik." *Archiv für Kirchenrecht* 93 (1913): 239–53.

Gryson, Roger. *Le Ministère des femmes dans l'Église ancienne.* Recherches et synthèses: histoire, 4. Gembloux, France: Duculot, 1972.

Harvey, Susan Ashbrook. "Women's Service in Ancient Syriac Christianity. Mother, Nun, Deaconess." In *Images of Women according to Eastern Canon Law* [= Kanon 16], edited by Carl G. Fürst and Richard Potz, 226–41. Egling, Germany: Kovar, 2000.

Jensen, Anne. *Gottes selbstbewußte Töchter. Frauenemanzipation im frühen Christentum?* Theologische Frauenforschung in Europa, 9. 2nd ed. Münster: Lit, 2003.

Katerelos, Evangelos. *Die Auflösung der Ehe bei Demetrios Chomatianos und Johannes Apokaukos: ein Beitrag zu byzantinischen Rechtsgeschichte des 13. Jahrhunderts.* Europäische Hochschulschriften, 23. Theology, 450. Frankfurt: Peter Lang, 1992.

Konidaris, Ioannis M. "Die Rechtsstellung monastisch lebender Frauen unter besonderer Berücksichtigung der Unterschiede zwischen Nonnen und Mönchen." In *Images of Women,* 131–43. *See above under* Harvey.

Le Bras, Gabriel, ed. *Histoire du droit et des institutions de l'Église en Occident.* Paris: Sirey, 1955–. [Some vols. have yet to appear].

L'Huillier, Peter. *The Church of the Ancient Councils. The Disciplinary Work of the First Four Ecumenical Councils*. Crestwood, N.Y.: St. Vladimir's Seminary Press, 1996.

Lutterbach, Hubertus. *Sexualität im Mittelalter: eine Kulturstudie anhand von Bußbüchern des 6. bis 12. Jahrhunderts*. Beihefte zum Archiv für Kulturgeschichte, vol. 43, Cologne, Germany: Böhlau, 1999.

Makowski, Elizabeth. *Canon Law and Cloistered Women. Periculoso and Its Commentators 1298–1545*. Studies in Medieval and Early Modern Canon Law, 5. Washington, D.C.: Catholic University Press of America, 1997.

Menuge, Noël James, ed. *Medieval Women and the Law*. Woodbridge, Suffolk, U.K.: Boydell Press, 2000.

Metz, René. *La Femme et l'enfant dans le droit canonique médiéval*. Reprint London: Variorum, 1985. [Collected articles published elsewhere 1951–1976].

Mitchell, Linda E. "Women and Medieval Canon Law." In *Women in Medieval Western European Culture*, edited by L. Mitchell, 143–55. Garland Reference Library of the Humanities, 2007. New York and London: Garland, 1999. [Concise general overview].

Müller, Daniela. *Vir caput mulieris. Zur Stellung der Frau im Kirchenrecht unter besonderer Berücksichtigung des 12. und 13. Jahrhundert. Vom mittelalterlichen Recht zur neuzeitlichen Rechtswissenschaft. Bedingungen, Wege und Probleme europäischer Rechtsgeschichte. Festschrift W. Trusen*. Edited by Norbert Brieskorn et al., 223–45. Rechts- und staatswissenschaftliche Veröffentlichungen der Görres-Gesellschaft, n.s., 72. Paderborn, Germany: Schöningh, 1994.

Osborne, Kenan B. *Lay Ministry in the Roman Catholic Church: Its History and Theology*. New York: Paulist Press, 1993.

Pitsakis, Constantin. *Clergé marié et célibat dans la legislation du Concile in Trullo: le point de de vue oriental/ The Council in Trullo Revisited*. Edited by George Nedungatt and Michael Featherstone, 263–306. Kanonika, 6. Rome: Pontificio Istituto Orientale, 1995.

Raming, Ida. *The Exclusion of Women from the Priesthood: Divine Laws or Sex Discrimination? A Historical Investigation of the Juridical and Doctrinal Foundations of the Code of Canon Law, Canon 968, 1*. Translated by Norman R. Adams. Preface by Arlene and Leonard Swidler. Metuchen, N.J.: Scarecrow Press, 1976. Original *Der Ausschluß der Frau vom priesterlichen Amt. Gottgewollte Tradition oder Diskriminierung?*[…]. Cologne: Böhlau, 1973.

Schäfer, K. H. "Kanonissen und Diakonissen." *Römische Quartalschrift* 24 (1910): 49–80.

Synek, Eva M. "Christliche Badekultur." In *Alltägliches Altertum*, edited by Edith Specht, 227–50. Frankfurt: Peter Lang, 1998.

———. "'Ex utroque sexu fidelium tres ordines'—The Status of Women in Early Medieval Canon Law." *Gender & History* 12 (2000): 595–621. Reprint in *Gendering the Middle Ages. A Gender and History Special Issue*, 65–91. Oxford: Oxford University Press, 2001.

———. "In der Kirche möge sie schweigen." *Oriens Christianus* 77 (1993): 151–64.

———. *Oikos. Zum Ehe- und Familienrecht der Apostolischen Konstitutionen*. Kirche und Recht, 22. Vienna: Plöchl, 1999.

———. "The Church as "oikos": Main Canonical Consequences." *Gender and Religion/Genre et religion*, edited by Karin E. Børresen, Sara Cabibbo, and Edith Specht, 143–53. Quaderni, 2. Rome: Carocci, 2001.

———. (2000b). "Zur Rezeption alttestamentlicher Reinheitsvorschriften ins Orthodoxe Kirchenrecht." In *Mother, Nun, Deaconess*, 25–70. See above under Harvey.

Theodorou, Evangelos. "I 'cheirotonia,' i 'cheirothesia' ton diakonisson" [The "Ordination," the "Consecration" of the Deaconess]. *Theologia* 25 (1954): 430–69, 576-601; 26 (1955): 57–76.

Ulrich, A. "Die Kanonissen: Ein vergangener und vergessener Stand der Kirche." *In Liturgie und Frauenfrage*, 184–94. See above under Berger.

Van der Meer, Haye. *Priestertum der Frau? Eine theologiegeschichtliche Untersuchung*. Quaestiones disputatae, 42. Freiburg: Herder, 1969.

Ysebaert, Joseph. "The Deaconesses in the Western Church of Late Antiquity and Their Origin." In *Evlogia. Mélanges offerts à Antoon A. R. Bastiensen*, edited by G. J. M. Bartelink et al., 421–36. Instrumenta Patristica, 24. Streenbrugis, Netherlands: Abbatia S. Petri; The Hague: Nijhoff, 1991.

EVA MARIA SYNEK

LAW, SALIC. *See* **Salic Law**

LAW, WOMEN IN, ANGLO-SAXON ENGLAND. Many of the law codes issued by Anglo-Saxon kings from the seventh to the eleventh centuries contain references to women, most commonly in connection with marriage customs, inheritance rights, and compensation for sexual and other crimes. The majority of such provisions occur in the seventh-century laws of Æthelberht of Kent, the ninth-century laws of Alfred (appended to which are the seventh-century laws of Ine of Wessex), and the eleventh-century laws of Cnut. These are supplemented by anonymous codes such as the late Old English text, *On the Betrothal of a Woman*, and by charters, place-names, and records of case law. The standard edition of the Anglo-Saxon laws is by Liebermann and includes variant readings from all extant manuscripts. Attenborough and Robertson provide editions with facing translations. The standard translation is by Whitelock.

Unfortunately, the sources offer many difficulties of interpretation. The early laws in particular are expressed very cryptically, and much of the vocabulary is now obscure. Further problems are presented by the mixture of old and new in the extant codes, since it is not always clear which clauses represent established custom and which were issued to cope with a changing situation or to modify existing procedures. The codes themselves are selective rather than comprehensive, and contain conflicting instructions that would have made them difficult to apply in a court of law. Wormald and others have suggested that their main purpose was political, designed to enhance the status of the king as law-giver, and that the information they contain may not be wholly reliable.

So far as women are concerned, the main emphasis in the earliest Anglo-Saxon laws is on monetary regulations for marriage and sexual relationships. Several clauses (here cited by number in parentheses) within Æthelberht's code deal with financial penalties for sexual relations with slaves, the amount of compensation being determined according to the class of slave and the rank of owner (10, 11, 14, 16). A man who committed adultery with the wife of a freeman was to provide another wife in her place in addition to paying the appropriate *wergild* (31), while compensation for adultery with the wife of an *esne* ([?] a hired laborer) is assessed at double an unspecified amount (85). Abduction of an unmarried girl is rated at fifty shillings in addition to payment of the usual bride price (82), and in aggravated circumstances a further twenty shillings were due (83). The earliest reference to a marriage contract in English occurs within a sequence of clauses discussing the payment to be made by the prospective bridegroom, the arrangements for annulling the agreement in the case of fraud, and the woman's inheritance rights in the event of being widowed (77–81). One of these clauses (79) alludes to the widow's right to custody of her children, a theme that recurs in the second series of Kentish laws (Hlothhere and Eadric 6) and in the West Saxon laws of Ine (38). A widow who remarried might lose custody as well as forfeit part of her inheritance from her first husband (Æthelberht 80), and this provision, like many others, is paralleled in continental Germanic legislation. *On the Betrothal of a Woman*, 4 states that a widow was entitled to half the joint property, and to all if she had borne a child, unless she married again; similar provisions occur in surviving wills. Several clauses in late Anglo-Saxon codes stipulate that widows were to remain unmarried for a year and then to be allowed a free choice of action (V Æthelred 21;

VI Æthelred 26; II Cnut 73); but the very fact that it was necessary repeatedly to legislate against widows being forced into remarriage suggests that in practice they may have been subject to coercion.

A number of laws specify penalties for crimes against women: manslaughter of a pregnant woman in Alfred 9, rape of an underage girl in Alfred 26, assault on a nun in Alfred 18, attack on a nun or widow in VI Æthelred 39, assault on a widow or girl in II Cnut 52, and so on. Taken together, these testify to a concern on the part of successive legislators to protect the more vulnerable members of society. However, it is rarely clear whether compensation for offences against a woman was paid directly to her or to one of her male relatives. An exception is Alfred 11, which identifies the woman herself as the recipient of compensation for sexual attack, and in the event that intercourse has taken place, allows her to bring oath-helpers to testify to her previous virginity and entitlement to maximum compensation. According to Alfred 8, the fine for removing a nun from her minster (monastery church) was to be divided between the king and the bishop, but it is uncertain whether this law deals with abduction or with a situation where the nun was a willing party.

An important point to emerge from the extant codes is that women were separately accountable under the law and had independent property rights, even after marriage. Æthelberht 73 stipulates that a free woman *locbore* (variously interpreted as "with long hair," or "in charge of the keys," or "able to be party to a contract") is to pay compensation of thirty shillings for an unspecified offense, variously interpreted as sexual, financial, or violent. Æthelberht 74 assesses the compensation payable by (or possibly to) an unmarried woman at the same rate as a free man. One of the harshest Anglo-Saxon laws is II Cnut 73, which stipulates that an adulterous wife is to lose her nose and ears and forfeit all her property to her husband. Even this, however, shows that a married woman possessed her own property distinct from that of her husband. Most strikingly, several laws make it clear that a woman was not necessarily implicated in a crime committed by her husband. Wihtred 12 stipulates that a man who makes offerings to devils without his wife's knowledge is to forfeit all his possessions, whereas if they both take part in the offence, both are to forfeit all their possessions. Ine 7 states that a man who steals without the knowledge of his wife and family is to pay a fine of sixty shillings; whereas if he steals with their knowledge, they are all to go into slavery. Ine 57 holds a woman partly responsible for her husband's theft of cattle only if she has eaten the stolen meat, and it allows her to clear herself on oath from such a charge. Both here and in VI Æthelstan 1, which similarly allows a woman to be dissociated from her husband's crime, her share of the joint property is defined as a third. II Cnut 76 states that a woman is not implicated by stolen goods brought home by her husband unless they are under her own lock and key, and it defines her areas of responsibility as the storeroom, chest, and coffer.

It has often been noted that the legal status of women appears to have been significantly higher in Anglo-Saxon times than during the later Middle Ages. Early scholars such as Buckstaff regarded the Norman Conquest as the turning point that led to a loss of independence, but in recent years Stafford and others have pointed to evidence of continuity between women's rights before and after 1066.

See also Dower; Dowry; Law, Canon, Women in; Marriage; Norse Women; Rape; Widows

BIBLIOGRAPHY

Primary Sources

Attenborough, F. L., ed. *The Laws of the Earliest English Kings.* Cambridge: Cambridge University Press, 1922.

Liebermann, Felix, ed. *Die Gesetze der Angelsachsen.* 3 vols. Halle, Germany: Max Niemeyer, 1903–1916.

Robertson, A. J., ed. *The Laws of the Kings of England from Edmund to Henry I.* Cambridge: Cambridge University Press, 1925.

Whitelock, Dorothy, ed. *English Historical Documents c.500–1042.* 2nd ed. London: Eyre Methuen, 1979.

Wormald, Patrick. "A Handlist of Anglo-Saxon Lawsuits." *Anglo-Saxon England* 17 (1988): 247–81.

Secondary Sources

Buckstaff, Florence Griswold. "Married Women's Property in Anglo-Saxon and Anglo-Norman Law and the Origin of the Common-Law Dower." *Annals of the American Academy of Political and Social Science* 4 (1894): 233–64.

Fell, Christine E. "A *Friwif Locbore* Revisited." *Anglo-Saxon England* 13 (1984): 157–65.

———, Cecily Clark, and Elizabeth Williams. *Women in Anglo-Saxon England and the Impact of 1066.* London: British Museum, 1984.

Hough, Carole. "A New Reading of Alfred, ch. 26." *Nottingham Medieval Studies* 41 (1997): 1–12.

———. "A Reappraisal of Æthelberht 84." *Nottingham Medieval Studies* 37 (1993): 1–6.

———. "Alfred's *Domboc* and the Language of Rape: A Reconsideration of Alfred, ch. 11." *Medium Ævum* 66 (1997): 1–27.

———. "The Early Kentish 'Divorce Laws': A Reconsideration of Æthelberht, chs. 79 and 80." *Anglo-Saxon England* 23 (1994): 19–34.

———. "Place-Name Evidence Relating to the Interpretation of Old English Legal Terminology." *Leeds Studies in English* 27 (1996): 19–48.

———. "The Widow's *Mund* in Æthelberht 75 and 76." *Journal of English and Germanic Philology* 98 (1999): 1–16.

———. "Two Kentish Laws Concerning Women: A New Reading of Æthelberht 73 and 74." *Anglia* 119 (2001): 554–78.

Klinck, Anne L. "Anglo-Saxon Women and the Law." *Journal of Medieval History* 8 (1982): 107–21.

Richards, Mary P., and B. Jane Stanfield. "Concepts of Anglo-Saxon Women in the Laws." In *New Readings on Women in Old English Literature,* edited by Helen Damico and Alexandra Hennessey Olsen, 89–99. Bloomington and Indianapolis: Indiana University Press, 1990.

Rivers, Theodore John. "Widows' Rights in Anglo-Saxon Law." *American Journal of Legal History* 19 (1975): 208–15.

———. "Adultery in Early Anglo-Saxon Society: Æthelberht 31 in Comparison with Continental Germanic Law." *Anglo-Saxon England* 20 (1991): 19–25.

Stafford, Pauline. "Women and the Norman Conquest." *Transactions of the Royal Historical Society* 6th series 4 (1994): 221–49.

———. "Women in Domesday." *Reading Medieval Studies* 15 (1989): 75–94.

Stenton, Doris Mary. *The English Woman in History.* London: George Allen & Unwin, 1957. Ch. 1: "The Anglo-Saxon Woman." 1–28.

Wormald, Patrick. "*Lex Scripta* and *Verbum Regis*: Legislation and Germanic Kingship, from Euric to Cnut." In *Early Medieval Kingship,* edited by P. H. Sawyer and I. N. Wood, 105–38. Leeds: School of History, University of Leeds, 1977.

CAROLE HOUGH

LAXDŒLA SAGA (c.1245). One of the most important Icelandic family sagas (*Íslendingasögur*), the *Saga of the Laxdœlir* was written in Old Norse and, some scholars believe, by a woman. Although some of the early Icelandic saga compilers are known to us by name, the identities of authors of what we now call "Icelandic family sagas" are now lost. This loss is particularly poignant considering that these are the sagas usually considered to be of highest interest to us today because of their anticipatory literary form—they are, in essence, early novels—their subtleness of characterization and their elegant plot development.

Although the authors of the family sagas are unknown, the environment that fostered all of early Icelandic saga-writing is not. Many writers of sagas and histories, including Snorri Sturluson (1178/9–1241), were sent at an early age to the early Icelandic church schools (most prominently, those associated with the monasteries at Oddi and Haukadal, at first, for men; later followed by the cloisters at Kirkjubær and Stadr, for women) for their education. These schools differed from their Continental counterparts in many ways, but perhaps most significantly in that the clerical authorities in charge of the men's schools were not celibate. The kinswomen of these men—wives, daughters, sisters—seem to have exerted a not inconsiderable influence on the students at these schools. From the attributions at the beginnings of various kings' sagas by Snorri Sturluson and others, in which these women are acknowledged as sources, it becomes apparent that there may have been two courses of study at these schools: a Latin education taught by men and a (probably unofficial) vernacular one, involving traditional and historical native lore taught by women. Thus the original, preliterary, authors of all the sagas we have can be said, in one sense, to be women, regardless of who finally put the material together and wrote it down.

However, there is one prominent Icelandic family saga marked by internal evidence as an extremely likely candidate for actual female authorship: *Laxdœla saga*, the saga of the inhabitants of the Lax River Valley. Unfolding over some two centuries, in the general region known as Breiðafjörður, particularly in the "Dales district," or Dalir, the story begins with the plight of a Norwegian chieftain, Ketill flatnefr (Ketill "Flat-nose"), forced to flee his homeland on the accession of King Harald hárfagri (Harald "Fair-hair") Halfdanarson in c.872. After Ketill dies in Scotland, his two sons, Bjorn and Helgi, and daughter, Unnr, settle in Iceland. The saga then recounts their descendants' adventures—especially their feuds—as the peace characterizing Unnr's regime disintegrates into conflict and bloodshed over ensuing generations. Set against this backdrop, the life and love affairs of a woman, Guðrún Ósvifrsdóttir, then forms the main theme.

The unique centrality and unusually sympathetic presentation of *Laxdœla*'s diverse array of female characters, as well as the sophisticated treatment of the saga's complex motivational structure—largely based on thwarted love and jealousy—have inclined modern researchers to suggest female authorship, rather than a male author such as Óláfr Þorðarson (d. 1259). The case becomes yet stronger when the saga is compared to its related saga, *Njáls saga* (the *Saga of Burnt Njal*), with which it shares some characters and situations. *Njáls saga* at least equals *Laxdœla* in literary sophistication, but *Njáls saga*'s female characters are stereotypes: they are either maleficent (Hallgerdr), or docile homemakers (Bergthora), while others are not even named (Njal's daughters; in contrast to his sons, who are not only named but more fully portrayed). In addition, *Njáls saga* glorifies the code of the warrior somewhat beyond what was the norm in the family sagas. *Laxdœla saga*, however, depicts a number of individually realized nonstandard female characters, including an indomitable woman warrior (and possible lesbian), "neither beautiful nor industrious," but eminently likable (Bróka-Audr = "Audr in breeches") and Guðrún, a willful beauty who changes husbands whenever it pleases her, admitting in the end: "Theim var ek verst, er ek unna mest" ("I was the worst to him I loved most"). Although she is Audr's enemy, Guðrún is portrayed with equanimity. As for the warrior's code, it is more parodied than revered in *Laxdœla saga*, as is demonstrated, for instance, by the stylish revenge Audr enacts, for her honor's sake, on her former husband. Finally, mother and foster mother figures are accorded more honor and demonstrative love by the other characters in the saga (as in Olaf Peacock's treatment of his mother, Melkorka, and her old nurse, for instance) than is common in the other family sagas; yet another reflection of a feminine worldview.

See also Jóreiðr Hermundardóttir í Midjumdal; Jórunn skáldmær; Norse Women; Scribes and Scriptoria; *Skáldkonur* (Old Norse-Icelandic Women Poets); Steinunn Refsdóttir

BIBLIOGRAPHY

Primary Sources
Laxdœla saga. Edited by Einar Ólafur Sveinsson. Íslenzk fornrit, 5. Reykjavík: Hid íslenzka fornritafélag, 1934.
The Laxdœla Saga. Translated by Margaret A. Arendt. Seattle: University of Washington Press; New York: American Scandinavian Foundation, 1964.
Laxdæla Saga. Translated by Magnus Magnusson and Hermann Pálsson. Harmondsworth, Middlesex, U.K.: Penguin Books, 1969. Reprint 1973.

Secondary Sources
Conroy, Patricia, and T. C. S. Langen. "*Laxdœla saga*: Theme and Structure." *Arkiv för nordisk filologi* 100 (1988): 118–41.
Dronke, Ursula. "Narrative Insight in *Laxdœla saga*." In *J. R. R. Tolkien, Scholar and Storyteller: Essays in Memoriam*, edited by Mary Salu and Robert T. Farrell, 120–37. Ithaca, N.Y. and London: Cornell University Press, 1979.
Kellogg, Robert. "Sex and the Vernacular in Medieval Iceland." *Proceedings of the First International Saga Conference, Edinburgh, 1971*, edited by Peter Foote, Hermann Pálsson, and Desmond Slay, 244–58. London: Viking Society, 1973.
Kress, Helga. "Ekki hofu vér kvennaskap: Nokkrar laustengdar athuganir um karlmennsku og kvenhatur í Njalu." *Sjötiu ritgerdar helgadar Jakobi Benediktssyni.* 1: 293–313. Reykjavík: Stofnun Árna Magnussonar, 1977.
Mundal, Else. "Women in Sagas." In *Medieval Scandinavia: An Encyclopedia*, edited by Phillip Pulsiano et al., 723–25. Garland Encyclopedias of the Middle Ages, 1. Garland Reference Library of the Humanities, 934. New York and London: Garland, 1993.
Mundt, Marina. "Kvinnens forhold til ekteskapet i Njáls saga." *Edda* 76 (1976): 17–25.
Tómasson, Sverrir. "*Laxdœla saga*." In *Medieval Scandinavia: An Encyclopedia*, edited by Phillip Pulsiano et al., 387–88. *See above under* Mundal, Else.

SANDRA BALLIF STRAUBHAAR

LE FÈVRE DE RESSONS, JEAN (c.1320–after 1380). Best known for his influential translations of moral works against and for women, Jean Le Fèvre—not to be confused with either his contemporary, the bishop of Chartres and jurist Jean Le Fèvre, or the later author, Jean Le Fèvre de Saint-Rémy (1396–c.1470)—was a *procureur* (attorney, justice) in the Parlement du Roi (King's parliament) at Paris. He was born in Ressons-sur-le-Matz in northern France. Based on the apparent dates of his poetry, particularly the *Respit de la Mort*, modern scholars A. G. Van Hamel and Geneviève Hasenohr place his birthdate at c.1320–1326. Even though his works display a solid knowledge of fourteenth-century civil, canon, and common law, his success in legal practice seems to have been minimal, as court records show his involvement in only seven cases between 1364 and 1375. This may have been the reason for the respectable poverty cultivated in his literary persona.

Le Fèvre's poems also reveal that he limped, and that he, like Socrates and—closer to home—Matheolus, whose work Le Fèvre would translate, had unfortunately married a shrew. A life-threatening illness on October 9, 1376, inspired Le Fèvre's *Respit de la Mort* (*Respite from Death*). According to Hasenohr's findings, he later composed his most influential work, the translation of Matheolus's *Lamentations* (*Laments* [*against Women*]) and its palinode, or rebuttal, *Le Livre de Leesce*, in the 1380s. Lacking further evidence, the chronology of these three poems remains conjectural, as does the date of the poet's death.

Seven of Jean Le Fèvre's works are extant. He began his career as a translator of Latin didactic works, including the *Theodolet*, a French reworking into decasyllabic couplets of the Latin-hexameter *Ecloga Theoduli* (*Eclogue of Theodulus*). The *Theodolet* was an example of the mysterious late-Latin works whose true authors often remain unknown while medieval schoolbooks found them useful as teaching aids for both style and moral content. This particular work is a pastoral moralizing poem attributed to Theodulus (ninth century). Le Fèvre's *Theodolet* pits Pseustis, a pagan shepherd from Athens, against Alithia, a Christian shepherdess who refutes the moral value of Pseustis's myths with examples from the Old Testament.

Another of Le Fèvre's early translation efforts was the *Disticha Catonis* (*Cato's Distichs*), attributed to the famous Roman statesman-censor Cato the Elder (234–149 B.C.E.) and even more acclaimed as a didactic work than the *Ecloga Theoduli*, which it sometimes accompanies in compilations. Le Fèvre replaced its Latin distichs (two-hexameter-line-verse units) with quatrains of decasyllabic couplets. He also translated a popular pseudo-Ovidian poem (in the manner of the famous Latin poet of love, Ovid [43 B.C.E.–c.17 C.E.]), the *Vetula* (*Old Woman*), into octosyllabic couplets with a prose prologue. The work describes Ovid's conversion from lechery to learning. Scholars also credit Le Fèvre with a French translation of the Latin hymns of the liturgy, found in Paris, Bibliothèque nationale de France MS fr. 964, and perhaps even the first *Danse macabre* (*Dance of Death*) (Hasenohr 1969, 1992).

The most famous of Le Fèvre's works is his translation/adaptation of Matheolus's *Lamentationes*, a 5,614-verse misogynous diatribe against marriage. Matheolus, the Latin diminutive for Mathieu or Maheu, was an unfrocked cleric from Boulogne, northern France (c.1298). His misogynistic persona was bolstered by his nickname, "Mathieu le Bigame" ("Mathew the Bigamist"). The four-book Latin poem describes marriage as an ordeal to prepare husbands for Paradise and contains a bold dream sequence in which Matheolus confronts God. Le Fèvre ensured the work's popularity by making, as scholar Gaston Paris put it, the "French verse clearer than the original." Le Fèvre made effective use of the long-winded and learned rhetorical technique known as *amplificatio* in his 9,842 octosyllables, since, to medieval readers, greater length meant greater authority. Most importantly, he gave the Latin poem a French flavor, imbuing it with the tone and techniques of the *fabliaux* (a thirteenth- to fourteenth-century collection of irreverent, often lewd tales) and enhancing its appeal by the comic use of proverbs.

Disturbed by the success of his translation of Matheolus's poem against women, Le Fèvre composed a personal legalistic rejoinder to all the embittered misogynist's arguments and evidence. This palinode, his *Livre de Leesce* (*Book of Joy* [*from Women*]), which is 3,391 octosyllabic verses in length, prefigures the antimisogynistic polemics and defenses of women by Christine de Pizan (c.1365–1430) and Martin Le Franc (c.1410–1461).

His remaining work, the *Respit de la Mort*—another original poem intertwining legalese with penitential discourse (death = debt)—is a 3,760 octosyllabic verse description of the poet's fictive appeal to the royal chancellery (= God) for a reprieve. As a debtor, owing his life to God, who is a merciful creditor, he pleads for a respite to mend his ways, deploying his abundant philosophical and legal knowledge. The anonymous early fifteenth-century *Règles de la Seconde Rhétorique* (*Rules for the Second Rhetoric* [i.e., for vernacular literature]) praises Le Fèvre's poems and literary technique.

See also Christine de Pizan; Le Franc, Martin; *Miroir de Mariage* (*Mirror of Marriage*); *Response du Bestiaire*; *Roman de la Rose*, Debate of the

BIBLIOGRAPHY

Primary Sources
Le Fèvre, Jean. [*Disticha Catonis* trans.] J. Ulrich, ed. "Die Übersetzungen der *Disticha des Pseudo-Cato.*" *Romanische Forschungen* 15 (1903): 41–149.
———. *Les Lamentations de Matheolus et Le Livre de Leesce de Jehan Le Fèvre de Ressons.* Edited by A.-G. Van Hamel. Bibliothèque de l'École des Hautes Études, 95: 1–2. Paris: E. Bouillon, 1892–1905.
———. *Le Respit de la Mort par Jean Le Fèvre.* Edited by Geneviève Hasenohr-Esnos. SATF. Paris: A. & J. Picard, 1969.
———. *La Vieille ou les dernières Amours d'Ovide, poème français du XIVe siècle traduit du latin de Richard de Fournival par Jean Lefèvre.* Edited by Hippolyte Cocheris. Paris: Aubry, 1861.
Règles de la Seconde Rhétorique. In *Recueil d'arts de Seconde Rhétorique*, edited by Ernest Langlois, 13. Paris: Imprimerie nationale, 1902.

Secondary Sources
Blumenfeld-Kosinski, Renate. "Jean Le Fèvre's *Livre de Leesce*: Praise or Blame of Women?" *Speculum* 69 (1994): 705–25.
Guglielminetti, Marziano. "Jean Le Fèvre et Machiavel: Matheolus et Belphegor." In *L'Aube de la Renaissance*, edited by Dario Cecchetti, Lionello Sozzi, and L. Terreaux, 225–32. Geneva: Slatkine, 1991.
Hamilton, George L. "*Theodulus*, a Medieval Textbook." *Modern Philology* 7 (1909–1910): 169–85.
Hasenohr, Geneviève. "Jean Le Fèvre." In *Dictionnaire des lettres françaises: Le Moyen Âge*, revised ed. by G. Hasenohr and Michel Zink, 802–4. Paris: Fayard/Livre de Poche, 1992.
———. "La Locution figée dans l'oeuvre de Jean Le Fèvre." *Le Moyen Français* 14–15 (1984): 229–81.
Heywood, Melinda Marsh. "Lady Philosophy and La Vieille: Old Women, Aging Bodies, and Female Authority in Late Medieval French Literature (Boethius, Guillaume de Lorris, Jean de Meun, Jean Le Fèvre, Christine de Pizan)." Ph.D. diss., University of Pennsylvania, 1997.
Pratt, Karen. "The Strains of Defense: The Many Voices of Jean Le Fèvre's *Livre de Leesce*." In *Gender in Debate from the Early Middle Ages to the Renaissance*, edited by Thelma S. Fenster and Clare A. Lees, 113–33. New York: Palgrave Macmillan, 2003.
———. "Translating Misogamy: The Authority of the Intertext in the *Lamentaciones Matheoli* and Its Middle French Translation by Jean Le Fèvre." *Forum for Modern Language Studies* 35 (1999): 421–35.
Ruhe, Ernstpeter. *Untersuchungen zu den altfranzösischen übersetzungen der Disticha Catonis.* Beiträge zur romanischen Philologie des Mittelalters, 2. Munich: Hueber, 1968.

Young, M. Joy. *Portraits of Woman: Virtue, Vice and Marriage in Christine de Pizan's* Cité des Dames. *Matheolus's* Lamentations *and Lefèvre's* Livre de Leesce. Washington, D.C.: Catholic University of America Press, 1992.

STEVEN M. TAYLOR

LE FRANC, MARTIN (c.1410–1461). Martin Le Franc, the author of *Le Champion des Dames* (*The Ladies' Champion*), an important defense of women, was born c.1410 in Aumale, Normandy (France). He studied at Paris with the brilliant but unprincipled Thomas de Courcelles—which is rather ironic since, while Thomas was one of Joan of Arc's most zealous prosecutors at her trial, his pupil would later help to exonerate her in his *Champion*. Le Franc earned his master's degree (thus becoming *maître-ès-arts*) and took religious orders. His works attest to his presence at the Treaty of Arras, northern France, in 1435 and at the Council of Bâle, or Basel (Switzerland) in 1431–1449, perhaps in the entourage of Amadeus VIII, count of Savoy. During the struggle reprising the Schism of the Church (1378–1418), which again produced two popes, the Council of Basel named Amadeus VIII anti-pope, under the name Felix V (1439–1449). Felix V appointed Le Franc papal secretary and protonotary apostolic, a member of the college of notaries attached to the papal court. On May 6, 1443, Felix V named him a canon of the cathedral of Lausanne (Switzerland). In September 1443, Le Franc was named provost of the Lausanne chapter and given the prebend (income-producing domain) of Dammartin. In October 1444, Felix V made him a canon of Torino (Italy) and in 1447, canon of Geneva. Later that year, Felix V made Le Franc apostolic legate (papal envoy) to the court of Philip, duke of Burgundy. Le Franc's signature is found on Felix V's renunciation of the papacy on April 7, 1449, at Lausanne. The legitimate pope, Nicholas V, subsequently reconfirmed Le Franc's appointments. Upon the death of Count Amadeus VIII in 1451, his son, Louis I of Savoy, made Le Franc his master of appeals, a post he filled from 1451 until 1459. In 1459, he was named abbot of the monastery of Novalese, Italy. He died in 1461 in Rome.

Martin Le Franc's earliest extant writings are two Latin epistles, composed c.1435, in which he claims that eloquence is the foundation of human civilization. Another Latin text, still unedited, is a dialogue on death between Le Franc and one "Johannes," who might be Jean Servion, the recipient of Le Franc's later translation of the prologue of the Old Testament Book of Jeremiah.

Le Franc's most important work, *Le Champion des Dames* (1440–1442), is a lengthy refutation of Jean de Meun's misogynous indictments of women in his continuation (c.1280) of Guillaume de Lorris's *Roman de la Rose* (c.1235) and possibly also Alain Chartier's *Belle Dame sans Merci* (1424). Le Franc's five-book allegory is composed of 24,336 octosyllabic verses grouped in octaves, each following the rhyme scheme abab-babc. In each book, Franc Vouloir (Free Will), the "champion" or defender of women's honor, refutes the attacks of one of Male Bouche (Evil Speech)'s henchmen; Male Bouche is a key negative character from Jean de Meun's *Rose*. Le Franc offers a veritable pantheon of famous virtuous women from the Bible and classical sources, adding contemporary individuals such as Christine de Pizan and Jeanne d'Arc (Joan of Arc). He rehabilitates infamous women including Cleopatra and Pope Joan by stressing their virtues and blaming their vices on male turpitude. His basic contention is that women are a source of all good unless corrupted by man. However, the *Champion des Dames* was coolly received, prompting Le Franc to compose a poetic rejoinder, the "Complainte du livre du *Champion des Dames* a maistre Martin Le Franc son acteur" ("Complaint of the Book of the *Ladies' Champion* to its Author, Master Martin Le Franc"), a witty 480-verse dialogue between the poem and its author, composed of sixty octaves (rhyme scheme: ababbcbc).

Martin Le Franc's other major work, *L'Estrif de Fortune et de Vertu* (*Strife* [*Debate*] *between Fortune and Virtue*, 1447–1448), is a *prosimetrum*—a work combining prose and verse sections—in the tradition of the sixth-century philosopher Boethius's popular *Consolatio Philosophiae* (*Consolation of Philosophy*). The work was suggested to Le Franc by Philip, duke of Burgundy. Probably also inspired by the great fourteenth-century Florentine poet Petrarch's *De remediis utriusque fortunae* (*Remedies for Good or Bad Fortune*), the *Estrif* features a debate between Lady Virtue and Lady Fortune. Twenty-three inserted poems, gleaned from such outstanding lyric-philosophical poets as Charles d'Orléans (1394–1465), reiterate the major prose arguments and demonstrate Le Franc's poetic skill. Modern scholar Oskar Roth credits Le Franc for introducing early Italian-humanistic ideas into France through this work.

See also *Belle Dame Sans Merci*; Christine de Pizan; Joan of Arc, St.; Joan, Pope; Le Fèvre de Ressons, Jean; *Roman de la Rose*, Debate of the

BIBLIOGRAPHY

Primary Sources
Le Franc, Martin. *Le Champion des Dames*. Edited by Robert Deschaux. 5 vols. Classiques Français du Moyen Âge, 127–31. Paris: Honoré Champion, 1999.
———. *L'Estrif de Fortune et Vertu*. Edited with notes and introduction by Peter F. Dembowski. Textes Littéraires Français, 513. Geneva: Droz, 1999.
Guillaume de Lorris and Jean de Meun, *Le Roman de la Rose*. Edited with notes and introduction by Félix Lecoy, vols. 1–3. SATF 92, 95, 98. Paris: Honoré Champion, 1976–1982.

Secondary Sources
Barbey, Léon. *Martin Le Franc, prévôt de Lausanne et avocat de l' amour et de la dame au XVᵉ siècle*. Fribourg, Switzerland: Éditions Universitaires, 1985.
Bidler, Rose M. "Les Locutions en Moyen Français. Martin Le Franc: Deux éditions récentes." *Le Moyen Français* 48 (2001): 147–250.
Dembowski, Peter F. "Martin Le Franc, Fortune, Virtue, and Fifteenth-Century France." In *Continuations: Essays on Medieval French Literature and Language in Honor of John L. Grigsby*, edited by Norris J. Lacy and Gloria Torrini-Roblin, 261–76. Birmingham, Ala.: Summa, 1989.
DuBruck, Edelgard E. "Pope Joan: Another Look upon Martin Le Franc's Papesse Jeanne (c.1440) and Dietrich Schernberg's Play *Frau Jutta* (1480)." *Fifteenth-Century Studies* 26 (2001): 75–85.
Gros, Gérard. "Le Livre du prince et le clerc: édition, diffusion et réception d'une œuvre (Martin le Franc lecteur de Charles d'Orléans)." *Travaux de Littérature (TraLit)* 14 (2001): 43–58.
Merkle, Gertrude H. "Martin Le Franc's Commentary on Jean Gerson's Treatise on Joan of Arc." In *Fresh Verdicts on Joan of Arc*, edited by Bonnie Wheeler and Charles T. Wood, 177–88. New York: Garland, 1996.
Martin, Robert, "Sur quelques passages difficiles du *Champion des Dames* de Martin Le Franc. Notes lexicographiques." *Revue de Linguistique Romane* 58.229–30 (Jan–June 1994): 143–52.
Merrilees, Brian. "Words in Favour of Women." *Florilegium* 18.1 (2001[2002]): 21–30.
Piaget, Arthur. *Martin Le Franc, prévot de Lausanne*. Lausanne: Payot, 1888. Reprint Caen, France: Paradigme, 1993.
Roth, Oskar. "Martin Le Franc et le 'De remediis' de Pétrarque." *Studi Francesi* 15 (1971): 401–19.
———. *Studien zum "Estrif de Fortune et Vertu" des Martin Le Franc*. Berne: Herbert Lang, 1970.

Taylor, Steven M. "Martin Le Franc's Rehabilitation of Notorious Women: The Case of Pope Joan." *Fifteenth-Century Studies* 19 (1992): 261–78.

———. "Le Procès de la sorcellerie chez Martin Le Franc: *Le Champion des Dames*, livre IV." *Wodan* 4.3 (spring 1994): 203–12.

Williams, Harry F., and Sylvie Lefèvre. "Martin Le Franc." In *Dictionnaire des lettres françaises: Le Moyen Âge*, new revised ed. by Geneviève Hasenohr and Michel Zink, 997–98. Paris: Fayard/ Livre de Poche, 1992.

———. "Structural Aspects of *Le Champion des Dames*." *Fifteenth-Century Studies* 11 (1985): 149–61.

Steven M. Taylor

LEOBA (700–780). Known also as Lioba, Leobgytha, and Leobgyda (= "beloved"), Leoba was an Anglo-Saxon nun who helped lead the illustrious St. Boniface Mission, renowned for their courageous efforts at converting northern Germany to Christianity. She not only read and taught widely but also composed religious poetry. Boniface testified that the Anglo-Saxon nuns who accompanied him to the Continent were avid readers and talented writers. Partly thanks to them we have a complete biography of Leoba composed by Rudolf of Fulda at the request of the famed abbot of Fulda, Rabanus Maurus (c.780–856). Because it was written after her death, her *vita* (life) drew from the written sources of those who knew her, especially four of her disciples with her in Germany: Agatha, Thecla, Nana, and Eoloba. Otloh of St. Emmeram (c.1010–c.1070) also mentioned her in his life of St. Boniface, composed for the monks at Fulda.

Leoba was born in Wessex, the daughter of an elderly couple who had given up the idea of having a child. Her mother, however, is said to have dreamed that in her bosom she bore a church bell, "which, upon being drawn out with her hand, rang merrily." An old nurse serving her mother interpreted the dream as the birth of a daughter. Indeed, the child Trutgeba, affectionately nicknamed Leoba, was born. The parents had her dedicated to God and when she became sufficiently grown, her mother sent her to the double monastery at Wimborne. There Mother Tetta trained her in the sacred sciences. Taking no pleasure in jests and romances, Leoba diligently studied the Scriptures. Whatever words she heard she committed to memory and put to practice. She ate sparingly, prayed continually, and worked with her hands. Loved by all the sisters, she imitated the good features of each. One night she dreamed that a purple thread came from her and there was no end to it, as if it were coming from her bowels. She had the dream interpreted by one of the old nuns as if it happened to one of her disciples. When the nun heard the story, she divined with ease the name Leoba as the person who had experienced the dream, and told her that with her knowledge she would instruct many people. Indeed, it was to Tetta that Boniface applied to send him Leoba as part of his mission to Germany (Bavaria, Frisia, Hesse, and Thuringia) and there set up a monastery for girls. Also, in a letter she herself wrote to St. Boniface (c.732), to whom she was related on his mother's side, Leoba stated that she had learned her poetry from Abbess Eadburga at the abbey of Thanet, who had her memorize divine laws in the forms of verses, and that she would now like to learn from him how to write better Latin and perfect her "little talents" (Letter 21, trans. Emerton) since Boniface's skill at Latin metrics was also well known.

Born in Wessex himself as Wynfrith, the future St. Boniface (c.675–754) was educated at the monastery at Exeter where he later became abbot. After an unsuccessful attempt to convert the Frisians in 716, Wynfrith was named Boniface by Pope Gregory II in 718–719 and ordered to try again. Boniface assisted St. Willibrord (658–739) in Frisia with far better results and then himself converted the Hessians. After summoning Boniface to return to Rome to ordain him bishop, Gregory again commissioned Boniface to organize an ecclesiastical settlement east of the Rhine in 732. Boniface was touched by Leoba's eager letter, and when Tetta obligingly sent her to him, he received Leoba very warmly and made her abbess of Tauberbischofsheim, a sizable double monastery, while other sisters ran abbeys and schools in other areas, for example: Thecla at Kitzingen, then Ochsenfurt, while Berthgyth and Chunihildt taught in Thuringia.

Intelligent, clever, and ambitious, she was most patient and universal in her charity. Rudolf, like most hagiographers (authors/compilers of saints' lives), emphasized her best qualities, stating outright his aim to celebrate her holiness, learnedness, and power by recounting the abovementioned omens of her holy destiny and a number of exemplary anecdotes from her career. Thus, for example, "one did not hear a bad word from Leoba's lips." She knew the Old and New Testaments, "the writings of the Church Fathers, the decrees of the church councils, and the whole ecclesiastical law." So enthusiastic about the Scriptures was she that she had the younger nuns read it to her while she was asleep. Whenever they skipped a word, she woke up and corrected them. There was also the case of a poor, crippled girl who would come begging for alms every day at the monastery. At one point, after committing fornication and then murdering the resulting child, she placed it in the water in a pool by the river flowing through the monastery. A local secular woman coming to fetch water found the corpse and spread the rumor accusing one of the nuns of the evil act (which Clarissa Atkinson rightly perceives as evidence of resentment, or at least suspicion, of the nuns by the surrounding community). When this reached Leoba's ears, she noted that one of the nuns had in fact been absent that day. When the nun, Agatha, returned, she refuted the accusation (she claimed to have been summoned home by her parents) and prayed to God to reveal the name "of the person who has committed the misdeed." Ordering the nuns to stand "in the form of a cross until each one of them sang the psalter," and then to process within the cloister three times a day, Leoba was certain that the Lord would hear them. Indeed, before the third procession, the wretched crippled girl gave up and confessed her sin. What is striking here to modern readers is how, for the nuns and Rudolf's readership, the public spectacle of the guilty woman's confession outweighed her private tragedy (they also feared their well's pollution by the baby's corpse). Rudolf was more interested in the larger drama of Leoba's miraculous wresting of the truth from falsehood to save her convent's reputation (Atkinson). And, as Rudolf assures us, Leoba performed many other deeds that endeared her to the people.

Her wisdom and diligent efficiency entranced Boniface as well. He promoted her to being his partner in the mission's affairs and trusted her implicitly, as reflected in his letters. He made her pledge that she would not abandon her adopted country, gave her his cowl, and promised her that her bones should be placed next to his in the tomb, so that they should await the day of Resurrection together. After Boniface's murder by some Frisians in 754, his relics (remains) were transported to Fulda. Leoba went frequently to Fulda to pray; the only woman admitted because "holy Boniface ordered that she be buried with him." She often frequented the palace of the future emperor Charlemagne (c.742–814), having been summoned by Queen Hiltigart. She also visited other monasteries, exhorting the nuns toward perfection. In old age, at the advice of Bishop Lull, she went to Scoranesheim, four miles south of Mainz, where she died in September 782, having taken the viaticum (Holy Communion given to those nearing death) from the English priest, Torhthat. Her body was transported to Fulda, but instead of being buried with Boniface, she was laid to rest on the north side of the altar.

See also Berthgyth; Boniface, St., Mission and Circle of; Bugga; Double Monasteries; Epistolary Authors, Women as; Scribes and Scriptoria

BIBLIOGRAPHY

Primary Sources

Boniface, St., and Bishop Lull. [Letters]. *Die Briefe des heilgen Bonifatius und Lullus.* Edited by Michael Tangl, 139–140. *Monumenta Germaniae Historica* (= MGH): *Epistolae Selectae*, 10. 2nd ed. Berlin: Weidmann, 1955. [Latin text only].

———. *The Letters of St. Boniface.* Translated by Ephraim Emerton. Records of Civilization, 31. New York: Columbia University Press, 1940. Reprint New York: Octagon, 1973. [Also contains Leoba's famous letter to him].

———. *The English Correspondence of Saint Boniface.* Translated by Edward Kylie. New York: Cooper Square, 1966.

Leoba. [Letters: (29) from her to Boniface; (96) from Boniface to her; (67) Boniface to Leoba, Tecla and Cynehilda]. In *Briefe des Bonifatius, Willibalde Leben des Bonifatius, nebst einigen zeitgenössischen Dokumenten,* edited by Reinhold Rau, 102–4; 318–21; 206–9, resp. Darmstadt, Germany: Wissenschaftliche Buchgesellschaft, 1968.

———. [Letter to Boniface, excerpted from Emerton's trans., *see above under* Boniface]. In *Women and Writing in Medieval Europe: A Sourcebook,* edited by Carolyne Larrington, 196–97. London and New York: Routledge, 1995.

Otloh of St. Emmeram. *Vitae Sancti Bonifatii.* Edited by Wilhelm Levison, 137. MGH. *Scriptores rerum germanicarum in usum scolarum.* Hannover and Leipzig, Germany: Hahn, 1905.

Rudolf of Fulda. *Leben des heiligen Bonifazius von Willlibald, der heilige Leoba.* Edited by Wilhelm Arndt et al., 121ff. 2nd ed. Leipzig: Dyksche Buchhandlung, 1883.

———. "The Life of Saint Leoba by Rudolf, Monk of Fulda." In *Anglo-Saxon Missionaries in Germany.* Edited and translated by Charles H. Talbot. London: Sheed & Ward, 1954. Reprint in *Medieval Women's Visionary Literature,* edited by Elizabeth Alvida Petroff, 106–14. New York and Oxford: Oxford University Press, 1986.

Secondary Sources

Atkinson, Clarissa. *The Oldest Vocation: Christian Motherhood in the Middle Ages.* Ithaca, N.Y.: Cornell University Press, 1991.

McLaughlin, Eleanor. "Women, Power, and Pursuit of Holiness." In *Women of Spirit: Female Leadership in the Jewish and Christian Traditions,* edited by Rosemary Reuther and Eleanor McLaughlin, 103–20. New York: Simon & Schuster, 1979.

McNamara, Jo Ann, and Suzanne Wemple. "Sanctity and Power." In *Becoming Visible: Women in European Society,* edited by Renata Bridenthal and Claudia Koonz, 90–118. 2nd ed. Boston: Houghton Mifflin, 1987.

Petroff, Elizabeth Alvida, ed. *Medieval Women's Visionary Literature.* New York and Oxford, 1986. [Useful commentary to above-cited translation].

Ranft, Patricia. *Women and Religious Life in Premodern Europe.* New York: St. Martin's, 1996.

SUZANNE FONAY WEMPLE

LEONOR LÓPEZ DE CÓRDOBA (1362/3–c.1412). The author of the first autobiography in Spanish literature, Leonor López de Córdoba was born in a period of political crisis. The fratricidal struggle between Pedro I "the Cruel" of Castile (1334–1369) and the future Enrique II "the Magnificent" (1333–1379) claimed Leonor's family as victims when she was a small child. This early descent from wealth and prominence into disgrace established the cyclical pattern of rise and fall that would characterize much of Leonor's life. We know of her fortunes and misfortunes from her own account: her *Memorias* (*Memoirs*) are the first extant autobiographical work by a writer of either gender in medieval Spain, and thus constitute a milestone. Further, when considered within a sociohistorical document, certain details of her memoirs attest to the autonomy of Spanish noblewomen at this time.

Leonor was the daughter of Martín López de Córdoba and Sancha Carrillo, nobles connected to King Pedro both politically and by blood. Sancha died when her daughter was very young, which may account for Leonor's marriage at age seven to the very wealthy Ruy Gutiérrez de Henestrosa. After their marriage, the young couple went to live with the king's daughters at Carmona, in southwestern Spain. When Pedro was murdered by his illegitimate half-brother Enrique in 1369, Leonor's father withdrew to Carmona to protect the princesses. The city would not be taken by force, but by treachery. Enrique agreed to two conditions: Carmona would be surrendered to him if he guaranteed safe passage of Pedro's daughters to England, and if he pardoned Martín López's family and accepted their allegiance. He fulfilled only the first condition. Martín López was seized and publicly beheaded in Seville; his entire family and household were stripped of their possessions and thrown into the Atarazanas prison.

From this period onward, Leonor's life, as represented in the *Memorias*, would be marked by tremendous losses and her struggle to overcome them. Plague decimated the family during their imprisonment. Leonor's description of the death of her thirteen-year-old brother reflects unmistakably her devastation and bitterness. When the family was finally released after King Enrique's death in 1379, only Leonor and her husband remained alive.

Enrique's will stipulated that the family's estates be restored, but this was not fulfilled. Consequently, Leonor was taken in by an aunt, while her husband disappeared for seven years, searching in vain for his lost fortune. On the return of her impoverished husband, the couple lodged in houses next to the aunt's in Córdoba. But each day, Leonor recalls, they suffered the indignity of having to return to her aunt's house for meals: her poverty was a public spectacle. She had also to endure the ill will of her cousins, jealous of their mother's favor toward Leonor.

Desperate for support, Leonor turned to the Virgin Mary. The *Memorias* contain numerous instances in which she documents the number of days and prayers she hopes will elicit the Virgin's aid; in fact, at the beginning of her work, Leonor presents herself as an example of one who commended her heart to the Virgin and was duly consoled and aided by Her. Leonor's first thirty-day invocation to the Virgin seems to end in failure: her prayers for a private entrance into her aunt's house are thwarted by conniving servants, the worst of whom is later silenced—either figuratively or literally—by Leonor's hands. But soon thereafter, a dream-vision of an arch opening into a flower-strewn expanse reveals to her that the Virgin will truly provide her with a house of her own. After seventeen years with her aunt, Leonor at last happens upon the very site shown to her in her dream; the aunt buys her the land, and Leonor proudly builds her home "by the labor of my own hands." All figurative language aside, this event offers a noteworthy example of a fourteenth-century noblewoman's financial autonomy, her right to own property and build on it (Kaminsky 1984).

Also in her account, Leonor believes that God has helped her because she took in a Jewish boy orphaned in the pogroms of 1391–1392. But her charity in adopting this boy, Alonso, is rewarded by bad fortune. Around the year 1400, plague strikes Córdoba, and Leonor seeks refuge for herself and her small children in Santa Ella, where Alonso, now an adult, resides. Her aunt and cousins follow her and displace Leonor's family from the best house in town. Meanwhile the plague ravages relentlessly: both families move on to Aguilar, where they are joined by Alonso, who is now infected. Despite her cousins' protests, Leonor's loyalty to her adopted son echoes that of her father's in protecting the slain King Pedro's daughters. Despite her good deeds, Leonor believes she must also answer for her sins: "and because of my sins, thirteen people, who watched over him that night, all died." Finally, there is no one else left to care for the ailing Alonso but Leonor's eldest son, a boy of twelve years. Ever practical, Leonor prays that if any more must die, let it be this boy, Juan, for he is sickly anyway. Juan indeed sickens and dies that night, while Alonso survives. More disgrace follows: Leonor's angry cousins, having attempted to eject her dying son, succeed in sending Leonor back to Córdoba. She leaves tearfully; her final words to her aunt show her patent despair: "Lady, may God not save me if I have deserved this."

The *Memorias* end with Leonor in disgrace. However, we know from contemporary historians that she was to rise once more to prominence before her final decline. As of 1406, she was installed at the royal court as principal advisor and favorite of Queen Catalina (Catherine) of Lancaster, granddaughter of Pedro I, leading the author of the *Crónicas de los reyes de Castilla* (*Chronicles of the Kings of Castile*) to write disdainfully of her influence on Castilian politics. At least one modern critic has examined possible lesbian overtones in Leonor's and Catalina's relationship and Leonor's friendships with other women (Hutcheson). Other critics have taken a more neutral stance, observing that, both as a child and as an adult, she lived in "what was essentially a gynocracy" because far more women than men govern her life, whether they are nobles or even servants (Kaminsky 1984; Ayerbe-Chaux). In any case, by 1412 Leonor had begun her last downward turn: she was displaced by another favorite, banished from court, and forbidden to return on pain of being burned alive.

The history of the *Memorias*' critical reception seems to share a similar cycle of disgrace and favor. While they were known and studied in the late nineteenth century, it was not until the1970s and 1980s that they received extensive critical attention. Unfortunately, such a surge in interest and enthusiasm can sometimes provoke a critical backlash, particularly in the case of noncanonical literature by women. Initially touted as new and exciting, the work also attracted insidious criticism: Leonor as author was judged as historically unreliable, subjective, incoherent, and finally, "garrulous, and inconsequential." Recent assessments, however, focus on previously unappreciated aspects of the *Memorias*: their unifying images and themes of loyalty, loss and death, vindication, the home and family, and Leonor's relationship with the divine. Analyses of the work's style, structure, autobiographical nature, and audience—her ability to "create a feminine space" (Mirrer)—continue to promote perspectives useful in evaluating other medieval works. Finally, the *Memorias* stand out as one of the few extant records of a woman who writes on her own authority and who speaks as a witness to historical events, whether as victor or victim.

See also Christine de Pizan; Comnena, Anna; Dower; Dowry; Lesbians in the Middle Ages; Mary, Blessed Virgin, in the Middle Ages; Murasaki Shikibu; Perpetua, St.

BIBLIOGRAPHY

Primary Sources
Crónicas de los reyes de Castilla. Edited by Cayetano Rosell. Biblioteca de Autores Españoles, 68. Madrid: Real Academia Española, 1953.
Leonor López de Córdoba. "Las memorias de Doña Leonor López de Córdoba." Edited by Reinaldo Ayerbe-Chaux. *Journal of Hispanic Philology* 2 (1977): 11–33. [Spanish text with critical and historical commentary].
———. "To Restore Honor and Fortune: 'The Autobiography of Leonor López de Córdoba.'" Translation and commentary by Amy Katz Kaminsky and Elaine Dorough Johnson. In *The Female Autograph*, edited by Domna C. Stanton, 70–80. Chicago and London: University of Chicago Press, 1984. [Complete English text].
———. [*Memorias*] "Autobiografía." In *Water Lilies/Flores del agua; An Anthology of Spanish Women Writers from the Fifteenth through the Nineteenth Centuries*, edited and translated by Amy Katz Kaminsky. Minneapolis: University of Minnesota Pres, 1996. [Bilingual (Old-Spanish and English) text].

Secondary Sources
Deyermond, Alan. "Las autoras medievales castellanas a la luz de las últimas investigaciones." In *Medioevo y literatura: Actas del V Congreso de la Asociación Hispánica de Literatura Medieval*, edited by Juan Paredes, 1: 31–52. Granada: Universidad de Granada, 1995.
———. "Spain's First Women Writers." In *Women in Hispanic Literature: Icons and Fallen Idols*, edited by Beth Miller, 27–52. Berkeley: University of California Press, 1983.
Estow, Clara. "Leonor López de Córdoba: Portrait of a Medieval Courtier." *Fifteenth-Century Studies* 5 (1982): 23–46.
Firpo, Arturo Roberto. "L'Idéologie du lignage et les images de la famille dans les *Memorias* de Leonor López de Córdoba." *Le Moyen Âge* 87 (1981): 243–62.
———. "Un ejemplo de autobiografia medieval: Las 'Memorias' de Leonor López de Córdoba (1400)." *Zagadnienia Rodzajów Literackich* 23 (1980): 19–31.
Ghassemi, Ruth Lubenow. "La 'crueldad' de los vencidos: Un estudio interpretativo de *Memorias de doña Leonor López, de Córdoba.*" *La Corónica* 18 (1989): 19–32.
Hutcheson, Gregory S. "Leonor López de Córdoba and the Configuration of Female-Female Desire." In *Same Sex Love and Desire among Women in the Middle Ages*, edited by Francesca C. Sautman and Pamela Sheingorn. The New Middle Ages. New York: Palgrave Macmillan, 2001.
Lauzardo, Aurora. "El derecho a la escrita: Las *Memorias* de Leonor López de Córdoba." *Medievalia* 15 (1993): 1–13.
Marimón Llorca, Carmen. *Prosistas castellanas medievales.* Alicante, Spain: Caja de Ahorros Provincial, 1990.
Mirrer, Louise. *Women, Jews, and Muslims in the Texts of Reconquest Castile.* Ann Arbor: University of Michigan Press, 1996.
Rivera Garretas, María-Milagros. *Textos y espacios de mujeres (EUROPA siglos IV–XV).* Barcelona: Icaria, 1990.
Suelzer, Amy. "The Intersection of Public and Private Life in Leonor López de Córdoba's Autobiography." *Revista Monográfica* 9 (1993): 36–46.

DENISE-RENÉE BARBERET

LESBIANS IN THE MIDDLE AGES. The word "lesbian," used to describe women whose primary erotic and emotional relationships are formed with other women, is of recent origin. It was unknown in the Middle Ages, as was the very notion of a self-conscious sexual identity or sexual preference. It can be used, however, as a convenient term for discussing medieval ideas and attitudes about women whose primary relationships, whether erotic, emotional, or perhaps even social, were with other women. There is very little evidence for the existence of lesbians in the Middle Ages and indeed, very little discussion of the possibility in the male-authored texts that survive from the period. However rare or invisible such women might actually have been, in the sources lesbians were generally either ignored or condemned according to the same strictures that prohibited male homosexuality, a phenomenon that received far more discussion from both medieval observers and modern scholars.

The foundation for medieval attitudes toward lesbians was the condemnation by St. Paul in his Epistle to the Romans 1: 26 of male and female homosexuality. Following the Apostle's lead, patristic writers such as Augustine (354–430) and John Chrysostom (c.347–407) also forbade female homoerotic activity. The patristic prohibitions made their way into the early penitentials, which prohibited sex acts between women, although generally they were viewed as less serious than sex acts between men. The *Penitential of Theodore* (attributed to Theodore of Tarsus [c.602–690]) provided penances for female/female sex acts and female masturbation. It also provided harsher penalties for a married woman than for a nun or girl who participated in such activities. The *Penitential of Bede* (c.700) condemned nuns who engaged in sexual relations using "an instrument" with other nuns. The harsher penalty in this canon appears to refer to the use of devices rather than to the religious status of the women.

The use of instruments such as dildoes, which replicated the penis, elicited harsher penalties from authorities than less specific sexual activities between women. Given the medieval phallocentric view of human sexuality, male authorities had difficulty conceiving of sexual activity in the absence of a penis and an active male participant. This may be one reason why lesbian sexual activity escaped notice and severe censure until the high Middle Ages. In the thirteenth century, in his *Summa Theologiae*, Thomas Aquinas (c.1225–1274) included both male and female homosexuality in the category of sodomy, which included other "unnatural acts" such as bestiality, masturbation, male homosexuality, and nonstandard heterosexual coital positions. This had two significant results. First, lesbian sexual activity was elided under the rubric of male homosexuality, rendering it even more invisible. Second, given the evaluation as sodomitical, lesbian sex acts were henceforth liable to the harshest legal penalties.

Despite the fact that lesbian sex acts came to be viewed as criminal and as serious as male homosexual acts, generally medieval secular law tended to ignore it. One notable exception is the French *Livres de jostice et de plet* (*Book of Justice and Litigation*, c.1260), which explicitly discussed sex between women, recommending that male and female homosexuality receive equivalent punishments. Perhaps because the prevailing social organization did not allow women to establish stable relationships and households outside the patriarchal family, secular laws and courts generally continued to ignore female/female sexual relations. Furthermore, lesbian sex neither challenged the patriarchal family nor threatened its need for stability and the legitimacy of heirs. This may help to account for the relative absence of discussions about lesbians in the sources.

On the rare occasions that lesbian sexual activity entered the sphere of the secular courts, such infractions were harshly punished. Some evidence suggests that prosecutors distinguished between the active "male" partner and the passive "female." The active woman received a much harsher sentence, usually death, while the passive woman was treated more leniently. So, too, secular courts harshly punished women who fashioned dildoes in an effort to replicate heterosexual intercourse. The apparent usurpation of male sexual prerogative, which in turn might threaten patriarchal social organization, appears to have been the foundation for such penalties, rather that lesbian sexual activity per se.

In medical writing, in contrast with theological and legal sources, lesbians were discussed in a slightly different way. Based on the writings of ancient Greek authorities and their Arabic translators and commentators, some medieval medical texts seem to admit the possibility of women who were "virile" and preferred to have sexual relations with other women. Such women were alleged to display other typically "masculine" characteristics such as intelligence, as well as being "masculine" in voice and bearing. Other treatises, influenced by astrology, discuss the possibility that women who were born under certain masculine configurations of the stars would prefer sexual relations with other women. Thus, in some medical treatises, there is the suggestion of something akin to an alternate sexual preference for women.

In light of the prevailing norms and sex-segregated social organization of medieval society, women had many opportunities to experience the company of other women. In village society, women frequently worked together in the fields and had the time and opportunity to develop their personal relationships. There is at least one case, cited in a fifteenth-century French royal register, in which two village women who worked together in the fields were charged with having sexual relations. Some of the lyrics of the women troubadours, in particular those of Bietris (or Bieris) de Romans, suggest something of the romantic relationships that might have developed between women in the higher ranks of courtly society.

The most obvious female communities in medieval Europe were convents. These religious communities allowed women to live in an almost exclusively female environment and to form intimate and long-term relationships with other women. The potential danger of lesbian sexual acts and homoaffective relationships was recognized very early. Writers of rules for nuns, from St. Augustine in the fifth century onwards, incorporated requirements that lights were to burn all night in the dormitories and that nuns should be modest and avoid nudity. Furthermore, they forbade "particular friendships," especially between older and younger nuns, a prohibition that suggests an awareness of the potential for homoaffective or homoerotic relationships within the exclusively female world of the convent.

Although convent life could have provided ready opportunity for relationships between women, and although nuns represented virtually the only literate group of women who could leave a record of their thoughts and emotions, there is remarkably little evidence attesting to relationships between these women. Significantly, there survives a love poem written by a twelfth-century nun, lamenting the absence of another woman. A letter between two nuns from the same period bespeaks a depth of emotion and passion that could be characterized as erotic love. Most of the epistolary evidence emanating from nuns and beguines, the two groups of literate women who lived in predominately female communities, is more opaque. Many, such as the writings of the mystic Hildegard of Bingen (1098–1179) and the beguine Hadewijch (c. 1260), suggest intense emotional relationships with other women. How these women understood their relationships and whether they encompassed an erotic or sexual dimension, however, remains problematic.

Alongside legal or prescriptive texts and the literature written by women, there is some evidence in male-authored sources that suggests an understanding of the possibility of sexual relationships between women. For example, in his *Livre des Manières* (*Book of Manners*), Étienne de Fougères (d. 1178), bishop of Rennes and chaplain to Henry II of England, included a description of sex acts between two women that, while assigning male and female roles, nevertheless, suggested mutual satisfaction, in stark contrast to the phallocentric view of human sexuality that prevailed in medieval thought.

As with all aspects of human emotions in the Middle Ages, research into the relationships between women remains fraught with difficulties. The scarcity of sources for the study of women remains a significant problem and those female-authored texts that have survived need to be reexamined and reinterpreted with an eye to the relationships hidden within them. The definition of sexual identity also remains problematic, especially for a period that discouraged all genital sexual activity—homosexual and heterosexual. Women's relationships need to be examined in a nuanced fashion encompassing emotional, erotic, and social bonds, even if genital sexual expression is absent or invisible.

Despite a growing body of research, there is still very little information available about lesbians in the Middle Ages. Most of the sources are male-authored and proscriptive; the evidence remains textual. Little is known of the women whose lives may be hidden behind this textual screen.

See also Bietris de Roman; Hadewijch; Hildegard of Bingen, St.; Law, Canon, Women in; Penitentials, Women in; Transvestism; Virginity

BIBLIOGRAPHY

Primary Sources
Bietris de Romans. In *Songs of the Women Troubadours*, edited and translated by Matilda Tomaryn Bruckner, Laurie Shepard, and Sarah White, 32–33. New York and London: Garland, 1995. Revised ed., 2000.

Étienne de Fougères. *Le Livre des Manières*. Edited by R. Anthony Lodge. Textes Littéraires Français, 275. Geneva: Droz, 1979.

Livres de justice et de plet. Edited by Henri Klimrath and Louis-Nicolas Rapetti. Glossary by P. Chabaille. Documents inédits sur l'Histoire de France: série I: Histoire politique. Paris: Firmin Didot, 1850.

Thomas Aquinas, St. *Summa Theologiae*. [Many editions and translations, notably the so-called "Blackfriars' *Summa*," with English trans., 60 vols. London, 1964–81].

Secondary Sources
Brooten, Bernadette J. "Paul's View on the Nature of Women and Female Homoeroticism." In *Immaculate and Powerful: The Female in Sacred Image and Social Reality*, edited by Clarissa W. Atkinson, Constance H. Buchanan, and Margaret R. Miles, 61–78. Harvard Women's Studies in Religion. Boston: Beacon Press, 1985.

———. *Love between Women: Early Christian Responses to Female Homoeroticism*. Chicago: University of Chicago Press, 1996.

Brown, Judith C. *Immodest Acts: The Life of a Lesbian Nun in Renaissance Italy*. New York: Oxford University Press, 1986.

Bennett, Judith M. "'Lesbian-Like' and the Social History of Lesbianisms." *Journal of the History of Sexuality* 9 (2000): 1–24.

Crompton, Louis. *Homosexuality and Civilization*. Cambridge, Mass.: Harvard University Press, 2003.

Holsinger, Bruce W. *Music, Body, and Desire in Medieval Culture: Hildegard of Bingen to Chaucer*. Stanford, Calif.: Stanford University Press, 2001.

Lochrie, Karma. "Between Women." In *The Cambridge Companion to Medieval Women's Writing*, edited by Carolyn Dinshaw and David Wallace, 70–88. Cambridge: Cambridge University Press, 2003.

Matter, E. Ann. "Discourses of Desire: Sexuality and Christian Women's Visionary Narratives." *Journal of Homosexuality* 18: 3/4 (1989-90): 119–31.

———. "My Sister, My Spouse: Women-Identified Women in Medieval Christianity." *Journal of Feminist Studies in Religion* 2: 2 (1986): 81–93.

Murray, Jacqueline. "Twice Marginal and Twice Invisible: Lesbians in the Middle Ages." In *Handbook of Medieval Sexuality*, edited by Vern L. Bullough and James Brundage, 191–222. New York: Garland, 1996.

Puff, Helmut. "Female Sodomy: The Trial of Katherina Hetzeldorfer (1477)." *Journal of Medieval and Early Modern Studies* 30 (2000): 41–61.

Sautman, Francesca Canadé, and Pamela Sheingorn, eds. *Same Sex Love and Desire among Women in the Middle Ages.* The New Middle Ages. New York: Palgrave, 2001.

Wiethaus, Ulrike. "Female Homoerotic Discourse and Religion in Medieval Germanic Culture." In *Gender and Difference in the Middle Ages*, edited by Sharon Farmer and Carol Braun Pasternack, 288–321. Minneapolis: University of Minnesota Press, 2003.

JACQUELINE MURRAY

LIOBA. *See* **Leoba**

LI QINGZHAO (1084–c.1151). Widely reputed to be China's greatest woman poet, Li Qingzhao wrote during the Song period and left a surviving opus comprising some seventy-eight poems, most of which were in the *ci* or song-lyric genre, at which she truly excelled, and five essays, including a treatise on the song-lyric (*Lun ci*).

Li Qingzhao was born in Licheng (now Jinan), Shandong province (on the east-central coast of China) into a highly educated family, and both her mother and father, a distinguished man of letters, wrote poetry. Li Qingzhao's success as a poet came early. She and her husband, Zhao Mingcheng, a minor government official and epigrapher, had an unusually companionate marriage, sharing interests in literature, art, and antiques, as celebrated or wistfully recalled in her poetry after Zhao Mingcheng's death. As a revealing example, she writes, "Whenever we obtained a book we would immediately inspect it together and organize our collected notes and labels. When we obtained a painting, calligraphy, or bronze vessel, we would view it and discuss its shortcomings, devoting to it the time it took for a candle to burn down." In fact, she and Zhao worked together on a vast archeological catalogue, the *Jin shi lu* (*Record of Stone and Metal*), so-called because it listed a multitude of art objects of stone and bronze and thus served as an important resource in the field.

Yet Li Qingzhao's life was not an easy one. She and her husband had to leave the capital when he fell out of political favor, then had to flee their home when the Jürchen armies attacked north China in 1127. Her husband died before they were able to resettle, and what we know of Li's life thereafter seems to have been hard. According to legend, she married a minor military official, Zhang Fuzhou, but divorced him soon thereafter because of his political malfeasance and mistreatment of her.

Li's poetry is admired above all for its ability to depict her emotional states by using everyday language and fresh imagery. Her early poems are full of vitality, depicting her as free to participate in drinking parties and poetry contests. The poems she wrote while in exile, however, portray her as grief-stricken, both for the country's loss of the north and her personal loss of her husband. She described herself as "thinner than a yellow flower," and "too lazy to comb her hair."

See also China, Women in; Christine de Pizan; *Trobairitz*

BIBLIOGRAPHY

Primary Sources

Li Qingzhao. [22 Poems and essay "On the Song-Lyric"]. In *Women Writers of Traditional China: An Anthology of Poetry and Criticism*, edited with introduction by Kang-i Sun Chang and Haun Saussy (various translators), esp. 89–100, 672–75. Stanford, Calif.: Stanford University Press, 1999. [English texts only, with useful background commentary, charts, and maps].

———. *Li Ch'ing-chao: Complete Poems*. Edited and translated by Kenneth Rexroth and Ling Chung. New York: New Directions, 1979.

Secondary Sources

Chung, Ling. "Li Qingzhao: The Moulding of Her Spirit and Personality." In *Women and Literature in China*, edited by Anna Gerstlacher, Ruth Keen et al. Bochum, Germany: Studienverlag Brockmeyer, 1985.

Dauber, Dorothee. *Geschliffene Jade: zum Mythos der Song-Dichterin Li Qingzhao*. Europäische Hochschulschriften, 17: Vergleichende Literaturwissenschaft, 94. Frankfurt, Germany and New York: Lang, 2000. [Critical analysis with Chinese texts and German, French, and English trans.].

PATRICIA BUCKLEY EBREY

LOMBARDA (early 13th century). Lombarda, a woman troubadour (*trobairitz*), exchanged a set of *coblas* (stanzas) in Occitan (language of southern France) with Bernart Arnaut of Armagnac: his two heterometric (mixed-verse patterned) stanzas plus *envoi* (closing, dedicatory stanza) are mirrored in her two responding stanzas (H, the single manuscript that records the exchange leaves space for but does not offer an *envoi* from Lombarda). Her identification as an early thirteenth-century Gascon *trobairitz*—that is, from Gascony, a southwestern province of France—is based on the historical evidence of Bernart Arnaut (d. 1226), the second son of Count Bernard IV of the Gascon domains of Armagnac and Fenzesac, who became count on his brother's death. In his second stanza, Bernart addresses his neighbor, Jordan III, lord of L'Isle-Jourdain, also attested in independent documents. Bernard plays humorously on proper names and geography, as he divides ladies and places between himself and his friend, a game that Lombarda picks up in her response. She turns his apostrophe to her as "Mirror of Worth" into a witty accusation that segues from motifs of sight to sound. While he complains that love delays too much, she does not know what mirror he gazes into: the paradox of mirror without seeing throws her out of tune and only the memory of her name (used in Bernard's opening verse) restores her to harmony. Lombarda's extended rhetorical play on the different forms of chord, discord, and accord, as well as her variations on the mirror (a common theme of troubadour lyric, often associated with the mirror of Narcissus) give a vigorous response to Bernart Arnaut's *coblas*, as each poet explores the image of self and other, whether imposed or self-created.

The single manuscript that records "Lombards volgr'eu eser per Na Lonbarda" ("I'd like to be a Lombard for Lady Lombarda") not only embellishes it with a miniature but embeds their exchange in a *razo* (commentary), a narrative that purports to explain the circumstances that gave rise to the song. Many such *razos* were composed in the thirteenth century to present troubadour lyric to new audiences. Songs that lived in the lively presence of poets and public brought together in Occitan courts and cities began to circulate in manuscript anthologies, especially in the courts and salons of Northern Spain and Italy. In this respect, it is interesting to note that Bernard Arnaut names Lombarda with two other ladies, one of whom (Alamanda) may be the *trobairitz* who participated in a *tenso* (debate poem) with Giraut de Bornelh. These songs set up a network of direct and indirect allusions that may connect them to the patterns of troubadour lyric in general or establish more specific links to individual songs in the repertoire.

See also Alamanda; *Trobairitz*

BIBLIOGRAPHY

Primary Sources
Boutière, Jean, and Alexander H. Schutz, eds. *Biographies des Troubadours: Textes provençaux des XIIIᵉ et XIVᵉ siècles*. Revised ed. with I.-M. Cluzel. Les Classiques d'Oc, 1. Paris: Nizet, 1964.
Lombarda. ["Lombards volgr'eu"]. In *Songs of the Women Troubadours*, edited and translated by Matilda Tomaryn Bruckner, Laurie Shepard, and Sarah White, 70–73, 169–70. New York: Garland, 1995. Revised ed. 2000.
———. In *Trobairitz: Der Beitrag der Frau in der altokzitanischen höfischen Lyrik. Edition des Gesamtkorpus*, edited by Angelica Rieger, 245–47. Beihefte der Zeitschrift für romanische Philologie, 233. Tübingen, Germany: Max Niemeyer Verlag, 1991.

Secondary Sources
Poe, Elizabeth W. *Compilatio, Lyric Texts and Prose Commentaries in Troubadour Manuscript H (Vat. Lat. 3207)*. The Edward C. Armstrong Monographs on Medieval Literature, 11. Lexington, Ky.: French Forum, 2000.
Sankovitch, Tilde. "Lombarda's Reluctant Mirror: Speculum of Another Poet." In *The Voice of the Trobairitz: Perspectives on the Women Troubadours*, edited by William D. Paden, 183–93. Philadelphia: University of Pennsylvania Press, 1989.

MATILDA TOMARYN BRUCKNER

LORD'S FIRST NIGHT. *See Jus Primae Noctis*

LOUISE OF SAVOY (1476–1531). Louise of Savoy (de Savoie), the countess, or duchess, of Angoulême, was an influential patron of the arts, the regent of France, and the mother of Francis I and Marguerite of Navarre. Louise summed up her passions in her motto: "Libris et Liberis" ("For my books and my children"). While historians typically restrict Louise's impressive activities to those of mother and regent, her artistic patronage merits equal attention because of her important role in promoting French humanist literature and the production of deluxe manuscripts and printed books. These books contain important textual and visual representations of women in medieval society, particularly as mothers and patrons.

Born at Pont-d'Ain in the Bresse region of France, daughter of Marguerite de Bourbon and Philip II, duke of Savoy, Louise was sent by her father to the court of Amboise after her mother's death in 1483 to be educated by Anne de Beaujeu (c.1461–1522), sister of Charles VIII of France. Louise's childhood was spent in the company of her brother Philibert le Beau and Marguerite of Austria. The three children's destinies would later intertwine when Marguerite, after two marital misfortunes, would marry Louise's brother in 1501; a happy union ending all too soon when Philibert died in 1504. Still later, Marguerite and Louise would join together in crucial international diplomatic negotiations. Both women's ability to withstand such challenges doubtless owed much to Anne de Beaujeu's teachings during their childhood at Amboise: most likely the lessons that Anne would later record in the conduct book composed for her own daughter, the *Enseignements* (*Teachings*), in which she emphasized that a true Christian princess should be modest, reserved, cultivated, indifferent to fashion, and impassioned by books rather than revelry. Most notably, however, was that despite also instructing her charges to avoid politics, Anne de Beaujeu overrode this precept by her own example as a major force in shaping events at the royal court, thus clearly providing an important model for Louise of Savoy's later entry into the political arena when appointed regent, as her mentor had been.

Therefore, when Louise parted from the Amboise court in February of 1488 at age twelve to marry Charles d'Orléans, count of Angoulême, she was already well prepared. Her marriage allowed her to pursue her literary interests, since the Cognac court prized books above all other possessions. A recognized bibliophile, Charles maintained a library of over two hundred manuscripts and deluxe printed editions (including works by such stellar medieval French and Italian authors as Boethius [d. c.524], Boccaccio [d. 1375], Dante [d. 1321], Jean de Meun [d. c.1303], Christine de Pizan [d. c.1429], and Petrarch [d. 1374]) and supported a troupe of artists, musicians, and writers. Louise's discriminating tastes quickly attracted the attention of the writers and artists at court. Robinet Testard, the court miniaturist, produced deluxe manuscripts of such classics as the thirteenth-century *Roman de la rose* (*Romance of the Rose*) and the *Echecs amoureux* (*Chess Game of Love*) from 1370–1380, in addition to a Book of Hours, the *Heures de Louise de Savoie*, in the countess's honor. For Louise as well, Testard and the scribe Jean Michel would produce elaborate copies of court poet Octovien de Saint-Gelais' 1496 French verse translation of the famous classical poet Ovid's *Heroides*, a collection of fictional letters by Greek and Roman heroines to their beloved heroes. In all, Testard's manuscripts provide us with multiple images depicting women engaged in activities both traditionally associated with them, such as spinning and reading, and in less common occupations including hunting, playing music, and writing. Women figure as frequent subjects even in a recognized misogynistic work such as the *Roman de la Rose*, in which Testard portrayed women as observers and key participants in the storyline. Scholars have identified some of the female representations in Testard's illuminations as possible likenesses of Louise of Savoy. While it is difficult to determine conclusively whether Testard really sought to portray Louise in these manuscripts, it is certain that she as patron inspired him and others at Cognac to revere women in their works. Louise would retain Testard and the scribe Jean Michel as part of her household until her death. Many of the works of Louise's protégés are today esteemed as national treasures.

While Louise de Savoy's early years as countess of Angoulême were filled with the reading of courtly works and occasional devotional texts, Charles's sudden death in 1496 led to a dramatic change in the types of books entering the Cognac library. Now a widow at nineteen, Louise found herself solely responsible for their two children, the future Marguerite de Navarre (1492–1549), celebrated author, and Francis I (1494–1547), king of France. Designated at her husband's death as the children's tutor, Louise immediately took charge of their education back at Amboise. Recognizing her strong maternal authority over the future king, publishers, writers, and artists strove to gain Francis's favor through Louise, who in turn appears to have been entirely absorbed in her son's upbringing and general welfare. This is evidenced both in authors seeking their support and in Louise's *Journal,* containing detailed records of Francis's life, while referring only rarely to her daughter. Louise also composed occasional verse in her son's honor, in which she explored their close relationship throughout her life.

The types of works dedicated to the countess reflect her maternal concerns, as leading writers of the early Renaissance—Symphorien Champier, François Demoulins, and Jean Thenaud—composed numerous works primarily for mother and son. From 1503 to 1508, renowned printer Anthoine Vérard dedicated at least seventeen books to Louise de Savoy, many of which duly intended for the dauphin Francis. Works such as *Les Hymnes en françoys* (*Hymnal in French*) and *Le Livre du Sainct Sacrement de l'autel* (*Book of the Holy Sacrament of the Altar*) valorized Louise's position as the dauphin's spiritual educator by portraying mother and son praying together. Vérard's edition of Octovien de Saint-Gelais' *Sejour d'Honneur* (*Sojourn of Honor*) shows the countess surveying the dauphin's receipt of the book from the publisher. Likewise, the anonymous *Compas du dauphin* (*The Crown Prince's Compass*) addresses the countess as Francis's "moral compass." Later, after François assumed the throne, the leading biblical humanist (an intellectual applying the methods of Classical humanism to revitalize interpretation of the Holy Scriptures), Jacques Lefèvre d'Étaples (1453–1536), would compose his learned Latin treatise on St. Anne, which would then be translated into French as the *Petit Livret faict à l'honneur de Madame Sainte Anne* (1518–1519), via an illuminated manuscript (Paris, Bibliothèque de l'Arsenal MS 4009) authored by the king's Franciscan tutor, François Du Moulin (or Desmoulins), specifically for Louise. The *Petit Livret* was a controversial work in that it dared to redefine the so-called Holy Kinship—a complex, hotly contested issue on the eve of the Protestant Reformation in Germany and France—favoring the primacy of St. Anne. For various political and devotional reasons, as encouraged by Du Moulin (a rather anti-Church cleric who questioned its practices and, like his idol, Lefèvre d' Étaples, sought to return to the Gospels as the core of belief, hence the term "evangelical humanism"), St. Anne became Louise and her family's favorite saint. Du Moulin was mainly trying to win royal patronage for the evangelical humanist, whose ideas would influence intellectual and spiritual life at court. Louise and her circle, though bright and cultivated, possessed limited Latin competence and thus greatly appreciated such texts in the vernacular, especially in manuscripts personalized for them, as Myra Orth has shown. Louise and her daughter, Marguerite, would protect Lefèvre d'Étaples for the rest of his life.

On the political and diplomatic side, once Francis I assumed the throne in 1515, he surprised no one by immediately naming his mother regent of France, a title that she maintained until her death in 1531, freeing him to pursue his dynastic dream of becoming Holy Roman Emperor by maneuvering with the pope and recommencing the Italian Wars, further encouraged by his stunning victory at Marignan (1515). The pope and Concordat nevertheless instead elected Charles V (Hapsburg) of Spain to the imperial crown (1519). Francis then waged repeatedly unsuccessful and costly wars in Italy against Charles, who was gaining control of much of Europe. Most disastrous was the battle of Pavia (1525), in which Francis was captured by Charles and imprisoned in Madrid, from whence he wrote moving letters to his mother. Louise consequently found herself involved in complex negotiations, along with her daughter, to resolve matters with Emperor Charles V, and Henry VIII of England, while papal and Protestant problems loomed in the background. This resulted in the Treaty of Madrid, which freed Francis and made peace between him and Charles (1526), only to be violated by her son on his return to France because of its harsh conditions imposed on him. Finally, only the women could put an end to the protracted wars. In 1529, Louise of Savoy, representing her son, Francis, and Marguerite of Austria, here representing her nephew Emperor Charles V, signed the Treaty of Cambrai, appropriately called the *Paix des Dames* (Ladies' Peace), which allowed Francis to keep Burgundy—a territory that the Madrid accord had ordered him to relinquish—while fulfilling all other requisites of the Madrid treaty.

Her son's military folly notwithstanding, Louise profoundly imbued her children with a love of literature, the visual arts, and classical-humanistic thought that enriched their Christian piety rather than excluded it (per the modern misunderstanding of the term "humanism"), as noted above. This philosophy is attested in the generous patronage of Francis I and Marguerite de Navarre, both of whom most scholars perceive as having embodied the fullest expression of the French Renaissance. Indeed, one of the storytellers (Dame Oisille) in Marguerite's famous *Heptaméron* (1540–1559), a collection of seventy-two tales resembling Boccaccio's *Decameron*, was modeled on Louise.

Louise of Savoy thus forged an important link between the medieval period and the Renaissance as royal mother and mentor, diplomat and patron.

See also Christine de Pizan; *Roman de la Rose*, Debate of the

BIBLIOGRAPHY

Primary Sources

Louise de Savoy. *Journal.* In *Collection complète des mémoires relatifs à l'histoire de France*, edited by M. [Claude Bernard] Petitot, vol. 16. Paris: Foucault, 1826.

———. *Journal.* In *Mémoires de Martin et Guillaume Du Bellai-Langei . . . pour servir à l'histoire du règne de François Ier.* Edited by L'Abbé Lambert, vol. 4. Paris: Nyon fils, 1753. [Houghton Library, Harvard University, holds Mme Du Barry's copy].

———. *Poésies du roi François Ier, de Louise de Savoie, duchesse d'Angoulême, de Marguerite, reine de Navarre, et correspondance intime du roi avec Diane de Poitiers et plusieurs autres dames de la cour.* Edited by Aimé Champollion-Figeac. Paris: Imprimerie royale, 1847.

Secondary Sources

Henry-Bordeaux, Paule. *Louise de Savoy, régente et "Roi" de France.* Paris: Plon, 1954. Reprint, Librairie Académique Perrin, 1972.

Kane, June. "Louise de Savoy, Poetess." *Studi Francesi* 65/66 (1979): 349–58.

Lecoq, Anne-Marie. *François Ier imaginaire. Symbolique et politique à l'aube de la Renaissance française.* Paris: Macula, 1987.

McCartney, Elizabeth. "The King's Mother and Royal Prerogative in Early-Sixteenth-Century France." In *Medieval Queenship*, edited by John Carmi Parsons, 117–41. New York: St. Martin's, 1993.

Mayer, Dorothy M. P. *The Great Regent: Louise of Savoy, 1476–1531.* London: Weidenfeld & Nicolson, 1966.

Norman, Joanne S. "Images and Image-Making at the Court of Francis I: Rondeaulx for Louise de Savoy." In *Proceedings of the Canadian Society for the Study of Rhetoric*, edited by Albert W. Halsall. Ottawa, Ont.: Carleton University, 1991–1992.

Orth, Myra D. " 'Madame Sainte Anne': The Holy Kinship, the Royal Trinity, and Louise of Savoy." In *Interpreting Cultural Symbols: Saint Anne in Late Medieval Society*, edited by Kathleen Ashley and Pamela Sheingorn, 199–227. Athens: University of Georgia Press, 1990.

Stone, Donald. *France in the Sixteenth Century: A Medieval Society Transformed.* Englewood Cliffs, N.J.: Prentice-Hall, 1969. [Esp. ch. 2].

Winn, Mary Beth. *Anthoine Vérard, Parisian Publisher, 1485–1512: Prologues, Poems and Presentations.* Geneva: Droz, 1997. [See especially 168–82].

DEBORAH McGRADY

LUNETE. Lunete is Laudine's confidante in Chrétien de Troyes's *Yvain, ou le Chevalier au lion* (*Yvain, or, The Knight with the Lion*, c.1177). She manipulates events and characters with humor and insight, arranging her mistress's marriage with the hero. As the "little moon" signified by her name, Lunete has earned a promise of protection from Gawain, whose origins as a sun god must have been known to Chrétien's audience. Related to the French *Yvain* is a Middle-Welsh tale, *Owein*, or *Chwedyl iarlles y ffynnawn* (*Owain*, or the *Lady of the Fountain*), contained in the collection called the *Mabinogion* (thirteenth century?). Lunete's Welsh counterpart is named Luned, intriguingly enough, and in the Middle-High German story inspired by Chrétien, Hartmann von Aue's *Iwein* (c.1210), she retains her exact name, Lunete.

See also Arthurian Women; Laudine

BIBLIOGRAPHY

Primary Sources

Chrétien de Troyes. *Yvain, ou le Chevalier au lion.* Edited and translated (Modern French) by David F. Hult. Lettres gothiques. Paris: Livre de Poche, 1994. [Bilingual Old-French-Modern French ed.].

Hartmann von Aue. *Iwein.* Edited and translated by Patrick M. McConeghy. Garland Library of Medieval Literature, 19A. New York: Garland, 1984.

Owein, or *Chwedyl iarlles y ffynnawn.* Edited by R. L. Thomson. Medieval and Modern Welsh Series, 4. Dublin: Dublin Institute for Advanced Studies, 1968. [Middle-Welsh text only].

———. In *The Mabinogion*, translated with introduction by Jeffrey Gantz, 192–216. Harmondsworth, U.K. and New York: Penguin, 1976. Reprint 1981.

———. In *Mabinogion*, translated by Gwyn Jones and Thomas Jones. Introduction by Gwyn Jones. Preface by John Updike. Everyman's Library, 168. New York: Knopf/Random House, 2001.

Secondary Source

Fenster, Thelma S., ed. *Arthurian Women: A Casebook.* Arthurian Characters and Themes, 3. New York: Garland, 1996. [Collection of critical essays on wide-ranging aspects, with introduction].

THELMA S. FENSTER

M

MACRINA THE ELDER, ST. (c.270–c.340). Macrina (or Makrina) the Elder was the grandmother of the more famous Macrina the Younger (c.327–380). She was born to a prominent family of Neocaesarea (Basil, Letter 204; Greg. Naz. Oration 43), the capital of Pontus Polemoniacus, in Asia Minor (now Niksar, Turkey). In her childhood she came into vital contact with the legacy of St. Gregory Thaumaturgus (c.213–c.270), apostle to Pontus, the first bishop of Neocaesarea and a disciple of the seminal Christian philosopher and interpreter of the Scriptures, Origen (185?–254?). Macrina became an important link in preserving the traditions of Gregory Thaumaturgus in the local church, and in relaying his moderate Origenism. Much of what we know of her life comes from Gregory of Nyssa *Vita Macrinae Junioris* (*Life of Macrina the Younger*, fourth century).

Macrina married—her husband's name does not survive—and became the mother of Basil the Elder, who was the father of Macrina the Younger, Basil, Gregory, and Peter. Macrina and her husband distinguished themselves as Confessors of the Faith during the last persecutions (303–313) visited on Christians during the reign of the emperor Diocletian, conducted with special savagery by Maxentius in the East. The couple's property was confiscated, and they fled to the forested mountains of Pontus where they endured many privations for seven years, according to the later fourth-century Gregory of Nazianzus (Oration 43.5).

As her grandchildren's teacher, Macrina exerted an important influence over their religious dispositions. When, in the wake of his bitter disillusionment over Eustathius of Sebaste, Basil had to rethink the basis of his whole engagement with the ascetic movement in relation to his Christian faith, he invoked his grandmother, whose memory was so highly regarded in Neocaesarea, as the guarantor of his own doctrinal authenticity (Letter 204). Implicitly, such a rethinking was also necessary for Macrina the Younger and Gregory of Nyssa. It may not be too much to say that Macrina passed on to her grandchildren a character of piety and faith grounded in the common tradition of the Church, which in the end, helped preserve them from the centrifugal forces of unrestrained ascetic enthusiasm or hyperimmersion in contemporary theological politics. Because she and her husband endured great hardship rather than deny Christ, and because she staunchly upheld local Church tradition in Neocaesarea while instilling her religious legacy within her vastly influential grandchildren, Macrina the Elder was in a real sense a Mother of the Church. Her feast day is January 14.

See also Desert Mothers; Macrina the Younger, St.

BIBLIOGRAPHY

Primary Sources
Basil. *Saint Basil: The Letters in Four Volumes*. Edited and translated by Roy J. Deferrari, 1: Letter 46, 288–89; 3: Letter 204, 168–69; Letter 223, 298–99. Cambridge, Mass.: Harvard University Press, 1926–1930.
Gregory of Nazianzus. *Oration 43* (On St. Basil). In *Patrologia Graeca*, edited by J.-P. Migne, 36: col. 493–606.
———. "On St. Basil the Great." In *Funeral Orations by Saint Gregory Nazianzen and Saint Ambrose*, translated by Leo P. McCauley, 27–99. Fathers of the Church, 22. Washington, D.C.: Catholic University Press of America, 1953. Revised ed. 1968.
———. *Panegyric on S. Basil*. In *Nicene and Post-Nicene Fathers*. Second Series, vol. 7: *Cyril of Jerusalem, S. Gregory Nazianzen*, edited by Philip Schaff and Henry Wace. Translated by Charles Gordon Browne, 395–422. New York: Christian Literature Publishing, 1894. Reprint Peabody, Mass.: Hendrickson, 1994.
Gregory of Nyssa. *Vita Macrinae Junioris*. In *Gregorii Nysseni Opera*, edited by Werner Jaeger, 8: 1: 345–416. Leiden, Netherlands: E. J. Brill, 1963.
———. "The Life of Macrina." In *Saint Gregory of Nyssa: Ascetical Works*, edited and translated by Virginia Woods Callahan, 164, 177. Fathers of the Church, 58. Washington, D.C.: Catholic University of America Press, 1967.

ANNA SILVAS

MACRINA THE YOUNGER, ST. (c.328–379). Revered as the "Mother of Greek Monasticism," Macrina (or Makrina) was the first born of the most remarkable family in Christian history. Not only was she the paternal granddaughter of Macrina the Elder (c.270–c.340?) and the maternal great-granddaughter of a Christian martyr, but her parents were also later recognized as saints, and her crop of siblings included four brothers recognized as saints, two of them as Doctors of the Church: Sts. Basil the Great of Caesarea (c.330–379) and Gregory of Nyssa (c.330–c.395), who has been called the Father of Mystical Theology. Basil and Gregory were instrumental in steering the resolution of the Arian crisis that had wracked the Church through much of the fourth century in favor of the neo-Nicene settlement at the Council of Constantinople in 381.

Macrina's parents were Basil the Elder, a renowned lawyer and rhetorician of Neocaesarea, the capital of Pontus Polemoniacus in northern Asia Minor (today Niksar, Turkey), and his wife Emmelia, who came from a family in the province of Cappadocia to the south. Much information about her family can be found in Gregory of Nazianzus's Panegyric on Basil. The chief sources for her life are Letter 19, the *Vita Macrinae Junioris* (*Life of Macrina the Younger*), and the dialogue *De Animae et Resurrectione* (*On the Soul and the Resurrection*), both by her brother Gregory of Nyssa, who had attended her last days and led her funeral. Gregory Nazianzus (fourth century) also wrote epigrams on her, her mother, and her siblings.

When she was twelve (c.340), her father chose a young man of good repute as her future husband, but he died within a very few years. The family was then living at Neocaesarea where the influence of Eustathius of Sebaste, a leader of the contemporary ascetic movement in Anatolia, was in the air. He became a friend of the family, and it seems Macrina was the first to catch the ascetic enthusiasm. With her fiancé dead, she rejected rearrangements for her marriage, claiming the status of a widow, even if a virgin one. She began her apprenticeship as an ascetic by serving at her mother's side, striving to have her life "witnessed" at all times.

It appears that not long after her father died (c.345/6), the family withdrew to its country estate on the river Iris called Annisa (modern Uluköy, near Tasova). Eustathius used to visit throughout the 350s and 360s (Basil, Letter 223). Here, as Macrina matured, her relationship with her mother underwent a subtle change: she became her mother's spiritual mother. In the mid-350s, her brother Naucratius died in a fishing accident. This was especially traumatic for Macrina because Naucratius had been the first of her brothers to follow her ascetic lead wholeheartedly, for which reason she regarded him as her "dearest" brother. After the tragedy she induced Emmelia to abandon the last vestiges of the aristocratic style and dedicate herself to a more ascetic community life. Slaves were treated as equals, menial work was undertaken by all, frugality was the rule, and the day was governed by a pattern of psalmody ordered to unceasing prayer.

Males and females originally associated in a way befitting an aristocratic household, with distinct men's and women's quarters. In such a setting, Macrina was the "father, teacher, attendant, mother, and counselor" of her youngest brother, Peter. By degrees, she steered this family-based Christian community toward a more formal monastic life, transcending its early Eustathian influence and bearing all the marks usually ascribed to Basil's reforms—whereas in truth it was Macrina who led the way. In fact, she played a pivotal role when Basil returned from Athens in 356, persuading him in no uncertain terms to forsake a secular career and choose baptism and the ascetic life instead. She had been living it already for years. By the time of Peter's profession in c.362, the transformation of Annesi into a classic "Basilian" community, with distinct houses for men, women, children, and guests, was complete. Basil himself was wholly converted from his earlier more independent type of ascetic life to this form of ordered community life and became its great expounder. After Emmelia died (c.370), Macrina, as the foundress and much revered spiritual guide, continued as the community's presiding genius, living in its female house; Peter, ordained by Basil in c.371, headed the male house and served all as a priest. Macrina and Peter hosted their brother Basil for a long retreat in 375/6, when he carried out a revision of his *Ascetikon*, or rule (guidelines for monastic life) for the Eastern Church that endures to this day. In c.380, Peter succeeded Eustathius as Bishop of Sebaste (now Sivas, Turkey).

Demonstrating the same practical charity we find so characteristic of Basil, Macrina and Peter went out during the great famine of 369 to rescue starving children abandoned by the roadside. She was also skilled and diligent in women's domestic crafts from her childhood. Her intellectual and doctrinal caliber, hinted at in the *Vitae Macrinae* and attested in *De Animae et Resurrectione*, shows her well able to engage in Greek philosophical discourse to persuade to orthodox Christian doctrine. She became renowned and much loved by the local population as a wonder-worker and even as an exorcist, though Gregory is loathe to provide examples. Many women, some of senatorial rank, looked to her as their spiritual guardian. The culmination of a lifetime of intense asceticism and prayer, voluntary poverty, charity, kindliness, and serenity shone in her dying days, which Gregory reports as an eyewitness.

Macrina's relationship with Gregory of Nyssa is intriguing. In the early 360s he had effectively declined Macrina's, Basil's, and Peter's ascetic ideal, married and taken on a secular career in Caesarea. Between then and his attendance at her deathbed in 379, no small transformation has taken place. It is a fair guess that by the time Basil had persuaded Gregory to service of the Church as bishop in c.372, Gregory had been to Annisa and drawn on Macrina as his coach in upgrading his spiritual life. He repeatedly calls her "the Great," and, in Letter 19, "the teacher of our life, a mother after our mother." He was prompted to write the *Vita Macrinae junioris* in c.380–381, precisely because he did not want his sister's memory to be lost in the shadow of their illustrious brother Basil.

Veneration of her as a saint sprang up quickly and became widespread as the large number of manuscripts of her life testify. Her feast day is July 19.

See also Desert Mothers; Double Monasteries; Hagiography (Female Saints); Macrina the Elder, St.; Thecla, St.

BIBLIOGRAPHY

Primary Sources

Gregory of Nazianzus. *Panegyric on S. Basil.* In *Nicene and Post-Nicene Fathers.* Second Series, vol. 7: *Cyril of Jerusalem, S. Gregory Nazianzen,* edited by Philip Schaff and Henry Wace, 395–422. Translated by Charles Gordon Browne. New York: Christian Literature Publishing, 1894. Reprint Peabody, Mass.: Hendrickson, 1994.

Gregory of Nyssa. *Vita Macrinae Junioris.* In *Gregorii Nysseni Opera,* edited by Werner Jaeger, 8: 1, 345–416. Leiden: E. J. Brill, 1963.

———. *Grégoire de Nysse: La Vie de Sainte Macrine.* Edited and translated by Pierre Maraval. Sources Chrétiennes, 178. Paris: Éditions du Cerf, 1971.

———. *Life of Macrina* and *On the Soul and the Resurrection.* In *Saint Gregory of Nyssa: Ascetical Works,* translated and annoted by Virginia W. Callahan, 161–91; 195–272, resp. Fathers of the Church, 58. Washington, D.C.: Catholic University of America Press, 1967.

———. *The Life of Saint Macrina.* Translated by Kevin Corrigan. Toronto: Peregrina, 1987.

Secondary Sources

Albrecht, Ruth. *Das Leben der heiligen Makrina auf dem Hintergrund der Thecla-Traditionen.* Göttingen, Germany: Vandenhoeck & Ruprecht, 1986.

Bouvy, Edmond. "Sainte Macrine." *Revue Augustinienne* (1902): 265–88.

Elm, Susanna. *Virgins of God.* Oxford and New York: Oxford University Press, 1994.

Luck, Georg. "Notes on the *Vita Macrinae* by Gregory of Nyssa." In *The Biographical Works of Gregory of Nyssa. Proceedings of the Fifth International Colloquium,* edited by Andreas Spira, 21–32. Patristic Monographs, 12. Cambridge, Mass.: Philadelphia Patristic Foundation, 1984.

McDonald, Durston. "Macrina: The Fourth Cappadocian." In *Prayer and Spirituality in the Early Church,* edited by Pauline Allen et al., 367–73. Everton Park, Queensland, Australia: Centre for Early Christian Studies/Australian Catholic University, 1998.

Momigliano, Arnoldo. "The Life of St. Macrina by Gregory of Nyssa." In *The Craft of the Ancient Historian: Essays in Honor of Chester G. Starr,* edited by John W. Eadie, 443–58. Lanham, Md.: University Press of America, 1985.

Stramara, Daniel F. "Double Monasticism in the Greek East, Fourth through Eighth Centuries." *Journal of Early Christian Studies* 6 (1998): 269–312.

Wilson-Kastner, Patricia. "Macrina: Virgin and Teacher." *Andrews University Seminary Studies* 17 (1979): 105–17.

ANNA SILVAS

MALATESTA, BATTISTA DA MONTEFELTRO. *See* **Battista da Montefeltro Malatesta**

MALMOJADES, LES. Catalan for "the unwilling nuns," the term *malmojades* for their songs belongs to a tradition of writing poetry from a female point of view that was well established in several Romance languages, as well as these languages associated with Spain, from the thirteenth century. Many anonymous poems collected and published in various medieval anthologies seem clearly to have been written by women. While in the Castilian *Romanceros* and *Cancioneros* a number of *malcasades* (unhappy housewives) can be found in Catalan; the greatest manifestation of these cycles of poetry can be seen in the poems by nuns lamenting their state in life, their lack of freedom and love. The *malmojades* date back to the Latin Middle Ages and are represented in both Castilian and Catalan. A variety of tones can be seen, from the simplest—"Agora que soy niña/quiero alegría,/que no se sirve Dios/de mi monjía" ("Now that I'm young/I want my fun,/I can't serve God/being a nun"; ed. Flores 1985: 8–9)—in Castilian to the angry words in Catalan of the "Monja per força," or "Forced Nun":

> Lassa, mays m'agra valgut/que fos maridada,
> O cortés amic agut/Que can suy monjada;
> Monjada suy a mon dan,/pecat gran
> Han fayt, segon mon albir,/Mas cels qui mesa m'i han,
> En mal an/los meta Déu e.ls ayr,
> Car si yo.u hagués saubut,/Mas fuy un poch fada,
> Qui.m donás tot Montagut/No hic fora entrada.
> (ed. Massó i Torrents 405–6)

(Alas! I wish I could have gotten married, or had a fine lover, instead of taking vows; My being a nun does me great harm; Those who put me here have committed a great sin, it seems to me; May God do them greater harm and despise them. For had I known—but I was a bit foolish—I would never have entered here, not even for all of Montagut.)

Some of the Catalan poems, many of which are to be found in the lyric collection in the Crown of Aragon Archive in Barcelona, titled the *Cançoneret de Ripoll* (Manuscript 129), are more complex, speaking of grief, fear, hope, and passion in the souls of women. These poems were widespread throughout Europe, both before and after attempts to suppress them in 789 by Charlemagne, king of the Franks and future emperor, a prohibition that clearly echoed the earliest ecclesiastical councils' condemnation of the *cantica puellarum* (young maiden's songs). The female poetic voice addressed another woman: her mother, sisters, or girlfriends, or in some cases, herself or an inanimate object. The *malmojades* constitute a poetic tradition created by women; even if the authors of surviving examples are unknown, their poems were gathered from popular tradition and rewritten.

See also Borja, Tecla; Catalan Women Poets, Anonymous; *Chanson de Femme* (Women's Song); *Frauenfrage*; Isabel de Villena; Reyna de Mallorques, La

BIBLIOGRAPHY

Primary Sources
"Alas! If I had Married" ["Lassa, mays m'agra valgut"]. In *An Anthology of Medieval Lyrics*, edited by Angel Flores. Translated by William Davis. New York: Modern Library, 1962.
Cançoneret de Ripoll. Ms. 129 of Ripoll. Archive of the Crown of Aragon, Barcelona.
Flores, Angel, and Kate Flores, eds. *The Defiant Muse: Hispanic Feminist Poems from the Middle Ages to the Present*. New York: The Feminist Press, 1985.
"Malmojades" [Selections]. "Observaciones sobre la poesía popular con muestras de romances catalanes inéditos." In *Manuel Milà i Fontanals. Obras completas*, vol. 6. Barcelona: Verdaguer, 1895.

"Malmojades" [Selections]. In *Repertori de l'antiga literatura catalana*, edited by Jaume Massó i Torrents. Barcelona: Alpha, 1932.

Romancerillo catalán. Barcelona: Verdaguer, 1882.

Secondary Sources

Duby, Georges. *Le chevalier, la femme et le prêtre: le mariage dans la France féodale*. Paris: Hachette, 1981.

Lapa, M. Rodrígues. *Liçoes de literatura portuguesa*. Coimbra, Portugal: Coimbra Editora, 1977.

Riquer, Martí de, Antoni Comas, and Joaquim Molas. *Història de la literatura catalana*, 2: 16–17. 11 vols. Barcelona: Ariel, 1964–1988.

Rubió i Balaguer, Jordi. "Del manuscrit 129 de Ripoll del segle XIV." *Revista de bibliografia catalana* 8 (1905): 285–378. Reprint Barcelona: L'Avenç, 1911.

Villas i Chalamanch, Montserrat. "Les Malmojades." *Double Minorities of Spain: A Bio-Bibliographic Guide to Women Writers of the Catalan, Galician, and Basque Countries*. Edited by Kathleen McNerney and Cristina Enríquez de Salamanca, 212–13. New York: Modern Language Association, 1994.

KATHLEEN MCNERNEY

MARCIA IN THE MIDDLE AGES. The historical "Marcia," the archetypal Woman as Self-Portraitist, was not a medieval woman at all. The textual source in which she first makes her appearance, and the set of culminating visual representations by which she is best known, sandwich most of the Middle Ages between them. Her name, however, is a fine medieval twist on a Classical text. Mentioned as the Hellenistic painter Iaia (or Laia, or Lala) of Kyzikos, in the *Historia Naturalis* (*Natural History*, 9: 35.40) of Pliny the Elder (23–79 C.E.), she is revived as Marcia in Boccaccio's *De Claris Mulieribus* (*Famous Women*, 1361–1362). Boccaccio likely misunderstood Pliny's reference to Iaia's contemporary, the grammarian Marcus Terentius Varro, and thus he has her as Varro's daughter, hence "Marcia" (feminized Marcus).

Whatever her correct name and proper time period, Marcia, the subject of various miniatures painted by Parisian illuminators at the dawn of the northern Renaissance, came to represent visually the creativity of medieval women and the working habits of medieval artists in general. The most famous representations of Marcia (and her sister artists Irene and Thamar—originally Timarete) appear in luxury manuscript editions of the anonymous French translation of Boccaccio (*Des Cleres Femmes*) fashioned around 1400 for dukes Philip the Bold of Burgundy (1342–1404) and Jean of Berry (1340–1416). These images of Marcia are interesting not only as representations of an artist at work (of which there exist other medieval exemplars) but also for the rather anomalous type of the artist at work on a self-portrait. The fascination of the genre informs much of the biographical literature on Marcia. In Boccaccio's *De Claris Mulieribus*, he infers from Pliny's comment that Marcia remained a *perpetua virgo* (perpetual virgin) and it was modesty that confined her in her choice of subject matter to herself and to other women. "I think that her chaste modesty was the cause of this," he writes, "for in Antiquity figures were for the greater part represented nude or half nude, and it seemed to her necessary either to make the men imperfect, or, by making them perfect, forget maidenly modesty." This argument bears a striking resemblance to the arguments of the French Academicians on the admission, in the waning years of the *Ancien Régime*, of Elisabeth Vigée-Lebrun (1755–1842), another celebrated painter of portraits. Capping the number of female Academicians at two, the Academy argued that women "cannot be useful" to the progress of the arts, since modesty prevented them from painting from "nature," that is, from the male nude. This logic typifies a long-standing double-bind by which women's creativity, restricted by social norms to a more limited range of experiences, is then disparaged as descriptive rather than inventive, as provincial and self-absorbed.

Images of Marcia, among them the "first representation of a frontal easel portrait known" (Miner), might conversely be viewed as an exaltation of the painter and the painter's craft, an expression of an interest in rendering the painter at work. Christine de Pizan (1364/5–1430?) borrows from Boccaccio in her *Livre de la Cité des Dames* (*Book of the City of Ladies*), but inserts a sly (and rather radical) revision of Boccaccio, explaining that Marcia painted a self-portrait out of desire for fame: "in order that her memory survive" (1:41). She also makes a point of praising a female illuminator of her acquaintance, Anastaise. As a woman writer and feminist, Christine was acutely aware of the predicament of the talented woman and her likely fate of historical oblivion.

Marcia painting her self-portrait. From Boccaccio, *Des Cleres Femmes BnF MS12420.* © Bibliothèque nationale de France, Paris.

These images may, then, mark a new attention to, and perhaps pride in, the craft of the painter. As representations of tools and working methods, they have been useful to scholars studying the practices of medieval artists, among them Millard Meiss, who begins the second volume of his monumental *French Painting in the Time of Jean de Berry* with a discussion of images of Marcia and other female painters. Despite the fact that they serve as the pretext for his introductory discussions of tools and methods, women painters are quickly dismissed from his survey. Still, he claims confidently that "the instruments and materials, like the subjects that engage them, must correspond" to contemporary workshops.

In the Burgundy manuscript (Paris, Bibliothèque nationale de France, fr. 12420), on fol. 101v, Marcia sits at her easel in a well-appointed chamber, wearing the fashionable gown, braids, and toque of a lady; her attitude is one of concentration, as she holds a small circular mirror in her left hand and paints delicately with her right. The image contains three versions of Marcia's face, the flesh-and-blood Marcia in profile, the others frontal. On a bench behind her are her brushes, pots, and small paintbox; a palette and several brushes lie on the easel nearby, while she is painting a frontal portrait. The Berry manuscript (Paris, BnF fr. 598) miniature (fol. 100v) shows us a more austere Marcia, wearing the garb of a lower social order (as might befit a craftswoman); it also adds a set of sculptor's tools. Other miniatures of women artists in the same manuscripts are similar, though they paint and sculpt Madonnas and Holy Faces. In one case, Thamar is given an assistant who is shown mixing paints in the background.

The Burgundy manuscript image of Marcia at her easel is as interesting for its later uses as for its contemporary significances. Marcia, Thamar, and Irene are frequently invoked, and their images reproduced, as founding "mothers" of a feminist genealogy of women artists. More often, they provide a mute background to the works of later artists. Marcia serves as the unattributed frontispiece to Edith Krull's *Kunst von Frauen*; as the unacknowledged prototype of Norman Rockwell's 1960 *Triple Self-Portrait* (a painting within which he more explicitly lays claim to the artistic legacies of Dürer, Rembrandt, Picasso, and van Gogh); as the cover girl of the first volume of a collection of essays on medieval artists (edited by Xavier Barral i Altet, 1990 [see under Bidon]), ironically subtitled *Les hommes* (*Men*). Linda Seidel has argued that Jan van Eyck (c.1390–1441) may have appropriated from the Burgundy miniature the juxtaposition of the scalloped shape of Marcia's palette, and the circular mirror, fusing them to create one of the hallmarks of his own famous mirrored self-portrait *en abyme* in his celebrated Arnolfini portrait (also known as *Jan Arnolfini and His Wife*). This nearly forgotten Hellenistic woman painter may thus, via Boccaccio, Christine, and the Parisian illuminators, stand behind one of the great monuments of Renaissance painterly self-awareness.

See also Artists, Medieval Women; Boccacio, Women in, *Des Cleres et Nobles Femmes*; Boccaccio, Women in, *De Claris Mulieribus*; Christine de Pizan; Scribes and Scriptoria

BIBLIOGRAPHY

Primary Sources

Boccaccio, Giovanni. [*Des claris mulieribus*, Middle French]. *Des cleres et nobles femmes*. Paris, Bibliothèque nationale de France, MS. fr. 12420 [esp. fol. 101v]; MS fr. 598[esp. fol. 100v]. This trans. or the original Latin version edited in items below:

———. *Boccace, Des cleres et nobles femmes: Ms. Bibl. nat. 12420*. Edited by Jeanne Baroin and Josiane Haffen. 2 vols. Paris: Les Belles Lettres, 1993–1995. [Original Middle–French text edited from Paris, BnF 12420 and facing Modern French translation; for English trans. *See under* Perkinson, *in* Secondary Sources, *below*].

———. *De mulieribus claris o Delle donne famose*. Edited by Vittore Branca. In *Tutte le Opere di Giovanni Boccaccio*, edited by Vittorio Zaccaria, vol. 10. Florence: Arnoldo Mondadori, 1967, 1970. [Original Latin text in modern ed.; notes in Italian].

———. *Famous Women*. Edited and translated by Virginia Brown. I Tatti Renaissance Library, 1. Cambridge, Mass.: Harvard University Press, 2001. [Bilingual Latin-English translation with notes].

Christine de Pizan. [*Le Livre de la Cité des Dames*]. *Città delle dame*. Edited by E. J. Richards. Translated (Italian) with commentary by Patrizia Caraffi. Revised ed. Milan: Luni, 1998. [Original Middle-French text].

———. *The Book of the City of Ladies*. Translated by Earl Jeffrey Richards. New York: Persea, 1982.

Pliny the Elder. *Natural History/Historia Naturalis*. Translated by H. Rackham. Loeb Classical Library. Cambridge, Mass.: Harvard University Press, 1952. [Bilingual Latin-English ed.]

Secondary Sources

Alexandre-Bidon, Danièle, and Monique Closson. "Scènes de la vie d'artiste au Moyen Âge: outils de travail et vie professionelle." In *Artistes, Artisans et Production Artistique au Moyen Âge*, edited by Xavier Barral i Altet, 3: 557–75. 3 vols. Paris: Picard, 1990.

Heller, Nancy G. *Women Artists: An Illustrated History*. 3rd ed. New York: Abbeville Press, 1997.

Kampen, Natalie. "Hellenistic Artists: Female." *Archeologia Classica* 27 (1975): 9–17.

Krull, Edith. *Kunst von Frauen* Frankfurt-am-Main: Weidlich, 1984.

Meiss, Millard. *French Painting in the Time of Jean de Berry: The Late Fourteenth Century and the Patronage of the Duke*. London: Phaidon, 1967.

Miner, Dorothy. *Anastaise and Her Sisters: Women Artists of the Middle Ages.* Baltimore: Walters Art Gallery, 1974.

Nochlin, Linda. "Why Have There Been No Great Women Artists?" In Nochlin, *Women, Art and Power,* ch. 7. New York: Harper & Row, 1988.

Parker, Rozsika, and Griselda Pollock. *Old Mistresses.* London: Routledge, 1981. [Esp. ch. 1, "Critical stereotypes: The Essential Feminine or How Essential is Femininity?"]

Perkinson, Stephen. "*Engin* and *Artifice*: Describing Creative Agency at the Court of France, ca. 1400." *Gesta* 41: 1 (2002): 51–67.

Seidel, Linda. *Jan van Eyck's Arnolfini Portrait: Stories of an Icon.* Cambridge: Cambridge University Press, 1993.

Sheriff, Mary. *The Exceptional Woman: Elisabeth Vigée-Lebrun and the Cultural Politics of Art.* Chicago: University of Chicago Press, 1996.

REBECCA E. ZORACH

MARGARET, LADY. *See* Beaufort, Margaret

MARGARET OF ANJOU

MARGARET OF ANJOU (c.1430–1482). Immortalized as the "she-wolf of France" by William Shakespeare, the French-born Marguerite d'Anjou, Margaret became queen of England in 1445 on her marriage to King Henry VI (1421–1471). Her husband's chronic mental illness made her the real leader of the House of Lancaster during the English civil war known as the Wars of the Roses (1455–1485). Margaret also composed many letters of social and political interest to historians.

Born at Pont-à-Mousson in Lorraine in eastern France, Margaret was the daughter of René, duke of Anjou (1409–1480) and later king of Naples and Sicily. René preferred cultivating the arts and letters to executing feats of arms or conducting diplomacy, tastes that rendered his claims to the thrones of Hungary and Jerusalem merely fanciful and reduced his ability to effectively hold or govern his other territories. Margaret's mother, Isabella, duchess of Lorraine, ruled and made war in René's place during his imprisonment from 1431 to 1437 following an unsuccessful challenge to Philip the Good, the powerful duke of Burgundy. Margaret likely inherited her later aptitude for the exercise of power and patronage from her mother and from her paternal grandmother, Yolanda of Aragon (c.1381–1442), another strong-minded woman who effectively replaced a weaker male ruler. Yolanda of Aragon, under whose tutelage Margaret spent eight years, was regent of Anjou and a major supporter of the Dauphin Charles of France (later Charles VII) during his dispossession from the French throne by the English between 1422 and 1429.

Margaret was betrothed to Henry VI in 1444. Her marriage secured an Anglo-French truce negotiated by Henry's ambassador, William de la Pole, earl of Suffolk (1396–1450), with her uncle, Charles VII (1403–1461), who was bringing the Hundred Years War (1337–1453) to a close by gradually expelling the English from France. Married to Henry on April 23, 1445, Margaret, aged about fifteen, was crowned queen at Westminster Abbey on May 30. Attractive and well educated, intelligent and energetic, the young queen at first took little part in politics, although she soon allied herself with Suffolk and the court faction that exerted paramount influence over Henry in the late 1440s. She continued the peace policy that had made her queen and helped to implement Henry's promise to cede the county of Maine in northwestern France to Charles in 1448.

Margaret of Anjou. Courtesy of the Perry Casteneda Library.

When the French finally expelled the English from Normandy in 1450, the war's severe financial toll, King Henry's inadequacy, and charges of treason leveled by such opponents as Richard Plantagenet, duke of York (1411–1460), caused Suffolk to fall from power as chief minister and led eventually to his assassination, perhaps by agents of York. As the childless king's most likely heir, Richard of York, then engaged in a bitter rivalry with Edmund Beaufort, duke of Somerset (d. 1455), Suffolk's successor as chief minister. Queen Margaret, viewing York as a threat to the Lancastrian crown, sided with Somerset. In August 1453, Henry VI went mad, falling into an uncommunicative state that rendered him totally incapable of ruling for over a year. In October 1453, Margaret gave birth to a son, Prince Edward, who displaced York as heir. Aware of the need to protect her child's rights, Margaret sought the regency, but Parliament chose York instead, naming him Protector in March 1454. King Henry's recovery ended York's protectorate in early 1455, but Margaret and Somerset persevered with their plan to neutralize York, who persuaded his new allies, Richard Neville, earl of Salisbury (c.1400–1460), and his son, Richard Neville, earl of Warwick (1428–1471), to take up arms against the Somerset and the court party. These actions launched the Wars of the Roses, a series of conflicts between the royal house of Lancaster and a rival branch of the royal family headed by York. (The wars were later named for the rose emblems of the two families—a red rose for Lancaster and a white rose for York.) During the inaugural confrontation of the wars, the first Battle of St. Albans in May 1455, the Yorkists killed Margaret's ally Somerset and captured her husband, the still-ailing king, thereby instituting York's Second Protectorate. Although Henry regained sufficient reason to dismiss York in 1456, the king was too enfeebled to rule effectively, leaving Margaret to assume leadership of the anti-York faction. Although she participated in Henry's so-called Love-day reconciliation of the factions in March 1458, the queen mostly withdrew her husband from London and kept him under her influence in the Midlands.

When the wars rekindled in 1459, Margaret's triumph at the Battle of Ludford Bridge forced York, Salisbury, and Warwick to flee England, leaving Margaret in control of the royal government. Summoning a Parliament to meet at Coventry in the autumn of 1459, the queen dominated the proceedings and successfully maneuvered through the houses several bills of attainder that stripped her exiled opponents of their lands and offices. However, when Warwick captured King Henry at the Battle of Northampton in July 1460, York returned from Ireland and laid formal claim to the crown before Parliament, which responded by passing the compromise Act of Accord. The act allowed Henry to remain king, but made York Henry's heir in place of Margaret's son Prince Edward. Margaret, who as then in Wales with her son, refused to recognize the prince's disinheritance and again mustered forces against York. At the Battle of Wakefield in December 1460, her armies slew York and Salisbury. They then defeated Warwick at the second Battle of St. Albans in February 1461 and restored Henry to Margaret's custody. Because the Lancastrian army had savagely attacked and sacked Yorkist towns and strongholds on its march south, frightened Londoners refused the queen admittance to the capital. Although negotiations involving several high-ranking noblewomen, including Lady Scales; the duchess of Buckingham; and Jacquetta of Luxembourg, duchess of Bedford, secured some supplies for her forces, Margaret eventually retreated from London, allowing York's son, Edward, earl of March, to enter the capital and be proclaimed king as Edward IV. On March 29, Edward defeated the Lancastrians at the Battle of Towton, forcing Margaret to flee to Scotland with her son, husband, and chief supporters. The regency government of King James III of Scotland, which maintained the longstanding Franco-Scottish alliance and was eager to turn the English civil war to Scottish advantage, gave refuge to the Lancastrians in return for the English surrender of Berwick, a town on the eastern coastal border between England and Scotland.

In 1462, Margaret returned to her native France and convinced Louis XI—the legendarily clever "Spider King" (1423–1483)—to provide her with a small army. With this she invaded Northumberland in northeaster England, capturing several castles, which she then lost, recaptured, and lost again over the following year. These costly forays reduced Margaret and her son to poverty and for a time forced them to wander lost and alone along the northern English coast. In the summer of 1463, Margaret and Prince Edward sailed back to France, leaving Henry in the custody of Lancastrians in Scotland and northern England until he was captured by the Yorkists in 1465. During the late 1460s, Margaret established a small court-in-exile at St. Mihiel-en-Bar. Neither the poverty nor the isolation of her court prevented the queen from plotting against the Yorkist regime, but it took her former enemy—Warwick—to revive the Lancastrian cause and restore Henry VI to power in 1470. In his change of allegiance Warwick acted less out love for Henry VI than out of anger over his loss of political dominance under Edward IV. Margaret still despised Warwick for having supported York and for questioning her son's legitimacy; however, she consented to negotiate with him after he humbly submitted to her on his knees. Prodded by Louis XI, Margaret finally accepted Warwick as an ally and assented to the marriage, arranged by her chancellor, Sir John Fortescue, of her son Edward to Warwick's daughter Anne Neville, which was celebrated at Amboise in December 1470.

Warwick, who is known to history as "the Kingmaker," overthrew Edward in October 1470, forcing the Yorkist king to flee to Burgundy. The earl then restored a befuddled Henry VI, who had been a prisoner in the Tower of London since 1465. Margaret and her son landed in England on April 14, 1471, the same day Warwick perished at the Battle of Barnet and her husband was again taken prisoner by Edward IV. Persuaded by her supporters to continue the fight in the pro-Lancastrian West Country, Margaret suffered both defeat and the death of her son at the Battle of Tewkesbury on May 4. Captured a few days later while hiding in a religious house, Margaret was paraded through London and came eventually to the Tower, where her husband was murdered on May 21. The House of Lancaster died with Henry VI. Margaret's imprisonment, some of which was more agreeably spent in the custody of Alice Chaucer, duchess of Suffolk, lasted until

1475, when Louis XI ransomed her for 50,000 crowns as part of the Treaty of Picquigny, by which Louis paid off Edward IV to avert further English invasion. The treaty forced Margaret to renounce all claims to the English throne, while Louis also made her surrender all rights to her French lands in return for a pension. The impoverished Margaret died on August 25, 1482, at the Château de Dampierre in Anjou. She was buried at the cathedral of St. Maurice in Angers, the capital of Anjou.

Some eighty-two of Margaret's letters survive; they cast little light on political matters but much on the queen's social and personal affairs. Modern scholarly opinion no longer accepts the extremely negative portrayal of her as a bloodthirsty adulteress found in Shakespeare's 1590s tragedy *Henry VI, Part 3* (1.4.111). Recent scholars including Diana Dunn and, in a more feminist mode, Helen Maurer, perceive a need to further revise her image through a less male-centered historical perspective. Maurer concludes that Margaret's queenship is memorable for its "anomalous circumstances," which "permitted and, indeed, forced her to act in unexpected ways" pushing at previously ill-defined boundaries that her rule would serve to redefine.

See also Chaucer, Alice; Jacquetta of Luxembourg; Joan of Arc, St.; Woodville, Elizabeth; Yolanda of Aragon

BIBLIOGRAPHY

Primary Sources
[See also bibliographies to secondary works below].
Margaret of Anjou. *Letters of Queen Margaret of Anjou and Bishop Bekington and Others*. Camden Society, o.s. 86. London, 1863.
Corporation of London Record Office. Journal VI, folio 10.
Myers, A. R., ed. "The Household of Queen Margaret of Anjou, 1452–3." *Bulletin of the John Rylands Library* 40 (1957–1958): 79–113; 391–431. Reprint in Myers, *Crown, Household and Parliament in Fifteenth-Century England*, edited by Cecil H. Clough, 135–229. London: Hambledon Press, 1985.
———. "The Jewels of Queen Margaret of Anjou." *Bulletin of the John Rylands Library* 42 (1959–1960): 113–31. For reprint *see above entry*.

Secondary Sources
Dunn, Diana. "Margaret of Anjou, Queen Consort of Henry VI: A Reassessment of Her Role, 1445–53." In *Crown, Government and People in the Fifteenth Century*, 107–43. New York: St. Martin's Press, 1995.
Erlanger, Philippe. *Margaret of Anjou: Queen of England*. London: Elek Books, 1970.
Griffiths, Ralph A. *The Reign of King Henry VI*. Berkeley: University of California Press, 1981.
Laynesmith, J. L. *The Last Medieval Queens: English Queenship 1445–1503*. Oxford and New York: Oxford University Press, 2004.
Maurer, Helen. *Margaret of Anjou: Queenship and Power in Late Medieval England*. Woodbridge, Suffolk, U.K.: Boydell Press, 2003.
Wagner, John A. *Encyclopedia of the Wars of the Roses*. Santa Barbara, Calif.: ABC-Clio, 2001.

JOHN A. WAGNER

MARGARET OF SCOTLAND, DAUPHINE OF FRANCE (1425–1445). Margaret was born in 1425, the eldest child of James I, Scotland's poet-king, and his English queen, Joan Beaufort. At the age of three, Margaret was promised in marriage to Louis (later Louis XI), son of Charles VII of France, who wished to renew the Auld Alliance with

Scotland: the 1295 treaty between Scotland and France against their "auld" enemy, England. However, it was not until 1436 that the young princess finally set sail for France. Margaret and Louis, who was then fourteen years old, were married in Tours on June 25, 1436, but Margaret remained for more than a year under the personal tutelage of her mother-in-law, Marie of Anjou, before the marriage was consummated. Louis's absence on military and political expeditions caused lengthy interruptions to their conjugal life. Meanwhile, the Dauphine took a full part in activities at court.

From the outset, Louis's neglect of his bride gave rise to speculation. It seemed that he neither loved nor respected Margaret. Perhaps the Dauphin's feelings for this bride—chosen for him by Charles VII—reflected the ambitious son's growing resentment of his father's authority. Whether she was systematically spied on or not, she certainly found herself vilified, the victim of malicious rumors put about by Jamet de Tillay, bailiff of Vermandois. Her childlessness, said to result from self-inflicted privations, was a fault; so also was her addiction to nocturnal versifying, and to fashionable literary and musical pursuits with courtiers and her ladies.

Despite the consistent affection and generosity of the king and queen, Margaret suffered progressively from these slanders. Following a brief illness, she died at Châlons-sur-Marne on August 16, 1445, aged only twenty. Death may well have come as a relief to the "Dauphine mélancolique" ("Melancholy Crown Princess"). To the end she had vigorously protested her innocence of all charges of marital infidelity. All her private papers having been destroyed—on Louis's orders—shortly after her death, written personal testimony is lacking. Although evidence of Jamet de Tillay's scandal-mongering was revealed in an official enquiry into the circumstances surrounding her death, strangely no public blame or punishment followed, and Jamet de Tillay retained his place and favor at court.

In her will, Margaret requested that she be buried in Thouars, in western France, at the chapel that she herself had commissioned in the abbey church of St. Laon. Initially, Abbot Nicolas Godard had received from the Dauphine half of the cost of the foundation, together with Margaret's Book of Hours as guarantee. In 1459, letters patent of Charles VII confirmed Margaret's donation to the abbey church, and allowed her Book of Hours to be restored to the king. However, it was not until 1479, thirty-four years after Margaret's death, that the ailing Louis XI acceded to the persistent requests of Abbot Nicolas Godard and agreed that the Dauphine's remains be transferred from Châlons to Thouars. Less than a century later, Margaret's tomb was desecrated by the Protestants. Prolonged neglect thereafter allowed all trace of her burial place to disappear. Thanks to local research, and to digging and restoration completed by the French-government-run Monuments Historiques in the mid-1990s, the Dauphine's tomb has been revealed, and she is once again fittingly honored in her chosen resting place.

Although none of Margaret's own poems appears to have survived, compositions by others of her circle are known. The most notable may be a St. Valentine's rondeau (roundel) by Blosseville that plays on the letter "M." A touching lament for the Dauphine survives in the Book of Hours of Margaret's sister Isabelle, duchess of Brittany; it has been added on a blank leaf, probably in Isabelle's own hand.

BIBLIOGRAPHY

Primary Sources
Paris, Bibliothèque nationale de France, MS. fr. 6955, fol. 259.
Paris, Bibliothèque nationale de France. MS. lat. 1369, fol. 56.

Blosseville et al. In *Rondeaux et autres poésies du XVe siècle*, edited by Gaston Raynaud. SATF, 29. Paris: Firmin Didot, 1889.

Secondary Sources
Balfour-Melville, E. W. M. *James I King of Scots*. London: Methuen, 1936.
Barbé, Louis A. *Margaret of Scotland and the Dauphin Louis*. London: Blackie, 1917.
Beaucourt, G[aston] du Fresne de. *Histoire de Charles VII*. Vols. 2–4. Librairie de la Société bibliographique, 2. Paris: A. Picard, 1881.
Bordonove, Georges. "Charles VII le Victorieux." In *Les Rois qui ont fait la France. Les Valois*, vol. 2. Paris: Pygmalion/Gérard Watelet, 1985.
Brown, Michael. "James I." In *The Stewart Dynasty in Scotland*, edited by Norman Macdougall. Edinburgh: Canongate Academic, 1994.
Champion, Pierre. *La Dauphine Mélancolique*. Paris: Marcel Lesage, 1927.
———. *Louis XI*. 2 vols. Paris: Édouard Champion, 1928.
Dictionary of National Biography. Vol. 12. London: Smith, Eder, 1909.
Heers, Jacques. *Louis XI: Le métier de roi*. Paris: Perrin, 1999.
Keay, John, and Julia Keay, eds. *Collins Encyclopaedia of Scotland*. London: Harper Collins, 1994.
Kendall, Paul Murray. *Louis XI*. London: George Allen & Unwin, 1971.

ELIZABETH LAIDLAW

MARGARET OF SCOTLAND, ST.

MARGARET OF SCOTLAND, ST. (c.1047–1093). The legendary queen, saint, and religious reformer of Scotland, Margaret was born in southern Hungary, daughter of the Anglo-Saxon Prince Edward the Exile, son of Edmund Ironside, and his wife, Agatha. She spent her first ten years at the Hungarian court, where the influence of the saintly King Stephen (d. 1038, canonized 1043) still prevailed. Margaret's second decade was spent in England. Her education continued in the cultivated and devout atmosphere of the court of Edward the Confessor, her uncle. A second Anglo-Saxon exile followed the Norman Conquest of 1066. Margaret and her family found refuge in Scotland at the court of King Malcolm III (Canmore), briefly in 1068 and again in 1070, after the defeat of the Northumbrian rebellion. She was queen of Scotland from 1070 to her death in 1093.

Most of what we know of her life comes from the early twelfth-century *Vita S Margaretae Scotorum Reginae* (*The Life of Saint Margaret, Queen of the Scots*), written by her first biographer, Turgot (Turgotus), prior-archdeacon of Durham and Bishop of St. Andrews, who also claimed to have been her confessor. Margaret's initial desire to devote her life to the Church may have been underscored by Turgot to associate her more closely with her namesake, St. Margaret of Antioch, whose legend, popular throughout Western Europe, depicted her as a servant of God who rejected marriage and was martyred for her faith. However, in 1070 the future Margaret of Scotland accepted the hand of King Malcolm III, the very Malcolm who had slain Macbeth, his father's murderer, before becoming king in 1058. Margaret was his second wife (after Ingibiorg). Turgot sought to commemorate her as Malcolm's "real" queen (effacing Ingibiorg as a mere concubine) and as a holy founding mother of Scottish kings.

Margaret's first decision as queen was to build a new church—of the Holy Trinity—on the site where she had been married, in Dunfermline, in Fife. Throughout her marriage she was revered for her rigorous religious observance and her gift of prophecy, so too for her lavish charity for the relief of the poor and the liberation of enslaved captives whose ransom she paid. She bore Malcolm six sons and two daughters, to whose strict upbringing and education Margaret herself attended. Three of her sons, Edgar, Alexander, and

David, were future kings of Scotland. Her daughter Edith, also known as Maud or Matilda, married Henry I of England. Turgot dedicated his biography to her as a "mirror," or model, for the ideal princess.

Through love and respect for his wife, Malcolm came to appreciate beauty, piety, and learning, although he remained illiterate. Margaret relied on him to interpret the Gaelic of the Scots, for example at councils in which she successfully argued for church reform in Scotland. Scholars dispute the extent of Margaret's reforming influence on the church, but evidence of her intentions is implicit in an extant letter (no. 50) addressed to her by Lanfranc, Archbishop of Canterbury (c.1010–1089), who, at her request, sent Benedictine monks to help her at Dunfermline. Reforms associated with her brought the church in Scotland into line with the Church in Rome in matters such as the observation of Lent, Easter communion, the Sabbath as a day of rest, and laws governing marriage. The introduction of a territorial and diocesan organization did not entirely eradicate the older independent Culdean settlements established in the eighth and ninth centuries by the Culdees, ancient monks of the Celtic church.

Under Margaret's influence, life at the Scottish court, both in Dunfermline and Edinburgh, grew more refined. The need for furnishings and rich adornments for Church and court encouraged international trade and brought about a revival of the Celtic artistic tradition. Margaret herself and the ladies of her court were expert embroiderers, who handed down their skills to succeeding generations. She also encouraged bookbinding and production. Her famous Gospel Book has survived (Oxford, Bodleian Library, MS Lat. liturg. f. 5): the volume that, according to Turgot, was retrieved—miraculously unscathed—from the river into which it had been unwittingly dropped by a page.

The queen's name lives on in the villages of South and North Queensferry, where Margaret made provision for pilgrims to St. Andrews to use her free ferry to cross the river Forth, and also in St. Margaret's Hope, a sheltered bay to the west of North Queensferry where she is said to have first set foot on Scottish soil.

Queen Margaret died in Edinburgh Castle on November 16, 1093, four days after learning of the deaths of her husband and her eldest son, Edmund, in battle in Northumberland. Later, her son David embellished her tiny chapel, now the oldest surviving building in Edinburgh Castle. She was buried at Dunfermline, which quickly became a place of pilgrimage. Margaret was canonized in 1251.

See also Hagiography (Female Saints); Ingibiorg; Matilda of Scotland; Place-Names, English, Women in

BIBLIOGRAPHY

Primary Sources

Anglo-Saxon Chronicle. Edited and translated by Dorothy Whitelock, David C. Douglas, and Susie I. Tucker, s.a. 1054. London: Eyre and Spottiswoode, 1961.

Gospel Book of St. Margaret. A facsimile reproduction [Oxford, Bodleian Library, MS. Lat. liturg. f. 5]. Edited by William Forbes-Leith S. J. Edinburgh: Douglas, 1896.

Lanfranc. *Letters of Lanfranc, Archbishop of Canterbury*. Edited and translated by Helen Clover and Margaret T. Gibson, 160–63. Oxford: Clarendon Press, 1979.

Turgot, Bishop. [*Vita S Margaretae Scotorum Reginae*] In *Symeonis Dunelmensis Opera et Collectanea*, edited by J. Hodgson Hinde, 234–54. Surtees Society Publications, 51. London, 1868.

———. [English translation of the *Vita*]. Translated by A. O. Anderson. In *Early Sources in Scottish History* A.D. *500–1286*, vol. 2. Edinburgh: Oliver & Boyd, 1922.

Secondary Sources

Baker, Derek. "'A Nursery of Saints': St Margaret of Scotland Reconsidered." In *Medieval Women*, edited by Derek Baker, 119–42. Studies in Church History, Subsidia, 1. Oxford: Basil Blackwell, 1978.

Barrow, G. W. S. "Benedictines, Tironensians and Cistercians." In Barrow, *The Kingdom of the Scots*, 188–211. New York: St. Martins, 1973. Revised version of "From Queen Margaret to David I: Benedictines and Tironensians." *Innes Review* 11 (1960).

Dickinson, W. C., G. Donaldson, and I. A. Miller, eds. *A Sourcebook of Scottish History*, vol 1. Edinburgh: Nelson, 1952.

Huneycutt, Lois L. "The Idea of the Perfect Princess: The Life of St Margaret in the Reign of Matilda II (1100–18)." *Anglo-Norman Studies* 12, edited by Marjorie Chibnall, 81–97. Woodbridge, Suffolk: Boydell Press, 1990.

Wall, Valerie. "Queen Margaret of Scotland (1070–93): Burying the Past, Enshrining the Future." In *Queens and Queenship in Medieval Europe. Proceedings of a Conference Held at King's College London, April 1995*, edited by Anne J. Duggan, 27–28. Woodbridge, Suffolk: Boydell Press, 1997.

Wilson, Alan J. *St Margaret of Scotland*. Edinburgh: John Donald, 1993.

ELIZABETH LAIDLAW

MARGARET OF YORK (1446–1503). Margaret of York, duchess of Burgundy, consort of Duke Charles the Bold (1433–1477), was one of the most influential women in English and French politics in the late fifteenth century and a noted patron of the arts and the Church. Born on May 3, 1446, probably at Fotheringhay in Northamptonshire, Margaret was the fifth of seven surviving children (out of twelve) of Richard Plantagenet, duke of York (1411–1460), and his wife, Cecily Neville (1415–1495). Like her siblings, Margaret was brought up in full awareness of her royal pedigree and its expectations. Margaret was born a decade before the start of the dynastic struggle for the royal succession known as the Wars of the Roses (1455–1485), which was fought between her family, the house of York (whose symbol was the white rose), and the reigning branch of the royal family, the house of Lancaster (whose symbol was the red rose). After 1450, the recurring mental instability of Henry VI (1421–1471) of Lancaster allowed noble factions led by Margaret's father and by Henry's wife, Queen Margaret of Anjou, to contend for control of the royal government. Although the duke of York was slain in battle in 1460, his eldest son and Margaret's eldest brother seized the Crown as Edward IV (1442–1483) in March 1461.

In March 1466, King Edward, seeking to strengthen political and commercial ties with Burgundy, one of the richest and most powerful states of western Europe, arranged Margaret's marriage with Charles, count of Charolais, a young widower who was son and heir to Duke Philip the Good of Burgundy (1396–1467). Besides the link with England, Charles needed a male heir, since his only child from his previous marriage was an infant daughter named Mary. In the late fifteenth century, the duchy of Burgundy was an independent state that encompassed modern Belgium and the Netherlands as well as portions of present-day France and Germany. Charles's cousin, King Louis XI of France, the fabled "Spider King" (1423–1483), sought to break the power of Burgundy and reabsorb into France the French parts of the Burgundian state. Seeking to prevent an Anglo-Burgundian alliance, Louis was able to stall negotiations until after Duke Philip's death in 1467, when Charles, now duke, concluded the alliance with Edward IV and agreed to the marriage with Margaret. Announced to Parliament in May 1468 and celebrated in Burgundy the following July, the wedding of Margaret and Charles, which

Christine Weightman, Margaret's biographer, has called the "marriage of the century," made Margaret duchess of Burgundy and created a formidable anti-French alliance that persuaded Louis XI to aid the house of Lancaster in regaining the English throne. In 1470, the French king brokered an unlikely alliance between Edward IV's disaffected supporter, Richard Neville, earl of Warwick, and Margaret of Anjou. Aided by the Lancastrians, Warwick overthrew Edward and restored Henry VI in October 1470. Edward IV fled immediately to the court of his sister and brother-in-law in Burgundy. When Warwick brought England into formal alliance with France, Duke Charles agreed to assist Edward in regaining the English throne. Margaret aided the Yorkist restoration by helping to persuade her favorite brother, George Plantagenet, duke of Clarence (1449–1478), to abandon his alliance with Warwick (formed when Clarence married Warwick's daughter in

Margaret of York being presented to Charles Le Téméraire (the Rash), Duke of Burgundy. From fifteenth-century French manuscript of *Life of Alexander the Great* by Quintus Curtius Rufus. © Bibliothèque nationale de France, Paris. The Art Archive/Bibliotheque Municipale Reims/Dagli Orti.

1469). Clarence reconciled with Edward IV when the latter returned to England in March 1471. By May 1471, Henry VI and his son were dead and Edward IV had regained the throne.

The dukes of Burgundy were renowned for their brilliant patronage of the arts and letters, and Margaret, as duchess of Burgundy—now the literary center of northern Europe—continued this tradition in grand style. Thanks to chroniclers like Olivier de La Marche (c.1426–1502), we have much eyewitness information on her milieu. Her documented library of twenty-five books was one of the largest traced to ownership by a woman at that time. She subsidized the earliest and most illustrious English printer, William Caxton, a merchant who entered her service by 1471, probably as a financial advisor. Caxton showed the duchess his half-finished English translation of Raoul Lefèvre's *Recueil des Histoires de Troie* (*Collection of the Histories of Troy*), a retelling of the legends of Troy, which Lefèvre had composed for Margaret's father-in-law, Duke Philip of Burgundy, in about 1465. More than a pretty volume, this work promoted two revealing ideological connections: first, that of the ancient Trojan nobility with fifteenth-century Burgundy as a model for chivalry (medieval moralists preferred Virgil's Trojan hero Aeneas, founder of Rome, to the Greeks, who, although victorious in the Trojan War, were thought too cunning to be properly noble), and, second, Burgundy's bond with England, which, validated by the Trojan heritage, guaranteed its rightness. Margaret corrected Caxton's English and encouraged him to complete the work. By late 1471, Caxton was in the duchess's service in Cologne, where he learned to use the new movable-type printing press and consequently was able to realize his momentous undertaking in 1476. Thus, thanks in part to Margaret, Caxton's *The History of Troy* became the first book ever printed in English—a milestone both in the technology of literacy and in the moral edification of the ruling class.

In January 1477, Duke Charles, earning his nickname "the Bold" (*le Téméraire*)—sometimes translated more aptly as "the Rash"—died in a major confrontation at Nancy with the duke of Lorraine, one of the web of international allies spun against Burgundy by Louis XI. Found half-eaten by wolves, Charles's corpse signaled the eventual end of the Valois line in Burgundy. By removing his most potent adversary, Louis was able to unify his kingdom, increasing its prosperity and influence. Even before the duke's death was certain, Margaret joined forces with Charles's daughter and heir, Mary of Burgundy (1457–1482), to save the duchy from French encroachment. She hoped for military assistance from her brother, Edward IV, but the king contented himself with warning Louis to respect his sister's property rights. Louis countered by accusing Margaret of complicity in a plot with her brother the duke of Clarence and other English lords to kidnap Mary and force her to wed the duke. Although Edward distrusted Clarence and rejected Margaret's efforts to promote a marriage between him and Mary, the king refused to believe Louis's charges against Margaret, and the duchess remained in favor with her brother.

Margaret was now the "duchess-mother of Burgundy" (but only symbolically, since she had no children) and dowager (denoting an entitlement in lands from her late husband), while her stepdaughter was the reigning duchess. Margaret tried to find a husband for Mary who could protect the interests of both women. After failing in her attempt to arrange a match with Clarence, Margaret supported Mary in her desire to conclude a marriage with the German Maximilian Habsburg (1459–1519), the son of the Holy Roman Emperor Frederick III and a future emperor in his own right. Duke Charles had pursued this same match years earlier. However, in 1477, Maximilian was in no position to provide substantial aid, leaving the two Burgundian duchesses to fend off the French on their own. Louis XI relentlessly manipulated alliances old and new to isolate Mary from her advisors and other support, forcing Margaret, who had been recruiting armies for Mary, to flee to Malines (Mechlin) in what is now northern Belgium. After making a public protest there, Margaret, escorted by three hundred archers, headed west to her dower town of Oudenaarde, where she sought to regroup the anti-French forces in Burgundy. Between 1477 and 1480 Louis also tried gentler tactics, offering Margaret protection in exchange for her lands, part of which he would later return to her. Margaret not only refused but also continued to press her brother Edward IV to renew the Anglo-Burgundian alliance, again frustrating many of Louis's designs. Over the years, Louis came to respect Margaret as a political force with which to be reckoned.

By the mid-1480s, Mary's marriage to Maximilian restored to Margaret her dower lands—a reward for her loyalty to her ducal family—and maintained most of Burgundy as an independent state under Mary's heirs. Margaret now set up her residence at Malines, already the prosperous administrative center of the Low Countries, where she gradually built a magnificent palace. Adorned with artistic treasures of the Burgundian court, the palace included paintings by Van Eyck, Van der Weyden, and Memlinc, and some of the finest tapestries and porcelains of the period. Margaret's role in fostering chivalric values, evidenced in her patronage of Caxton's *History of Troy*, resurfaced in 1501, when she presided over a ceremony restoring the Order of the Golden Fleece, an order linking feudal service with service to God. Once a trademark of the dukes of Burgundy, the order had almost disappeared between 1477 and 1501.

Margaret was extremely pious, a trait inherited from her mother, and generously supported the local monastery of the Recollects. Most of the books she chose for her library, in contrast to Charles's antique-pagan tastes, were religious. Malines benefited immensely from her careful management of her lands and revenues, whose defense she also handled when necessary by raising troops and enforcing law and order, the latter in a reformist spirit. She would spend most of the rest of her life in Malines, maintaining contact with Maximilian and looking after her grandchildren following Mary's death in a hunting accident in 1482. Her grandson, Archduke Philip of Austria and duke of Burgundy in succession to his mother, further secured Margaret's possessions when he came of age. Margaret's last few years were spent mainly at Binche in Hainault (southwestern Belgium).

Although she returned only once to England, Margaret nonetheless maintained contacts there (and also in Scotland and Ireland), alternately seeking and lending aid to her brother Edward IV. After the death of her brother, Richard III, and the overthrow of the House of York at the Battle of Bosworth Field in August 1485, Margaret became a zealous supporter of efforts to overthrow Henry VII (1457–1509), the first monarch of the House of Tudor and Richard's supplanter. Despite Henry's marriage to her niece Elizabeth of York, Margaret gave men and funding to an impostor named Lambert Simnel (d. c.1525), who pretended to be her nephew Edward Plantagenet, earl of Warwick, the son of Clarence. Her court at Malines served as a refuge for Yorkist exiles, many of whom joined Simnel, who had himself crowned as "Edward VI" in Ireland in 1487 and then led an unsuccessful invasion of England. In the 1490s, Margaret supported another Yorkist pretender, Perkin Warbeck (d. 1499), who claimed to be Richard Plantagenet, duke of York, the younger son of Edward IV. In 1492, Margaret met and publicly acknowledged Warbeck as the real York, whom she had last seen in 1480, three years before he disappeared in the Tower of London with his brother Edward V. Presumed murdered by their uncle Richard III, the missing boys have become a historical cause célèbre as historians still debate the fate of the "Princes in the Tower." Whether Margaret actually believed the pretenders to be her nephews or was simply using the movements they inspired to restore the House of York and perhaps recover her English holdings is now unclear. Whatever her reasoning, by writing letters to the courts of Europe affirming his identity as York, she helped maintain Warbeck as a significant threat to Henry VII and the House of Tudor for six years. In 1497, Warbeck's capture and confession of his ruse forced Margaret to ask Henry for pardon, which she received. She nonetheless remained a steadfast Yorkist until her death in November 1503 at Malines, where she was buried at the monastery of the Recollects.

See also Elizabeth of York; Margaret of Anjou; Woodville, Elizabeth

BIBLIOGRAPHY

Primary Sources

La Marche, Olivier de. *Mémoires d'Olivier de la Marche, maître d'hôtel et capitaine des gardes de Charles le Téméraire.* Edited by H. Beaune and J. d'Arbaumont, 3: 101–201; 4: 95–144. 4 vols. Paris: Renouard, 1883–1888.

Stevenson, Joseph, ed. *Letters and papers illustrative of the wars of the English in France during the reign of Henry the Sixth, king of England.* 2 vols. Rerum britannicarum medii aevi scriptores, 22. London: Longman, Green et al., 1861–1864. [e.g., William Worcester's *Annales*, in 2: 2.]
[See also notes to Weightman, below].

Secondary Sources

Weightman, Christine. *Margaret of York, Duchess of Burgundy 1446–1503.* Gloucester, U.K.: Alan Sutton; New York: St. Martin's, 1989. Revised ed. Stroud, U.K.: Alan Sutton, 1993.

JOHN A. WAGNER

MARGARETA VON SCHWANGAU (c.1390–1451/1459). Margareta von Schwangau was a German noblewoman who wrote significant letters. Born in Hohenschwangau, she was the wife of the famous South Tyrolean poet Oswald von Wolkenstein (1376/77–1445), whom she married in 1417.

In contrast to her husband, who was a knight and *minnesinger* (the medieval German counterpart to the southern-French troubadour), Margareta gained access to a new form: epistolary literature. It took a long time for her to begin corresponding with her husband, relatives, and friends, but her letters soon proved to be excellent examples of this literary genre. Keeping to his own literary forte, her husband composed a number of songs about Margaret that are considered outstandingly realistic and erotic songs of the late German Middle Ages. The couple lived in the castle Hauenstein near Brixen in Southern Tyrol (Brixen = Italian: Bressanone, since South Tyrol is now technically in Northern Italy) until Oswald's death in 1445. In 1447, Margareta handed the castle's administration over to her sons and settled in Brixen, where she died sometime between 1451 and 1459. Her letters present her as a very pragmatic and farsighted person. In her occasional expression of strong emotion for her husband in her letters, she transcended the stylistic and formalistic barriers of traditional medieval epistolary literature. Her letters also represent the new, higher level of literacy then recently made available to women of both the lower nobility and the bourgeoisie. In addition, her letters acutely mirror the actual South Tyrolean economic and political situation. Even though they do not provide us with sufficient data to flesh out a more detailed biography of Margareta, they still give us some idea of her as a writer and loving wife of a revered poet.

See also Epistolary Authors, Women as; *Minne*

BIBLIOGRAPHY

Primary Sources

Margareta von Schwangau. [*Letters*]. In *Deutsche Privatbriefe des Mittelalters*, edited by Georg Steinhausen, vol. 1. Berlin: Königliche Preussische Akademie, 1899.
———. *See* Pörnbacher, Hans *below in* Secondary Sources.

Secondary Sources

Classen, Albrecht. "Margareta von Schwangau: Epistolary Literature in the German Late Middle Ages." *Medieval Perspectives* 1.1 (spring 1986): 41–53.

Pörnbacher, Hans. *Margareta von Schwangau. Herrn Oswalds von Wolkenstein Gemahlin.* Weissenhorn, Germany: Konrad, 1983.
Schwob, Anton. *Oswald von Wolkenstein. Eine Biographie.* 3rd ed. Bozen, Tyrol: Athesia, 1979.

ALBRECHT CLASSEN

MARGUERITE D'OINGT (c.1260–c.1310). The visionary Marguerite d'Oingt was the prioress of the Carthusian (Benedictine) convent of Pelotens (modern Poleteins) near Lyons, France. She authored three texts, each in a different language, and a number of letters. Her major work, the *Speculum* (*Mirror*), was written in French; the *Pagina meditationum* (*Page of Meditations*) in Latin, and *La Vie de Sainte Beatrix d'Ornacieux Vierge* (*The Life of the Virgin St. Beatrice of Ornacieux*) in Franco-Provençal. Her writings were well known in the fourteenth century and were translated into Provençal (southern-French language). Very little is known of her life besides what she says in her writings. She is one of the mystical writers who developed the theology of God as Mother.

From among the few established facts concerning her life, we know that she was the prioress of the Carthusian convent of Pelotens by 1288, and that she had begun to write her Latin *Pagina meditationum* two years earlier. She is mentioned in her parents' wills in 1297 and 1300, and the anonymous copyist of her works gives her death as occurring in 1310. Her family was one of the most ancient and powerful families in the Lyonnais/Beaujolais region, ruling the fiefdom of Oingt since 1093. An intriguing Christian-historical coincidence is that when the Romans founded the village of Oingt (58 B.C.E.), they called it Iconium—the same name as that of the Near-Eastern town, now Konya, Turkey, in which St. Paul would establish an important church and conversion center. Marguerite had two brothers and three sisters, two of whom entered convents as she did.

According to the modern editors of Marguerite's works, she became a writer inadvertently and continued to write only under pressure from her superiors. After falling ill as the result of a number of powerful visionary experiences, apparently in 1286, she was cured by the act of writing down her experiences. In one of her surviving letters, perhaps to her spiritual director, Marguerite speaks of her writing as the only way in which she could relieve what she felt in her heart after her visions. But there is more to her motivation than this; she is not simply saying she had to write. Two unique characteristics of her writing point to a strong authorial consciousness: the fact that she writes in three languages suggests that she composed with a specific audience in mind, and her dominant use of metaphors associated with writing and book production indicates that for her, all communication was a form of writing, of inscription. German mystics such as Hildegard of Bingen (1098–1179) heard God tell her to speak and write her visions, Gertrude the Great of Helfta (1256–c.1302) wrote down what she had memorized in her heart, but Marguerite writes what is *written* in her heart.

Marguerite d'Oingt brought two new perspectives to mystical writing by women. The first is the idea that the visionary is not a vessel but a text: a body in whom or on whom a text is inscribed. The second point is her emphasis on the act of writing, as she physically transfers the text written within her to the pages of a book—"as soon as she put a word in that book, it left her heart." In her *Speculum*, Christ is also a text; His wounds are inscribed on His body, and she reads the message of His Passion. This view of writing implies that the body and its experiences will also be central to her expression, which comes through very clearly in her first written work, the *Pagina meditationum*.

The *Pagina meditationum* begins with her conversion experience in 1286. As she was listening to the words of the Mass, certain phrases stood out to her, and she began to meditate on them. She decided to write down her *cogitationes* (thoughts) in order to remember them better and return to them more easily during prayer. She then addresses herself directly to God; in the course of re-creating Christ's Passion, she reflects on the love God manifests to human beings. It is near the close of this section that she speaks of God as her mother: "For are you not my mother and more than my mother? The mother who bore me labored in delivering me for one day or one night but you, my sweet and lovely Lord, labored for me for more than thirty years" (see Bynum 1982, 1992). The conclusion of this meditation is a statement of her love for God and her desire to be saved by him when she dies. The meditation is almost entirely in Latin, but occasionally, as here, she breaks into dialect to express her desire to leave the body and be with Christ. The second meditation works through her thoughts on sin and the fear of Hell. This leads her to a fierce attack on the vices of religious people in her day. From this she moves to a contemplation of what will happen to such people in hell. She visualizes sinners before the throne of God on the Day of Judgment, their sins parading before them and their consciences suddenly awakening to realize with horror the judgment of God. After this, Marguerite's attention turns to God's judgment for the elect, and she has a glimpse of heaven. The meditation closes with thanks to God for the spiritual gifts He has sent her and a request: "Sweet Master, write in my heart that which you wish me to do; write your laws there; write your commandments so that they can never be erased."

In the *Speculum*, her major work, we find a remarkably concise use of visionary experience as the ground for instruction in meditation. Marguerite, who composed this work in the last decade of the thirteenth century (we know the book was presented to the Carthusian General Chapter in 1294 by Hughes, prior of Valbonne), organizes her *Speculum* into three chapters, each based on a different vision. In each chapter she first tells the content of her vision, its central images and metaphors, and then shows how she meditated on the details, with the results of those meditations presented as models to be followed by her readers. She speaks of the self as having the visions in the third person and uses the first person for her reflective narration. She addresses her readers directly as *vous*, often using imperatives: "think about this," "meditate on this." The central image of the *Speculum* is the book; in the first chapter she sees Christ holding a closed book in His hand as if to preach from it. On the clasp of the book (where the title would usually be written) she notes letters in three colors: white, black, and silver-gilt. The book in toto suggests a number of themes for meditation: Christ's generosity in joining His divinity to our human misery; His humility; His desire to be persecuted; His poverty, patience, and obedience. These meditations cause her to turn to another book, the book of her conscience, in which she finds her own inadequacies. In the second chapter she sees the book open, and in or on its mirror-like pages is a vision of Paradise; this place is the source of all good: wisdom power, charm, strength, kindling of love, unthinkable joy. In the third vision, as Marguerite attempts again to meditate on Christ seated next to God the Father, she is ravished into heaven itself, again a place larger than the world, filled with a brilliant light, full of handsome and glorious beings. She sees that Christ is there, and that His wounds transmit the light, and she sees how He has made His friends like himself.

The third text attributed to Marguerite d'Oingt is *La Vie de Sainte Beatrix d'Ornacieux*. Here Marguerite narrates the life of a young saint whom she knew well because Beatrice had been her student when she was novice mistress. Beatrice died on November 25, 1303, a few years before Marguerite. Although Marguerite felt great admiration for her, she comments that her austerities were often "senz grant discretion" ("without moderation"), and she notes that the saint tormented herself "outra reyson" ("senselessly"), on Good Friday. This biography too is a visionary work, which retells and analyzes the mystical experiences of Beatrice.

Although the works of Marguerite d'Oingt had been virtually ignored by modern scholarship until the 1980s, her writings were apparently widely read in her time. She is one of the first women writers to describe the motherhood of God and to see the visionary as not a vessel but a text. She is also unusual in the fact that she wrote in both the vernacular (French and Franco-Provençal) and in Latin. Her prose is simple, concise, and lyrical. Whether she is writing in Latin or in the vernacular, the rhythms of her phrases are incantatory. In the *Pagina meditationum*, she demonstrates a remarkable ear for colloquial speech, while it is her visual imagination that dominates the *Speculum*.

Marguerite's descendants and any surviving relatives died out during the Black Death in 1348, or shortly thereafter, for her family line, at least in terms of male heirs, was deemed extinct by 1382. Marguerite was venerated locally as a saint until the French Revolution and is still touted as part of the village of Oingt's tourist attractions. Her canonization is still pending.

See also Gertrude the Great, of Helfta, St.; Hagiography (Female Saints); Hildegard of Bingen, St.

BIBLIOGRAPHY

Primary Sources
Marguerite d'Oingt. *Marguerite d'Oingt: édition critique de ses œuvres*. Critical ed. by Antonin Durrafour, Pierre Gardette, and Paulette Durdilly. Lyons. Faculté catholique. Institut de linguistique romane, 21. Paris: Les Belles Lettres, 1965.
———. *The Writings of Margaret of Oingt, Medieval Prioress and Mystic (d. 1310)*. Translated, with introduction and notes, by Renate Blumenfeld-Kosinski. Focus Library of Medieval Women. Newburyport, Mass.: Focus, 1990. New ed. Cambridge: D. S. Brewer, 1997.
———. "The Mirror of St. Marguerite d'Oingt." Translated by Richard J. Pioli. In *Medieval Women's Visionary Literature*, edited by Elizabeth Petroff, 290–94. New York: Oxford University Press, 1986.

Secondary Sources
[See also notes to above translations].
Bynum, Caroline W. *Fragmentation and Redemption: Essays on Gender and the Human Body in Medieval Religion*. New York: Zone Books, 1992.
———. *Holy Feast and Holy Fast: The Religious Significance of Food to Medieval Women*. Berkeley: University of California Press, 1987.
———. *Jesus as Mother: Studies in the Spirituality of the High Middle Ages*. Berkeley: University of California Press, 1982.
http://home.infionline.net/~ddisse/oingt.html [Useful, updated site for bibliography and translated texts, etc.].
http://oingt.free.fr/Histoire/Histoire.htm#Marguerite [Informative on the history of Marguerite's family and hometown].
McGinn, Bernard. *The Flowering of Mysticism: Men and Women in the New Mysticism (1200–1350)*, 3: 288–92.The Presence of God, 3. New York: Crossroad, 1998.

Müller, Catherine M. "How to Do Things with Mystical Language: Marguerite d'Oingt's Performative Writing," In *Performance and Transformation: New Approaches to Late Medieval Spirituality*, edited by Mary A. Suydam and Joanna E. Ziegler. New York: St. Martin's Press, 1999.

———. *Marguerite Porete et Marguerite d'Oingt de l'autre côté du miroir*. Currents in Comparative Romance Languages and Literatures, 72. New York: Peter Lang, 1999.

Petroff, Elizabeth. "Writing the Body: Male and Female in the Writings of Marguerite d'Oingt, Angela of Foligno and Umiltà of Faenza." In Petroff, *Body and Soul: Essay on Medieval Women and Mysticism*, 204–24. Berkeley: University of California Press, 1994.

ELIZABETH A. PETROFF

MARÍA DE AJOFRÍN (d. 1489). A Spanish Hieronymite visionary, María de Ajofrín was the daughter of fairly well-off commoners from the town of Ajofrín near Toledo, an important city in central Spain. She showed signs of unusual piety from an early age. María had many suitors and her relatives made plans to marry her off, but when she got wind of their intentions, at the age of thirteen she made a vow of chastity and determined to enter a religious order. Finally, when she was fifteen, María convinced her father to take her to Toledo, where a divine vision inspired her to join a group of holy women closely associated with the Hieronymite Order, an order of hermits dedicated to St. Jerome (fourth century). She continued to receive visions and prophecies until her death in 1489, and such miraculous phenomena were recorded in the hagiographic text written by her confessor, Juan de Corrales.

María was often called on to mediate between the living and the dead by bearing messages from the souls in purgatory to their still-living friends and relatives. In that way, the living could know if their relatives in Purgatory needed more suffrages or some other task performed to ascend to paradise. But it was a series of political messages and prophecies that established María's credentials as a visionary and led to her collaboration with the Church authorities.

María's early visions deal above all with the need for ecclesiastical reform in Toledo. In particular, in a vision she received on All Saints' Day (November 1) in 1484, Christ appeared to her seated on a throne, holding a double-edged sword in his mouth. In her vision, Christ instructed her to tell the archbishop of Toledo to eradicate those five sins by which immoral clergymen were daily crucifying Christ: lack of faith, greed, lust, ignorance, and lack of reverence for sacred things. Christ also gave her a sign to authenticate the divine source of her message for the archbishop: the sword that Christ held would pierce her heart and the blood that flowed from it would be a living testimony for all.

The wound that then appeared on María's breast was not just any sign, for as both a replication of the Passion of Christ (as in the lance wound in Christ's side) and a replication of the *compassio* (cosuffering with Christ's Passion) of the Virgin Mary at the Crucifixion (Simeon's prophecy of a sword piercing Mary's soul in Luke 2:35), it was a crucial element in the construction of María's holiness. By thus assimilating María to both himself and his mother, Christ seemed to establish her authority and to prepare her for her role as prophetess and message-bearer. However, it was the notarial document that her confessor ordered drawn up, stating how he and the other witnesses saw the wound on María's body, that finally convinced the archbishop of Toledo of the authenticity of María's extraordinary experiences. From then on, she could be reasonably assured that her messages would be considered to be of divine origin and that attention would be paid to them.

It is difficult to assess the effectiveness of María de Ajofrín's mediumistic role, first, because her biographers are primarily interested in the miraculous favors she enjoyed and not in their tangible results, and second, because her task was merely to bear such messages, not to carry them out. Nonetheless, it is probably no accident that Cardinal Mendoza (1428–1495), the archbishop of Toledo, was singled out as the primary receiver of the messages intended to convey God's anger at clerical immorality, for the cardinal himself seemed more interested in furthering the political and economic interests of the powerful Mendoza clan, which included two of his own illegitimate children, than in reforming the clergy of Toledo.

In succeeding visions, María continued to convey God's wrath at clerical immorality and at the presence of heretics in Toledo. With its large population of converts from Judaism, some of whom were secret Judaizers, there must have been hostility toward the implantation of the Inquisition in Toledo. There is further evidence that Cardinal Mendoza himself may have been personally opposed to its establishment. Particularly scandalous was the discovery of Judaizers in the very heart of the Hieronymite order and in the very same city of Toledo. Inquisitorial documents from the years 1486 until 1488 reveal that some of the monks from the Hieronymite monastery of La Sisla had engaged in especially outrageous Judaizing (crypto-Jewish) practices. In 1488, three years after the establishment of the Inquisition in Toledo, María received a vision in which the flagellated Christ claimed that his shoulders had been made bloody by the heretics. In this vision, Christ instructed María to encourage the Holy Office to pursue such Judaizers with greater vigor. While we have no knowledge of María de Ajofrín's role, if any, in the establishment of the Inquisition in Toledo, her part in encouraging its operation is clearer. With her divinely inspired messages, she conveyed to the Church hierarchy God's divine approval of the tribunal's unrelenting eradication of heresy.

Thanks to her visions, María, although of humble birth, was empowered to reproach the sinfulness of the clergy and, more concretely, to sermonize none other than Cardinal Mendoza, the highest ecclesiastical authority in Spain. Once her experiences were validated, she became a sort of collaborator with the Church hierarchy. Her status as woman and as visionary was enhanced by that official support, while her visions were put to political use by the ecclesiastical establishment to enhance its own agenda of rigorous extirpation of heresy.

See also Constance of Castile; Hagiography (Female Saints); Jewish Women in the Middle Ages; Teresa de Cartagena

BIBLIOGRAPHY

Primary Source
Corrales, Fray Juan de. *Vida de María de Ajofrín*. Escorial, MS C-III-3, fols. 193r–231v.

Secondary Source
Surtz, Ronald E. *Writing Women in Late Medieval and Early Modern Spain: The Mothers of Saint Teresa of Avila*. Middle Ages. Philadelphia: University of Pennsylvania Press, 1995.

RONALD E. SURTZ

MARIA OF VENICE (Maria Sturion) (1379–1399). Born Maria Sturion, Maria of Venice was a Dominican penitent (member of the Order of Penance of St. Dominic).

When compared with the dramatic stories of other putative saints, the life of Maria Sturion seems remarkably ordinary. Born around 1379 to a well-to-do, though not noble, Venetian family, she grew into a proper young lady, polite and well-mannered, with a normal interest in worldly display. At the age of fifteen or so, she married a man of similar social background, Giannino della Piazza, and moved into the house of her husband's family. The marriage, however, was not a great success. Maria's husband soon went off to the wars near Mantua, abandoning her to the care of his father. Unhappy with this arrangement, Maria returned to her family home. It was at this point that she began to frequent the Dominican church of Sts. Giovanni and Paolo, where she passed her time listening attentively to the sermons of Tommaso d'Antonio "Caffarini" of Siena, who became her spiritual director and eventually granted her the habit of a Dominican penitent. She did not get to wear it for long as her short life came to an end when she died of the plague in 1399 at age twenty.

Out of this unpromising material, Tommaso crafted a model of sanctity that would be not just admirable in his readers' eyes but also applicable to their lives. Maria was modest and humble, chaste and obedient. She was pious, but not heroically so. One of the greatest signs of her holiness, according to Tommaso, was that she always arrived early at the church where he was to preach and stayed awake throughout his interminable sermons. She renounced her youthful worldliness, stripped her clothing of every superfluous ornament, and devoted herself to charitable activities, though with the moderation urged by her spiritual advisor. He warned Maria against going about the city to tend the sick, since that would expose an attractive young woman like her to slander and scandal—or worse. And he persuaded her to turn over all her possessions to her mother so that the family patrimony would be safeguarded against impulsive excesses of generosity.

In Tommaso's carefully crafted biography, Maria served a dual purpose. She transformed into imitable form the inimitable sanctity of her own model, Catherine of Siena. In the place of Catherine's extravagant self-mortifications, Maria performed measured austerities; instead of being rapt in ecstatic visions, she walked to church with modestly downcast eyes. In short—and this was Tommaso's second point—she exemplified the way in which any pious woman could live by the rules governing the Dominican Order of Penance, which Tommaso was eagerly promoting in the very years that he was counseling Maria and writing her biography. Anyone who wanted to know what the rule's precepts meant in practice could turn to Tommaso d'Antonio's *Leggenda di Maria da Venezia* (*Legend of Maria of Venice*) and find there a living model of decent, well-bred, and nondisruptive piety. In Tommaso's hands, this sad relic of a broken marriage became the very embodiment of the primly devout young lady.

See also Catherine of Siena, St.; Hagiography (Female Saints); Penitentials, Women in; Rules for Canonesses, Nuns, and Recluses

BIBLIOGRAPHY

Primary Sources
Tommaso Caffarini [Thomas of Siena]. *Leggenda di Maria da Venezia*. In Fernanda Sorelli, *La santità imitabile: "Leggenda di Maria da Venezia" di Tommaso da Siena*, 151–225. Deputazione di storia patria per le Venezie, Miscellanea di studi e memorie, 23. Venice: Deputazione di storia patria per le Venezie, 1984. [Ed. plus historical study].

————. "The Legend of Maria of Venice." Translated by Daniel Bornstein. In *Dominican Penitent Women*, edited by Maiju Lehmijoki-Gardner. Classics of Western Spirituality. New York: Paulist Press, (2005).

Secondary Sources

Bornstein, Daniel. "Spiritual Kin and Domestic Devotions." In *Gender and Society in Renaissance Italy*, edited by Judith C. Brown and Robert C. Davis, 173–92. London and New York: Longman, 1998.

Sorelli, Fernanda. "Imitable Sanctity: The Legend of Maria of Venice." In *Women and Religion in Medieval and Renaissance Italy*, edited by Daniel Bornstein and Roberto Rusconi, 165–81. Chicago: University of Chicago Press, 1996.

DANIEL E. BORNSTEIN

MARIA DE VENTADORN (c. 1165–c. 1221). A celebrated patron and poetess, Maria, viscountess of Ventadorn, coauthored a *tenso* (dialogue poem) with the male troubadour Gui d'Ussel (or d'Uisel). She was one of the less prolific among the *trobairitz* (woman troubadours), yet because of her exalted social position at the court of Ventadorn—renowned for fostering troubadours—Maria is mentioned more frequently any other woman who composed verse in Occitan, the language of southern France, in the twelfth and thirteenth centuries.

She was born presumably in Turena, the Occitan name for Turenne, in the province of Limousin (now in the Corrèze region, south-central France). The daughter of Raimon II, viscount of Turena (c.1143–1191), and Hélis de Castelnau, Maria married Eble V, viscount of Ventadorn (Corrèze), as his second wife, before 1191. They had two sons. Within Eble's court, already an established center of troubadour culture, Maria's literary patronage inspired the songs of a dozen troubadours, including the Monk of Montaudon, Savaric de Mauleon, Guiraut de Calanson, Gausbert de Poicibot, and Bertran de Born (c.1140–1194). Gaucelm Faidit (c.1150–1205) alone addressed thirteen songs to her between c.1188 and 1195. The *razo* (prose introduction) to two of Gaucelm's songs recounts a complicated and almost certainly apocryphal story of how Maria rid herself of the troubadour's unwelcome attentions (ed. Boutière and Schutz, 170–79). She is last attested in an act of 1221, in which she witnessed her husband's monastic vows and joined him in entering the Cistercian abbey of Grandmont (Stronski, 44; ed. Rieger, 262–73).

Her only extant work, a *tenso* known by its opening verse, "Gui d'Uisel, be.m pesa de vos" ("Gui d'Ussel, I'm troubled about you") composed c.1208 (Schultz-Gora, 10) and exchanged with the troubadour Gui d'Ussel, is preserved in no fewer than ten manuscripts. In one, called *H* (Rome, Vatican Library, lat. 3207), its folio 53 is adorned with a portrait miniature of Maria wearing a narrow diadem and gold-embroidered robe while holding in her hand a rod or scepter whose meaning, while obscure, seems to be associated with the poetic arts (Rieger 1985, 391–92). In this same manuscript and another (called *P*, f. 48), the *tenso* is introduced by a *razo* purporting to explain the circumstances of its composition, the unhappy love that had caused Gui to renounce singing and the chance remark that sparked their debate. The traditional *tenso* is a dialogue poem composed jointly by two real authors, each of whom speaks in his or her own voice and is accorded rigorously equal space in the text. The poem of Maria and Gui is a *partimen* (debate poem), a subgenre of the *tenso* in which the first interlocutor proposes a problem and offers the second speaker his or her choice of positions to defend, the first speaker then takes the opposing position.

Maria's persona, who laments Gui's renunciation of song, asks if, in his opinion, a lady who loves a man should do as much for him as he for her. Gui's persona's decision to join this poetic debate and thereby end his silence seems a reluctant accession to Maria's unspoken command. He replies that in love there must never be a greater and a lesser and that the lady should act as does her lover, without regard to her superior wealth and station. Maria retorts that the lady ought to be for her lover as both beloved *and* lady (*domna*), while he should be for her a beloved but never a lord (*seignor*). Asserting that every love affair begins with the suitor pledging to serve the lady, she remarks that he who professes to be a servant but then seeks to become an equal betrays his words. Gui, who, having spoken second, is given the concluding speech, argues again for equality of the sexes, observing that love is the process of making two hearts one and reminding Maria that the suitor is obligated to his lady only through love. This credo is underscored by the fact that the language of their love-fidelity oaths echoes that of feudal oaths between lord and vassal. If there is a resolution to this tense and witty debate over sexual politics, it is a highly ambiguous one, since each ignores the other's attempts to re-define *fin'amor* (re-fined, courtly love) in a standoff. On the one hand, Maria, acting the part of the haughty domna, has obliged Gui to break his self-imposed silence; on the other, lady and poet have engaged in a poetic game (a frequent metaphor in the Occitan lyric for the game of love) in which each has participated as an equal, their equality ensured by the rigid limits of the poetic form (ed. Bruckner, xxvi–xxviii; Bruckner 1994, 882–83).

See also Capellanus, Andreas; *Trobairitz*

BIBLIOGRAPHY

Primary Sources
Gaucelm Faidit. [Songs to Maria]. In *Les Poèmes de Gaucelm Faidit, troubadour du XIIe siècle. Édition critique*, edited by Jean Mouzat, 303–4. Les Classiques d'Oc, 2. Paris: Nizet, 1965.
Gui d'Ussel. [Poems]. In *Les Poésies des quatre troubadours d'Ussel*, critical ed. with translation (modern French) by Jean Audiau, 73–75, 141–42. Paris: Delagrave, 1922. Geneva: Slatkine, 1973.
———— and Maria de Ventadorn. "Gui d'Ussel be.m pesa de vos." In *Songs of the Women Trou-badours*, edited and translated by Matilda Tomaryn Bruckner, Laurie Shepard, and Sarah White, 38–41, 157–58. New York and London: Garland, 1995. New ed. 2000. [Most recent, authoritative: original texts, notes, introduction, and English trans.].
————. "Gui d'Uisel be.m pesa de vos." In *Trobairitz: Der Beitrag der Frau in der altokzitanischen höfischen Lyrik. Edition des Gesamtkorpus*, edited by Angelica Rieger, 260–73. Beihefte der Zeitschrift für romanische Philologie, 233. Tübingen, Germany: Max Niemeyer Verlag, 1991. [Most authoritative, German trans. and commentary].
[*Vidas* and *razos* mentioning Maria, including two *razos* of her *tenso*]. In *Biographies des troubadours. Textes provençaux des XIIIe et XIVe siècles*, edited by Jean Boutière and Alexander H. Schutz, revised with I.-M. Cluzel, 75–77, 170–79, 208–9, 212–14, 314–20, 456–61. Les Classiques d'Oc, 1. Paris: Nizet, 1964.

Secondary Sources
[See also notes to above editions].
Bruckner, Matilda Tomaryn. "Debatable Fictions: The *Tensos* of the *Trobairitz*." In *Literary Aspects of Courtly Culture: Selected Papers from the Seventh Triennial Congress of the International Courtly*

Literature Society, edited by Donald Maddox and Sara Sturm-Maddox, 19–28. Cambridge: D. S. Brewer, 1994.

Eméric-David, Toussaint-Bernard. "Marie de Ventadour." *Histoire Littéraire de la France*, 17: 558–61. Paris: Firmin Didot; Treuttel & Wurtz, 1832.

Rieger, Angelica. "'Ins e.l cor port, dona, vostra faisso:' Image et imaginaire de la femme à travers l'enluminure dans les chansonniers des troubadours." *Cahiers de Civilisation Médiévale* 28 (1985): 385–415.

———. "La *mala canso* de Gui d'Ussel, un exemple d'intertextualité de pointe." In *Contacts de langues, de civilisations et intertextualité: Actes du IIème Congrès international de l'Association Internationale d'Études Occitanes. Montpellier, 20–26 septembre 1990*, edited by Gérard Gouiran, 2: 1071–88. Montpellier, France: C. E. O. de l'Université de Montpellier, 1993.

Schultz-Gora, Oskar. *Die provenzalischen Dichterinnen*. Leipzig: Gustav Foch, 1888. Reprint Geneva: Slatkine, 1975.

Stronski, Stanislaw. *La Légende amoureuse de Bertran de Born*. Paris: Édouard Champion, 1914. [The most authoritative historical commentary on Maria before ed. Rieger, see above, under Primary Sources].

MERRITT R. BLAKESLEE

MARIE DE BOURGOGNE/MARY OF BURGUNDY. *See* Margaret of York

MARIE DE BRABANT (1254–1321). Queen of France and literary patron, Marie's charm, refinement, and controversial political activity have made her the stuff of legend. Born in Louvain (now in Belgium), May 13, 1254, she was the daughter of Adelaide of Burgundy (d. 1273) and Duke Henry III of Brabant. Intelligent and attractive, she received the education customary for noblewomen and, like her father, gave evidence of a distinct taste for poetry. In 1275 she became the second wife of the French king, Philip III the Bold (1245–1285), son of Louis IX (St. Louis, 1214–1270) and Blanche of Castile (1188–1252). Marie and Philip would have three children: Marguerite, Blanche, and Louis.

The dynamic young queen soon surrounded herself with a court that cultivated literature. The poet Adenet le Roi (c.1240–c.1300) was one of her favorites and dedicated to her his most highly regarded poem, the lengthy romance *Cléomadès,* based in part on an *Arabian Nights* tale and on his travels through Italy, and ends in praise of Marie and her sister-in-law, Blanche of France. That Blanche was the widow of Ferdinand (d. 1275), son of the illustrious King Alfonso X (*El Sabio* = "the Wise") of Spain (1221–1284), may explain *Cléomadès*'s Spanish hero and link with Arabic literature.

A rather weak-willed monarch, Philip was dominated by his chamberlain, Pierre de la Broce, an ambitious and unscrupulous man who had already worked himself into an important position at court under Louis IX. Jealous of Marie's influence over the king, Pierre circulated rumors that she had poisoned the king's heir, a son by his first marriage. Because this slander was believed, Queen Marie was shut up in a tower of the Château of Vincennes, near Paris. Threatened also with execution, she was saved by the exposure before the king of Pierre de la Broce's treachery. Pierre was arrested and, largely due to the efforts of the Marie's brother and other supporters, was speedily found guilty and executed (1278).

Adenet le Roi, the chronicler Guillaume de Nangis (d. 1300), and other writers defended Marie's complete innocence in the affair, but none was able to overcome the contradictory force of the great Florentine poet Dante Alighieri (1265–1321) in the second part of his *Divina Commedia* (*Divine Comedy*). Dante's allusion to the event, which had occurred in his youth, in his *Purgatorio* (6: 22–24), represents Marie as the villain whom the poet seeks to warn in his verses for having caused the death of "Pier della Broccia," a victim of false charges: "Pier della Broccia dico, e qui proveggia,/mentr'è di qua, la donna di Brabante,/sì che però non sia di peggior greggia" ("Pierre de la Broce I mean: and here let the Lady of Brabant take heed, while she is on earth, that she be not of a worse herd for this").

After the death of her husband, she continued to live for a time at court, but eventually retired to the Château de Murel in Picardy (in northern France), where she devoted herself to literature and to good works. One of her children, Louis, count of Evreux, married Marguerite of Artois, founding the line that produced the kings of Navarre, patrons of the arts in their turn. Marie died at the Château de Murel January 10, 1321.

Her story inspired several literary works in the late eighteenth through early twentieth centuries.

See also Blanche of Castile

BIBLIOGRAPHY

Primary Sources
Adenet le Roi. *Cléomadès*. In *Oeuvres d'Adenet le Roi*, edited by Albert Henry, vol. 5. Université Libre de Bruxelles. Travaux de la Faculté de philosophie et lettres, 46. Bruges, Belgium: De Tempel, 1951.
Ancelot, François. *Marie de Brabant: drame historique en cinq actes et en vers*. Brussels: Ode & Wodon, 1829.
———. *Marie de Brabant, poème en six chants*. Paris: U. Canel, 1825. 3rd ed. 1826.
Dante. *Purgatorio*. Edited and translated by John D. Sinclair. Galaxy Books, 66. New York: Oxford University Press, 1970. Original 1939.
Guillaume de Nangis. *Gesta Philippi III*. In *Recueil des Historiens de la France*, 20 (1820): 466–539. [Latin text and French translation].
Imbert, Barthélémy. *Marie de Brabant, reine de France. Tragédie*. Paris: Prault, 1790. [Presented by the Comédiens du roi in 1789].
Maugenet, F. P. A. [pseudonym of A. P. F. Ménégault]. *Marie de Brabant, reine de France. Roman historique*. Paris: L. Collin, 1808
Riche, Daniel. *Marie de Brabant, la royale magicienne*. Paris: Baudinière, 1932.

Secondary Sources
Langlois, Charles-Victor. *Le Règne de Philippe III, le Hardi*. Paris: Hachette, 1887. Reprint Geneva: Mégariotis, 1979.
Lecoy de la Marche, Albert. *La France sous Saint Louis et Philippe le Hardi*. Paris: Librairies-imprimeries reunies, 1894.
Sivéry, Gérard. *Philippe III le Hardi*. Paris: Fayard, 2003.

CHARITY CANNON WILLARD

MARIE DE CHAMPAGNE (1145–1198). An outstanding French patron of poets and courts of love, Marie was once identified by some scholars as the actual Marie de France. The daughter of King Louis VII of France (c.1120–1180) and Eleanor of Aquitaine (1122–1204), Marie was the elder of two princesses born to the French royal family. Scholars including John Benton suggest that her contact with her legendary mother was virtually nonexistent, given Marie's parents' divorce in 1152; June McCash argues for a less extreme view of the relationship between two of the greatest female literary patrons in France. We do have evidence that Marie was educated by a *magistra* (teacher), Alix de Mareuil, a native of Champagne from the convent of St-Pierre-d'Avenay. A charter from 1153 records Marie's childhood engagement to Henri I le Libéral, count of Champagne, who had already distinguished himself in the service of Marie's father, Louis, during the Second Crusade. In accordance with local Champenois custom, Marie then probably left Louis's court to be brought up in her future husband's domain until her marriage to Henri le Libéral in 1164. Except for a possible extended visit to her mother's court at Poitiers in west central France c.1168–1174, Marie spent most of the rest of her life in Champagne, in northeastern France. She bore Henri four children— Henri II, Marie (who would also be known as Marie de Champagne, but also countess of Flanders), Scholastique, and Thibaut III—all of whom apparently stayed with her until they married or came of age.

Although Henri spared Marie many of the administrative burdens precociously endured by her mother, Marie acted as regent on several occasions both during Henri's lifetime, during his participation in the Crusades (1179), and after his death in 1181; her longest

Seal for Marie de Champagne as shown in Chartres Cathedral portal. Photo courtesy Janet Snyder.

regency extending from 1190 to 1197. She had considered remarriage to Philip, count of Flanders, a distant relative and also son of a friend of Henri's, her deceased husband. However, this was never finalized and she never remarried. Among her chief advisors was Geoffroi de Villehardouin, marshal of Champagne from 1189 and later author of the prose chronicle *La Conqueste de Constantinople* (*Conquest of Constantinople*), an eyewitness account of the Fourth Crusade.

Despite residual support for the theory that she wrote the celebrated *Lais* under the name Marie de France, there is no real evidence that Marie, countess of Champagne, was herself ever an author. Her importance lies rather in her patronage of a constellation of poets, her interest and participation in courtly love casuistry, and her enduring role as initiator and transmitter of literary taste. Twelfth-century Champagne was a marketplace for textiles from the north and for exotic goods shipped through southern ports and passes. The annual Champagne fairs, held by the count's authority and under his protection, were known throughout Europe. Similarly, Marie's court at Troyes emerged as a meeting place for northern lyric-poetic (*trouvère*) tradition and the southern-French, or *Provençal*, love poets called *troubadours*. This she accomplished through both patronage—a well-established tradition in her family—and pedigree, since she was great-granddaughter to founding troubadour Guillaume IX de Poitiers (1071–1127) and grandmother of noted *trouvère* Thibaut IV of Champagne, king of Navarre (1201–1253). Unlike her mother's well-documented history, Marie's life is more difficult to reconstruct because of the absence of extant personal correspondence and pertinent cartularies. Marie's influence is therefore best examined in the light of her family ties and the many highly esteemed literary works she inspired or commissioned. For example, none less than Chrétien de Troyes composed his famous romance, *Lancelot* or *Le Chevalier de la Charrete* (*The Knight of the Cart*) at her behest. He addresses her in his prologue as "my lady of Champagne" and credits her with developing the romance's plot and inner meaning as it relates the trials of love service at King Arthur's court and Lancelot's long-suffering loyalty to Queen Guinevere. The trouvère Gautier d'Arras also mentions the countess of Champagne in his *Eracle* (*Heracles*), a romance set in the Near East in which the hero advises the Emperor Phocas to release his wife, Empress Athanais, thus permitting her to marry her lover. Significantly, the details of this love triangle recall the unhappy relationship of Marie's own parents and her mother's subsequent remarriage to Henry II Plantagenet (1133–1189). Another beneficiary, Andreas Capellanus, in his *De arte honeste amandi* (*On the Art of Honest Loving*), expounds the theory and practice of love at all levels of society, particularly in aristocratic circles. Such were the so-called courts of love: ceremonious, highly refined debates and games among nobles and writers, convening at various courts of patronage, like Marie's, around France. Book 2 of Andreas's work records nine of Marie's verdicts on issues of love, judgments she must have offered during her stay at Poitiers while taking part in courtly debates on how best to behave in various love situations. For example, in one case, "a certain knight loved his lady beyond all measure and enjoyed her full embrace, but she did not love him with equal ardor." Marie's judgment censures the lady for shortchanging her suitor. But her most momentous, explicitly documented judgment as recorded by Capellanus was that love cannot exist between husband and wife—a tenet of courtly love doctrine justifying the triangle. Marie also sponsored the *trouvères* Conon de Béthune and Gace Brulé, as well as such lesser-known poets as Guillaume de Garlande, Huon de Valery, Gilles de Vieux-Maisons, and Pierre II de Molins. While we may judge Marie's tastes by the works of the many poets she promoted, only in Andreas's manual of love does she speak directly to us, which validates the notion that his *Arte* served as the conduct manual of Marie's court. As often happens, the countess felt increasingly drawn to religious works in old age, making the court of Champagne an important center for translation of Scripture from Latin into French. Marie also commissioned a rhymed translation of Psalm 44, the *Eructavit* (*He uttered*) and, in 1192, asked the little-known poet Everat to translate the Old Testament metrically, of which he finished only the Book of Genesis: more an adaptation than a translation in the modern sense; laced with praises of Marie and Henri as well as profuse explanatory-moralizing notes, or glosses; the entire work totaling about 21,000 verses.

Because of the talented, productive array of poets whom Marie attracted and protected, especially after 1180, the court of Champagne rivaled both the French and English royal courts in breadth and brilliance of literary activity.

See also Arthurian Women; Capellanus, Andreas; Eleanor of Aquitaine; Guinevere; Marie de France

BIBLIOGRAPHY

Primary Sources
Capellanus, Andreas. [On Marie] In Pascale Bourgain. "Aliénor d'Aquitaine et Marie de Champagne mises en cause par André le Chapelain." *Cahiers de civilisation médiévale* 19 (1986): 29–36.

Chrétien de Troyes. *Le Chevalier de la Charrete*. Edited by Mario Roques. Classiques Français du Moyen Âge, 86. Paris: Honoré Champion, 1967.

———. *Lancelot, or, The Knight of the Cart*. In *Chrétien de Troyes: Arthurian Romances*, edited and translated by William W. Kibler. New York and London: Penguin, 1991.

[See also notes to Benton and McCash below]

Secondary Sources

Benton, John F. "The Court of Champagne as a Literary Center." *Speculum* 36 (1961): 551–91.

Evergates, Theodore. "Aristocratic Women in the County of Champagne." In *Aristocratic Women in Medieval France*, edited by T. Evergates, 74–110, esp. 76–80. Philadelphia: University of Pennsylvania Press, 1999.

Krueger, Roberta L. "Desire, Meaning, and the Female Reader: The Problem in Chrétien's *Charrete*." In *Lancelot and Guinevere: A Casebook*, edited by Lori J. Walters, 229–45. Arthurian Characters and Themes, 4. Garland Reference Library of the Humanities, 1513. New York: Garland, 1996. Reprint New York: Routledge, 2002.

Labande, Edmond-René. "Les Filles d'Aliénor d'Aquitaine: étude comparative." *Cahiers de civilisation médiévale* 19 (1986): 101–12.

Lejeune, Rita. "Le Rôle littéraire de la famille d'Aliénor d'Aquitaine." *Cahiers de civilisation médiévale* 1 (1958): 319–37.

McCash, June Hall. "*Eructavit cor meum*: Sacred Love in a Secular Context at the Court of Marie de Champagne." In *Earthy Love, Spiritual Love, Love of the Saints*, edited by Susan J. Ridyard, 159–78. Sewanee Mediaeval Studies, 8. Sewanee, Tenn.: Press of the University of the South, 1999.

———. "Marie de Champagne and Eleanor of Aquitaine: A Relationship Reexamined." *Speculum* 54 (1979): 698–711.

Petersen Dyggve, Holger. "Trouvères et protecteurs de trouvères dans les cours seigneuriales de France." In *Commentationes Philologicae in honorem Arthur Långfors*. Suomalaisen Tiedakatemian Toimituksia (Annales Academiae Scientiarum Fennicae), B: 50. Helsinki, 1942.

WILLIAM PROVOST

MARIE DE COMPIÈGNE (12th–13th centuries). Marie de Compiègne is a mysterious figure in medieval literature written for and against women. She is referred to in the opening lines of three of the numerous versions of the *Evangile aux Femmes*, an Old French satire against women (versions C, D, and G, in the edition by George Keidel). The scholar Léopold Constans thought that she was not only the author of this poem but was actually the famous twelfth-century Anglo-Norman poetess, Marie de France. However, Eduard Mall, a Marie de France specialist, demonstrated in 1877 that these two suppositions are false and that the references to Marie de Compiègne are later interpolations. The poem is probably to be regarded as anonymous, in spite of the allusion in several versions to a certain Jehan Durpain of Vaucelles, who has been seen as the author. The oldest copy of the poem dates from around 1300 (Paris, Bibliothèque nationale de France, MS fr. 1553), but there are several later manuscripts. The *Evangile* lent itself readily to the addition and subtraction of lines and stanzas (version A, for example, contains 131 lines, version B 64 lines, and version H 53 lines). The material itself seems far more likely to have been written by a man than a woman. In the text women are in general somewhat harshly treated:

A woman is in all things of changeable disposition; by nature the more one forbids her something the keener she is to do it; she thinks one thing and says another; one minute she wants something, the next she changes her mind: she speaks with the stability of smoke in the wind. It is not right or just to speak ill of women; they are wise, full of assurance, and exceedingly courtly; and whatever one says about them, it is wrong not to trust them, like a shepherd trusts the wolf who has eaten his sheep. (version A, vv. 41–48)

See also Marie de France; *Miroir de Mariage* (*Mirror of Marriage*)

BIBLIOGRAPHY

Primary Sources

[*Evangile aux femmes*]. Constans, Léopold. *Marie de Compiègne d'aprés l'Evangile aux Femmes.* Paris: Franck, 1876. [Ed. of version A].

————. Keidel, George C. *The Evangile aux femmes.* Baltimore: The Friedenwald Company, 1895–96. Reprint Geneva: Slatkine, 1974. [Eds. of versions A–J].

————. Jodogne, Omer. "L'Édition de l'*Evangile aux femmes.*" In *Studi in onore di Angelo Monteverdi,* edited by Giuseppina Gerardi Marcuzzo, 1: 353–75. Modena, Italy: Società Tipografica Editrice Modenese, 1959. [Ed. of version B].

Secondary Sources

[See also notes to above critical eds.].

Mall, Eduard. "Noch einmal: Marie de Compiègne und das *Evangile aux femmes.*" *Zeitschrift für romanische Philologie* 1 (1877): 337–56.

GLYN S. BURGESS

MARIE DE FRANCE (12th century). The first known woman writer in French, Marie is the author of twelve short stories (the *Lais*), a collection of around a hundred fables (the *Fables*), and a hagiographic text on the theme of the Purgatory of St. Patrick (the *Espurgatoire seint Patriz*). Born in France, as the term was understood in the twelfth century, she wrote under the name of Marie, the name Marie de France being derived from a line in the Epilogue to the *Fables*: "Marie ai nun, si sui de France" ("Marie is my name and I am from France"). She wrote in French and probably flourished during the period 1160–1190. It seems likely that she spent part of her life in Britain, where she probably composed the *Fables*, the *Espurgatoire*, and some of the *Lais*.

Marie wrote in the wake of the development of the romance form toward the middle of the twelfth century. She was doubtless acquainted with the *romans antiques* (twelfth-century romances of Antiquity, based on Latin authors such as Statius [first century C.E.] and Virgil [70–19 B.C.E.]), Wace's *Roman de Brut* (*Romance of Brutus*, mid-twelfth century), stories derived from the Roman poet Ovid (43 B.C.E.–17 C.E.), and the Tristan legend. She used the normal meter of romance, the octosyllabic rhyming couplet, and developed the themes of these early romances, which were largely adaptations from Latin. The *Lais* in particular revolve around the themes of love and adventure, and Marie continued romance writers' exploration of the relationship between the individual and society. But on the one hand, she shunned the romance as a genre in favor of the *lai*, a short narrative in verse, equivalent to the modern short story. On the other hand, as she tells us in the Prologue to the *Lais*, she decided against translating a Latin text into French because others had done so and it would therefore not be to her advantage (vv. 28–32). She turned instead to the vernacular, folkloric lays of which she had heard ("Des lais pensai k'oï aveie," v. 33), poems originally composed to perpetuate the memory of things that happened to their protagonists, their *aventures* (adventures). Marie claims to have heard some of these lays herself. None survive, but we know them to have been short lyrical compositions sung to the accompaniment of a harp or a five-stringed instrument called the *rote*. Several times in the *Lais* Marie informs us that they were originally composed by the Bretons, whose Celtic language and culture were distinct from the French.

The lays attributed to Marie de France are preserved in five manuscripts, but the principal collection is in London, British Library MS Harley 978. Here twelve poems are found in the order: *Guigemar, Equitan, Le Fresne* (*The Ash Tree*), *Bisclavret* (*The Werewolf*), *Lanval, Les Deus Amanz* (*Two Lovers*), *Yonec, Laüstic* (*The Nightingale*), *Milun, Chaitivel, Chevrefoil* (*The Honeysuckle*), and *Eliduc* (many of these titles are not directly translatable, as they are the Breton names of their protagonists). In all, these poems, which are preceded by a fifty-six-line General Prologue, contain a little under six thousand lines of text. They vary considerably in length: *Chevrefoil*, the shortest, has 118 lines, and *Eliduc*, the longest, 1,184 lines. It is possible that around half of the lays were composed in France, the other half after Marie had come to Britain, either as a result of marriage or to further her professional career. The lays of *Guigemar, Lanval, Yonec, Milun, Chevrefoil*, and *Eliduc* contain British place names, or suggestions that their composition was associated with Britain (particularly southwest England and South Wales).

The stories, centering on knights and the ladies they fall in love with, are closely linked to contemporary feudal and courtly society, and they were clearly intended for an aristocratic audience. The heroes are brave, strong, and handsome men from the lower or upper nobility. The women are beautiful, intelligent, and sociable creatures. Both men and women are *curteis* (courtly) and *franc* (noble). They know how to handle themselves in society, and they speak well and behave in a responsible manner. Marie evidently wishes her heroes and heroines to enjoy a happy marriage together. But when the woman has been married off to a man on account of her child-rearing capability, Marie is willing to allow her an adulterous relationship with a man to whom she is more suited, something that would no doubt have shocked the feudal lords in her audience.

One of the most notable features of the poems is the wide variety of marital and amorous situations. Five of Marie's heroes have relationships with married women: Guigemar and Muldumarec in *Yonec*, the young knight in *Laüstic*, Milun, and Tristram in *Chevrefoil*. In five lays the heroines are unmarried: Le Fresne, Lanval's *amie*, the king's daughter in the *Deus Amanz*, the lady in *Chaitivel*, and the daughter of the King of Exeter in *Eliduc*. In *Equitan* and *Bisclavret*, there is a happy marriage at the outset of the story, and the plot is based on the unjustifiable affair with another man conducted by the wife. Five lays end with a happy relationship (*Guigemar, Le Fresne, Lanval, Milun, Eliduc*), whereas the other seven poems end more or less unhappily.

The supernatural (*le merveilleux*) is another of Marie's trademarks. For example, she allows two heroines (the ladies in *Guigemar* and *Yonec*) and one hero (Lanval) to enjoy some happiness thanks to a nonrational element in the text. Guigemar is led to his beloved as a result of an encounter with a talking, androgynous hind—a female red deer—who has the power to outline his destiny to him. Lanval's mistress is a supernatural being from Avalon. She possesses exceptional beauty, immense wealth, and the power to impose a taboo on Lanval and to know when it has been broken. The lady in *Yonec* prays for a lover, and he duly arrives in the form of a hawk with the ability to transform himself into a handsome knight; like the talking hind, he can predict the future. But Marie does not overdo the merveilleux element. The hawk in *Yonec* turns out to be the king of the area around Caerleon in South Wales. The supernatural permits the author to arrange for her favored characters to escape the impasse and frustration of the real world. But this real world is never far away. The activities of the twelfth-century knight (tournaments, hunting, and war), the problems of the relationship between lord and vassal, questions of social status, and even such matters as the feeding of a baby on a long journey (*Milun*, vv. 109–14) are among the many aspects of contemporary life touched on by Marie in the course of her poems.

An attractive example from the *Lais* is *Laüstic* (*Nightingale*). The setting for this 160-line lay is the region of Saint-Malo, on the coast of Brittany. The story tells of a wise and courtly girl who is married to a knight for whom she has no affection. The girl falls in love with a knight, called a *bacheler* (young man), who lives next door to her. He is a man of great prowess and generosity, always willing to perform honorable deeds. The lovers are never able to meet, their communication limited to nocturnal rendezvous at which they toss gifts from one house to the other and gaze longingly at each other. One summer, during which they stand with particular frequency at their windows, the lady's husband becomes suspicious and asks why she leaves his bed so repeatedly. "My lord," replies the lady, "there is no joy in this world for anyone who does not hear the nightingale sing. This is the reason I come to stand here. I hear it sing so sweetly at night and it seems to cause me such pleasure" (vv. 83–88). The angry husband makes plans to catch the bird, which is brought to him alive by the household servants. "I have ensnared the nightingale, which has kept you awake so much," he says to his wife. "Now you can rest in peace" (vv. 107–9). The lady asks him for the bird, but the husband breaks its neck with his two hands and throws the body at his wife breast, staining her white tunic with blood over her heart. Fearing that her lover will think she has become faint-hearted, the lady arranges for the bird to be wrapped in a piece of embroidered silk and taken to her beloved with a message explaining what has happened to her (the *aventure*). The young knight, who is neither uncourtly nor slow ("Mes ne fu pas vileins ne lenz," v. 148), has a little *chasse* (casket) created out of pure gold and encrusted with precious stones. The corpse of the nightingale is placed within, and the knight carries it with him wherever he goes.

To the bare outline of this lay one can add the comment that, in choosing the nightingale as symbol of her love, the lady can be seen as condemning the relationship to a speedy extinction. The nightingale is an excellent symbol of something that can never be, an unrealizable dream. The famous Roman scientific author Pliny the Elder (23–79 C.E.), in his *Natural History*, reports that the nightingale, after a brief period of rapturous song, sings itself to death. The lay ends unhappily, but by sending the bird to her beloved the lady takes a form of revenge on her husband. She is one of Marie's many likable and intelligent heroines who are resourceful enough to win victories over the men who oppress them.

Two of the lays, *Le Fresne* and *Eliduc*, have heroines who, by their inspired gestures, permit the stories to turn out more happily. Le Fresne spreads her precious brocade, symbol of her nobility of birth, onto the marriage bed of her beloved as he is about to succumb to pressure from his vassals and take a wife of acceptable social standing. Through this action, she is recognized by her mother and in due course allowed to take her rightful place as her lover's wife. Eliduc's first wife, Guildelüec, revives his beloved Guilliadun, who had lapsed into a coma, with a red flower snatched from the mouth of a weasel. She commits the sublimely self-sacrificial act of withdrawing into a convent to permit her husband to marry his beloved.

We do not know when the lays were completed and arranged as they are in MS Harley 978. Did Marie arrange them herself with a specific thematic intent? We do know that the collection was offered to a "noble king" (Prologue, v. 43). He is described, like one of Marie's heroes, as "pruz e curteis" ("valiant/skilled at arms and courtly," v. 44), and he is said to be a man "before whom all joy bows down and in whose heart all *biens* [goodness, virtue] has taken root" (vv. 45–46). This king is normally identified as Henry II of England (1154–1189), but plausible claims have been made for his son Henri au Cort Mantel ("Henry of the Short Coat"—crowned 1170, d. 1183), who may have merited the adjectives pruz and curteis more than his father. But flattery is part of the technique of prologues and there is flattery too in the prologue to the *Fables*. Marie must have enjoyed a good reputation in literary circles, for the *Fables* were actually commissioned by a certain Count William (Epilogue, v. 9), said to be the flower of chivalry, learning and *curteisie* (courtliness/courtesy; Prologue, vv. 31–32). Unfortunately, this Count William is frustratingly difficult to pinpoint. A precise identification would give a good idea of the date of composition of the *Fables*. If they were composed fairly early, in the 1170s or early 1180s, William of Mandeville, earl of Essex (d. 1189) or William of Gloucester (d. 1183), a boyhood friend of Henry II, are good candidates. If the *Fables* were written after the death of Henry II in 1189, the count could have been the illegitimate son of Henry II and Rosamund Clifford, William Longsword, who became earl of Salisbury in 1196 and who is described on his tomb as "the flower of counts" (*flos comitum Willelmus*). But one could certainly not rule out William Marshal who became earl of Striguil and Pembroke in 1189 and was regent of England from 1216 until 1219. William Marshal's reputation as a knight was outstanding, and Marie's ideal knight in the *Lais* bears more than a passing resemblance to William. The collection of fables itself was translated into French, Marie tells us, from a collection in English, which she attributes to King Alfred ("reis Alvrez," Epilogue, v. 16), but which was doubtless by an unknown fabulist rather than by the king of that name. The same holds true for a more ancient source she mentions, called the *Romulus* (fourth century), wrongly thought by Marie and others to be from the Roman Emperor Romulus (Prologue, v. 12). Marie's collection contains 102 fables and it has survived in twenty-three manuscripts, including MS Harley 978. The first forty correspond closely to the fables in the *Romulus Nilantii*, a branch of the *Romulus* compilation. Other fables come from a variety of sources and some are of unknown origin. The morals to the *Fables* show that Marie is interested in society at all levels and in different forms of human relationships: vassal–lord, husband–wife, mother–son, and so forth. She is particularly concerned with the feudal hierarchy and with the concept of loyalty binding man to man. Fables 6 and 7 tell us about evil lords (*mals seignurs*) who should never been given any chance to obtain greater power and who will never thank anyone who does them a favor. The bad or evil lord treats others worse the stronger he becomes, and he is constantly on the lookout for a chance to do them down ("Cum plus est fort, [e] pis lur fet;/Tuz jurs lur est en mal aguet," Fable 6, vv. 31–32). The concepts of justice and personal responsibility are central to the fables, but Marie is capable of including a fable that shows a woman hoodwinking her husband. A peasant looks through his door and sees his wife in bed with another man. "What have I seen?" he says. "What do you see, my lord?" says the wife. "Another man, and it appears he is holding you in tight embrace on my bed." "You're mad," she says, "if you think everything you see is true." She takes him to a tub of water and makes him look into it. He tells her he sees in it his own image. "You are not in the tub fully clothed. You must not believe your eyes, which often lie." "I repent," says the husband. Marie seems to support the woman in her trickery and comments on the usefulness of sense and intelligence (Fable 44).

The *Espurgatoire seint Patriz* is a 2,300-line account of a descent into the Other World by a knight named Owein via a cavern on Station Island in Lough Derg, county Donegal. Marie's text is based on the *Tractatus de purgatorio sancti Patricii* (*Treatise on Saint Patrick's Purgatory*), written probably around 1180, if the dedicatee, named as H. de Sartis, is Hugh, abbot of Old Wardon in Bedfordshire from 1173 to 1185–1186. If, as is less likely, the abbot is Henry, the date would be around 1215, which would make Marie's translation unrealistically late. Marie probably wrote her *Espurgatoire* in the 1180s. During his visit to the Other World, Owein is taken by devils through a series of *champs* (fields), where he gets a taste of the torments awaiting sinners. In the fourth champ he sees all manner of suffering: "Many people were hanging there by their feet, in burning chains; a number by their hands and arms, in painful nooses. And there were many hanging by their hair; many were hanging head down in infernal flames [. . .] [others by] burning hooks; some by their eyes, their noses, their ears— the number of these was quite astonishing—some by their necks, their mouths, their chins, their breasts" (vv. 1073–94). Owein escapes the unpleasant fate of these victims by calling on the name of Jesus, and he is rewarded by a visit to the Terrestrial Paradise, a place of great light ("granz clartez," v. 1580), where there is an abundance of flowers and trees, sweet-smelling herbs and fine fruits, a place of joy and tranquility. He even gets a glimpse, from the top of a mountain, of the entrance to Heavenly Paradise, set in a sky in which again there is great light and an impression of glittering gold.

The knight's visit to the Other World is a cautionary tale, an inspiration for those prepared to live a life of virtue, and in some ways a form of aventure reminiscent of the *Lais*, in particular of the lady's visit in *Yonec* to the magic kingdom of Muldumarec, whose every building seemed to be made of solid silver. But the *Espurgatoire* lacks the depth of the *Lais*. Marie is at her best in such *Lais* as *Laüstic*, the *Deus Amanz*, and *Eliduc*, in which the characters are beset by human problems and in which she can be said to have shown an awareness of human psychology unknown in earlier writers.

But who, then, was this Marie de France? She was definitely from a good family and had received a sound education. She knew Latin and contemporary vernacular literature, and possessed the linguistic ability to acquire a thorough knowledge of English. She has been seen as Marie, abbess of Shaftesbury in Dorset and half-sister to Henry II, and also as another Marie who was a nun at the monastery of Reading. She has been identified as Marie de Boulogne, daughter of Stephen of Blois (who is mentioned in the *Espurgatoire*, v. 503). Particularly tempting is the identification by Urban T. Holmes Jr. as Marie de Meulan, daughter of Waleran de Meulan (also called Waleran de Beaumont), one of the great noblemen of the times and a dedicatee in several manuscripts of the *Historia regum Britanniae* of Geoffrey of Monmouth. This Marie married Hugh Talbot, baron of Cleuville and owner of lands in Herefordshire and Buckinghamshire. One thing is certain: she is the Dame Marie mentioned by a contemporary, Denis Piramus, in his *Vie seint Edmund le rei*. Denis tells us that Dame Marie composed verse lays in verse that are not at all true ("Vers de lais,/Ke ne sunt pas del tut verais," vv. 37–38). These lays were greatly admired at court and particularly liked by the ladies who listened to them joyfully and willingly.

Marie herself saw her work not only as entertainment—"K'il seit pleisibles a la gent" ("so that it will bring pleasure to people," *Milun*, v. 4)—but also as something beneficial (a "granz biens," Prologue to *Lais*, v. 5). She wanted, like earlier fable writers, to improve people (*amender*, Prologue to *Fables*, v. 9), to provide them with something important that would be "entendables/A laie gent e cuvenables" ("within the comprehension of lay people and appropriate for their needs," *Espurgatoire*, vv. 2299–300). The notion has been expressed that Marie progressed "from entertainment through moralization to edification" (Ewert, *Lais*, vii). However, the fact is that these ingredients are found in each of Marie's works, albeit in different doses. Like the morals attached to the fables, each work has its own *philosophie* (wisdom, moral lesson, *Fables*, Prologue, vv. 24–25). All together they make Marie one of the foremost women writers in the French language.

See also Arthurian Women; Christine de Pizan; Eleanor of Aquitaine; Enchantresses, Fays (*Fées*), and Fairies; Murasaki Shikibu; Rosamond, Fair

BIBLIOGRAPHY

[For a full bibliography see Glyn S. Burgess, *Marie de France: An Analytical Bibliography* Research Bibliographies and Checklists, no. 21 (London: Grant and Cutler, 1977), Supplement no. 1 (1986), Supplement no. 2 (1997)].

Primary Sources

Denis Piramus. *La Vie seint Edmund le rei*. Edited by Hilding Kjellman. Göteborg, Sweden: Elanders Boktryckeri Aktiebolag, 1935.

Geoffrey of Monmouth. *Historia regum Britanniae*. Edited by Neil Wright et al. 5 vols. Cambridge and Dover, N. H.: D. S. Brewer, 1985–.

Marie de France. *L'Espurgatoire Saint Patriz: nouvelle édition critique*. Edited by Yolande de Pontfarcy. Ktemata, 13. Louvain, Belgium and Paris: Peeters, 1995.

———. *Saint Patrick's Purgatory: A Poem by Marie de France*. Translated with introduction and notes by Michael J. Curley. Medieval & Renaissance Texts & Studies, 94. Binghamton, N.Y.: CEMERS, 1993.

———. *Lais*. Edited by Alfred Ewert. Blackwell's French Texts. Oxford: Blackwell, 1944. Reprinted with a new introduction and bibliography by Glyn S. Burgess. Bristol, U.K.: Bristol Classical Press, 1995.

———. *Les Lais de Marie de France*. Edited by Karl Warke. Annotated and translated (Modern French) by Laurence Harf-Lancner. Lettres gothiques. Paris: Livre de Poche, 1990.

———. *Lais*. Edited and translated by Philippe Walter. Paris: Folio classique/Gallimard, 2000.

———. *The Lais of Marie de France*. Translated by Glyn S. Burgess and Keith Busby. Penguin Classics. Harmondsworth, Middlesex, U.K.: Penguin Books, 1986; 1999.

———. *Les Fables*. Critical ed. by Charles Brucker. Ktemata, 12. Louvain: Peeters, 1991, 1998.

[Romulus. *Romulus Nilantii*]. In Léopold Hervieux. *Les Fabulistes latins, depuis le siècle d'Auguste jusqu'à la fin du moyen âge*. 2nd ed. Paris: Firmin-Didot, 1893.

Secondary Sources

Amer, Sahar. *Esope au feminin: Marie de France et la politique de l'interculturalité*. Amsterdam: Rodopi, 1999.

Bloch, R. Howard. *The Anonymous Marie de France*. Chicago: University of Chicago Press, 2003.

Bruckner, Matilda T. *Shaping Romance: Interpretation, Truth, and Closure in Twelfth-Century French Fictions*. Philadelphia: University of Pennsylvania Press, 1993.

Burgess, Glyn S. *The Lais of Marie de France: Text and Context*. Athens: University of Georgia Press; Manchester: University of Manchester Press, 1987.

Clifford, Paula. *Marie de France: Lais*. Critical Guides to French Texts, 16. London: Grant & Cutler, 1982.

Holmes, Urban T., Jr. "New Thoughts on Marie de France." *Studies in Philology*, 29 (1932), 1–10.

Krueger, Roberta L. "Marie de France." In *The Cambridge Companion to Medieval Women's Writing*, edited by Carolyn Dinshaw and David Wallace, 172–83. Cambridge: Cambridge University Press, 2003.

Maddox, Donald. *Fictions of Identity in Medieval France*, Cambridge: Cambridge University Press, 2000.

Ménard, Philippe. *Les Lais de Marie de France: contes d'amour et d'aventure du moyen âge*. Paris: Presses Universitaires de France, 1979, 1995.

Mickel, Emanuel J., Jr. *Marie de France*. Twayne's World Authors Series, 306. New York: Twayne, 1974.

GLYN S. BURGESS

MARIE D'OIGNIES. *See* **Beguines;** *Mulieres Sanctae*

MARRIAGE. More than any other social institution, marriage governed the lives of most medieval women and men on multiple levels. It combined the most personally intimate (sexual intercourse), biologically practical (producing children and maintaining a household), and publicly political of events (socioeconomic advancement of either or both spouses and families; perpetuation of ruling dynasties). Only funerals were accorded equal importance in that, like marriage, though in another way, they reflected the culmination of a person's life in society. Little wonder then that religion learned early on to control what was originally a secular custom, regardless of national culture. In the Christian world, the early Church Fathers (founders of early Christian doctrine) devised matrimonial rules while protesting that, ideally, marriage was second best to virginity. And as religion came to govern marriage, it also sought to regulate women and their most menacing component, sexuality. The following discussion focuses primarily on Western Christendom (see cross-references and bibliography for other cultures).

Christian marriage, while claiming its principles to be rooted in natural law as defended by Gratian's canon law (c.1142), deliberately differentiated itself from pagan, Jewish, and later Muslim ideals, primarily in stressing monogamy and lifelong permanency of the marital union. Early Hebrew law affirmed the custom of marriage through purchase, and woman's status as her husband's property with no autonomous rights of inheritance or divorce (Deut. 21: 14; 24: 1; Ex. 21: 7)—a characteristic the Christian Middle Ages would perpetuate in varying degrees. Jews at first practiced polygamy, but then switched to monogamy as a more sacred bond. Christian doctrine also borrowed from Jewish and especially Roman law, the latter having contributed the ideal of *consortium omnis vitae, divini et humani juris communicatio* (lifelong partnership sharing civil and religious rights; cited in Cross and Livingstone). Emperor Justinian, founder of civil law (sixth century), tolerated divorce in special cases, as did, by his influence, the Eastern Church.

Already in the teachings of Jesus one finds matrimony perceived as part of the divine plan of creation, the prohibition of divorce and remarriage (Mk. 10: 6–9; Mt. 19: 4–6), and also the recommendation of celibacy, especially in time of crisis (Mt. 19: 10–12). The Apostle Paul (first century), while revering chastity as superior to marriage and forbidding divorce, nonetheless in his practice among his followers allowed separations and even remarriage. Basically, Paul seems to advocate that whichever celibate or married status a man or woman chooses, he or she must then wholeheartedly meet its specific responsibilities in compliance with God's plan (1 Cor. 7).

The inevitable question confronting this ecclesiastical glorification of chastity concerns human continuity—how else if not through sex and procreation? In attempting a simplified version, as with all the other complex issues covered here, perhaps a useful summary response may be distilled from John Chrysostom, bishop of Constantinople (d. 407), who, while offering much positive advice on marriage, also states that marriage was founded after the Fall to console humankind for its mortality by enabling humans to procreate. But because the Resurrection of Christ vanquished death, and mankind is on its way to a better life, "the world is full," there is no further need for offspring (cited in Shahar).

Church Fathers such as Augustine (d. 430) strengthened the aspect of indissolubility by proposing the idea of marriage as an earthly reflection of Christ's union with the Church. This last comparison, originating with Paul, also reiterated woman's subordination to man taken and refined from Roman law: "As the church is subject to Christ, so let wives also be subject in everything to their husbands" (Eph. 5: 24). Augustine also proclaimed marital sex to be nonsinful only if the couple did so just to have children, and if their intercourse were as devoid of pleasure as possible (as in *City of God*, 14: 22 in Kearney; McCarthy). For after virginity, and nonmarried (celibate) chastity—the latter having become the rule for the clergy by the late eleventh century—chastity within marriage, or spiritual marriage (Elliott 1993) was best, followed by sex for procreation, but exclusive of lust. The marriage of Mary and Joseph became the ideal Christian marriage in that it was a spiritual, sexually unconsummated bond and also elevated marriage beyond the goal of procreation (Gold; Brooke; Elliott 2003); later, French theologian Robert de Sorbon (d. 1274) would extol the marriage of Tobias and Sarah (from the Apocryphal book of Tobit 10: 12–13) for similar reasons. The intensified spiritualization of the marriage bond led to its becoming one of the seven sacraments (ninth century)—along with Baptism, Confirmation, the Eucharist (body and blood of Christ via the communion wafer and wine), Penance, Extreme Unction (last rites), and Orders—the most holy means by which Christ communicates His grace to mortals.

There is a tendency among modern readers—given all the strictures, underlying misogyny, and other attitudes incompatible with marital happiness prevalent in Paul and the Church Fathers—to neglect the unique, more positive aspects of Christian teaching on marriage, as when Paul also urges that men love their wives just as Christ loved the Church (Eph. 5: 25). That most influential high-medieval theologian, Thomas Aquinas (thirteenth century), emphasized marriage as the *maxima amicitia* (greatest friendship), an unbreakable union of two hearts (Shahar). For such reasons, Christian apologists pride themselves on having infused the element of love into the otherwise ultra-practical institution of marriage.

Many nuns, having committed to lives of chastity and service on earth, considered themselves Brides of Christ through a mystical union also based on love. Later (twelfth century), various lay orders or groups allowed women members to be married and even, like the Donnés, permitted married couples (Miramon).

The Church's favoring of virginity and chastity, and its effect on marriage, has prompted moderns to suspect the notion of medieval sexuality to be an oxymoron. Fortunately, in practice, the clergy were more forgiving of married couples and even couples about to be married in sexual matters. But by the late Middle Ages, unmarried couples caught fornicating were forced by the Church to swear marriage vows in the future, with a repetition of the offense resulting in marriage, which legalized any offspring from these acts (Karras in Linehan and Nelson). In the other direction, canon law (law governing Church and clergy) would allow unconsummated marriages to be dissolved on condition that the sexually retentive spouse (usually the bride) joins a monastery, or if, after two months of resistance the groom had the right to consummate the marriage, collecting his "conjugal debt."

Ecclesiastical domination of the rite, fully asserting itself by c.1200 throughout Europe, both reinforced what is now called patriarchal domination—the husband's commanding role over the wife—and tempered it to protect women without diminishing the husband's or clergy's control. English common law referred to married women as *femmes coverts* (from Middle-French, literally covered women), signifying the wives' legal dependence and subordinate position to their husbands—as opposed to *femmes soles* (single women), a complex group comprising widows, virgins, and women who never married, who enjoyed more freedoms, including the right to initiate court actions by themselves. This meant that a married woman was a legal minor, "covered" by her husband in any important matter; she had little free agency and could not even draw up her own will without a male guardian. Even a married urban businesswoman needed a male guardian, usually her husband, to initiate legal proceedings; by the same token, he was held responsible for her actions and debts, although married women could be sued. Only in cases of rape or spousal abuse, or in determining delicate feminine conditions such as pregnancy, virginity, or sterility, could a woman go to court without her husband's consent. Many of these pro-patriarchal common-law tendencies were supported by canon law. In other words, wives had more autonomy in the early Middle Ages than after c.1100. Noblewomen, except for the fortunate, resourceful, and strong-willed, probably enjoyed the least freedom and also the least permanency in marriage, since, aside from facing widowhood, they could be repudiated by husbands powerful enough to attempt to bypass, or buy off, the clergy to form a better political alliance elsewhere (Livingstone, in Mitchell).

Another of the paradoxes arising from the ecclesiastical encouragement of male dominance is that, despite this belief, the clergy simultaneously urged wives to correct the moral behavior of their husbands (including spending habits), often by using their feminine wiles and enticements—the same lust-arousing aspect of women condemned by the Church Fathers. Thus even though husbands, because they were deemed intellectually and morally superior, were vested with official power over their wives' spiritual, legal, and financial lives—not to mention the prohibition against women as public religious teachers—women were expected to "preach" to their husbands within the domestic context, and it would be through penitentials (manuals of penance) by priests including Thomas of Chobham (c.1215) (see Farmer) and Pierre Dubois (d. 1321) (see Vecchio in Klapisch-Zuber 1992) that wives would learn how to accomplish this. Given this unofficial role, women, especially queens and other nobles, proved essential to the Christianization of early Europe, as queens such as Clotilde, wife of Clovis, king of the Franks (sixth century), converted their husbands, and consequently entire kingdoms, via a process known as "domestic proselytization," to invoke the term coined by historian Jane Schulenburg.

A decisive turning point in Christian marital ideology was the notion of consent on the part of each of the betrothed, heralded in the policy of Pope Alexander III (d. 1181; see Noonan), and more fully formulated by Peter Lombard (c.1100–1160), so that *consensus facit nuptias* (consent makes the marriage). This supplanted the Germanic principle of marriage as entirely arranged by parents or guardians, entitled by the *mundium* (German concept of guardianship over women and other "incompetents"), and perhaps also the groom, if older. The new mutual consent law allowed couples to marry over the objections of their parents, although parental consent was preferable. While displacing parental power, it also facilitated private marriage—marriage not solemnized within a church—which the Church tended to recognize nonetheless, in a reversion to early secular days; it was more important to preserve the sacrament (Shahar). One would expect this new development to bode well for women as part of the general surge toward individualism characterizing the supposed twelfth-century Renaissance, yet Dyan Elliott demonstrates, via the example of Christina of Markyate (d. post-1155)—a dutiful, but also intensely pious, bride parentally pushed into marriage, which she refused to consummate and escaped by becoming a religious hermit—that respect for a bride's consent was slow to take hold (Elliott 2003). Using another approach, Janet Nelson has found that, according to evidence, the higher the social position, the lower this consent appears to have been valued, particularly the bride's consent, as the young couples (usually in their teens) were often instruments of their families' political policies, with the groom having more say than the bride, if any. Age is also a factor here, since older royal widowers tended to marry younger brides. Brides could only escape distasteful arrangements (either the groom or the "yoke of marriage" itself) respectably by entering a convent and thus gaining protection from the Church, as in the case of Margaret of Hungary (Nelson 1999). But the Church could also dictate marriage patterns among nobles, primarily for reasons of exogamy (prohibiting marriages between close relatives), and also to hinder or thwart the dissolution of royal marriages (French civil law prescribed six degrees of separation). The only category of noble bride who could have a say appears to have been divorcees and widows about to remarry. Notable examples of women (usually older, previously married) who chose their (usually younger) mates include Matilda of Tuscany (1046–1115), in choosing her second husband, Welf V of Bavaria, and Eleanor of Aquitaine (1122?–1204), freshly divorced by Louis VIII, who married the future Henry II of England (1133–1189) (Livingstone, in Mitchell).

In early medieval Christian societies, the old custom of polygyny (multiple wives and concubines) prevailed among the wealthy nobles, for example, in Ireland (Herlihy 1985) and among the Franks (France and Germany), whose King Charlemagne—before the pope crowned him Emperor in 800—married four wives and took six concubines. Little distinction was evident between wives and concubines in such societies during the sixth through eighth centuries, even in matters of inheritance rights for offspring, although legitimate children were preferred in Germanic law. Eventually, through a combination of the political pragmatics of determining succession and moral law provided by the Church, wives—then monogamy—finally won out (Stafford).

Regardless of the society (although Christian marriage traditions again borrow most directly from the Roman in this regard), the marriage rite consists in two main parts: the betrothal and the marriage ceremony itself. In England, the legal age for marriage was twelve for women and fourteen for men. In societies that secluded their aristocratic women, as in Byzantium and possibly Russia (Muscovy and the Steppes), bride-shows were arranged before the prospective groom, enabling him to meet and choose from eligible women of his class. Several imperial bride-shows are recorded for the eighth and ninth centuries in Russia (Ostrowski). The first phase, betrothal, included the arrangement and gift-giving between the two prospective spousal families and the fixing of the brideprice (paid by the husband to the bride's kinsmen) and/or dowry (paid by the bride's family to the groom) and dower (assets designated by the husband for the wife and minor children on the husband's death, predicated on the dowry), the first two of which had to be commensurate with the families' status and financial means. Diane Hughes has confirmed that, although the more Mediterranean-based dowry eventually replaced brideprice and other gifts, for a time these gifts coexisted in some form in parts of Europe and still in Asia. The other medieval Germanic wedding gifts, along with brideprice, were: after the wedding-night, the *morgengabe* (German = morning gift: a groom's payment to his bride as a reward for surrendering her virginity to him) and the father's send-off gift to his daughter about to leave her parental home. The shift in emphasis from brideprice to dowry is significant in that the assets move from the bride's family to the bride herself, since her dowry at marriage usually comprised her dower in widowhood (Hughes).

Dress—the bride's and groom's ceremonial clothing, varying from culture to culture, reflecting their social class and especially how well dowered the bride was—and even architecture also played important roles in symbolizing marriage as a rite of passage, since betrothals took place at the parish church door or narthex (a sort of front porch, originating in Byzantine churches, where penitents and candidates for baptism also congregated): threshold structures. The marriage ceremony itself also took place at the church door, or outside the church premises, as chronicled in parts of fifteenth-century England. Precisely what proportion of marriages were in fact contracted completely outside local churches has been difficult to determine (Brooke).

The second phase, the marriage service intended primarily to bless the couple, centered on the Nuptial Mass, as of the time of the African Church Father Tertullian (d. c.225), or a simpler blessing ceremony at the altar (thus within the church). This replaced the sacrificial rites practiced by the Romans. In the Eastern Church (the Christian religion observed in Byzantium), an elaborate blessing ceremony replaced the Nuptial Mass of the Roman Church: the couple donned crowns (symbolizing the glory of the martyrs) and shared a cup of wine. Certain services also blessed the marital bed chamber, as in Salisbury, England's, Sarum Liturgy (eleventh century on).

Wives of all classes, but especially among the nobility (for whom the most evidence exists), moved to their husband's place of residence for the wedding and to live for the remainder of their lives, or at least for the length of the marriage. Upper-class wives brought their own entourage of ladies in waiting and also had schooled themselves in the language of the husband's court (one thinks of the challenges confronting Anne of Bohemia in resettling at Richard II's court in London). A widowed queen about to remarry, or an orphaned crown princess, in Merovingian times (sixth to seventh centuries) passed her inherited domain automatically to her new husband, as in the cases of Brunhild and Emma, whose remarriages helped protect their kingdoms with a new male ruler, thereby defusing potential aristocratic resentment of female succession (Nelson 1999). In Byzantium, influential women knew how to arrange marriages to create a veritable nexus of power, most successful is the role of marriage in consolidating the eleventh-century Komnenos dynasty (see James and Hill, in Mitchell).

A wife brought a dowry to the union and was endowed by the husband at marriage via the dower to be used to support herself and their children in widowhood. In urban societies, the bride's dowry included material goods and capital, more than the landholdings associated with feudal marriages, which paid for most of the initial expenses involved in establishing and furnishing the couple's household. Such material comforts among townspeople could compensate for the (at least initial) emotional emptiness in a union formed more as a partnership than a love match. Marriages between tradespeople and artisans could also succeed if spouses worked either together or separately toward increasing the couple's financial solidarity (Hanawalt and Dronzek, in Mitchell). These unions produced children who, it was hoped, would carry on the family profession and continue its good name.

Queens, as wives of kings, had an exceptional dower that truly required attention: their husband's kingdoms, which, should the widowed queen remarry, would transmit to her new husband. Frankish legal thinkers were the first to set down rituals for queen-making immediately after the marriage and the queen's specific political roles, all the way to the sanctity of her burial service: from altar to grave, as it were. In so doing they helped eliminate polygamy in Europe—since these Frankish rules would spread throughout the Continent—and, by sanctifying the king's wife in a monogamous marriage, the Church gave her more power as her husband's heir, since, in polygamous royal families, the king's mother had more influence, because she was a more stable entity than her son's varying bedmates. Also by condoning royal monogamy, the Church helped to strengthen the dynastic line of succession (Stafford; Nelson 1999).

Litigation concerning marriage, in England at least, in the ecclesiastical courts focused less frequently on divorce and dissolution than on one party's suing to enforce a marriage denied by the other spouse. Cases involving bigamy were also numerous (Helmholz; Sheehan; Esmein). Adultery constituted one the very few grounds for divorce as permitted by the Church. In local practice, women adulterers of all social categories were usually punished more harshly than men, especially in Mediterranean societies including southern Italy and Spain, where the penalty could be death. In other parts, punishment was almost as severe: the convicted woman would be humiliated by being forced to run a race naked in public—the "course" (Hughes).

Remarriages for widows, let alone divorcees, were more problematical than for widowers because of dower difficulties and presumptive heirs, although in principle the laws encouraged widows to remarry. In fact, the Latin Kingdom of Jerusalem made remarriage of widows mandatory after the requisite mourning period; otherwise, the government would confiscate their lands. Secular law codes often required widows to wait for a prescribed period of time before remarrying. Canon law permitted them to remarry, though it always considered second or third marriages less sacred than the first (Mitchell, in Mitchell; Brundage).

Wives, priests, and lawgivers were not the sole effective means of disseminating virtuous ideals into the real world. Just as priests had their penitential manuals, women were provided with conduct manuals or courtesy books, almost all of which were written by men, with the shining exception of Christine de Pizan's *Livre des Trois Vertus* (*Book of the Three Virtues*, 1405–1406). Courtesy books taught women good manners, proper hygiene and dress, and other basic social survival skills (including how to please one's husband, or put up with a brutish one), addressing themselves either to one or various classes of women. The more encyclopedic manuals like the *Mesnagier de Paris* (*The Householder of Paris*, c.1393) also informed her on how to run a household, from balancing finances to dressing game. Another example, less familiar but recently rediscovered by scholars, the

Llibre de les dones (*Book for Ladies*, c.1396) by the Catalan Francesc Eiximenis, stresses both Catholic education and practical skills, learned from the girl's mother, as essential to forming a good Spanish townswoman. The *Llibre* was very influential in its day and translated into several languages (Peláez, Batlle, and Viyoles, in *La Femme* 1995). The French moralist and statesman, Philippe de Mézières, in his *Vertu du Sacrement du mariage* (1384–1389), underscores the sanctity of marriage while inserting the famous tale of Griselda, the archetypal long-suffering wife, from Boccaccio's *Decameron* (c.1352), as does Chaucer in his *Clerk's Tale* (c.1390). By contrast, the bitter tone of Eustache Deschamps's *Miroir de Mariage* (*Mirror of Marriage*, 1381–1389), often misunderstood, belongs to a long tradition of misogamistic (anti-marriage) literature harking back to Classical Antiquity (Wilson and Makowski; Blamires), in reaction to which were produced such promarital texts as the *Quinze Joyes de Mariage* (*Fifteen Joys of Marriage*) (early fifteenth century) and much of Christine de Pizan's literary career. In between these two attitudes, Heloise's eloquent and keenly intelligent reply to her beloved Abelard (early twelfth century) in essence decries marriage as an abasement of their transcendent love (Brooke). The relentless discrepancies, whether humorous, poignant, or tragic, between the Church's teachings and the everyday citizen's attempts to incorporate them into real life have inspired a multitude of literary works displaying a range of marital and wifely characterizations (Elliott 2003; Cartlidge; Brooke). When not moralizing or revising female history, Christine de Pizan, also a gifted lyric poet, composed one of the rare poems celebrating erotic love within marriage (*Autres Ballades*, 26, 1399–1402). Literature thus joins secular and religious moral manuals and treatises, legal and financial archives, historical chronicles, and demographic statistical data in enabling family historians to gain a more complete picture of medieval marriage and family life.

Among the major scholars of medieval marriage, Dyan Elliott, using a variety of secular (mainly English) and religious primary sources and current research, has most recently, in concise but comprehensive form, discussed marriage as a multileveled institution for containing both spouses, especially women, via oscillating trends in consent and coercion. Christopher Brooke, in what may be the best book-length synthesis, builds upon a "chain" of disciplines developed by previous specialists, devoting chapters to individual questions, influences, and especially individual literary and historical persons and works (even visual arts) as case studies. Georges Duby's books focus on inheritance and masculine dominance in case studies; Diane Hughes has provided several key articles, among which the most definitive study of the evolution of the dowry and its ramifications. Jack Goody has contributed an invaluable anthropological approach to the history of family development, while David Herlihy and Christiane Klapisch-Zuber base their theories on painstaking statistics, taken primarily in northern Italy, although Herlihy's *Medieval Households* mentions other European cultures as well.

See also Anne of Bohemia; Bride of Christ/*Brautmystik*; Brunhild; Chaucer, Geoffrey, Women in the Work of; Celibacy; Childhood and Child-Rearing in the Middle Ages; China, Women in; Christina of Markyate; Christine de Pizan; Comnena, Anna; Concubines; Courtesy Books; Dorothea of Montau, St.; Dower; Dowry; Eleanor of Aquitaine; Emma/Ælfgifu; Fatimid Egypt, Women in; Griselda; Hagiography (Female Saints); Heloise; Ingeborg/Isambour of France; Ingibiorg; Jewish Women in the Middle Ages; *Jus Primae Noctis*; Kempe, Margery; Law, Canon, Women in; Law, Women in, Anglo-Saxon England; Mary, Blessed Virgin, in the Middle Ages; Matilda of Tuscany/Canossa; *Miroir de Mariage* (*Mirror of Marriage*); Norse Women; Paston, Margaret; Penitentials, Women in; Rape; *Sachsenspiegel* and *Schwabenspiegel*; Slaves, Female; Syrian-Christian Women; *Vertu du Sacrement de Mariage, Livre de la*; Virginity; Widows; Zoe Karbounopsina

BIBLIOGRAPHY

Primary Sources
[See also bibliographies to Secondary Source entries, esp. Elliott 2003; Hughes; Brooke].

Abelard and Heloise. [Letters]. "Abelard's Letter to a Friend (*Historia Calamitatum*)"; "The Letter of Heloise on the Religious Life and Abelard's First Reply"; "The Personal Letters between Abelard and Heloise." Edited by James T. Muckle. *Medieval Studies* 12 (1950): 163–213; 17 (1955): 240–81; 15 (1953): 47–94, respectively. [Latin text and notes].

———. *The Letters of Abelard and Heloise.* Translated by Betty Radice. Harmondsworth, U.K.: Penguin, 1974.

Amt, Emilie, ed. *Women's Lives in Medieval Europe: A Sourcebook.* New York and London: Routledge, 1993. [Contains translated selections from texts pertinent to the canon law, marriage blessing, and debate on chastity vs. marriage, 79–94].

Augustine, St. *De bono coniugali, De sancta uirginitate.* Edited, translated, and introduced by P. G. Walsh. Oxford Early Christian Texts. Oxford: Clarendon Press; New York: Oxford University Press, 2001. [See also in Kearney; in McCarthy, see below].

———. *Marriage and Virginity.* Translated by Raymon Kearney. Edited and introduced by David G. Hunter. Words of St. Augustine: A Translation for the 21st Century, 1: 9. Hyde Park, N.Y.: New City Press, 1999. [Contains treatises on marriage, virginity, widowhood, adultery, continence].

Blamires, Alcuin, et al., eds. *Woman Defamed and Woman Defended: An Anthology of Medieval Texts.* Oxford: Clarendon Press, 1992. [English translations of wide range of key texts, plus commentary].

[Christina of Markyate]. *The Life of Christina of Markyate, a Twelfth-Century Recluse.* Edited and translated by Charles H. Talbot. Oxford: Clarendon Press, 1959. Reprint 1987. [Latin original and English translation with notes].

Christine de Pizan. *Autres Balades 26.* In *Œuvres poétiques*, edited by Maurice Roy, 1: 237–38. Société des Anciens Textes Français, 24. Paris: Firmin Didot, 1886. Reprint New York: Johnson, 1965. [French text only].

———. *Le Livre des Trois Vertus.* Critical ed. by Eric Hicks. Introduction and notes by Charity C. Willard. Bibliothèque du XVᵉ siècle, 50. Paris: Honoré Champion, 1989.

———. *The Treasure of the City of Ladies, or Book of the Three Virtues.* Translated and introduced by Sarah Lawson. Harmondsworth, U.K. and New York: Penguin, 1985.

Eiximenis, Francesc. *Lo Llibre de les dones.* Edited by Franck Naccarato. 2 vols. Barcelona: Curial, 1981.

[England, Marriage Service. Sarum Missal, etc.]. Translated extracts in Amt, 83–89. *See above.*

[England, various documents]. McSheffrey, Shannon, ed. and trans. *Love and Marriage in Late Medieval London.* Documents of Practice. Kalamazoo, Mich.: TEAMS/Medieval Institute, 1995.

[France]. Philippe (de Remi) de Beaumanoir. *Coutumes de Beauvaisis.* Critical ed. by Amédée Salmon. Textes pour servir à l'étude et à l'enseignement de l'histoire, 24, 30. 2 vols. Paris: Picard, 1899–1900.

[France]. *Registre criminel de la justice de St-Martin-des-Champs à Paris au XIVᵉ siècle.* Edited by Louis Tanon. Paris: Willem, 1877. [See, e.g., pp. 143, 189].

[Gratian]. *Corpus iuris canonici.* Edited by Emil L. Richter. Revised by Emil Friedberg. 2 vols. Leipzig, Germany: Tauchnitz, 1879. Reprint Graz, Austria: Akademische Druck, 1955. [Latin text only, German notes. See esp. vol. 1: *Decretum*, Case 33 question 2.10 (cols. 1154–55) and question 5 *passim* (cols. 1254–56)].

———. [*Decretum*]. *The Treatise on Laws: (Decretum, DD. 1–20).* Translated by Augustine Thompson. With the Ordinary Gloss translated by James Gordley. Introduction by Katherine Christianson. Washington, D.C.: Catholic University of America Press, 1993. [See esp. ch. 7.2–3 (pp. 6–7)].

————. [*Decretum*, ch. 27 q. 2; ch. 30 qq. 2, 5; ch. 31 q.1, 2; ch. 32 qq. 1–2, 5–7; chap. 33 q. 2.] Translated extracts in Amt, 79–83. *See above.*

[Justinian]. *Corpus iuris civilis.* Edited by Paul Krüger, Theodor Mommsen, Rudolf Schoell, Wilhelm Kroll. 3 vols. Berlin: Weidmann, 1954. Reprint Hildesheim, Germany: Weidmann, 1989–1993. [Latin and Greek texts only; see, e.g., vol. 1: 4 (*Institutiones* 1.9.1)].

————. *The Digest of Justinian.* Edited by Paul Krüger and Theodor Mommsen. Translated by Alan Watson. 4 vols. Philadelphia: University of Pennsylvania, 1985. [The *Digest* is part of the above *Corpus.* Latin and English ed.; also in McCarthy, see next entry].

McCarthy, Conor, ed. *Love, Sex and Marriage in the Middle Ages: A Sourcebook.* London and New York: Routledge, 2004.

Paston Letters and Papers of the Fifteenth Century. Edited by Norman Davis. 2 vols. Oxford: Oxford University Press, 1971, 1976.

Robert de Sorbon. *De matrimonio.* In *Notices et extraits* [. . .] *Bibliothèque nationale,* edited by Jean B. Haureau, 1: 200. Paris: Klincksieck, 1890.

[Scandinavia]. Ebel, Else. *Der Konkubinat nach altwestnordischen Quellen.* Ergänzungsbände zum Reallexikon der germanischen Altertumskunde, 8. Berlin and New York: de Gruyter, 1993. [Studies and includes source materials on Scandinavian marriage customs].

[Spain]. Bethune, Brian. "Text of the Christian Rite of Marriage in Medieval Spain." Ph.D. diss., University of Toronto, 1987.

Tertullian. [*Ad uxorem*]. *À son épouse.* Edited and translated (French) by Charles Munier. Sources chrétiennes, 273. Paris: Éditions du Cerf, 1980. [Latin and French texts and notes].

————. [*De exhortatione castitatis*]. *Exhortation à la chasteté.* Critical ed. and commentary by Claudio Moreschini. Translation (French) by Jean-Claude Fredouille. Sources chrétiennes, 319. Paris: Éditions du Cerf, 1980. [Latin and French texts and notes].

————. [*De monogamia*]. *Le marriage unique.* Critical ed. and translation (French) by Paul Mattei. Paris: Éditions du Cerf, 1988. [Latin and French texts and notes].

————. *Treatises on Marriage and Remarriage: To His Wife, An Exhortation to Chastity, Monogamy.* Translated by William P. Le Saint. Westminster, Md.: Newman Press, 1951.

Thomas of Chobham. *Summa confessorum.* Edited by F. Broomfield. Analecta medievalia Namurcensia, 25. Louvain, Belgium and Paris: Nauwelaerts, 1968.

Secondary Sources

Bennett, Judith. *Women in the Medieval Countryside: Gender and Household in Brigstock before the Plague.* New York: Oxford University Press, 1987.

Brooke, Christopher N. L. *The Medieval Idea of Marriage.* Oxford and New York: Oxford University Press, 1989.

Brundage, James A. *Law, Sex and Christian Society in Medieval Europe.* Chicago: University of Chicago Press, 1987.

————. "Widows and Remarriage: Moral Conflicts and Their Resolution in Classical Canon Law." In Walker, 17–31. *See below.*

Cartlidge, Neil. *Medieval Marriage: Literary Approaches, 1100–1300.* Woodbridge, U.K. and Rochester, N.Y.: D. S. Brewer, 1997.

Cross, F. L., and E. A. Livingstone, eds. *The Oxford Dictionary of the Christian Church.* 3rd ed. Oxford: Oxford University Press, 1997. [See esp. entries "Divorce" and "Matrimony"].

Davis, Isabel, Miriam Müller, and Sarah Rees Jones, eds. *Love, Marriage, and Family Ties in the Later Middle Ages.* International Medieval Research, 11. Turnhout, Belgium: Brepols, 2003.

Donahue, Charles. "The Canon Law on the Formation of Marriage and Social Practice in the Later Middle Ages." *Journal of Family History* 8 (1983): 63–78.

Duby, Georges. *Mâle Moyen Âge: de l'amour et autres essais.* Champs, 216. Paris: Flammarion, 1990. Original, 1988.

————. *Love and Marriage in the Middle Ages.* Translated by Jane Dunnett. Chicago: University of Chicago Press, 1994. [Translation of above entry, which collects Duby's pertinent essays first published 1967–1986].

Elliott, Dyan. "Marriage." In *The Cambridge Companion to Medieval Women's Writing*, edited by Carolyn Dinshaw and David Wallace, 40–57. Cambridge: Cambridge University Press, 2003.

———. *Spiritual Marriage: Sexual Abstinence in Medieval Wedlock*. Princeton, N.J.: Princeton University Press, 1993.

Esmein, Adhémar. *Le Mariage en droit canonique*. Paris, 1891. 2nd ed. Revised by Robert Génestal and Jean Dauvillier. 2 vols. Paris: Sirey, 1929–1935. Reprint (1st ed.) New York: Burt Franklin, 1968.

Falcón-Pérez, Maria Isabel. "Le Mariage en Aragon au XVe siècle." In *La Femme dans l'histoire et la société méridionales (IXe–XIXe siècles). Actes du 66e congrès de la Fédération historique du Languedoc-Rousillon (Narbonne, 15 et 16 octobre 1994)*, 151–86. Montpellier: Ville de Narbonne/l'Aude, 1995. [Also contains texts of relevant archives].

Farmer, Sharon. "Persuasive Voices: Clerical Images of Medieval Wives." *Speculum* 61 (1986): 517–43.

La Femme dans l'histoire et la société méridionales (IXe–XIXe siècles). Actes du 66e congrès de la Fédération historique du Languedoc-Rousillon (Narbonne, 15 et 16 octobre 1994), 187–218. Montpellier: Ville de Narbonne/l'Aude, 1995. [Important collection on southern-French women by major scholars].

Fradenburg, Louise O. *City, Marriage, Tournament: Arts of Rule in Late Medieval Scotland*. Madison and London: University of Wisconsin Press, 1991.

Friedman, Mordechai A. "Developments in Jewish Marriage and Family Law as Reflected in the Cairo Geniza Documents." In *Judaeo-Arabic Studies: Proceedings of the Founding Conference of the Society for Judaeo-Arabic Studies*, edited by Norman Golb, ch. 9. Amsterdam, Netherlands: Harwood, 1997.

Gold, Penny S. "The Marriage of Mary and Joseph in the Twelfth-Century Ideology of Marriage." In *Sexual Practices in the Medieval Church*, edited by Vern Bullough and James A. Brundage, 102–17. Buffalo: Prometheus, 1982.

Goody, Jack. *The Development of the Family and Marriage in Europe*. Cambridge: Cambridge University Press, 1983.

Hanawalt, Barbara. *The Ties that Bound: Peasant Families in Medieval England*. New York: Oxford University Press, 1986.

———. "Widows." In Dinshaw and Wallace, 58–69. *See above under* Elliott 2003. [Excellent concise view, with most up-to-date essential bibliography].

Heene, Katrien. *The Legacy of Paradise: Marriage, Motherhood and Woman in Carolingian Edifying Literature*. Frankfurt, Germany and New York: Peter Lang, 1997.

Helmholz, Richard H. *Marriage Litigation in Medieval England*. Cambridge Studies in Legal History. Cambridge: Cambridge University Press, 1974. Reprint Holmes Beach, Fla.: W. Gaunt, 1986.

Herlihy, David. *Medieval Households*. Cambridge, Mass.: Harvard University Press, 1985.

———, and Christiane Klapisch-Zuber. *Les Toscans et leurs familles: une étude du "catasto" florentin de 1427*. Paris: CNRS/FNSP/EHSS, 1978. [Both above are classics].

———. *Tuscans and Their Families: A Study of the Florentine Catasto of 1427*. Yale Studies in Economic History. New Haven, Conn.: Yale University Press, 1985. [Abridged, rearranged translation of above].

Hughes, Diane Owen. "From Brideprice to Dowry in Mediterranean Europe." *Journal of Family History* 3 (1978): 262–96. Reprint in Kaplan, 25–58. *See below*.

Jochens, Jenny. "Marriage and Divorce." In *Medieval Scandinavia: An Encyclopedia*, edited by Phillip Pulsiano and Kirsten Wolf et al., 408–10. Garland Reference Library of the Humanities, 934. New York and London: Garland, 1993.

Journal of Family History. Minneapolis: National Council of Family Relations, 1976–. [Often contains valuable articles for the Middle Ages].

Kaplan, Marion A., ed. *The Marriage Bargain: Women and Dowries in European History*. New York: Harrington Park Press, 1985.

Klapisch-Zuber, Christiane, ed. *Histoire des femmes en Occident, 2: Le Moyen Âge*. Paris: Plon, 1992. Original *Storia delle donne nell'Occidente*. Rome-Bari: Laterza, 1990. [Important, innovative essays by major scholars, many pertaining to medieval marriage].

————. *Silences of the Middle Ages. A History of Women in the West*, 2 vols. Edited by Georges Duby and Michelle Perrot, vol. 1. Cambridge, Mass.: Harvard/Belknap Press, 1993. [English translation of above].

————. *Women, Family and Ritual in Renaissance Italy*. Translated by Lydia G. Cochrane. Chicago: University of Chicago Press, 1985. [Translated classic essays].

Kirshner, Julius. "Wives' Claims against Insolvent Husbands in Late Medieval Italy." In *Women of the Medieval World: Essays in Honor of John Hine Mundy*, edited by J. Kirshner and Suzanne F. Wemple, 256–303. Oxford and New York: Basil Blackwell, 1985.

Linehan, Peter, and Janet L. Nelson, eds. *The Medieval World*. New York and London: Routledge, 2001. Reprint 2003. [Innovative collection of essays, several touch on marriage].

Lochrie, Karma. *Covert Operations: The Medieval Uses of Secrecy*. Middle Ages. Philadelphia: University of Pennsylvania Press, 1999.

Mitchell, Linda E., ed. *Women in Medieval Western European Culture*. Garland Reference Library of the Humanities, 2007. New York and London: Garland, 1999.

Molho, Anthony. *Marriage Alliance in Late Medieval Florence*. Cambridge, Mass.: Harvard University Press, 1994.

Molin, Jean-Baptiste, and Protais Mutembe. *Le Rituel de mariage en France du XIIe siècle au XVIe siècles*. Théologie historique, 26. Paris: Beauchesne, 1974.

Miramon, Charles de. *Les "donnés" au Moyen Âge. Une forme de vie religieuse laïque v. 1180–v. 1500*. Paris: Éditions du Cerf, 1999.

Nelson, Janet L. "Medieval Queenship." In Mitchell, 179–208. *See above*.

Noonan, John T. "Power to Choose." *Viator* 4 (1973): 419–34.

Parsons, John Carmi, ed. *Medieval Queenship*. New York: St. Martin's, 1993.

Ostrowski, Donald. *Muscovy and the Mongols: Cross-Cultural Influences on the Steppe Frontier, 1304–1589*. Cambridge: Cambridge University Press, 1998.

Pollock, Frederick, and Frederick W. Maitland. *The History of the English Law before the Time of Edward I*. 2nd ed. 2 vols. Cambridge: Cambridge University Press, 1923. Reprint Washington, D.C.: Lawyer's Literary Club, 1959.

Reynolds, Philip L. *Marriage in the Western Church: The Christianization of Marriage during the Patristic and Early Medieval Periods*. Supplements to Vigiliae Christianae, 24. Leiden: E. J. Brill, 1994.

Rouche, Michel, ed. *Mariage et Sexualité au Moyen Âge. Accord ou crise? (Colloque international de Conques)*. Paris: Presses de l'Université de Paris-Sorbonne, 2000.

Schulenburg, Jane T. *Forgetful of Their Sex: Female Sanctity and Society, ca. 500–1100*. Chicago: University of Chicago Press, 1998.

Sellar, W. H. D. "Marriage, Divorce and Concubinage in Gaelic Scotland." *Transactions of the Gaelic Society of Inverness* 51 (1981): 463–78.

Shahar, Shulamith. *The Fourth Estate: A History of Women in the Middle Ages*. Translated by Chaya Galai. Revised ed. London and New York: Routledge, 2003.

Sheehan, Michael. "The Formation and Stability of Marriage in Fourteenth-Century England: Evidence of an Ely Register." *Medieval Studies* 33 (1971): 228–63.

Skinner, Patricia. *Women in Medieval Italian Society, 500–1200*. Women and Men in History. Harlow, U.K.: Longman/Pearson, 2001.

Stafford, Pauline. *Queens, Concubines and Dowagers: The King's Wife in the Early Middle Ages*. Athens: University of Georgia Press, 1983.

Uitz, Erika. *Women in the Medieval Town*. Translated by Sheila Marnie. London: Barrie & Jenkins, 1988. Original Leipzig, Germany: Edition, 1988. [Especially good for Germany].

Walker, Sue S. *Wife and Widow in Medieval England*. Ann Arbor: University of Michigan Press, 1993.

Wilson, Katharina M., and Elizabeth Makowski. *Wykked Wyves and the Woes of Marriage: Misogamous Literature from Juvenal to Chaucer*. SUNY Series in Medieval Studies. Albany: State University of New York Press, 1990.

NADIA MARGOLIS

MARY, BLESSED VIRGIN, IN THE MIDDLE AGES.

The preeminent female figure in all of medieval Christendom, the Blessed Virgin Mary is the mother of Jesus Christ the Redeemer and supreme among saints and intimate of angels; intercessor and mediator in both word and deed for those who devote themselves to her. During the Middle Ages, her image evolved through a multitude of theological, historical, literary, and visual-arts interpretations.

Despite Mary's position, which would rival that of Christ during the Middle Ages, actual historical information about her in the New Testament is scarce. The gospels of Mark and John begin their story when Christ is an adult; Matthew mentions that Mary was found to have conceived a child of the Holy Spirit, but spends more time with the comforting of Joseph; it is only Luke who reveals Mary as a person and records her words and reactions to the events happening around her. Otherwise, we must look beyond the canonical Bible. The names of Mary's parents, Joachim and Anne, along with the concept of her perpetual virginity first appeared in the Apocryphal (noncanonical) Book of James (sometimes called the "Protoevangelium" ["proto-Gospel"]), one of the "Infancy Gospels," compiled by a Jewish Christian (2nd century) from Matthew, Luke, and other sources, supposedly by Christ's brother, James. From James's Gospel sprang, almost inevitably, the apoc-

The Virgin Mary as the Queen of Heaven, fourteenth century. She is depicted wearing a crown as befits her status as queen of heaven and is standing on a crescent moon, which represents chastity. From a biblical poem. © The British Library/Topham-HIP/The Image Works.

ryphal Gospel of the Birth of Mary, written in Latin rather than Hebrew or Greek, narrating Mary's life from birth through early adolescence. Because this was in truth a much later work than the canonical Gospels and even James (some attribute it to St. Jerome [d. 420] basing it on a Hebrew original, but it may have been later), the Gospel of the Birth of Mary includes more developed "facts" on Mary's life, including, her parents' names (as in James: Joachim and Anne) details of her childhood in the Temple, betrothal to Joseph, Annunciation, and the Virgin Birth of Christ.

Marina Warner points out that it is precisely the lack of real factual knowledge that has allowed for the creation (and re-creation) of the figure of the Virgin throughout the Christian era: "she belongs to a vast community of people and represents a gradual accretion of their ideas, the deposit of popular belief interacting with intellectual inquiry" (Warner, xxiv). As such, rather than being a projection or embodiment of any personal philosophical stance, the Virgin serves as recipient and vessel of the hopes and prayers of those who worship her. While it can be argued that such a portrayal reduces the Virgin—and symbolically all women—to a mere passive figure, it must also be acknowledged that in the medieval period she was elevated to an extremely powerful position, and that further, despite the fact that she is a woman, her authority and her right to exercise it are simply never questioned.

Patristic authors (the "Fathers of the Church": the early doctrinal founders, second through seventh centuries) concerned themselves first with presenting Mary as theobedient counterpoint to the disobedient Eve, as illustrate in the writings of Justin Martyr (d. c.165) and Irenaeus (d. c.202). More important, the concept of her perpetual virginity was probably being advocated prior to the Book of James by Irenaeus and Clement of Alexandria (d. c.215), with Athanasius (d. 373) referring to her as *aeiparthenos*, the "ever virgin." The principal opponent of this concept was Jovinian (d. c.405), who refused to believe in Mary's perpetual virginity; he also denied that virginity should be accorded higher status than marriage. But Jovinian was a twice-condemned unorthodox monk, and from the fifth century onward, both Eastern and Western Churches accepted the doctrine of Mary's perpetual virginity.

This doctrine of her virginity was essential to setting Mary apart from all other women. While it was generally agreed that men and women were equal in theological terms, both having been created by God and given immortal souls, it was women who were ruled not by reason but by the urgings of their own flesh. Treatise after treatise in the Middle Ages warns of how womanly flesh will use its terrifying power to wreak havoc on and wrest control from its rightful male holders. It is therefore logical that Mary be further elevated above and freed from the corrupted bonds of the flesh. Four dogmas of the Western Church constituting Marian doctrine do precisely that: she is not only the mother of the Son of God (*Theotokos*), she as well conceived and gave birth as a virgin (the Annunciation) and was herself conceived without the stain of original sin (the Immaculate Conception); finally, she was spared the final degradation of the flesh in death (and perhaps death itself) by being taken up into heaven (the Assumption). These doctrines highlighting phases of her life were not established in the same chronological order. Her standing as Theotokos, most likely developed among Alexandrian theologians since the influential yet controversial Origen (d. c.254) and defended by Cyril in c.430 against the view that Mary was mother only of Christ's humanity affirmed by Nestorius (d. c.451), was upheld at the Council of Ephesus (431). St. Ambrose (d. 397) added that, in giving birth to Christ she also yielded Christians borne in her womb with Him, and thus could be equated with the figure of the Church (*Ecclesia*) itself, an aspect that would make her at once mother, daughter, and wife of Christ—allowing her pure, spiritual parenting to supplant her (potentially sin-prone) biological one. The doctrine of the corporeal Assumption of Mary was "officialized" by Gregory of Tours (d. 594), after gathering momentum since the fourth century among less orthodox theologians, together with increasingly widespread observance of the Feast of the Assumption, during which Germanus of Constantinople (d. c.733), among others (sixth to eighth centuries), preached sermons extolling Mary's power in heaven. The Immaculate Conception proved to be the most difficult doctrine to stabilize, since, though it had many supporters, it was nevertheless disputed throughout the Middle Ages. Anselm of Canterbury (d. 1109) denied it, as would most of the keenest intellects of twelfth- through thirteenth-century West. Theologians including Albert the Great, Bonaventure, and Thomas Aquinas agreed with Anselm's denial because, they reasoned, all beings conceived naturally (sexual intercourse) bear the stain of original sin, and because Mary was conceived naturally—Theotokos status notwithstanding—she is not exempt from original sin. Because the Eastern Church—even though its theologians proclaimed Mary's implicit sinlessness since the seventh century—did not share the Western Church's concept of original sin, it never accepted the doctrine of Immaculate Conception, nor has it made a dogma of the Assumption. Mary's Immaculate Conception as doctrine had a primary defender in the English historian and theologian Eadmer (d. 1128), who opposed his teacher, Anselm of Canterbury, by attempting to disprove the idea that original sin was transmitted by sexual intercourse. Instead, Eadmer asserted, Mary was born by "passive conception": a unique state apparently reserved for Mary alone, leaving the biological parental act unspecified, which only God could and did effectuate. Later, Duns Scotus (d. 1308) enhanced Eadmer's theory via more rigorous scholastic logic, yet controversy continued at length thereafter. The very vital and influential Franciscans (founded 1209) defended it, as did the resourceful Jesuits (1540), until finally, the Western, Roman Catholic Church, after centuries of conciliar and papal decrees concerning various phases of the doctrine and feast days, approved Immaculate Conception as a doctrine in 1854.

Official doctrine lagged far behind popular belief and even localized Church practice, and Mary had probably been successfully set apart both physically and spiritually from all other women by the High Middle Ages (twelfth to thirteenth centuries). While she is different from all other women, her power is precisely the highest manifestation of the traditionally female virtues of compassion, mercy, justice, and intercession available to all those who devote themselves to the Virgin, no matter their previous deeds or misdeeds.

Miracles are Mary's most potent form of self-manifestation. They underscore her role as intercessor: a divinity hearing and answering direct prayers. The first recorded vision of Mary is believed to have been experienced by the Greek Church Father Gregory Thaumaturgus (d. 270), as noted in a panegyric by the theologian Gregory of Nyssa (d. c.395). This suggests that belief in Mary as intercessor had already existed in the Near East. After the Council of Ephesus determined her status as mother of God (Theotokos) in 431, devotion to Mary only intensified; her name sometimes even came to replace the Lord's in some prayers. In the West, when Gregory of Tours penned his eight *Libri Miraculorum* (*Books of Miracles*, later sixth century), he in a sense opened up hagiography—the writing of saints' lives (focusing on the local favorite St. Martin of Tours among others)—as a historical and literary genre largely defined by the saints' working of miracles. The flourishing of hagiography and simultaneous cult of the Virgin (eleventh through twelfth centuries) merged to produce accounts of Mary's and other saints' miracles as historical and, by the later thirteenth century, theatrical genres. Churches dedicated to the saints and to Mary sought records of miracles as part of their (retroactive) historical validation and also as a complement to preaching for the edification of their congregations. Particularly in England, home of the Feast of Mary's Conception, we find works such as William of Malmesbury's treatise on the miracles of the Virgin (c.1140), together with his compilation *Gesta pontificum Anglorum* (*Deeds of the English Popes*, 1125). In France, too, authors including Vincent of Beauvais (d. 1264) and lesser-knowns such as Gilon, Herman of Laon, and Hugues Farsit made collections of miracles for their respective northern-French churches. Modern expert Benedicta Ward details the voluminous number of miracles said to have occurred at shrines such as Laon, Soissons, and Chartres in the twelfth century. Ward categorizes these into three basic types: "vengeance, protection, and cures." In the flesh-and-blood medieval world, it was the cures of bodily illness that abounded, especially among the poor and destitute. In the vast *Miracles de Nostre-Dame* (*The Miracles of Our Lady*) by Gautier de Coinci, prior of Soissons (d. 1236), the miracle form reaches its artistic zenith while offering a universal breadth of social commentary in which Mary functions as constant mediator: between God and the individual, between the individual and society, and between the individual and herself. Another Frenchman, Rutebeuf (d. 1285) would be the first to convert these narratives into true theater in his celebrated *Miracle de Théophile* (*Theophilus's Miracle*), in which Mary intervenes to save a Devil-dealing cleric, Théophile (note that it means "lover of God"), from damnation. Rutebeuf inspired other dramatists of Mary's miracles, as exemplified in the *Miracles de Notre Dame par personages* (*Our Lady's Miracles by Characters*, fourteenth century), a manuscript containing the "scripts" for forty miracles, half of which contain sermons. In these records and dramas, the Virgin appears as a very real and forceful presence in both the idealized spheres of theology and artistic creation and also in the practical, physical space of everyday men and women. She was, in effect, a figure that bridged and joined the divine and human, and spiritual and physical worlds.

To envision the Virgin as such raises interesting and complex questions about the relationship of ordinary women to her. The Virgin's most significant act—conceiving and giving birth to Christ—is the embodiment of the most physical and exclusively female act possible. And yet, representative of all women as she is, the Virgin is absolutely unlike any of them for doctrinal reasons, a distant and always unattainable paragon for women. But how aloof is she toward both men and women, as reflected in medieval literature and the arts? Furthermore, how do the above-described doctrines, dogmas, and miracle traditions interact in this regard? Do they make Mary more distant or do they humanize her? Some sample representations of the Virgin in music, various literary genres, and the visual arts from across the medieval centuries may shed light on this question.

Returning to the twelfth century, we find the image of Mary revered in many poems, hymns, and liturgical songs by the famous German abbess and visionary, Hildegard of Bingen (1098–1179). As Margot Fassler remarks, Hildegard valued singing as an essential part of monastic spirituality and life more than any of her predecessors. She thus left a larger corpus of music than any other composer—man or woman—of her century. One genre at which she excelled was the antiphon, usually a short chant sung by a choir together with the intonation of psalms and canticles (Fassler, in Newman 1998). She composed them often to the glory of Mary, as, for example, in her Antiphon 11:

> What a great wonder it is
> That into the humble form of a woman
> The King entered.
> God did this,
> Because humility rises above everything.
> And what great fortune is contained
> In this feminine form,
> Because the malice that flowed from one woman,
> This woman has wiped away hereafter,
> She has established the sweetest odor of virtues,
> And she has honored and adorned heaven
> Far more than she earlier disordered the earth. (trans. Barbara Grant)

Hildegard first presents the Virgin as she is often portrayed in scenes of the Annunciation: a humble, passive figure who does not react but rather accepts with wonder this great mystery. Such humility figures among the list of traditional virtues for medieval women. But then, Hildegard tells us, it is precisely such humble lowliness that opens the way to great heights: her Virgin is transformed into an active and powerful establisher of virtue by her own hand. Her goodness has wiped away Eve's "malice" as origin of the world's disorder. But after making this obligatory (for her patristic-traditional readers), she shows Mary as the redeemer of Eve. In the final verse, Hildegard reconciles not only Eve and Mary, but also makes Mary the prototype "feminine form" for all mortal women, replacing Eve (whom the misogynistic Church Fathers decried as the negative, and sole, model for women). Women, as earthly manifestations of Mary, therefore become active participants in their own redemption, and in that of the world.

The thirteenth century in Europe beheld a world of abundant artistic creation dedicated to the Virgin, in conjunction with the above-discussed authors of miracle plays. She is publicly honored in the soaring magnificence of the cathedrals erected in her name and privately revered the miniatures in illuminated prayerbooks and other manuscripts. In music, following Hildegard's legacy, we need only look to the *Cantigas de Santa María* (*Songs of St. Mary*) composed by none less than the king of Castile and Leon, Alfonso X, El Sabio ("The Wise," 1221–1284). The *Cantigas* were a collection of over four hundred songs in Galician combining music, poetry, and illumination to form one of the most remarkable artistic collaborations of the medieval period.

Slightly earlier came Gonzalo de Berceo (c.1180–c.1246), perhaps the first Spanish poet known by name. A secular priest at a Benedictine monastery, Gonzalo's contribution to Marian literature is his collection of miracle tales of the Virgin, the *Milagros de Nuestra Señora* (*Miracles of Our Lady*). This work merits a somewhat longer analysis than our other sample authors, partly because Gonzalo has received less critical attention than they (though see Kelley), and also because his *Milagros*, coming at the chronological and thematic midpoint in the evolution of the medieval Mary, may be examined as an exceptionally complete inventory of the Virgin's attributes by this time in wonderfully readable form. Gonzalo introduces his work by depicting a weary pilgrim who, in the midst of his journey, happens on a lovely green meadow full of sweet-scented flowers and trees laden with lush, perfect fruits. Birds sing so beautifully that no human voice could hope to equal them. And most mysteriously of all, four fountains flow through the meadow, providing cool, refreshing water in summer, warm water in winter. The pilgrim, wonderstruck, lies down in the shade of the beautiful groves, where he finds release from all his worldly cares. This is no ordinary earthly meadow, we soon learn. Like him, Gonzalo, we too are pilgrims on our way to our eternal dwelling in Paradise; like him, we too can avail ourselves of this goodly meadow, this refuge, which is none other than the Virgin Mary. Gonzalo goes on to interpret the darker points of his initially paradisiacal scene as an allegory: the meadow's eternal green freshness is the Virgin's incorruptible virginity; the four wondrous fountains are the four Gospels, written by the evangelists but amended and approved by the Virgin; the refreshing shade of the trees are the prayers that she offers up night and day for sinners. The trees themselves are her miracles, the birds amidst their branches the Fathers of the Church, and finally, the sweet flowers filling the meadow are the numberless names of the Virgin: "of the heavens queen,/temple of Jesus Christ, morning star,/liege lady and compassionate neighbor,/of bodies and souls health and medicine." Thus does he introduce us to his image of Mary. Gonzalo's *Milagros* were likely read out loud for the entertainment and edification of a lay audience. Miracle 21, "Of how an abbess became pregnant," takes many of the traditional misogynist charges against women and uses them not only to exemplify the power and glory of the Virgin but as well to show the positive workings of a community of women. A young and virtuous abbess governs her convent wisely until she one day goes on the wrong path and finds herself pregnant. Some in her convent share her distress, but others take delight in her misdeed and summon the bishop. Alone, pregnant, and in tears, the abbess begs for the Virgin's help and mercy. And an amazing miracle occurs: the Virgin appears and delivers the abbess's baby effortlessly and painlessly, then gives it to two waiting angels who deliver the child into the custody of a hermit. Best of all, the Virgin removes all signs of pregnancy from the abbess's body. When the bishop arrives, the nuns denounce their abbess. She is examined by the bishop's clerics, and her innocence declared, after which the bishop turns his wrath on what he believes to be the scheming nuns. Had the tale ended here, it might have been simply one more in the tradition of misogynist warnings about women who gleefully carry out grand deceptions. Instead, the abbess reveals both the truth and the wonderful miracle the Virgin has accomplished, and the tale ends as one of mutual aid, understanding, and reconciliation among women, thanks to the intervention of the Virgin. She deceived only so that the authority of a powerful female figure—herself a sinner like all earthly women—could be reestablished and peace restored to the community.

Berceo's collection of miracles documents the state of this key aspect of Marian belief by the early thirteenth century. He enumerates an assortment of sins and sinners, ranging from the relatively minor infraction of a canon who is persuaded by his family to leave the Church and to marry, to an inveterate thief sentenced to be hanged, to the extreme case of a monk who, having yielded to the temptations of the flesh while on a pilgrimage, is persuaded by the Devil first to castrate and then to kill himself. In the first two instances, each man is devoted to the Virgin: the canon recites her Hours each day, even though it is not contemporary Church practice; the thief always remembers to say "Ave Maria" and to kneel before her image. In the third instance, the monk is a pilgrim of Saint James, who will seek the Virgin's intercession on his pilgrim's behalf. This devotion is all that is needed for the Virgin to come to her supplicants' aid. The canon, chastened by the Virgin for leaving her service, goes through with the wedding, only to later slip away back into her protective arms, never to be seen again; the thief finds himself held up on the gallows by the hands of the Virgin, who also comes again to his rescue by placing her hands between his neck and the knives of his frustrated castigators. The foolish pilgrim sets the stage for the most spectacular miracle: at Saint James's request, the Virgin retrieves the poor man's soul from the clutches of devils, returns it to his body, and heals the man's wounds—although she chooses not to replace what was cut off. The Virgin's power is supreme, transcending all laws, including those of nature.

Far better known than Gonzalo Berceo is Dante Alighieri (1265–1321), who frequently invokes Mary in the *Inferno, Purgatorio,* and *Paradiso* of his *Divina Commedia (Divine Comedy)*. Moreover, his fifteen verses opening the *Paradiso*'s final canto, as spoken by the great mystic and preacher St. Bernard of Clairvaux (twelfth century), reveal structurally as well as spiritually that, for Dante, Mary is the gateway to glimpsing the Beatific vision of the Divine Essence of his pilgrimage, apparent even in the first two lines, in which operates a telling reversal of parental roles: "Vergine madre, figlia del tuo figlio,/umile e alta più che creatura" ("Virgin mother, daughter of your Son,/more humble and sublime than any creature"). Scholars such as Jaroslav Pelikan have judged Dante's verses to Mary in Canto 33 in particular as the "high point in Marian poetry." It is Mary, "gentle lady in heaven," whom Dante has order the poet's beloved and guide, Beatrice, to come to Dante the pilgrim's aid and explain to him the degrees toward salvation. Dante has won Mary's favor by loving Beatrice nobly, thus separating himself from the "vulgar crowd." If Beatrice is Dante's beloved *donna* (lady) on earth, Mary is the *bella sposa* (beautiful wife) in heaven, as prefigured in the "beautiful muse" of the *Inferno* (2: 85–114). Dante the pilgrim sings *Salve Regina* in her honor to sustain himself through Purgatory. Mary is also the "fair flower" he invokes every morning and evening (*Paradiso* 23: 88–89). For Dante, then, Mary is both intimate and distant, loving and gentle, and yet a goddess; a transcendent feminine force sufficient to overcome all Patristic misogyny, thanks to her incarnation on earth, Beatrice, and vice versa.

Christine de Pizan (1365–c.1430?) was, like Hildegard, a prolific woman visionary who inveighed against the corruption of her time, except Christine was secular and in the world. Born of the northern Italian intelligentsia before migrating with her family to the French court, she also knew and admired Dante, whose encyclopedic pilgrimage, the *Commedia*, she sought to infuse into French letters as an antidote to the *Roman de la Rose*, particularly Jean de Meun's continuation of it (c.1265), a learned but anticlerical, misogynistic pilgrimage toward an kind of love depressingly inferior to Dante's. Christine composed several works in which Mary plays a major role, the most obvious being her early-career (1402–1403) *Les XV. Joyes Nostre Dame* (*The Fifteen Joys of Our Lady*) and *Une Oraison Nostre Dame* (*Prayer to Our Lady*). Her *XV. Joyes*, which participates in a preexisting devotional genre tradition enumerating the various ways in which Mary comforts and inspires miserable mortals (again, as intercessor), also redeems the Marian genre, as well as women, from parodic blasphemy, since a popular anticonjugal satire, the *Quinze Joyes de Mariage* (*The Fifteen Joys of Marriage*, in which "joy" is sarcastic) had recently appeared (c.1400). In the *Oraison*, by its title an intimate, devotional genre, Christine, calling herself "moy, pecharesse" ("I, female sinner"), prays to Mary on behalf of all levels of society (including praying for a cure to King Charles VI's madness), especially women ("le devot sexe des femmes"—"the devout gender of women"), citing the Church Fathers yet without losing her fresh, fervent edge. In her less personal, secular revisionist history of women, the well-known *Cité des Dames* (*City of Ladies*, 1404–1405), Christine, speaking not as herself as she did in the *Oraison* but through the figures of Justice and Reason, echoes several phrases from the earlier prayer but in a more stately, almost bombastic, tone, to lend more authority to her ideas. She describes Mary in the *Cité* as women's "defendaresse" and "protectarresse"; she is also the "fontaine des vertus." Mary's presence also affords Christine the opportunity to quote positive things said about women by theologians. Even more than in Dante's *Paradiso*, the Virgin Mary dominates the last chapter of the *Cité*, radiantly presiding over the edifice's (the *Cité* as castle) exalted completion. Later, at a sad time in her old age, after the death of her promising son, Christine would return to religion, composing the *Heures de contemplacion sur la Passion de Nostre Seigneur* (*Hours of contemplation on the Passion of Our Lord*, 1420), which she self-effacingly introduces as a translation from the Latin. Her "translation" is not without her own personal touches as she emotionally self-identifies alternatingly with Christ on the Cross and the weeping Mary, each grieving His or her loss. Given that Christine had earlier (1403) signaled her awareness of her name, "Christ-ine," as containing that of the "most perfect of men" (*Mutacion de Fortune*, vv. 374–78), she imparts a unique kind of authority to her relationship to the Virgin. To return briefly to the *Heures de contemplacion*, we note various verbally re-created tableaux that were or would become standard in medieval visual representations of Mary and Christ: the *mater dolorosa* (grieving mother) and *pietà* (seated Mary mourning Christ, down from the Cross). By contrast, in Christine's earlier religious works, we see Mary and Christ reigning together in glory.

One of the great literary-historical coincidences is that Christine would be one of the very rare named French authors to celebrate Joan of Arc in the heroine's lifetime, in her last known work, the *Ditié de Jehanne d'Arc* (*Tale of Joan of Arc*, 1429). Joan pertains to our discussion most strikingly in the fact that she headed many of her letters "Jhesu Maria" ("Jesus Mary"), which was also inscribed on her military banners. Joan also understood the indispensable significance of her virginity in setting herself apart from other women and fulfilling her mission to save France—just as theologians did with Mary—and called herself not "Jeanne d'Arc" but "Jean la Pucelle" ("Joan the Maiden"), or simply "La Pucelle." Joan's virginity would help her redeem France, a country allegedly (according to English propaganda) lost through Queen Isabel's promiscuity (nullifying Charles VII's claim to the throne). Although Mary's presence was important to her religious education, Joan has been associated more closely with Jesus and her saints (Michael, Margaret, and Katherine).

Moving toward the end of the Middle Ages, and from among the innumerable visual portraits of Mary, we have selected a miniature from the Hours of Engelbert of Nassau, a work of the Master of Mary of Burgundy (c.1480). Books of Hours—so-called because the prayers contained within were divided for recitation according to the eight canonical hours of each day—were intended for the private contemplation and spiritual connection of their viewers. The Master of Mary of Burgundy, in a manner analogous to Christine de Pizan's "translation" in her *Heures de contemplacion* (again, a book of hours), re-created the standard scenes from canonical Books of Hours, art historian Jonathan Alexander observes, "as dramatizations of a lived psychological experience with which he was able to empathize." In describing the lovely miniature of Mary on her way to share the news of the Annunciation with her cousin Elizabeth, Alexander notes the specific purpose of such an intimate view into the Virgin's life: "we are made aware of the effect of the Annunciation on her. She feels she must tell someone about it, and by showing her walking by herself the artist suggests her loneliness. The need for the Christian to put himself in the place of Christ and of His mother [. . .] was constantly emphasized by late medieval pious writings directed to the laity" (note to ed. Master of Mary of Burgundy, 26). In this particular miniature, Mary is no mere willing vessel for the worldly entrance of the Son of God; by showing her as a pregnant woman alone with her physical state, the image invites the viewer, male or female, into a spiritual identification with Mary through her own body. Contemplation, and thus personalization of this sacred image by a male patron devoted to Mary, may have been a consideration in the making of this work. If Engelbert of Nassau, the book's patron, were indeed such a "sensitive male," it would imply that even the most privileged men could be vulnerable to their wives' pregnancy and its primal emotions: surprise, joy, unease, fears for their child's and their own future, the feeling of solitary responsibility for the creation of a new human life; the loftiest life born in a humble stable. Or maybe, as Alexander seems more inclined to believe, it is the artist Master's sensitivity being reflected here; Engelbert would merely content himself with the manuscript miniatures' lavish execution rather than their deeper message.

Even in this necessarily limited sampling, the medieval Mary can be seen as a rare comforting, positive force, born of desiccated and deliberate doctrines, exalted yet humanized by the talents and devotion of her believers. Her cult, whether through Mariology (study of the person of Mary and her place in the Incarnation) or Mariolatry (erroneous attribution of divine aspects to Mary, according to Church dogma) would continue to grow and transform throughout the Renaissance and into the modern era, as represented in new feast days, religious orders, and similar commemoration of phases of her life and person.

See also Artists, Medieval Women; Christine de Pizan; Hagiography (Female Saints); Hildegard of Bingen, St.; Jeanne d'Evreux; Joan of Arc, St.; Katherine of Sutton; Music in Medieval Nunneries; *Natura*; Virginity

BIBLIOGRAPHY

Primary Sources

Alfonso X, el Sabio. *Cantigas de Santa María.* Edited with introduction and notes by Walter Mettmann. Clásicos Castalia, 134–36. Madrid: Castalia, 1986–1989.

Christine de Pizan. [*Livre de la Cité des Dames*]. *La Città delle Dame.* Edited by E. J. Richards. Translated (Italian) with introduction by Patrizia Caraffi. Biblioteca Medievale. Revised ed., Milan: Luni, 1998.

———. *The Book of the City of Ladies.* Translated by E. J. Richards. Foreword by Natalie Z. Davis. Revised ed., New York: Persea, 1998.

———. *L'Oroyson Nostre Dame; Les XV. Joyes Nostre Dame.* In *Œuvres poétiques de Christine de Pisan*, edited by Maurice Roy, 3: 1–14. Société des Anciens Textes Français [= SATF]. Paris: Firmin Didot, 1896.

———. *"L'Oroyson Nostre Dame": Prayer to Our Lady.* Translated by Jean Misrahi and Margaret Marks. New York: Kurt Volk, 1953.

———. "Christine de Pizan: The XV Joys of Our Lady." Translated by Glenda Wall. *Vox Benedictina* 2 (1985): 134–47.

Dante Alighieri. *Paradiso.* Edited and translated by John D. Sinclair. Galaxy Books. New York: Oxford University Press, 1966. Original 1946. [Bilingual Italian-English ed.].

Gautier de Coinci. *Les Miracles de Nostre Dame.* Edited by Frédéric V. Koenig. Textes Littéraires Français, 64, 95, 131, 176. 4 vols. Geneva: Droz, 1955–1970.

Gonzalo de Berceo. *Los milagros de Nuestra Señora.* Edition and study by Brian Dutton. 2nd ed., revised. London: Tamesis Books, 1980.

———. *Miracles of Our Lady.* Translated by Richard Terry Mount and Annette Grant Cash. Studies in Romance Languages, 41. Lexington: University Press of Kentucky, 1997.

Hildegard of Bingen. *Lieder.* Edited by Pudentiana Barth et al. Salzburg, Austria: Otto Müller, 1969.

———. "Antiphon 11." In *Medieval Women's Visionary Literature*, edited by Elizabeth A. Petroff. New York: Oxford University Press, 1986.

Master of Mary of Burgundy. *A Book of Hours for Engelbert of Nassau: The Bodleian Library, Oxford.* Introduction and legends by J. J. G. Alexander. New York: G. Braziller, 1970.

Miracles de Nostre Dame par personages. Edited by Gaston Paris and U. Robert. SATF. 8 vols. Paris: Firmin Didot, 1879–1893.

Rutebeuf. *Le Miracle de Théophile.* Edited, translated (Modern French), and introduced by Jean Dufournet. Paris: Garnier-Flammarion, 1987. [Bilingual Old–French-Modern French ed.].

Secondary Sources

Ackerman, Jane E. "The Theme of Mary's Power in the *Milagros de Nuestra Señora.*" *Journal of Hispanic Philology* 8 (1983): 17–31.

Boss, Sarah Jane. *Empress and Handmaid: On Nature and Gender in the Cult of the Virgin Mary.* London and New York: Cassell, 2000.

Carroll, Michael P. *The Cult of the Virgin Mary: Psychological Origins.* Princeton, N.J.: Princeton University Press, 1986.

Clayton, Mary. *The Cult of the Virgin Mary in Anglo-Saxon England.* Cambridge: Cambridge University Press, 1990.

Cuneen, Sally. *In Search of Mary: The Woman and the Symbol*. New York: Ballantine Books, 1996.

Durham, Michael S. *Miracles of Mary: Apparitions, Legends, and Miraculous Works of the Blessed Virgin Mary*. San Francisco: Harper, 1995.

Ellington, Donna Spivey. *From Sacred Body to Angelic Soul: Understanding Mary in Late Medieval and Early Modern Europe*. Washington, D.C.: Catholic University of America Press, 2001.

Flory, David A. *Marian Representations in the Miracle Tales of Thirteenth-Century Spain and France*. Washington, D.C.: Catholic University of America Press, 2000.

Frey, Winfried. "*Maria Legens-Mariam Legere*: St. Mary as an Ideal Reader and St. Mary as a Textbook." In *The Book and the Magic of Reading in the Middle Ages*, edited by Albrecht Classen. New York: Garland Publishing, 1998.

Gold, Penny Schine. *The Lady & the Virgin: Image, Attitude, and Experience in Twelfth-Century France*. Chicago: University of Chicago Press, 1985.

Graef, Hilda. *Mary: A History of Doctrine and Devotion*. 2 vols. New York: Sheed and Ward, 1963–1965.

Grieve, Patricia E. "The Spectacle of Memory/Mary in Gonzalo de Berceo's *Milagros de Nuestra Señora*." *Modern Language Notes* 108 (1993): 214–29.

Gros, Gérard. "'Mon oroison entens . . .': Étude sur les trois opuscules pieux de Christine de Pizan." *Bien dire et bien aprandre* 8 (1990): 99–112.

Guitton, Jean. *The Madonna*. Illustrations selected by Chantal Renaudeau d'Arc. New York: Tudor Publishing Company, 1963.

Iannace, Florinda M., ed. *Maria vergine nella letteratura italiana*. Fililibrary Series, 19. Stony Brook, N.Y.: Forum Italicum Publishing, 2000.

Katz, Melissa R. *Divine Mirrors: The Virgin Mary in the Visual Arts*. With essays by Melissa R. Katz and Robert A. Orsi. Oxford and New York: Oxford University Press, 2001.

Kelley, Mary Jane. "Ascendant Eloquence: Language and Sanetity in the works of Gonzalo de Berceo." *Speculum* 79 (2004): 66–87.

Krause, Kathy M. "Virgin, Saint, and Sinners: Women in Gautier de Coinci's *Miracles de Nostre Dame*." In *Reassessing the Heroine in Medieval French Literature*, edited by Kathy M. Krause. Gainesville: University Press of Florida, 2001.

Livingstone, E. A., ed. *Oxford Dictionary of the Christian Church*. Original editor F. L. Cross. Oxford: Oxford University Press, 1997.

McHugh, John. *The Mother of Jesus in the New Testament*. Garden City, N.Y.: Doubleday, 1975.

Newman, Barbara. *God and the Goddesses: Vision, Poetry and Belief in the Middle Ages*. Middle Ages. Philadelphia: University of Pennsylvania Press, 2003.

———, ed. *Voice of the Living Light: Hildegard of Bingen and Her World*. Berkeley: University of California Press, 1998.

O'Carroll, Michael. *Theotokos: A Theological Encyclopedia of the Blessed Virgin Mary*. Wilmington, Del.: M. Glazier, 1982.

Pelikan, Jaroslav. *Eternal Feminines: Three Theological Allegories in Dante's Paradiso*. New Brunswick, N.J. and London: Rutgers University Press, 1990.

———. *Mary Through the Centuries: Her Place in the History of Culture*. New Haven, Conn.: Yale University Press, 1996.

Reed, Teresa P. *Shadows of Mary: Reading the Virgin Mary in Medieval Texts*. Cardiff: University of Wales Press, 2003.

Ruether, Rosemary Radford. *Mary, the Feminine Face of the Church*. Philadelphia: Westminster Press, 1977.

Saupe, Karen, ed. *Middle English Marian Lyrics*. Kalamazoo: TEAMS/University of Rochester/ Medieval Institute Publications, Western Michigan University, 1998.

Scarborough, Connie L. *Women in Thirteenth-Century Spain as Portrayed in Alfonso X's Cantigas de Santa Maria*. Hispanic Literature, 19. Lewiston, N.Y.: E. Mellen Press, 1993.

Tavard, George H. *The Thousand Faces of the Virgin Mary*. Collegeville, Minn.: Liturgical Press, 1996.

Ward, Benedicta. *Miracles and the Medieval Mind: Theory, Record and Event, 1000–1215*. Philadelphia: University of Pennsylvania Press, 1982.

Warner, Marina. *Alone of All Her Sex: The Myth and the Cult of the Virgin Mary*. New York: Knopf, 1976.

Witt, Elizabeth A. *Contrary Marys in Medieval English and French Drama*. Studies in the Humanities, 17. New York: Peter Lang, 1995.

DENISE-RENÉE BARBERET

MASCHERONI, LUCIA. *See* **Catherine of Bologna, St.**

MATILDA OF FLANDERS. *See* **Adela of Blois**

MATILDA OF SCOTLAND (1080–1118). Also called Edith, Eadgyth, or Good Queen Maud/Mold, Matilda of Scotland composed epistles in Latin to Anselm and Pope Paschal and was the first wife of Henry I, king of England (1068–1135). Edith, who would take the name Matilda on her marriage and coronation, was born to the queen and future saint, Margaret (c.1047–1093), and King Malcolm (Canmore) III of Scotland (d. 1093)—the same Malcolm who regained the throne from Macbeth. Orphaned at age thirteen, she received an excellent, if strict, education from an aunt, Christina of Hungary, a nun at either Wilton or Romsey. Her aunt gave her the firm grounding in Classical literature that later enabled her to compose erudite and thoughtful letters. She also instilled within Matilda a profound Christian piety and impeccable conduct at Wilton, though the latter's cloistered status made her ineligible for marriage to her eager suitor, King Henry. She thus appealed to Anselm, Archbishop of Canterbury who, together with an assembly of bishops, nobles, and clergy, after some reluctance, declared her free to marry the king in 1100.

Now Queen Matilda, she seems to have expressed her gratitude to Anselm through a correspondence conducted with him despite his conflict with her husband over the critical issue known as investiture determining whether the king or the Church had more power to appoint, or "invest" bishops and other lay and Church officials—a conflict resulting in Anselm's forced exile from England to the Vatican until King Henry finally relented. Her efforts to reconcile conflicts between Church and state extended even farther: she founded the first Austin Priory in 1108 and, among other public-works projects, constructed a bridge across the river Lea, to be maintained by the nuns of Barking abbey with her subvention through a land grant. Henry's marriage to Matilda, or "good queen Maud/Mold," increased his popularity among his subjects. The couple had three children: two boys, the first dying in infancy and the second named William (1103–1120), and a girl, the future empress Matilda, wife of Henry V. Matilda thereby fulfilled the prophecy of her ancestor and by then cult-figure, Edward the Confessor (d. 1066), of "regrafting the green tree" of English succession (*Vie d'Edouard le Confesseur* [*Life of Edward the Confessor*], vv. 4977–90), together with her generous patronage of musicians, scholars, and poets—particularly those of religious works—despite the possibly suspicious sources of these funds. Astutely aware of the value of hagiography in ensuring her family's continuity, because of her descent from the Confessor and also from St. Edith, she commissioned her mother's biography by her scholarly prior, Turgot. Very much her mother's daughter, despite limited contact due to Margaret's early death in 1093, Edith/Matilda also did much to shape the outlook of her younger brother, the pious yet powerful lord and patron, David, who in turn helped his brothers, the future King Edgar of Scotland, and Alexander.

Of her own literary works we retain only seven letters: six to Archbishop Anselm, the future saint (1093–1109), and one to Pope Paschal on Anselm's behalf, all devoted to healing the rift caused by Anselm's disagreement with King Henry. Matilda's letters are highly literate: full of quotations from Classical Roman authors such as Cicero and Virgil (both first century B.C.E.), the Scriptures, and Church Fathers including Gregory (d. 604) and Augustine (d. 430), and allusions to many other learned authorities. Her writing is as versatile as that of Abelard (d. 1142/3) or Montaigne (d. 1592) in that she is clearly at home in a variety of contexts while preferring, as in her patronage, scriptural or patristic subjects—those dealing with the early Church founders ("Fathers"). Letter 242 to Anselm is a model of twelfth-century epistolary writing. Deploying a rationale reminiscent of Alan of Lille (d. 1203), she begs Anselm to end his fast since it is ultimately a transgression against nature, depleting him, she argues, for his real mission, in body as well as spirit, citing from Cicero's *De senectute* (*On Old Age*): "the gift of the orator is not intelligence alone but breadth and strength." She substantiates her advocacy of moderation in fasting, as in all things, by referring to John, who wanted to outlive his Lord so that the Virgin would have someone to turn to; likewise all pastors must eat for their flocks to feed. Matilda then lists a number of other figures from ancient and scriptural sources who first fasted, then ate: just as Daniel, Moses, Pythagoras, and Socrates taught both fasting and eating so did Christ at the wedding feast whereupon he turned water into wine.

Other letters, while not as overtly humanistic—merging pagan-classical and scriptural wisdom—nonetheless betray an impressive breadth of learning. Letter 320 thanks Anselm for his letter that, as she says, "chased the clouds of sadness away, his words shining through like rays of new light." In the same letter she implores him not to give up hope as she herself is still hopeful that he will ultimately be forgiven, a confidence based more on her faith in God and man than on any particular action taken by her husband. In yet another epistle (384), Matilda likens the acumen found in Anselm's letters to that characterizing the writings of Cicero, Quintilian, Paul, and Augustine. Always concerned about Anselm's welfare, Matilda makes a special appeal to Pope Paschal in the former's defense (Letter 323). Notable for its "periodic style"—that most elegant and complex of Classical Latin sentence structures used to discuss difficult subjects—her epistle none-theless refrains here from mentioning any pagan Latin authors. Matilda restricts herself to an allusion from Peter and images drawn from the patristic tradition, particularly the parable of sheep seeking nourishment just as Anselm's flock need him. Matilda's letters, on the whole, reflect a woman so conversant with the learning of the past that she is able to draw from it and adapt it readily and effectively, whatever the circumstance or audience. The humanistic and humane content of her writing also expressed itself in her many charitable and civic-minded works, from issuing writs in her husband's absence to building roads, founding the lepers' hospital of St. Giles, and aiding the poor.

See also Epistolary Authors, Women as; Margaret of Scotland, St.

BIBLIOGRAPHY

Primary Sources
Anonymous. *La Vie d'Edouard le Confesseur: poème anglo-normand du XIIe siècle.* Critical edition by Östen Södergård. Uppsala, Sweden: Almqvist & Wiksell, 1948.

[Matilda, Queen of England]. [Letters]. In *S. Anselmi Cantuariensis Archiepiscopi Opera Omnia*, vol. 2. Edited by Frances S. Schmitt. Edinburgh: Thomas Nelson, 1946–1961 [Original Latin texts only].

———. "Good Queen Maud [Letters]." In *The Writings of Medieval Women: An Anthology*. Edited and translated by Marcelle Thiébaux. 2nd ed. New York and London: Garland, 1994.

Pinkerton, John. *Life of St. Margaret*. In *Ancient Lives of Scottish Saints*, translated with an introduction by W. M. Metcalfe, vol. 2. Paisley: Gardner, 1895. Reprint Lampeter, Wales: Llanerch, 1998.

Turgot. *Vita S. Margaretae Scotorum Reginae*. In *Symeonis Dunelmensis Monachi Opera et Collectanea*. Edited by H. Hinde. Surtees Society, 51. London, 1868.

Secondary Sources

Baker, Derek. "'A Nursery of Saints': St Margaret of Scotland Reconsidered." In *Medieval Women*, edited by Derek Baker, 119–42. Studies in Church History, Subsidia, 1. Oxford: Basil Blackwell, 1978. Reprint 1981.

Chibnall, Marjorie. *Empress Matilda: Queen Consort, Mother and Lady of the English*. Oxford and Cambridge, Mass.: Basil Blackwell, 1991.

Huneycutt, Lois L. *Matilda of Scotland: A Study in Medieval Queenship*. Woodbridge, Suffolk, U.K. and Rochester, N.Y.: Boydell Press, 2003.

Thiébaux, Marcelle. "Good Queen Maud." In *The Writings of Medieval Women: An Anthology*, edited and translated by Marcelle Thiébaux. 2nd ed. New York and London: Garland, 1994. [Good, concise biographical notes].

WILLIAM PROVOST

MATILDA OF TUSCANY/CANOSSA (1046–1115). Known as the "Great Countess," and also referred to as Matilda of Canossa, Matilda was a powerful Italian landholder and military strategist who supported Pope Gregory VII during the infamous Investiture controversy—a significant, prolonged confrontation between Church and Empire—against the Holy Roman Emperor Henry IV. She exemplifies certain women rulers who, because their domains were small enough, could rule directly and personally in a way that queens rarely could, and thereby "override abstract anxieties about female governance" (Hollister and Bennett).

Matilda was the youngest child of Bonifazio—marquis of Tuscany and count of Reggio and several other major northern-Italian areas, especially Lombardy—and Beatrice of Lorraine, daughter of Frederick II, duke of Lorraine and Matilda of Swabia, an extensive south-German duchy. However, soon after Bonifazio was murdered (1052), her older sister and brother died, leaving the eight-year-old Matilda heiress to an important domain with her mother as guardian. Partly to shield her daughter's birthright, Beatrice remarried (1056), to a cousin, Gottfried (the Bearded), a duke of Upper Lorraine who had rebelled against Holy Roman Emperor Henry III (r. 1039–1056). Such pro-papal, anti-imperial policies would mark Matilda and her family for life.

Henry III not only militarily intervened in papal politics but also sought to reform the corrupt papacy by deposing Benedict IX, the incumbent, and his rivals (anti-popes) in Rome and replacing them with German-born reform popes, the ablest being Leo IX (r. 1049–1054). Matilda's family also involved themselves in the complex papal elections of Leo's successors: her stepfather, Gottfried's, brother Frederick became pope (Stephen IX/X) and his successors hailed from Tuscany. Matilda's parents' armies imparted the necessary clout to these papal claims and staved off the anti-popes. According to legend (in the absence of historical evidence), the young Matilda herself engaged in battle during this time.

Matilda of Canossa, Italian countess of Tuscany and ally of
Pope Gregory VII. Allegorical portrait. © The Art Archive/Museo
di Castelvecchio Verona/Dagli Orti.

Also at this time (c.1065), Matilda married Gottfried the Bearded's son by his first marriage, Gottfried the Hunchback, but the couple separated after the elder Gottfried's death (1069), with his son returning to Germany to his patrimony, the duchy of Lower Lorraine, where he died in 1076. On her mother's death that same year, Matilda, now thirty, came into her formidable inheritance: her parents' northern-Italian domains and her husband's in Lorraine, so that her lands extended to both sides of the Alps and Appenines.

The high point of Matilda's renown converged with one of history's most dramatic encounters to decide which was more powerful, the papacy or the Holy Roman Empire—that is, the Church or the state—and thus resolve the so-called Lay Investiture Controversy. Until this time, the Germanic Holy Roman emperors reserved the right to appoint or "invest" bishops. Although these emperors were fundamentally lay rulers, they had considered themselves divinely ordained ever since Charlemagne was crowned by the pope at Rome in 800.

Furthermore, as noted previously, Emperor Henry III had even taken to appointing the popes himself. Pope Gregory VII (1073–1085) worked to ban this practice on the part of Henry III's son and successor, Henry IV (1056–1106), denying the divinity of lay rulers and their control over the clergy. After a heated exchange of insulting letters between Gregory and Henry, the pope excommunicated the emperor, which, together with secular political unrest among the German princes, gravely threatened Henry's throne. To retain his position, Henry had to reconcile with Pope Gregory in a most humbling fashion: the emperor showed up, walking barefoot in the snow and dressed in a coarse penitent's robe, at Matilda's Appenine mountain castle in Canossa (January 1077) to beg forgiveness of Pope Gregory and promise to respect his authority. Gregory reluctantly lifted his excommunication, allowing the emperor to regain his standing among his princes.

As moving a moment as this was, its consequences were short lived; Gregory again had to excommunicate Henry for his behavior (1080), and Henry crossed the Alps and into Rome with an army intending either to force the pope to lift the excommunication or to depose Gregory and install his own pope. Throughout this conflict, Matilda vigorously supported Gregory against Henry. Because of her land holdings and her own army, she controlled western access to Rome and thus posed a constant obstacle to Henry's strategy. Although Henry eventually triumphed and Gregory was forced to take refuge in the

Vatican hideout, Castel Sant'Angelo, then to die in exile in Salerno (1085), Matilda remained faithful to the pope as his communications agent for northern Europe, even after Henry seized the pope's official seal, which Matilda managed to bypass in corresponding with German pro-papal allies. After installing his own pope, anti-pope Clement III, who would in turn consecrate him as emperor, Henry then focused his attention on deposing Matilda through his Italian allies, but Matilda defeated them at Sobara (near Modena) in 1084. The following year she led her armies to aid Gregory's successor, Pope Victor III (1086–1087).

Three years later (1089), Matilda took a new husband, Welf V of Bavaria, ancestor to the pro-papal party, Italianized as "Guelphs," which the Florentine poet Dante would later join and commemorate in his *Divina Commedia* (*Divine Comedy*, 1321). Henry again tried to drive out Matilda, only to suffer defeat by her armies, appropriately near Canossa (1092), and never again regain his influence in Italy. The phrase "to go to Canossa" would ever thereafter indicate submission to the Catholic Church, particularly once Germany's modern unifier, Otto von Bismarck (1815–1898) coined it as such.

After some fifty years as one of the papacy's most ardent warriors and aides, Matilda did reconcile with Henry's more diplomatic successor, Henry V (r. 1106–1125) in 1111, when the latter came to Italy. Since she had no children or other heirs, she willed her lands to him. However, prior to this understanding, she had promised her vast holdings to the pope, and died of gout in 1115 without revoking her earlier bequest. This confusion resulted in Henry V seizing her lands right away and then, also since Henry died without heirs, led to a further lengthy struggle between papacy and empire to win the so-called Mathildine Inheritance, from which the Tuscan cities eventually emerged as independent communes and the Papal States took over the rest.

As of the seventeenth century, Matilda is one of only three women whose remains lie in St. Peter's Basilica at the Vatican. The modern Italian playwright Luigi Pirandello would enshrine her in a different way, incorporating her persona in his play *Enrico IV* (*Henry IV*—usually translated as *The Living Mask*, 1922).

Our primary sources for Matilda's life include a poem by Donizone, a monk of Canossa, praising her life, while Emperor Henry IV's advocate, Bishop Benzo of Alba, provides less favorable but valuable additional details in his book to Henry. Both are therefore contemporary and to some extent eyewitness accounts (Eads 2000; 2002; Web site). Pope Gregory's letters and of course Matilda's own letters are also informative.

See also Dower

BIBLIOGRAPHY

Primary Sources

Benzo of Alba. [*Ad Henricum IV. Imperatorem libri VII*]. *Sieben Bücher an Kaiser Heinrich IV.* Edited and translated (German) by Hans Seyffert. *Monumenta Germaniae Historica* [= MGH]. *Scriptores rerum Germanicarum in usum scholarum separatim editi*, 65. Hannover, Germany: Hahn, 1996. [Original Latin text with German translation and notes].

Donizone of Canossa. *Vita Mathildis: celeberrimae principis Italiae.* Edited by Luigi Simeoni. *Rerum Italicarum Scriptores*, 5: 2. Torino: Bottega d'Erasmo, 1973. Original Bologna: N. Zanichelli, 1930–1940.

———. [*Vita Mathildis*]. *Matilda di Canossa, il poema di Donizone.* Edited and translated (Italian) by Ugo Bellocchi and Giovanni Marzi. Le Antiche Provincie Modenese. Monumenti, 24. Modena, Italy: Aedes Muratoriana, 1970. [Original Latin with Italian trans. and mss. facsimiles].

————. *Vita di Matilde di Canossa*. Translated (Italian) by Paolo Golinelli. Introduction by Vito Fumagalli. Milan: Jaca, 1987. [Italian only].

Gregory VII. [Letters]. *Das Register Gregors VII*. Edited by E. Caspar. MGH. *Epistolae Selectae*, 2. 2 vols. Berlin: Weidmann, 1920–1923.

————. *The Registry of Pope Gregory VII, 1073–1085*. 2 vols. Translated by H. E. J. Cowdrey. Oxford: Oxford University Press, 2002.

———— et al. [Investiture Controversy Documents]. In *Quellen zur Investiturstreit*. Edited and translated by E. Caspar et al. Ausgewählte Quellen zur deutsche Geschichte des Mittelalters, 12. Darmstadt, Germany: Wissenschaftliche Buchgesellschaft, 1978–.

Matilda of Tuscany/Canossa. [Letters, charters, etc.]. *Die Urkunden und Briefe der Markgräfin Mathilde von Tuszien*. Edited by Elke and Werner Goez. MGH. *Diplomata*, 5. Laienfürsten- und Dynastenurkunden der Kaiserzeit, 2. Hannover: Hahn, 1998. [Latin original, German notes] /

Secondary Sources

Blumenthal, Uta-Renate. *The Investiture Controversy: Church and Monarchy from the Ninth to the Twelfth Century*. Medieval Studies. Philadelphia: University of Pennsylvania Press, 1991.

Cowdrey, H. E. J. *Pope Gregory VII: 1073–1085*. Oxford and New York: Oxford University Press, 1998.

Eads, Valerie. "Mighty in War: The Campaigns of Matilda of Tuscany." Ph.D. diss., City University of New York, 2000.

————. "The Geography of Power: Matilda of Tuscany and the Strategy of Active Defense." In *Crusaders, Condottieri and Cannon: Medieval Warfare in Societies around the Mediterranean*, edited by L. J. Andrew Villalon and Donald Kagay. Leiden: Brill, 2002.

————. http://hungrysamuraionline.com [Impressive Web site devoted entirely to Matilda, with translations of extracts from above-listed primary sources, secondary material, and images].

Ferri, Edgarda. *La Grancontessa: vita, avventure e misteri di Matilde di Canossa*. Le Scie. Milan: Mondadori, 2002.

Fraser, Antonia. *The Warrior Queens*. 2nd ed. London: Weidenfeld & Nicolson, 1994. Original eds.: *Boadicea's Chariot: The Warrior Queens*. London: Weidenfeld & Nicolson, 1988; *The Warrior Queens*. New York: Knopf, 1989.

Hollister, C. Warren, and Judith M. Bennett. *Medieval Europe: A Short History*. Boston: McGraw-Hill, 2002. [See esp. 246, 254, 362].

Overmann, Alfred. *Gräfin Mathilde von Tuscien: ihre Besitzungen, Geschichte ihres Gutes von 1115–1230 und ihre Regesten*. Frankfurt: Minerva, 1965. Original Innsbruck, Austria, 1895.

NADIA MARGOLIS

MAUDE OF SCOTLAND. *See* **Matilda of Scotland**

MECHTHILD OF HACKEBORN (1241–1299). A German mystic sometimes confused with her famous contemporary at Helfta, Mechthild of Magdeburg, Mechthild of Hackeborn was one of the most influential women mystics of the thirteenth century in her own right. Her visions, prayers, and songs, next to those of St. Gertrud the Great, had a crucial impact on catholic piety for centuries.

At age seven, Mechthild, accompanied by her parents, visited her sister Gertrud in the Cistercian nunnery of Rodersdorf, in the diocese of Halberstadt, founded in 1229 by Elisabeth, countess of Mansfeld. At that time the monastery was governed by the abbess Kunigunde of Halberstadt. Despite her parents' resistance, Mechthild finally obtained their permission to enter the order. Her sister, Gertrud of Hackeborn (1232–1292), became abbess in 1251 and in 1258 moved the convent from Mansfeld to Helfta (or

Helpede), ruled by the lords Albrecht and Ludolf von Hackeborn. In 1343, Helfta was destroyed in a feud between Brunswick and Mansfeld and refounded near Eisleben, in Saxony. Guided by the Dominicans from nearby Halle, Gertrud of Hackeborn promoted the study of liberal arts (grammar, logic, rhetoric, arithmetic, astronomy, geometry, music), liturgy (the prescribed Church services), and exegesis (multilevel commentary on the Scriptures). Thus the outstanding Dominican philosophers Albert the Great (d. 1280) and Thomas Aquinas (d. 1274) were well known to Mechthild (*Liber Specialis Gratiae*, 5: 9). She excelled in liturgical chorals and singing Mass, earning her the positions of *magistra* ([choir-] mistress) and *cantrix* (chantress). Both musical activities deeply influenced her early mystical visions.

At the age of fifty, after a prolonged period of sickness, the intensity of her visions increased and she began to discuss them. One of her students, Gertrud, who had entered the convent as a five-year-old and who would later become known as St. Gertrude the Great (1256–1301/2), and at least one other anonymous nun, sometimes called the Third Nun (Voaden), wrote down her accounts and compiled them as the *Liber Specialis Gratiae* (*Book of Special Grace*) at the behest of Abbess Sophie of Querfurt. These scribes left personal comments in the text, thus demonstrating that the *Liber* was truly the product of a communal effort to preserve Mechthild's visionary experiences. The manuscript of the original text, in German, is lost, leaving only the later, Latin version, copied by the priest Albert, vicar of St. Pauli at Erfurt. Of this version there are four manuscript traditions in varying degrees of completeness: A (containing nine manuscripts), B (thirty-six mss.), C (seventeen mss.), and D (twenty-sixfragments). In all, there are 250 manuscripts containing either the complete text or extracts from Mechthild's *Liber*.

Mechthild's spiritual sisters did not reveal to her their *Liber Specialis Gratiae* until much later, at which point Mechthild hesitantly agreed to make her visions public via this book. Except for a few letters addressing a matron, scarcely any of this book was written by Mechthild herself (Book 4, ch. 59).

The *Liber Specialis Gratiae* contains the following chapters: (1) Mechthild's visions in close parallel to the liturgy, (2) Her personal contacts with Jesus, (3) The right way to praise God, (4) Prayers for people and promises of salvation, (5) Her visions of the Afterlife, (6) The virtue and blessedness of her sister Gertrud of Hackeborn, and (7) Mechthild's blessed transfiguration at her death on November 19, 1292. As had Gertrude the Great, Mechthild devoutly cultivated the Sacred Heart of Christ: a powerful, almost shockingly carnal, recurrent vision intermingling Christ's throbbing, bleeding heart and chest wound with female anatomy—hence, in certain manuscript illustrations, this Wound of Christ resembles a vagina. Mechthild too borrowed from the Song of Songs' images of kissing, resting at the Lord's side, of His wounds and Passion, and of death as a ceremonial walk into the bedroom of the Lord. Convent life also receives considerable attention, particularly emphasizing virtue and discipline. Mechthild assumes not only the female roles of spiritual counselor, teacher, and intermediary between God and man, but also the masculine one of priest.

She sees herself as God's bride because He has given her a ring with seven jewels representing the stages of his early life (3: 1). She depicts herself as either a bird or a rabbit in Christ's lap, but each time the author turns to her audience and explains the allegorical meaning of such images. Most important are her visions of union with God and the dying, or rather of her body's disappearance (2: 35). Often the image of a beautiful house serves to evoke the *unio mystica* (mystical union) with Christ.

Both Gertrud the Great's *Legatus divinae pietatis* (*The Herald of God's Loving-Kindness*) and Mechthild's visions were often copied and printed together. Mechthild has been seen as the model for Dante's Matelda in his *Divina Commedia* (*Divine Comedy*, 1321): the mysterious fair lady bathed in sweet grace—unnamed despite her commanding presence in the *Purgatorio* (28, vv. 40–148), but later coyly named by Beatrice in canto 33 (v. 119; ed. Sinclair). Likewise, in Boccaccio's *Decameron* (1351–1353), we find another "donna Matelda" similarly described (7: 1), but more recent critics have demonstrated that such attributions represent nothing more than wishful thinking.

Various schools of thought have considered Mechthild's emphasis on justification of divine grace and on the notion of predestination as harbingers of the Reformation (sixteenth century). Together with the Gertrude the Great's prayers and visions, Mechthild's enjoyed enormous popularity (there was even a Middle-English translation and a sixteenth-century French one) into modern times, as exemplified by the success of Martin van Kochem's 1668 *Gebetbuch der heiligen Gertrudis und Mechtildis* (*Prayer Book of the Holy Gertrude and Mechthild*), which by 1694 had sold 30,000 copies. Mechthild's texts have been reprinted until the present time.

See also Boccaccio, Women in, *Des Cleres et Nobles Femmes*; Bride of Christ/ *Brautmystik*; Convents; Gertrude the Great, of Helfta, St.; Mechthild of Magdeburg; Music in Medieval Nunneries

BIBLIOGRAPHY

Primary Sources
Alighieri, Dante. *Dante's Purgatorio*. Edited and translated with commentary by John D. Sinclair. Galaxy Books, 66. New York: Oxford University Press, 1939. [Editor's commentary echoes nineteenth-century theories identifying Mechthild with Matelda].

Mechthild of Hackeborn. [*Liber spiritualis gratiae*]. In *Revelationes Gertrudianae et Mechthildianae*. Edited by the Benedictine Monks of Solesmes: Part 2 edited by Dom Louis Paquelin. Poitiers and Paris: Oudin, 1877.

———. *The Booke of Gostlye Grace*. Edited by Teresa Halligan. Toronto: Pontifical Institute of Medæval Studies, 1979. [Middle English translation with modern notes].

———. *Das Buch vom strömenden Lob*. Translated (German) by H. U. von Balthasar. Einsiedeln, Germany: Johannes, 1955.

Secondary Sources
Bangert, Michael. "*Vor dir steht die leere Schale meiner Sehnsucht:*" *die Mystik der Frauen von Helfta*. Leipzig: Benno-Verlag, 1998.

Finnegan, Sr. Mary Jeremy. *The Women of Helfta: Scholars and Mystics*. Athens: University of Georgia Press, 1991.

Hamburger, Jeffrey. *The Visual and the Visionary: Art and Female Spirituality in Late Medieval Germany*. New York: Zone Books, 1998.

Holsinger, Bruce W. *Music, Body and Desire in Medieval Culture: Hildegard of Bingen to Chaucer*. Figurae: Reading Medieval Cutlture. Stanford, Calif.: Stanford University Press, 2001.

Hubrath, Margarete. *Schreiben und Errinern: zur "memoria" im* Liber Specialis Gratiae *Mechthilds von Hackeborn*. Paderborn, Germany: Schöning, 1996.

Laughlin, M. F. "Mechthild of Hackeborn." In *New Catholic Encyclopedia*, 9: cols. 545–46. New York and St. Louis: McGraw-Hill, 1967.

Petroff, Elizabeth Alvilda. *Medieval Women's Visionary Literature*. New York and Oxford: Oxford University Press, 1986.

Ruh, Kurt. *Geschichte der abendländischen Mystik. II: Frauenmystik und Franziskanische Mystik der Frühzeit*. Munich: Beck, 1993.

Schmidt, Margot. "Elemente der Schau bei Mechthild von Magdeburg und Mechthild von Hackeborn. Zur Bedeutung der geistlichen Sinne." In *Frauenmystik im Mittelalter*, edited by Peter Dinzelbacher and D. R. Bauer, 123–51. Ostfildern, Germany: Schwabenverlag, 1985.

———. "Mechthild de Hackeborn." In *Dictionnaire de Spiritualité*, 10: cols. 873–77. Paris: Beauchesne, 1980

———. "Mechthild von Hackeborn." In *Mein Herz schmilzt wie Eis im Feuer: Die religiöse Frauenbewegung des Mittelalters in Porträts*, edited by Johannes Thiele, 87–99. Stuttgart: Kreuz Verlag, 1988.

Voaden, Rosalynn. "All Girls Together: Community, Gender and Vision at Helfta." In *Medieval Women in their Communities*, edited by Diane Watt, 72–91. Cardiff: University of Wales Press, 1997.

Weissbrot, Johannes, and Margot Schmidt, eds. *Die Grundwerke der drei grossen Frauen von Helfta: Perlen deutscher Mystik.* Introduction by Hans Urs von Balthasar. Freiburg-im-Breisgau, Germany: Herder, 2001.

ALBRECHT CLASSEN

MECHTHILD OF MAGDEBURG (c.1207–c.1282/94). Mechthild composed an influential volume of revelations, poems, and treatises in German, rather than in Latin, as one of three important interconnected nuns writing at Helfta; she is not to be confused with her fellow sister, Mechthild of Hackeborn. Hardly anything is known of her early childhood, but she was probably born to wealthy aristocratic parents living in the vicinity of Magdeburg, Lower Saxony (today, northeastern Germany). Although she must have received a thorough education, she often identified herself by a humble persona of illiterate simplicity: the standard "humility topos" exploited by medieval women writers. When twelve years old, she experienced her first revelation, which she described as the Greeting of the Holy Spirit. This spirit urged her to devote her life to God, so Mechthild became a Beguine (female religious leading pious but noncloistered lives) at Magdeburg in 1230 under the direction of the Dominicans.

Although soon venerated as a saint, because of her harsh criticism of the clergy's debaucheries and the upper Church hierarchy, and also because of growing disapproval of the Beguines, she immediately faced much hostility and suffered public slander. In old age, she took refuge in the nunnery of Helfta, Saxony, a Cistercian-inspired convent (one following the Benedictine rule more austerely), in around 1270–1271, where she was warmly welcomed by the accomplished abbess Gertrud of Hackeborn, her sister Mechthild of Hackeborn, and the future St. Gertrude the Great—both of the latter being younger mystical authors. By this time Mechthild of Magdeburg was already ailing and half blind.

In about 1250, according to her own testimony, she began to record God's words under the Low German title of *Das fliessende Liecht der Gotheit* (Modern German: *Das fliessende Licht der Gottheit* = *The Flowing Light of the Godhead*) to bear witness of God's glory to mankind, at the urging of her confessor, Heinrich of Halle, once he had learned of her revelations. Heinrich and his fellow Dominicans supported Mechthild in her writing over the ensuing decades. This book became the first major literary document of German female mysticism in the high Middle Ages. It excels in its astounding degree of subjectivity and spirituality, unprecedented in religious texts. To attain such spiritual-emotional heights, she borrows from the language and imagery of the Song of Songs and, more daringly (since she is taking from secular love poetry to express sacred themes) frequently applies dialogues in the form of the *Wechsel* (exchange) a courtly poetic genre cultivated in the *Minnesang*, the medieval German counterpart of troubadour lyrics. She also demonstrates a familiarity with the writings of such noteworthy theologians and spiritual authors as St. Bernard of Clairvaux (1090–1153), William of Saint-Thierry (1075/80–1148), the Victorines (twelfth-century group of Parisian scholars and mystics influenced by St. Bernard), the German evangelical preacher David of Augsburg (c.1200–1272), the prolific visionary abbess Hildegard of Bingen (1098–1179), and the reformer and pope Gregory the Great (c.540–604). She particularly emphasizes her closeness to God and that her words are His own, as she recreates a variety of (now, classic) mystical experiences: her quasi-erotic union with God; intense feelings of fire, heat, and light searing within her, the vision of the Trinity, of Christ's heart, and of her journeys through Hell, Purgatory, and Heaven. Even though *Das fliessende Liecht* lacks a specific theological argument—a trait not uncommon in mystical texts—it reveals Mechthild's profound understanding of the mystery of Christ's love and mercy as a dynamic process of transfiguration. Such ideas are heightened by her remarkable talent at a variety of literary forms evidenced in *Das fliessende Liecht*: spiritual poems, love songs, allegories, visions, and polemical admonitions against the clergy and worldly sins. Furthermore, her frequent reliance on bridal imagery and nuptial metaphors, extending to fervent expressions of eroticized love of Christ, drew much criticism, since these normally male-articulated feminizations, now penned by a woman, cast her in a disturbingly authoritative position, a trans-sexual theological-political paradox analyzed by modern scholars like Caroline Bynum and Barbara Newman.

Mechthild's Books 1 through 6 were translated into Latin shortly after her death; however, the translators were unaware of the *existence* of Book 7, which she had composed at Helfta. The secular priest Heinrich of Nördlingen (c.1310–c.1387) translated the work into Middle-High German (*Das Fliessende Licht*), perhaps with the assistance of the *Gottesfreunde* ("Friends of God"—an informal group of mystical writers) at Basel, Switzerland, in about 1345. These later Latin and vernacular efforts turned out to be even more valuable once the original Low German text of *Das fliessende Liecht* was lost sometime in the late Middle Ages. Still extant manuscripts include the sole complete one, at Einsiedeln (MS 277), and partial manuscripts at Würzburg (MS Nr. 1 110, fol. 40a–62b), Wolhusen (a German translation of a Latin version), and Basel (MSS B IX 11 and A VIII 6). In addition to its immediate impact on Gertrude the Great and Mechthild of Hackeborn, Mechthild's book met with enthusiastic, widespread reception in southern Germany from the fourteenth to the sixteenth centuries, particularly among the Dominicans. It was first critically edited by Morel in 1869, which has recently been updated by Neumann and Vollmann-Profe. Never canonized, Mechthild nonetheless died with the renown of sanctity between 1282 and 1294.

See also Beguines; Bride of Christ/*Brautmystik*; *Frauenlied*; Gertrude the Great, of Helfta, St.; Hildegard of Bingen, St.; Mechthild of Hackeborn; *Minne*

BIBLIOGRAPHY

Primary Sources

Mechthild of Magdeburg. *Offenbarungen der Schwester Mechthild von Magdeburg oder Das Fliessende Licht der Gottheit*. Edited by G. Morel. Regensburg, Germany, 1869. Reprint Darmstadt: Wissenschaftliche Buchgesellschaft, 1963. Reprint 1976.

———. *Revelationes Gertrudianae et Mechtildianae*. Edited by the Benedictine Monks of Solesmes. Pt. 2. 2: *Sororis Mechtildis Lux Divinitatis*. Edited by Dom Louis Paquelin. Poitiers and Paris: Oudin, 1877.

———. *"Das fliessende Licht der Gottheit" nach der Einsiedler Handschrift.* Edited with notes by Hans Neumann and Gisela Vollmann-Profe. 2 vols. Münchener Texte und Untersuchungen, 100–101. Munich and Zurich: Artemis Verlag, 1990–1993.

———. *Flowing Light of the Godhead.* Translated with introduction by Frank Tobin. Preface by Margot Schmidt. Classics of Western Spirituality. New York: Paulist Press, 1998.

———. *Flowing Light of the Divinity.* Translated by Christiane Mesch Galvani. Edited with an introduction by Susan Clark. Garland Library of Medieval Literature, 72. New York: Garland, 1991.

———. *Selections from "The Flowing Light of the Godhead."* Translated by Elizabeth A. Andersen. Library of Medieval Women. Woodbridge, U.K. and Rochester, N.Y.: Boydell & Brewer, 2003.

———. [Excerpts]. *Beguine Spirituality: Mystical Writings of Mechthild of Magdeburg, Beatrice of Nazareth, and Hadewijch of Brabant.* Edited and introduced by Fiona Bowie. Translated by Oliver Davies. New York: Crossroad, 1990.

Secondary Sources

Bynum, Caroline W. *Jesus as Mother: Studies in the Spirituality of the High Middle Ages.* Berkeley and Los Angeles: University of California Press, 1982.

Classen, Albrecht. *"Flowing Light of the Godhead*: Binary Oppositions of Self and God in Mechthild von Magdeburg." *Studies in Spirituality* 7 (1997): 79–97.

Cross, F. T., et al. "Mechthild of Magdeburg." In *The Oxford Dictionary of the Christian Church.* 3rd ed. Oxford and New York: Oxford University Press, 1997.

Howard, John. "The German Mystic Mechthild of Magdeburg." In *Medieval Women Writers,* edited by Katharina M. Wilson, 153–85. Athens: University of Georgia Press, 1984.

Neumann, Hans. "Problemata Mechthildiana." *Zeitschrift für deutsches Altertum und deutsche Literatur* 82 (1948–1950): 143–72.

Newman, Barbara. *God and the Goddesses: Vision, Poetry, and Belief in the Middle Ages.* Philadelphia: University of Pennsylvania Press, 2003.

———. "WomanSpirit, Woman Pope." In B. Newman, *From Virile Woman to WomanChrist: Studies in Medieval Religion and Literature,* 182–223. Philadelphia: University of Pennsylvania Press, 1995.

Schmidt, Margot. "Mechthild de Magdebourg." In *Dictionnaire de Spiritualité,* 10: cols. 877–85. Paris: Beauchesne, 1980.

Strauch, Gabriele. "Mechthild von Magdeburg and the Category of *Frauenmystik.*" In *Women as Protagonists and Poets in the German Middle Ages,* edited by Albrecht Classen, 171–86. GAG 528. Göppingen, Germany: Kümmerle, 1991.

Tobin, Frank. "Audience, Authorship and Authority in Mechthild von Magdeburg's *Flowing Light of the Godhead.*" *Mystics Quarterly* 23.1 (1997): 8–17.

Voaden, Rosalynn. "All Girls Together: Community, Gender and Vision at Helfta." In *Medieval Women in their Communities,* edited by Diane Watt, 72–91. Cardiff: University of Wales Press, 1997.

ALBRECHT CLASSEN

MEDEA IN THE MIDDLE AGES

MEDEA IN THE MIDDLE AGES (1150–1400). An ancient Greek mythological figure reborn in medieval European literature, Medea was a princess, priestess, and sorceress, and wife of Jason. Her name in Greek (*Medeia*), associated with the Greek verb *medesthai* meaning "to devise," aptly presages her Classical-mythological image as the archetypal scheming woman, capable of turning her talent for magical healing or rejuvenating potions into poison and painful consequences because of her susceptibility to wickedness. The best-known ancient legend about her, immortalized in the Greek tragedian Euripides's drama (431 B.C.E.), shows her, a semi-divine princess, at first ingeniously helping her beloved Jason to steal the Golden Fleece, and then bearing him children, only to deploy her artfulness, after he abandons her, to kill their children and his new bride in a

637

Medea. Courtesy of the North Winds Picture Archives.

jealous rage. Despite Euripides's psychological sensitivity, rendering his Medea more sympathetic, as would Apollonius of Rhodes in his *Argonautica*, the tragedian's version would serve to type her as a beguiling but witchlike barbarian. During the Middle Ages, however, her courtly and Christianized avatars would depart significantly from Antiquity's negative portrayals in works by male and female authors alike.

Ancient and Late Antique Medea: A Composite Legend. Since there is no single Classical work presenting Medea's complete story, and also for purposes of comparison with the various medieval Medeas to be discussed below, the following preliminary section attempts a summary composite of all details from the various Greek and Latin plays, histories, narrative poems, and learned allusions in commentaries pertaining to her, from Hesiod's *Theogony* (fl. c.700 B.C.E.) to Hyginus's *Fabulae* (second century). Of course, many of these authors were not yet known in the Middle Ages, or were read only in paraphrase or extracts in anthologies. The principal classical sources for the medieval versions of Medea's story are Ovid's *Heroides* and *Metamorphoses*. Seneca's dramas, *Medea* and *Thyestes* may also have been known. Cicero's *De Natura Deorum* (*The Nature of the Gods*) may have been another source. Chaucer refers to Valerius Flaccus's *Argonautica* as a source of his legend of Medea. The connection of the Argonautic expedition to the plunder of Troy is taken from Dares the Phrygian's sixth-century prose narrative, *De Excidio Troiae Historia* (*History of the Fall of Troy*). But this last removes us from the Classical period and into Late Antiquity and early Middle Ages, the heyday of Christianized mythographical compendia in the manner of Fulgentius (late fifth century) and others. For example, one of the authors to be discussed, Benoît de Sainte-Maure (or Sainte-More) (twelfth century) found information on the order and types of tasks demanded of Jason in the work of the so-called First Vatican Mythographer (c.eighth century), one of several mythological compilations interspersed with Christian allegories.

Medea is a barbarian sorceress, princess of Colchis, a land in the eastern extremity of Jason's world. She is also niece of the goddess-enchantress Circe, and granddaughter of Helios (the Sun), who saves the lives of Jason and his Argonauts by supplying the hero with a magic potion to enable him to perform the impossible tasks imposed by her father, Aeëtes, King of Colchis (on the east coast of the Black Sea, now in the Georgian Republic), to capture the Golden Fleece. In aiding Jason, Medea betrays her father and her homeland. When Medea accompanies Jason in his escape from Colchis, she murders, or assists Jason in murdering, her brother. The double-edged ethics of her deeds for the love of Jason would prove problematic for Classical authors in judging her character. On the favorable side, she deploys her skills as sorceress to restore youth to Jason's aged father, Aeson; on the more questionable side, she dupes the daughters of Jason's detestable uncle, Pelias, into murdering their father, a crime for which she and Jason have to flee to Corinth to escape punishment (some versions also have her earlier murdering her infant brother Apsyrtus and scattering his limbs to divert the Colchians from pursuing the Argonauts). Sometime during this period, Medea bears Jason two sons. In all of these actions, she demonstrates her love for Jason by placing her knowledge and her body at his disposal, and that her attachment to him surpasses all other personal loyalties, bringing her to the height of her powers as a loving healer and to the depths of perfidy as a vengeful schemer.

While at Corinth, Jason succumbs to his lust for power and also for a younger Greek princess in the bargain. He has already forsaken Hypsipyle, queen of Lemnos, pregnant with his twin sons, when he accepts the love and protection of Medea. The opportunity for Jason's self-advancement arises when Creon, the current king of Corinth, who is without male issue, deems Jason an appropriate successor to the throne of Corinth and suitor for the hand of his daughter, Glauce. Medea's barbarian origins now apparently exclude her from consideration in Jason's new plan, a betrayal culminating in the banishment of Medea and his two sons. Banishment, even in the relatively civilized eras of Athens and Rome when Medea's story was dramatized and narrated, meant certain death.

When Medea is informed of Jason's betrayal, she raves in outrage and anguish, and then she deliberates. Her plan includes the slaying of her rival by means of a golden robe and diadem that she has infected with her poisons, and the killing of her two sons by Jason. The fact that Creon is also consumed by the flames engulfing his daughter, Glauce, is an added bit of unexpected justice. As she weaves her plot for revenge, Medea realizes that she lacks only a refuge to complete her victory over Jason and his allies. This appears in the form of Aegeus, king of Athens, then woefully childless. With her promise to aid Aegeus in his quest for a son, Medea enlists his aid by exacting his oath that, if she can leave Corinth on her own, he will provide her with asylum in Athens. Unaware of Medea's scheme of revenge, Aegeus listens sympathetically as Medea recounts her story of her ambitious and faithless Jason, whose banishment of Medea and her children has imperiled their lives. However, because Aegeus's protection will not include her sons, Medea must murder them, or so she believes. Her most monstrous act of vengeance—her slaying of her sons by Jason—she therefore carries out in anguish to protect them from a crueler end at the hands of the Corinthians and other potential enemies of fatherless sons. But vengeance is the overriding motive. For Jason the widower, deprived of the possibility of sons by Glauce, his future rests with his sons by Medea (two major authors, Euripides and Seneca, both ignore his twins by Hypsipyle). The death of her sons will therefore complete Medea's revenge on Jason at the cost of her own maternal grief. Medea chooses to endure every sorrow to show men that they break their vows to women only at the greatest cost to themselves.

When Medea flees Corinth—the main version holds, in a chariot drawn by dragons sent by grandfather Helios—she arrives at Athens and receives the promised assistance from Aegeus in spite of her prior actions. In Hyginus's version of the story, she bears Aegeus a son, Medus. However, in earlier versions, Aegeus manages to father Theseus with the princess of Troezen, and without Medea's aid. When the maturing Theseus arrives at Athens, Medea tries to poison him. Theseus is saved only at the moment of raising the poisoned cup to his lips: his cloak is thrown back to free his arm, revealing the ancestral sword Aegeus had left behind to be claimed by his son. On seeing the sword, an outraged Aegeus drives Medea out of Athens. In another version she has Theseus sent off to fight the bull of Marathon; still other versions contain both of her unsuccessful attempts to eradicate Theseus as a threat to her position.

According to Hyginus (*Fabulae*, 21–27), Medea's story concludes with her propitiation of her murdered brother (little Apsyrtus)'s shade and her reconciliation with her father Aeëtes, now living exiled and in abject poverty, having been driven from his throne by his treacherous brother Perses. Medea restores her father to his throne by means of her still formidable magic. She also provides the kingdom with an heir in the person of her son, Medus. This ending emphasizes the reconciliation of Medea with the family she had betrayed for Jason, and the restoration of order and harmony to Aeëtes's kingdom through Medea's efforts. Though barely known throughout most of the Middle Ages because of the delayed accessibility of manuscripts of his work, Hyginus would nonetheless be read as a principal authority for Classical mythology from the later fourteenth century and throughout the Renaissance.

Benoît de Sainte-Maure's *Roman de Troie*. The first fully developed medieval characterization of Medea, or, in Old French, *Medee*, appears in Benoît de Sainte-Maure's monumental romance retelling of the fall of Troy, *Le Roman de Troie* (c.1165). Benoît recounts the narrative of the commencement of Medea's love for Jason, his oath of loyalty to her, her resultant rescue of him and his Argonauts through her extensive knowledge of unguents, enchantments, and other tools of sorcery, and their departure for Greece with the blessing of her father, King Oëtes of Jaconites (just as in the original Greek myth: the capital city of Colchis, or Colchos). Benoît employs the story of Jason's winning of Medea and the Golden Fleece as a prologue to the rape of Helen and Troy's subsequent punishment at the hands of the avenging Greeks. From this point onward in medieval narrative or lyric (there are no dramas about Medea from the Middle Ages), the portrait of Medea as skillful sorceress and loyal lover becomes a staple of poets and mythographers.

What makes Benoît's portrayal of Medea so noteworthy is that the French poet transforms the classical heroine by contextualizing her narrative in the matrix of themes and meanings which comprise the concept of *fin'amor* (*Troie*, v. 1266), the refined, individualistic love, also called courtly love—as distinct from the feudal marriage contract—celebrated by medieval poets. In such a context Medea is described as a maiden, "que mout fu sage e gente e bele" ("who was very wise and slender and lovely," v. 556). The most important aspect of Medea's character is her overt fidelity to Jason. Medea's love for and loyalty to Jason motivate her every act. In Benoît's portrait, Medea's actions are always beneficial and nurturing.

Benoît makes a number of other adjustments to the story and character of Medea as found in the Latin sources most likely available to him. For example, Benoît calls Jason's inimical uncle Peleus instead of Pelias, confusing him with the father of Achilles, who conquered Troy. Thus Benoît has Jason's exploits prefigure Achilles's humbling of Troy. Furthermore, Benoît eliminates from his narrative two of Medea's crimes committed for Jason's sake that are found in the Classical sources: the betrayal of her father and the murder of her brother, Benoît's Medea being an only child. Jason and Medea part on good terms with the courteous Oëtes in *Le Roman de Troie*. Also, there is no mention of any of Medea's other violent acts. The only sinister note is Benoît's prediction of Jason's betrayal of Medea, the cause of their future tragedy. Jason's preliminary dalliance with Hypsipyle is not included in Benoît's version. Benoît's Medea is prepared to love Jason because his reputation for beauty and virtue have preceded him to Jaconites. The conflict between *amor* (passion) and *pudor* (maidenly modesty), of which the the Roman poet Ovid (d. 17 C.E.) makes so much, is transformed in Benoît's heroine into mere concern over how to initiate her relationship with Jason.

Benoît's Medea has Jason summoned to her bedchamber where she informs him of the dangers that confront his quest. There she exacts from him his oath of marriage and presents him with five gifts with which to accomplish his tasks safely (a talisman against fear, an unguent against fire, a magic ring of invisibility that has power to protect the bearer from venom, a written enchantment with which to propitiate Mars who owns the ram that Jason must kill for its fleece, and a compound with which to stop up the nostrils of the fire-breathing bulls Jason must subdue as one of his feats). These are all part of Medea's "leial consel" ("faithful counsel," *Troie*, v. 1308), which she will tender Jason if he accepts her proposal of marriage.

Unlike any of the Classical sources, which defer physical consummation of their relationship until they depart from Colchis, once Medea has exacted Jason's promises of loyalty, love, and marriage, she takes him into her elaborately adorned bed in which they spend the night, "Tot nu a nu e braz a braz" ("Completely naked, body to body, arm in arm," v. 1631). At this point the narrator wryly comments that Jason deflowered Medea that night because she wanted it as much as he (vv. 1633–35).

Another medieval touch is the order of actual tasks that Jason must perform to win the Fleece. These exploits take place on an island in a river flowing past Medea's paternal domain of Jaconites. As does many a medieval heroine, Medea observes Jason's deeds from a tower window. Perhaps the most astounding aspect of Medea's character is that she expresses her self-confidence with the words, "quant que jo vueil, tot puis faire" ("whenever I wish, I can do anything," v. 1409), language that asserts the identity of her will and her ability to realize it through her sorcery. Such language resembles that applied by medieval theologians and poets to the powers of God.

Later Medieval Troy Legends. Whenever the story of Troy is told, whether in the vernacular, *Le Roman de Troie en prose*, or in Latin, *Historia Destructionis Troiae* (*History of the Destruction of Troy*), Medea's tale is included. Two prose redactions of Benoît's Troy legend are extant, Codex Bodmer 147 and a version edited by Léopold Constans and Edmond Faral titled *Le Roman de Troie en prose*. In both versions, the general structure and content of Benoît's poem are retained, but descriptive detail and *fin'amor* emphasis are all but eliminated. This results in a much flatter narrative and a more culpable Medea, whose main objective is a lust for power over Jason through matrimony. The narrative of Jason and Medea in *Le Roman de Troie en prose* concludes with Jason abandoning a pregnant Medea on a desert island where she gives birth to twin boys. Medea escapes from this predicament, tracks Jason down, dismembers her children, and serves them to her husband, "Por quoi les sages jugent que ceste fu la plus cruël mere qui onques fuste" ("This is why wise men judge her the cruelest mother who ever was," *Troie en prose*, v. 18).

Through the intermediary of the thirteenth-century prose redactions of his work, Benoît's narrative functions as the initial source of the Medea's appearances in such works as Guido delle Colonne's *Historia Destructionis Troiae* (1287), Jean de Meun's continuation of the *Roman de la Rose* (*Romance of the Rose*, c.1270), the *Ovide moralisé* (*Moralized*

Ovid, late thirteenth century to the early fourteenth century), Boccaccio's *Il Filocolo* (*Love's Labor*, c.1340) and *De mulieribus claris* (*Famous Women*, c.1361–1375), Chaucer's *Legend of Good Women* (c.1386), Gower's *Confessio Amantis* (*The Lover's Confession*, 1386/90), and Christine de Pizan's *Epistre Othea* (*Epistle of the Goddess Othea*, 1400–1401) and *Le Livre de la Cité des dames* (*Book of the City of Ladies*, 1404–1405).

Guido's *Historia* goes much further than *Le Roman de Troie en prose* in presenting a negative portrait of Medea. The Sicilian judge makes Medea an example of feminine instability and dissolute desire. Although Guido reintroduces the story of Medea's rejuvenation of Aeson to the narrative, he debunks magic and blames Medea for trusting in her sorcery and her lover. Guido also reintroduces the conflict between *amor* and *pudor* in Medea's conscience, which had been an essential aspect of Ovid's portrait of her in *Metamorphoses*, Book 7.

In Jean de Meun's continuation of *Le Roman de la Rose*, a fairly elaborate account of Medea's tale is used by La Vielle (The Old Woman) to defend the treacheries perpetrated by women against men. Jean de Meun also includes a reference to Medea's magical restoration of youth to Aeson, but shows the act was motivated by Medea's desire to control Jason by his sense of obligation to her. La Vielle mentions Medea's killing of her children as a punishment for Jason's disloyalty and perjury, but has Medea strangle them, "worse than if she were a cruel stepmother" (v. 13232).

The huge fourteenth-century vernacular (Middle-French) version of the multicentury compilation of Ovid's works in Christianized form, the *Ovide moralisé*, is an encyclopedic account of Medea's story blending not only elements from Ovid's *Metamorphoses*, Book 7, but also from his *Heroides*, Letters 6 and 12, plus details from the first-century Roman tragedian Seneca's *Medea*, and Benoît's *Roman de Troie* overlaid with Christian allegorical glosses. Jason's sojourn on Lemnos returns to the narrative, as well as all of the Ovidian material. In addition, there is a detailed description of the burning of Creusa (= Glauce), but not Creon, developed with touches from Seneca. The Golden Fleece becomes a symbol of Mary's holy, salvific virginity. The severing of Pelias's head is an allegory of Christ defeating the devil, while Aeson's dismemberment and rebirth is an allegory of Christ's martyrdom for mankind. The burning of Creusa (1644–1672) symbolizes the vengeance inflicted by God on those who would deceive the virtuous through the false beauties of the world. The *Ovide moralisé* thus includes the entire legend, but reasserts the positive characterization of Medea and places the onus of blame on Jason's treachery as does Benoît's narrative.

Among the several works of Boccaccio in which Medea appears, two are worthy of mention here. In *Il Filocolo*, Book 3, Jason's abandonment of Medea is justified because of her cruelty, or, in Boccaccio's Italian: "Medea poi per la sua crudeltà fu giustamente da lui lasciata, trovando egli Creusa più pietosa di lei" (3: 18.23). Perhaps following the ending of *Le Roman de Troie en Prose*, another reference to Medea identifies her with Procne in the murderer of their children (*Filocolo*, 3: 35.7). Identification of Medea and Procne as cruel mothers may be traced to Ovid (*Amores*, 2: 14.39–40, *Ars Amatoria* [*Art of Love*], 2.381–86, *Remedia Amoris* [*Love's Cure*, 59–62]), and Hyginus (*Fabulae*, 239). In Book 4, references to Medea's story appear in the debates concerning the nature of love, the "questioni d'amore." In discussion of Question Two, Fiammetta uses Medea to prove her point that a person who wins and then loses her (or his) love suffers more than one who never attains fulfillment of her desire (*Filocolo*, 7: 24.3). Most important is the reference to Medea in the seventh question (4: 43–46), which debates whether love is good or evil. Medea is cited as an example of someone experiencing *amore per diletto* (love for the sake of pleasure). Fiammetta argues that such passion deprives the lover of honor and freedom, leads him or her into difficulties, awakens vices in the lover, and drives the lover into hopeless situations. Caleon attempts to use Medea's bestowing her skills and her person on Jason as an example of how amore per diletto ennobles the lover, in Medea's case inspiring generosity or liberality, but Fiammetta counters that Medea was deprived of her reason by her passion for Jason and prodigal, not liberal. Medea foolishly wasted her arts and her person on her undeserving lover. It is significant that both Geoffrey Chaucer and Christine de Pizan will apply the term "delight" in their respective condemnations of Jason and defenses of Medea.

In *De mulieribus claris* (17: 2), Medea is "formosa satis et malefitiorum longe doctissima" ("quite beautiful and by far the cleverest of witches"). Boccaccio uses the term *maleficium* (evil deed), an offense against God that was punishable by burning, to the describe powers of Medea (see also *Genealogia Deorum Gentilium* [*Genealogy of the Pagan Gods*], 4: 12.24–25). His description continues, in his *De mulieribus*, "Nec illi—quod longe peius—ab artibus fuit dissonus animus; nam, deficentibus eis, ferro uti arbitratibatur levissimum" ("Far worse, her character was in keeping with her arts, for, if those failed, she thought nothing of resorting to the sword," 17: 1–3), as her ancient Greek version already demonstrated. Boccaccio's brief but incisive narrative depicts Medea as the prime agent of all evil intention as she makes Jason her innocent pawn. For example, Medea restores Aeson to youth only to obligate Jason more completely as in the *Roman de la Rose*, and it is Medea who plots to murder Pelias because she wants Jason to have a throne (27: 6–9). Finally, Boccaccio uses Medea as an example of the sin born through sight in the souls of those who worship appearances rather than inner virtue (27: 11–14). Nevertheless, Boccaccio's *De mulieribus claris*, asserts that Medea is reconciled with Jason, and together they restore Aeetes to his throne. This emendation to her legend probably comes from Boccaccio's reading of Hyginus—who, we recall, also incorporates reconciliation into his account—or some similar mythographical source.

Among the references to Medea by Geoffrey Chaucer, several are worthy of note. In *The Book of the Duchess*, Medea is mentioned among the stained glass portraits from *Le Roman de Troie* adorning the narrator's dream chamber (326–31). More significantly, the dreamer-narrator advises the man in black that if he murders himself, commits suicide in grief over the loss of his beloved, he will be damned as was Medea, "That slough hir children for Jason" (727). In pantheon of historical figures called *The Hous of Fame*, Medea is mentioned among the suffering women abandoned by faithless lovers whose fate resembles that of Dido (1: 401). Medea is also found among the famous magicians and sorcerers who inhabit Fame's castle (3.1259–82). These "tregetours" are capable of making "a man ben hool or syk" (1270) with their magic, a reduction of the complementary episodes of Aeson and Pelias in Medea's narrative. In *The Legend of Good Women*, Chaucer sets Medea in the context of those faithful women who suffer martyrdom in the service of the god of Love. Chaucer uses the term "fyn lovyng"—his translation of Benoît's and the French courtly poets' *fin'amors*—in both manuscripts' (called F and G) versions of the Prologue to the poem (v. 534; 544, resp). The narrator accuses Jason of "foul delyt, which that thou callest love!" (v. 1380, see also 1585–86). Following Benoît and Guido, Chaucer retains the medieval order of narrative while omitting the specifics of Medea's powers or gifts to Jason. Chaucer's sympathies become evident when he mentions Jason's abandonment of Medea for Creon's daughter, but not Medea's subsequent revenge. His selective use of Classical sources (he also mentions Ovid and Valerius Flaccus) focuses most completely on Jason's perfidious nature and actions, "as evere in love a chef traytour he was" (1659). Chaucer's secular martyrology reduces Medea to the status of victim, denying her any interest or power as a character. However, when, in the introduction to "The Man of Laws' Tale," Harry Bailey enumerates Chaucer's works, the Host includes a reference to the "Seintes Legendes of Cupide" ("Holy Legends of Cupid," 2.B.61) with the following apostrophe: "The crueltee of the, queene Medea,/Thy litel children hangynge by the hals,/For thy Jason, that was of love so fals!" (72–74). The tone of these lines resembles more that of Medea in *The Book of the Duchess* than *The Legend of Good Women*. They indicate Chaucer's awareness of the diversity of sources of Medea's story, in this case, *Le Roman de la Rose*, and characterizes Chaucer's martyrology as a literary exercise.

More complex, because it is more comprehensive, is John Gower's version of the narrative in *Confessio Amantis*, Book 5. Gower's narrator uses the story of Jason and Medea as an exemplum of the consequences of perjury in love. Gower's narrative follows that of *Le Roman de Troie*, and Guido's *Historia*, with significant additions from Ovid, the *Ovide Moralisé*, and Boccaccio. Gower has Medea retain her powers of sorcery and her violent acts of revenge. A significant variation in Gower is that he has both Jason and Medea fall in love at their first encounter. Also, Gower's is the first narrative to present a detailed description of Jason's passion for Medea (5: 3375–92, 3407–20). Most significantly, on completion of her revenge on Jason and informing him of his sins, Gower has Medea ascend to the heaven of Pallas, Goddess of Wisdom, in her escape, leaving a desolate Jason behind (5: 4218–22).

In Christine de Pizan's *L' Epistre Othea a Hector*, an illuminated collection of one hundred tales from mythology glossed with allegory and moral explanation, bestowed by a goddess named Othea for the education of a prince or high official (Hector of Troy, Christine's sons, the French princes), Othea warns the youthful Hector against becoming like Jason, who used Medea to obtain the Golden Fleece and then abandoned her. Jason is an example of ingratitude. Christine refers to Hermes Trismegistus (a cumulative collection of scientific and philosophical writings in Greek, Latin, and Coptic), the Cistercian mystical preacher St. Bernard (twelfth century) and the Old Testament Book of Wisdom in developing her moral message. Medea's foolish delight in Jason's beauty and her prodigality (ch. 58), the very charges leveled against Medea by Boccaccio's Fiammetta, are used as negative examples from which Hector must learn the value of reason, restraint, and moderation. The good knight must use his moral strength to curb his senses to maintain his virtue. Christine's discursive style in the *Epistre Othea* resembles that of the *Ovide Moralisé* and Boccaccio's works. *Le Livre de la Cité des dames* (1: 32) places Medea with Circe among those women who are possessed of learning and wisdom, as Medea's powers, but not her crimes, are catalogued. The enumeration of Medea's magical talents is a conflation of Classical and medieval sources. Medea also appears in another part of the *Cité* as an example contradicting the accusation made by men that few women are faithful in love. Christine's comforter, Rectitude, appearing before the author in a vision, comments that Jason's perjury and abandonment of Medea for another woman left her despondent and incapable of feeling joy (2: 56). Rectitude is silent about Medea's anger and her revenge on Jason. In addition to the sources cited above, Rectitude's comments make use of the material developed by *Le Roman de Troie* and the tradition it initiates.

See also Boccaccio, Women in, *De Claris Mulieribus*; Boccaccio, Women in, *Des Cleres et Nobles Femmes*; Boccaccio, Women in, Works Other than *De Claris Mulieribus*; Chaucer, Geoffrey, Women in the Work of; Christine de Pizan; Dido in the Middle Ages; Enchantresses, Fays (*Fées*), and Fairies; Judgment of Paris; Witches

BIBLIOGRAPHY

Primary Sources

Benoît de Sainte-Maure. *Le Roman de Troie*. Edited by Léopold Constans. 6 vols. Paris: Firmin Didot, 1904–1912.

Boccaccio, Giovanni. *Famous Women/De mulieribus claris*. Introduced, edited, and translated by Virginia Brown. I Tatti Renaissance Library. Cambridge, Mass.: Harvard University Press, 2001. [Bilingual Latin-English ed.].

———. *Il Filocolo*. Edited by Enzo Quaglio. In *Tutte le opere di Giovanni Boccaccio*, general editor Vittore Branca, vol. 1. Milan: Mondadori, 1967.

Chaucer, Geoffrey. *The Riverside Chaucer*. Edited by Larry D. Benson et al. 3rd ed. Boston: Houghton-Mifflin, 1987.

Christine de Pizan,. *La Città delle dame*. Edited by E. J. Richards. Introduction and Italian translation by Patrizia Caraffi. Biblioteca Medievale. Revised ed. Milan: Luni, 1998. [Bilingual Middle French-Italian ed.].

———. *The Book of the City of Ladies*. Translated with commentary by Earl Jeffrey Richards. Foreword by Natalie Zemon Davis. Revised ed. New York: Persea, 1998.

———. *Epistre Othea*. Critical ed. by Gabriella Parussa. Textes Littéraires Français, 517. Geneva: Droz, 1999.

———. *Letter of Othea to Hector*. Translated with introduction, notes, and an interpretive essay by Jane Chance. Newburyport, Mass.: Focus, 1990.

Dares Phrygius and Dictys. *De Excidio Troiae Historia*. Edited by Ferdinand Meister. Leipzig: Teubner, 1873.

———. *The Trojan War*. Translated by R. M. Frazer. Bloomington: Indiana University Press, 1966.

Gower, John. *Confessio Amantis*. *The Complete Works of John Gower*, vol. 3. Edited by G. C. Macaulay. Oxford: Clarendon Press, 1901.

Guido delle Colonne [Guido de Columnis]. *Historia Destructionis Troiae*. Edited by Nathaniel Edward Griffin. Cambridge, Mass.: The Medieval Academy of America, 1936.

Guillaume de Lorris, and Jean de Meun. *Le Roman de la Rose*. Critical ed. by Félix Lecoy. Classiques Français du Moyen Age [=CFMA], 92. 3 vols. Paris: Champion, 1965–1970 [Later reprints].

Hyginus. *Fabulae*. Critical ed. by Peter K. Marshall. Bibliotheca Scriptorum Graecorum et Romanorum Teubneriana. New ed. Munich and Leipzig: K. G. Saur, 2002.

Ovide Moralisé. Edited by Cornelis de Boer et al., vols. 1, 3. 5 vols. Amsterdam: Johannes Müller, 1915–1938.

Le Roman de Troie en prose. Edited with commentary by Léopold Constans and Edmond Faral. CFMA, 29. Paris: Édouard Champion, 1922. [Old-French text, Modern French commentary].

———. *Version du Codex Bodmer 147*. Edited by Françoise Vielliard. Bibliotheca, Bodmeriana, 4 Geneva: Fondation Martin Bodmer, 1979.

Secondary Sources

Delany, Sheila. *The Naked Text: Chaucer's Legend of Good Women*. Berkeley: University of California Press, 1994.

Dinshaw, Carolyn. *Chaucer's Sexual Poetics*. Madison: University of Wisconsin Press, 1989.

Dominguez, Frank. *The Medieval Argonautica*. Potomac, Md.: Studia Humanitatis, 1979.

Feimer, Joel N. "The Figure of Medea in Medieval Literature: A Thematic Metamorphosis." Ph.D. diss., City University of New York, 1983.

———. "Jason and Medea in Benoît de Sainte-Maure's *Roman de Troie*: Classical Theme and Medieval Context." In *Voices in Translation: The Authority of "Olde Bookes" in Medieval Literature. Essays in Honor of Helaine Newstead*. Edited by Deborah Sinnreich-Levi and Gale Sigal, 35–52. New York: AMS Press, 1992.

———. "Medea in Ovid's *Metamorphoses* and the *Ovide Moralisé*: Translation as Transmission." *Florilegium* 8 (1986): 40–55.

Hagedorn, Suzanne C. *Abandoned Women: Rewriting the Classics in Dante, Boccaccio, and Chaucer*. Ann Arbor: University of Michigan Press, 2003.

McCracken, Peggy. *The Curse of Eve, the Wound of the Hero*. Middle Ages. Philadelphia: University of Pennsylvania, 2003. [See esp. ch. 3].

Morse, Ruth. *The Medieval Medea*. Cambridge: D. S. Brewer, 1996. [Excellent comprehensive study].

Peters, Edward. *The Magician, the Witch, and the Law*. Philadelphia: University of Pennsylvania Press, 1978.

JOEL N. FEIMER

MEDICINE AND MEDIEVAL WOMEN. In his early thirteenth-century *Ancrene Riwle* or *Ancrene Wisse* (*Guide for Anchoresses*), an anonymous English author recommended that "anchoresses," religious women living in solitary enclosure, be bled (phlebotomized) at least four times a year. Less than a century earlier, Peter Abelard had recommended to Heloise that her nunnery have an inmate who knew how to bleed, "in order that it not be necessary for a man to come among the women for this purpose" (Letter 7). These two passing comments are doubly suggestive. On the one hand, they raise the question of how the physiology and pathology of the female body were conceptualized in medieval medical theory. Why was regular phlebotomy thought to be salubrious? What constituted "disease" in women? Issues of theory, in turn, led to those of practice. The frequency with which even healthy medieval women were expected to interact with medical practitioners raises the question of the gender of the phlebotomist who would have carried out the bleeding. If these anchoresses and nuns are to shun intimate contact with men (as they are repeatedly exhorted to do), then the prospect of being bled by a male barber or surgeon four times a year would certainly prove problematic. Both the author of the *Guide* and Abelard were describing ideal situations, of course, ones that may not have been realized for all women religious, let alone for the majority lay female populace. Yet their remarks remind us that in the gendered society of medieval Europe, it was with the body itself that the process of "gendering" began. The topic of "Women and Medicine," therefore, involves issues not only of how the female body was theorized, but how and by whom those theories were created and effectuated as diagnostic and therapeutic practices. It is necessary to examine women's participation in medieval medicine as practitioners before turning to their experiences as patients.

Women as Practitioners. Medieval European women—Christian, Muslim, and Jewish—practiced medicine in any number of capacities, many of them treating both male and female patients. We find women working under such generic titles as *medica*, *metgesse*, *miresse*, or *leche*: terms that can loosely be translated as "physician" or simply "healer." Women also practiced as surgeons. Indeed, surgeons constitute the majority of women who received formal licenses to practice medicine (licensing having been introduced in various localities from the twelfth century on). At least twenty-seven such women have been documented in the southern Italian kingdom of Naples, and four in eastern Spain

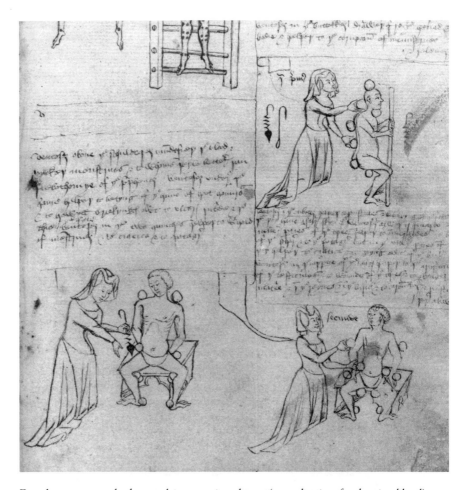

Female surgeon or barber applying cupping glasses (a mechanism for drawing blood) and cauterizing a male patient. From a fifteenth-century English collection of surgical texts. London, British Library, MS Sloane 6, f. 177r. Reprinted by permission of The British Library.

prior to the mid-fourteenth century. Women are also found as barbers (who would have often done minor surgical operations, such as setting bones and bloodletting), as apothecaries (who would have prepared and dispensed medications), and as midwives. Perhaps the largest number of women who practiced medicine are designated by none of these professional labels in historical sources but are referred to instead (often derogatively) as "empirics" or *vetule*, "old women."

While the range of women's medical practices was large, as a percentage of all documented practitioners, their numbers have remained quite small. For every one woman surgeon or barber thus identified, there may be ten, twenty, even a hundred men. The reasons for this lie partly in the documentation and the categories used by historians for identifying and classifying medieval practitioners. For example, given the near universality of childbirth as a repeated event of women's lives and the near monopoly that women (apparently) had on assisting at it, the paucity of references to midwives is suspicious: in published studies, only 157 have thus far been identified in France and only a scant half dozen in England. At the moment, these numbers are essentially meaningless as no historian has yet thoroughly searched local records for all evidence of midwives. It remains questionable, however, how much even an exhaustive local search would turn up. Unlike physic (general internal medicine) and surgery, midwifery only began to be regulated toward the end of the medieval period when it came to the attention of the ecclesiastical and secular legal establishments (both male-controlled), which were responsible for producing the bulk of the documentary evidence that still exists. From the early thirteenth century on, theological concerns surrounding infant baptism led to stipulations that priests should instruct the laity (not necessarily midwives) on how to perform emergency baptisms should the newborn's life seem at risk. This same concern led Church councils to mandate that caesarian sections be performed (the fetus was to be removed from its dead mother's womb to baptize it before it, too, expired). It was thus primarily because of religious and not medical concerns that, at least in northern France (where we currently have the most evidence), the appointment or oversight of midwives was initiated. Elsewhere, a few municipalities began appointing midwives to serve the needs of the town's women (especially indigent ones) from 1302; official licensing of midwives did not begin, however, until over a century later (the earliest example now known coming from Brussels in 1424).

Little is known about how specialist midwives would have been trained; once licensing was implemented, the oaths probably sworn by midwives stress their moral character, not their medical competence. Indeed, it may well be asked to what extent specialized midwives existed prior to the institution of formal ecclesiastical and municipal regulation, and to what extent midwifery functions were performed not by trained specialists but by female neighbors and kinswomen. In the southern French town of Manosque (a community of some 3,000–4,000 people), at least three women are delivering babies c.1265. They seem to be specialist midwives, though what they are actually called is *bajule*, the feminine equivalent of bailiff, and a term that was also used in Manosque for wet-nurses. The vague professional identity of these women is likewise suggested by the fact that when legal testimony is needed on issues surrounding childbirth, the court turns to neighbor women more often than to midwives. In fact, throughout Christian Europe it was customary to call in "upright and mature women" (*honestae mulieres et veteranae*) to do physical inspections in cases of rape, pregnancy, and so forth. Historians have often assumed these women to have been midwives, yet Pope Honorius III had been explicit in asserting that the testimony of these women (to whom no medical expertise is attributed) was preferable to that of midwives. It was probably only toward the end of the Middle Ages that the category of midwife was elided for legal purposes with that of "upright and mature woman."

As with Manosque, much of our information about medieval women's medical practices comes from court cases, where women are more often seen as defendants being prosecuted for illegal medical practice than as expert witnesses. The case of Jacoba Felicie in Paris in 1322 is the most famous of these, but others have been documented. While we should note that many prosecutions of unlicensed practice involved male practitioners as well, there was developing in the later medieval period a rhetoric that women, simply because they were women, were unsuited for medical practice. There is some exaggeration in modern claims that the witch hunts of the late fifteenth through seventeenth centuries were really attempts to eradicate midwives. Yet there is also no question that the gradual imposition of medical licensing, on the one hand, and the continued exclusion of women from the universities and other formal avenues of education, on the other, did have a constraining and ultimately suffocating effect on women's medical practices. Midwives, often highly respected members of their communities, will still be the chief birth attendants well into the early modern period, but they will be heavily regulated and circumscribed into a narrow range of practice. Empiric practitioners, however, caricatured as simple and ignorant "old women" by physicians and clerics alike since the thirteenth century, will be pushed closer and closer toward what will ultimately serve as the stereotype for the heretic and the witch.

Women as Patients. Medieval medicine as experienced by women as patients is even more imperfectly understood than the experiences of female practitioners. As yet, we know little about the basic demographic facts or morbidity patterns of medieval women. It has been speculated that changes in diet around the eleventh and twelfth centuries may have not only increased women's life span but also improved their health during their childbearing years. Recent osteological research, however, while confirming that the childbearing years were indeed dangerous (accounting for the mortality of

Male physician taking the pulse of a female patient, from a late-thirteenth-century German manuscript. London, British Library, MS Arundel 295, f. 256r. Reprinted by permission of The British Library.

nearly 17 percent of women, as compared to a rate of 13 percent mortality for men of the same age group), nevertheless suggest that barring certain crises (e.g., migration and epidemics) early medieval women tended to live as long as their European counterparts well into the modern period, that is, into their sixties and seventies. Beyond this, little can be said about changing incidences of perinatal (near time of birth) mortality, degenerative diseases of the reproductive organs (cancers and the like), varying bacterial and viral infections, and most other aspects of women's health.

Medieval gynecological literature is of little help in assessing such issues. Historians' estimates of the ages of menarche (onset of menstruation) and menopause, for example, have relied solely on textual evidence. This, however, is highly formulaic and tradition-bound and, to that extent, suspect. Medical literature is likewise of limited value in assessing the prevalence or rarity of diseases as they are conceived in modern Western medicine. While the eleventh-century writer Constantinus Africanus says that cancers can occur in any organ but develop most frequently in the womb and breasts (a statement that would certainly accord with modern medical observations), for the most part it is virtually impossible to "translate" medieval descriptions of disease into modern medical language of ovarian tumors, uterine fibroids, endometriosis, and the like. The only symptoms that could have been perceived beyond the woman's own report of her pain were such external signs as swelling or emissions from the vagina, or the absence of expected functions as in infertility or the cessation of menstruation. Beginning in the late thirteenth century, Italian physicians began to perform forensic autopsies, and by the fifteenth century, patrician families regularly requested them, focusing their attention particularly on women, they claimed, to prevent hereditary disease. As historians of anatomy are wont to point out, however, these new dissection practices probably served more to reinforce traditional concepts of pathology than to change them. The changes in disease categorization and description that do take place in gynecological literature during the medieval centuries, therefore, probably have more to do with differing theoretical perspectives and expository forms than with any identifiable changes in the biological realities of women's lives.

It is, in any case, the way in which a culture itself viewed and interpreted the "biological realities" is most important to understanding how medical thinking and medical practice interacted historically. It is thus in documenting medieval conceptions of disease and therapeutic responses that the real value of medieval medical writings lies. Most were written in Latin, though substantial numbers of texts still survive in the various vernacular languages (including, for the early medieval period, Anglo-Saxon), in Hebrew (which after the eleventh century was the chief written language of educated European Jews), and in Arabic (which was used in parts of Spain). Many of these texts, whether large encyclopedic works of medical theory or small works of *praxis* like herbals and recipe collections, would have included information pertinent to women's health care: from general medical matters (cures for internal diseases, treatments for wounds, instructions on how and when to phlebotomize) to more specifically female concerns (how to provoke menstruation, expel the dead fetus, etc.). Writings devoted exclusively to women's conditions—gynecological diseases, obstetrical matters, and cosmetics—also existed in Latin and the vernacular languages. In the early medieval period, these either derived from ancient Greek texts (particularly the writings of the Hippocratics and Soranus) or they collected empirical cures from random sources. From the late eleventh century on, gynecological writings tended (like most medical literature) to show influences of Arabic medicine, which adhered to the rather different theoretical precepts of a second-century C.E. Greek writer, Galen of Pergamon. Only two female medical writers have thus far been documented: Trota of Salerno and Hildegard of Bingen. Reflecting the range of practice we have already noted for other women, both wrote on medical matters generally and not simply matters to do with women.

The gynecological disease concepts articulated in medieval medical writings differ in many respects from modern disease categories. Chief among them was concern to maintain regular menstruation, either because it was seen as the necessary prelude to fertility (a notion reinforced by the common designation of menstruation as "the flowers"), or because it was seen as a regular purgation needed to keep the female body healthy. (The regular phlebotomizing of premenopausal anchoresses and nuns was, then, in a certain sense redundant.) Menstruation could be either excessive or too scanty; either way, the objective was to restore it to its "natural" balance. A second striking disease concept found in most medieval medical writings is that of "uterine suffocation" or "suffocation caused by the womb." This condition involved epileptic-like fits of falling, fainting, contortions of the body, gritting or grinding of the teeth, and, in its most extreme form, death. Medieval writers disagreed whether this condition was actually caused by the womb wandering to the upper part of the body (thereby physically blocking the respiratory organs) or by the "action at a distance" of toxic substances from the uterus affecting the vital organs. Either way, the uterus was the culprit, usually because menstruation was disrupted somehow, or because the woman was not sexually active. Other gynecological concerns included uterine and breast disorders (cancers, lesions, etc.), infertility, contraception, and conditions consequent to childbirth.

How all this lore about women's health was "translated" into actual therapeutic practice is as yet unclear. We have little that approaches the historical specificity of the modern medical case history. Perhaps most important in assessing the way issues of gender were played out in medieval Europe are questions of how medical knowledge was disseminated and who had the most control in the patient–practitioner encounter. Most medical texts were written in highly technical Latin, which was only accessible to those having advanced training in scholastic discourse. Even many vernacular translations are intended for professional audiences, in many cases for surgeons who would be less likely to be literate in Latin than university-educated physicians. While some female practitioners may have figured among these audiences, it is male practitioners who are most frequently documented to be in possession of medical books, including gynecological texts.

Literate male practitioners thus had privileged access to medical literature, and various kinds of evidence show that they put their textual precepts directly into practice, treating female patients in a variety of situations for a variety of diseases. Contracts, for example, still exist for southern Europe showing male physicians agreeing to treat all the members of a household—male and female—for a fixed annual fee. Learned male physicians in Italy were writing personalized diagnoses and prescriptions called *consilia* from the late thirteenth century on; many of these discuss female patients, who as often as not are being treated for gynecological ailments. Iconographical evidence likewise shows male practitioners treating female patients. Male involvement in women's health care seems to have stopped short of the birthing chamber, though even here we find male physicians taking it on themselves to instruct female attendants. Indeed, it has been suggested that male surgeons, particularly in France, increasingly performed caesarean sections at the end of the medieval period. It is likely, however, that surgical excision of the fetus was only the most dramatic of male surgical practices on women; virtually all later medieval French gynecological texts are found in surgical compendia known to have been owned by men.

Male medical practice on female patients was not without its tensions, both for the male practitioner whose reputation (or so tracts on medical ethics sometimes warned) might be put at risk by intimate contact with women, and for female patients whose social honor (or, in the case of the anchoresses and nuns, sacral chastity) might be compromised. Male practitioners often avoided these problems by employing female assistants to perform manual examinations and operations under their instructions, though even they sometimes admitted that certain complicated procedures (such as cutting for bladder stones) were virtually impossible.

One solution to this problem was to empower women with medical knowledge. Several vernacular gynecological texts, both from the late Antique period (when "vernacular" meant Latin) and from the late medieval period, are addressed to female audiences: in late Antiquity to professional midwives, and in the later Middle Ages to concerned laywomen. (The first known medieval tract primarily for midwives dates only from the end of the fifteenth century; this German tract, in turn, was a prelude to Eucharius Rösslin's famous *Rosegarden for Pregnant Women and Midwives*, published in German in 1513 and frequently reprinted and translated thereafter.) Employing various rhetorical formulae, these texts exhort women to share information among themselves; they warn that women should not take offense at these texts, nor should men use them for slandering women. Even these "women's texts," however, were often appropriated by men, who continued to consider women's health care a proper and lucrative aspect of their practice.

In a world populated primarily by illiterates, there must necessarily have been alternative explanatory mechanisms and therapies, and alternate modes of dissemination beyond the written text. Prayer and pilgrimage, charms and miraculous cures at the graves and shrines of saints undoubtedly accounted for much of what medieval people themselves considered health care. There are, in fact, many relatively untapped sources for reconstructing the history of both the mental and the physical experiences of health and disease of medieval women. The long testimony before the court of the Inquisition of an accused heretic, one Beatrice de Planissoles (1310–1320s), is woven across the biological threads of a woman's life: she excuses herself from visiting someone because she is still "lying-in" after a birth; she retains the umbilical cords from the births of her daughters' sons because she has been told they will aid her in any future lawsuit; she can tell that another daughter has entered menarche because her face is congested (Beatrice keeps a rag bloodied with this first flow to perform love magic later); she describes a contraceptive amulet that her lover, the priest Pierre Clergue, was accustomed to use; she suspects another lover-priest of having bewitched her because her love for him seemed inordinate for a woman who had already entered menopause. Sources like Beatrice's testimony are by no means transparent witnesses to "real life." Still, they may some day be analyzed with sufficient interpretive nuance to create a history of women's own experiences of their biological existence and their encounters with the systems of medical care in medieval Europe.

See also Ancrene Riwle; Guilds, Women in; Heloise; Hildegard of Bingen, St.; Trota and "Trotula"

BIBLIOGRAPHY

Primary Sources
[Because of their number and complexity, only those primary sources directly cited in text are given here. For others, see works under Secondary Sources, below.]
Abelard, Pierre, and Heloise. *The Letters of Abelard and Héloise*. Translated with an introduction by Betty Radice. Harmondsworth, U.K. and Baltimore: Penguin Books, 1974.
Ancrene Wisse: Guide for Anchoresses. Translated by Hugh White. London: Penguin, 1993.
[Beatrice of Planisolles]. In Jacques Fournier. "Inquisition Records." In *Readings in Medieval History*, edited by Patrick J. Geary, 540–58. Lewiston, N.Y.: Broadview Press, 1989.
Rösslin, Eucharius. *Eucharius Rösslin's "Rosengarten," gedruckt im Jahre 1513*. Edited by Gustav Klein. Alte Meister der Medizin und Naturkunde in Facsimile-Ausgaben und Neudrucken nach Werken des 15.–18. Jahrhunderts, 2. Munich: C. Kuhn, 1910.
———. *When Midwifery Became the Male Physician's Province: The Sixteenth-Century Handbook* The Rosegarden for Preganant Women and Midwives. Translated with an introduction by Wendy Arons. Jefferson, N.C.: McFarland, 1994. [English trans. of above].

Secondary Sources
Agrimi, Jole, and Chiara Crisciani. "Savoir médical et anthropologie religieuse: Les représentations et les fonctions de la vetula (XIIIe–XVe siècles)." *Annales: E.S.C.* 48 (1993): 1281–1308.
Cabré, Montserrat. "From a Master to a Laywoman: A Feminine Manual of Self-Help." *Dynamis: Acta Hispanica ad Medicinae Scientiarum Historiam Illustrandam* 20 (2000): 371–93.

Cadden, Joan. *Meanings of Sex Difference in the Middle Ages: Medicine, Science and Culture* Cambridge: Cambridge University Press, 1993.

Green, Monica H. "Bibliography on Women and Medicine." *Medieval Feminist Newsletter* 10 (fall 1990): 23–24; 11 (spring 1991): 25–26; 13 (spring 1992): 32–34; 15 (spring 1993): 42–43; 19 (spring 1995): 39–42; 21 (spring 1996): 39–41; 26 (fall 1998): 8–11; *Medieval Feminist Forum* [retitled] 30 (fall 2000): 44–49; 32 (fall 2001): 50–53; 34 (spring 2003): 19–23.

———. "From 'Diseases of Women' to 'Secrets of Women': The Transformation of Gynecological Literature in the Middle Ages." *Journal of Medieval and Early Modern Studies* 30 (2000): 5–39.

———. *Women's Healthcare in the Medieval West: Texts and Contexts.* Aldershot, U.K.: Ashgate, 2000. [Includes as an appendix a comprehensive list of more than 150 medieval gynecological texts].

Harley, David. "Historians as Demonologists: The Myth of the Midwife-witch." *Social History of Medicine* 3 (1990): 1–26.

Kruse, Britta-Juliane. *Verborgene Heilkünste: Geschichte der Frauenmedizin im Spätmittelalter.* Quellen und Forschungen zur Literatur- und Kulturgeschichte, 5 (Berlin and New York: Walter de Gruyter, 1996). Summarized in English in "Women's Secrets: Health and Sexuality of Women in Unpublished Medieval Texts." In *Sex, Love and Marriage in Medieval Literature and Reality: Thematische Beiträge in Rahmen des 31th International Congress on Medieval Studies an der Western Michigan University (Kalamazoo-USA) 8.–12. Mai 1996,* 33–40. Griefswald, Germany: Reinecke Verlag, 1996.

McVaugh, Michael R. *Medicine before the Plague: Practitioners and Their Patients in the Crown of Aragon, 1285–1345.* Cambridge: Cambridge University Press, 1993.

Park, Katharine. "Medicine and Society in Medieval Europe, 500-1500." In *Medicine in Society: Historical Essays,* edited by Andrew Wear, 59–90. Cambridge and New York: Cambridge University Press, 1992.

Rawcliffe, Carole. "Hospital Nurses and their Work." In *Daily Life in the Late Middle Ages,* edited by Richard H. Britnell, 43–64, 202–6. Stroud: Sutton, 1998.

Siraisi, Nancy. *Medieval and Early Renaissance Medicine: An Introduction to Knowledge and Practice.* Chicago: University of Chicago Press, 1990.

Taglia, Kathryn. "Delivering a Christian Identity: Midwives in Northern French Synodal Legislation, c.1200-1500." In *Religion and Medicine in the Middle Ages,* edited by Peter Biller and Joseph Ziegler, 77–90. York Studies in Medieval Theology, 3. York: York Medieval Press, 2001.

MONICA H. GREEN

MELANIA THE ELDER, ST. (c.342–c.410). The early Christian ascetic and founder of a double monastery on the Mount of Olives, Melania formed an important link between the Eastern and Western Churches. Most of our knowledge of her life comes from Palladius's *Lausiac History* (c.419) and references to her in the writings of St. Jerome (c.345–420), St. Paulinus of Nola (353/5–431), and Rufinus of Aquilea (c.345–411).

Antonia Melania was born in Spain of a wealthy senatorial family, granddaughter of the Consul Marcellinus (341), and a relative of Paulinus of Nola. She was educated to a high degree of literacy in both Latin and Greek. At about age fifteen she married Valerius Maximus, a Roman prefect (361–363). She suffered several miscarriages, and then in a single year (364), lost both her husband and two children, being left with one son, Publicola. As a widow, she frequented the ascetic circles of Rome for some years, then entrusted her son's education to the local prefect, distributed some of her wealth, and sailed for Egypt in 372. Befriended by the priest Isidore of Alexandria, who introduced her to the local monks, she soon did the rounds of the desert thoroughly, sponsoring the monks and helping them during the persecutions of the Arians (early Christians deemed heretical by the Church) and later, those under Archbishop Theophilus of Alexandria (d. 412). While working as the monks' servant she confronted the prefect of Egypt (Palladius, 46). In Alexandria she also met and befriended Rufinus (Rufinus Tyrannius or Turranius) of Aquileia. Moving to Palestine in about 378, Melania founded a double monastery on the Mount of Olives—the highest point on the hills east of Jerusalem—where Rufinus joined her as head of the male section (381). The monastery's sound economy was based on a thriving book workshop (Rufinus, 2: 8), becoming a center of hospitality, works of mercy, and Christian reconciliation (Palladius, 46: 6). Through all of these activities the influence of the cenobitic (of religious communal life) doctrine of St. Basil of Caesarea (Basil the Great, c.330–379) may be discerned, which Rufinus relayed to the West on returning to Italy (397) in the form of the *Asceticon*, or "Rule of St. Basil," the basis for the future rule (guidelines for monastic life) of the Eastern Church. Thus Melania and Rufinus served as key intermediaries between the Greek East and Latin West. It was here at Melania's monastery that the historian Palladius came to know her. He testifies to the extent and depth of Melania's reading in the Christian classics (Palladius, 55: 3) and to her asceticism and force of character, calling her "that female man of God" (55: 9). When the uproar over Origenism—the complex and often misrepresented theology based on the lost, but highly provocative writings of Origen (early third century)—broke out in the 390s, Melania allied herself with Bishop John of Jerusalem and Rufinus against Jerome and St. Epiphanius (c.315–403), and in Rome, the renowned ascetic St. Marcella (c.325–411).

Melania possessed a certain gift for spiritual direction and was not to be toyed with. At one time (c.382) she took in hand a confused young deacon on the run from Constantinople, upon whom she conferred the monastic habit and who, at her bidding, joined the monks in the Nitrian Desert of Egypt, where he became one of the most famous among them: the spiritual writer and preacher Evagrius of Pontus (346–399).

Returning to Rome in 400, she encouraged the ascetic ideal in her granddaughter, Melania, and others, and converted and instructed a certain Apronianus (LH 54). She visited Sicily in 404, and from there went on to Hippo (now in northeast Algeria) to meet the great Augustine, where, also in 405, she sustained the news of her son's death. She seems to have returned to Italy and then, in 409–410, returned to Jerusalem, where she soon died.

We know that Melania corresponded with noted early Christian figures such as Evagrius, Rufinus, and Palladius, but whatever collection of her letters may have existed did not survive. We may attribute this to Jerome's "blackening" of her name (*melania* = black in Greek, see Jerome's Letter 133), for her support of Rufinus and defense of Origen. But then, to incur Jerome's ire was to find oneself in some excellent company.

See also Desert Mothers; Double Monasteries; Macrina the Elder, St.; Macrina the Younger, St.; Melania the Younger, St.; Rules for Canonesses, Nuns, and Recluses

BIBLIOGRAPHY

Primary Sources
Evagrius of Pontus. "Evagrius of Pontus' *Letter to Melania*." Edited by M. Parmentier. *Bijdragen* 46 (1985): 2–38.
Jerome, St. [Chronicle]. *S Hieronymi Chronicon*. In *Patrologia Latina*, vol. 27: year 377, col. 698. 221 vols. Paris: Migne, 1844–1864.

————. [Letters]. In *Patrologia Latina*, vol. 22: 325-1197. 221 vols. Paris: Migne, 1844–1864.

Palladius. *The Lausiac History of Palladius*. Edited by Cuthbert Butler. Texts and Studies: Contributions to Biblical and Patristic Literature 6. 2 vols. Cambridge: Cambridge University Press, 1898–1904. Reprint Hildesheim, Germany: Olms, 1967. [Prolegomena and Greek text edited with notes].

————. *The Lausiac History*. Edited and translated by Robert T. Meyer. Ancient Christian Writers, 34. Westminster, Md.: Newman Press; New York: Paulist Press, 1965. [English trans with notes].

————. "Melania the Elder." In *Handmaids of the Lord: Contemporary Descriptions of Feminine Asceticism in the First Six Christian Centuries*, edited and translated by Joan M. Peterson, 299–308. Kalamazoo, Mich.: Cistercian Publications, 1996. [Excerpted from the *Lausiac History*, with commentary].

Paulinus of Nola, St. *Epistula*. Edited by Wilhelm von Hartel. *Corpus Scriptorum Ecclesiasticorum Latinorum*, 29. Vienna: Tempsky, 1894.

————. *Letters*. Translated by Peter G. Walsh. Ancient Christian Writers 35, 36. New York: Newman Press, 1975. [See nos. 28, 29, 31, 45].

Rufinus of Aquileia, *Apologia contra Hieronymum*. In *Tyranni Rufini Opera*, edited by Manlio Simonetti, 2: 26. 105. *Corpus Christianorum Series Latina*, 20. Turnhout, Belgium: Brepols, 1961. [Latin text only].

Secondary Sources

Adkin, Neil. "'Alii discunt - pro pudor!—a feminis': Jerome, *Epist.* 53.7.1." *Classical Quarterly* n.s. 44 (1994): 559–61.

Coon, Lynda L. *Sacred Fictions: Holy Women and Hagiography in Late Antiquity*. The Middle Ages. Philadephia: University of Pennsylvania Press, 1997.

Moine, Nicole. "Melaniana." *Recherches Augustiniennnes* 5 (1980): 3–79.

————. "Mélanie l'Ancienne." In *Dictionnaire de Spiritualité ascétique et mystique*, 10: 955–60. Paris: Beauchesne, 1980.

Murphy, Francis X. "Melania the Elder: A Biographical Note." *Traditio* 5 (1947): 59–77.

————. *Rufinus of Aquileia (345–411): His Life and Works*. Washington, D.C.: Catholic University of America Press, 1945.

Petersen, Joan M. *Handmaids of the Lord, Contemporary Descriptions of Feminine Asceticism in the First Six Christian Centuries*. Kalamazoo, Mich.: Cistercian Publications Inc, 1996. [Good introductions and commentary to translated texts].

Schwartz, Eduard. "Palladiana." *Zeitschrift für neutestamentliche Wissenschaft* 36 (1937): 166–67.

ANNA SILVAS

MELANIA THE YOUNGER, ST. (383–439). A founder of several monasteries in North Africa and the Holy Land, Melania the Younger was the granddaughter of Melania the Elder (c.342–c.410), born of the union of Publicola, son of Melania the Elder, and the patrician Albina Caionia (378). In 397, at age fourteen, Melania married her cousin Valerius Pinian, as prearranged. "Continually stung by stories of her grandmother" (Palladius, 61), she was for married celibacy from the outset, but Pinian wanted them at least to secure heirs. After a son was stillborn, followed by the death of their little girl, he consented, at first reluctantly, but then wholeheartedly, to live with her as brother.

After her father's death (405), with the support of her grandmother and the consent of Emperor Honorius, they began the lifelong project of dispersing their immense wealth for the benefit of the poor, despite opposition by the Senate, bankers, and relatives. They withdrew from the city to their villa on the Via Appia in Rome, converting it into a hostel for pilgrims—where they also received the historian Palladius (c.364–c.425)—set free many slaves (though many did not wish it), and gave over their wardrobe of silks for liturgical use. Melania took to zealous fasting, poring over the Scriptures and the lives of the saints, and doing her share of slaves' work (Palladius, 61), entirely winning her mother over to the ascetic life.

As the Goths advanced from the north, they, together with her mother, headed south, stopping with Paulinus at Nola (407) then settling in Sicily (408) with Rufinus of Aquileia. After his death (410) they moved on to Africa, making the acquaintance of St. Augustine (354–430) at Hippo (now northeast Algeria) and his companion, Alipius—immortalized in the former's *Confessions*—in Thagaste, south of Hippo, where Melania founded and presided over a community of sisters for seven years.

In 417 they moved to Jerusalem, from where they set out on a tour of the Egyptian monks, "who received her as though a man," and met St. Cyril of Alexandria (d. 444). After the deaths of her mother (420) and husband (431), Melania gave herself to periods of seclusion and more intense asceticism. In 432, she founded a monastery for women on the Mount of Olives, atop the hills east of Jerusalem, but refused to become mother superior, wishing instead only to minister to the sisters as a slave, and in 436 founded a monastery for men nearby. That same year year she also journeyed to Constantinople, where she effected the conversion of her uncle Volusian, with whom Augustine had corresponded. She also joined in the Nestorian controversy—so named for Nestorius (post-351–post-451), patriarch of Constantinople, who held that the Incarnate Christ consisted of two separate Persons (Divine and Human), for which he was condemned by the pope and Cyril in 430—defending of the unity of Christ's person. Melania's meeting with the Empress Eudokia (c.400–460), wife of Theodosius II (408–450), impressed the empress sufficiently to cause her to journey to Jerusalem acknowledging Melania as her spiritual mother in 438. The *vita* (biography) by Gerontius provides examples of Melania's preaching, wonderworking, and exorcism. Her death day on December 31 (439) is her liturgical feast day.

The Greek Church began to venerate Melania soon after she died, but historically knew her only through the reworked vita in the *Menologion* of Simeon Metaphrastes (fl. 960), a collection of "metaphrased" (reworked) saints' lives. Until Melania's *vita* was translated in the sixteenth century, she was little known in the West. In the latter part of the nineteenth century, the great flurry of textual research and discovery further increased her popularity: the Bollandists established a premetaphrastic Greek text from a manuscript discovered in the Barberini library (Delahaye). Meanwhile, Cardinal Rampolla, while papal nuncio in Madrid, discovered the ancient Latin *vita* in the Escorial (palace and monastery) near Madrid, giving the fullest account of all. Although scholars are undecided as to which version came first, Rampolla's publication in 1905 of both the Latin and Greek texts, with much supplementary material, remains a cornerstone of studies in Melania the Younger.

See also Desert Mothers; Eudocia; Macrina the Elder, St.; Macrina the Younger, St.; Melania the Elder, St.; Rules for Canonesses, Nuns, and Recluses

BIBLIOGRAPHY

Primary Sources
Augustine, St. *Epistulae*. In *Patrologia Latina*, vol. 33: 124, 125, 126. 221 vols. Paris: Migne, 1844–1864. [Latin text only].
Gerontius. "S. Melaniae Iunioris acta Graeca." Edited by H. Delahaye. *Analecta Bollandiana* 22 (1903): 5–50. [First ed. of the Greek text, but *see below, next entry*].

————. *Vita Melaniae Iunioris.* Critical ed. with [French] translation and notes by Denys Gorce, Sources Chrétiennes 90. Paris: Éditions du Cerf, 1962. [Authoriative Greek text].

————. *The Life of Melania the Younger.* Introduction, translation, and commentary by Elizabeth A. Clarke. Studies in Women and Religion 14. Lewiston, N.Y.: Edwin Mellen Press, 1984. [Based on the Greek text, with notes on the Latin version].

————. *Santa Melania giuniore, senatrice Romana: documenti contemporanei e note.* Edited by Cardinal Rampolla del Tindaro. Rome: Vatican, 1905. [Contains the Latin *vita* discovered by Rampolla (see also Laurence's ed. below), and reprints Delahaye's ed. of the Greek *vita*, cited above].

————. *The Life of St Melania, by His Eminence, Cardinal Rampolla.* Translated by Ellen M. A. Leahy and edited by Herbert Thurston S.J. London: Burns & Oates, 1908.

————. *La Vie latine de Sainte Mélanie.* Critical ed. with [French] translation and commentary by Patrick Laurence. Collectio minor/Studium Biblicum Franciscanum, 41. Jerusalem: Franciscan Press, 2002. [Authoritative Latin text].

————. "The Life of the Holy Melania." In *Handmaids of the Lord: Contemporary Descriptions of Feminine Asceticism in the First Six Christian Centuries*, edited and translated by Joan M. Peterson, 311–62. Kalamazoo, Mich.: Cistercian Publications, 1996. [English trans. with notes].

Palladius. *The Lausiac History of Palladius.* Edited by Cuthbert Butler. Texts and Studies: Contributions to Biblical and Patristic Literature 6. 2 vols. Cambridge: Cambridge University Press, 1898–1904. Reprint Hildesheim, Germany: Olms, 1967. [Prolegomena and Greek text edited with notes].

————. *The Lausiac History.* Edited and translated by Robert T. Meyer. Ancient Christian Writers, 34. Westminster, Md.: Newman Press; New York: Paulist Press, 1965. [English trans. with notes].

————. "Melania the Younger." In *Handmaids of the Lord*, 308–10. See above under Gerontius, "The Life of the Holy Melania."

Secondary Sources

Coon, Lynda L. *Sacred Fictions: Holy Women and Hagiography in Late Antiquity.* The Middle Ages. Philadephia: University of Pennsylvania Press, 1997.

Courcelle, Pierre. "Date, source et genèse des *Consultationes Zacchei et Apollonii*." *Revue d'histoire des religions* 146 (1954): 174–93. [The *Consultations* depend on correspondence of Augustine with Volusian].

Elliott, Dyan. *Spiritual Marriage: Sexual Abstinence in Medieval Wedlock.* Princeton, N.J.: Princeton University Press, 1993.

Leclerq, Henri. "Mélanie la Jeune (sainte)." In *Dictionnaire d'Archéologie chrétienne et de liturgie*, 11: 1. cols. 209–30. Paris: Letouzey, 1933.

Martain, Philip. "Une conversion au 5e s., Volusien." *Revue Augustiniennne* 1 (1907): 145–72.

McNabb, Vincent. "Was the Rule of St Augustine written for St Melania the Younger?" *Journal of Theological Studies* 20 (1918–1919): 242–49.

Moine, Nicole. "Melaniana." *Recherches Augustiniennnes* 15 (1980): 3–79.

————. "Mélanie la Jeune (sainte)." In *Dictionnaire de Spiritualité ascétique et mystique*, 10: cols. 960–65. Paris: Beauchesne, 1980.

Salisbury, Joyce E., Robert Woytowicz, and M. Parmentier. "The Life of Melania the Younger: A Partial Re-evaluation of the Manuscript Tradition." *Manuscripta* 33 (1989): 137–44.

ANNA SILVAS

MELUSINE (12th–15th centuries). The figure of Melusine, half fairy by birth and intermittently half serpent, is associated with medieval folklore and fairy tales as well as with historically informed genealogical narrative. In the two French romances that bear her name, the *Roman de Mélusine* by Jean d'Arras (1393) and the *Roman de Mélusine* by Coudrette (c.1400), she is depicted as the supernatural founder of the powerful medieval dynasty of Lusignan in Poitou. The latter achieved its greatest prominence during the twelfth century by bringing the kingdoms of Cyprus and Jerusalem within its purview. In these romances, however, the marvelous figure of Melusine becomes linked with a legendary, often fanciful account of the Lusignan fortunes, one redolent of the Crusades and of conquests in remote areas of Europe and the Near East. Relatively neglected by scholars until recent decades, Melusine has emerged as one of the most compelling female personages of medieval French fiction.

The myth of Melusine antedates these written versions by several centuries. It has been traced to Gallo-Roman and Celtic prototypes, in legends of a female figure who effected marvelous feats of construction and became "the fairy of medieval economic growth" (Le Goff). She is also related to a variety of creatures who undergo periodic transformations to assume animal forms, legendary beings recorded in Latin texts by twelfth-century clerical authors such as Walter Map (*De nugis curialium* [*Of Trifles at Court*]) and Gervaise of Tilbury (*Otia imperialia* [*Imperial Leisure*]). In the two vernacular French narratives recounting the extraordinary deeds of Melusine and her progeny, elements of myth and folklore are blended with epic, Crusade narrative, romance, and theological doctrine to form a text that represents itself as historical: a fuller, more serious representation of Melusine than her idly intriguing twelfth-century forerunners.

Composed during a critical phase of the Hundred Years War (1337–1453), the *Roman de Mélusine* shades from history into fiction to uphold the proprietary claims to Lusignan of illustrious patrons. Jean d'Arras's prose romance claims to be based on a Latin chronicle furnished by his powerful patron, Jean Duc de Berry, at whose behest the work was undertaken, undoubtedly to enhance his claim to the Lusignan heritage in Poitou. The slightly later version by Coudrette, in octosyllabic verse, was composed for similar reasons, again on behalf of a patron, the lord of Parthenay, a Lusignan descendant. The latter part of the story recounted in both versions centers primarily on Melusine's ten sons, most of them possessed of extraordinary prowess that will distinguish them throughout Europe and the Middle East. Through conquest or alliance, they will reign as kings in Cyprus and Lesser Armenia and assume lordships not only in key cities of Poitou but in Alsace, Luxembourg, and Bohemia as well.

Many of the accomplishments attributed to Melusine are in conformity with the desires and aspirations of late feudal society: agrarian prosperity, inexhaustible wealth and luxury, nobiliary privilege and prestige, and political advantage. Melusine is both supernaturally beautiful and extraordinarily bountiful; like her fairy precursors in the narrative lays and romances of earlier centuries, she promises to fulfill every desire of the man who becomes her husband; she produces, in a short span of time, ten male heirs. Through her fairy prescience and her wise counsel, she enables her husband to escape death and to reclaim his heritage in Brittany; her sagacious addresses to various of her ten sons as they depart for conquest or Crusade contain a wealth of instruction concerning the ethics of government, chivalric conduct, and military strategy. We are invited to admire both the effective design of the fortresses and cities she erects with amazing dispatch and the sumptuousness of her attire and jewels; long passages detail the extravagance of celebrations and festivities she organizes, at which she epitomizes courtly ideals of grace, feminine elegance, and largesse.

But Melusine's arresting story features much more than these often-cited functions as founder and genetrix. The story of her life with her husband, Raymondin, like that of her fairy mother and mortal father whose telling precedes it, conforms in its large outline to a pattern familiar from lay and romance: a fairy meets and marries a mortal, only to disappear following the mortal partner's violation of an interdict she has set as a condition of their union. Jean d'Arras in his exordium (prologue) mentions a number of liaisons of this type, citing both learned and popular opinion. But Melusine is only half fairy. She and her sisters, along with her mother, were cast into "great misery" by the father's violation of the mother's interdiction against seeing her in childbed. The daughters avenge this misdeed by imprisoning their father forever inside a mountain, and are in turn punished by their mother; she tells them that had it not been for their vengeful act, they would soon have been drawn, by the power of the paternal seed, to abandon "the ways of nymphs and fairies." Now she subjects each of them to a unique form of punishment, in the case of Melusine that of assuming the form of a serpent from the waist down every Saturday. The possibility of abandoning the fairy state is made contingent on the outcome of her eventual marriage to a mortal, but with high stakes: if he respects her interdict against seeking to see her on Saturday or speaking of it to anyone, she will live naturally and die as a "normal" woman; if he should violate this prohibition, she will be compelled to return to her former "great misery" and torment.

Fundamental to Melusine's story, then, is the desirability of escape from her fairy state and the uncertainty of her ultimate destiny. Throughout the life shared with her mortal husband, indices of her supernatural status are prominent: fairy prescience, extraordinary feats of construction and display of riches of unknown origin, and the grotesque facial deformities borne by all but the last two of her ten sons. But she voluntarily proclaims her religious orthodoxy to her husband before their marriage and maintains a virtuous Christian profile of piety, religious observance, and good works. The betrayal by her mortal spouse is prompted by false allegations that her Saturday absences are a ruse to conceal her regular infidelity. Suspicious, her husband voyeuristically watches her bizarre metamorphosis in her bath and eventually proclaims in public the truth about her semiserpentine transformation. Though he repents at once of his misdeed and pleads with her to remain, she is compelled to depart, assuming the guise of a flying reptile. Having lost her, he makes a pilgrimage to Rome to confess his misdeed to the pope, then retires to a hermitage in Montserrat.

Thus the characterization of Melusine is ambiguous, combining mysterious and potentially disquieting traits with others that present the reassuring figure of a feudal matriarch devoted to the advancement of husband and sons. Just prior to her definitive transformation, she voices a poignant lament for the lost joys of her former life as a "normal" woman, and in her airborne, serpentine state she circles Lusignan uttering piteous human cries; following her departure, there are reports that she returns to nurture her infant children, and she is seen on the highest tower of the fortress days before a death is to occur within the dynasty or before Lusignan itself is to change hands.

In his exordium, Jean d'Arras insists that such creatures as fairies are among God's *merveilles*, and that their ways are therefore not susceptible to human understanding. His presentation of Melusine's story nonetheless raises questions, also variously raised by clerical authors, concerning the status of fairies in a mortal world governed by the laws of divine Providence; the prominence accorded issues of culpability and penance has prompted some readers to speculate concerning Melusine's damnation or salvation. Yet Melusine herself remains an opaque character: her achievements occasion great wonderment and curiosity, but her affective state is undisclosed until the final scene preceding her departure, when it assumes extraordinary novelistic prominence. The text itself is silent on the question of her ultimate fate: we know only that she returns to a former state of suffering to be endured until the High Judge sits in judgment.

This complex and enigmatic figure has engendered widely divergent readings, both negative and positive. Among the former, some focus on Melusine's intermittent monstrosity and identify traces of clerical attitudes toward monsters as demonic creatures, while others discern an ambivalence toward the female gender characteristic of a medieval misogyny that associated women with the serpent of Genesis. On the positive side, readings attentive to the global configuration of the romance highlight her courtly profile and her status as victim of her husband's betrayal, and cite evident efforts to divest her of potential malefic associations.

Melusine's story met with immediate and remarkable success, as attested by numerous manuscripts and by an unusually consistent history of printed versions through the nineteenth century. A mid-fifteenth-century German prose version of Coudrette's verse romance, by Thüring von Ringoltingen in 1456, was the first to appear in print, in 1474 in Augsburg, and it became extremely popular through the nineteenth century via more than eighty editions. Two printed Spanish translations of the *Historia de la linda Melosina* (*Story of the Fair Melusine*) soon followed, with an English edition first appearing around 1510. During the early modern period, Melusine was revered as a vigilant, beneficent overseer of climatic functions and agricultural enterprises in various sectors of medieval France (Le Roy Ladurie). The variable perceptions over time, in both learned and popular culture, of her quasi-mythic capacities and achievements attest to her remarkably enduring collective appeal as a nurturant facilitator of human designs and aspirations. Even today she retains her prominence. Her story reached a vast public as part of A. S. Byatt's recent best-selling novel, *Possession*, while the medieval narratives that first brought her extraordinary story into being are now available to a wider public through English and modern French translations.

See also Enchantresses, Fays (*Fées*), and Fairies

BIBLIOGRAPHY

Primary Sources
Coudrette. *Le Roman de Mélusine, ou Histoire de Lusignan*. Edited by Eleanor Roach. Paris: Klincksieck, 1982.
Historia de la linda Melosina. Edited by Ivy Corfis. Madison, Wisc.: Hispanic Seminary of Medieval Studies, 1986.
Jean d'Arras. *Mélusine: Roman du XVe siècle par Jean d'Arras*. Edited by Louis Stouff. Dijon: Bernigaud & Privat, 1932. Reprint Geneva: Slatkine, 1974.
———. *Le Roman de Mélusine ou l'Histoire des Lusignan*. Modern French translation by Michèle Perret. Paris: Stock, 1979.
———. English translation by Donald Maddox and Sara Sturm-Maddox, forthcoming.
Thüring von Ringoltingen. *Mélusine*. Edited by Karin Schneider. Texte des späten Mittelalters, 9. Berlin: E. Schmidt, 1958 [Modern French trans. with introduction by Jean-Marc Pastré. Greifswald: Reineke-Verlag, 1996].

Secondary Sources
Byatt, A.S. *Possession: A Romance*. New York: Random House/Vintage, 1990.
Clier-Colombani, Françoise. *La Fée Mélusine au Moyen Âge: Images, Mythes et Symboles*. Paris: Le Léopard d'Or, 1991.
Harf-Lancner, Laurence. *Les Fées au Moyen Âge: Morgane et Mélusine*. Paris: Honoré Champion, 1984.

———. "Mélusine." In *Dictionnaire des mythes littéraires*, edited by Pierre Brunel, 999–1003. Monaco: Du Rocher, 1988. [English trans. Wendy Allatson et al., *Companion to Literary Myths, Heroes and Archetypes*. London and New York: Routledge, 1992].

Lecouteux, Claude. "La Structure des légendes mélusiniennes." *Annales: Economies, Sociétés, Civilisations* 33 (1978): 294–306.

Le Goff, Jacques. "Mélusine maternelle et défricheuse." *Annales: Economies, Sociétés, Civilisations* 26 (1971): 587–603. Reprinted in *Pour un autre Moyen Âge*. Paris: Gallimard, 1979. English translation: "Melusina: Mother and Pioneer." In Le Goff, *Time, Work and Culture in the Middle Ages*, 205–22. Translated by Arthur Goldhammer. Chicago: University of Chicago Press, 1980.

Le Roy Ladurie, Emmanuel. "Mélusine ruralisée," *Annales: Economies, Sociétés, Civilisations* 26 (1971): 604–22. [*See* English trans., next entry].

———. "Mélusine Down on the Farm: Metamorphosis of a Myth." In Le Roy Ladurie, *The Territory of the Historian*, 203–20, translated by Ben Reynolds and Siân Reynolds. Brighton: Harvester Press, 1979.

Lundt, Bea. *Melusine und Merlin im Mittelalter: Entwürfe und Modelle weiblicher Existenz im Beziehungs-Diskurs der Geschlechter*. Munich: Wilhelm Fink, 1991.

Maddox, Donald, and Sara Sturm-Maddox, eds. *Melusine of Lusignan: Founding Fiction in Late Medieval France*. Athens: University of Georgia Press, 1996.

Markale, Jean. *Mélusine*. Paris: Retz, 1983. Reprint Albin Michel, 1993.

Perret, Michèle. "L'Invraisemblable Vérité: témoignage fantastique dans deux romans des 14e et 15e siècles." *Europe* 654 (1983): 25–35.

Pillard, Guy-Édouard. *La Déesse Mélusine: Mythologie d'une fée*. Maulévrier, France: Hérault, 1989.

Stouff, Louis. *Essai sur Mélusine, roman du XIVe siècle par Jean d'Arras*. Publications de l'Université de Dijon, 3. Dijon: Bellais/Paris: A. Picard, 1930.

SARA STURM-MADDOX AND DONALD MADDOX

MENSTRUATION AND MENOPAUSE. *See* **Medicine and Medieval Women**

MERICI, ANGELA, ST. (1470/75–1540). The Italian visionary Angela Merici founded the Ursulines, the last major women's religious order of the Middle Ages, or one of the first major early-modern orders. She spent most of her career in Brescia, in the province of Lombardy, northern Italy.

Born to a modest family in Desenzano, also in Lombardy, she was orphaned as a child and went to live with her uncle until the age of twenty-two, whereupon she returned Desenzano to become a teacher of young girls. She began as a Franciscan Tertiary: a member of the Franciscan Third Order who dedicated herself to the apostolic life and who wore a habit. Some tertiaries did take vows by this time but were not cloistered, living rather in their own homes according to their orders' rules, and functioning in the real world. Other tertiaries joined her in her mission, and Angela's school earned considerable esteem. Because of her success, the Franciscans sent her, in 1516, to Brescia to establish a lay charitable association for women, a female counterpart to the men's confraternity, the Company of Divine Love, which had been formed to minister to victims of syphilis—an unfortunate import during this Age of Exploration—to care for women sufferers. Such charitable movements recruited from among wealthy townswomen eager to help the less fortunate and who had already been trying to save poor women from prostitution. At the same time their good works, directed by orders like the Franciscans, helped bring about religious reform within the Catholic Church on the eve of the Protestant Reformation.

In 1524–1525, Angela made a pilgrimage to Palestine, in the course of which, like Paul on the road to Damascus (Acts 9), she was struck blind. During this period of blindness, she experienced visions that convinced her to found her own order, a resolve that she was able to fulfill once she regained her sight.

Around 1535, Angela returned to Brescia and gathered eight women of humble origins to help educate and care for poor, sick women. To maintain discipline as well as a separate sense of lay identity within her group, Angela formulated her own rule, tailored to meet the needs of a religious society far more complex than those envisioned by the much earlier Benedictine and Augustinian monastic rules, while retaining these communities' basic aura of piety, virginity, and good works. Again, Angela's mission at Brescia, like her earlier, lesser one at Desenzano, was highly successful, in great part because of her well-conceived rule. Her group became known as the Company of St. Ursula, named for her patron saint. One of the salient features of Angela's rule was its incorporation—rather than exclusion— of the city of Brescia and its prosperity. She integrated her company's administrative framework within the municipal plan of Brescia, then enlisted the good-hearted upper-class women, after careful selection, to serve as lady governors of each neighborhood. Townsmen were appointed to help with protection. Each lady governor carefully attended to her neighborhood's problems and requirements and periodically reported to the mother general. Members of the Company of St. Ursula had to be virgins; much like other ter-tiaries, they lived and dressed simply (though they wore no official habit) in their own homes and took no vows. They met frequently with their governors. The company's central purpose was to perform some kind of charitable work and Christian instruction.

As ideal as this all may seem, particularly since the Church was in dire need of effective teachers to preserve its doctrines, Ursula's innovative order in deliberately drab dress— which had never intended to be a real order—aroused suspicion among those already concerned to prohibit women preachers (teaching resembled preaching) in accordance with Scripture (citing, for example, 1 Cor. 11: 2–16). But Angela's gift for public relations with local religious and secular hierarchies managed to allay any serious opposition. In 1536, her company was approved by the bishops; she was elected mother superior in 1537. After her death in 1544, Pope Paul III issued his bull of approbation.

The Company of St. Ursula did not assume the identity of Ursulines until 1582, under Charles Borromeo, the influential bishop of Milan, who negotiated the new order's papal approbation. Although, Borromeo's Catholic counterreformation measures transformed the company into a more traditional women's order, the Ursulines continued to thrive, particularly in the New World. Angela was canonized in 1807. Her feast day is January 27.

See also Beguines; Clare of Assisi, St.; Convents; Hild (Hilda), St.; Rules for Canonesses, Nuns, and Recluses

BIBLIOGRAPHY

Primary Sources
Angela Merici. *Regola, Ricordi, Legati.* Critical ed. and trans. (Italian) by Luciana Mariani and Elisa Tarolli. Introduction by Ansgario Faller. Spiritualità, 7. Brescia: Editrice Queriniana, 1976.
————. [Rule, etc.]. In *Angela Merici and Her Teaching Idea, 1474–1540,* translated with commentary by Sr. Mary Monica. New York: Longman, Green, 1927. [Contains trans. of key documents, including the papal approbation].
————. [Rule, etc.]. In *Angela Merici and the Company of St. Ursula: According to the Historical Documents,* edited with commentary by Teresa Ledóchowska. Translated by Mary T. Neylan.

Rome: Ancora, 1970. Original *Angèle Merici et la Compagnie de Ste Ursule à la lumière des documents*. Preface by Eugène Tisserant. Rome: Ancora, 1967.

Bertoletti, G. *Storia di S. Angela Merici, 1474–1540*. Brescia, 1923. [Rare; compiled from early lives; partially prints the earliest (1568) by Giovanni Battista Nazari].

Secondary Sources

[See also above works].

Caraman, Philip. *Saint Angela: The Life of Angela Merici, Foundress of the Ursulines (1474–1540)*. New York: Farrar, Straus, 1964.

Livingstone, E. A., ed. *The Oxford Dictionary of the Christian Church*. Original edited by F. L. Cross. 3rd ed. Oxford: Oxford University Press, 1997.

Margoni, Alberto. *Angela Merici: l'intuizione della spiritualità secolare*. Preface by Pietro Borzomati. Spiritualità e promozione humana, 19. Soveria Mannelli (Catanzaro): Rubbettino, 2000.

Ranft, Patricia. *Women and the Religious Life in Premodern Europe*. New York: St. Martin's, 1996.

NADIA MARGOLIS

MÉZIÈRES, PHILIPPE DE. *See Vertu du Sacrement de Mariage, Livre de la*

MIDWIFERY. *See Medicine and Medieval Women*

MINNE (12th–14th centuries). The term *Minne* originally meant "memory," then "in loving memory" (from the German *meinen* = "to think of"), and finally, "love," a kind of caring, helping love, or caritas, and much later, love for the opposite sex, but of the ennobling kind; refined away from *concupiscentia* ("lust"). *Minne* became personified as "Lady Love" or "Lady Venus"—in contrast to the male Cupid or God of Love—by the thirteenth century.

In the courtly literature of the twelfth and thirteenth centuries, Minne was the overwhelming experience of medieval lyric poets, especially the troubadours and their female counterparts (*trobairitz*) in their cultivation of *fin'amors* (varied spellings), meaning "refined, good love," and *amor de lonh* (love from afar), and the German *Minnesänger*, whose very name, meaning "singers of/to Minne," derives from *Minne*, which is their topic and vocation. The *Minnesänger* also celebrated the concept of *Frauendienst* ([Love-] service to one's Lady] as part of their brand of love, for, as Stephen Jaeger characterizes it, the moral aspect of collections like the Regensburg Songs (c.1106) "was one-sided: the women 'trained the man'" to be a good lover (Jaeger, 162).

On the religious front, alongside the *hohe Minne* (lofty love) of the poets and troubadours, developed the *minnente Herze Gotes* (the loving, mystical heart of God), the divine love emulated by the mystics, both male and female, in seeking to unite their souls with God. The appearance and flowering of both courtly love and mystical love were roughly contemporaneous. While the erotic love of the troubadours would strike us as the opposite of the *caritas* (charity) and *amicitia* (friendship), the basis of Christian doctrine, a crossover does seem to have taken place at the expressive-linguistic level, in that both categories strove for union with the lady or God through love, in fleeting periods of union amid longer intervals of burning desire from afar enunciated by courtly and contemplative authors alike. The Minne of the courtly poets, inspired by the desire for carnal union of

Medieval lovers, fourteenth century. A lover takes leave of his lady. An illustration based on a picture of the poet/minstrel Bruno von Hornberg. Engraving from *Big Heidelberg Book of Lovers*, University Library of Heidelberg. © Mary Evans Picture Library.

the lover (the *fin amant*) with his beloved Lady (*amie*). Yet the rhetoric of reverence, echoing religious writing, was preceded by previous crossovers: among love poetry, religious devotional writing, and feudal loyalty oaths, for example when the poet addresses his lady as *Domna*, the female counterpart of Lord (*Dominus*), whether a feudal lord or the Lord God. This sort of deliberate blurring attempts to render mortal love as something greater and more transcendent, not only as a strategy of seduction to win the woman but also as a means of attaining some sort of immortality for poet and beloved. Conversely, the mystics of the twelfth century onward "carnalized" their antithetically pure love of God in such a way as to make it more immediate, engulfing all possible senses, both spiritual and physical. Both courtly and religious authors converged on the question of "knowledge": the *gai saber* (joyful wisdom) of the troubadours (so intriguing to nineteenth-century philosophers such as Nietzsche) and the *Sapientia*, or divine wisdom, plus related concepts, of the mystics. The blurring of boundaries between the two registers—sacred and profane—seems to have revitalized each side in its expression of desire. Each also fostered an art of love: the sacred inspired primarily by the Song of Songs and the secular poets by the Roman poet Ovid (the chief influence in Andreas Capellanus's *De amore* [*Art of Love*], late twelfth century). But medieval commentators like Gérard of Liège (thirteenth century) did their part in promoting crossover thematics by mixing the Song of Songs and the works of the Fathers of the Church with courtly writings into a single "art," or sometimes a "rule"—not monastic, but amorous, quasi-imperceptibly—as in the contemporaneous, anonymous *Règle des fins amants* (*Rule for Good Lovers*; Newman 1995).

In demonstrating the defiant similarities between the two fundamentally opposite loves (religious and courtly *Minne*), Barbara Newman recently analyzed the role of *Minne* in three significant medieval mystical women authors: Hadewijch of Brabant (thirteenth century), Mechthild of Magdeburg (d. 1282) and Marguerite Porete (d. 1310)—beguines (pious laywomen living as a community) versed in courtly literature in addition to the Scriptures and commentaries on them. The differences among the three are based on how each author situates *Minne*, often in relation to *Brautmystik* (the concept of Christ as bridegroom and the adoring mystic's soul as the bride), within the particular dynamic of her "mystical love affair," in which the chivalric *aventure* of courtly romance becomes a divine aventure for the soul. Of the three, Hadewijch's development of *Minne*, throughout its 987 occurrences in her *Strophische Gedichten* (*Stanzaic Poems*), is the most complex (Newman 1995; 2003).

Newman's interpretation supplements, and even refreshingly counters at times, the more traditional view, in which scholars point to differences between sacred and profane poetics as evidenced in literature. For example, often in courtly love poetry the lover desires a lady who is often cold and indifferent, to be wooed and besought by the poet's prayers. According to the mystics, this is merely desire, because true *Minne* is a mutual love of the soul for God and of God for the soul. To the mystics of the Middle Ages, God is love, and He has loved him/her first: to desire God is to love Him, to be on the way of possessing Him and being possessed by Him. Thus, courtly love contents itself with less than mystical love. It lives and endures without ever attaining its end, whereas mystical love is the embracing of the object, God. The mystic desires, too, but not because he is not loved of God, nor because he loves, but because he desires to give yet more love for love. He suffers, too, from his desires, but his sufferings arise not from unrequited love, but from his inability to return enough love for love. Moreover, the *Minne* of the courtly poets, to remain pure, must avoid union with the beloved or separate the fulfillment of his love from the love itself. Such is the quandary dividing the two sections of the *Roman de la Rose* (*Romance of the Rose*, thirteenth century): first authored by Guillaume de Lorris, a respectful, mystical fin'amors poet (for whom the aspiring good lover could desire but never pluck, the Rose), and then, some fifty years later, Guillaume's allegorical quest for the Rose was completed by Jean de Meun, an urban secular intellectual who, sneering at such doctrines of love in favor of the more fashionable scientific rationalism, allows the Rose to be possessed, in keeping with Nature's, if not the Church's (or *fin'amor's*), plan.

In late medieval times, like Meun's rose in the ongoing *Roman*, the term *Minne* became degraded by a more jaded mentality and even obscenity. *Minne* was thus eventually replaced by the modern German for love, *Liebe* (Newman 1995; Wiercinski).

See also Alba Lady; Bride of Christ/*Brautmystik*; Capellanus, Andreas; Hadewijch; Marie de France; Mechthild of Magdeburg; Porete, Marguerite; *Roman de la Rose*, Debate of the; *Trobairitz*

BIBLIOGRAPHY

Primary Sources

Capellanus, Andreas. [*De amore*]. Walsh, P. G., ed. and trans. *Andreas Capellanus on Love*. Duckworth Classical, Medieval and Renaissance Editions. London: Duckworth, 1982. [Bilingual Latin-English ed.].

Des Minnesangs Frühling. Edited by Hugo Moser and Helmut Tervooren, revised from ed. by Karl Lachmann et al. 38th ed. 2 vols. Stuttgart, Germany: Hirzel, 1988.

Gérard of Liège. "Quinque incitamenta amoris." Edited by André Wilmart. *Revue d'ascétique et de mystique* 12 (1931): 349–430.

Hadewijch. *Strophische Gedichten*. Edited with commentary by J. van Mierlo. Leuvense Studiën en Tekstuitgaven 13. Antwerp, Belgium: Standaard-Boekhandel, 1942.

———. *Poetry of Hadewijch*. Edited and translated by Marieke van Baest. Louvain, Belgium: Peeters, 1998.

Lorris, Guillaume de, and Jean de Meun. *Le Roman de la Rose*. Edited by Daniel Poirion. Paris: Garnier Flammarion, 1974.

————. *The Romance of the Rose*. Translated by Frances Horgan. The World's Classics. Oxford: Oxford University Press, 1994.

Mechthild of Magdeburg. *Das fliessende Licht der Gottheit*. Edited by Hans Neumann. Munich: Artemis, 1990.

————. *The Flowing Light of the Divinity*. Translated by Christiane Mesch Galvani. New York: Garland, 1991.

Porete, Marguerite. *Le Mirouer des simples ames*. Edited by Romana Guarnieri and Paul Verdeyen. *Corpus Christianorum Continuatio Medievalis*, 69. Turnhout: Brepols, 1986.

————. *The Mirror of Simple Souls*. Translated with commentary by Ellen Babinsky. New York: Paulist Press, 1993.

[Regensburg Love Songs]. *Carmina Ratisponensia*. Edited by Anke Paravicini. Editiones Heidelbergenses, 20. Heidelberg, Germany: Winter, 1979.

Règle des fins amants. "La Règle des fins amants: Eine Beginenregel aus dem Ende des XIII. Jahrhunderts." Edited by Karl Christ et al. In *Philologische Studien[...] Festgabe Karl Voretsch*. Halle, Germany: Max Niemeyer, 1927.

Secondary Sources

Bladel, Franz van. *Hadewijch: Die Minne es al*. Louvain, Belgium: Davidsvons/Literair, 2002.

Bräuer, Rolf. *Der helden Minne: Triuwe un Êre: Literaturgeschichte der mittelhochdeutschen Blütezeit*. Geschichte der deutschen Literatur, 2. Berlin: Volk und Wissen, 1990.

Haferland, Harald. *Hohe Minne: zur Beschreibung der Minnekanzone*. Beihefte zur Zeitschrift für deutsche Philologie, 10. Berlin: Erich Schmidt, 2001.

Müller, Ulrich, ed. *Minne ist ein swaerez Spil: neue Untersuchungen zum Minnesang und zur Geschichte der Liebe*. Göppinger Arbeiten zur Germanistik, 440. Göppingen, Germany: Kümmerle, 1986. [Essays by Peter Dinzelbacher and other major German scholars].

Newman, Barbara. *God and the Goddesses: Vision, Poetry and Belief in the Middle Ages*. Middle Ages. Philadelphia: University of Pennsylvania Press, 2003.

————."*La mystique courtoise*: Thirteenth-Century Beguines and the Art of Love." In Newman, *From Virile Woman to WomanChrist: Studies in Medieval Religion and Literature*, 137–81. Middle Ages. Philadelphia: University of Pennsylvania Press, 1995.

Petroff, Elizabeth Alvilda. *Medieval Women's Visionary Literature*. New York: Oxford University Press, 1986. [Anthology of excerpts with useful commentary and introductions].

Philipowsky, Katherina-Silke. *Minne und Kiusche im deutschen Prosa-Lancelot*. Europäische Hochschulschriften, 1: Deutsche Sprache und Literatur, 1842. Frankfurt: Peter Lang, 2002.

Sziráky, Anna. *Éros, Lógos, Musiké: Gottfrieds "Tristan" oder eine utopische renovatio der Dichtersprache und der Welt aus dem Geiste der Minne und Musik?* Wiener Arbeiten zur germanischen Altertumskunde und Philologie, 38. Berne and New York: Peter Lang, 2003.

Wentzlaff-Eggebert, Friedrich-W. *Deutsche Mystik zwischen Mittelalter und Neuzeit*. 3rd ed. Berlin: de Gruyter, 1969. Original 1947.

Wiercinski, Dorothea. *Minne: Herkunft und Anwendungsschichten eines Wortes*. Cologne, Germany: Böhlau, 1964.

EDITH BRIGITTE ARCHIBALD

MIRABAI (c.1498–c.1565). Mirabai is the best-known woman poet among the *bhakti* singer-saints of North India. Her legend has been transmitted throughout India in songs from a largely oral tradition, and more recently in films, plays, novels, recordings, comics, and popular art. Her devotional songs, *bhajans*, are sung in Gujarati, Hindi and its dialects, Punjabi, Bhojpuri, Bengali, and Oriya. Much of her biography has been gleaned from Nabhadas's skeletal account in the *Bhaktamal*, composed in 1600, followed by the enlarging historical detail of Priyadas's commentary in 1712, and the songs themselves. Considering the lateness of Priyadas's hagiography and the absence of reliable manuscript sources for the poetry, the tradition of oral stories and songs may be as important as the historical figure of Mirabai, who is also called Meerabai, Mira, or Meera (*bai* is a feminine suffix).

This vernacular oral tradition is rooted in the *bhakti* movements, which started in south India around the sixth century and spread to the north. *Bhakti* saints stressed a personal relationship with their god based on humility, devotion, and feeling rather than on learning. They rejected caste and wealth, used regional languages rather than Sanskrit (the religious and classical literary language), and challenged the established authority of rulers and priests. In their "countersystem," they created a space of rebellious religious expression for women and those of the lower castes (Ramanujan).

Like other women *bhakti* saints, Mirabai rejected earthly marriage and wealth at an early age. In Priyadas's account, Mira was born and married into leading Rajput princely families in Rajasthan, a parched, largely desert region in western India, whose dusty plains, craggy hills, and fortresses bear witness to a history of war and conflict. According to legend, when she saw a wedding procession as a little girl, she asked her mother who her bridegroom was and her mother pointed to an image of the god Krishna. From them on, she became a fervent devotee of Krishna. When her family, the rulers of Merta, arranged her marriage to a Rana, possibly the crown prince of Mewar, she went through the ceremony thinking that she was truly wedded only to Krishna. When she parted with her family, she did not want to take her wealth of jewels and clothes, but instead wanted only her image of Krishna.

On arrival at her husband's home, she refused to bow to the family goddess, *kuldevi*, claiming that Krishna was her only master. This angered her mother-in-law and began the protracted struggles with her husband and his family that are a dominant theme in the songs. She refused to consummate her marriage, insisting that Krishna was her only husband. She sought out the "company of saints," wandering mendicants devoted to Krishna (Hawley). Her sisters-in-law tried to dissuade her from what was seen as inappropriate company. She also sang and danced for Krishna in the public space of the temple, which was considered shocking behavior. Her husband's family eventually tried to lock her in and even wanted to kill her.

At least two attempts were made on her life by the Rana, and accounts vary as to whether the Rana was her husband, brother-in-law, or father-in-law. The first attempt came in the form of poison that supposedly turned to nectar as she drank it. The second attempt came in the form of a snake that, in variants of the story, turned either into a garland of flowers or a stone sacred to Krishna called a *salagram*.

Mira soon left her husband's family and traveled west in the company of mendicant ascetics to Brindavan and Dwarka, pilgrimage places associated with the life of Krishna. According to some accounts, she was accompanied by her maid, companion, and amanuensis Lalita throughout her travels.

Mira's responses to male ascetics show a sense of humor and a canny instinct for survival. In Brindavan she confronted Jiv Gosvami, a great theologian who refused to meet her because she was a woman and could be a distraction to his asceticism. She responded that before Krishna everyone is female, and he relented. She stayed there for some time, acquiring a large following, until she moved on to Dwarka. In another story, an ascetic demanded that Mira submit to his sexual advances because, he claimed, Krishna had sanctioned them. Mira cleverly drew the situation into the public space of the gathering of devotees. There she laid out a bed and asked the man to proceed. Thus shamed, he turned white, and converted to a believer, begging her to be his spiritual guide. Both incidents show Mira's handling of some of the real obstacles and harassment that dogged female ascetics.

Accounts of the manner of her death are ambiguous. The Rana sent a delegation of Brahmins for her, either because he was doing penance for her inauspicious exile or because he was angry and possibly blamed her for political and military problems that his kingdom was facing (Bahadurshah attacked and ransacked Chittor in 1534 and about 13,000 women are said to have committed a kind of collective suicide, *jauhar*, rather than face conquest). When Mira refused to return, the Brahmins went on a hunger strike. She finally prepared to go home with them, but as she prayed in the temple, the story holds, she was drawn into the image of Krishna. The only remains found were her clothes draped around the icon of Krishna.

For a Rajput princess to shed the protection, finery, and luxuries of her royal family, to wander, singing and dancing among devotees with disregard for public opinion would hardly be acceptable, as it would not be even for upper-class urban women today. It took fearlessness, and *bhakti* provided "a creative framework" for her unconventional behavior and "alternative way of life" (Kishwar and Vanita, 83–84). Hers was not a secluded devotion in the women's quarters. She sought a community of devotees, *bhaktas*, who at the time often included those from lower castes and Muslims. According to tradition, she chose Ravidas, the *bhakti* saint from the low caste of leatherworkers, as her guru. The Mughal emperor Akbar, a Muslim, is said to have traveled to Dwarka to pay her homage along with his chief musician, Tansen, who is supposed to have sung a *bhajan* with her.

Mira's poetry is meant to be sung. In the absence of reliable manuscripts, scholars suggest that her signature in the last line, frequently "Mira's Lord is the Lifter of the Mountain, *Giridhar Naagar*," may have been added to songs composed by others. Fourteen hundred short compositions are attributed to her. They are in the languages of the areas where she lived, western Rajasthani, Vraj bhasha, and Gujarati. They are characterized by lyrical simplicity, marked rhythm, and recurring refrains.

Krishna is evoked in a heroic, protective aspect, as the one who lifted a mountain on his fingertip to shield the cowherds from a storm sent by Indra, the god of rain. He is also the beautiful beloved who gives ephemeral delight as the cowherd flute player of Brindavan. Like Radha and the other cowherding women, the *gopis*, she is his consort. In many songs, separation from him provokes pain and longing, even madness. Many poems are addressed to a woman friend while she waits. Many others begin with the active pronoun "I" who forges a relationship with Krishna, chiding, pleading, demanding, dancing, and singing (Kishwar and Vanita, 88). Her yearning is echoed in nature, in the cry of the cuckoo or thirsting rain-bird, in the gathering of clouds, and the onset of monsoon rain. Bridal imagery abounds as she wears a red sari and jewelry for Krishna. In one song, she recounts a dream sequence in which she marries him. By contrast, marriage here on earth is part of a cruel world of slander, gossip, and persecution that provokes her asceticism.

As Parita Mukta's and Lindsey Harlan's fieldwork has shown, Mira's rupturing of the feudal social order is remembered in Rajasthan even today, where her name is used as a term for a "loose woman" and was suppressed in manuscripts and respectable society. However, Parita Mukta shows that the "people's Mira" perseveres in the oral bardic tradition and in the collective singing of peasants and artisans. To them her songs are a symbol of resistance against the rule of the Rana, the authority of a husband, and Rajput privilege in the caste system.

Mukta asserts that congregational singing of Mira *bhajans* among the lower castes in Saurashtra and Rajasthan, such as weavers, leatherworkers, and sweepers, serves as a means of building community and class consciousness. The songs become a vehicle for their prevailing concerns and anxieties. In discussions after *bhajan* gatherings that she attended, Mukta notes the slippage between the messages of the songs and themes such as the social experience of women or caste privilege. Further, these gatherings provide an occasion for villagers to discuss relief works during a period of drought or to bring migrant communities within the fold.

Mira is shorn of her connections to this community in most modern texts. Colonel James Tod's nineteenth-century colonial account sentimentalizes her as an isolated romantic mystic (289–90). Gandhi saw her as a symbol of nonviolent resistance and her inclusion in his prayers and writings, as well as the film *Meera* from the early days of Indian cinema, brought her to a pan-Indian middle-class audience. M. S. Subbalakshmi's influential recording from the film and Vishnu Digambar Paluskar's renditions integrated Mira bhajans into a restrained and virtuosic classical style. In commercial media today, Mira has been both eroticized and domesticated. The central change in her story in films, comics, and popular art is an alteration of her rebellion against marriage to make her a pious housewife and a pure widow often depicted in white plaster of Paris images in urban households. Even in Rajasthan, she has been through something of a revival where her courage is now claimed as a symptom of her Rajput heritage (Harlan).

Her strong appeal in popular culture remains part of her legacy. Mira's life and works did not lead to the establishment of a collective movement or sect. However, the enduring power of her songs lies in the suffering and devotion they convey and her inspiring struggle to follow her chosen path in the face of intense societal pressure that many see mirrored in their own experience today.

See also Chanson de Femme (Women's Song); *Frauenlied*; Hagiography (Female Saints); Music in Medieval Nunneries; Music, Women Composers and Musicians; *Skáldkonur* (Old Norse-Icelandic Women Poets)

BIBLIOGRAPHY

Primary Sources
Mirabai. *The Devotional Poems of Mirabai*. Translated by A. J. Alston. Delhi: Motilal Banarsidass, 1980.
———. *Mirabai ki Padavali*. Edited by Parasuram Caturvedi. Allahabad, India: Hindi Sahitya Sammelan, 1973.

Secondary Sources
Harlan, Lindsey. *Religion and Rajput Women: The Ethic of Protection in Contemporary Narratives*. Berkeley: University of California Press, 1992.
Hawley, John Stratton, and Mark Juergensmeyer. *Songs of the Saints of India*. New York: Oxford University Press, 1988.
Kishwar, Madhu, and Ruth Vanita. "Modern Versions of Mira." *Manushi* 50–52 (January–June 1989): 100–101.
———. "Poison to Nectar: The Life and Work of Mirabai." *Manushi* 50–52 (January–June 1989): 74–93.
Mukta, Parita. *Upholding the Common Life: The Community of Mirabai*. Delhi: Oxford University Press, 1997.
Ramanujan, A. K. "Talking to God in the Mother Tongue." *Manushi* 50–52 (January–June 1989): 9–14.

Sangari, Kumkum. "Mirabai and the Spiritual Economy of Bhakti." *Economic and Political Weekly.* 25. 26 (July 7, 1990): 1464–75; 25. 27 (July 14, 1990): 1537–52.

Subbalaxmi, M. S. *Meera Bhajans.* EALP 1297. Dum Dum, India: Gramophone Company of India, 1965.

Tod, James. *Annals and Antiquities of Rajast'han, or the Central and Western Rajpoot States of India,* vol. 1. London: Smith, Elder and Co., 1829.

Tharu, Susie, and K. Lalitha, eds. *Women Writing in India 600 B.C. to the Present. Vol. I: 600 B.C. to the Early Twentieth Century.* New York: Feminist Press, 1991.

PRATEETI PUNJA BALLAL

MIROIR DE MARIAGE (*Mirror of Marriage*) (1381–1389). The *Miroir de Mariage* is a well-known yet usually misunderstood poem by its often equally misunderstood author, Eustache Deschamps (c.1346–c.1406), the prolific, influential courtier-poet conversant with Geoffrey Chaucer and Christine de Pizan. Although characterized as Deschamps's primary work on women and one of the principal marriage treatises of the French Middle Ages, the *Miroir* is seldom read in its entirety because of the lack of a convenient modern edition and translation. As a result, only its antifeminist sections have been widely cited, and these often secondhand, thereby causing the *Miroir* and its author to be branded as examples of clerkly misogyny. However, a closer examination of the complete *Miroir* and other works among Deschamps's 1,500 writings reveals his ideas on women to be more varied and sympathetic in tone and substance; the result of his complex poetic personality as nurtured by his education, family and social status, and intriguing literary-political career.

Despite his lack of university degree and any clear evidence of noble rank, Deschamps managed to attain posts usually accorded only those of noble birth during his successful lifelong career serving the high nobility and later, the royal retinue: first as squire (*escuyer*) at the court of Charles V (d. 1380), then Charles VI (d. 1422) and Louis d'Orléans (d. 1407), and later as a bailiff (*bailli*)—in those days a sort of circuit-court judge and revenue collector. The broad spectrum of humanity encountered in such capacities provided ample material for his highly varied writings as he became an esteemed and popular poet whose other most famous work, would be the more predictably instructive *Art de dictier* (*Art of Poetic Composition*, 1392).

Le Miroir de mariage (Poem 1498 in the Queux de Saint-Hilaire and Raynaud edition) opens with a highly ornate rhetorical discussion of true friendship: only real friends will persist in adversity and tell the truth. After this initial demonstration of his poetic-rhetorical virtuosity, Deschamps soon appears far more interested in human peculiarities, and accordingly changes to a more accessible, colorful, and sometimes even comic style to engage the reader. The *Miroir*'s central debate focuses on whether the allegorical main character, Franc Vouloir (Free Will), a well-off male figure, should marry. The influence of Jean de Meun's *Roman de la Rose* (*Romance of the Rose*, c.1265), particularly in its use of irony and learned enumeration, resonates here, as Franc Vouloir's false friends—Desir (Desire), Folie (Foolishness), Servitude (Servility), and Faintise (Deceit)—urge marriage and the perpetuation of his line, noting that even animals marry and procreate, that the Bible exhorts men to marry, and that the young and wealthy Franc Vouloir should decide while still eligible. Franc Vouloir ponders the validity of his friends' continued allusions to biblical, classical, and medieval defenses of marriage as he formulates his own ideal mate: young and pretty but also humble, silent, chaste, wise, genteel, and prepared to raise many children. Yet his enthusiasm fades as he contemplates this ideal's unattainability and the potential horrors of an unhappy union. Unable to decide, Franc Vouloir writes his one true friend, Repertoire de Science (Repository of Wisdom), for help. Repertoire de Science's lengthy, learned reply interests us today because it inventories the entire known canon of classical and medieval misogyny (against women) and misogamy (against marriage), including the Bible, the classical Roman poet Ovid's *Ars amatoria* (*Art of Loving*), the fourth-century St. Jerome's *Adversus Jovinianum* (*Against Jovinianus*), a popular antimatrimonial epistle containing a fragment from the ancient Greek satirist Theophrastus' *Liber Aureolus de Nuptiis* (*Little Golden Book of Marriage*), and Matheolus' *Lamentaciones* (*Lamentations*, c.1300). Echoes of the *Roman de la Rose* again recur in the catalogue of wicked wives (Wilson and Makowski). Marriage may not technically be a sin, states Repertoire, but it distracts the knight and the nobleman from their duties; renown will do more for a man than children, and history is replete with accounts of many a disastrous marriage. Among the false friends rushing to refute these points, Folie asserts that, on the contrary, all religions sanction marriage to preserve the offspring's rights and social order; history also records deeds of heroic, virtuous biblical women such as Judith and Esther, whereas children can also bring great joy. Desir then adds that less danger of sin exists within marriage than within a monastery, while Servitude contends that marriage is the very goal of life and Faintise points out that no social life is possible without the family. Franc Vouloir, his mind assailed from all sides, finally abjures carnal marriage and declares his spiritual marriage by dedicating himself to God. Folie objects, provoking Franc Vouloir to launch into an amplified list, taken from vast historical compilation called the *Grandes Chroniques de France* (*Great Chronicles of France*, thirteenth through fifteenth centuries), of recent historic misfortunes presumably caused by Folie. It is in the middle of this recitation that the text breaks off, without conclusion.

Though unfinished, the *Miroir* remains Deschamps's longest work at 12,103 verses, and unlike Guillaume de Lorris's *Roman de la Rose*, the *Miroir* attracted no later continuator to finalize its message. Its incompleteness, along with other factors, may counter claims by some scholars that Chaucer borrowed from it for his *Canterbury Tales*, especially the "Wife of Bath's Prologue," the "Franklin's Tale," and "Merchant's Tale," though certain close parallels are undeniable (Wimsatt; Edwards). In compiling the canonical evidence for both sides while alternatingly advocating and criticizing the institution of marriage, the *Miroir* actually functions as the record of a debate—an *altercatio*—rather than as either a defense or condemnation of marriage (Wilson and Makowski). Its occasional equanimity also defies the common notion of its uniform misogyny, for example when it holds marriage to be as difficult for women as for men. In addition, this "mirror" deserves closer examination for its numerous images drawn from other aspects of daily life. Such elements, their sources and purpose, are also part of satire: Deschamps may have been too clever and worldly wise to state a serious, single-minded position on such dangerously difficult questions as women in general and marriage in particular. He may have intended this treatise as a more ambitious than usual exercise in poetic experimentation, as heralded by his other writings, rather than a true manual for achieving marital bliss.

Deschamps's posterity offers additional clues toward his true ideas on women, or at least how such ideas were received. That proto-feminist author Christine de Pizan openly lauded Deschamps balances Chaucer's mixed messages and helps to offset his misogynistic recurrence in that most brilliant, though scarcely profeminist, Renaissance author

Rabelais, for whom Franc Vouloir served as both motto and character inspiration (for Panurge) in his omnivorously satirical *Pantagruel* episodes (mid-1500s). Christine read Deschamps's work differently from the way Rabelais and Chaucer did, in part because of her woman's sensibility. Yet far from condemning him as one might expect, she addressed him as "mentor and friend" in the *Epistre a Eustace Morel* (*Epistle to Eustache Deschamps*; "Morel" being his other name) of 1404. Earl Jeffrey Richards observes that Christine admired Deschamps's moralizing poems, as if ignoring his *Miroir*, citing him as a potent alternative to Jean de Meun against whose immorality she attacked in the *Debat sus le Rommant de la Rose* (*Debate of the* Romance of the Rose) (Richards, in Sinnreich-Levi 1998). Deschamps replied to Christine with equal respect, praising her as the "most eloquent of the muses" and with the refrain, "Seule en tes faiz au royaume de France" ("Alone in your exploits within all the French kingdom"; *Balade* 1242). Despite his obvious incorporation of the *Roman de la Rose* in his work, in this poem Deschamps agrees with Christine on the evil effects of the insidious popularity of its "false doctrine."

The *Miroir*'s inconclusiveness prompts us to read Deschamps's many other allusions to women, whom his writings depict in scenes from the everyday lives of all classes: nuns and ladies, maidens and crones; their occupations and their fashions. In these, Deschamps's tone ranges from raucous to moralizing; his persona varies from that of simple observer to the *mal marié* (unhappily married man) or this figure's female counterpart, the *mal mariée*. Indeed, his more interesting moralizing and political poems—perhaps the same ones admired by Christine de Pizan—deplored contemporary sociopolitical ills, sometimes even using women's voices. Deschamps mal mariées complain in wry tones: the wife of *Balade* 1232 decides to take a lover of her own since her unfaithful husband has wasted their community property on his "fillettes" (girlies) and thus already broken their marriage vows; another wife bemoans marriage to a poor man (*Balade* 1235); another wife vents her wrath over her husband's diminished sexual capacity (*Balade* 892; *Rondeau* 670); and in *Rondeau* 853, a wife curses the matchmaker who saddled her with a jealous husband. Similarly, women's fashions and ways provide Deschamps with an opportunity to poke fun at human foibles (of both sexes) like vanity, for instance when he begs women to stop confining their breasts by the taut brassiere, "Dame, aiez pitié de la tettine" ("Lady, take pity on your tits"; *Balade* 1469), or condemns excessively elaborate hairstyles (*Balades* 1209 and 1210), not so much for the standard clerkly prudish reasons of *luxuria* (self-indulgence, narcissism), but because daily styling of such impractical coiffures wastes time.

However, the poems of greatest gendered interest embody fresher, less formalized voices. In *Virelais* 751 and 742, for example, we find novices who have fled the convent explaining their plight; young and vital, they yearn to take lovers in the fields beyond rather than be imprisoned behind the convent's walls fit only for the disabled and de-formed. In *Balade* 1144, a servant laments the difficulties of her job; she has learned not to judge anything at first glance. All three of these poems express women's complaints without a hint of sarcasm. Since the voices of the working and lower classes are heard so infrequently in medieval literature, any occurrence, especially a sympathetic one, is noteworthy. In a lighter vein, among Deschamps's female types is the alluring fifteen-year-old of *Rondeau* 554—"Sui je belle?" ("Aren't I beautiful?")—who catalogs her physical charms and other assets, fantasizing about the courtly men who will seek her love and to all of whom she will swear fidelity.

In real life, the two women closest to Deschamps were his wife and daughter. Deschamps wrote poignantly of his family, mourning the death of his wife in childbirth, waxing philosophical at his daughter's marriage, and guiding his two sons' careers. He lovingly addresses his daughter on her wedding day, while also eulogizing his late wife in *Balade* 1151 by enclosing a veritable rule for wives based on her example: to speak little, obey and be loyal to her husband, and to behave as a good woman; to govern her body and her household (including the cattle and horses) so as to avoid gossip, injury, and loss. If little is known of Deschamps's daughter, less is known of his wife, touchingly remembered in *Balade* 1184 for the abovementioned traits and also as his "amie" ("female friend") bestowed by God, signifying his love for her in courtly terms alongside those of domestic practicality. Before dismissing both poems for their formulaic vision of feminine perfection, we should remember that Deschamps need not have written of his family at all, let alone so affectionately. He may well have been the first French poet to write positively of family life.

By contrast, his writings about nonspecific women, those outside his family and friends, conform more to ill-tempered stereotype, as in *Balade* 269, also a rule for wives, but harshly humorless and misogynistic as it orders women to behave and obey as serfs. *Balade* 862, read by nineteenth-century critic Amédée Sarradin as a condemnation of the poet's wife and children, has been reinterpreted by Ian Laurie as a metaphorical comment on Deschamps's service to Blanche d'Orléans and the infant Charles VI (in Sinnreich-Levi 1998). *Balade* 1149, a rollicking complaint about the problems of marrying off a daughter, might be spoken by any modern father of the bride, simultaneously loving his daughter and bewailing the expense and uproar of a big wedding. In the final tally, for every stereotypically misogamous or misogynistic poem (see also, for example, *Balade* 1486: "Femme est plus fort lien qui soit" ["Woman is the strongest of all forms of bondage"]), Deschamps has also left us more appealing female-voiced counterparts, about sixty in all. Among these poems, some are courtly love dialogues in which a lady and knight either debate their love or discuss some topic of mutual interest (*Balades* 1026, 1302). In *Rondeau* 691, a lady bids her love farewell, and in *Virelai* 719, the lady withdraws her love from a disloyal lover. *Balade* 1159 presents the advice sought by a young man of a lady.

Woman as word itself, whether euphoniously or grammatically symbolic, also enters into Deschamps's female portraiture. After unsuccessfully wooing Peronne, the beloved of his deceased poetic idol, Guillaume de Machaut (1300–1377), as chronicled in the latter's *Voir Dit* (*True Tale*), Deschamps consoles himself, at least in rhyme, by winning the heart of one "sweet Gauteronne" (*Balades* 447, 493). The name-game ingeniously intertwines Deschamps's conflicting emotions and stylistic modes, as recently elucidated by James Wimsatt. The poet also capitalizes on the female force of allegorical figures such as France, Mother Church, Fortune, Necessity, and even the (human) Head imparted by their grammatical gender. In *Lay* 312, France, a woman first by grammar, then by Deschamps's talent for emotional evocation, as he shows the personified nation lamenting the death of Bertrand du Guesclin (1380), great hero of the Hundred Years' War, much as a woman might mourn the death of her lover.

Also as a poet of history, Deschamps was one of the first to invent a list of Nine Worthy Women, or *Neuf Preuses*, to complement the fourteenth-century French tradition of the *Neuf Preux* (Nine Worthy Men) epitomizing biblical, classical, and medieval heroism. Deschamps attempts to balance these by citing brave Amazons and powerful queens from

Antiquity and the Old Testament (*Autres Balades* 93 and 403). Appearing alongside the men, these women Worthies captivated popular imagination in poetry, tapestry, and courtly spectacle. Given this and other aforementioned aspects of his writings on women, Deschamps merits recognition as perhaps the most comprehensive, and comprehending, offered by any medieval French poet of women in all their perceived dimensions, both negative and positive, during this significant cultural period.

See also Chaucer, Geoffrey, Women in the Work of; Christine de Pizan; Griselda; Le Fèvre de Ressons, Jean; Marriage; Nine Worthy Women; *Roman de la Rose*, Debate of the; *Vertu du Sacrement de Mariage, Livre de la*

BIBLIOGRAPHY

Primary Sources
Christine de Pizan. "Une epistre a Eustace Mourel." In *Œuvres complètes de Christine de Pisan*, edited by Maurice Roy, 2: 295–301. Société des Anciens Textes Français [=SATF]. Paris: Firmin Didot, 1891.
———. "A Letter to Eustache Morel [and Morel's Answer]." In *The Selected Writings of Christine de Pizan*, edited and translated by Renate Blumenfeld-Kosinski and Kevin Brownlee, 109–13. New York: W. W. Norton, 1997.
Deschamps, Eustache. *L'Art de dictier*. Edited and translated by Deborah M. Sinnreich-Levi. East Lansing, Mich.: Colleagues Press, 1994.
———. "Le *Miroir de mariage* d'Eustache Deschamps: édition critique accompagnée d'une étude littéraire et linguistique." Edited by Monique Dufournaud-Engel. Ph.D. diss., McGill University, 1975. Abstract in *DAI* 36 (1975): 6734A.
———. *Œuvres complètes d'Eustache Deschamps*. Edited by Gaston Raynaud and the Marquis de Queux de Saint-Hilaire, 9. SATF. 11 vols. Paris: Firmin-Didot, 1878–1903. Reprint New York: Johnson, 1966.

Secondary Sources
Becker, Karin. *Eustache Deschamps: l'état actuel de la recherche*. Orléans: Paradigme, 1996.
Boudet, Jean-Patrice, and Hélène Millet, eds. *Eustache Deschamps en son temps*. Paris: Publications de la Sorbonne, 1997. [Annotated anthology of thematically grouped extracts from Deschamps's works].
Edwards, Robert R. "Some Pious Talk about Marriage." In *Matrons and Marginal Women in Medieval Society*, edited by Robert R. Edwards and Vickie L. Ziegler, 111–27. Woodbridge, U.K. and Rochester, N.Y.: Boydell & Brewer, 1995.
Grossel, Marie-Geneviève. "Sainte paysanne et épouse fidèle: l'image de Griseldis à l'épreuve des Miroirs de mariage." In *Autour d'Eustache Deschamps: Actes du Colloque de l'Université de Picardie, Amiens, 5–8 Novembre 1998*, edited by Danielle Buschinger, 103–26. Amiens, France: Presses du Centre d'Études Médiévales, Université de Picardie, 1999.
McMillan, Ann. "Men's Weapons, Women's War: The Nine Female Worthies, 1400–1600." *Medievalia* 5 (1979): 113–39.
Sinnreich-Levi, Deborah M., ed. *Eustache Deschamps, Courtier Poet: His Work and His World*. New York: AMS Press, 1998.
Wilson, Katharina M., and Elizabeth Makowski. *Wikked Wyves and the Woes of Marriage: Misogamous Literature from Juvenal to Chaucer*. Albany: State University of New York Press, 1990.
Wimsatt, James I. *Chaucer and His French Contemporaries: Natural Music in the Fourteenth Century*. Toronto: University of Toronto Press, 1991.

DEBORAH M. SINNREICH-LEVI

MONTEFELTRO, BATTISTA. *See* **Battista de Montefeltro Malatesta**

MORGAN LE FAY. The lady of the enchanted island of Avalon, Morgan (also Morgain la Fee, Fata Morgana, etc.) was King Arthur's formidable sister whose reputation, from her first appearance in the middle of the twelfth century until the end of the Middle Ages, suffers a remorseless decline. Her beauty and many talents, so warmly admired in the earliest texts, either fade or are applied to evil ends in later works until she seems the very antithesis of her former self. The only exception to this pattern is the account of the mortally wounded Arthur being taken to her for healing on the Isle of Avalon. This tale, which preserves her primary role as a healer, has firmly resisted change.

Morgan is first mentioned in the *Vita Merlini* (*Life of Merlin*) of Geoffrey of Monmouth, a long poem in Latin (c.1150). There the bard Taliesin describes how nine sisters rule benevolently over the "Fortunate Isle," which produces all kinds of food without cultivation. Morgan alone is described in detail:

Morgan le Fay, King Arthur's fairy sister, who reveals Lancelot and Guinevere's intrigues to him. Engraving by J. Dobie after painting by G. F. Watts. © Mary Evans Picture Library.

She who is first of them is more skilled in the healing art, and excels her sisters in the beauty of her person. Morgen [*sic*] is her name, and she has learned what useful properties all the herbs contain, so that she can cure all sick bodies. She also knows an art by which to change her shape, and to cleave the air on new wings [. . .] And men say that she has taught mathematics to her sisters.

It is to her that Arthur is brought for healing after the Battle of Camlann. This she promises to accomplish with her healing art if he remains with her for a long time.

In *Erec et Enide* and *Yvain*, two French verse romances (later twelfth century), Chrétien de Troyes also refers to the healing powers of Morgan, to whom he gives the title "le Fay." He adds, in the former poem, that she rules in the Isle of Avalon with her lover Guingamar and, in the latter, that she is the sister of Arthur, a relationship rapidly adopted by later writers. The *Gesta Regum Britanniae* (*Deeds of the Kings of Britain*), a Latin poem (mid-thirteenth century), establishes a romantic link between Morgan and Arthur, but this is not found elsewhere in medieval literature. Her appetite for lovers was widely recognized, however, extending even outside of Arthurian tradition to include figures such as Ogier le Danois (Ogier the Dane). In the *Roman d'Auberon* (fourteenth century), she marries Julius Caesar, and their son Auberon becomes king of Faery. In French Arthurian verse romance of the thirteenth century, Morgan remains a powerful and generally benevolent fay: in *Floriant et Florete*, for example, she is the hero's protector.

By contrast, in French Arthurian prose romance of the thirteenth century, Morgan's reputation erodes progressively. Although accounts conflict, she is usually identified as one of the daughters of the Duke and Duchess of Tintagel, and thus a half-, rather than full, sister of Arthur. Even though Arthur's father, King Uther, is responsible for the death of Morgan's father in the course of his ultimately successful attempt to sleep with the Duchess Igerne (or Ygerna), in the Vulgate Cycle (c.1215–1235), Morgan remains friendly with her half-brother, whom she carries off to Avalon in a boat after the Battle of Camlann. After her affair with Guiomar is broken up by Arthur's cousin Queen Guinevere, however, Morgan becomes the queen's bitter enemy and constantly seeks either to seduce Lancelot from her side or to expose their relationship. In the Prose *Tristan*, she tries to accomplish this latter design by sending to Arthur's court a magic drinking horn from which no unfaithful lady can drink without spilling, but she is foiled when one of Arthur's knights diverts it to King Mark's court in Cornwall.

In the Post-Vulgate Cycle (1230–1240), Morgan, here the wife of King Urien and mother of Yvain, becomes Arthur's enemy as well after he executes one of her lovers, and she incites another lover, Accolon, to try to kill the king with his own sword, Excalibur. Although this plot is foiled, she does manage to steal and dispose of the magical sheath that protects Arthur from injury. Seeking to take advantage of his vulnerability, she later sends her brother a poisoned mantle.

From a fay impervious to the passage of time, Morgan degenerates into a mere sorceress who must conceal her age through magic arts. These arts themselves are no longer linked to her supernatural powers as a fay, but are learned from wise men like Merlin, whom she seduces for his knowledge; nor do they extend beyond deception and illusion. Her once-prized favors are condemned as promiscuity and evidence of a hot and lustful nature in romances that celebrate the single-minded devotion of courtly lovers: in the *Prophecies de Merlin* (*Merlin's Prophecies*), Alexandre l'orphelin ("Alexander the orphan") even threatens to cut off his private parts rather than submit to her advances. The wise healer now seeks the death of others, especially the brother for whose care she first won fame, but her schemes are invariably and humiliatingly frustrated.

This harsh portrait begins to affect the treatment of Morgan in later verse romance. Thus in *Claris et Laris*, a French poem from the late thirteenth century, she kidnaps the two heroes (Claris and Laris) and imprisons them in an enchanted valley, a stratagem she widely employs in prose romance. Her enmity against Guinevere is offered as one motive for the action in *Sir Gawain and the Green Knight*, the great English poem from the late fourteenth century, but she is paid little attention elsewhere in Middle English literature until Sir Thomas Malory's prose *Le Morte Darthur* (1469–1470). Malory adopted the negative attitude toward Morgan that he found in his French prose sources, and since his is the version of Arthurian legend most widely known among English-speaking people, this accounts for the widespread perception of Morgan le Fay as little more than an evil witch.

Scholars who have studied the figure of Morgan have focused their attention on two main areas: her origins and the decline of her reputation. Some perceive the influence of Classical antecedents such as the Three Fates, from whose name is derived the word "fay," and allegorical females including Boethius's Lady Philosophy (c.524). Others have sought Morgan's origins in oral tradition and Celtic literature, identifying her variously with the Irish Muirgen (one of the names of the mermaid Liban); with the Morrigan, an Irish goddess of war and fertility noted for her shape-shifting powers and for her love–hate relationship with Cuchulainn (the great hero of the Ulster Cycle); with the Irish Macha who is linked with both the Morrigan and Badb (perhaps triple aspects of the one goddess); and with Modron, the Welsh version of the Old Celtic divine mother, Matrona. Morgan may indeed be able to trace her roots back to more than one of the above, as well as to others like the Irish Fand, who has Cuchulainn brought for healing to her island realm, then rewards him with her love for fighting on her behalf. It has also been argued that Morgan originates in Sicilian tradition, where the mirage known as Fata Morgana was believed to be a vision of Morgan's castle in the Otherworld.

While acknowledging that a number of motifs may have been borrowed from these sources, some scholars reject claims for Morgan's direct descent from such figures, seeing her rather as a creation of medieval literature. They argue, moreover, that the focus on antecedents has distracted attention from the role that Morgan plays in the medieval romances themselves. Close scrutiny of this role reveals the extent to which her reputation declines, in part because of the changing context in which she is placed. Because she acts the convenient part of the antagonist, she is aligned with villains such as Mark and Brehus Sans Pitie ("Merciless Brehus") against first Lancelot and Guinevere, then Arthur and all good knights.

Recognition of Morgan's degeneration has, in its turn, prompted attempts to explain it. Protagonists require antagonists, but why should a benevolent healer like Morgan be moved into the latter category? Three main theories have been advanced to account for Morgan's demise. First of all, the sympathy with which individual romances view the lovers who are their heroes and heroines inevitably casts their enemies in an unattractive light. In the Vulgate Cycle not only Morgan, but also Arthur and Gawain, behave badly at times, thus overshadowing the adultery of Guinevere and Lancelot. This technique of blackening the reputation of the offended parties is repeated in subsequent romances, particularly the Prose *Tristan*. Because Morgan takes Arthur to her Otherworld realm, she soon becomes associated with the widespread tradition of the fay who falls in love with a human and lures him to her realm. She thus is used as a temptress, the rejection of whose advances serves to demonstrate the loyalty of the knight to his lady. Moreover, since Morgan's name is linked with more than one lover, her promiscuity makes the unswerving commitment of the courtly lovers look admirable by contrast.

Another cause for the negative portrayal of Morgan and her sister fays is the growing hostility of the Church toward magic. Folk belief in fairies and other supernatural creatures, the survival of worship of pagan deities, and even herbal cures were originally tolerated as usually harmless superstitions. By the thirteenth century, however, they were increasingly seen as part of witchcraft that was linked to devil-worship and heresy. As the attitude of the Church toward these threats grew more severe, as witnessed by the rise of the Inquisition, so, it is surmised, writers grew more cautious about treating magic favorably in case they themselves became objects of suspicion.

The third explanation for Morgan le Fay's decline is male disapproval of a well-educated, powerful, and independent woman. She was perceived as a threat, not only by misogynistic clerics, but also by the patriarchal establishment. Whereas heroines such as Guinevere and Isolde rely on knights like Lancelot and Tristan to champion their cause, Morgan exercises power more directly, abducting and confining others by means of her own magic. She wields her power, moreover, for her own purposes, not for the greater good of Arthur and his kingdom.

The widespread tradition of the fay's affair with her lover in the Otherworld is thus perceived initially as a precious gift to be gained only by escaping from a hostile world in poems like Marie de France's *Lanval* (late twelfth century), a Breton *lai* (short romance). It is later reinterpreted, however, as the imprisonment of a good knight by an evil sorceress. The Grail romances carry this process one step farther when devils in the guise of beautiful women try to seduce the questing knight and damn his soul.

The process of decline is facilitated by fragmenting Morgan into a number of related figures or "avatars." The most important of these is the Lady of the Lake, a designation that seems to apply to more than one person. Her primary role is that of protector, initially of Lancelot, but later of Arthur as well. In earlier texts including the Vulgate Cycle and Ulrich von Zatzikhoven's *Lanzelet* (c.1194–1205), a Middle-High German verse romance composed in what is now Switzerland, she rears Lancelot as his foster mother in her watery realm; in the later prose romances, she gives advice to Arthur and protects him against Morgan's schemes on several occasions, most notably in warning that the mantle sent by his sister is poisoned and in aiding him in his fight against Accolon. In this role, she succeeds Merlin, who is imprisoned by another avatar (known variously as Nimue, Niniene, Niviene, and Viviane) after she has learned the secrets of his magic.

In her role as protector, the Lady of the Lake embodies the nurturing side of woman. Morgan, by contrast, comes increasingly to represent the devouring side, unrestrained in her sexual appetites, vengeful when crossed. Only the story of her bearing her mortally wounded brother at the last to the Isle of Avalon for healing recalls what she once was.

See also Arthurian Women; Enchantresses, Fays (*Fées*), and Fairies; Guinevere; Igerne; Lady of the Lake; Marie de France; Medea in the Middle Ages; Melusine; Witches

BIBLIOGRAPHY

Primary Sources

Chrétien de Troyes. *Erec et Enide*. Edited and translated [Modern French] with commentary by Michel Rousse. GF-Flammarion, 763. Bilingue. Paris: Garnier-Flammarion, 1994. [Bilingual Old-French-Modern French ed.].

———. *Erec and Enide*. Translated by Ruth H. Cline. Athens: University of Georgia Press, 2000.

———. *Yvain*. Edited and translated with commentary by David F. Hult. Lettres gothiques. Paris: Livre de Poche, 1994. [Bilingual Old-French-Modern French ed.].

———. *Complete Romances of Chrétien de Troyes*. Translated with introduction by David Staines. Bloomington: Indiana University Press, 1990.

[*Claris et Laris*]. *Li Romans de Claris et Laris*. Edited by Johann Alton. Bibliothek des literarischen Vereins in Stuttgart, 169. Tübingen, Germany: Literarischer Verein in Stuttgart, 1884. Reprint Amsterdam 1966.

Floriant et Florete. Edited by Harry F. Williams. University of Michigan Publications in Language & Literature, 23. Ann Arbor: University of Michigan, 1947.

Geoffrey of Monmouth. *Vita Merlini/ Life of Merlin*. Edited with translation and commentary by Basil Clarke. Cardiff: University of Wales Press/Board of Celtic Studies, 1973.

Gesta regum Britanniae. Critical ed. by Francisque Michel. Bordeaux: Gounouilhou, 1862.

[Grail Legends, French]. *Le Livre du Graal*, vol.1. Critical ed. and translation [Modern French] by Philippe Walter et al. 2 vols. Paris: Éditions de la Pléiade/Gallimard, 2001–2003.

Lancelot: roman en prose du XIIIᵉ siècle. Edited by Alexandre Micha. 9 vols. Textes Littéraires Français [=TLF], 247, 249, 262, 278, 283, 286, 288, 307, 315. Geneva: Droz, 1978–1983.

Malory, Thomas. *Le Morte d'Arthur.* In *Malory: Complete Works.* Edited by Eugène Vinaver. Originally 1954. 2nd ed. Oxford and New York: Oxford University Press, 1971.

Marie de France. *Lais.* Edited and translated by Philippe Walter. Paris: Folio classique/Gallimard, 2000. [Bilingual Old-French-Modern French ed.].

————. *The Lais of Marie de France.* Translated by Glyn S. Burgess and Keith Busby. Original ed. 1986. New ed. Harmondsworth, Middlesex, U.K. and New York: Penguin, 1999.

[*Les Prophecies de Merlin*] *Merlin: 1498.* 3 vols. London: Scolar Press, 1975. [Facsimile reprint of Antoine Vérard's 1498 Paris ed.].

[Prose *Tristan*]. *Le Roman de Tristan en prose.* Edited by Joël Blanchard et al. 3 vols. Classiques Français du Moyen Âge, 123, 133, 135. Paris: Honoré Champion, 1997.

Le Roman d'Auberon. Critical ed. by Jean Subrenat. TLF, 202. Geneva: Droz, 1973.

Ulrich von Zatzikhoven. *Lanzelet, eine Erzählung.* Edited by K. A. Hahn. Afterword and bibliography by F. Norman. Deutsche Neudrucke. Texte des Mittelalters. Berlin: De Gruyter, 1965. Originally Frankfurt: H. L. Bronner, 1845.

————. *Lanzelet.* Translated by Kenneth G. T. Webster. Revised by R. S. Loomis. New York: Columbia University Press, 1951.

Sir Gawain and the Green Knight. Edited and translated by William Vantuono. Notre Dame, Ind.: University of Notre Dame Press, 1999. [Bilingual Middle English-Modern English ed.].

Secondary Sources

Berthelot, Anne. "Merlin and the Ladies of the Lake." *Arthuriana* 10 (2000): 55–81. Reprint in *Merlin: A Casebook*, edited by Peter H. Goodrich and Raymond H. Thompson, 162–85. New York and London: Routledge, 2003.

Bogdanow, Fanni. "Morgain's Role in the Thirteenth-Century Prose Romances of the Arthurian Cycle." *Medium Aevum* 38 (1969): 123–33.

Fries, Maureen. "From the Lady to the Tramp: The Decline of Morgan le Fay in Medieval Romance." *Arthuriana* 4 (1994): 1–18.

Harf-Lancner, Laurence. *Les Fées au moyen âge: Morgane et Mélusine. La Naissance des fées.* Geneva: Slatkine, 1984.

Jennings, Margaret, C. S. J. "'Heavens defend me from that Welsh Fairy' (Merry Wives of Windsor, V, 5, 85): The Metamorphosis of Morgain la Fee in the Romances." *Court and Poet.* Edited by Glyn S. Burgess, 197–205. Liverpool: Cairns, 1981.

Loomis, Roger Sherman. "Morgain la Fee and the Celtic Goddesses." *Speculum* 20 (1945): 183–203. Reprint in Loomis, *Wales and the Arthurian Legend*, 105–30. Cardiff: University of Wales Press, 1956. Reprint Folcroft, Pa.: Folcroft Press, 1969.

Olstead, Myra. "Morgan le Fay in Malory's Morte Darthur." *Bibliographical Bulletin of the International Arthurian Society* 19 (1967): 128–38.

Paton, Lucy Allen. *Studies in the Fairy Mythology of Arthurian Romance.* Boston: Ginn, 1903. 2nd ed. by Roger Sherman Loomis. New York: Burt Franklin, 1960.

Thompson, Raymond H. "The First and Last Love: Morgan le Fay and Arthur." In *Arthurian Women: A Casebook*, edited by Thelma S. Fenster, 331–44. Arthurian Characters and Themes, 3. Garland Reference Library of the Humanities, 1499. New York and London: Garland, 1996.

Wais, Kurt. "Morgain amante d'Accalon et rivale de Guenievre." *Bibliographical Bulletin of the International Arthurian Society* 18 (1966): 137–49.

Wathelet-Willem. Jeanne. "La Fée Morgan dans la chanson de geste." *Cahiers de Civilisation Médiévale* 13 (1970): 209–19.

RAYMOND H. THOMPSON

MOTHERING. *See* **Childhood and Child-Rearing in the Middle Ages**

MULIERES SANCTAE (early to mid-13th century). A term most closely associated with Jacques de Vitry in his biography of Marie d'Oignies, *Mulieres sanctae* or *mulieres religiosae* literally means "holy" or "religious women." These terms were applied to loosely knit communities of noncloistered, pious women who first emerged in the early thirteenth century, usually in urban centers. In northern Europe, such groups would eventually be known as the beguines, which found their counterparts in groups like the Humiliati ("the Humbled Ones," a preaching movement practicing self-mortification, care of the sick and poor as means of doing penance) of Italy. Jacques de Vitry (c.1160/70–1240), an Augustinian canon regular (a semi-monastic cleric, as opposed to "secular canon"), preacher, crusader, historian, one-time bishop of Acre (now Akko, in Israel), and eventual cardinal bishop of Tusculum (near Rome), became an avid advocate and defender of these groups in northern Europe and was particularly influenced by the *mulieres sanctae* of Oignies in the diocese of Liège, in what is now Belgium. His chief work on the subject is a biography of Marie d'Oignies (c.1177–1213), considered to be a prototypical beguine.

Jacques de Vitry was probably born in the north of France into a wealthy upper-middle-class family. He was educated in Paris, and from Paris went to Oignies where he became an Augustinian canon in the monastery of Saint Nicholas from 1211 to 1216. During these years, Jacques became familiar with the groups of holy women proliferating in the Low Countries. He was impressed by their simple and austere lifestyle as well as their profound spirituality. These women, living either in communities or at home, were committed to the *vita apostolica* (apostolic life). They supported themselves by their own labor (very often hospital work) and pledged themselves to lives of poverty and chastity, all without taking a solemn, lifetime vow, as is required in monasticism. They practiced extreme asceticism, and their religious experiences often assumed a mystical form. It is important to stress, however, that these women were strictly orthodox: their spirituality had a "Christocentric" orientation (focused on the figure of Jesus), with a deep reverence for the priesthood and the sacraments. The use of mental imagery in describing their mystical raptures, as well as an intense Eucharistic devotion (focused on the Body and Blood of Christ), was especially characteristic of their spirituality.

Jacques was particularly affected by Marie d'Oignies, the spiritual nucleus of a group of clerics, laypeople, and female mystics. He wrote a biography of Marie shortly after her death (1213) at the request of Bishop Fulk of Toulouse, who had been driven from his see (official domain) by Cathar heretics. Jacques accordingly presents Marie as a model of a new kind of sanctity—a female sanctity capable of exorcising the heresy afflicting the Church in his time. In addition to providing a lively account of these communities of *mulieres sanctae*, Jacques explores the depth of Marie's piety, describes her religious observances, and reveals the extent of his own indebtedness to her. Although Jacques served as Marie's confessor, she was, by his own admission, his "spiritual mother" who assisted him immeasurably in his preaching, allaying his nervousness, assisting in preparation, and providing inspiration. In fact, Jacques describes himself as Marie's instrument in preaching. But Thomas de Cantimpré, the Dominican canon regular who wrote a supplement to Jacques's biography of Marie (c.1230), goes much farther: according to

Thomas, Jacques was drawn initially to Oignies by reports of Marie's sanctity; he became a canon regular at her request and was ordained at her behest.

Jacques intended the biography of Marie as a propagandistic tool aimed at gaining official recognition for these women as an independent female order. While recognizing the spiritual merits of the *mulieres sanctae*, he was also aware of the harsh economic realities that made groups of pious women a necessary option; there was insufficient room in convents to absorb the number of surplus, unmarriageable women (part of the phenomenon historians have labeled *Frauenfrage*). Even so, Jacques realized that without the protection of an official rule validating their way of life, these unaffiliated groups of laywomen would be open to slanderous attacks. In 1216, Jacques acted as advocate for the *mulieres sanctae* before the Papal Curia (papal court in Rome), but he only received verbal approbation from Honorius III (d. 1227) that they could continue to live in common, assisting one another by mutual exhortation. Gregory IX (c.1148–1241), a friend of Jacques de Vitry's who had actually read his biography of Marie, made the papal recognition more formal in the bull *Gloriam virginalem*, but this still did not constitute the rule that Jacques had hoped for. Ultimately, his efforts on their behalf were defeated by Canon 13 of Lateran IV (1214), which forbade the formation of new orders.

Jacques de Vitry's biography of Marie is important from a historical standpoint in that it is the first biography of a female mystic and thus inaugurated a new kind of hagiography. He also provides an eyewitness account bearing on the origins of the beguine movement. While his thoughts on the *mulieres sanctae* are concentrated within this biography, Jacques makes fleeting references to them in his other works. Furthermore, his letters, histories, and sermons—all of which are informed by his extensive travels—indicate a comprehensive interest in popular piety and provide valuable insights regarding parallel movements of holy women such as the early Franciscans or the Humiliati. Finally, because of Marie's influence on his preaching, Thomas's sermons provide an intriguing source in that respect as well.

Although Thomas de Cantimpré's supplement casts doubt on Jacques de Vitry's commitment to the cause of the *mulieres sanctae* as he rose within the ecclesiastical hierarchy, it is nevertheless clear that Jacques remained faithful to the memory of Marie, carrying a relic of her with him everywhere. He showered rich gifts on Oignies, and granted indulgences to all those who would revere Marie's relics. He was eventually buried at Oignies per his expressed wishes.

See also Beguines; Clare of Assisi, St.; *Frauenfrage*; Guglielmites; Hagiography (Female Saints); Relics and Medieval Women; Rules for Canonesses, Nuns, and Recluses

BIBLIOGRAPHY

Primary Sources

Jacques de Vitry. *Vita Mariae Oigniacensis*. Edited by Daniel Papebroeck. In *Acta Sanctorum*, June, vol. 4 (Antwerp, 1707): 636–66; In *Acta Sanctorum . . . editio novissima*, June, vol. 5 (Paris, 1867): 542–72.

Thomas de Cantimpré. *Supplementum*. Edited by Arnold Rayssius. In *Acta Sanctorum* June, vol. 4 (Antwerp, 1707): 666–76; In *Acta Sanctorum . . . editio novissima*, June, vol. 5 (Paris, 1867): 572–81.

Jacques de Vitry and Thomas de Cantimpré. *Two Lives of Marie d'Oignies*. Translated with introduction and notes by Margot King. 4th ed. Toronto: Peregrina, 1998. [Both Jacques's and Thomas's *Lives* in English].

Jacques de Vitry. *Historia Occidentalis*. Critical ed. by John F. Hinnebusch. Spicilegium Friburgense, 17. Fribourg, Switzerland: University Press, 1972. [Latin only. See esp. pp. 27, 116–18, 144–48].

———. *Historia Occidentalis*. Translated (French) by Gaston Duchet-Suchaux. Introduction and notes by Jean Longère. Sagesses chrétiennes. Paris: Éditions du Cerf, 1997.

———. [*Letters*]. *Les Lettres de Jacques de Vitry*. Critical ed. by R. B. C. Huygens. Leiden: E. J. Brill, 1960. [See letter of October 1216 describing the *mulieres sanctae* of Lombardy and Umbria, pp. 71–78].

———. *Sermones in epistolas et evangelia dominicalia*. Edited by Damianus a Ligno. Antwerp, 1575.

———. *Sermones de sanctis*. Cologne, MS Starch GB, fol. 181. [These have never been edited].

———. *Sermones vulgares* or *Ad status*. Paris, Bibliothèque nationale de France, MS lat. 17509. [Partially edited, *see next entry*].

———. *Sermones vulgares* or *Ad status*. Edited by by J. B. Pitra. In *Analecta novissima spicilegii Solesmensis, Altera continuatio*, vol. 2: *Tusculana*. Paris, 1888. [See esp. pp. 449–50].

———. *The Exempla, or, Illustrative Stories from the Sermones vulgares of Jacques de Vitry*. Edited with introduction and notes by Thomas F. Crane. Folk-Lore Society, 26. London: D. Nutt, 1890. Reprint Nendeln, Liechtenstein: Kraus, 1967. [Latin text only, see esp. p. 36].

———. *Sermones feriales et communes*. Brussels, Bibliothèque Royale MS 1122–1124 f.1ra–80rb.

———. *Die Exempla aus den Sermones feriales et communes des Jakob von Vitry*. Edited by J. Greven. Heidelberg: Carl Winter, 1914. [Latin text. See p. 32].

———. *Ad virgines* Edited by J. Grevens. "Der Ursprung de Beginenwesens." *Historisches Jahrbuch* 35 (1914): 43–49. [Sermon probably written for a community of *mulieres sanctae*].

———. [*Sermons* relevant to women]. *The Faces of Women in the Sermons of Jacques de Vitry*. Edited and translated with commentary by Carolyn Muessig. Toronto: Peregrina, 1999. [Select sermons from the above groups; English texts only].

Secondary Sources

Bolton, Brenda M. "*Mulieres sanctae*." *Studies in Church History* 10 (1973): 77–97. Reprint in *Women in Medieval Society*, edited by Susan Mosher Stuard, 141–58. Philadelphia: University of Pennsylvania Press, 1976.

———. "*Vitae Matrum*: A Further Aspect of the *Frauenfrage*." In *Medieval Women*, edited by Derek Baker, 253–73. Subsidia, 1. Ecclesiastical History Society. Oxford: Basil Blackwell, 1978. Reprint 1981.

Devlin, Dennis. "Feminine Lay Piety in the High Middle Ages: The Beguines." *Distant Echoes. Medieval Religious Women*. Edited by J. A. Nicholas and Lillian Shank. 1: 183–96. Cistercian Studies, 71. Kalamazoo, Mich.: Medieval Institute, 1984.

Geyer, Iris. *Maria von Oignies. Eine hochmittelalterliche Mystikerin zwischen Ketzerei und Rechtgläubichkeit*. Europäische Hochschulschriften, 454. Frankfurt: Peter Lang, 1992.

King, Margot II. *The* Mulieres religiosae *of the Diocese of Liège: A Select Bibliography*. Toronto: Peregrina, 1998.

McGinn, Bernard. "*Mulieres religiosae*: Experiments in Female Mysticism." In McGinn, *The Flowering of Mysticism. Men and Women in the New Mysticism, 1200–1350*. New York: Crossroads, 1998.

Simons, Walter. *Cities of Ladies: Beguine Communities in the Medieval Low Countries, 1200–1565*. Philadelphia: University of Pennsylvania Press, 2001.

Wiethaus, Ulrike. "The Death Song of Marie d'Oignies: Mystical Sound and Hagiographical Politics in Medieval Lorraine." In *The Texture of Society: Medieval Women in the Southern Low Countries*, edited by Ellen E. Kittell and Mary A. Suydam, ch. 7. The New Middle Ages. New York: Palgrave Macmillan, 2004.

DYAN ELLIOTT

MURASAKI SHIKIBU (c.973–c.1015). Lady Murasaki, as she is usually called in English, authored what is arguably the world's first novel, *Genji Monogatari* (*The Tale of*

Genji), *Murasaki Shikibu nikki* (*The Diary of Murasaki Shikibu*), and a set of poetic memoirs (*kashu*). Like other aristocratic women of her time, she is known by a so-briquet because her personal name is not recorded. *Shikibu*, meaning "secretariat," derives from the office of a male member of her family, and *Murasaki* is the name of the fictional Genji's young wife, which tradition has attached to the author. In her diary, Murasaki relates a playful exchange between herself and a courtier, which may be the origin of the pseudonym.

Murasaki's father was Fujiwara no Tametoki, a governor of Echizen known for his Chinese poetry. From an early age she studied the strictly male subject of Chinese literature with him. According to her diary, she was so much more adept than her brother Nobunori that her father wished she had been born a boy. In a set of autobiographical poems, she tells of travels with her father in the summer of 996, and soon after that she entered a brief but happy marriage to a much older man, Fujiwara no Nobutaka (d. 1001), who already had number of other wives. Her husband is described by their famous contemporary, Sei Shonagon (966–c.1017) in her *Makura no soshi* (*The Pillow Book*) as distinctive and flamboyant. Mur-

Murasaki Shikibu, Japanese court lady and author of *Genji Monogatari* (*Tale of the Genji*). © The Art Archive.

asaki's only daughter, Kenshi, born in 999, went on to rise in the aristocracy, becoming a major poet in her own right. During the years 1005–1007, Murasaki became a lady-in-waiting to Empress Shoshi, the second consort of Emperor Ichijo.

Beginning in around the early ninth century, imported Chinese influences underwent a native transformation into new Japanese patterns; these became known as Heian Court Culture, named after the Japanese capital Heian-kyo. In the Heian period (794–1192), the most highly esteemed literature was poetry and prose in *kanbun*, a method of writing classical Chinese embellished with Japanese reading symbols. In contrast to the public nature of kanbun, which was used exclusively by men, Heian women used their own gendered literary mode, called *kana* (Okada), then *hiragana* writing, a phonetic syllabary (list of written characters, each representing a syllable) developed to transcribe the sounds of vernacular Japanese and to provide a private or supplementary mode of social communication and artistic expression. Murasaki Shikibu's hiragana writings are product of the aristocratic culture characterizing the eleventh century, the height of the Heian period.

The early Heian *nikki* (diary), was a carefully dated kanbun record of weather, nature, and recent public events with little personal comment. However, the female-authored diaries of middle-ranking aristocratic women from prominent literary families became prevalent between the mid-tenth to mid-twelfth centuries. This *nyobo bungaku* (court lady literature) reflects the women's deeply nuanced feelings about their limited and closeted existence. *Murasaki Shikibu nikki*, is both a chronological record of her own private life and an intimate account of the various court ceremonies centering on the birth of the second son of the Emperor Ichijo. Written about 1008–1010, it retrospectively covers the three previous years when she was in attendance on the second consort, following the death of her husband. *Murasaki Shikibu nikki* contains three major sections: a microscopic description of the birth of Prince Atsuhira, the first child of the Empress Shoshi; a letter to a friend that describes people in the court and relates jealous peer reaction to Murasaki's scholarship; and a collection of court anecdotes revealing the realities of life at the Heian court during the period of its greatest glory. Although some early twentieth-century critics disparaged the seemingly trivial concerns of female diaries, many readers now appreciate the ways in which they reflect the gender restrictions at that time.

While the *Murasaki Shikibu nikki* reflects the realities of court life as a diary should, the *Genji Monogatari*, being a novel, describes the court as it should ideally be. *Monogatari* meant either gibberish, idle talk, or a work of prose fiction in the vernacular, as opposed to kanbun. While Murasaki probably was not the first woman to compose prose fiction in the vernacular, she was the first to write a *tsukur monogatari* (fabricated tale), of lasting literary value. No earlier Japanese prose fiction by a woman survives. *Genji Monogatari* relates the amorous career of the courtly ideal, Genji, the Shining Prince. The story begins with his first love affair with his stepmother, Lady Fujitsubo (whom his emperor father married because she resembled Genji's dead mother), and ends with the adultery of his young wife, Onna San-no-miya. In between these two milestones are his relationships with two wives and a long series of ladies. Twice as long as the Russian Lev Tolstoi's monumental *Voina i Mir* (*War and Peace*, 1864–1869), the English translation of *Genji* runs 1,090 pages and presents 430 characters ranging over four generations. The various romantic interludes seem like separate episodes and amount to independent short stories within the main theme of the novel. The action of *Genji* can be divided roughly into four parts: Part 1 (chapters 1–21) describes the world of the Shining Prince, his coming of age, and his first disappointments; Part 2 (chapters 22–33), shows Genji at the height of his happiness, surrounded by the several women he loves; In Part 3 (chapters 34–44), Genji suffers retributive justice; and Part 4 (chapters 45–54), describes the attenuation of Genji's line.

Genji can be considered the first novel, if by novel we mean a work of narrative fiction in which the chief interests are plot and character. Remarkably sophisticated when compared to European works of the same century, *Genji* is notable for its psychological realism, narrative voice, and literary critical acumen. From the time of its composition c.1002 through today, *Genji* has received wide acclaim. Murasaki tells how the book came to the attention of the court soon after its composition, and its established fame fifty years later is attested in diaries. At some point in the twelfth century, scholars became engaged in producing "authoritative" versions of *Genji*, and from that time on, its place in the canon was secure despite occasional Buddhist and Confucian attacks on fictional works. One of the first literary works to be printed using moveable type in Japan, *Genji* appeared in five printed editions in 1650. The text was first fully translated into English by Arthur

Waley in 1935; a critically acclaimed translation by Edward Seidensticker appeared in 1976. This novel, representing the essence of Japanese culture to generations of Japanese and comparative literary scholars, continues to inspire literary commentaries to this day.

See also Abutsu-ni; Christine de Pizan; Izumi Shikibu; Leonor López de Córdoba; Marie de France; Perpetua, St.; Sei Shonagon

BIBLIOGRAPHY

Primary Sources
[All are English texts only unless specifically noted otherwise].
Murasaki Shikibu. [*Murasaki Shikibu nikki*]. *Diary.* Translated with introduction by Richard Bowring. Penguin Classics. London and New York: Penguin, 1996.
———. [*Murasaki Shikibu Nikki; Kashu*]. *Her Diary and Poetic Memoirs: A Translation and Study* by Richard Bowring. Princeton Library of Asian Translations. Princeton, N.J.: Princeton University Press, 1982. Reprint, 1985. [English translation with excellent introduction and notes].
———. [*Genji Monogatari*]. *The Tale of Genji.* Translated by Royall Tyler. 2 vols. New York: Viking, 2001.
——— *The Tale of Genji.* Translated by Edward G. Seidensticker. New York: Alfred A. Knopf, 1976. Reprint 1978. Abridged eds. New York: Vintage, 1985, 1990.
———. *The Tale of Genji. A Novel in Six Parts.* Translated by Arthur Waley. Boston: Houghton Mifflin, 1935.
———. [*Tale of Genji*, selections]. *A String of Flowers: Untied Love Poems from the* Tale of Genji. Translated by Jane Reichold with Hatsue Kawamura. Berkeley, Calif.: Stonebridge Press, 2003.

Secondary Sources
Bargen, Doris G. *A Woman's Weapon: Spirit Possession in the* Tale of Genji. Honolulu: University of Hawaii Press, 1997.
Bowring, Richard. *The Tale of Genji.* Landmarks in World Literature. Cambridge: Cambridge University Press, 1988.
Cranston, Edwin. "Murasaki's Art of Fiction." *Japan Quarterly* 18 (1971): 207–13.
Field, Norma. *The Splendor of Longing in the* Tale of Genji. Princeton, N.J.: Princeton University Press, 1987.
Harding, Carol E. "'True Lovers': Love and Irony in Murasaki Shikibu and Christine de Pizan." In *Crossing the Bridge: Comparative Essays on Medieval European and Heian Japanese Women Writers,* edited by Barbara Stevenson and Cynthia Ho, 153–73. New York and Houndmills, U.K.: Palgrave St. Martin's, 2000.
Ho, Cynthia. "Words Alone Cannot Express: Epistles in Marie de France and Murasaki Shikibu." In *Crossing the Bridge,* 133–52. See above.
Keene, Donald. *Seeds in the Heart: Japanese Literature from Earliest Times to the Late Sixteenth Century.* New York: Henry Holt, 1993.
———. *Travelers of a Hundred Years. The Japanese as Revealed through 1,000 Years of Diaries.* New York: Henry Holt, 1989.
McCullough, Helen C. *Brocade by Night: "Kokin Wakashu" and the Court Style in Modern Japanese Court Poetry.* Stanford, Calif.: Stanford University Press, 1985.
Miner, Earl. ed. *Principles of Classical Japanese Literature.* Princeton, N.J.: Princeton University Press, 1985.
Morris, Ivan. *The World of the Shining Prince: Court Life in Ancient Japan.* New York: Penguin, 1964.
Okada, H. Richard. "Speaking for: Surrogates and the *Tale of Genji.*" In *Crossing the Bridge,* 5–27. *See above under* Harding.
Pekarik, Andrew, ed. *Ukifune. Love in the Tale of Genji.* New York: Columbia University Press, 1982.
Schalow, Paul G., and Janet A. Walker, eds. *The Woman's Hand: Gender and Theory in Japanese Women's Writing.* Stanford, Calif.: Stanford University Press, 1996.

Shirane, Haruo. *The Bridge of Dreams. A Poetics of the* Tale of Genji. Stanford, Calif.: Stanford University Press, 1987.

CYNTHIA HO

MUSCOVY, WOMEN IN (c.1300–c.1450). The situation of women in Muscovy (the center of medieval Russia: first confined to what is now modern Moscow and greatly expanding from the 1300s to the 1600s) encapsulates an important cross-cultural interaction involving early Rus' (indigenous), Byzantine Christian and Mongol cultures (the Mongols, ruled by khans, having originated in the steppes of central Asia and who brutally overran much of China and continued all the way to Eastern Europe, thirteenth century)—and also of how historians have learned to interpret the impact of these influences on women's lives. Elite secular women in Muscovy were allegedly secluded; that is, wives and daughters lived under the same roof as their husbands and fathers but in separate rooms, and aristocratic Muscovite women were forbidden to be seen on urban streets unless they wore veils or traveled in closed carriages. Examination of the extent to which this seclusion actually occurred, why, and from which cultural influences revises several longstanding assumptions about Muscovite, Mongol, and related cultures and their verifiable treatment of women, within the broader system of cultural stereotyping, old and new.

Donald Ostrowski, in his recent penetrating analysis of the Mongol presence in medieval Muscovy overall, portrays medieval Russian history as a special case, in comparison to medieval Europe, because of its merging of Eastern and Western cultures in a manner quite distinct from the better-known cultural fusion and fission between Rome (West) and Byzantium (East) and the added Mongol (or, less correctly, Tatar) element. In addition, the Mongol domination (the fabled "Tatar Yoke") under the Qipchaq Khanate (traditionally called the "Golden Horde": the portion of the Mongol Empire allotted to Jochi, son of Chingiz [Genghis] Khan in c.1227), lasting from 1237 to c.1448 in Muscovy, has, since c.1445, been stereotyped by the Russian Church and the Ukrainian nationalist historians as a period of unrelenting barbarism, utterly devoid of enlightenment of any sort and from which all bad aspects of Russian culture originate. In terms of women's lives, this anti-Mongol viewpoint held that the practice of their seclusion derived from the Mongols and represented yet another example of barbaric (i.e., non-Western) oppression of women, or, that because seclusion was strictly ill intentioned, it must have come from the "evil" Mongol invaders. But Ostrowski and others have found neither notion to be true.

At some point respectable Muscovite women were indeed secluded, based on the record of one of the first European visitors there, Sigmund von Herberstein (d. 1566), in his *Rerum Moscoviticarum commentarii* (*Notes upon Russia*), when he affirms, "they consider no woman virtuous unless she live shut up at home, and so closely guarded that she could go out nowhere" (*Notes upon Russia*, trans. Major, 1: 93; Ostrowski, 64). But just when this custom first began in Muscovy has not yet been determined. In any case, it could not have come from the Mongols, since, as several historians, both early—Marco Polo (d. 1324) and Willem van Ruysbroeck (William of Rubruck, d. c.1270)—and modern, have noted, Mongol women enjoyed a prominent role in the activities of their encampment. Not only were their elite women not secluded, but their husbands included them in decision making and heeded their political advice. This is related via several examples in the *Yuan chao bi shih* (*Secret History of the Mongols*) and in the Mamluk historian al-'Umarī (fourteenth century; cited in Ostrowski, 65). No level of Mongol steppe-nomadic culture seems to have secluded its women. Upper-class women were neither secluded nor veiled, yet they received much respect during this time—a unique juxtaposition, as shall be explained later—even after adopting Islam, until after the fall of the Qipchaq Khanate (sixteenth century) when veiling among Muscovite women was attested. While men were still superior, women commoners and aristocrats were certainly better off than they would be later, when Mongol civilization supposedly "progressed" and consequently stratified, and when, inevitably, with stratification came patriarchy. Ostrowski's affirmations in this regard for Russia, along with those of historians of the ancient Mediterranean and Near East, unknowingly parallel those of Joan Kelly and others concerning Western European women's autonomy and rights, most prevalent in the early Middle Ages, and their decline as they moved closer to the Renaissance.

Returning to the question of seclusion and its origins, it did not come from the Mongols. Some modern scholars suggest that it probably grew out of indigenous Rus' culture (itself a mix of Slavic, Viking, and other mores) or through contact with Muslim Near Eastern traders. Muscovite women were probably not secluded until the late fourteenth century or perhaps even the sixteenth century (Kollmann 1983; Halperin). However, Ostrowski points to the more likely Byzantine influence, citing a variety of firsthand sources and modern findings (Laiou; Runciman), since elite Byzantine women were secluded probably up until the eleventh century, after which the custom remained more as a nostalgic ideal than a reality. The practice of veiling—more liberating because it "enclosed" women while allowing them to interact with the outside world (though on a restricted basis)—continued. But the Byzantine practice of seclusion differed from the Russian version and may well have disappeared some five hundred years before the Muscovite Churchmen adopted it. This leads Ostrowski to the at least provisory conclusion that these theologians formulated their version out of a learned, retrospective, but flawed, ideal notion of Byzantium, at that time the supreme ecclesiastical (Church-centered) culture.

What the Muscovite seclusion issue does cause us to ponder is that a historically more advanced, Christian civilization (Byzantium) once again proves to be more restrictive of women than a more primitive one (the Mongols). Yet the framework for such judgments reflects a modern pro-Western-Christian bias. As Ostrowski reminds us, from the medieval Rus's more Eastern perspective, Byzantium may have been the ideal Christian state, but it had "sold out" to the Romans and was thus punished by destructive Turkish invasions (fifteenth century). By contrast, the Mongols represented the ideal secular elite empire by this time.

The purpose of seclusion itself—and its more mobile variation, veiling—may require a less negative interpretation than moderns usually and understandably accord it. In Muslim society, for example, it gauged the degree of respect due to women proportionate to the husband's wealth and position: a good, successful man was a strong protector of his women; his prosperity enabled him to afford extra living space for them. On the darker side, in cases where husbands abused their wives (as tolerated and even condoned in Muslim law), it furnished the woman some separation. The Muscovite version improved on this aspect by making women's quarters a safety zone that men could not enter, thereby distinguishing it from a harem (Runciman). Despite the latter, and although Christians battled them as murderous infidels through much of the Middle Ages, Muslim society rightly considered itself an advanced society with all the attendant paradoxes for women's lot; seclusion and veiling were part of its stratification. Likewise in China, footbinding was practiced, though not among the "rougher" Mongols there. Similar tendencies prevailed in Muscovy, whether out of primal dominating instincts or conscious emulation of superior cultures: secluding women had become a mark of cultural prestige. When we examine the attitudes of the Church Fathers toward women, we find that, in attempting to implement their misogyny in social practice, advanced medieval Christian societies did no better. Around the world, women tolerated and even helped to perpetuate these confining practices because they did minimize the danger of rape and other unwelcome advances. It is also important to remember that in unabashedly primitive, aggressive societies, there was no point in secluding or veiling women, since their men were too crude to have obeyed the practice.

Finally, although Muscovite women were undeniably second-class citizens, they were not slaves, and therefore were entitled to property and legal rights (Levy). Also, a man desiring a woman could not abduct and rape her and then expect to legitimize his crime through marriage: this was not allowed by the c.1280 Novgorod code, the *Zakon sudnyj ljudem* (*Court Law for the People*). All of which pales, as reality invariably does, beside the mythical power of women in the vast concept of "Mother Russia" in folktale, literature, spirituality, and art originating in Slavic lore since the early Middle Ages, as Joanna Hubbs has surveyed.

See also Concubines; Footbinding; Marriage; *Periculoso*; Rape; Slaves, Female; Virginity

BIBLIOGRAPHY

Primary Sources

Herberstein, Sigmund von. *Rerum Moscoviticarum commentarii.* [Facsimile reprint of 1571 Basel ed.]. Frankfurt, Germany: Minerva, 1964.

———. *Notes upon Russia.* Translated, edited and introduced by R. H. Major. Works issued by the Hakluyt Society, 10, 12. 2 vols. London: Hakluyt Society, 1851–1852. Reprint New York: Burt Franklin, 1963.

Polo, Marco. *Il milione.* Critical ed. by Ruggero Ruggieri. Biblioteca dell'Archivum Romanicum, 1: 200. Florence: Olschki, 1986.

———. *Travels of Marco Polo.* Translated by Henry Yule. Revised with notes by Henri Cordier. 2 vols. New York: Dover, 1993. [Reprints Yule's complete English trans. (1903) with Cordier's copious notes and addenda (1920)].

———. *Travels of Marco Polo.* Translated by William Marsden. Edited and revised by Manuel Komroff. Introduction by Jason Goodwin. New York: Modern Library, 2001. [Abridged ed.].

Secret History of the Mongols. Translated with commentary by Francis W. Cleaves. Harvard-Yenching Institute. Cambridge, Mass.: Harvard University Press, 1982.

Willem van Ruysbroeck. *Itinera et relationes Fratrum minorum, saeculi XIII et XIV.* In *Sinica franciscana*, 1, edited by Anastasius van den Wyngaert. Florence (Quaracchi): College of St. Bonaventure, 1929.

———. *The Mission of Friar William of Rubruck: His Journey to the Court of the Great Khan Möngke, 1253–1255.* Translated, introduced, and annotated by Peter Jackson with David Morgan. Works issued by the Hakluyt Society, 2nd ser., 173. London: Hakluyt Society, 1990. [English text only; replaces the 1900 Rockhill trans. in same series].

Zakon sudnyj ljudem (*Court Law for the People*). Translated, introduced, and annotated by Horace W. Dewey and Ann M. Kleimola, esp. 12–13, 34–35. Michigan Slavic Materials, 14. Ann Arbor: [Univ. Michigan] Department of Slavic Languages and Literatures, 1977. [Old Church Slavonic versions and English trans. and commentary].

Secondary Sources

Halperin, Charles J. *Russia and the Golden Horde: The Mongol Impact on Medieval Russian History.* Bloomington: Indiana University Press, 1985.

Hubbs, Joanna. *Mother Russia: The Feminine Myth in Russian Culture.* Bloomington: Indiana University Press, 1988.

Kelly, Joan. "Did Women Have a Renaissance?" In *Becoming Visible: Women in European History,* edited by Renate Bridenthal and Claudia Koonz. Boston: Houghton-Mifflin, 1977. Reprint in Kelly, *Women, History and Theory,* 19–50. Chicago: University of Chicago Press, 1984.

Kollmann, Nancy S. "The Seclusion of Elite Muscovite Women." *Russian History* 10 (1983): 170–87.

———. "Women's Honor in Early Modern Russia." In *Russia's Women: Accommodation, Resistance, Transformation,* edited by Barbara E. Clements, Barbara A. Engel, and Christine D. Worobec, 60–73. Berkeley: University of California Press, 1991.

Laiou, Angeliki E. "The Role of Women in Byzantine Society." *Jahrbuch der österreichischen Byzantinistik* 31 (1981): 233–60.

Lerner, Gerda. *The Creation of Patriarchy.* New York: Oxford University Press, 1986.

Levy, Sandra J. "Women and Control of Property in Sixteenth-Century Russia." *Russian History* 10 (1983): 201–12.

Ostrowski, Donald. *Muscovy and the Mongols: Cross-Cultural Influences on the Steppe Frontier, 1304–1589.* Cambridge: Cambridge University Press, 1998. [See esp. ch. 3].

Runciman, Stephen. "Some Notes on the Role of the Empress." *Eastern Churches Review* 4 (1972): 119–24.

NADIA MARGOLIS

MUSIC IN MEDIEVAL NUNNERIES. Nunneries offered women in the Middle Ages an arena for leadership, scholarship, and musicianship. Many women, both unmarried and widowed, found the nunnery a place where their talents and creativity could be used.

The emergence of Christian communities of virgins in late Antiquity led to the formation of communal worship patterns regularly including the singing of psalms and the offering of prayers by the fourth century . As early as the late fourth century, St. Gregory of Nyssa describes the singing of the nuns on the occasion of the death of his sister, Macrina. With the creation of the Benedictine Rule (c.540) by St. Benedict of Nursia, communities of both monks and nuns had a guidebook for their communal living. At the heart of the rule is the outline for the Divine Office, which is the same regardless of the gender of the monastic community. Each day the nuns chant matins, lauds, prime, terce, sext, none, vespers, and compline—the canonical hours dividing their entire day—as well as the daily Mass. Benedict carefully sets forth the distribution of the psalms in each service so that all 150 psalms are chanted weekly. Additionally, the repertoire includes antiphons (generally short chants that particularize the psalms to the liturgical occasion), responsories (liturgical chants that include a solo section and are often more musically elaborate than antiphons), and hymns (strophic, versified chants with syllabic musical settings). Benedict's rule remained the standard throughout the Middle Ages; even many of those communities that were not Benedictine based their practices on the Benedictine Rule.

Within the monastic structure there was a hierarchy of positions, several of which have a bearing on musical practices. At the head of an abbey was the abbess in whom resided the major decision-making authority for the abbey. She was assisted by a prioress and possibly subprioresses. The person most directly responsible for the musical life was the *cantrix* or chantress. Her responsibilities included training novices in singing, balancing the two sides of the choir, taking care of the liturgical books, making sure that the music

The nun's choir. Detail from fresco in chapel. © The Art Archive/ Palazzo Comunale Perugia/Dagli Orti.

appropriate to each liturgical occasion was sung, and delegating responsibility for a job that rotated weekly for intoning the chants. In a large establishment, the cantrix/chantress would be assisted by a *succentrix* or subchantress.

The choir in a medieval nunnery sat in two halves that usually faced each other. Much of the music that was sung, especially the psalms, was sung in alternation between the two sides of the choir. The chantress had to be sure that the two sides were approximately equal in musical strength and in the balance of senior and junior members of the order. She had the authority to move people from side to side as she deemed necessary.

The music sung by the nuns was primarily that known as plainchant or "Gregorian" chant. This repertoire is unaccompanied, monophonic (one melody line), and, at least by the later Middle Ages, in basically equal note values with no metric regularity. The chant notation indicates pitch relationships but was not intended to indicate specific pitches. Therefore, part of the job of the person who intoned the chant was to indicate the pitch and tempo at which it would be sung. Contemporary records caution against being too extreme in either pitch or tempo. There is nothing in the musical notation of manuscripts that survive from nunneries to indicate a difference from those used in monasteries, although the rubrics (instructions in red in the manuscript) are often customized to indicate women by such terms as cantrix or *abbatissa*.

The chant repertoire varied somewhat from place to place depending on local customs. An especially important factor was the saint for whom the nunnery was named. If it was a saint whose feast was already celebrated as a major feast day (indicated in red on the church calendar), then no additional repertoire was probably needed. If, however, the saint was a relatively minor one to the church at large, (e.g., St. Ethelburga at Barking Abbey, England), the local nunnery would celebrate the patronal feast day as a red-letter day, necessitating additional antiphons, responsories, and hymns. It would be the chantress's responsibility to be sure that this repertoire was available, and it is likely that on many occasions she composed such music herself. The repertoire of the great nun-composer Hildegard of Bingen (1098–1179), for example, includes many chants specifically for the nuns in her abbey.

In addition to the chant repertoire, there are a few indications that nuns did sing polyphony (multipart music) on occasion. The largest manuscript collection comes from the Monasterio de las Huelgas ("Monastery of Repose") in Burgos, Spain. A large and wealthy establishment, this house drew much of its membership from the royalty and many royal weddings and funerals were held there. A fourteenth-century polyphonic manuscript from this abbey offers clear evidence that these nuns did sing polyphony.

Several other sources with a few polyphonic pieces in them can be connected to nunneries; however, there is no evidence to suggest that nunneries were as much in the vanguard of compositional techniques as monasteries in the later Middle Ages.

There was one liturgical occasion for which the service in nunneries differed considerably from that in monasteries: the service for consecrating virgins. Whereas the service in monasteries emphasized "putting on the new man in Christ," the consecration of virgins stressed the image of the nun as the "bride of Christ." The service took on the importance and some of the trappings of a wedding. By the twelfth century this service had become quite elaborate including the blessing of the clothing and the ring as well as the nun herself. Instructions in the bishop's pontificals give detailed information on the ceremony.

Despite the anonymity in which most medieval nuns lived and worked, there are a few individuals whose accomplishments in music are worth mentioning. Although this article deals with Western Christianity, it would be remiss not to mention the Byzantine nun-composer, Kassia (b. c.810, C.E.). Her sacred compositions were written for the Byzantine Rite. Many of them are *sticheron*, long compositions sung for both the morning and evening services. Some of her forty-nine liturgical compositions continue to be sung in the Eastern Orthodox Church today.

Herrad of Landsberg (c.1130–1195), abbess of Hohenburg, compiled the knowledge of her day into an encyclopedic volume known as the *Hortus Deliciarum* or *Garden of Delights*. Several selections of her poetry and music were included as part of this beautifully illuminated volume. Unfortunately, only two of these, one of them polyphonic, were copied prior to the destruction of the manuscript in a fire in 1870.

Studies of specific monastic establishments are perhaps more likely to yield insight into women's musical lives. The great houses in England of Barking Abbey, Shaftesbury Abbey, and Syon Abbey all had rich musical lives. A manuscript from the Abbey of Origny-Sainte-Benoîte in northern France details the production of musical dramas by nuns of that house. The Monasterio de las Huelgas in Burgos, Spain, and several German houses all give evidence that many nuns were active and talented musicians.

See also Birgitta of Sweden, St.; Bride of Christ/*Brautmystik*; Herrad of Hohenberg/Landsberg; Hildegard of Bingen, St.; Katherine of Sutton; Macrina the Younger, St.; Music, Women Composers and Musicians; Rules for Canonesses, Nuns, and Recluses

BIBLIOGRAPHY

Primary Sources

Anderson, Gordon A. *Las Huelgas manuscript: Burgos, Monasterio de Las Huelgas.* Neuhausen-Stuttgart, Germany: American Institute of Musicology/Hänssler-Verlag, 1982.

Collett, Barry, ed. *Female Monastic Life in Early Tudor England with an Edition of Richard Fox's Translation of the Benedictine Rule for Women, 1517.* Burlington, Vt. and Aldershot, U.K.: Ashgate, 2002.

Kock, Ernest A., ed. *Three Middle-English Versions of the Rule of St. Benedict and Two Contemporary Rituals for the Ordination of Nuns.* Early English Text Society, o.s. 120. London: Kegan, Paul, Trench, Truebner, 1902.

Tolhurst, J. B. L., ed. *The Ordinale and Customary of the Benedictine Nuns of Barking Abbey.* Henry Bradshaw Society, 45. London: Harrison, 1927.

Secondary Sources

Bagnall, Anne D. "Musical Practices in Medieval English Nunneries." Ph.D. diss. Columbia University, 1975.

Edwards, J. Michele. "Women in Music to ca. 1450." In *Women and Music: A History*, edited by Karen Pendle, 8–28. Bloomington and Indianapolis: University of Indiana Press, 1991.

Holsinger, Bruce W. *Music, Body, and Desire in Medieval Culture: Hildegard of Bingen to Chaucer.* Figurae: Reading Medieval Culture. Stanford, Calif.: Stanford University Press, 2001.

Marshall, Kimberly. "Symbols, Performers, and Sponsors: Female Musical Creators in the Late Middle Ages." In *Rediscovering the Muses: Women's Musical Traditions*, edited by Kimberly Marshall, 140–68. Boston: Northeastern University Press, 1993.

Neuls-Bates, Carol, ed. *Women in Music: An Anthology of Source Readings from the Middle Ages to the Present*, 3–20. New York: Harper & Row, 1982.

Rokseth, Yvonne. "Les Femmes Musiciennes du XIIᵉ au XIVᵉ Siècle." *Romania* 61 (1935): 464–80.

Touliatos-Banker, Diane. "Women Composers of Medieval Byzantine Chant." *College Music Symposium* 24/1 (1984): 62–80.

Yardley, Anne Bagnall. "Bridgettine Spirituality and Musical Practices at Syon Abbey." In *Studies in St. Birgitta and the Brigittine Order*, edited by James Hogg, 2:199–214. Salzburg: Universität Salzburg, 1993.

———. "'Ful weel she soong the service dyvyne': The Cloistered Musician in the Middle Ages." In *Women Making Music: The Western Art Tradition, 1150–1950*, edited by Jane Bowers and Judith Tick, 15–38. Urbana and Chicago: University of Illinois Press, 1986.

———. "The Marriage of Heaven and Earth: A Late Medieval Source of the *Consecratio virginum*." In *Studies in Medieval Music: Festschrift for Ernest H. Sanders*, edited by Peter M. Lefferts and Brian Seirup, 305–24. New York: Columbia University Department of Music, 1990. Originally *Current Musicology* 45–47 (1988).

———. *Performing Piety: Music in Medieval English Nunneries*. The New Middle Ages. New York: Palgrave, 2005.

ANNE BAGNALL YARDLEY

MUSIC, WOMEN COMPOSERS AND MUSICIANS (c.300–c.1450). Developing a portrait of the musical activities of women, particularly in Western Europe but also in other parts of the world, from the fourth to the fifteenth centuries is rather like creating a tapestry from a variety of fibers and textures. No single type of resource provides comprehensive information on the range of their participation. We can, however, bring together an array of resources: iconographic and literary references, wills and financial accounts, guild records and religious documents, didactic treatises and chronicles by travelers, tax records and song texts, and music treatises and manuscripts. Each resource category carries its own insights, limitations, and problems for the study of women in medieval music.

Music as Women's Mode of Expression and Social Exchange

Ecclesiastical Society. Women's activities in music paralleled their overall opportunities in the early Christian church. During the early centuries of Christianity both women and men sang during worship. In her account of the service at the Church of the Holy Sepulcher in Jerusalem, the pilgrim Egeria (c.386) described singing—perhaps in antiphonal style (alternately, responsively by two choirs)—by monks, virgins, laywomen, and laymen. However, by the late fourth century many church councils and individual churchmen sought to silence women's singing during the worship service. Patristic literature—writings by the early Church Fathers—frequently sought to justify the exclusion of women from singing and preaching activities by citing the injunction "women should keep silence in the churches" (1 Cor. 14: 34), an admonition which scholarly consensus now identifies as a later insertion to Paul's Epistle to the Corinthians. In 379, the Synod of Antioch forbade women to sing with men. About the same time, the *Didascalia of the 318*

Fathers stated: "nor should they [women] sing along or take part in the responses, but they should be silent and pray to God" (Quasten, 157). Cyril of Jerusalem (313–386) wrote: "The virgins should sing or read Psalms very quietly during divine worship. They should speak with their lips alone so that nothing is heard" (Quasten, 157). In a dialogue entitled *Contra Pelagianos* (*Against the Pelagians*), St. Jerome (c.347–420) reacted very negatively to the singing of women in public. Many, but not all, early Christian writers continued to encourage extraliturgical—outside of Mass and the Divine Office—singing of psalms by women as a deterrent to singing secular music. However, both Gregory of Nazianzus (c.329–c.389), one of the three principal Fathers of the Greek Church, and Arsillos, an Iberian ruler, advocated that, even in private worship at home, only men should sing. From the fourth century, the opportunity for women in public churches was further inhibited when congregational singing shifted to music provided by select choirs, solely of men and boys.

Women playing a bowed viol and a pandeiro. From *Nobles' Songbook*, 1275 manuscript. © The Art Archive/Bibliotecha Nacional Lisbon/Dagli Orti.

The gradual suppression of singing by Christian women can be linked to various factors: a reaction to the singing among women in other religious groups, the characterization of women musicians as prostitutes and courtesans, the identification of women with the arousal of sexual desire and worldly temptation, and, chiefly, the political victory of the Roman Church over heretics and Gnostics. The Gnostics professed a special "knowledge" (Greek = *gnosis*) of God and human destiny distinct from Church teachings, and also treated women and men in an egalitarian fashion. The Gnostics were the dominant Christian community in Egypt and northern Syria from the third century until the time of Augustine (354–430) and posed the greatest threat to the Roman Church. The subjugation of women by the Roman Church occurred simultaneously with its suppression of the Gnostic community. The exclusion of women from the music of public worship was also deeply rooted in patriarchy. The domination of women was a means of retaining and enhancing the power of the Latin Church Fathers and of institutional Christianity as a state religion.

Separately then, Christian women's communities took on new significance from the fourth century, when the nunneries offered women virtually their only opportunity to sing and compose music in praise of God. The convent nourished leadership and creativity among women: "The impulse toward leadership which kept the men in the world sent the women out of it" (Putnam, 78). Between 500 and 1500, the convent was the only acceptable alternative to marriage for European women and "fostered some of the best sides of intellectual, moral and emotional life" (Eckenstein, vii). Especially during the eleventh and twelfth centuries, Christian convents were among the major centers of culture. Singing liturgical music was the central communal activity in most convents. Education of novices focused around reading and singing to encourage participation in collective worship. In singing eight Offices plus Mass together each day, making and sharing music was at the very core of women's communal lives. The visions of Mechthild of Hackeborn (c.1241–1299) and Gertrude the Great (1256–1302), both nuns at the convent of Helfta in Germany, attest to the power of music, its subversive potential, and its integral position in their theological understandings (Holsinger, 240–53). In medieval nunneries women found an outlet for creativity in singing and sometimes in musical composition. Additionally, one woman provided leadership as *cantrix* (chantress), assuming a leadership role not open to medieval women outside the convent. She served as conductor with responsibilities for choosing repertoire, conducting rehearsals, overseeing the copying of music and illumination work, library management, and supervising liturgy.

Secular Society. Women participated in many aspects of secular music as amateur and professional singers, dancers, and instrumentalists; composers; benefactors; and educators. The hierarchy in Western cultures that exalts composers today can also be seen, although to a lesser extent, in the Middle Ages. No clear division between composers and performers yet existed, and some social mobility was possible. In a late fourth-century sermon St. John Chrysostom (c.347–407), patriarch of Constantinople, described the importance of popular song in the lives of working people, specifically mentioning lullabies sung by wet-nurses and songs performed by women while weaving—"sometimes individually and to themselves, sometimes all together in concert" (Strunk, 68). *The Book of the Pious*, by thirteenth-century Rhenish Jews (from lands along the Rhine), almost certainly referred to singing by women when it condemned the singing of Gentile lullabies to Jewish infants.

Women are especially visible in descriptions of social dancing. Their participation in dance-songs is known from the beginnings of Christianity in both liturgical and non-liturgical situations. The two most common forms of medieval dance-song preserved in writing are the *carole* and the *rondeau*, enjoyed by workers and nobility alike. Both include a refrain so that all the dancers could participate in the singing. Although neither form has a single defining shape, each dance type can be identified by a common feature: rondeaux include the refrain within the stanzas, and caroles utilize a *vuelta*, or "turning line," that is, the final line of the stanza rhymes with the refrain. Song texts—for example, those in *Carmina Burana* or in an eleventh-century manuscript called the *Cambridge Songs*—frequently refer to circle dancing, one of the oldest styles. A woman is most often cited as dance leader. Peter Dronke has reconstructed a possible recitation-performance of the Latin dance-song "Tempus est iocundum, O virgines modo congaudete" ("The time is joyful; O girls, rejoice now!") from *Carmina Burana* (fol.70v; no. 179). The narrative presents a social event. In the first strophe, the chorus leader calls the young women and men together and introduces the refrain, which the chorus sings at the end of the remaining seven strophes. Women soloists are featured in the second, fifth, and sixth strophes; men, in the others. Typically, this carole employs a vuelta. Each stanza ends with the Latin word "*floreo*" ("I blossom out of love"), which rhymes with the refrain's "*pereo*" ("I die of love"). This constant element signaled the entrance for the chorus. Singing is the most documented music for dance-songs; however, instrumentalists are also mentioned. Thirteenth-century French manuscript illuminations reflecting contemporaneous practices support the literary evidence. These illustrations include genre scenes in the margins of secular manuscripts as well as decorations in *chansonniers* (songbooks) and collections of *romans* (romances). The instruments most associated with dancing were pipe and tabor (a frame drum often with a snare) along with the vielle (a bowed string instrument with an oval-shaped body). An illumination from a thirteenth-century Book of Hours (London, British Library MS Stowe 17, f. 112) shows a woman playing a vielle while a young man dances.

Another example of music as part of the social exchange between women and men comes from a biography of St. Jón (d. 1121), the first bishop of northern Iceland. "There was a favourite game of the people—which is unseemly—that there should be an exchange of verses: a man addressing a woman, and a woman a man—disgraceful strophes, mocking and unfit to be heard" (Dronke 1984, 105). These love songs retained their popularity despite Bishop Jón's admonition against them. This game of love songs, as they were called by the biographer, likely presented an opportunity for women and men to sing simple improvised dialogues.

Women as Patrons, Poet-Composers, and Scribes. Prominent women were frequent benefactors of music, and several connected with French courts during the late Middle Ages were especially important. Eleanor of Aquitaine (c.1122–1204) exerted substantial political power first as wife of Louis VII, king of France, and later of Henry II, king of England. She and her daughters, Marie and Aelis, countess of Blois, influenced their courts, shaping aristocratic values and behavior in various cultural centers. Eleanor and Henry subsidized the troubadours at her court in Anjou and later transplanted their literature to England. While at her court in Poitiers, Eleanor and her daughter Marie disseminated French courtly manners—including music, singing, and the new vernacular literature—to women and men who became the ruling nobility in various areas of France, England, Sicily, and Spain. With Marie's support, Eleanor's court at Champagne was active in the diffusion of the troubadour and *trobairitz* (women troubadours) lyric and became the most active *trouvère* (northern-French counterpart to southern-French troubadours) center in northern France during the last third of the twelfth century and the first half of the thirteenth century. Eleanor's other daughter, Aelis, is reported to have inspired the trouvère Gautier d'Arras, and Eleanor's granddaughter, Blanche of Castile, was a *trouvère*. In southern France during approximately the same time period, Marie de Ventadorn (c.1165–c.1221), herself a *trobairitz*, also supported troubadours. Her marriage to the viscount of Ventadorn placed her in one of the centers of troubadour activity. Among the men receiving her support was Gui d'Ussel, and one of their *tensos* (love-debate lyrics)—more specifically, a category of *tenso* called a *partimen*, because each lover speaks his/her "part"—has been preserved (ed. Bruckner et al., 39–41).

Study of the European medieval lyric, to be treated in more detailed fashion later, reveals much concerning gender systems. Repeatedly, the texts of songs pronounce what it meant to be a woman or a man, and women and men differed in their perspectives. Women's choice and treatment of form also differed from that of their male contemporaries. To gain a more comprehensive understanding of medieval Western Europe, the views of women must be added to such male concepts as that of *fin'amors*, in Old French, and *Minne*, in Middle-High German—what we call in English, for want of a better term, "courtly love": a covert, out-of-wedlock love affair supposedly for true love (rather than by legal contract) and thus highly erotic, which usually benefited the man more than the woman, especially as the woman suffered more from vile gossip than the man after public discovery of the affair.

Writings by a fifteenth-century Dominican friar provide confirmation of women as skilled copyists or scribes. He cites at least a dozen convents with active scriptoria, and singles out two nuns at Colmar in Alsace, northeastern France, who were especially proficient at copying choir books. In his eulogy for Sister Lukardis of Utrecht, the friar praises her work as a copyist: "she busied herself with [...] writing, which she had truly mastered as we may see in the large, beautiful, useful choir books which she wrote and annotated for the convent and which has caused astonishment among many fathers and priests who have seen the missal she prepared, written in a neat, correct script" (Labarge, 224).

Music and Poetry: International Traditions. The medieval lyric, continuing traditions that had flourished throughout Western Europe for centuries, was part of a performing/aural tradition rather than a written/visual one, with poetry and music being inseparable. During the late Middle Ages the lyric was international in scope yet formed a diverse repertoire, making simple definitions impossible. Indeed, late fourteenth-century literary doctrinaires such as Eustache Deschamps dubbed poetry "musique naturelle," in contrast to music as "musique artificielle." Though women appear to have participated in smaller numbers than men as composers of the medieval lyric, they were more active than has often been reported.

Southern France: The **Trobairitz.** Current scholarship about lyric traditions has produced the most information about the *trobairitz* and troubadours of southern France. The *trobairitz*, or women composer-poets of Occitania, wrote lyric in Provençal (*langue d'oc*) and flourished during the late twelfth and thirteenth centuries. To establish a definitive list of *trobairitz* and the corpus of their work is not possible as scholars differ considerably on what was actually composed by a woman. Recent scholarship has begun to focus more attention on interpretative analysis. The music of the *trobairitz* and troubadours was less frequently written down than their poetry. The melodies were short and easily remembered, in contrast with many of the lengthy strophic poems. The modest interest in written preservation of the music might also be attributable to other factors: (1) the medieval lyric was an outgrowth of earlier traditions of improvisation, (2) precise repetition in the musical renditions was not valued, (3) the short, repeated melodies were easily learned by rote, or (4) the participants sometimes lacked notational skill.

Among the *trobairitz* materials, only "A chantar m'er de so q'ieu no volria" ("I have to sing of what I would not wish") by the Countess of Die (Comtessa de Dia) includes musical notation. This poem is preserved in more than one manuscript; however, the music appears only in the *Manuscrit du roi*, a *chansonnier* (songbook) copied in around 1270 for Charles of Anjou, brother of Louis IX. Literary scholars have particularly high praise for this lyric, in which a woman grapples to understand rejection by her lover. Even in her lament, her affirmed self-worth, as she proclaims "ma beltatz" ("my beauty"), in both the first and last stanzas, is rare for her time.

Like their male counterparts, *trobairitz* wrote *tensos*—debate songs or dialogues involving questioning and an exchange of views—and *cansos*—songs or, more specifically, love songs. The form of the tenso, highlights the battle of the sexes, and in them the *trobairitz* remain close to the troubadours' language and imagery. Using the more open form of the canso, women found more distinctive voices, and their distance from *fin'amors* is more apparent. Neither the women nor the men in the poems are as idealized, but instead exhibit lived experience. The *trobairitz* lyric most often speaks directly to the beloved rather than to a general audience. The women's poems articulate their desire for recognition as individuals and for a voice in their relationships with men. Perhaps the most substantial transformation of *fin'amors* is the *canso* by Bietris de Roman (early thirteenth century). In addressing itself to "Na Maria, pretz e fina valors" ("Lady Maria, of virtue and pure worth"), this work may be an expression of lesbian love. Scholars' interpretations vary considerably: some read this work as female friendship (Rieger 1989); some consider it to have been actually authored by a man (Schultz-Gora; Poe); or that Bietris is a spokesperson for a man (Sainte-Palaye, vol. 3), a religious poem in which Maria is the Virgin Mary, and an expression of lesbian love (Bec 1984; Bogin; Nelli; Boswell). Read in this latter way, language of the courtly tradition elevates the beloved through Bietris's words of praise and speaks of physical desire. The tone of this love lyric, however, is more positive than much of the repertoire of either the *trobairitz* or troubadours: there is no deceit, no infidelity, no bitterness or anger toward the beloved. For example, stanza two reads:

> For this I beg you, please, to let pure love,
> delight, and sweet humility
> give me the help I need with you
> so you will grant me, lovely lady, please,
> what I most hope to enjoy;
> for in you lie my heart and my desire:
> I have all my happiness because of you,
> I'm sighing many sighs because of you. (Bruckner ed. and trans.)

Northern France: Women Trouvères. By the early thirteenth century, the women *trouvères*, writing in *langue d'oïl*, developed as the northern-French counterparts to the *trobairitz*. Although scholars are not in agreement about the actual number or even existence of historical women trouvères, one recent study by Eglal Doss-Quinby et al., identifies eight historical women trouvères by name, notably Blanche of Castile (1188–1252, wife of Louis VIII of France), the duchess of Lorraine (probably Marguerite de Champagne, daughter—not wife—of Duke Thibaut IV), and Dame Margot, among others. Among thirteen known debate songs (*jeux-partis* and *tensons*, the northern analogue of the Occitan *tenso*) that appear to have women authors or coauthors, six survive with music. There is an anonymous *jeu-parti* set to music of the most widely known troubadour canso: "Can vei la lauzeta mover" ("When I see the lark moving") by Bernart de Ventadorn. The debate by Dames Margot and Maroie survives in two manuscripts with very different melodies—perhaps by one of these women—and suggesting its admiration. The abovementioned *Manuscrit du roi* (Paris, BnF MS fr. 844) contains pieces by women trouvères as well as for the *trobairitz*, including ones set to music. Several other monophonic lyric genres represented besides the *jeu parti* and *tenson* are the *chanson d'amour* (love song), the *aube* (erotic dawn-song, like the Provençal *alba*), Crusade song, a *chanson pieuse*, or nonliturgical devotional song and a *plainte*, or lament—this last without music and often attributed to two different men, but Dronke (1968) tentatively ascribes it to a woman *trouvère* on the basis of textual and linguistic analysis of it as a woman's lament.

Like the *trobairitz*, most of the women *trouvères* and other French poets were noblewomen. Marie de France, famed twelfth-century author of narrative *lais*, could be considered a kind of *trouvère*. We know she accompanied herself on the harp and that music for her compositions did exist, though manuscript(s) of it no longer survive (Maillard, 66).

In a discussion of the documented singing of women at court, Kimberly Marshall suggests that new questions are needed to assess female creativity in an oral culture like that of the *trouvères*. She counters the general assumption by scholars that women sang music conceived by men and music that was notated by suggesting instead that women may have created their own monodies (one-part vocal compositions), most frequently without reference to written materials. Furthermore, she speculates that some songs attributed to men are actually just the written formalization of songs created and transmitted orally by women.

Latin as Musical Lingua Franca: The Carmina Burana. The pregnancy song, "Huc usque, me miseram!" ("How miserable am I!"; fol. 52v; no. 126), although anonymous like most of the poems in the *Carmina Burana*, was most likely written by a woman and serves as an example of a Latin lyric. *Carmina Burana*, a thirteenth-century anthology preserving over two hundred poems, shows the diversity of the medieval Latin lyric as well as poems in a German dialect. Although these poems were meant to be sung, only a few include music in staffless, unheighted neumes (nondiastematic notation, that is, one using graphic signs instead of the now conventional stemmed and/or heighted "notes" on a staff), while others have space left for a melody. "Huc usque, me miseram!" which resembles poems about pregnancy written in other European languages, does not include musical notation.

Spain as a Multicultural Marvel. Available documentation suggests considerable literary and musical activity at the major Spanish courts during the late Middle Ages, in which women participated in various ways. The Iberian Peninsula had come to harbor a highly cosmopolitan culture: integrating Muslims, Jews, and Christians, even forming distinctive hybrid cultures including the Mozarabs (Christians adopting the customs of their Islamic conquerors), since the seventh- and eighth-century Islamic invasions and gradual, intermittent Christian reconquest from after 1000 through 1492. For example, in Castile at the court of Sancho IV (r. 1284–1295), palace account books show salaries for twenty–seven minstrels: two Arabic women, twelve Arabic men, a Jewish man, and twelve Christian men. The association of dark skin with *jougleresses* (women *jougleurs* [various spellings] = minstrels; so called because they "juggled" and performed music) suggests a special prominence of Moors among women minstrels, even beyond the borders of Spain. Frederick II, Holy Roman Emperor and king of Sicily, employed Moorish musicians in his Norman-Saracen court at Palermo. Several medieval romances include episodes in which a noblewoman disguises herself as a *jougleresse* by darkening her face and becoming a traveling musician who plays an instrument and sings. These are found in such popular works as *Aucassin et Nicolette* (late twelfth century)—the unique example of *chantefable* (tale for singing and recitation)—and the slightly later *Bevis of Hampton* (*Bueve de Hantone* in French and Provençal; *Bove d'Ancona* in Italian), a chanson de *geste*, or heroic epic "song" (poem).

From at least the eleventh century onward, women singers at the courts of Andalusia entertained with bilingual lyrics. They concluded their *muwashahāt* (love poems in classical Arabic or Hebrew) with vernacular stanzas using colloquial Arabic or Spanish. These final stanzas or *kharjas* talk directly and frankly of complex feelings and present women as active lovers. They are the earliest known examples of so-called "women's songs" (*cantiga de amigo* or *chanson de femme*), where male authors attempted to write from a woman's subject position.

Accounts of Arabic and Jewish women who wrote lyrics in medieval Spain indicate the importance of being in a creative environment. Most of these women can be linked with other accomplished poets, for example, a father or lover, a woman teacher, or in one instance a slave master. Although not all were noblewomen, they were usually connected with a court. Kasmūnah (Qasmūnah), daughter of a Jewish poet, studied with her father and was considered an outstanding writer. Her two-part dialogues with her father parallel some Provençal tensos. A lyric exchanged between an Arabic woman, Hafsah bint al-Hājj al-Rakūnïyah (d. 1184 or 1190), and her beloved, Abū Ja'far, also resembles the tenso.

While a resident of Cordova, Zeynab al-Murabiyyah (d. 1009), who never consented to marriage, composed several verses praising al-Mudhfer, a son of Mansŭr ibn Abī 'Āmir, who eventually usurped the throne of Cordova. Wallādah (d. 1087/1091), daughter of the King of Cordova and for a time the beloved of poet Ibn Zaydūn, rivaled the most famous male poets of her day. At least one of Wallādah's female students, Bahjah, was also well known for lyric writing. A freed slave, al-'Arūdhiyyah (d. eleventh century), learned grammar and rhetoric from her master in Valencia, then surpassed him as a poet. Hind, a slave woman in mid-twelfth-century Xativa, who excelled in poetry and music as an 'ūd (short-necked Arabic lute) player and singer, was praised by a famous Arabic poet in an invitation to his house: "The nightingale, after hearing thy performance, envies thee, and wishes to hear again the deep intonations of thy lute" (al-Makkari, 1: 166–67). Unfortunately, manuscripts of neither medieval Arabic music nor secular music attributed to medieval women on the Iberian Peninsula are known to have survived.

Italy. Earlier scholars identified three thirteenth-century women as contributors to the Italian secular lyric; however, modern scholarship has found no evidence of poetry by Gaia da Camino (mentioned in Dante's *Divina Commedia* [*Divine Comedy*] of 1321) and now considers Nina Siciliana merely a legend. Two sonnets with religious overtones and part of a secular tenzone (debate poem) are still tentatively attributed to a woman known only as "the accomplished damsel"—La Compiuta Donzella. Her identity has been extensively investigated although nothing concrete has been established. Her poetry has been variously evaluated in terms of quality but is now generally accepted as the earliest Italian verse by a woman (see Cherchi in Paden). Until at least the mid-fourteenth century, no music for the Italian secular lyric has survived.

Asia: Japan. A distinctive tradition of women's participation in music has also been documented in Japan; however, many details about medieval Japanese women singers remain contested by scholars. Kwon describes a group of women singers (*asobi*) strongly linked with the performance of *imayō*, a popular song genre that emerged in the late tenth century, flourished during the next two centuries, and died out by the late thirteenth century. Superb singing skills distinguished the asobi from other courtesans. Barbara Ruch, however, has challenged the conventional view of these entertainers as a single, low-status group linked with prostitution. She provisionally suggests three types of women as the most significant artistically: the *kugutsu*, who were traditionally associated with puppet theater and especially with *imayō*; the *shirabyōshi*, dancers cross-dressing in white costumes and perhaps originally among the kugutsu; and *yūjo* (or *asobime*), literally meaning "female entertainer" but often translated as "courtesan" or "prostitute." Regardless of specific details, women entertainers markedly influenced "every major vocal and choreographed genre of literature and music from the twelfth century on" (Ruch, 530), including Noh and later kabuki. Court diaries and letters from the Heian period (794–1192) establish that singers entertained prominent members of court, including emperors. Emperor Goshirakawa (1127–1192) launched a particularly striking student–teacher relationship in 1157 when he called Otomae (1085–1169) to court to teach him her repertoire of *imayō*. An esteemed singer, Otomae traced her musical ancestry back through four generations of female teachers and required the Emperor to relearn his repertoire according to her musical style. Although the *imayō* collection titled *Ryōjin Hishō* ("Secret Selection of Songs that Make the Rafter Dust Dance") is generally attributed to Emperor Goshirakawa, the material was surely Otomae's whether she composed the songs or passed along earlier material. Compiled over two decades, the anthology was completed in 1179; today 566 texts from this collection are extant. The lyrics juxtaposed a diversity of topics, ranging from Buddhist doctrine to songs about nature. Unfortunately, all of the music is lost and virtually nothing is known about the performance of *imayō* except that singers often accompanied themselves with a small drum (*tsuzumi*) or by tapping a closed fan against the palm of the hand.

Women Composers and Genres. Despite actions that would likely thwart their creativity, some women did emerge as composers. They contributed to the major genre of Byzantine chant: hymns, including *troparia*, *stichēra*, and *kanōnes*. Like a *troparion*, a *stichēron* was originally a monostrophic stanza sung between psalm verses. A Byzantine *kanōn* is a verse form of nine sections, each alluding to one of the nine biblical canticles. Each section contains several stanzas with a repeated melody. Palaeologina, a cultured and educated member of the Imperial family, composed *kanōnes* in honor of Saints Dimitri, Theodora, and others. Music by only two of the women is preserved: one song is ascribed to the daughter of Ioannes Kladas, and numerous liturgical compositions are attributed to Kassia, or Kassianē (b. 810), although not all are considered authentic. Many of her known works are stichēra; however, her most famous piece, "The Fallen Woman," is a *troparion*.

Although the names of individual composers—women or men—were rarely known during the first millennium of Christianity, at least seven women can be identified as composers of Byzantine Christian chant between the ninth and fifteenth centuries. During the ninth century there flourished Martha, an abbess at Argos; Thekla, an abbess near Constantinople and known for a *kanon* praising Theotokos or the Virgin Mary; Kassia, a well-educated poet-composer and the most significant of these Byzantine women musicians, and Theodosia, another composer and abbess known for her *kanōnes*. During the thirteenth century, Kouvouklisena performed as a singer and *domestikena* (or leader) of a women's choir, while an anonymous daughter of Ioannes Kladas—himself a leading composer of Byzantine chant—sang and composed in the late fourteenth century. Somewhat later came the nun Palaeologina, who probably founded the convent of St. Theodora in Thessalonika.

Religious music-drama was one of the most interesting accretions to medieval Christian rituals. The dramas developed largely beginning in the tenth century, or perhaps as early as the reign of Charlemagne (768–814), during an era when there was an impulse to embellish and humanize the rituals of Christianity. During the next several centuries, the dramas grew in length, and some manuscripts provide detailed rubrics about the enactment, indicating costumes and props or giving directions for dramatic gestures and movement. Women characters play especially significant roles in the Easter drama, reenacting the dialogue between the angel and the women visiting Christ's empty tomb, *Quem quaeritis* (*Whom seek ye?*) or *Visitatio Sepulchri* (*Visit to the sepulcher*), the earliest and most popular story. Additional music-dramas recounting other biblical stories may not have been as prevalent at nunneries. For example, at the abbeys of Origny-Sainte-Benoîte (near St. Quentin, France), Barking (England), and Wilton (England) only the Easter drama with its prominent roles for women was apparently incorporated into their repertoires. Although clerics and choirboys generally took the roles of both female and male characters, nuns also participated, creating more realistic, mixed casts. In at least six different versions of *Visitatio*, women portrayed the three Marys (Mary Magdalene and the other two Marys at Christ's tomb). A late thirteenth-century manuscript at Troyes, largely in French, documents a performance by the nuns and clergy of Notre Dame. Three nuns took the Mary roles in fourteenth-century performances at the collegiate church at Essen and at Barking Abbey in Essex during the time when Lady Katherine of Sutton was abbess (1363–1376). Participation by nuns is indicated in the rubrics of the *Wilton Processional*, in the fourteenth-century St. Quentin drama from the nunnery of Origny-Sainte-Benoîte, and in a fifteenth-century *Quem quaeritis* from Brescia in the Lombardy region of Italy. The St. Quentin drama and the *Visitatio Sepulchri* in the Wilton Processional, a manuscript created for and by Benedictine nuns c.1300, led to a rethinking of the traditional conclusion that development in music-drama was accomplished through the inclusion of additional scenes and characters. The story in the *Wilton Processional* focuses on the single scene of the three Marys and the angel at the tomb, but is longer and more complex than many others with this plot. Clearly, adding characters was not the only way to enrich and enlarge the Easter drama. That nuns should have retained the emphasis on women rather than adding scenes in which men predominated is not surprising. William Smoldon described the anonymous creator of the St. Quentin manuscript—including music, French rubrics, and versified French for some extended scenes—as "a writer, arranger, and musician of ability and dramatic imagination," and continued: "The versifications are skilful and varied in form, and we have noted quite a number of instances of independent thinking. [. . .] We must include St. Quentin 86 as being among the most successful of the Church music dramas; one surely worthy of revival" (Smoldon).

In addition to the many anonymous nuns who provided religious leadership and who created embroidery, tapestries, sculpture, illuminations, and songs, a few identifiable individuals stand out during the period of intense creative activity in the twelfth century. In music and other disciplines, Hildegard of Bingen was exceptional in both the depth and breadth of her intellectual and creative scope. A twelfth-century visionary theologian, Hildegard composed seventy-seven religious songs and a lengthy music-drama, *Ordo virtutum* (*Play of the Virtues*), which has no medieval parallel. Disavowing any serious educational background, she claimed that all her writings and music came to her in visions. Yet her works reveal a familiarity with two medieval music theorists: the statesman-philosopher Boethius (c.480–524) and Benedictine monk Guido of Arezzo (c.991–after 1033). Her need to deny human instruction can be understood in the context of medieval gender politics, the visionary tradition of the Rhine mystics, and a deep awareness of biblical dreamers. For Hildegard, music was an avenue of access to mystical experience and composition a way to make palpable God and divine beauty. Her poetry and music, dating from as early as the 1140s, was written largely for the Offices and Mass at her convent. A few pieces celebrated saints important in nearby Trier and were perhaps written on commission. Her chant cycle, *Symphonia armonie celestium revelationum* (*Symphony of the Harmony of Celestial Revelations*), is preserved in two different versions, one manuscript from 1175 containing fifty-seven chants and a second manuscript from the 1180s containing seventy-five pieces. These chants are distinctive and idiosyncratic, though also linked with the medieval chant repertory. Her texts, modeled on the prayers and songs of the liturgical Office, "contain some of the most unusual, subtle, and exciting poetry of the twelfth century" (Dronke 1970, 151). Their resulting free-verse or prose quality is echoed in her freely spun melodic lines with their irregular, unpredictable gestures. Like her contemporaries, Hildegard constructed her works from a small number of melodic formulae; however, her development process was different. In comparison with Adam of St. Victor (d. 1192), who used stock figures to assemble music in a patchwork quilt fashion, Hildegard's elaboration and embellishment of melodic formulas resulted in more continuous, through-composed (that is, not strophic but with different music for each stanza) musical lines. Musical stability arises from organic melodic unity rather than from external factors such as strophic form or regular poetic meter. Hildegard's songs often encompass a wide range, covering two octaves or more. Her frequent use of ascending and descending leaps of a fifth is also exceptional for chant. Though Hildegard's hymns and sequences are not bound by traditional forms, her works in other genres—the Kyrie (from Greek: *kyrie eleison* = "Lord have mercy"; a prayer), an alleluia-verse, eighteen responsories, and many of the forty-three antiphons—have identifiable precedents in Gregorian chant repertory.

Analysis of "O virga" ("O branch") shows both Hildegard's independence and her connections with contemporaries and tradition. Textually, "O virga" has ties with the typical formal pattern of sequences from the tenth and eleventh centuries, in which first and last verses stand alone while other verses are paired. Hildegard balances the salutation in the first strophe with a prayer to Salvatrix (a feminine savior) in the last. The central strophes are grouped in threes, not twos, by their content, though melodically, "O virga" retains the couplet form common in the sequences of her contemporaries. Hildegard's strophes are neither rhymed nor alike structurally: they do not contain the same number of syllables or the same pattern of stresses. In "O virga" each pair of verses employs a single melodic idea, transformed to fit the differing texts. The resulting sound is unified through recurring melodic fragments both within and across pairs, but literal repetition is avoided.

Recent scholarship by Holsinger positions Hildegard's music and poetry within a female-centered religious experience that includes homoerotic desire. This contrasts with traditional accounts (Newman; Dronke) that view medieval devotion to the Virgin Mary as asexual. While not suggesting that Hildegard was a lesbian, Holsinger explores how her music "sexualized the entire body" (Holsinger, 128) and how the music and poetry when read in connection with her scientific writings present a powerful expression uniting body, voice, and spirituality.

Women's actual participation in medieval polyphony as singers or composers is a matter of scholarly debate. Three manuscripts of polyphonic music from fourteenth- and fifteenth-century England have slim ties with nunneries but at least suggest the possibility that nuns in England sang in parts. Continental sources, on the other hand, give strong evidence that nuns sang polyphony: sixteen manuscripts from convents span over three hundred years from as early as the twelfth century and originated in Spain, France, Germany, Italy, Switzerland, Austria, and the Netherlands. The primary genres of this period are represented: conductus, motet, Mass movements, sequence, and hymn. The Las Huelgas Codex, in the Monastery of Las Huelgas near Burgos (Spain), containing 136 pieces, is the most extensive source of polyphony known to have been owned by a nunnery. The manuscript, dating from the fourteenth century, was copied from a manuscript that María González de Aguero had transcribed earlier in the century. The complex music apparently reflects the skill of the nuns and girls in the choir of Las Huelgas monastery, and consuetudinary (pertaining to customs) records indicate that nuns sang in three parts. This convent had a trained choir of young girls similar to the boys' choirs in cathedral schools. From 1241 to 1288, the time of Abbess Berenguela, daughter of Beatrix of Spain and Ferdinand III, one hundred nuns sang in the choir and forty girls were in training. A conventional explanation maintains that women did not participate in church polyphony as performers or composers since their education was insufficient. Indeed the education, even in convents, varied considerably and declined for women in the later medieval period. As the intellectual centers shifted in the late twelfth and thirteenth centuries from convents and monasteries to urban universities that were closed to women, the artistic and intellectual activity of nuns declined. However, even if women performing polyphonic music was not a common occurrence, the evidence substantiates that it was widespread in terms of time period and geographic range. Paula Higgins notes "the perplexing absence of a single musical composition attributed to a woman between c.1300 and 1566, followed by a proliferation of publications of polyphonic music by women from 1566 on" (1993, 180). She concurs with Howard Mayer Brown that women were probably composing music but not admitting such authorship due to social pressures.

Women as Minstrels and Performers. When the functions of composer and performer were distinguished, traveling performers (minstrels or jougleresses in southern France) were accorded less status and were often from a lower social class than composer-poets (e.g., *trobairitz*). While information on performance by medieval men and women is lacking in detail, evidence indicates that women engaged in many of the same secular performing activities as their male counterparts. Distinct musical activities appear to be due at least as much to class as to gender. For example, medieval French literary sources identify aristocratic women as singers of dance-songs, troubadour and trouvère chansons, motets, and lais. In Cordova during the reign of al-Mansūr ibn Abī 'Āmir (939–1002), well-educated women played instruments such as the organ to entertain their husbands. Didactic treatises, such as the anonymous fourteenth-century *Clef d'amors* (*Key of Love*), aimed toward middle- and upper-class women, encouraged singing and playing some instruments as a pastime. *Del reggimento e costumi di donna* (*Rules of Conduct for Ladies*) by Francesco da Barberino (1264–1348) addressed dance and music as appropriate components of a noblewomen's education. French treatises do not generally condemn public performance by women, but Barberino's early fourteenth-century Italian treatise seeks to limit women's musical activity to the private sphere. On the other hand, women from lower social classes are known largely as professional performers, either traveling minstrels or servants at court.

Provençal, Old French, Spanish, Galician-Portuguese, and Middle English each have words which refer specifically to women minstrels: *jougleresse, menestrelle, juglaresa* or *juglara, jograresa,* and *gliewméden*. In addition to singing and instrument-playing, minstrels possessed an array of entertainment skills—tumbling, juggling, reciting, dancing, performing magic tricks, acrobatics, exhibiting trained animals, and mime. Some minstrels were slaves; others were hired by courts of the nobility. The eleventh-century court of Poitiers in Occitania (southern France) included hundreds of Moorish *jograresas*, received as remuneration for assistance given Aragon in the campaign against the Moors in 1064.

Payment records verify the presence of women singers and instrumentalists at various courts, especially in France. For example, in 1239, Louis IX paid Mélanz, a *cantatrix* (woman singer) to the Countess of Blois. Mahaut d'Artois employed a woman singer for Christmas 1319 and a woman organist named Jehanne in 1320. Mahaut's granddaughter, a princess of France, employed three female singers and a woman bellringer. Female musicians from various locales—Lyons (1372), Paris and Puy (1374)—were employed by the eminent patron Jean de France, duke of Berry (at Paris), along with a husband–wife team in 1377. The earliest documented organization of musicians was a lay religious guild in Arras, France around 1175, which admitted both women and men. Women and men were treated equally in the articles of incorporation for the earliest trade guild of minstrels organized in Paris in 1321. The articles, which regulated such activities as apprenticeships and hiring until 1773, consistently refer to *menestreus* and *menestrelles* or *jougleurs* and jougleresses. Seven of the thirty-seven people to sign the original articles as registered in 1341 were women.

Women's Musical Instruments. Iconography, French literary sources, and financial accounts of the English court all indicate that a single instrument, rather than an ensemble, most frequently accompanied voice(s) in European monophonic music of the twelfth and thirteenth centuries. Medieval sources represent women as performers of percussion instruments, organ, and especially string instruments, while wind instruments, specifically discouraged as unfeminine (inappropriate even for aristocratic men) during the Renaissance, must already have been a rarity. Percussion instruments, also viewed as unsuitable for women by the fifteenth century, were linked earlier with two activities in which women were prominent: processionals and dancing This is depicted in a late fourteenth-century manuscript illumination, at Vienna's Österreichische Nationalbibliothek, portraying five women in a procession, singing and playing small drums and handbells, two of the most common medieval percussion instruments.

Evidence that medieval women most frequently played string instruments—vielle, harp, psaltery, gittern, rote, lyre, rebec, and citole—can be found in French romances and didactic treatises. Illuminations in thirteenth-century French sources show women playing a similar group of strings: vielle, harp, rebec, and gittern. Iconography from the Iberian Peninsula offers some of the richest sources on medieval instruments and instrumentalists, and women are quite visible in these sources. For example, in a Galician-Portuguese manuscript called *Cancioneiro da Ajuda* (*Songbook of Succor*), twelve of the sixteen miniatures include women performers, most frequently singers who often accompany themselves with castanets or tambourine.

Women are also linked with the organ from very early on in music history. In fact, the earliest known organist, Thaïs, was a Greek woman (third century, B.C.E.). In Hungary, the tomb inscription for Aelia Sabina (probably third century to fourth century) reads: "She herself remaining, as she was seen among the people, playing the hydraulis [an early organ] so well" (Hettrick, 40). Since the early Christian church rejected the use of instruments in worship as pagan, the organ was not widely used in church services until the fourteenth century. However, wealthy monasteries owned and used organs much earlier, and perhaps this was true for convents as well. Beginning in the Middle Ages, small organs—called portative and positive—were signs of accomplishment and deemed appropriate instruments for domestic entertainment by women. A particularly detailed account by Apostolic Protonotary Teodoro da Montefeltro describes organ performances of Bianca de' Medici, a fourteen-year-old Florentine woman who entertained the entourage of Pope Pius II in early 1460. Montefeltro's letters, which indicate that Bianca performed intabulations (arrangements of vocal music for keyboard, employing a special system of notation using letters and numbers instead of notes on a staff) of well-known polyphonic vocal works by Binchois and others, favorably describe her playing "with fine phrases and proportion and impressive rhythm" (Prizer, 3–4). In keeping with the largely unwritten performance tradition of instrumental music during the fourteenth and fifteenth centuries, these arrangements were probably more likely her own than performances from notated intabulations by another composer. Thus, the close relationship among the roles of performer, improviser, and composer for organists during the late medieval period suggests an area in which women may have participated in creating polyphonic music.

In medieval China, the Tang dynasty (618–907), which sustained one of the greatest eras of Chinese poetry, is also considered a peak in music history. Several paintings, created in various eras, depict an all-women court orchestra performing for a nobleman and his wife, most likely representing events during the Tang dynasty. Perhaps the earliest and most exquisite of these is a scroll from the Sung dynasty (960–1279) imitating a tenth-century work by the famous painter Chou Wên-chü (Chicago Art Institute). The nineteen musicians shown conform to general expectations of the *li-yüan* ensemble introduced by Ming Huang in 714. The illustration shows precisely the instruments used during the Tang dynasty in the ensemble to accompany a genre of refined art songs called *fa-chü*: pairs of four-stringed *p'i-p'a* (lute), *k'ung-hou* (harp), *chêng* (zither), *shêng* (mouth organ), *ti* (transverse flute), *ch'ih-pa* (vertical flute) or *pi-li* (oboe), *chieh-ku* (side drum), *fang-hsiang* (gong-chime), and *p'ai-pan* (clapper), plus one *ta-ku* (large drum). Although these paintings claim to depict Emperor Ming Huang and his wife, Yang Kuei-fei (or Guifei), the evidence is insufficient to verify this. In any case, the paintings portray a nobleman—emperor, aristocrat, or high-level official—and his wife enjoying the music of their private orchestra. Ming Huang, an exceptionally charitable sponsor of music and dance, doubled China's official music departments by creating two new conservatories. In addition to a training center for his favorite music, *fa-chü*, he established another school primarily for female court musicians, often called singing girls. This institution, called *chiao-fang*, served more than three thousand women performers during this period. Hundreds of the women who were trained at the *chiao-fang* came to teach at the li-yüan conservatory. All of the musicians in these departments were government slaves.

Conclusion. Throughout the centuries of the European Middle Ages and contemporaneously in China and Japan, music was viewed as a powerful enterprise as well as a source of entertainment and pleasure. The spiritual power and moral persuasion ascribed to music gave it special significance and encouraged its regulation. Thus an institution such as the Christian Church, which proclaimed the psalms' seductive musicality as sacrosanct, also suppressed the voices of women. Because music functioned as a significant means to articulate status it is closely connected with both class and gender systems in the secular world as well. The presence of skilled musicians at court along with the creation of elaborate melodies and complex forms were marks of power and prestige. Middle- and upper-class women were restricted from public performance, yet their education and leisure gave them the opportunity to cultivate music as a personal accomplishment. At the lower end of the hierarchy, women musicians among slave and servant groups enjoyed considerable visibility as professional performers, while suffering abuse in other aspects of their lives. Gender and class differences thus contributed to and mostly defined the varied musical activities between women and men or among women during the medieval era.

See also *Alba* Lady; Bietris de Roman; Birgitta, of Sweden, St.; Blanche of Castile; *Chanson de Femme* (Women's Song); Compiuta Donzella; Comtessa de Dia; Courtesy Books; *Daina*; Desert Mothers; Egeria; Eleanor of Aquitaine; *Frauenlied*; Gertrude the Great, of Helfta, St.; Guilds, Women in; Hildegard of Bingen, St.; Katherine of Sutton; *Kharja*; Law, Canon, Women in; Lesbians in the Middle Ages; Maria de Ventadorn; Marie de France; Mary, Blessed Virgin, in the Middle Ages; Mechthild of Hackeborn; Mechthild of Magdeburg; Music in Medieval Nunneries; *Muwashshah*; Scribes and Scriptoria; *Skáldkonur* (Old Norse-Icelandic Women Poets); Transvestism; *Trobairitz*; *Trouvères*, Women; Wallādah; Yang Guifei

BIBLIOGRAPHY

Primary Sources
[See also Discography below].
Bec, Pierre. *Chants d'amour des femmes-troubadours: Trobairitz et "chansons de femme."* Paris: Stock, 1995.
Briscoe, James. *Historical Anthology of Music by Women.* Bloomington: Indiana University Press, 1987.
Bruckner, Matilda Tomaryn, Laurie Shepard, and Sarah White, eds. and trans. *Songs of the Women Troubadours.* New York: Garland, 1995. Revised ed. 2000.
Doss-Quinby, Eglal, Joan T. Grimbert, Wendy Pfeffer, Elizabeth Aubrey, eds. and trans. *Songs of the Women Trouvères.* New Haven, Conn. and London: Yale University Press, 2001.
Hildegard von Bingen. *Ordo virtutum*, etc.—*see* Discography *below.*
Kassianē. *Thirteen Hymns for Voice.* Edited by Diane Touliatos. Bryn Mawr, Pa.: Hildegard Music, 2000.
Klinck, Anne L., ed. *An Anthology of Ancient and Medieval Woman's Song.* New York: Palgrave Macmillan, 2004.
al-Makkari [al-Maqqari], Ahmed Ibn Mohammed. *The History of the Mohammedan Dynasties in Spain.* Translated and edited by Pascual de Gayangos. 2 vols. 1840. Reprint, New York: Johnson Reprints, 1964.
Newman, Barbara, ed. *Symphonia: A Critical Edition of the* Symphonia armonie celestium revelationum [by Hildegard]. Ithaca, N.Y. and London: Cornell University Press, 1988. 2nd ed. 1998.
Rieger, Angelica. *Trobairitz: Der Beitrag der Frau in der altokzitanischen höfischen Lyrik. Edition des Gesamtkorpus.* Beihefte der Zeitschrift für romanische Philologie, 233. Tübingen, Germany: Max Niemeyer, 1991.
Rosenberg, Samuel N., Margaret Switten, and Gérard Le Vot, eds. *Songs of the Troubadours and Trouvéres: An Anthology of Poems and Melodies.* New York: Garland Publishing, Inc., 1998. [CD included].
Strunk, Oliver. *Source Readings in Music History.* New York: W. W. Norton, 1950.

Secondary Sources
Bagnall, Anne D. "Musical Practices in Medieval English Nunneries." Ph.D. diss. New York: Columbia University, 1975.
Bec, Pierre. "'Trobairitz' et chansons de femme. Contribution à la connaissance du lyrisme féminin au moyen âge." *Cahiers de civilisation médiévale* 22 (1979): 235–62.
———, ed. *Burlesque et obscénité chez les troubadours: Pour une approche du contre-texte médiéval.* Paris: Stock, 1984.

Bogin, Meg. *The Women Troubadours*. New York: W. W. Norton, 1980. 1st ed. as *Les femmes troubadours*. Paris, 1978.

Bonse, Billie Ann. "'El son de n'alamanda': Another Melody by a *Trobairitz?*" M.A. thesis, Ohio State University, 1998.

Boswell, John. *Christianity, Social Tolerance and Homosexuality. Gay People in Western Europe from the Beginning of the Christian Era to the Fourteenth Century*. Chicago: University of Chicago Press, 1980.

Brown, Howard Mayer. "Women Singers and Women's Songs in Fifteenth-Century Italy." In *Women Making Music*, edited by Jane Bowers and Judith Tick, 62–89. Urbana: University of Illinois Press, 1986.

Bruckner, Matilda Tomaryn. "A Subgroup: The Women Troubadours." In *A Handbook of the Troubadours*, edited by F. R. P. Akehurst and Judith M. Davis, 201–33. Berkeley: University of California Press, 1995.

Cheyette, Fredric L., and Margaret Switten. "Women in Troubadour Song: Of the Comtessa and the Vilana." *Women & Music: A Journal of Gender and Culture* 2 (1998): 26–45.

Coldwell, Maria V. "*Jougleresses* and *Trobairitz*: Secular Musicians in Medieval France." In *Women Making Music*, edited by Jane Bowers and Judith Tick, 39–61. Urbana: University of Illinois Press, 1986.

Curne de Sainte-Palaye, Jean Baptiste de la. *Histoire littéraire des troubadours*, 3 vols. Paris, 1774. Reprint Geneva: Slatkine, 1967.

Dronke, Peter. *The Medieval Lyric*. London: Hutchinson University Library, 1968. 3rd ed. Cambridge: D. S. Brewer, 1996.

———. *Poetic Individuality in the Middle Ages. New Departures in Poetry 1000–1150*. Oxford: Oxford University Press, 1970. 2nd ed. London: Westfield College, 1986.

———. *Women Writers of the Middle Ages: A Critical Study of Texts from Perpetua (†203) to Marguerite Porete (†1310)*. Cambridge: Cambridge University Press, 1984.

Eckenstein, Lina. *Woman under Monasticism*. 1896. Reprint New York: Russell & Russell Inc., 1963.

Edwards, J. Michele. "Women in Music to ca. 1450." In *Women & Music: A History*, edited by Karin Pendle, 8–28. Bloomington: Indiana University Press, 1991. 2nd ed. 2001, 26–53.

Foster, Gennette. "The Iconology of Musical Instruments and Musical Performance in Thirteenth-Century French Manuscript Illuminations." Ph.D. diss., City University of New York, 1977.

Folena, Gianfranco. "Tradizione e cultura trobadorica nelle corti e nelle città venete." In *Storia della cultura veneta: Dalle Origini al Trecento*, 453–562. Venice: Neri Pozza, 1976.

Hettrick, Jane Schatkin. "She Drew an Angel Down: The Role of Women in the History of the Organ 300 B.C. to 1900 A.D." *The American Organist* 13.3 (March 1979): 39–45.

Higgins, Paula. "The 'Other Minervas': Creative Women at the Court of Margaret of Scotland." In *Rediscovering the Muses: Women's Musical Traditions*, edited by Kimberly Marshall, 169–85. Boston: Northeastern University Press, 1993.

———. "Parisian Nobles, a Scottish Princess, and the Woman's Voice in Late Medieval Song." In *Early Music History* 10, edited by Iain Fenlon, 145–200. Cambridge: Cambridge University Press, 1991.

Holsinger, Bruce W. *Music, Body and Desire in Medieval Culture: Hildegard of Bingen to Chaucer*. Figurae: Reading Medieval Culture. Stanford, Calif.: Stanford University Press, 2001.

Kishibe, Shigeo. "A Chinese Painting of the T'ang Court Women's Orchestra." In *The Commonwealth of Music: In Honor of Curt Sachs*, edited by Gustave Reese and Rose Brandel, 104–17. New York: The Free Press, 1965.

Klinck, Anne L., and Ann Marie Rasmussen, eds. *Medieval Woman's Song—Cross-Cultural Approaches*. Philadelphia: University of Pennsylvania Press, 2002.

Kwon, Yung-Hee Kim. "The Female Entertainment Tradition in Medieval Japan: The Case of Asobi." *Theatre Journal* 40.2 (May 1988): 205–16. Reprint in *Performing Feminisms: Feminist Critical Theory and Theatre*, edited by Sue-Ellen Case, 316–27. Baltimore: Johns Hopkins University Press, 1990.

Labarge, Margaret Wade. *Women in Medieval Life: A Small Sound of the Trumpet*. London: Hamish Hamilton, 1986.

Maillard, Jean. *Evolution et esthétique du lai lyrique, des origines à la fin du XIVème siècle*. Paris: Centre de Documentation Universitaire, 1963.

Marshall, Kimberly. "Symbols, Performers, and Sponsors: Female Musical Creators in the Late Middle Ages." In *Rediscovering the Muses: Women's Musical Traditions*, edited by Kimberly Marshall, 140–68. Boston: Northeastern University Press, 1993.

Nelli, René, ed. *Ecrivains anticonformistes du moyen-âge occitan: I. La femme et l'amour*. Paris: Phébus, 1977.

Newman, Barbara. *Sister of Wisdom: St. Hildegard's Theology of the Feminine*. Berkeley and Los Angeles: University of California Press, 1987.

———, ed. *Voice of the Living Light: Hildegard of Bingen and Her World*. Berkeley and Los Angeles: University of California Press, 1998.

Paden, William D., ed. *The Voice of the Trobairitz: Perspectives on the Women Troubadours*. Philadelphia: University of Pennsylvania Press, 1989.

Page, Christopher. *The Owl and the Nightingale: Musical Life and Ideas in France 1100–1300*. Berkeley and Los Angeles: University of California Press, 1989.

Poe, Elizabeth Wilson. "A Dispassionate Look at the *Trobairitz*." *Tenso* 7 (1992): 142–64.

Pollina, Vincent. "Melodic Continuity and Discontinuity in 'A chanter m'er' of the Comtessa de Dia." In *Miscellanea di studi romanzi offerta a Giuliano Gasca-Queirazza per il suo 65° compleanno*, edited by Anna Cornagliotti et al., 2: 887–96. Alessandria: Edizioni dell' Orso, 1988.

Prizer, William F. "Games of Venus: Secular Vocal Music in the Late Quattrocento and Early Cinquecento." *Journal of Musicology* 9.1 (1991): 3–56.

Quasten, Johannes. "The Liturgical Singing of Women in Christian Antiquity." *Catholic Historical Review* 27.2 (1941): 149–65.

Rieger, Angelica. "Beruf: *Joglaressa*. Die Spielfrau im okzitanischen Mittelalter." In *Feste und Feiern im Mittelalter*, edited by Detlef Altenburg, Jörg Jarnut, and Hans-Hugo Steinhoff, 229–42. Sigmaringen: Jan Thorbecke Verlag, 1991.

Rieger, Angelica. "Was Bieiris de Romans Lesbian? Women's Relations with Each Other in the World of the Troubadours." In *Voice of the Trobairitz*, 73–94. *See above, under* Paden.

Rokseth, Yvonne. "Les Femmes musiciennes du XIIe au XIVe siècle." *Romania* 61 (1935): 464–80; also as "Die Musikerinnen des 12. bis 14. Jahrhunderts," translated by Birgit Salomon and Freia Hoffmann. In *Von der Spielfrau zur Performance-Künstlerin*, edited by Freia Hoffmann and Eva Rieger, 40–59. Kassel, Germany: Furore-Verlag, 1992.

Ruch, Barbara. "The Other Side of Culture in Medieval Japan." In *The Cambridge History of Japan*, 3, edited by Kozo Yamamura, 500–543. Cambridge: Cambridge University Press, 1990.

Sankovitch, Tilde. "*Trobairitz*." In *The Troubadours: An Introduction*, edited by Simon Gaunt and Sarah Kay. New York: Cambridge University Press, 1999.

Scheifer, Martha Furman, and Sylvia Glickman, eds. *Composers Born before 1599*. Vol. 1 of *Women Composers: Music through the Ages*. New York: G. K. Hall, 1996.

Schultz-Gora, Oscar. "Nabieiris de roman." *Zeitschrift für romanische Philologie* 15 (1891): 234–35.

———, ed. *Die provenzalischen Dichterinnen. Biographien und Texte nebst Anmerkungen und einer Einleitung*. Leipzig: Fock, 1888. [His original stance favored a lesbian interpretation, but he shifted his position under heavy criticism; see above.]

Slocum, Kay Brainerd. "Confrérie, Bruderschaft and Guild: The Formation of Musicians' Fraternal Organisations in Thirteenth- and Fourteenth-Century Europe." *Early Music History* 14, edited by Iain Fenlon, 257–74. Cambridge: Cambridge University Press, 1995.

Smoldon, William L. *The Music of the Medieval Church Dramas*. London: Oxford University Press, 1980.

Touliatos, Diane. "The Traditional Role of Greek Women in Music from Antiquity to the End of the Byzantine Empire." In *Rediscovering the Muses:*, 11–123. *See above, under* Marshall.

Touliatos-Banker, Diane. "Medieval Women Composers in Byzantine and the West." In *Musica antiqua VI: Acta scientifica. pod patronatem UNESCO*. [Proceedings of the VIth International Congress of Musicology "Musica Antiqua Europae Orientalis"], 687–712. Bydgoszcz, Poland: Filharmonia Pomorska im. I. Paderewskiego w Bydgoszczy, 1982.

———. "Women Composers of Medieval Byzantine Chant." *College Music Symposium* 24 (spring 1984): 62–80.

Yardley, Anne Bagnall. "'Ful weel she soong the service dyvyne': The Cloistered Musician in the Middle Ages." In *Women Making Music*, 15–38. *See above, under* Brown.

Zufferey, François. "Toward a Delimitation of the *Trobairitz* Corpus." In *The Voice of the Trobairitz*, 31–43. *See above under* Paden.

Discography

The Ancient Miracles. Ensemble für frühe Musik Augsburg. Christophorus CD 77178.

Ancient Music for a Modern Age. Sequentia, directed by Barbara Thornton and Benjamin Bagby. Deutsche Harmonia Mundi 09026-61868-2. Also RCA 61868.

Ave Eva: Songs of Womanhood from the 12th and 13th Centuries. Brigitte Lesne, voice, harp and percussion. Opus 111 OPS30-134.

Bella Domna: The Medieval Woman: Lover, Poet, Patroness and Saint. Sinfonye, directed by Stevie Wishart. Hyperion CDA66283.

Calamus: Medieval Women's Songs. Pneuma Classics 50. [Anonymous from Arabic-Andalusian tradition; from Martin Codex]

Carmina burana, vol. 2. Studio der Frühen Musik, directed by Thomas Binkley. Teldec 8.44012 ZS.

La Chambre des Dames: Chansons et Polyphones de Trouvères (XIIe & XIIIe siècles). Diabolus in Musica, directed by Anroine Guerber. Aquitaine D2604.

Chansons der Troubadours. Studio der Frühen Musik, directed by Thomas Binkley. Telefunken SAWT 9567-B.

Chanterai: Music of Medieval France. Sonus. Dorian DIS-80123.

A Feather on the Breath of God. Gothic Voices, directed by Christopher Page. Hyperion CDA66039. [Hildegard hymns and sequences]

Forgotten Provence: Music-making in the South of France, 1150–1550. The Martin Best Consort. Nimbus Records NI 5445.

Gesänge der hl. Hildegard von Bingen. Schola der Benediktinerinnenabtei St. Hildegard in Eibingen, directed by Maria-Immaculata Ritscher, OSB. Psallite 242/040 479 PET.

Geistliche Musik des Mittelalters und der Renaissance. Instrumentalkreis Helga Weber, directed by Helga Weber with Almut Teichert-Hailperin. Teldec 66.22387. [Hildegard].

Hildegard von Bingen and her Time: Sacred Music of the 12th Century. Ensemble für frühe Musik Augsburg. Christophorus CD 74584.

Hildegard von Bingen: Canticles of Ecstasy. Sequentia, directed by Barbara Thornton. Deutsche Harmonia Mundi 05472 77320 2. Also RCA 77320.

Hildegard von Bingen: 11,000 Virgins: Chants for the Feast of St. Ursula. Anonymous 4. Harmonia Mundi France 907200.

Hildegard von Bingen: Heavenly Revelations. Oxford Camerata, directed by Jeremy Summerly. Naxos 8.550998.

Hildegard von Bingen: 900 Years. Sequentia. RCA 77505. [8-CD boxed set of complete works].

Hildegard von Bingen: O Jerusalem. Sequentia, directed by Barbara Thornton and Margriet Tindemans. RCA 77353.

Hildegard von Bingen: O Nobilissima Viriditas. Emmanuel Bonnardot, Catherine Schroeder, Catherine Sergent. Musisoft [Media 7] 6.

Hildegard von Bingen: O vis aeternitatis. Schola of the Benedictine Abbey of St. Hildegard. Ars Musici 1203.

Hildegard von Bingen: Ordo virtutum. Sequentia, directed by Barbara Thornton and Margriet Tindemans. EMI CDS7492498; also Deutsche Harmonia Mundi (Editio Classica) 2-77051-2-RG. Also RCA 77394.

Hildegard von Bingen: [Sacred Songs]. Instrumentalkreis Helga Weber, directed by Helga Weber; Almut Teichert-Hailperin, soprano et al. Entrée CHE0041-2.

Hildegard von Bingen: Saints. Sequentia, directed by Barbara Thornton and Margriet Tindemans. RCA 77378. [2 CDs].

Hildegard: Symphonia Armonie Celestium Revelationum; Birgitta: Cantus Sororum. Les Flamboyants. Raum Klang 9802. [St. Birgitta of Sweden was a fourteenth-century nun].

Hildegard von Bingen: Symphoniae. Sequentia, directed by Barbara Thornton. EMI/Deutsche Harmonia Mundi (Editio Classica) 77020-2-RG. Also RCA 77020.

Hildegard of Bingen: Symphoniae. Benedictine Abbey, Rudesheim. Bayer BYR 100116.

Hildegard von Bingen: Voice of the Blood. Sequentia, directed by Barbara Thornton. Deutsche Harmonia Mundi 05472 77346 2. Also RCA 77346.

Historical Anthology of Music by Women, I. Compiled by James R. Briscoe. Bloomington: Indiana University Press, 1991. [Kassianē; Hildegard]

The Lauds of Saint Ursula: Hildegard of Bingen (1098–1179). Musicians of the Early Music Institute, Indiana University School of Music, directed by Thomas Binkley. Focus 911.

Luminous Spirit: Chants of Hildegard von Bingen. Rosa Lamoreaux with Hesperus. Koch International Classics 7443.

The Medieval Lady. Andrea Folan with Elizabethan conversation. Leonarda LE340.

A Medieval Tapestry: Instrumental and Vocal Music from the 12th through 14th Centuries. The Folger Consort. Bard BDCD1-9003.

Monk and the Abbess. Musica Sacra, directed by Richard Westenburg. Catalyst CAT 68329.

Ordo Virtutum after Scivias. Directed by Stefan Morent with Monika Mauch and Andrea von Ramm. Bayer BYR100249. [Hildegard; slightly condensed version with added narration in German]

Sacred Women: Women as Composers and Performers of Medieval Chant. Sarband, directed by Vladimir Ivanoff. Dorian DOR-93235. [Byzantine, Christian, and Arab chant; Kassianē; Hildegard; Anonymous from Codex Las Huelgas].

The Sweet Look and the Loving Manner: Trobairitz, Love Lyrics and Chansons de Femme from Medieval France. Sinfonye, directed by Stevie Wishart. Hyperion CDA66625.

Troubadours. Clemencic Consort, directed by René Clemencic. Harmonia Mundi HMC 90396.

J. MICHELE EDWARDS

MUWASHSHAH. The *muwashshah* (plural *muwashshahāt*) is a lyric genre of Hispano-Arabic poetry originating in Muslim Spain (al-Andalus) during the late ninth century. It was written by men but often performed by women. These lyrics are prosodically intricate and rhetorically elaborate songs of praise, of life's pleasures, and, especially, of love's problematics.

The earliest extant texts in Arabic date from c.1000, and in Hebrew not appreciably later. However, they appear to have originated before these examples, back to the late ninth century. The *muwashshahāt* flourished at the splendid courts of al-Andalus, then spread to more popular audiences, soon to be adopted by Andalusian Jews for both secular and liturgical Hebrew poetry (Rosen-Moked). Later they were imported to North Africa and the Middle East, where they are sung to this day (Liu and Monroe).

Usually divided into five stanzas, which categorize the *muwashshah* as "strophic," the *muwashshah* contains two types of rhyme alternating through its five stanzas and therefore differs from the dominant form of Arabic verse, which is monorhythmic. Each stanza divides into two sections: the *ghuṣn*, whose rhyme was unique to that particular stanza, and the *simṭ* or *qufl*, whose rhyme echoed that pervading the entire poem. The *muwashshah*'s rhyme scheme can vary; the simplest being aaabb cccbb, and so forth, while the more complex include internal rhyme, in which the word ending a midsection (hemistich) of a verse would rhyme with that of a preceding verse. The most complete *muwashshah* also contained a prelude, called the *matla'*. The last *simṭ*, called *kharja*, (meaning literally "exit") forms the parting message of the poem. The *kharja* has received particularly wide attention in recent decades because of its provocative sociolinguistic departures from the body of the *muwashshah*; it uses a colloquial dialect while the rest of the *muwashshah* is composed in more learned registers of Arabic or Hebrew. The *kharja* (both in Arabic and Hebrew poems) was often written in the Andalusi vernaculars (Arabic or Mozarabic; the latter a hybrid dialect made up of Arabic and Romance elements). Within the total *muwashshah*, the main part of the poem is for the man's voice, while the *kharja* is often sung in the women's voice, thus affording a glimpse of the woman's view of love, often at odds with the man's.

Particularly since the brilliant discoveries made by Samuel Stern in the late 1940s, scholars have been debating the origins of the *muwashshah*. The so-called Romance advocates, perceiving its structural affinities with such peninsular (Spanish) genres as the *villancico* and the *canción*, advanced the hypothesis that all these forms stem from lost peninsular, pre-Arabic (pre-eighth century) strophic prototypes. By contrast, the Arabist theory claims Arabic roots for this genre and for a related genre, the *zajal*. The *muwashshah* and the *zajal* are also involved in another debate, one concerning the origins of Provençal troubadour poetry and more generally the European theme of courtly love (Menocal 1987).

Despite their popularity, and although they were written by professional poets and performed at court, the *muwashshahāt* were considered noncanonical poetry. They were thus often omitted from the *dīwān* (collected works) of esteemed poets and have survived only in collections dedicated to the genre itself. Though the great majority were composed by male poets for male audiences, a small number of *muwashshahāt* were written by Andalusian women. One was Nazhun, from Granada in the eleventh century, reported by the historian al-Maqqari (or at Makkari, d. c.1603) to have possessed "extraordinary talents for poetry." Another was Qasmuna, the daughter of Isma'il Ibn Bagdala (supposedly the Hebrew poet Samuel Ibn Naghrela), who, according to al-Maqqari, composed *muwashshahāt* together with her father.

The performance of the *muwashshahāt*, on the other hand, was more definitely a woman's art. As Stern (1946, 1974), Monroe (1974), and Compton have shown, the three most influential early critics formulating medieval Arabic literary canon pertaining to the *muwashshah* were Ibn Bassam in his *Dhakira* (d. 1147), Ibn Sana' al-Mulk (d. 1211), in his *Dār al-tiraz*—the closest to a true poetics of the genre—and Ibn Khaldūn (d. 1406), in his *Muqaddimah*, all noted this role. Ibn Khaldūn observes that the *muwashshahāt* were sung by a female soloist accompanied by a women's choir. So powerful was their effect that the Jewish philosopher and jurist Maimonides (Egypt, thirteenth century) prohibits Jews from listening to *muwashshahāt*, especially when sung by women, because "they aroused the desire to fornicate."

See also Chanson de Femme (Women's Song); Jewish Women in the Middle Ages; Kharja; Music, Women Composers and Musicians

BIBLIOGRAPHY

Primary Sources
Ghazi, Sayyid, ed. *Dīwā;n al-muwashshahāt al-Andalusiyah*. 2 vols. Alexandria, Egypt: Munshaat al-Maarif, 1979. [Ed. in Arabic with facsimiles].
Monroe, James T., ed. and trans. *Hispano-Arabic Poetry: A Student Anthology*. Berkeley: University of California Press, 1974. [Good introduction, bilingual texts of some *muwashshahāt*].
Ibn Bassam. *Ad Dakhira fi mahasin ahl al-Yasira*. Edited by Ihsan Abbas. Beirut, Lebanon: Dār al-Taqafa, 1979.
Ibn Khaldun. *Min Muqaddimat Ibn Khaldūn, nusus jamaaha wa-rattabaha wa-qaddama laha Albir Nasri Nadir*. Beirut, Lebanon: Dār al-Mashriq, 1967.

———. *The* Muqaddimah: *An Introduction to History. Ibn Khaldun.* Edited and translated by Franz Rosenthal. 3 vols. Bollingen series, 43. New York: Pantheon Books, 1958. Reprint, Princeton, N.J.: Princeton University Press, 1967.

Ibn Sanā'al-Mulk. *Dār al-tirāz fī amal al-muwashshahāt talīf al-Sa'īd Abī al-Qāsim Hibat Allah ibn Jafar ibn Sana al-Mulk/Dār al-Tiraz, poétique du muwassah.* Edited by Jawdat al-Rikābī. 2nd ed. Damascus, Syria: Dār al-Fikr, 1977. [Critical ed. of Arabic text based on Cairo and Leiden manuscripts, with facsimiles].

———. English translation in extracts *see* Compton, *below.*

Maqqari, Ahmad ibn Muhammad. *Analectes sur l'histoire et la littérature des Arabes d'Espagne/Nafh al-tib min ghusn al-Andalus al-ratib.* Edited and translated into French by Reinert P. A. Dozy et al. 2 vols. Leiden: Brill, 1855–1861. Reprint Amsterdam, Netherlands: Oriental Press, 1967.

Sola-Solé, Josep M., ed. *Corpus de poesí mozárabe (las hargas anadalusies).* Barcelona, Spain: Hispam, 1973.

———. *Los Jarchas romances y sus moaxajas.* Madrid: Taurus, 1990. [Revised version of above: transliterations of original text and Spanish translations of sixty-four known *kharjas* and their corresponding *muwashshahāt*].

Stern, S. M. "Les Vers finaux en espagnol dans les muwashshahs hispano-hébraïques." *Al-Andalus* 13 (1948): 299–346.

Secondary Sources

Alvarez, Luis. "muwashshah." In *The Encyclopedia of Arabic Literature,* edited by Julie Meisami and Paul Starkey, 2: 563–66. London: Routledge, 1998.

Armistead, Samuel G., and James T. Monroe. "Beached Whales and Roaring Mice: Additional Remarks on Hispano-Arabic Strophic Poetry." *La Corónica* 13 (1985): 206–42.

Compton, Linda. *Andalusian Lyrical Poetry and Old Spanish Love Songs: The* muwashshah *and Its* Kharja. New York: New York University Press, 1976.

García-Gómez, Emilio. "La Poésie lyrique hispano-arabe et l'apparition de la lyrique romane." *Arabica* 5 (1958): 113–44.

Hitchcock, Richard, and Consuelo Lopez-Morillas. *The* Kharjas: *A Critical Bibliography.* Supplement, 1. Research Bibliographies & Checklists, 20.1. London: Grant & Cutler, 1996.

Latham, D. "The Prosody of an Andalusian Muwassah Re-examined." In *Arabian and Islamic Studies in honor of R. B. Serjeant,* edited by Robin L. Bidwell and Gerald R. Smith, 86–99. London: Longman, 1983.

Jones, Alan. *Romance Kharjas in Andalusian Arabic Muwassah Poetry. A Paleographical Analysis.* London: Ithaca Press/Oxford University Oriental Studies, 1988.

———. "Romance Scansion and the Muwassahat: An Emperor's New Clothes?" *Journal of Arabic Literature* 11 (1980): 36–55.

Liu, Benjamin M., and James T. Monroe, eds. *Ten Hispano-Arabic Strophic Songs in the Modern Oral Tradition.* University of California. Publications in Modern Philology, 125. Berkeley: University of California Press, 1989.

Menocal, María Rosa. *The Arabic Role in Medieval Literary History.* Philadelphia: University of Pennsylvania Press, 1987.

———, Raymond Scheindlin, and Michael Sells, eds. *The Literature of Al-Andalus.* Cambridge and New York: Cambridge University Press, 2000.

Rosen, Tova. "The Muwashshah." In *The Literature of Al-Andalus,* edited by Menocal et al., 165–89. *See above entry.*

Rosen-Moked, Tova. *Le-ezor shir: al shirat ha-ezor ha-Ivrit bi-yeme ha-benayim/The Hebrew Girdle Poem (muwashshah) in the Middle Ages.* Haifa, Israel: University of Haifa, 1985.

Spitzer, Leo. "The Mozarabic Lyric and Theodor Frings' Theories." *Comparative Literature* 4 (1952): 1–22.

Stern, Samuel M. *Hispano-Arabic Strophic Poetry.* Edited by Leonard P. Harvey. Oxford: Clarendon, 1974. [Includes reprints of his seminal articles and 1946 dissertation].

TOVA ROSEN

N' ALAIS. *See* **Alaisina Yselda**

NA BIETRIS. *See* **Bietris de Roman**

NA CARENZA. *See* **Carenza, Na**

NA CASTELLOZA. *See* **Castelloza, Na**

NA ISELDA. *See* **Alaisina Yselda**

NATURA. One of the great and meaningful allegorical figures of the Middle Ages, Natura (Nature) was often characterized as a goddess because of the cosmic and moral ramifications of her activities. Like two other related major personifications, Philosophia and Fortuna, Natura emerges as an allegorized form out of the intellectual and cultural legacy of Classical Antiquity to medieval Europe. Because of the complex and various meanings of the word *physis* in Greek and *natura* in Latin, however, one finds in both Classical languages many instances of unallegorized, or, more precisely, grammatical personification of her—that is, cases in which she is a woman simply because "natura" is a feminine noun, without further characterization. Yet much of the significance of the fully allegorized medieval Natura figure derives from these unallegorized, or less-allegorized, personifications representing the meaning and actions of nature in the world. Throughout the following overview of the medieval literary history of Natura, therefore, "Natura" will signify the fully allegorized forms and "nature" the less allegorized, grammatical evocations.

In general terms, Antiquity bequeathed three major ideas of nature to the Middle Ages. First, nature could stand for the order of all creation as a single, harmonious whole, whose study would lead to the recognition and comprehension of the divine model that gave it form. Second, it could stand for the Platonic, and later, Neoplatonic, concepts of the cosmic intermediary between the intelligible and material worlds. Third, it could stand for the creative principle, ordained and directly subordinated to the mind and will of God, that presides over the continuity and preservation of all life in the world. A primary contribution to these ideas of nature originated in the writings of the Athenian (Greek) philosopher Plato (c.427–c.348 B.C.E.). His concept of the "world-soul" as the bridge between the material and immaterial worlds gave rise to the Neoplatonist, most notably Plotinian (after the third-century Greek philosopher Plotinus), placement of nature in a second world-soul, the offspring of the first, more powerful world-soul that contemplates the divine mind. This second world-soul, which Plotinus calls nature, imparts life, including the desire for self-perpetuation, to matter by transmitting to it images of the ideal world received from the first world-soul. These concepts, often combined with the fourth-century B.C.E. Greek philosopher Aristotle's ideas of nature as a principle of universal order and as the specific realm below the sphere of the moon—the so-called "sublunary world"—were conveyed to the medieval world through various sources, but none more telling than the commentaries of Macrobius and Chalcidius. The latter's early fourth-century Latin translation of approximately the first half of Plato's *Timaeus* was the only direct source of Plato's thought in the Middle Ages. Chalcidius's extensive commentaries on the work provided knowledge of other Platonic dialogues and of Neoplatonic thought in general. His commentary represented nature as the vivifying force specifically of the sublunary world. In addition, echoing Aristotle, he defined nature as the second of three kinds of creativity or work, after God's and preceding the human artist's. Chalcidius's ideas played a major role in medieval characterizations of Natura. Similarly, the very popular early fifth-century commentary on Cicero's *Somnium Scipionis* (*Dream of Scipio*) by Macrobius not only communicated aspects of the Neoplatonic world picture but it also reinforced the Aristotelian division between the immortal heavens and the mutable sublunary world of nature. It also offered a personified locution of nature as a craftsman or artist (*artifex*) participating in the biology of human creation and reproduction.

Many of these ideas of nature passed into medieval culture through the *De consolatione Philosophiae* (*Consolation of Philosophy*) of Boethius (c.480–524), an important link to the thought of the ancient world. Especially significant in the discourse of Philosophia's prose lectures to Boethius are the concepts of nature's dependence on Providence for its power and direction, and that of nature's presiding over procreation and providing a guide for right behavior. Later Boethian commentators, like pseudo-John Scotus Erigena (ninth century) and William of Conches (early twelfth century), would further define and shape these ideas in terms of the medieval Natura as intermediary between God and the world and as God's steward over procreation and human artistry. But Boethius also contributed significantly to the allegorized figure of Natura the goddess through his poetic representation of nature, especially in the second meter of the Consolatio's third book, in which he describes "Natura potens" ("powerful Nature") driving the universe as a charioteer would his team of horses. Descending in part from Orphic and Eastern sources of the Great Mother, this kind of figure of nature as cosmic power also appears in the works of many Latin poets, despite the considerable range of philosophical and religious persuasion among them, including Ovid (43? B.C.E.–17 C. E.), Lucretius (98?–55 B.C.E.), and, of particular importance to the Middle Ages, Statius (c.45–96) and Claudian (d. 408?). These various personifications of Natura by the poets of Antiquity provided medieval authors with a prototypical model on which to base their characterizations of the goddess.

However, individual features were also drawn from other major personified figures, of which there is no better example than Boethius's own Philosophia, whose torn tunic was to be handed down eventually to the Natura of Alan of Lille, in his major books, *De planctu naturae* (*Complaint of Nature*, 1160–1172) and *Anticlaudianus* (*Treatise Against Claudian*, 1181–1184).

But just prior to Alan's portrayal, the central and most influential characterization of the personified figure in the period, stands the Natura of the early twelfth-century Chartrian (from the philosophical School of Chartres, France) intellectual, Bernard, or Bernardus Silvestris (Bernard Silvestre, Bernard Sauvage). His poem of the cosmogony, *Cosmographia* (*Cosmography*), also known as *De mundi universitate* (*On the Whole Universe*), composed (as was the *De planctu naturae*) in the prosimetrum form: so-called because of its characteristic alternating sections of prose and verse made popular by Boethius and Martianus Capella (fifth century), represents a culmination of several centuries of medieval Christian Neoplatonism. Written between 1145 and 1156, the *Cosmographia* consists of two books: "Megacosmos"—on the universe—and "Microcosmos"—on humankind—in which Natura plays a key role in the creation. She is subordinate to Noys, Bernard's name for the Greek *nous* (divine wisdom), a figure with strong parallels to but never explicitly identified with the second person of the Trinity. In the first book ("Megacosmos"), Natura complains of matter's shapelessness and disorder and pleads with Noys to put it in order. After the process of creation is under way, she produces bodies to house the souls provided by Endelechia (entelechy), Bernard's term for the world-soul. In the second book ("Microcosmos"), at the behest of Noys, Natura embarks on a journey of epic proportions in which she travels through the heavens to the uppermost sphere to met the goddess Urania, where Natura is entrusted with the soul for the ultimate act of creation, that of the microcosm in emulation of the celestial order. After descending with the new soul and Urania to earth, Natura joins the soul to the body prepared for it by Physis, an intriguing figure who both mediates Natura's power in the sublunary world and represents the progress of the physical sciences in the theory and practice of the time, perhaps as a result of the introduction of some Aristotelian notions of nature into the Platonic tradition.

An extremely complex work, Bernard's *Cosmographia* demands that it be understood as a presentation—*sub fabulosa narratione* (narration in the manner of a fable), wrapped in the Timaean myth of creation—of the Scriptural truth of Genesis. This may explain why it contains only a few, relatively briefly and at times obliquely made, allusions and references to Christianity. Among these, however, are explicit references to the Trinity, to which Natura and Urania pray before beginning their descent to earth, and to the virgin birth of Christ, included in the history of the human race as it is written in the stars. Bernard weaves the doctrine of the Fall of Man and its consequences particularly in his account of the inferiority and instability of the sublunary world. It is this doctrine that relates to the activity of his Natura figure in a manner heralding one of the most important features of the medieval goddess as she was developed in the work of later writers. The work closes with the actual shaping of man's body out of the four elements left over from the creation of the macrocosm, whereupon the fate of this paragon of creation, its moment of pre-lapsarian (before the Fall) status programmed apparently for an early end, is announced through special praise for the sexual organs' combat against death. Here, in the closing verses of the *Cosmographia*, the object is not the restoration of the lost state through

Christ's Incarnation, but rather the continuation of human life; for through the perpetuation of the race nature is restored. Natura herself is depicted as artfully molding the seminal fluid through which the forms of ancestors may be revived.

Bernard's naturalistic vision anticipated the major functions of Alan of Lille's goddess Natura as God's vicegerent, the *vicaria Dei*, and as "overseer of procreation and marriage" ("procreatrix et pronuba"): features that Jean de Meun (*Roman de la Rose*) and Geoffrey Chaucer (*Book of the Duchess, Parliament of Fowls, Canterbury Tales*) would develop over the next two centuries. As if continuing the narrative begun by Bernard, Alan of Lille (Alain de Lille, Alanus de Insulus) in his *De planctu naturae* and *Anticlaudianus*, pursues the theme of Natura and her creation beyond that of origins as the allegory of cosmogony yields to one of cosmology and salvation history. Like the Philosophia of Boethius, Natura appears in the *De planctu* before a troubled narrator, in this case over humanity's departures from Natura's decrees, and offers a lengthy complaint and allegorical description of the causes and consequences of these departures, followed by a scene in which Hymen, the god of marriage, and other allegorized virtues in her retinue, meet with Natura and her priest, Genius, who condemns as excommunicate all those who practice unlawful love or other vices of intemperance. In this vision of Natura complaining, a motif echoing Claudian's *De raptu Proserpinae* (*The Rape of Proserpina*), Natura herself, the fashioner of the human race, laments in detail how humanity has strayed from her principles, primarily but not exclusively through its acts of perverted and unproductive love. In her account, she explains that God had ordained her to provide the mutable world with continuity through procreation and to this end she had enlisted the aid of Venus, her husband Hymen, and their son Cupid. After first following Natura's instructions in the proper use of the hammers and anvils turned over to her, also equated metaphorically with obeying the rules of grammar, Venus soon grew bored with her task and committed adultery with a figure named Antigenius in some manuscripts and Antigamus in others, producing a son named Jocus (Mirth, or Sport). As a result, all manner of intemperate, adulterous, and unnatural love was released in the world, followed by numerous other vices, identified as the daughters of old idolatry.

This complicated, fabulous depiction of fallen human nature was prompted in the first place by the narrator's inquiry about a tear in one of Natura's garments. Reminiscent of the tear, noted by Boethius, in Philosophia's garment that represented the violence men have done to her truth, this tear appears in a tunic that is only one part of Natura's elaborate dress and represents the violence the human race has done to the truth of its own rational nature. The extraordinary, lengthy *descriptio per vestimentum* (description through clothing) of Natura's appearance covers the entire created universe from the fixed stars in her crown to the flowers on her shoes as she rides in her chariot, continuously drawing with her pen on tablets pictures that shortly and persistently fade away. Through this sustained rhetorical tour de force, Alan has incorporated into a single portrait Natura's major cosmological features, especially her position as *vicaria Dei* (vicar of God) and her function as *procreatrix* of the transitory sublunary world. The concluding episode of the *De planctu naturae*, the most important aspect of which is the arrival at the convocation of virtues of the goddess's priest Genius, suggests a resolution to the problems raised in Natura's complaint and also prepares the way for the argument of the *Anticlaudianus*. Based on a cosmic figure who assigns form and individuality to all that is created in the lower world in Bernard's *Cosmographia*, Alan's Genius is described as Natura's priest and "other self," with whom she has had a daughter named Truth. Joining the company at her invitation through a letter delivered to him by Hymen, Genius arrives in robes on which the images of things appear evanescently, and, like Natura, he draws with either hand on a piece of parchment images that continuously fade. Putting on his priestly robes and delivering his excommunication of all behavior that is *contra naturam* (against nature), Genius offers a corrective to the moral depravity that has marred her tunic and the possibility of restoration to a state of virtue.

The realization of this restoration is the major theme of Alan's *Anticlaudianus*, in which Natura calls for the creation of a new and perfect human—a *novus homo*—a figure suggesting a prelapsarian version of Adam or Christ. Though it is Natura who convenes the virtues and initiates the proposal for the making of a new human whose effectuation will redeem the hitherto defective creation, the figure of Prudence actually carries out the central epic action of the over 4,000-line narrative. Yet Natura, in her various cosmic functions, is never far away from the center of the complex and elaborate process in which the construction of the new man occurs. It is she who fashions his body out of the elements and, after the creation is complete, leads the virtues in his defense against the attack of the vices, the psychomachic (war of intellectual abstractions: here, good against evil) triumph of man's renewed integrity confirming the renewal of her own moral authority.

This characterization of the medieval Natura throughout the twelfth century as a feminine personification of not merely one, but a constellation of cosmic abstractions, produced a powerful symbolic image of woman as an important part of the order of things. But as a figure performing her roles in Bernard and Alan's fables—what the later Dante called "allegories of the poets"—she takes on an even greater significance by virtue of the allegorical implications of her literal actions. Nature's cumulatively redemptive role—initiated in Bernard with her role of countering death by ensuring the survival of humanity, and continuing in Alan with her added capacity, as aided by the priestly presence of Genius, to introduce the possibility of moral reformation, then finally, through her cooperation with other divine and cosmic figures, the attainment of perfection—suggests that of the Church (*Ecclesia*) and its founder. These phases of her appearance, particularly her advent in the *De planctu naturae* to reverse the course of events symbolized by the temporary victory of old Idolatry, present strong resonances of the Incarnation and the coming of Christ. While the gender-consistent typological association of Natura/Ecclesia offers immediate accessibility, that of Natura/Christ claims a more profoundly meaningful figural affinity and strikes a still deeper cultural resonance. If it is true that at roughly the same time, the medieval mind could conceive of Jesus as Mother, then it could also conceive of Mother Nature as Jesus. As an allegorical figure who comes as Christ, Natura is, therefore, a forerunner of Dante's Beatrice who comes as Christ in the *Divina Commedia* (*Divine Comedy*, 1321). Yet Dante invokes this parallelism first and most strikingly in the twenty-fourth chapter of the *Vita Nuova* (*New Life*, c.1293), with the vision of Primavera (Spring)/Giovanna leading Beatrice. Such an analogy between John the Baptist and the True Light and the figures of two young women loved by him and his best friend, Guido Cavalcanti, results, at least partly, from the later medieval poets' tendency to appropriate earlier poets' symbolic abstractions and transform them into actual persons, both good and bad. In this vein, just as the allegorical figures named Faux Semblant (False

Seeming) and La Vieille (the Old Woman) of the *Roman de la Rose* provided foundations for Chaucer's characterizations of his Pardoner and Wife of Bath, so did Natura provide Dante with a prototype through which he could imagine redemption coming in the form of a woman.

It is noteworthy that the literature of the later Middle Ages basically preserved the majestic allegorized image of Natura as a cosmic and moral force, though not without some serious departures. While the portrayal of Natura in a Latin allegorized lament like Jean de Hauville (or Hanville, or Johannes de Altavilla)'s *Architrenius* (c.1184) depended directly on Alan of Lille's, her later representation in a work like the *Pèlerinage de Vie Humaine* (*Pilgrimage of Human Life*) of Guillaume de Deguilleville (fl. 1330–1358), derived primarily from that of Jean de Meun's continuation of the *Roman de la Rose* (*Romance of the Rose*, c.1275). Jean de Meun, in turn, had based his goddess—perhaps the most widely circulating Natura figure of the later medieval period—on that of Alan and even translated him in places verbatim. Yet in the course of the roughly five thousand lines devoted to the contribution of Natura and Genius to the grand debate and narrative concerning love, Jean radically reworked both figures to suit the action and theme of his poem. Besides concentrating more than Alan on the human qualities of his personified goddess Natura, portraying her at times as petulant and distraught and subjecting her to a thinly veiled ironic sermon by her priest Genius on the prolixity of women, Jean introduced a number of fundamental changes to her representation as a cosmic and moral force. Retaining her status as *vicaria Dei*, he especially emphasized her work as procreatrix, giving posterity an enduring picture of her working at her forge; however, he eliminated her role as pronuba, thus removing marriage as the legitimizing context of reproduction, and dissociated Natura from reason, thus denying it as one of her gifts to humanity. In fact, Jean shifts much of task of preaching the doctrine of love taught by Alan's Natura onto another of his *Rose*'s allegorical characters, Raison (Reason), to simplify his Natura into a morally neutral figure whose overriding concern is to prevent the life-sustaining, procreative urge she inspires from being blocked in any way. It is a position that Venus and the God of Love are quite ready to exploit to achieve their end, and Jean de Meun, in a stunning parodic reversal of the traditional excommunication ceremony near the final scene of his *Roman de la Rose*, puts Genius through a double costume change and sends him with Natura's message to Love's camp. As he leaves Natura, Genius sheds his priestly robes and puts on secular clothes, only to have them removed by the God of Love, who then re-dresses him as his own bishop. The new meaning of Natura, thus, has been symbolically as well as literally wrapped anew in a narrative that places the natural inclination toward reproduction in the service of a religion of love devoted only to the act and not the procreative end of sexual union.

Like Dante, Chaucer had read both Alan of Lille and Jean de Meun, as reflected in his treatment of Natura. Natura as *artifex*, particularly as incomparable creator of feminine human beauty, is mentioned in the *Book of the Duchess* by the grieving Knight in Black in his description of the departed "goode faire White." She reappears likewise as artist, and also as *vicaria Dei* and queen of the sublunary world in the Physician's Tale of *The Canterbury Tales* in a passage praising the beauty of Virginia, a work of Nature's art superior to that of any of the greatest of human artists. But the most important appearance of Natura in Chaucer comes near the end of the *Parliament of Fowls*, in the scene casting her as "vicaire of the almighty Lord" to preside over the mating rites of the birds on

St. Valentine's Day. Thus Chaucer restores to the goddess what Jean had deleted: the role of *Natura pronuba et procreatrix*, the divinely appointed overseer of marriage and procreation—and not merely the sexual act—a combination so important in Alan of Lille.

Because the grammatical gender of nouns did not apply to the English of Chaucer's time as it did in other Western languages, the feminine personification of Alan's Natura directly follows the characterization established by his French and Latin *auctores* (authors/authorities). It is instructive to remark the contrast in the way Chaucer's contemporary, William Langland, handled the personification of the Middle-English synonym for nature, *kynde*, in his visionary political and moral satire, *Piers Plowman* (c.1362–1387). While some functions of nature and natural law alluded to in the poem are denoted by the personified term kynde, it is the allegorical figure of Kynde himself—appearing in the middle of the work—the creator, father, and former of all things, who both compares and contrasts with Natura. Since the word itself left Langland free to assign either gender to its personification, it was his decision to identify it with God the Creator that determined Kynde's masculine gender. This choice, however, does not necessarily imply Langland's unawareness of or resistance to the Chartrian Natura tradition, especially if one recalls that, in the Holy Trinity, the figure of God as creator must also reflect Christ, for whom Natura had served as a type in Alan of Lille's allegories. The absence of grammatical gender allowed Langland the freedom to shape a new and different but not altogether alien Natura figure.

Similarly, Dante, in the third part of his *Commedia*, the *Paradiso*, canto 13, through the discourse of St. Thomas Aquinas, would depict Natura directly in line with her former representations. Dante the poet thereby exploited the new setting and perspective of his true history of a living man's journey through the otherworld to produce a highly condensed and original, though still traditional, portrayal. Prompted by Dante the narrator-pilgrim's question about the wisdom and perfection of Solomon, Aquinas lectures him on the creation of eternal and temporal things. Describing the descent of the divine creative light from its source in the Trinity through the angelic hierarchies and the heavens and finally down to matter, Aquinas explains the principle of creation that directly made Adam and Christ, who are thus more perfect than Solomon, and indirectly made all earthly creatures, those brief contingencies generated with or without seed. Out of this distinction between God's primary and nature's secondary creative causes, there suddenly emerges a singular and acute image of the goddess that captures an important part of her centuries-in-the-making significance. On the lowest sublunary level of creation, Dante's Aquinas continues, "the wax of things" is imperfect, for nature always stamps it with the seal defectively, "working like an artist who has the skill of his art and a hand that trembles." With a swift stroke of minimal personification, Dante the poet manages to invoke the concept of the *vicaria Dei*, the secondary cause that imprints matter with the seal of the idea, but he most brilliantly summons and transforms the traditional threefold division of creativity—God's, nature's in imitation of God, and the human artist's in imitation of nature—into a context suited to Dante the pilgrim's new "trans-humanized" state. The *Paradiso* poet suppresses the explicit statement of the third category but retains it, nonetheless, through the simile of his description of nature working like an artist. In one way, Nature may be perceived as the artist who knows the perfect form, being close to the source of divine light, but who always falls short in execution, being the creative principle of a physical and fallen world. In another, perhaps more important, way, it is an apt description of Dante himself, who, by virtue of the journey to which he has been called, has risen above his earthly nature to see things of which, on his return to this world, he must write as best he can, a burden, he confesses ten cantos later, that causes him to "tremble." In the wake of this first stage of his restoration, this human artist—Dante—must strive to emulate the nature that mediates between his world and that of the light that gave them both their being. The assimilation of redeemed human nature to the station of Natura has become a condition of his writing.

See also Beatrice; Chaucer, Geoffrey, Women in the Work of; Laura; *Roman de la Rose, Debate of the*; Virginity

BIBLIOGRAPHY

Primary Sources
Alan of Lille. *Anticlaudianus, or, The Good and Perfect Man*. Translated with commentary by James J. Sheridan. Toronto: Pontifical Institute of Mediaeval Studies, 1973.
———. [*De planctu naturae*] *Complaint of Nature*. Translated with commentary by James J. Sheridan. Mediaeval Sources in Translation, 26. Toronto: Pontifical Institute of Mediaeval Studies, 1980.
Bernard Silvestris. *Cosmographia*. Critical ed. by Peter Dronke. Leiden: E. J. Brill, 1978.
———. *The Cosmographia*. Translated with commentary by Winthrop Wetherbee. Records of Western Civilization. New York: Columbia University Press, 1990.
Boethius. [*De consolatione Philosophiae*] *Consolation of Philosophy*. Translated with commentary by Joel C. Relihan. Indianapolis, Ind.: Hackett, 2001.
Claudian. *De raptu Proserpinae*. Critical ed. and translation by Claire Gruzelier. Oxford Classical Monographs. Oxford: Clarendon Press; New York: Oxford University Press, 1993.
Chalcidius. *Timaeus. Plato; a Calcidio translatus commentarioque instructus*. Edited by Jan H. Waszink and Povl J. Jensen. Corpus Platonicum Medii Aevi, Plato latinus, 4. London: Warburg Institute & E. J. Brill, 1975.
Chaucer, Geoffrey. *Canterbury Tales*. In *The Riverside Chaucer*, edited by Larry D. Benson. 3rd ed. Boston: Houghton Mifflin, 1987.
Dante Alighieri. *Divina Commedia*. Edited and translated by Charles Hall Grandgent. Revised by Charles Singleton. Cambridge, Mass.: Harvard University Press, 1972. [Bilingual ed.].
———. *Vita nuova*. Critical ed. by Luca Carlo Rossi. Introduction by Guglielmo Gorni. Milan: Arnoldo Mondadori, 1999.
———. *Vita nuova*. Translated with introduction by Mark Musa. World's Classics. Oxford and New York: Oxford University Press, 1992.
Guillaume de Deguilleville. *Pèlerinage de vie humaine*. Edited by J. J. Stürzinger. Publications of the Roxburghe Club, 124. London: Nichols & Sons, 1893.
———. *Pilgrimage of Human Life*. Translated by Eugene Clasby. Garland Library of Medieval Literature, B76. New York: Garland, 1992.
Guillaume de Lorris and Jean de Meun. *Roman de la Rose*. Edited by Félix Lecoy. 3 vols. Classiques Français du Moyen Âge, 92, 95, 98. Paris: Honoré Champion, 1965–1970. Reprinted 1970–1976, 1982.
———. *The Romance of the Rose*. Translated by Frances Horgan. World's Classics. Oxford and New York: Oxford University Press, 1994.
Jean de Hauville. *Architrenius*. Edited and translated by Winthrop Wetherbee. Cambridge Medieval Classics, 3. Cambridge: Cambridge University Press, 1994.
Langland, William. *Piers Plowman. C text*. Edited by Derek Pearsall. York Medieval Texts, 2nd series. Berkeley: University of California Press, 1978.
———. *Piers Plowman*. Verse translation by George D. Economou. Middle Ages. Philadelphia: University of Pennsylvania Press, 1996.
Macrobius. [*Commentarii in Somnium Scipionis*]. *Commentary on the Dream of Scipio*. Translated with notes by William H. Stahl. New York: Columbia University Press, 1990.

Plato. *Timaeus*. Translated with introduction by Donald J. Zeyl. Indianapolis, Ind.: Hackett, 2000.

Plotinus. [*Enneads*, selections] *The Essential Plotinus*. Translated with commentary by Elmer O'Brien. Indianapolis, Ind.: Hackett; New York: New American Library, 1964.

Secondary Sources

Bennett, J. A. W. *The Parlement of Foules: An Interpretation*. Oxford: Clarendon Press, 1957.

Bynum, Caroline Walker. *Jesus as Mother: Studies in the Spirituality of the High Middle Ages. Publications of the Center for Medieval and Renaissance Studies, UCLA, 16. Berkeley: University of California Press, 1982.*

Chenu, Marie-Dominique. *Nature, Man, and Society in the Twelfth Century*. Translated by Jerome Taylor and Lester K. Little. Chicago: University of Chicago Press, 1968.

Economou. George D. *The Goddess Natura in Medieval Literature*. Cambridge, Mass.: Harvard University Press, 1972.

Ferrante, Joan M. *Woman as Image in Medieval Literature: From the Twelfth Century to Dante*. New York: Columbia University Press, 1975.

Fleming, John V. *The* Roman de la Rose: *A Study in Allegory and Iconography*. Princeton, N.J.: Princeton University Press, 1969.

Gunn, Alan M. F. *The Mirror of Love*. Lubbock: Texas Tech Press, 1952.

Huot, Sylvia. *The Romance of the Rose and Its Medieval Readers: Interpretation, Reception, Manuscript Transmission*. Cambridge Studies in Medieval Literature, 16. Cambridge: Cambridge University Press, 1993.

Newman, Barbara. *God and the Goddesses: Vision, Poetry, and Belief in the Middle Ages*. Middle Ages. Philadelphia: University of Pennsylvania Press, 2002.

Raynaud de Lage, Guy. *Alain de Lille*. Paris: Librairie Philosophique J. Vrin, 1951.

Stock, Brian. *Myth and Science in the Twelfth Century: A Study of Bernard Silvester*. Princeton, N.J.: Princeton University Press, 1972.

Wetherbee, Winthrop. *Platonism and Poetry in the Twelfth Century: The Literary Influence of the School of Chartres*. Princeton, N.J.: Princeton University Press, 1972.

White, Hugh. *Nature and Salvation in Piers Plowman*. Cambridge: D. S. Brewer, 1988.

———. *Nature, Sex, and Goodness in a Medieval Literary Tradition*. Oxford and New York: Oxford University Press, 2000.

Ziolkowski, Jan. *Alain de Lille's Grammar of Sex: The Meaning of Grammar to a Twelfth-Century Intellectual*. Cambridge, Mass.: Mediaeval Academy of America, 1985.

GEORGE D. ECONOMOU

NINE WORTHY WOMEN (14th–15th centuries). The motif of the Nine Worthy Women, or, in French, the *Neuf Preuses*, refers to a specific late fourteenth- and fifteenth-century grouping of nine female warriors, established as a pendant to the better-known Nine Male Worthies (*Neuf Preux*) who, as a group, constituted the epitome of chivalric prowess. These pantheons were inspired by the parades of heroes episodes contained in Ancient Greek and Roman epics, which not only provided models of public virtue and military honor, but also helped to reinforce cultural and artistic continuity from one civilization to another across the ages. The Nine Worthy Women represents a perhaps more daring additional crossover, that between conventions of gender. The common goal became one to provide models for ideal heroes, then heroines, to counteract the threatened extinction of chivalry within what many moralists perceived as an unraveling of late-medieval European social codes.

However, the adoption of the term *Neuf Preuses* to parallel the title of the male canon somewhat exaggerates the similarities between the two groups. Jacques de Longuyon, a poet from Lorraine, France, invented the male motif in his *Les Voeux du paon* (*Vows of the*

Peacock), a poem from 1312 belonging to the extended group of epics and romances comprising the *Roman d'Alexandre* (*Romance of Alexander the Great*). Longuyon, in formulating this thematic list, frankly proclaimed it to identify the nine best exemplars of chivalric honor the world had ever known, culled from ancient and near-contemporary myth, legend, and history. This enumeration first names three pagans—one Greek (from Homer's *Iliad*), one Trojan, one Roman—Hector, Alexander, Julius Caesar; then three Old Testament, thus Jewish, heroes (Joshua, David, Judas Maccabeus), followed by three Christians—the ninth-century Frankish emperor Charlemagne, the more mythical King Arthur, and Godefroi de Bouillon, the crusader-hero of the 1356 epic poem, *Le Chevalier au cygne et Godefroi de Bouillon* (*The Knight of the Swan and Godfrey of Bouillon*), part of the group of twelfth- through fifteenth-century French poems known as the *Crusade Cycle* (*Cycle de la Croisade*). Longuyon contributed no female counterparts to these male Worthies. In fact, his heroines exemplify traditional feminine traits, and the *Voeux* ends with their marriages. The *Voeux du paon* were soon translated into Scottish by the archdeacon of Aberdeen, John Barbour (d. 1395), as part of his *Buik of Alexander*.

There is little evidence of the existence of the Worthy Women until the 1380s, but their sudden appearance and immediate popularity in that decade are rather astonishing. Although a 1388 royal inventory cites the need to repair a tapestry of "les presses" (a variant spelling of "les preuses"), implying much earlier origins, the first literary references to the female Worthies, both French, occur in Jean Le Fèvre's *Le Livre de leësce* (*Book of Joy*, c.1380–1389) and in two undated ballads (c.1380s) by Eustache Deschamps in his *Autre Balades* (*Other Ballades*) sequence: nos. 93 "Il est temps de faire la paix" ("It Is Time to Make Peace") and 403.

In contrast to the fixed nature of the male canon, the members of the female canon varied. Apparently attempting to parallel the *Neuf Preux* by selecting women who showed "manly courage," the anonymous formulator(s) of the female canon ignored the strict triadic division by faith of the males and honored only pagan women warriors, predominantly Amazons. That the male grouping was divided into threes must have made the list easier to remember (in addition to the sacred Trinitarian connotation of the number three to the Christian Middle Ages), and thus more resistant to change, than the less familiar names and unstructured list of the female grouping. But changes in the list of *Preuses* are circumscribed and understandable: the name Antiope alternates with the variant Sinope, Lampedo substitutes for co-ruler Marpesia, and the popular tapestry subjects, Teuta from Pliny's *Historia naturalis* (*Natural History*), Deiphyle, and sister Argia from Statius's *Thebaid* (or its twelfth-century French version, the *Roman de Thèbes* [*Romance of Thebes*]), sometimes replace one or two Amazons. A comparison of Le Fèvre's and Deschamps's lists shows Sinope, Hippolyta, Menalippe, Semiramis, Thomyris, Penthesilea, Teuta, and Deiphyle in common, but where Le Fèvre gives Lampedo, Deschamps names Marpesia. But examination of the names of female *exempla*, or moral examples, in Deschamps's ballads suggests that he might have preferred a canon of less warlike women as his *Preuses*—Lucretia, Penelope, Esther, and Judith, or an array of Christian saints.

The question of exact sources for the women is also hazier than that for the male tradition. The third-century Roman author Justin (Justinus) composed an *Epitome*, a sort of digest condensing the forty-four books of the *Historia Philippicae* (*History of the Macedonians*) by the earlier, Augustan-age (27 B.C.E.–14 C.E.) Roman historian Trogus Pompeius.

Justinus's work, typical of the genre known as "epitome," lists and describes exemplary personages and names the Amazon mainstays of the burgeoning Nine Worthy Women canon. Many manuscripts of the *Epitome* have been traced to scholarly libraries throughout the European Middle Ages, from Charlemagne's time (ninth century) to France and Italy in the early fourteenth century. It is thus not surprising that at least one such manuscript ended up at Laon, in northern France, where the female motif seems to have gathered its first impetus. Another disseminating medium was the tapestry industry, centered in nearby Arras, which often adopted series of eight or nine figures from literature to create a room of tapestries. Knowledge of at least some of the Worthy Women as part of Classical Antique (Greek and Roman) lore, if a bit garbled and fragmented, was also transmitted through various medieval intermediaries. These were usually patchwork compilations of learning and commentaries, sometimes moralized, for vernacular Christian readers, often school-boys. A major catalog of women, more deftly done than those just described, is that by the great Italian humanist writer Giovanni Boccaccio (c.1313–1375), especially in his c.1361 *De claris mulieribus* (*Famous Women*), for which Justin served as a basis. Boccaccio's catalog, which was soon translated from Latin into French (*Des cleres femmes*), cites several of the Worthy Women.

It seems certain that these nine illustrious women, like their male counterparts, were intended originally as a rhetorical and iconographical topos, or theme, emphasizing women's noble traits to be equal to men's. Nonetheless, the authors and poets who popularized these women warriors were not blind to their double reputations. In fact, Boccaccio combined Justin's generally positive image of the Amazons with negative sources to create the ambiguous, indeed rather tongue-in-cheek, praise of Antique women characterizing the *De claris mulieribus*. But however subtle and diverting, Boccaccio's double-edged histories carried a potentially detrimental charge not lost on one woman reader, Christine de Pizan (1364/5–1430?). A staunchly prolific Franco-Italian champion of her gender, Christine rewrote Boccaccio to defend women wholeheartedly in the *Cité des dames* (*City of Ladies*) in 1404–1405.

The representation of the Amazons in the visual arts, however, reflects more unanimity in its tendency to highlight only their positive side. In sculpture, frieze, manuscript illumination, tapestry, pageantry, and early playing cards, whether armed and mounted or standing in ornate gowns in courtly repose, the women give no hint of their darker side. (The woodcuts of the 1473 Ulm edition of Boccaccio's *De claris mulieribus* offer a striking exception to this characterization, since these portraits of women are cast in more sinister fashion.) Nevertheless, literate audiences knew of Semiramis's incest as well as her conquests; of Thomyris's cruelty as well as her valor. They knew too that the very concept of the worthy female warrior was self-contradictory by Christian moral standards, since it ignored traditional feminine virtues. The uncertainty of the Middle Ages over which virtues female heroism should glorify recalls Deschamps's poetry. He recognized that the Amazons had "cruel hearts," but he glorified their conquests, ability to govern, and other remarkable feats in verse to his patron, Louis, duke of Orléans, a nobleman so taken by the Worthy Women that it is likely he who had them sculpted in colossal proportions as part of the mantelpiece of Coucy castle.

A broader-based debate on the concept of female heroism, intensified by the arrival of Joan of Arc, is played out in the iconography of the Worthy Women over whether to depict them in armor or feminine dress. Such pre-Joan portraits of the Neuf Preuses as the splendid miniature c.1404 in the Paris, Bibliothèque nationale de France manuscript 12559 of Thomas of Saluzzo's verse-prose narrative, the *Chevalier errant* (*Knight Errant*), bear witness to this quandary: all the women bear weapons and shields, but all wear decidedly feminine dress from head to toe, save for gauntlets and elbow protection; only the exceptionally helmet-coiffed Menalippe is also allowed a breastplate over her dress. Joan's insistence in 1429 that she lead the French army dressed in men's armor drew attention to the moral symbolism of the two dress codes. Technically, Joan was condemned for violating the Old Testament Book of Deuteronomy's prohibition against women in male attire. Yet despite the moral condemnation of women in male dress inherent in Joan's conviction, the historical reality of the Maid in male armor apparently caused a shift in the iconographic tradition of the Worthy Women. This transformation may have been fostered, at least partly, by Joan's first literary apologist, Christine de Pizan, in her last known work, the *Ditié de Jehanne d'Arc* (*Tale of Joan of Arc*) in 1429. Christine's homage to the heroine of Orléans not only served to dispel lingering doubts concerning the Maid's divine inspiration, it also asserted Joan's surpassing example, "more worthy [*preux*] than any man in Rome!" In this verse (199) and ones soon following (217–24), Joan's exploits outshine those of biblical heroines (Judith, Esther, and Deborah) and other "worthy women" (*preuses*) thus implying her status as more than equal to that of tenth Worthy Woman.

Thanks to Christine's poem, Joan's various other defenders, and the warrior Maid's own real-life presence and charisma, these heroines were henceforth depicted in armor. An important example appeared in Sébastien Mamerot's *L'Histoire des Neuf Preux et des Neuf Preuses* (*History of the Nine Worthy Men and Nine Worthy Women*, 1461), a work commissioned by Louis de Laval. Laval's grandfather, the redoubtable military leader Bertrand Du Guesclin (c.1315–1380), was once named the Tenth (Male) Worthy; Laval's brothers André and Guy rode with Joan of Arc. An illumination in Mamerot's manuscript offers a vivid example of armed, mounted Amazons without a trace of femininity. Ironically, although Joan is elevated in this work to the status of Tenth Female Worthy, the smiling but somehow pitiful figure drawn in the book's margin alongside that passage—quite possibly intended as a portrait of the Maid—shows her not in armor but in the dress and conical cap of her condemnation and burning.

Another innovation in Christine's *Ditié* to reinforce the female heroic tradition via Joan's example proved equally short-lived. Ever since Deschamps, French poets entertained the possibility of restructuring the canon of the *Neuf Preuses* along the lines of the threefold divisions of the male canon. Christine came closest when she invoked Esther, Judith, and Deborah (a perfect Jewish triad). However, the national culture that invented the Worthy Women and experienced Joan of Arc was never able to follow through, and the perfect blend of martial prowess and Christian humility represented in Joan was never translated into a new, triadically divided canon of nine women for a variety of political and artistic reasons. In a final irony, however, such a change did occur in sixteenth-century Germany, probably due to the Maid's influence. Selected and regrouped were Lucretia, Veturia, and Virginia; Esther, Judith, and Jael (for Deborah); followed by St. Helena, St. Birgitta, and St. Elizabeth. But by the time the motif had become the structural equivalent of Longuyon's Worthies, the motif, renamed along the German guidelines as the *Three Good Heathens, Three Good Jews and Three Good Christians*, had lost not only its French character but also the concept of martial prowess from which it originated.

See also Boccaccio, Women in, *De Claris Mulieribus*; Christine de Pizan; Joan of Arc, St.; Le Fèvre de Ressons, Jean; Valkyries

BIBLIOGRAPHY

Primary Sources

Boccaccio, Giovanni. [*De claris mulieribus*]. *Famous Women*. Edited and translated by Virginia Brown. I Tatti Renaissance Library, 1. Cambridge, Mass. and London: Harvard University Press, 2001. [Latin text with English trans. and notes].

Christine de Pizan. *Le Ditié de Jehanne d'Arc*. Edited and translated by Angus J. Kennedy and Kenneth Varty. Medium Aevum Monographs, n.s. 9. Oxford: Society for the Study of Mediaeval Languages and Literature, 1977.

Deschamps, Eustache. *Oeuvres complètes*. Edited by A. Queux de Saint-Hilaire. Société des Anciens Textes Français, 1: 199–201 and 3: 192. Paris: Firmin Didot, 1878–1883.

Jacques de Longuyon. *Les Voeux du paon* [original Old French and Old Scottish trans.]. In *The Buik of Alexander: or, The Buik of the most noble and valiant conquerour Alexander the Grit*, by John Barbour, edited by R. L. Graeme Ritchie, vols. 2–3. 4 vols. Scottish Text Society, n.s., 17, 12, 21, 25. Edinburgh and London: W. Blackwood, 1921–1925.

Justinus, Marcus Junianus. *Epitoma historiarum Philippicarum Pompei Trogi*. Edited by Otto Seel. Bibliotheca scriptorum Graecorum et Romanorum. 2nd ed. Stuttgart, Germany: B. G. Teubner, 1972.

———. *Epitome of the Philippic History of Pompeius Trogus*. Translated by John C. Yardley. Introduction and notes by Robert Develin. Classical Resources, 3. Atlanta, Ga.: Scholars Press, 1994.

Le Fèvre, Jean. *Les Lamentations de Matheolus et le Livre de Leësce de Jehan le Fèvre de Ressons*. Edited by Anton-Gérard Van Hamel. Bibliothèque de l'École des Hautes Études, Sciences philologiques et historiques 95/96. 2 vols. Paris: Émile Bouillon, 1892–1905.

Mamerot, Sébastien. *Histoire des Neuf Preux et des Neuf Preuses*. Vienna, Austria. Hofbibliothek, Latin manuscripts 2577–78.

Thomas III, Marquis of Saluzzo. Marvin J. Ward. "A Critical Edition of Thomas III, Marquis of Saluzzo's *Le Chevalier errant*. Ph.D. diss., University of North Carolina, Chapel Hill, 1984. Printed on demand, Ann Arbor, Mich: UMI, no. 8415876.

———. *Le Chevalier errant*. Paris, BnF ms. fr. 12559, fol. 125v. [Best reproduction of the illumination of the Nine Worthy Ladies]. In Meiss, see below, vol. 1 (text): 12–15; vol. 2 (plates), fig. 47.

Secondary Sources

Ancona, Paolo d'. "Gli affreschi del Castello di Manta nel Saluzze." *L'Arte* 8 (1905): 94–106; 183–98.

Dulac, Liliane. "Un mythe didactique chez Christine de Pizan: Sémiramis ou la veuve héroïque (Du *De mulieribus claris* de Boccace à la *Cité des dames*)." In *Mélanges de philologie romane offerts à Charles Camproux*, 1: 315–43. Montpellier, France: C. E. O., 1978.

Fraioli, Deborah. "Why Joan of Arc Never became an Amazon." In *Fresh Verdicts on Joan of Arc*, edited by Bonnie Wheeler and Charles T. Wood, 189–204. Garland Reference Library of the Humanities, 1976. New York and London: Garland, 1996.

Guiffrey, Jules. "Note sur une tapisserie représentant Godefroy de Bouillon et sur les représentations des preux et des preuses au quinzième siècle." *Mémoires de la Société Nationale des Antiquaires de France*, ser. 4, 10 (1879): 97–110.

Lecourt, Marcel. "Notice sur *L'Histoire des neuf preux et des neuf preuses*." *Romania* 37 (1908): 529–37.

Luce, Siméon. *La France pendant la guerre de Cent Ans. Épisodes historiques et vie privée au XIVe et XVe siècles*. 2 vols. Paris: Hachette, 1890.

Meiss, Millard. *French Painting in the Time of Jean de Berry: The Limbourgs and Their Contemporaries.* 2 vols. New York: George Braziller, 1974.

McMillan, Ann. "Men's Weapons, Women's War: The Nine Female Worthies, 1400–1640." *Mediaevalia* 5 (1979): 113–39.

Schroeder, Horst. *Der Topos der Nine Worthies in Literatur in der bildender Kunst.* Göttingen, Germany: Vandenhoeck & Ruprecht, 1971. [The most exhaustive treatment of the topic].

DEBORAH A. FRAIOLI

NOGAROLA, ANGELA (early to mid-15th century). Angela Nogarola, aunt of the Italian humanist writer Isotta Nogarola (1418–1466) and of her sister, Ginevra Nogarola (b. 1417), who also composed, was a literary person in her own right. Although apparently not nearly as prolific as her niece Isotta, she nonetheless composed a *Liber de Virtutibus* (*Book of Virtues*) in 342 lines, as well as other poems and letters in Latin. She addressed one of her poems to the skillful but ruthlessly ambitious Giangaleazzo Visconti (1351?–1402) and one of her letters to Maddalena Scrovegni (1356–1429), considered the earliest humanist woman writer.

See also Humanists, Italian Women, Issues and Theory; Nogarola, Ginevra; Nogarola, Isotta; Scrovegni, Maddalena

BIBLIOGRAPHY

Primary Sources

Nogarola, Angela. [Works]. *Isotae Nogarolae Veronensis Opera quae supersunt omnia accedunt Angelae et Zeneverae Nogarolae epistolae et carmina.* Edited by Eugen Abel. 2 vols. Vienna: Gerold, 1886.

———. See Parker, below, esp. 250–60. [Sizable excerpts in Latin and English trans. with commentary].

Secondary Source

Parker, Holt. "Latin and Greek Poetry by Five Renaissance Italian Women Humanists." In *Sex and Gender in Medieval and Renaissance Texts: The Latin Tradition*, edited by Barbara K. Gold, Paul Allen Miller, and Charles Platter, 247–85, esp. 250–60. SUNY Medieval Studies. Albany: State University of New York Press, 1997.

THELMA S. FENSTER

NOGAROLA, GINEVRA (1417–?). Sister to Isotta Nogarola (1418–1466), Ginevra Nogarola wrote letters and poems in Latin. A former pupil of the important educator Guarino of Verona (1370–1460) trained both Ginevra and her sister in Latin. Guarino of Verona himself praised her style. She also copied at least one manuscript, that containing Justinus's Roman history, now held by Yale University Library and inscribed: "Cenevra anogarolis scripsi manu mea immaculate" ("I, Ginevra Nogarola, wrote [this] in my immaculate hand"). Ginevra apparently ceased writing when she married. Her letters are published in volume 2 of her sister's *Opera* (*Works*).

See also Humanists, Italian Women, Issues and Theory; Nogarola, Angela; Nogarola, Isotta; Scrovegni, Maddalena

BIBLIOGRAPHY

Nogarola, Ginevra. [Works]. *Isotae Nogarolae Veronensis Opera quae supersunt omnia accedunt Angelae et Zeneverae Nogarolae epistolae et carmina.* Edited by Eugen Abel. 2: 327–42. Vienna: Gerold, 1886.

THELMA S. FENSTER

NOGAROLA, ISOTTA (1418–1466). Isotta Nogarola, among the earliest women writers of the Italian fifteenth century, or Quattrocento, pursued the type of epistolary, literary exchange characteristic of European Renaissance humanism, corresponding in a notably accomplished Latin with leading humanist figures of her day. As the daughter of a noble and enlightened Veronese family—her aunt Angela (early to mid-fifteenth century) and sister Ginevra (b. 1417) also wrote—Isotta learned Latin and Greek. Her mother had secured the services of Martino Rizzoni, erstwhile pupil of the famous Guarino of Verona (1370–1460), whose grammar curriculum formed young men, many of them future state leaders, in the finer points of Classical Latin style (as opposed to the medieval "lower" Latin), the basis of the humanistic education. When Isotta was eighteen, she began corresponding with humanists of Guarino's circle (for example, Girolamo, Guarino's son, and two of Guarino's disciples, Ludovico Cendrata, whose orations and letters were noted for their abundant classical citations, and Giorgio Bevilacqua). After Isotta's Latin composition had come to the attention of Guarino himself through the son of the Venetian Doge, Giacomo Foscari, she took the step of writing directly to Guarino. He did not reply, however, and Isotta, feeling publicly shamed, was moved to ask Guarino for a response, which he finally sent.

Isotta never married, having chosen to pursue a life of scholarship; nor did she enter the convent. In 1438 she was accused, in an anonymous letter, of having committed incest with her brother. Deploying a then-common argument, the letter claimed that an eloquent woman could never be chaste (a view apparently shared by both men and women, given that women were among those who had ridiculed Isotta over Guarino's failure to reply to her). Whatever the letter-writer's motives, the allegation forced Isotta to leave Verona for Venice. When she returned three years later, she took up the course she would follow for the rest of her life, living at home with her mother and engaging, as did other humanists, in both the fashionable *studia humanitatis* (humanistic studies)—that is, the cultivation of ancient pagan Greek and Roman authors rather than medieval ones— and in sacred studies, dealing with Christian religious topics.

At a time when the status of one's correspondents could help to make known (thus, in a sense, to "publish") one's letters, Isotta corresponded with a number of important men, including Ermolao Barbaro the Elder, a former Guarino student who led an active political and ecclesiastical life and was the nephew of Francesco Barbaro, author of *De re uxoria* (*On marriage*, 1415). Another of her correspondents, Nicholas Barbo, was a lawyer and man of letters who, in a letter to a friend, defended Isotta from the charge of incest. The humanist Lauro Quirino addressed a letter to her in which he outlined a reading curriculum. Costanza Varano (1426–1447), another of the first-generation Italian humanist women, was also one of Isotta's correspondents.

Among the abundant writings that Isotta left, the Latin debate called "Of the Equal or Unequal Sin of Adam and Eve," which she undertook between 1451 and 1453 during an exchange with her frequent correspondent, the Venetian nobleman, humanist, and diplomat, Ludovico Foscarini, has most interested modern readers. The two friends argued the individual responsibility of Adam and Eve for the Fall, and the result, which Isotta recast as a dialogue, was a clever, early example of a topic that flourished, though not always with the same sparkle, long into the *Querelle des femmes* (Quarrel about Women). The precedent for such a debate lay in medieval tradition, for Peter Lombard and his commentators, as well as St. Thomas Aquinas (c.1225–1274), among others, had already considered whether Adam or Eve was the more responsible for the Fall—that is, how sin was related to gender. Isotta and her interlocutor set themselves the task of proving true or not Augustine's proposition that Adam and Eve "sinned unequally according to sex, but equally according to pride." Both undeniably enjoyed the exercise of their debating skills, but Isotta's approach especially seemed to announce the type of Renaissance paradox in which the writer attempted to defend the apparently indefensible— in this instance, Eve.

A few examples may help to illustrate the point. In the course of the debate Ludovico holds that Eve sinned out of pride; she wanted to be equal to God. Eve was the cause of Adam's sin, and thus her sin was greater than his. Moreover, he says, Eve tricked her husband. Isotta proceeds by trying to turn Eve's weakness into a strength, concomitantly making Adam's perceived strength into a weakness. She maintains that Eve ate the apple out of simple frailty and would have hurt only herself, but when Adam, who knew better, followed suit, he brought down all of humanity. By arguing that Adam was in fact created perfect, whereas Eve was not, Isotta claims that Adam was therefore guiltier, for he should have known better. He broke God's commandment, but Eve, because she received no such order, sinned less. In fact, says Isotta, God did not even bother talking of Eve's redemption, so small was her sin! Further, we cannot say that Eve led Adam into sin, for if Adam had free will, then he would have been guiltier than Eve; if not, only God could have taken it away from him, not "simple" Eve.

As in medieval debates on this topic, no clear verdict emerges; or rather, because the medieval church never seriously entertained a change in the status of women, the conclusion had largely been determined before the debate began. Instead, the idea was to display one's erudition and wit, at which Isotta excels. She deploys already-tested arguments with new sparkle, and she manages further to insert what is arguably an indirect personal note when she portrays Eve as one who desires knowledge. That is, when Foscarini accuses Eve of pride in seeking knowledge to make her the equal of God, Isotta emphasizes through incremental repetition Eve's wish to know, especially about good and evil. Echoing perhaps the first sentence of the Greek philosopher (fourth century B.C.E.) Aristotle's *Metaphysics*, Isotta affirms that it is human nature to want to know; but in her view, this is especially true of the female. First, she paraphrases what the devil said to Eve: "You will not die; but God knows that the day you eat the apple, your eyes will be opened, and you will be like gods, knowing good from evil" (Gen. 4–5; all translations from the debate itself from King and Rabil; see Bibliography). She cites Genesis 3–6: "And the woman saw that the fruit of the tree was good to eat, and that it was pleasant to the eye, and that the tree was desirable for becoming intelligent." Then she comments: "Nevertheless, desiring the knowledge of good and evil is clearly a smaller sin than to transgress a divine commandment, since the desire for knowledge is a natural thing, and every man, by his nature, desires to know." And she says finally: "Supposing that inordinate desire is a sin, as in Eve's case, yet she did not desire to equal God in respect of power but only in regard to the knowledge of good and evil, *a knowledge that by her nature she was inclined to desire*" (emphasis added). Repetition eventually succeeds in bringing forward what must otherwise remain unsaid: that the first *woman*, but not the first *man*, sought knowledge of good and evil. And in fact, some modern scholarship has agreed, finding that Genesis 3 may well be part of biblical "wisdom literature" and that the woman, not the man, plays the central role in the acquisition of that knowledge. Isotta's extant work is collected in her *Opera* (*Works*), along with the writings of her sister and aunt.

See also Humanists, Italian Women, Issues and Theory; Nogarola, Angela; Nogarola, Ginevra; Scrovegni, Maddalena; Varano, Costanza

BIBLIOGRAPHY
[Essential bibliography may be found in the appendix to King 1978, listed below in Secondary Sources].

Primary Sources
Nogarola, Isotta. [Works]. *Isotae Nogarolae Veronensis Opera quae supersunt omnia accedunt Angelae et Zeneverae Nogarolae epistolae et carmina.* Edited by Eugen Abel. 2: 327–42. Vienna: Gerold, 1886. Budapest: F. Kilian, 1886. Microfilm: History of Women reel 472, no. 3527, Research Publications, 12 Lunar Drive, Woodbridge, Conn.
———. Translated in King and Rabil (*see below*).
———. [Sizable excerpts in Latin and English] in Parker, 260–66, see Secondary Sources, *below.*
———. *Isotta Nogarola: Letters, Dialogu on Adam and Evee, Orations.* Edited and translated by Margaret L. King and Diana Robin. The Other Voice in Early Modern Europe. Chicago: University of Chicago Press, 2004.
Varano, Costanza. "Ad Dominam Isotam Nogarolam/To the Lady Isotta Nogarola." In Parker, 266–67. See under Secondary Sources, below. [Homage to Isotta by older illustrious female contemporary].

Secondary Sources
Benson, Pamela Joseph. "Introduction" and ch. 2, "From Praise to Paradox: The First Italian Defenses of Women." In Benson, *The Invention of the Renaissance Woman: The Challenge of Female Independence in the Literature and Thought of Italy and England,* 1–8, 33–64. University Park: Pennsylvania State University Press, 1992.
Fenster, Thelma. "Christine de Pizan et Isotta Nogarola sur la culpabilité d'Eve." In *Une femme de lettres au Moyen Âge: Études autour de Christine de Pizan,* edited by Liliane Dulac and Bernard Ribémont, 481–93. Orléans: Paradigme, 1995.
———. "Strong Voice, Weak Mind? Isotta Nogarola's Defense of Eve." In *Strong Voices, Weak Histories?* edited by Pamela J. Benson and Victoria Kirkham. forthcoming.
Grafton, Anthony, and Lisa Jardine. "Women Humanists: Education for What?" In *From Humanism to the Humanities: Education and the Liberal Arts in Fifteenth- and Sixteenth-Century Europe,* ch. 2. Cambridge, Mass.: Harvard University Press, 1986. Revision of Lisa Jardine, "Isotta Nogarola: Women Humanists—Education for What?" *History of Education* 12 (1983): 231–44.
Grendler, Paul F. *Schooling in Renaissance Italy: Literacy and Learning, 1300–1600.* Johns Hopkins Studies in Historical and Political Science, 107th ser. Baltimore and London: Johns Hopkins University Press, 1989.
King, Margaret L. "Book-Lined Cells: Women and Humanism in the Early Italian Renaissance." In *Beyond Their Sex: Learned Women of the European Past,* edited by Patricia H. Labalme, 66–90. New York: New York University Press, 1980.
——— "The Religious Retreat of Isotta Nogarola (1418–1466): Sexism and Its Consequences in the Fifteenth Century." *Signs: Journal of Women in Culture and Society* 3 (1978): 807–22.
——— "Thwarted Ambitions: Six Learned Women of the Italian Renaissance." *Soundings* 59 (1976): 280–304.

———————— *Women of the Renaissance*, 194–98. Chicago: University of Chicago Press, 1991.

———————, and Albert Rabil Jr. *Her Immaculate Hand: Selected Works by and about the Women Humanists of Quattrocento Italy*, 57–69. Binghamton, N.Y.: Center for Medieval and Renaissance Texts and Studies, 1983. 2nd ed. 1992.

Meyers, Carol. *Discovering Eve: Ancient Israelite Women in Context*. New York: Oxford University Press, 1988.

———————. *See* Parker, *below*, esp. 250–60 [Sizable excerpts in Latin and English trans. with commentary].

Parker, Holt. "Latin and Greek Poetry by Five Renaissance Italian Women Humanists." In *Sex and Gender in Medieval and Renaissance Texts: The Latin Tradition*, edited by Barbara K. Gold, Paul Allen Miller, and Charles Platter, 247–85, esp. 250–60. SUNY Medieval Studies. Albany: State University of New York Press, 1997.

Ulbrich, Claudia. "Literaturbericht: Frauen- und Geschlechtergeschichte. 1: Renaissance, Humanismus und Reformation." *Geschichte in Wissenschaft und Unterricht* (February 1994): 108–20.

THELMA S. FENSTER

NONNENBÜCHER. *See* **Sister-Books** *(Schwesternbücher)*

NORSE WOMEN. The literature of medieval Norway and Iceland, known as Old Norse, provides rich opportunities for the study of women. Because the Nordic peoples participated in a vast cultural continuum introduced by the German tribes who entered the Roman Empire by the end of the fourth century, these writings are important for understanding the Norse-Germanic world for nearly a millennium.

An early form of script known as the runic alphabet common to all Germanic peoples was used extensively throughout the Nordic world from the second to the early fourteenth century. Intended primarily to commemorate men, the terse runic inscriptions have been used for linguistic study but can also be exploited for uncovering inheritance patterns and women's property rights, marriage, and family size, although they are silent on many other issues of concern to women.

Pagan Norwegian colonists began to settle Iceland by the late ninth century and their descendants accepted Christianity in the year 1000. Not until the early twelfth century, however, did the Norse begin to commit their experiences to writing in their vernacular language. Although the authors were Christians, they nonetheless preserved the fullest and most authentic evidence of the previous pagan culture. Iceland possesses few runic inscriptions, but it produced the largest body of vernacular literature. It is this abundant corpus from which we shall draw representations of female images found mainly in myth and poetry and descriptions of mortal women and their roles in society furnished by laws and prose narratives known by the generic term *sagas*. From the linguistic evidence of the names of the week in English, German, and the Scandinavian languages, we may assume that all the Germanic peoples at some point worshipped a common pantheon that included the male gods Tyr (Tuesday), Ódinn (Wednesday), and Thor (Thursday), as well as the goddess Freyja and Frigg (Friday). The chief information about this pantheon derives from the so-called *Poetic Edda*, best preserved in a single manuscript known as the Codex Regius. Written in Iceland about 1270, it is divided between eleven mythological poems portraying a divine cosmos and eighteen mythological lays (short romances) describing a heroic world of Germanic heroes and heroines, some of whom were connected with the momentous events when the Continental tribes first entered the Roman Empire.

Landing of Norsemen by E. Leutze. From the original painting in the Academy of Fine Arts, Philadelphia. Courtesy of North Wind Picture Archives.

The mythological poems reveal tantalizing glimpses of powerful but shadowy female figures, particularly knowledgeable about the future, who may have been worshipped in the distant past by the inhabitants of continental and northern Europe. The classical Germanic pantheon, however, probably of Indo-European origin and exemplified by the gods retained in the names of the week, was strongly patriarchal. Although equal in numbers to the male gods, most goddesses were mere names. Frigg, the wife of the chief god Óðinn and the only goddess displaying maternal interest, may have been more powerful on the Continent, but in the north she was replaced by Freyja, goddess of love and a specialist in magic. Furthermore, the mythological cosmos was permeated with misogyny. Often equated with evil, femaleness was associated with the hostile world of the giants who lived beyond the realm of the gods.

The compiler of the Codex Regius provided a biological and textual connection between the divine and heroic worlds by making Helgi, the first hero described in the heroic lays, the great-grandson of Óðinn. Helgi was unhistorical, but with his half-brother Sigurðr we enter the territory of the famous Nibelung story based on verifiable events among the Burgundians of the fifth century. Compared to the mythological lays, a remarkable aspect of the heroic poems is the fact that women were numerous and powerful. Cycle valkyries and shield-maidens are prominent in the Helgi cycle, and the Sigurðr cycle contains the oldest representations of Brynhildr and Gudrún, the famous Germanic-Nordic heroines personifying female revenge. From this ancient poetry, well known long before inscription, later poets and prose authors distilled four female images that they elaborated and amplified in their own writings. These include the warrior, the prophetess or sorceress, the avenger, and the inciter.

It is possible, as claimed by Classical Roman authors and reinforced by archaeology, that Germanic women fought in desperate moments during the earliest Germanic migrations. In the Norse tradition, the most authentic female warrior historically is the Gothic Princess Hervor, allegedly in charge of the army defending her country against the invasions of the Huns in the late fourth century. The story is told in *Hlodskvida*, the oldest preserved heroic lay (not found in the Codex Regius). Despite this evidence, however, Germanic women do not seem to have fought regularly in wars. The woman warrior, nonetheless, became the special Nordic contribution to the gallery of female portraits within world literature. Women in arms appeared as supernatural valkyries, human shield-maidens and maiden warriors, and even as maiden kings who both fought and ruled as long as they remained virgin. The most fully drawn portraits of these figures are found in the genre known as the heroic sagas. Thus, the Gothic Princess Hervor, from the ancient poem, became the inspiration for a younger poem about her alleged foremother, also named Hervor, and the two poems were inscribed in a long saga named *Hervarar saga ok Heidreks konungs* (*The Saga of King Heidrek the Wise*), which focused on the story of the new Hervor. The figure of the maiden king is exemplified in the Swedish Princess Thornbjorg in *Hrolfs saga Gautrekssonar* (*Hrolf Gautrekson: A Viking Romance*).

Already the first-century Roman historian Tacitus had commented on the prophetic capabilities of ancient Germanic women, and Icelandic and Norwegian laws bristled with prohibitions against pagan magic. As confirmed by the narrative genre known as the family sagas, it is therefore likely that the sorceress is better anchored in the social fabric of the Norse world than is the female warrior. The performance of prophesy and magic may in fact have been female specialties to which men gained entry only belatedly and never obtained the proficiency of women. The best illustration of female prophesy is the alleged performance by Thornbjorg who predicted the cessation of a famine in Greenland in the early eleventh century, described in *Eiriks saga rauda* (*Eirik the Red*); and the sorceress is best exemplified by Thorveig in *Kormaks saga*.

The female avenger is personified in the Burgundian Gudrún. Suffused with revenge for kin, her life is known in the north almost exclusively from the heroic lays, but, named Kriemhilt or Kriemhild, she appears prominently in the *Nibelungenlied* (c.1200), the great medieval German epic derived from the Old Norse sagas. When young, she used her own physical strength, and when older, she obtained vengeance indirectly through verbal inciting. The most interesting aspect of her revenge is its changing focus as it moved from natal to marital kin. In the oldest versions, she was depicted as enacting revenge on behalf of her brothers although they had murdered her first husband Sigurdr. The story is told in *Atlakvida*, the oldest version of the Nibelung story, perhaps composed in Norway in the late ninth century, and this focus was retained in later lays also written in the north. In the German *Nibelungenlied*, however, she (Kriemhilt) instigated revenge against her brothers for having killed her first husband, and she was entirely responsible for their deaths. Gudrún's story was elaborated in prose in *Volsunga saga*, a narrative retelling the entire Nibelung story, and she remained a potent force in the Icelandic imagination as suggested by subsequent naming patterns. More than a hundred women in Norse literature and countless ordinary women in charters and documents bore her name, and Gudrún is still the most common name in modern Iceland.

The ratio between the singular role of the Burgundian Gudrún in Norse literature and the proliferation of her name in the Icelandic consciousness is reversed by the inciter Brynhildr, known in the heroic poetry for having goaded her husband Gunnar to kill her first love Sigurdr. Her name was practically unknown outside the poetry, but the activity of goading men modeled on her behavior became the role most frequently ascribed to Norse women in all walks of life. Like the prophetess figure, the inciter may have been rooted in the social fabric of the Germanic world at some point. Before the acceptance by the continental tribes of primogeniture and legitimacy as principles governing royal succession, women associated with leading families used their sexual attraction and verbal facility—including inciting—to gain power for themselves and to work for the acceptance of their sons as new leaders, as Gregory of Tours (538/9–594) demonstrates among the Merovingians. Portrayed in numerous texts, the Norwegian Queen Gunnhildr from the late ninth century fits this model. From this plausible environment among royalty and leading chieftains the inciting woman spread in Icelandic literature to all levels of society; mothers and housewives and even milkmaids and washing women constantly goaded men. *Njáls saga*, the most famous of the Icelandic family sagas, thus contains more than thirty cases of inciting women, but this frequency suggests that the figure had become a literary motif.

Although these images, especially the sorceress and the inciter, may have possessed a possible social base, they reveal less about women's real lives in Norse society than about the male authors' perceptions of females, a subject pertinent to the study of gender. The Old Norse sources also yield detailed information about ordinary women's lives in the areas of marriage, sexuality, reproduction, and production during pagan times as well as in the Christian era. The evidence is found in two genres of prose narratives and in Norwegian and Icelandic laws. Most important in the former group is the family sagas or sagas of Icelanders, which depict the last years of the future Icelanders in their homeland in Norway, their immigration and settlement in Iceland, the lives of their descendants during the saga age, a period extending into the early eleventh century thus encompassing the conversion. This group also includes the contemporary sagas that portray medieval Iceland from the early twelfth to the middle of the thirteenth century when the country lost its independence to Norway. Most important among the laws is the Icelandic *Grágás* (*Grey Goose*), the largest of all Germanic law codes, which was committed to writing in 1117 but had been conveyed orally since its acceptance in the early tenth century.

As among the Continental tribes, pagan marriage in the North was a commercial contract between two families intended to regulate the flow of property from one generation to the next and to identify a man's legitimate children for whom he was economically responsible. Only the groom or his family could initiate the marriage contract. The first step consisted of the engagement in which the two families agreed on the property each would relinquish to the new couple and determined the day for the wedding. At the celebration the bride—who was not normally consulted—and her dowry were handed over to the groom. In addition to his wife, a man often had other sexual partners, including established concubines and casual encounters with slaves and servants. Divorce was easy to obtain, and women kept their property, thus retaining their attractiveness as future marriage partners.

Churchmen tried to modify this pagan marital behavior by introducing the notions of fidelity and indissolubility, but with little effect. They were willing to accept the availability of divorce, but were frustrated in their inability to curb extramarital affairs. Reversing native tradition, therefore, they now attributed sexual initiative to women and thus heightened the inherited misogyny. They had better success with their proposal of female consent, and Christian law obligated a man to consult the woman he wanted to marry before negotiating financial arrangements with her family.

Although protected by their native and marital families, Norse women were exposed to male sexual violence and harassment in both pagan and Christian contexts. If impregnation resulted, the law authorized the father or guardian of an unmarried pregnant woman to torture her—without causing wounds and blue marks—until she revealed the name of her seducer, to ensure that the man would be made to take financial responsibility for the child. Information about lovemaking is sparse, but, not surprisingly, reveals universal and age-old patterns, as is also the case for childbirth. The baby was received from behind by female helpers while the mother knelt on the floor. Icelandic women nursed their babies during the Middle Ages, but by the Early Modern period they came to consider their own milk inferior and substituted it with cows' milk and cream. Inevitably, the island suffered from an unusually high infant mortality rate.

In the Norse world, however, birth was not a sufficient guarantee for life; equally important was the father's acceptance of the infant. The Norwegian laws state categorically: "every child must have a father." Immediately after birth the baby "was carried" to the father in a formal ceremony that determined its fate. Examining the infant, the man looked for family resemblances; if he liked what he saw, he accepted paternity, gave the child a name chosen from notable but deceased members of the family on either side, sprinkled it with water, and allowed it to be returned to the mother for its first feeding. If he did not accept the child it was "carried out," that is, it was exposed out of doors and thereby destined to die in the harsh climate. The opening words of the Icelandic law announced the abolition of this pagan control of demographic growth through infanticide: "This is the beginning of our law that all people in this country must be Christian [...] Every child that is born shall be brought to baptism as soon as possible, regardless of how deformed it may be." While Christian mothers were thus spared the fear of having their child exposed, they continued to live with the tradition of fostering, according to which a father might decide to send his child away during its formative years to be raised elsewhere. Ancient infanticide and continued fostering may explain that maternal feelings rarely surfaced in the literature; nevertheless, the Icelandic law required grown children to take care of their mother in old age if she was in need.

In addition to their traditional domestic tasks, the most important contribution of Icelandic women to production was their labor of spinning and weaving. The resulting homespun clothed the entire population from cradle to grave and was put to every imaginable use, ranging from packs, bedding, and wall hangings to sails. Most remarkable is the fact that a certain length (the *alin* or ell) of this cloth became the standard of measurement for commercial exchange and was employed as currency in payments of taxes, fines, and trade. Until the fourteenth century, when it was replaced by dried fish, homespun was the most important item of export through which Iceland obtained the necessary grain, flour, and other commodities that could not be produced locally. Women's indispensable contribution to the economic life in traditional societies is no longer questioned, but in medieval Iceland their share was truly extraordinary.

See also Childhood and Child-Rearing in the Middle Ages; Law, Women in, Anglo-Saxon England; *Skáldkonur* (Old Norse-Icelandic Women Poets); Spinners and Drapers; Valkyries

BIBLIOGRAPHY

Primary Sources (in translation)
The Complete Sagas of Icelanders. Edited by V. Hreinsson et al. 5 vols. Reykjavik, Iceland: Leifur Eiríksson, 1997.
The Earliest Norwegian Laws. Translated by Laurence M. Larson. New York: Columbia University Press, 1935.
Hrolf Gautreksson: A Viking Romance. Edited and translated by Hermann Palsson and Paul Edwards. Toronto: University of Toronto Press, 1972.
Laws of Early Iceland: Gragas, I. Translated by Andrew Dennis, Peter Foote, and Richard Perkins. Winnipeg: University of Manitoba Press, 1980.
Poems of the Elder Edda. Translated by Patricia Terry. Revised ed. Philadelphia: University of Pennsylvania Press, 1990.
The Poetic Edda. Vol 1: Heroic Poems. Edited and translated by Ursula Dronke. Oxford: Clarendon, 1969.
The Saga of King Heidrik the Wise. Edited and translated by Christopher Tolkien. London: Nelson, 1960.
The Saga of the Volsungs: The Norse Epic of Sigurd the Dragon Slayer. Translated by Jesse L. Byock. Berkeley: University of California Press, 1990.

Secondary Sources
Andersson, Theodore M. *The Legend of Brynhild*. Islandica 43. Ithaca, N.Y.: Cornell University Press, 1980.
Clover, Carol. J. "The Politics of Scarcity: Notes on the Sex Ratio in Old Norse Society." *Scandinavian Studies* 60 (1988): 147–88.
———. "Maiden Warriors and Other Sons." *Journal of English and Germanic Philology* 85 (1986): 35–49.
Grundy, Stephan. "The Viking's Mother." In *Medieval Mothering*, edited by Bonnie Wheeler and John C. Parsons, 223–35. Feminea Medievalia, 4. New York: Garland, 1996.
Jesch, Judith. *Women in the Viking Age*. Rochester, N.Y.: The Boydell Press. 1991.
Jochens, Jenny. *Old Norse Images of Women*. Philadelphia: University of Pennsylvania Press, 1996.
———. *Women in Old Norse Society*. Ithaca, N.Y.: Cornell University Press, 1995.
———. "Old Norse Motherhood." In *Medieval Mothering*, edited by Bonnie Wheeler and John C. Parsons, 201–22. Feminea Medievalia 4. New York: Garland, 1996.
———. " 'Med Jákvaeði Hennar Sjálfrar:' Consent as Signifier in the Old Norse World." In *Consent and Coercion to Sex and Marriage in Ancient and Medieval Societies*, edited by Angeliki Laiou, 271–89. Washington, D.C.: Dumbarton Oaks, 1993.
———. "The Illicit Love Visit: An Archaeology of Old Norse Sexuality." *Journal of the History of Sexuality* 1 (1991): 357–92.
———. "Old Norse Sources on Women." In *Medieval Women and the Sources of Medieval History*, edited by Joel T. Rosenthal, 155–88. Athens: University of Georgia Press, 1990.
———. "*Voluspá*: Matrix of Norse Womanhood." *Journal of English and Germanic Philology* 88 (1989): 344–62.
———. "The Female Inciter in the Kings' Sagas." *Arkiv för nordisk filologi* 102 (1987): 100–19.
Kalinke, Marianne E. *Bridal-Quest Romance in Medieval Iceland*. Islandica, 46. Ithaca, N.Y.: Cornell University Press, 1990.

Larrington, Carolyne. "Scandinavia." In *The Feminist Companion to Mythology*, edited by Carolyne Larrington, 137–61. London: Pandora, 1992.

Motz, Lotte. *The Beauty and the Hag: Female Figures of Germanic Faith and Myth*. Philologica Germanica, 15. Vienna: Fassbaender, 1993.

Ross, Margaret Clunies. *Prolonged Echoes: Old Norse Myths in Medieval Northern Society, vol. 1: The Myths*. Odense, Denmark: Odense University Press, 1994.

———. "Women and Power in the Scandinavian Sagas." In *Stereotypes of Women in Power*, edited by Barbara Garlick, Suzanne Dixon, and Pauline Allen, 105–19. Contributions in Women's Studies, 125. New York: Greenwood Press, 1992.

Sawyer, Birgit. *The Viking-Age Rune-Stones: Custom and Commemoration in Early Medieval Scandinavia*. Oxford: Oxford University Press, 2000.

JENNY JOCHENS

NORSE WOMEN POETS. *See* **Skáldkonur (Old Norse-Icelandic Women Poets)**

NOVELA SENTIMENTAL/**SENTIMENTAL ROMANCE** (mid-1300s–early 1600s). The Spanish *Novela Sentimental* was a late medieval European "best seller" revealing much about women and social mores. In Spain it influenced Fernando de Rojas's *Tragicomedia de Calisto y Melibea* (Comedia 1499; *Tragicomedia* 1502–1503), (*Tragicomedy of Calistus and Melibee*)—usually known as *La Celestina*, itself highly influential—and Miguel de Cervantes (1547–1616) in his prose fiction. In translation, the *novela sentimental* genre helped shape sentimental prose style in French and English. Pascual de Gayangos and José Amador de los Ríos were among the first to recognize sentimental romance as a sub-genre of the chivalric romance, known in Spanish as *libros de caballerías* (knights' books) or *libros de aventuras* (adventure books). Alan Deyermond has shown that the lack of an equivalent term for romance in Spanish has impeded wide acceptance of this position.

Regula Rohland de Langbehn has identified three phases in its development. The first phase comprises Juan Rodríguez del Padrón's *Siervo libre de amor* (*Slave of Love*, c.1440) and Dom Pedro, constable of Portugal's *Sátira de infelice e felice vida* (*Satire of Unhappy and Happy Life*, Castilian version, 1450–1453); both are erotic pseudo-autobiographies with strong allegorical elements. A transitional work, *Triste deleytaçión* (*Sad Delectation*, 1458–1470), possibly by the Catalan Fra Artal de Claramunt, combines elements of the first and second phases but has a more developed plot. The sentimental romances of Juan de Flores (fl. 1470–1480s) and Diego de San Pedro represent the peak of the genre. It became static in its third phase, from the late 1490s to 1550—probably due to the impact of *Celestina*, a hybrid text drawing on sentimental romance.

Sentimental romances are narratives of frustrated love that end in violence and death. The narrator is usually either the protagonist or an actor in the plot who gives a first-hand account. Nevertheless the narrative is frequently presented in lengthy monologues or exchanges of letters assigned to individual characters and rubricated—highlighted in red by the manuscript's scribe—to indicate speaker, addressee, and mode of communication. Sentimental romance is a complex genre often containing debates, letters, and lyrics within a single work.

Outside the narrative, women functioned as patrons and readers, while within the stories, they appear as objects of desire and as speaking subjects whose worldview is largely unmediated. Through a critique of the viability of the courtly experience as a mode of negotiating gender relations, sentimental romances are central to the fifteenth-century literary debate on the moral worth of women. The role played by female characters increased from the first to the second phase, and this process culminated in *Celestina*. Patricia E. Grieve has argued that the malevolent Celestina usurps the role of mother, important in the second-phase sentimental romances, with destructive results.

In the first phase, female characters are given cursory treatment. In *Sátira*, for example, the beloved is an abstraction whose qualities are debated by the lover/narrator and a College of Virtues. Nonetheless, many of its glosses relate the tragic deaths of lovers. *Siervo* comprises a frame story and an intercalated sentimental romance, *Estoria de dos amadores* (*Story of Two Lovers*), in which Ardanlier and Liessa flee the wrath of King Croes, his father, through the courts of Europe before the pregnant Liessa is brutally murdered by Croes and grief-stricken Ardanlier kills himself. Yrena, unrequited lover of Ardanlier, founds a Temple of Vesta in their memory. Liessa and Yrena are noble women who participate actively in courtly love. The sexually initiated Liessa is contrasted with Yrena and her frustrated sexual, and later chaste, love. As Vera Castro Lingl argues, each stands for one of the paths of loving described in the *accessus*, or introductory gloss: reciprocated love (Liessa), unrequited love (Yrena), with the third (Synderesis), neither loving nor being loved, appearing in the frame.

In *Triste deleytaçión*, the hero Enamorado (Enamored One) pursues and successfully approaches his beloved, Senyora, before the two are forcibly and violently parted. Senyora receives a sentimental, physical, and philosophical education on relations between sexes from Madrina and vows to adhere to *amor con firmeza* (steadfast love). While Françoise Vigier has indicated that Andreas Capellanus's *De amore* was a general source, Louise Haywood has shown that Madrina's speeches generally make uncritical use of both pro- and antifeminist traditions. During Madrina's discussion of the deceptions of men, more emphasis is put on men's guilt and lack of fear and *verguença, pudeur* (shame, modesty), and the women are largely exculpated. Olga Tudorica Impey has also studied this portion of the narrative.

Flores's *Grisel y Mirabella* deals explicitly with the debate about the moral worth of women. Mirabella and Grisel are caught *in flagrante delicto* and penalized under the law of Scotland: death to the guiltier and exile for the other. However, since both claim primary responsibility, a court of love is established to resolve the general point. The judges are Torrellas (author of a misogynist treatise) and Braçayda (Criseyde of the Trojan legend). Women are judged the guiltier party. Finally, Torrellas's attempted seduction of Braçayda leads him to a secret rendezvous where the court ladies tortured him to death, perhaps eating his flesh. He meets a just death that nonetheless reveals women's bestial nature. Lillian von der Walde Moheno has shown that the conduct of both genders is thus roundly condemned.

In his *Grimalte y Gradissa*, Flores uses the techniques of metafiction to explore the relationship between fiction and gender. Flores, who changed his name to Grimalte to tell this story, gives Gradissa a copy of the fourteenth-century Italian Boccaccio's *L'Elegia di Madonna Fiammetta* (*Elegy of Lady Fiammetta*)—"Fiometa" in Spanish—hoping it will persuade her to reciprocate his love. Instead she orders him to reconcile its protagonists but his intervention ends with Fiometa's suicide, and Pánfilo's and his own exile. *Grimalte y Gradissa* exposes the fact that women are the victims of sexual love whether or not they yield. Gradissa is able to exercise power over Grimalte but only because he has chosen to love her. Her status as courtly lady prevents her from acting in her own right and, by extension, from effecting the reconciliation herself as either author or actor. Fiometa's reciprocation of Pánfilo's love reverses the power dynamic. Nonetheless this loss of status empowers her to write (Flores makes no mention of Boccaccio), to act, to rebel against male dominion and against the narrator's wishes. Finally, the selection of Fiometa as a female "author"/character emphasizes the subordinate role of women in Spanish sentimental romance.

Diego de San Pedro's romances are heavily dependent on one another. In *Arnalte y Lucenda* (published 1491), the first-person narrator makes Arnalte's love story known to the ladies of the court. Arnalte's approaches to Lucenda were largely unreciprocated, despite the intervention of his sister. Lucenda's marriage to a rival led to his death at Arnalte's hand in a duel. In distress Arnalte retired to the country where the narrator discovered him. Aspects of Arnalte's conduct have lead critics to suggest the presence of comic elements. In *Cárcel de Amor* (*Prison of Love*, 1492), the Auctor (author) acts as a go-between for Leriano. His unreciprocated love becomes public, and Laureola is imprisoned by her father. When diplomatic negotiations fail, Leriano forcibly frees her. Restored to her previous position, Laureola severs relations, and, after a spirited defense of women, Leriano dies.

San Pedro's sentimental romances reveal the conflict between the expectations of male characters who engage in courtly love and societal norms regarding acceptable standards of behavior for women. The conflict arises in part from the apparent inability of male characters to subject their will to reason and then to accept the words of women at face value. Like Flores's sentimental romances, San Pedro's contain many intertexts (borrowings from or allusions to other literary works) that point to the high literary consciousness of their authors.

See also *Belle Dame sans Merci*; Boccaccio, Women in, Works Other than *De Claris Mulieribus*; Capellanus, Andreas; Criseyde; Griselda; *Roman de la Rose*, Debate of the

BIBLIOGRAPHY

Primary Sources
[F.A.d.C.]. *Triste deleytaçión: novela de F.A.d.C., autor anónimo del siglo XV.* Edited by Regula Rohland de Langbehn. Morón: Universidad, 1983.
Flores, Juan de. *Grimalte y Gradisa.* Edited by Carmen Parrilla García. Monografías da Universidade de Santiago de Compostela, 140. Santiago de Compostela, Portugal: Universidade, 1988.
———. *Grisel y Mirabella.* In *The Novels of Juan de Flores and Their European Diffusion: A Study in Comparative Literature*, edited by Barbara Matulka, 331–70. New York: Institute of French Studies, 1931. Reprint Geneva: Slatkine Reprints, 1974.
Pedro de Portugal, Condestável Dom. *Sátira de infelice e felice vida.* In his *Obras completas*, edited by Luís Adão da Fonseca, x–xiv, 1–175. Lisbon: Fundação Calouste Gulbenkian, 1975.
Rodríguez del Padrón, Juan. *Siervo libre de amor.* In *Obras completas*, edited by César Hernández Alonso, 153–208. Biblioteca de la Literatura y el Pensamiento Hispánicos, 48. Madrid: Editora Nacional, 1982.
San Pedro, Diego de, *Obras completas*, I: *"Tractado de amores de Arnalte y Lucenda" y "Sermón"*, edited by Keith Whinnom. Clásicos Castalia, 54. Madrid: Castalia, 1973.
———. *Obras completas*, II: *Cárcel de Amor*, edited by Keith Whinnom, Clásicos Castalia, 39, 3rd ed. Madrid: Castalia, 1985.

Secondary Sources

Amador de los Ríos, José, *Historia crítica de la literatura española*, 6: 338–51. Madrid: the author, printed by José Fernández Cancela, 1865. Reprint Madrid: Gredos, 1969.

Castro Lingl, Vera, "Assertive Women in Medieval Spanish Literature." Ph.D. diss., Queen Mary & Westfield College, University of London, 1995.

Deyermond, Alan D. "The Lost Genre of Medieval Spanish Literature." *Hispanic Review* 43 (1975): 231–59.

Gayangos, Pascual de. "Discurso preliminar." In *Libros de caballerías*, Biblioteca de Autores Españoles, 40, iii–lxii. Madrid: Rivadeneyra, 1857.

Grieve, Patricia E. "Mothers and Daughters in Fifteenth-Century Spanish Sentimental Romances: Implications for *Celestina*." *Bulletin of Hispanic Studies* 67 (1990): 345–55.

———. *Desire and Death in the Spanish Sentimental Romance (1440–1550)*. Newark, Del.: Juan de la Cuesta, 1987.

Haywood, Louise M. "Female Voices in Spanish Sentimental Romances." *Journal of the Institute of Romance Studies* 4 (1996): 17–35.

———"Gradissa: A Female Reader in/of a Male Author's Text." *Medium Aevum* 64 (1995): 85–99.

Impey, Olga Tudorica. "Un doctrinal para las doncellas enamoradas en la *Triste deleytación*." *Boletín de la Real Academia Española*, 66 (1986): 191–234.

Rohland de Langbehn, Regula. "Argumentación y poesía: función de las partes integradas en el relato de la novela sentimental española en los siglos XV y XVI." In *Actas del IX Congreso de la Asociación Internacional de Hispanistas, 18–23 agosto 1986, Berlín*, edited by Sebastian Neumeister, 1: 575–82. Editionen der Iberoamericana, 3. Monographien und Aufsätze, 28. Frankfurt am Main, Germany: Vervuert for AIH, 1989.

———. "Desarrollo de géneros literarios: la novela sentimental española de los siglos XV y XVI." *Filología* 21 (1986): 57–76.

———. "El problema de los conversos y la novela sentimental." In *The Age of the Catholic Monarchs, 1474–1516: Literary Studies in Memory of Keith Whinnom*. [Special Issue] *Bulletin of Hispanic Studies*, edited by Alan Deyermond and Ian Macpherson, 134–43. Liverpool, U.K.: Liverpool University Press, 1989.

———. "Fábula trágica y nivel de estilo elevado en la novela sentimental española de los siglos XV y XVI." In *Literatura hispánica: Reyes Católicos y el Descubrimiento: Actas del Congreso Internacional sobre Literatura Hispánica en la Época de los Reyes Católicos y el Descubrimiento. Pastrana, julio 1986*, edited by Manuel Criado de Val, 230–36. Barcelona: PPU, 1989.

Vigier, Françoise. "Le *De arte amandi* d'André le Chapelain et la *Triste deleytación*, roman sentimental anonyme de la seconde moitié du XVᵉ s." *Mélanges de la Casa de Velázquez* 21 (1985): 159–74.

Walde Moheno, Lillian von der. *Amor e ilegalidad: 'Grisel y Mirabella' de Juan de Flores*, Medievalia, 12. Estudios Lingüísticos y Literarios, 34. Mexico City: UNAM & Colegio de México, 1996.

Whinnom, Keith. *The Spanish Sentimental Romance, 1440–1550*. Research Bibliographies and Checklists, 41. London: Grant & Cutler, 1983.

LOUISE M. HAYWOOD

NOVELLA D'ANDREA (fl. early–mid-14th century). Novella d'Andrea is the beautiful woman lecturer in law at Bologna made famous by Christine de Pizan (1364–1430?). Identifying her as the daughter of Giovanni d'Andrea, a professor of canon law at the University of Bologna (1275–1347), Christine refers to her as a recent, illustrious example of the validity and appropriateness of educating women in her *Livre de la Cité des dames* (*Book of the City of Ladies*, 2: 36.3). According to Christine, Giovanni d'Andrea saw fit not only to educate his daughter but to send her on occasion to lecture in his stead when other duties detained him. He even supposedly collected her lectures on law and titled it *Novella super Decretalium* (*Novella on the Decretals*). She is said to have lectured from behind a curtain to keep her audience from being distracted by her loveliness. Unfortunately, Christine's account is not confirmed by histories of the Bolognese Studium, even by sources contemporary to Giovanni (and Novella) d'Andrea, although Christine could have heard it from her father, Tommaso da Pizzano (Thomas de Pizan, d. 1387), who frequented that milieu and may even have known Giovanni d'Andrea personally (Caraffi and Richards, notes to ed.). More concretely, Jean Le Fèvre (c.1320–c.1380) cites the same glowing account in his *Livre de Leesce* (*Book of Joy*), vv. 1140–1154. Whether true or false, the story circulated in Christine's time and she accepted it as true: Novella d'Andrea's usefulness in Christine's argument would have been diminished notably were it widely known to be false or invented for this occasion. Furthermore, as legal historian Mary Ann Case recently concludes, the fact of Novella's acceptance by Christine's contemporaries, and the "remarkable coincidence" of her father's most famous work bearing her name, lend credibility to her status.

See also Christine de Pizan; Humanists, Italian Women, Issues and Theory; Law, Canon, Women in; Le Fèvre de Ressons, Jean

BIBLIOGRAPHY

Primary Sources

Christine de Pizan. *La Città delle dame*. Edited by E. J. Richards. Translated [Italian] with introduction by Patrizia Caraffi. 2nd ed. Milan: Luni, 1998. [Bilingual Middle-French and Modern Italian ed. with useful notes].

———. *Le Livre de la cité des dames*. Translated by Eric Hicks and Thérèse Moreau. Paris: Stock, 1986. [With excellent introduction by Moreau].

———. *The Book of the City of Ladies*. Translated with commentary by Earl Jeffrey Richards. Foreword by Natalie Zemon Davis. Revised ed. New York: Persea, 1998. [Excellent notes].

Le Fèvre, Jean. *Le Livre de Leesce*. In *Les Lamentacions de Matheolus et le Livre de Leesce*, edited by A. G. Van Hamel, vol. 2: 1–44. 2 vols. Paris: Émile Bouillon, 1905.

Secondary Sources

Case, Mary Anne. "Christine de Pizan and the Authority of Experience." In *Christine de Pizan and the Categories of Difference*, edited by Marilynn Desmond, 71–87. Medieval Cultures, 14. Minneapolis and London: University of Minnesota Press, 1998.

Sarto, Mauro, and Mauro Fattorini. *De claris professoribus Archigymnasii Bononiensis a saeculo XI usque ad saeculum XIV*. Bologna: Merlani, 1878–1896. Reprint 1962.

REGINA PSAKI

NUNNERIES, MEROVINGIAN (6th–8th centuries). The institution of the Merovingian nunnery—nunneries existing during the reign of the Frankish dynasty, in what is now mostly France and Germany, from Meroveus (mid-fifth century) until Charlemagne (crowned 800)—emerged in barbarian Europe from Antique origins in the cult of virginity and from the early Christian practice of consecrating women to a chaste life within their family home. Christianity's espousal of spiritual equality in addition to the Church's attempts to impose monogamy gave Merovingian nunneries a dual objective: to create a monastic foundation for female spirituality and to provide an alternative life for those women who would no longer be supported by multiple marriage. In practice, providing the social outlet of the nunnery's second purpose often negated dedicated attempts to attain its primary purpose.

Pope Gregory the Great (Gregory I, c.540–604) was an especially dynamic promoter of monasticism throughout much of Europe, both to consolidate his papal power and to spread Christian theology. For the Germanic aristocracy and the Gallo-Roman ecclesiastical establishment, there were reciprocal benefits from an institution for women. The Church, in addition to attracting aristocratic men, could maintain both unmarried and religious women. From the aristocracy the Church acquired first of all the endowments and resources of the women entering the nunneries, and second, the long-range benefit of simplifying and consolidating inheritances, making property donations and usufruct (usage rights of others' property) more profitable for the Church. The male clerics cooperated with the women in propagating the monastic way of life, as dictated by certain *regulae* (rules, guidelines). Although women could not participate in pastoral or ministerial functions, they were identified by lives of abstinence and prayer.

Merovingian women turned the nunneries into centers of teaching, textual scholarship, medicine, and charity toward the outside community. The cultural initiatives of the Merovingian nunneries belied the institution's ambiguous origins as a spiritually equal, but socially restrictive establishment.

The exemplary lives of the nunneries' patron saints generated powerful cults within the kingdom. The popular use of hagiographies for women like St. Clotilda, or Clothild (d. 544), wife of the Frankish King Clovis (d. 511), and her daughter-in-law through her oft-married son King Clothar I (d. 561), St. Radegund (520–587), enabled the nunneries to compete in the commerce surrounding saintly relics and shrines. The saints' *vitae* (biographies), written either in the nunneries or through the nunnery's patronage, also provided the means to add women's roles to the canon of the Church.

See also Aldegund, St.; Clotilde, St.; Gertrude of Nivelles, St.; Hagiography (Female Saints); Radegund, St.; Relics and Medieval Women; Rules for Canonesses, Nuns, and Recluses

BIBLIOGRAPHY

Primary Sources

Gregorii I papae registrum epistularum. Edited by Paul Ewald and Ludo Hartmann, passim. *Monumenta Germaniae Historica. Epistularum tomus 1–2.* 2 vols. Berlin: Weidmann, 1889. Reprint 1957.

Mayo, Hope. "Three Merovingian Rules for Nuns." 2 vols. Ph.D. diss., Harvard University, 1974. [Latin texts of the Rules of Aurelianus, Donatus, and the anonymous Rule of Certain (Church) Fathers for Virgins, with commentary].

McNamara, Jo Ann, and John E. Halborg, et al. *Sainted Women of the Dark Ages.* Durham and London: Duke University Press, 1992. [English trans. of many key lives with excellent commentary].

Secondary Sources

Bitel, Lisa M. "Women's Monastic Enclosures in Early Ireland: A Study of Female Spirituality and Male Monastic Mentalities." *Journal of Medieval History* 12 (1986): 15–36.

Hochstetler, Donald. *A Conflict of Traditions: Women in Religion in the Early Middle Ages, 500–840.* Lanham, Md.: University Press of America, 1992.

McNamara, Jo Ann, and Suzanne Wemple. "Sanctity and Power: The Dual Pursuits of Medieval Women." In *Becoming Visible: Women in European History*, edited by Renate Bridenthal and Claudia Koontz, 90–118. 2nd ed. Boston: Houghton Mifflin, 1987.

Millinger, Susan. "Humility and Power: Anglo-Saxon Nuns in Anglo-Norman Hagiography." In *Distant Echoes: Medieval Religious Women*, edited by John Nichols and Lillian Shank, 115–129. Kalamazoo, Mich.: Cistercian Publications, 1984.

Schulenburg, Jane Tibbetts. "Strict Active Enclosure and Its Effects on the Female Monastic Experience (500–1100)." In *Distant Echoes*, 51–86. *See above entry.*

Wemple, Suzanne F. *Women in Frankish Society: Marriage and the Cloister, 500–900.* Philadelphia: University of Pennsylvania Press, 1985.

SUZANNE FONAY WEMPLE

OBSTETRICS. *See* **Medicine and Medieval Women**

PASTON, MARGARET (c.1426–1484). Margaret Paston was the most representative member of a prominent Norfolk-based family known for prolific and revealing correspondence in English. Margaret Paston is the author of 104 letters, addressed largely to members of her family between 1441 and 1478. The Paston documents as a whole comprise nearly a thousand items, including letters by fourteen members of the family dated between 1422 and 1509. Besides Margaret—the most prolific correspondent in the Paston family—three other Paston women authored letters: Agnes Paston (d. 1479), Margaret's mother-in-law, composed thirteen letters; Elizabeth Paston Poynings (1429–1488), Margaret's sister-in-law, wrote two letters; and Margery Brews Paston (c.1448–1478), Margaret's daughter-in-law, leaves six letters. The Paston papers vividly record the struggles and concerns of a rising family in fifteenth-century England. The letters of these Paston women in particular document the responsibility and commitment of English gentlewomen to the preservation of family and property.

Born Margaret Mautby in Norfolk, Margaret Paston, an heiress, married John Paston I (1421–1466) in 1440. Throughout her marriage, and during the almost two decades of widowhood that followed, Margaret Paston assumed tremendous responsibilities for the management, protection, and sometimes the actual defense of her family's manors. John Paston's life was complicated, if not compromised, by his determination to win his claims to the formidable estate of Sir John Fastolf (d. 1459), Margaret's cousin, battle Margaret continued after John's death in 1466. She bore five sons and two daughters who reached adulthood. Her husband's frequent absences from home on business, to which his Fastolf involvement contributed greatly, occasioned the seventy-seven letters she wrote to him. Most of her other letters were written to her two sons, John Paston II (1442–1479) and John Paston III (1444–1504). Having written or dictated her will on February 4, 1482, she died November 4, 1484.

As her biography suggests, Margaret Paston emerges from her letters as a woman completely defined by and solely concerned with the fortunes of her family. In the letters addressed to her husband, Margaret generally adopts a businesslike tone; she reports with anecdotal detail and carefully plotted narrative on the recent events that have affected the Paston holdings. She chronicles her own decisions and the roles she has to assume, often at great risk, in her husband's absence. For instance, in February 1448, she relates to John how she dealt with a kidnapping threat (Davis, no. 132) and other dramatic moments she faced alone, such as her expulsion from Gresham, her jointure—a settlement of land she received for her marriage—(nos. 128, 129, 130, 131), or the destruction of another disputed property, Hellesdon, by the Duke of Suffolk (nos. 188, 189, 193, 194), all narrated in colloquial prose of straightforward simplicity. Now greatly valued by historians for information on manners, customs, diet, estate management, and other details of daily life during this one family's rise to prominence during the Hundred Years War (1337–1453) and the Wars of the Roses (1455–1485), her letters were originally intended to keep her husband apprised of life at home in Norfolk. Beyond the financial, political, and business matters occupying the bulk of her letters, Margaret also reports items of gossip, along with the births, deaths, and marriage arrangements among local inhabitants. Except for occasional expressions of affection, her tone seldom varies from the detached and matter-of-fact: "the logge and the remenaunte of your place was betyn down on Tuesday and Wednesday" ("the main lodge and remainder of your place was beaten down ..."), she writes of the destruction of Hellesdon (no. 194), where she had gone to live in 1465. Her letters also contain requests, usually placed toward the closing, for goods John could send or bring to Norfolk from London, such as lace (no. 127), almonds and sugar (no. 130), hats for their sons (no. 138), trenchers (no. 144), dates, and cinnamon (no. 151), as well as frequent requests for girdles and cloth of various descriptions. But she makes her most urgent request in letter no. 130, uncharacteristically placed immediately after the salutation, when she requires her husband "to gete som crosse bowis, and wyndacis to bynd them with" ("to get some crossbows and special winches to bend them with [for stringing]"). In her elegant summary of the Paston letters, Virginia Woolf notes that Margaret Paston "neither bewailed her lot nor thought herself a heroine ... the long, long letters she wrote so laboriously ... to her husband who was (as usual) away, make no mention of herself." Woolf characterizes the tone: "For the most part her letters are the letters of an honest bailiff to his master, explaining, asking advice, giving news, rendering accounts" (p. 7).

However, the rhetorical pattern of these letters, and the political and social circumstances generating them, would leave little room for a woman like Margaret Paston to cultivate a true, intimate self. As Norman Davis has shown, the variety and number of scribal hands represented in the letters of the Paston women suggest that the women of the family could not write, or could not write well, and consequently dictated their letters. The letters of each the Paston men, in contrast, are generally restricted to a single hand presumed to be autograph. Thus Margaret Paston, not surprisingly, dictates letters that represent her public, social position as a married and later widowed gentlewoman, a position with which she appears absolutely comfortable. She structures her letters around rhetorical conventions employed formulaically. For example, the salutations in the letters Margaret addresses to her husband are all slight variations on one rhetorical formula: "Ryght wyrshypfull hosbonde, I recomaunde me to you. Please it you to wyte" ("Right worshipful husband, I commend myself to you. May it please you to know," no. 183)—reminiscent of the language and posture of homage. This frequently repeated address suggests the hierarchical structure of marriage and the wife's subordinate position within the structure. By contrast, Margaret addresses her sons, John Paston II and John Paston III, no less formulaically but much less deferentially ("I grete you wele and send you Goddes blissyng and myn, letyng you wete that" ["I greet you well and send you God's blessing and mine, letting you know that"; no. 210]). Her letters to her sons are somewhat imperious on the topics of finance and property, and she demonstrates continual concern for potentially profitable marriages for her children. Her daughter Margery thwarted Margaret's marital designs and stubbornly pledged below herself, to the Paston's bailiff, Richard Calle in 1469—an unsuitable match that Margaret laments to her son in letter no. 203. In her account, Margaret emphasizes Margery's rebellious use of language to subvert her mother's wishes for a more proper and advantageous match; as when she describes to her son the bishop's interrogation of Margery: "he wished to know the words that she had said to him, whether they made matrimony or not. So she repeated what she had said, and said boldly that if those words did not ensure it, then she would make this surer before going there, for she thought that in her conscience she was bound, whatever the words were." Margaret thus describes, via epistolary rhetoric, her daughter's rhetorical defiance of the social conventions and family hierarchy: "These lewd word grieve me and her grandmother as much as all the rest." The bishop finally decided in favor of Margery and Richard's marriage (1429). Yet the daughter's discursive independence, however brutal, did nothing to challenge the security of her mother's opposite convictions, whose strength derived from her acceptance of, and not rebellion against, the position assigned to noblewomen in her world. If Margaret Paston "makes no mention of herself," her letters, along with those of her female descendants including Margery Brews, wife of John Paston III, nonetheless testify to the social construction of the female self in late medieval culture.

See also Dower; Dowry; Epistolary Authors, Women as; Humility Topos; Marriage; Medicine and Medieval Women; Rhetoric, Women and

BIBLIOGRAPHY

Primary Sources
Paston Letters and Papers of the Fifteenth Century. Edited by Norman Davis. 2 vols. Oxford: Oxford University Press, 1971, 1976 [All citations taken from the 1976 ed.].

The Paston Letters: A Selection in Modern Spelling. Edited with introduction by Norman Davis. Oxford and New York: Oxford University Press, 1999.

The Paston Letters, A.D. *1422–1509*. Edited by James Gairdner. Revised ed. 4 vols. Westminster: Archibald Constable & Co., 1900–1908; 6 vols. London: Chatto & Windus, 1904. Reprint New York: AMS Press, 1965.

The Paston Letters: A Selection in Modern Spelling. Edited by Norman Davis. Oxford: Oxford University Press, 1963. Reprint 1978, 1983.

Secondary Sources
Davis, Norman. "Margaret Paston's Uses of Do." *Neuphilologische Mitteilungen* 73 (1972): 55–62.

Gies, Frances, and Joseph Gies. *A Medieval Family: The Pastons of Fifteenth-Century England*. New York: HarperCollins, 1998.

Haskell, Ann S. "Marriage in the Middle Ages: The Paston Women on Marriage in Fifteenth Century England." *Viator* 4 (1973): 459–71.

Krug, Rebecca. *Reading Families: Women's Literate Practice in Late Medieval England*. Ithaca, N.Y.: Cornell University Press, 2002.

Richmond, Colin. *The Paston Family in the Fifteenth Century: The First Phase*. Cambridge: Cambridge University Press, 1990.

———. *The Paston Family in the Fifteenth Century: Fastolf's Will*. Cambridge: Cambridge University Press, 1996.

———. *The Paston Family in the Fifteenth Century: Endings*. Manchester, U.K.: Manchester University Press; New York: PalgraveMacmillan, 2000.

Rosenthal, Joel T. *Telling Tales: Sources and Narration in Late Medieval England*. University Park: Pennsylvania State University Press, 2003.

Watt, Diane. "'No Writing for Writing's Sake': The Language of Service and Household Rhetoric in the Letters of the Paston Women." In *Dear Sister: Medieval Women and the Epistolary Genre*, edited by Karen Cherewatuk and Ulrike Wiethaus, 122–38. Middle Ages. Philadelphia: University of Pennsylvania Press, 1993.

Whitaker, Elaine. "Reading the Paston Letters Medically." *English Language Notes* 31 (1993): 19–27.

Woolf, Virginia. "The Pastons and Chaucer." In *The Common Reader*. 1st ser., 3–23. New York: Harcourt, Brace & World, 1925.

MARILYNN DESMOND

PATRISTIC ATTITUDES TOWARD WOMEN. *See* **Desert Mothers; Eustochium, St.; Virginity**

PAULA, ST. *See* **Eustochium, St.**

PENITENTIALS, WOMEN IN. Penitentials were handbooks written to assist priests to hear confession and assign penance. These handy reference guides were designed to be consulted by the confessor in the field. The handbooks were written in Latin and, while the Old-Irish Penitential (late eighth century) was in the vernacular, it was heavily dependent on earlier Latin manuals. Such manuals contained lists or tariffs of sins and the penance appropriate to each. The practices recommended by these manuals were gender defined, either overtly or covertly, and reflect a variety of shifting perspectives over the course of the early Middle Ages.

The practice of confessing sins and performing penance to expiate guilt and receive forgiveness was established in the early Church. Originally penance was a public rite and available to the sinner only once in a lifetime. The penitent was readmitted to the community of the faithful on completion of the assigned penance but she or he also bore certain prohibitions such as the inability to marry for the remainder of his or her life. Gradually, the practice of penance modified, and by the sixth century there is evidence that the penitential discipline had loosened enabling private, repeatable penance to coexist with the older, public nonrepeatable form. The impetus for this innovation came from Celtic Ireland, where monasteries were the local religious centers and the abbot and monks exercised moral and spiritual leadership. The monastic practice of frequent private confession and penance for minor faults spread outward to the laity (nonreligious) who sought spiritual guidance from the monks. The practice of private and repeatable penance extended rapidly to Anglo-Saxon England and, by the seventh century to continental Europe, where it was introduced by Irish missionaries.

These intrepid Irish missionaries carried penitentials with them across Europe. The earliest penitentials include works attributed to Finnian (late sixth century), Columbanus (sixth to seventh centuries), and Cummean (seventh century). The Penitential of Columbanus was the earliest to be taken to the Continent. It influenced later Frankish penitentials such as those of Bobbio (early eighth century), Fleury (late eighth century), and St. Gall (ninth century), as well as Visigothic ones such as the Penitential of Silos (ninth century) and the Penitential of Vigila of Alveda (ninth century). Irish penitentials also influenced the Anglo-Saxon tradition, which included works attributed to Theodore (eighth century), Bede (eighth century), and Egbert of York (late tenth century).

The reaction to the introduction of penitentials in continental Europe varied. Originally they were embraced enthusiastically and inspired the appearance of indigenous handbooks. However, during the Carolingian reforms, councils such as those of Châlon (813) and Paris (829) condemned penitentials as uncanonical and inconsistent. Such criticisms seem to have had little effect, for penitentials frequently appeared on lists of books that a priest ought to own. In addition, new penitentials were written to reconcile the need for consistency and authority with the practical problems addressed by penitentials. This new approach was seen in Haltigar of Cambrai's *Roman Penitential* (c.830), Hrabanus Maurus's *Penitential Addressed to Otgar* (842) and *Penitential Addressed to Heribald* (856), and Regino of Prüm's *Ecclesiastical Discipline* (c.906).

The canonical collections such as those of Ivo of Chartres and Gratian tended to dominate the eleventh and twelfth centuries and overshadowed the penitentials. However, Burchard of Worms's *Decretum* (*Decree*) Book 19, *Corrector et medicus* (*Corrector and Doctor*) is a confessional treatise that continued the tradition of the penitentials. The influence of the penitentials is also seen in the works of Bartholomew of Exeter (c.1150–1170), the noted French authority Alan of Lille (c.1175–1200), and Robert of Flamborough (1208–1213). By the beginning of the thirteenth century, there was a more developed understanding of the sacrament of penance as a result of the influence of scholastic methodology (cultivating a form of reasoning based on meticulous logic rather than direct experimentation) and a growing interest in sacramental theology (religious thought dealing with the rituals the Church recognized as the visible signs of invisible grace). This, coupled with the Fourth Lateran Council (1215) decree *Omnis utriusque sexus* (*For Everyone of Either Sex*), which required annual confession by every adult Christian, resulted in the appearance of a new type of manual, the *summa confessorum* (the confessors' authoritative compilation). These works placed confession and penance within a sophisticated theological and canonical framework. The *summae* ultimately superseded and supplanted the penitentials, with their simple lists of sins and penances.

In theory, the literature of penance and confession pertained equally to all Christians, male and female. In practice, however, there were great discrepancies in the treatment of men and women. The earliest penitentials, produced as they were in a monastic environment, were concerned with the sins of male religious. When the manuals treated the sins pertaining to the laity, this male perspective continued. Women are presented primarily as passive objects, objects of men's sins, objects whose status could exacerbate the seriousness of men's sins. For example, the *Penitential of Finnian* discusses the relative seriousness of the sin if a man defiled a virgin, a widow, a married woman, or a nun, and whether or not a child were conceived as a result. The penances prescribed for the man vary with the woman's status, but the penitential does not admit the possibility of the woman as actor or initiator of the sin and thus one who is morally culpable. Women are presented as active sinners only in two areas. Penances are recommended for women who practice magic and for wives who desert their husbands. This relative neglect of women as independent moral agents is perpetuated in later Irish penitentials and reflects something of the realities of the surrounding society. For example, the *Penitential of Columbanus* required a man to make restitution for committing adultery. If the women were married, the restitution was to be made to her husband; if she were a widow or young girl it was made to her parents. Such a penance clearly shows the influence of the custom of bride-price and reflects something of the prevalent secular evaluation of women. Over time, the penitentials expanded the scope of their treatment and those of Anglo-Saxon origins present a fuller discussion of female penitents than do their Irish precursors. The *Penitential of Theodore*, for example, prescribes penances for a woman who masturbates and distinguishes the relative seriousness of the sin depending on the woman's status as married, single, or widowed. Although the Irish penitentials treated male homosexual activity in some detail, it is only with Theodore and Bede that lesbian activity is mentioned.

While exhibiting a broader understanding of the activities of women, the penitentials of the eighth and ninth centuries continue to reflect the subordinate position of women in early medieval society. Theodore underscored a wife's subordination to her husband and allowed a married woman to be disinherited for her adultery. If a husband wanted to reconcile with an adulterous wife, the *Penitential* then advises that her punishment is no longer the concern of the clergy, but rather is to be determined solely by her husband. Women were also under the control of their parents, although Theodore states that after a girl is sixteen or seventeen years old, her father may no longer marry her to someone against her will. Presumably there were no restrictions on the father's right to marry off a daughter younger than sixteen.

As penitential literature became more sophisticated and refined, women were treated in greater depth and detail. Yet penitentials of necessity had a limited perspective and understanding of women. The genre continued to be written by men and primarily for men. A male penitent was assumed as the norm. While it may be argued that the spiritual advice and penances were applicable to any penitent, regardless of sex, the penitentials present a male perspective of the nature and role of women. Consequently, they do not provide a balanced view of women as moral agents or as active in their world.

The discussion of women and the sins specific to them continued to receive more attention in later penitentials and in the *summae confessorum* that superseded them. But women also continued to be perceived through the eyes of the male cleric who wrote such works, and to some degree they continued to be viewed as an object or occasion for men to sin. Thus, while penitential literature was not overtly misogynistic, it was influenced and shaped by the perspective of its male authors and the values of secular society. For this reason, it is useful as a source for tracing the development of attitudes toward women in the Middle Ages. It is not a source in which women speak in their own voices.

See also Law, Canon, Women in; Law, Women in, Anglo-Saxon England; Lesbians in the Middle Ages; Norse Women; Rules for Canonesses, Nuns, and Recluses; Witches

BIBLIOGRAPHY

Primary Sources
Alan of Lille, *Liber Poenitentialis*. Edited by Jean Longère. 2 vols. Analecta Mediaevalia Namurcensia, 17. Louvain, Belgium: Nauwelaerts, 1965.
Bieler, Ludwig, ed. *The Irish Penitentials*, Scriptores Latini Hiberniae, 5. Dublin: Institute for Advanced Studies, 1963. Reprint 1975. [English and Latin texts].
McNeill, John T., and Helena M. Gamer, *Medieval Handbooks of Penance*. New York: Columbia University Press, 1938. Reprint 1990. [English trans. of excerpts from the major Irish, Anglo-Saxon, and Frankish penitentials].

Robert of Flamborough, *Liber Poenitentialis*. Edited by J. J. F. Firth. Studies and Texts, 18. Toronto: Pontifical Institute, 1971.

Secondary Sources

Biller, Peter, and A. J. Minnis, eds. *Handling Sin: Confession in the Middle Ages*. York, U.K.: Boydell & Brewer, 1998.

Frantzen, Allen J. *The Literature of Penance in Anglo-Saxon England*. New Brunswick, N.J.: Rutgers University Press, 1983.

Michaud-Quantin, Pierre. *Sommes de casuistique et manuels de confession au moyen âge (XII–XVI siècles)*, Analecta Mediaevalia Namurcensia 13. Louvain: Nauwelaerts, 1962. [Good introduction to *summae confessorum*].

Morey, Adrian. *Bartholomew of Exeter, Bishop and Canonist*. Cambridge, Mass.: Harvard University Press, 1937.

Payer, Pierre J. *Sex and the Penitentials. The Development of a Sexual Code 500–1150*. Toronto: University of Toronto, 1984.

Schmitz, Hermann Joseph. *Die Bussbücher und die Bussdisciplin der Kirche*. 2 vols. Mainz, Germany: F. Kirchheim, 1883. Reprint Graz, Austria: Akademische Druck, 1958.

———. *Die Bussbücher und das kanonische Bussverfahren*. Düsseldorf, Germany: L. Schwann, 1898. Reprint Graz: Akademische Druck, 1958.

Smith, Julie Ann. *Ordering Women's Lives: Penitentials and Nunnery Rules in the Early Medieval West*. Aldershot, U.K.: Ashgate, 2001.

Tentler, Thomas N. *Sin and Confession on the Eve of the Reformation*. Princeton, N.J.: Princeton University Press, 1977.

Vogel, Cyrille. *Les "Libri Paenitentiales."* Typologie des Sources du Moyen Âge Occidental, 27. Turnhout, Belgium: Brepols, 1978. Revised fascicle, "Mise à jour" (same title and series) by A. J. Frantzen. 1985. [Essential bibliography].

JACQUELINE MURRAY

PERICULOSO (1298). "For the perilous and detestable state of certain nuns," *Periculoso* is the decree (1298) of Pope Boniface VIII imposing strict cloister—claustration—on all women living under religious rules (Friedberg). In his preamble, the pope mentioned the shameless immodesty of certain nuns (*moniales*) who, wandering away from their monasteries (sometimes in secular clothing) and permitting suspect persons to enter, caused grief to God (to whom they had vowed their virginity), disrepute to the religious life, and set a bad example to many others. So that they might devote all their time to the service of God and keep their souls and bodies holy, all professed nuns of every order everywhere were to remain in permanent cloister (*clausura*). They could never go out, unless gravely ill with an infectious or shameful disease, nor allow anyone in except, for reasonable cause and by special license, an honorable person. No religious house should take in more sisters than it could maintain on its endowment in this economically unproductive cloister, except Franciscan, Dominican, and Carmelite convents, which supported themselves in part by begging. An abbess or prioress could go out, with a proper escort and no dallying, to perform homage for some property she might hold as a fief. All judges were commanded to permit nuns to appear and litigate by proxy or attorney instead of compelling them to come out of their cloister into court in person. The pope committed the enforcement of nuns' claustration to their bishops.

Boniface VIII (c.1234–1303) had been a lawyer by profession, and the code of canon law that he commissioned, the Liber Sextus (Sixth Book), contained all the useful decrees that had come into being since the Decretals of Gregory IX in 1234. He also took this opportunity, combining his legal knowledge and the papal legislative authority, to make new laws, settle legal questions, and correct disorders in the Church according to his own ideas. *Periculoso* injected a papal law into the customary life of dedicated religious women, a life that until then had been governed by the discipline of the orders, the houses, and the women themselves. The "peril" that moved Boniface to legislate may have been the appearance of religious groups of women who preached and appropriated other clerical functions, and some of whom, for example the Guglielmites of Milan, seemed to be linked with the Spiritual Franciscans and with the pope's bitter rivals, the Colonna cardinals, as Makowski shows. *Periculoso* contains no reflection of the Council of London's Canon 52, "Nuns should not go outside certain places" (Powicke and Cheney), although Boniface had been a secretary to the papal legate presiding there in 1268. Acting on his own sense of right order, without consultation, recognizing none of the activities to which the religious women of his time were devoting their energy and their specifically Christian motivations, such as service in hospitals, teaching, and feeding the poor, Boniface VIII made an inapplicable law. Lay Christians continued to give nuns who were active in the world the honor and privileges that *Periculoso* would have reserved to the strictly cloistered.

See also Convents; Guglielmites; Law, Canon, Women in; Rules for Canonesses, Nuns, and Recluses

BIBLIOGRAPHY

Primary Sources
Friedberg, Emil, ed. *Corpus iuris canonici*, 2nd revised ed. after E. L. Richter. 2 vols. Leipzig, Germany: Tauchnitz, 1879–81 and reprints.
Powicke, F. M., and C. R. Cheney, eds. *Councils and Synods; with other documents relating to the English Church (1205–1265); (1265–1313)*. Vol. 2 in 2 parts. Oxford: Clarendon, 1964.

Secondary Source
Makowski, Elizabeth. *Canon Law and Cloistered Women: Periculoso and Its Commentators 1298–1545*. Washington, D.C.: Catholic University of America Press, 1997.

DANIEL WILLIMAN

PERPETUA, ST. (d. 203). Vibia Perpetua was a legendary African martyr of the Roman Empire who composed one of the earliest first-person accounts of civil disobedience and protest. The main source for her life is the *Passio Sanctarum Perpetuae et Felicitatis* (*The Passion of Sts. Perpetua and Felicity*), a contemporary document written in Latin that underwent multiple versions and translations. It differs from other acts of the martyrs, which are usually written by witnesses or those having interviewed eyewitnesses, because it also is partly written by Perpetua herself; it contains her intensely personal and spiritual diary from the last days of her life in prison, during which she experienced visions and decided to become a martyr, a form of liberation and self-fulfillment (Rader).

Her story may be outlined as follows. Perpetua, a well-educated Roman matron of an elite family, aged twenty-two, living in Carthage, North Africa—then part of the Roman Empire—is married with one infant son whom she was nursing. We know virtually nothing of her husband. She and four companions, all catechumens (those training to be Christians in preparation for baptism): two slaves, Revocatus and Felicitas, and two others, Saturninus and Secundulus, were arrested for openly professing and practicing their Christian faith, in that they refused to sacrifice to the emperor, Geta Septimius Publius (189–211), during his birthday celebrations according to pagan Roman custom. During her prison stay, she kept a diary recording her sentiments about her religion and its affect on her and her family. She also recounts four visionary dreams that she deemed prophetic in her determination to die for her beliefs despite her family ties: (1) a bronze ladder of inestimable length, perilously festooned with sharp weapons of all kinds and a snake skulking at its foot, which she must climb; the ladder portends future suffering for her and her companions. They undergo a hearing in which she is warned by the Roman governor of the consequences of her adherence to Christianity, and how her father and infant wish her to recant as well. But Perpetua remains adamant; her father claims her child, who no longer wishes her breast, and yet she feels no physical discomfort from this. (2) She sees her brother Dinocrates, who had died at seven of a horrid facial cancer, standing in a pool, dirty, pallid, and thirsty because the pool's edge was too high for him to drink from it (Dinocrates died unbaptized). She prays for his suffering. (3) Her brother reappears in this vision, experienced by Perpetua while chained; this time he is clean and refreshed, happily drinking from a golden vessel beside the pool. A Roman officer, the prison warden, visits her and her fellow catechumens, but strangely, looks on them with respect, as if to sense a special power within them. Her father comes to her and flings himself on the ground before her, screaming regret over his life and tearing out his beard. She sympathizes with his sorrow. (4) The deacon comes to her the day before she is to face the murderous beasts in the arena and reassures her of his support during her ordeal. Before entering the arena to combat not the beasts, but a loathsome-looking Egyptian adversary, Perpetua is stripped and then turns into a man. A towering male arbiter, wearing a purple tunic and gold and silver sandals, carrying a huge baton and a branch laden with apples, appears and promises a different reward to each—Perpetua-man and the Egyptian—in the event of his victory. After a struggle, Perpetua-man wins and receives her reward of a branch from the giant arbiter, who then kisses her. She then enters the "Portal of the Living," the way accorded only to victorious gladiators. This dream Perpetua interprets as a premonition of her combat—again, not with beasts, but with the Devil—from which she will emerge triumphant.

Within the *Passio*, consisting of twenty-one sections divided into four main parts, these visions, which modern critics have found vastly intriguing (von Franz, ed.; Dronke; Salisbury) occupy the central portion (sections 3–10). Part 1 (sections 1–2) contain the introduction and report by an eyewitness—many believe the famous African Church Father Tertullian (c.160–c.225) or a member of his circle. Part 2 (sections 3–10), Perpetua's prison diary—has been characterized by Peter Dronke as including an "outer" depiction of what befell her and an "inner" one of her visions based on her secret thoughts—ending with her self-conscious remark that she ceases writing on the eve of her fatal combat and that it must be left to another to relate, if he will, what was to take place in the amphitheater. Part 3 (section 11–13) presents the account given by a fellow prisoner, the priest Saturus (who had later voluntarily joined Perpetua and the other catechumens in prison), of his own vision and providing testimony for Perpetua. Part 4 (sections 14–21) contains the conclusion by the eyewitness: the account of the final struggle in the amphitheater and the inevitably gory deaths of Perpetua and her companions, enclosed by the compiler—possibly a third party, in conjunction with Perpetua and Saturus, and the eyewitness—in a moral and religious exhortation.

At least two voices are therefore discernible in the *Passio*: that of the compiler and that of the martyrs themselves. Dronke also reminds us to consider that Perpetua's record of lived experience is also affected by her literate experience: her own readings as an educated person and catechumen. Nevertheless, St. Augustine (354–430), in his *De Doctrina Christiana* (*On Christian Doctrine*, 4: 20. 39–44) observes no aesthetic distinction between Perpetua's diary and the redactor's hagiographic frame. Tertullian is regarded as a possible compiler for linguistic and intertextual reasons, such as when he refers to the visions of Perpetua and quotes phrases from the vision of Saturus, echoing the *Passio*, in his treatise, *De testimonio animae* (*On the Testimony of the Soul*). The language of the Latin text of the *Passio* is colloquial and homely, without any stylistic ornaments, associated by scholars with the *sermo humilis* (humble style) of Perpetua's writing. The *Acta* (the *Passio* in its various forms, shorter and longer; one, slightly later, was actually called the *Acta minora*) of Perpetua have had a strong influence on the later martyrologists (Harris). The *Passio/Acta*, first published by P. Poussin in 1663, has come down to us without a title and without naming its author, its locality, or its date. In 1889, James Rendel Harris discovered a complete Greek text of the martyrdoms in a convent in Jerusalem, which he believed to be the original text. However, the current tendency among scholars has dismissed Harris's thesis and regards the Greek text as a translation of the Latin, since the martyrdoms of the Latin Church are expected to have been chronicled in the Latin tongue.

The *Passio* does not furnish us with a great deal of historical information beyond what bears on the incident of the prison and the arena, although both Rosemary Rader and Joyce Salisbury have recently shown that there is much to be learned by reading the *Passio* in light of the social, religious, and political dynamic of that time. For we have not only the overall cultural conflict between late Roman imperial power and that of burgeoning Christianity (and its resultant subculture of martyrs as activists and protesters of their day), but also the father–daughter confrontation fused with the pagan–Christian problem (Perpetua's father was non-Christian; even early Christian society was male dominated), and the bond between mother and child (would her father have raised him to be Christian, and thus save her son's soul?), as well as the gender-role vs. self-expectation tension exhibited in Perpetua's sexual change in her fourth vision.

Because the basilica erected to enshrine the remains of Sts. Perpetua and Felicity at Carthage became extremely important and highly revered, as has her *Passio* by scholars, the prophecy of Perpetua's fourth dream can be said to have come true. Her feast day is March 7.

See also Hagiography (Female Saints); Humility Topos; Relics and Medieval Women

BIBLIOGRAPHY

Primary Sources
Acts of the Christian Martyrs. Edited and translated by Herbert R. Musurillo, 106–31. Oxford: Clarendon Press, 1972. [Authoritative Latin text, English trans. and commentary]. Reprint in Petroff, 70–77. See below, Secondary Sources.
"A New Version of the Acts of Perpetua and Felicitas." Edited by James Rendel Harris and S. K. Gifford. *Haverford College Studies* 3 (1890): 1–73. [Greek and Latin texts].
Passio Sanctarum Perpetuae et Felicitatis. Edited by Cornelius J. M. J. van Beek. Nijmegen, Netherlands: Dekker & Van de Vegt, 1936. [Larger ed., Latin].
Passio Sanctarum Perpetuae et Felicitatis, Latine et Graece. Edited by C. I. M. I. van Beek. Florilegium Patristicum, 43. Bonn: P. Hanstein, 1938. [Shorter ed.: authoritative Greek and Latin texts].

The Passion of St. Perpetua. Critical ed. by J. A. Robinson. Text and Studies (Contributions to Biblical and Patristic Literature), 1. 2. Cambridge: Cambridge University, 1891. [Latin text].

The Passion of Perpetua. Translated by Marie-Louise von Franz. Jungian Classics, 2. Irvington, Texas: Spring, 1980. Original German version "Die Passio Perpetua." In Carl Jung, *Aion*, 389496. Zürich: Roscher, 1951. [Trans. with Jungian analysis of Perpetua's visions].

———. [*Passio*]. "Perpetua." Introduced and translated by Rosemary Rader. In *A Lost Tradition*, edited and translated by Patricia Wilson-Kastner et al., 1–32. Washington, D.C.: University Press of America, 1981. [Entire, English only; excellent introduction].

———. [*Passio*]. "Prisoner, Dreamer, Martyr." In *The Writings of Medieval Women: An Anthology*, edited and translated by Marcelle Thiébaux, 3–22. Garland Library of Medieval Literature, 100B, 2nd ed. New York and London: Garland, 1994. [Entire text in English only, useful commentary].

[*Passio*, 3–10]. In *Women Writers of the Middle Ages: A Critical Study of Texts from Perpetua (†203) to Marguerite Porete (†1310)*, translated by Peter Dronke. Cambridge: Cambridge University Press, 1984. [English trans. with excellent commentary].

Secondary Sources
[See also notes to above critical texts and translations].

McInerney, Maud B. *Eloquent Virgins from Thecla to Joan of Arc.* The New Middle Ages. New York: Palgrave Macmillan, 2003.

Petroff, Elizabeth A., ed. *Medieval Women's Visionary Literature*. New York: Oxford University Press, 1986.

Salisbury, Joyce E. *Perpetua's Passion: The Death and Memory of a Young Roman Woman*. New York and London: Routledge, 1997.

Smith, Lacey B. *Fools, Martyrs, Traitors: The Story of Martyrdom in the Western World*. New York: Knopf, 1997.

Vitz, Evelyn Birge. "Gender and Martyrdom." *Medievalia et Humanistica* n.s. 26 (1999): 79–99.

Walters, Lori J. "Metamorphoses of the Self: Christine de Pizan, the Saint's Life, and Perpetua." In *Sur le chemin de longue etude...Actes du Colloque d'Orléans, juillet 1995*, edited by Bernard Ribémont, 158–81. Études christiniennes, 3. Paris: Honoré Champion, 1998. [In both authors' accounts (Perpetua's visions, Christine's *Mutacion de Fortune*), the narrator-heroine must change into a man to confront crisis, etc.].

ARISTOULA GEORGIADOU

PETRONILLA OF CHEMILLÉ (1115–1149).

Petronilla, or, in French, Petronille de Chemillé, was the first abbess of Fontevraud, a French monastery of nuns and monks. Petronilla, a native of Anjou in western France, was born in the later eleventh century. She married into the family of the lords of Chemillé, vassals of the count of Anjou. In the last few years of the eleventh century, Petronilla joined the followers of the charismatic Robert of Arbrissel (c.1045–1116). Robert had been a parish priest, diocesan official, hermit, and founder of a house of regular canons when in 1096 Pope Urban II charged him to preach the gospel far and wide. Robert quickly attracted a crowd of male and female disciples and settled together in 1101 at Fontevraud, some forty miles east of Chemillé. Robert's followers first lived in huts at Fontevraud, but overcrowding soon demanded the construction of the customary substantial buildings of a monastery. Robert desired to return to his traveling evangelism. Not wanting to supervise Fontevraud, he put two women in charge of the building and other management: Hersende, a local widow, and Petronilla, whom he recognized as an "experienced estate manager." These two women, then, directed a mixed monastic community of male and female religious seekers.

With Hersende and Petronilla in charge, Fontevraud expanded its model of nuns and monks together under female supervision was imitated at numerous priories. Hersende died in about 1112; soon after, Robert referred to Petronilla as "handmaid of the hand-maids of God," a reference to the popes' self-designation as "servant of the servants of God." Sensing death approaching, Robert named Petronilla first abbess of his burgeoning monastic order in October 1115. When Robert died a few months later, Petronilla assumed her duties as spiritual and practical director of Fontevraud and its approximately fifteen daughter houses.

The choice of Petronilla as abbess caused some consternation at the time and has drawn extensive and sometimes critical commentary ever since because Petronilla, unlike many female monastic superiors, was not a virgin. The surviving documentation does not call her a widow, either. She may have been one of the company of wives fleeing their marriages whom Robert of Arbrissel protected and refused stubbornly to return to their husbands. Robert chose Petronilla specifically for her practical acumen, commenting that one who had spent her whole life in the cloister might not manage mundane affairs very effectively, and further that it was fitting for one who had endured early trials along-side him to shoulder responsibility for present prosperity. Petronilla more than justified Robert's confidence. As abbess she presided over further expansion of the order, which included more than fifty monasteries in France and Spain by the time of her death. It was probably at Petronilla's order that hundreds of documents concerning the properties of the abbey and its priories were copied into one register, the so-called Great Cartulary of Fontevraud. Petronilla's determination to protect the rights of her congregation remained undiminished right to the end. Only a few weeks before her death she attained favorable settlement of a five-year quarrel over properties that had come to the attention of Bernard of Clairvaux, the best-known monk of the twelfth century, and the pope. Petronilla saw no conflict between spiritual aims and temporal necessities, noting that "Often putting aside the glory of reading and prayers, we turn to management of temporal goods for the advantage of our successors, which indeed we do for this reason: when we are sleeping in our tombs, we may be helped by their prayers before God."

When Petronilla, called in a Fontevraud record "our incomparable and irrecoverable mother," died in 1149, the Order of Fontevraud under her guidance had become what it remained until the French Revolution: the largest and wealthiest federation of monas-teries for women in Catholic Europe. Pope Calixtus II personally dedicated the abbey church in 1119. This handsome and impressively large Romanesque structure remains at Fontevraud today, along with a twelfth-century dormitory and a unique octagonal kitchen, lasting reminders of Petronilla's accomplishments.

See also Catherine of Bologna, St.; Convents

BIBLIOGRAPHY

Primary Sources
Grand cartulaire de Fontevraud, vol. 1, edited by Jean-Marc Bienvenu. (Collection des archives historiques de Poitou 63). Poitiers: Société des antiquaires de l'Ouest, 2000.
Patrologia cursus completus. Series latina, ed. J.-P. Migne, vol. 162: 1043–1118. 221 vols. Paris, 1844–1864. [Latin biographies of Robert of Arbrissel and numerous documents concerning the early history of Fontevraud].

Secondary Sources

Bienvenu, Jean–Marc. *L'étonnant fondateur de Fontevraud, Robert d'Arbrissel*. Paris: Nouvelles Éditions Latines, 1981.

Tunc, Suzanne. *Les Femmes au Pouvoir: Deux Abbesses de Fontevraud aux XIIe et XVIIe siècles*. Paris: Éditions du Cerf, 1993.

Venarde, Bruce L. "*Praesidentes Negotiis*: Abbesses as Managers in Twelfth-Century France." In *Portraits of Medieval and Renaissance Living: Essays in Memory of David Herlihy*, edited by Samuel K. Cohn Jr. and Steven A. Epstein, 189–205. Ann Arbor: University of Michigan Press, 1996.

———. *Women's Monasticism and Medieval Society: Nunneries in France and England, 890–1215*. Ithaca, N.Y.: Cornell University Press, 1997.

BRUCE L. VENARDE

PHILIPPA OF LANCASTER. *See* Filipa de Lencastre

PINAR, FLORENCIA (late 15th century). One of a small number of women writers active in Spain during the Middle Ages, Pinar composed poetry that is recognized today for its innovative and linguistically anomalous style, and for the attention it draws to women's social, political, and doctrinal identities during the late medieval period. Little is known about Pinar except that she can be placed at the court of Ferdinand and Isabella, whose rule in Spain dates from 1479, and that she was a well-educated woman, conversant in the composition of courtly lyrics.

Pinar's works appear in three *cancioneros* (poetry collections of the fifteenth and sixteenth centuries), including Hernando del Castillo's well-known *Cancionero General* of 1511. Although she appears as author of a number of cancionero poems, only three are universally attributed to her: "Ay!, que ay quien más no bive" ("Alas! There is one who no longer lives"), "Otra canción de la misma señora a unas perdizes que le embiaron bivas" ("Another song by the same lady, to some partridges that were sent alive to her") and "Canción de Florencia Pinar" ("A Poem by Florencia Pinar"). Florencia was probably the sister of the male poet, "Pinar," who wrote a gloss, or commentary, on her poem, "Canción de Florencia Pinar," along with many other glosses and *cancionero* poems.

For years Pinar's poetry was dismissed by critics as trivial, perhaps as a result of its distinction from other poems found in the vast poetry collections of her period. Unlike most *cancionero* texts, Pinar's work relies more on concrete imagery (e.g., birds, worms) than on abstractions. Her work is also plainly erotic and contains several rather clear references to female sexuality. Indeed, Pinar's style can be aggressively feminine, incorporating, for example, rhyme schemes that depend on feminine grammatical gender (with verses ending exclusively in feminine nouns or pronouns) and a female speaking subject. This latter characteristic is particularly unusual in *cancionero* poetry where women are more often poetic themes than voices.

Pinar's fourteen-line "Ay! que ay quien más no bive" is a *canción*, consisting of octosyllabic verse. The form is a common one used in *cancionero* poetry. The poem's first stanza contains five lines with the rhyme scheme abbab. Its second stanza contains nine lines following certain distinct formulae of repeated rhyme: a *redondilla* (cddc: that is, the third rhymed verses enclose two verses of the same fourth rhyme) and a *quintilla* (five lines following the rhyme scheme abbab), the whole of which mimics the first five lines of the poem. The text's repetitive wordplay on the sigh (*ay*) presents an intellectual puzzle more akin to the courtly poetry in vogue at the time than Pinar's other poems, which are far more concrete. Like those other poems, however, it dwells on the suffering and captivity that ensue from love and sexual passion.

Suffering and captivity are in fact what is explicitly concrete in "Otra canción de la misma señora a unas perdices que le embiaron bivas." This poem, also a *canción*, is introduced by a five-line *quintilla* (abaab), followed by a four-line *redondilla* (cddc), coupled with another five-line *quintilla* possessing the same rhyme scheme as the first stanza. The poem focuses on sexual division, in particular masculine aggression against women, through the imagery of female birds held captive by male hunters. The poem also hints at women's sexual initiative and erotic fantasy through the symbolism of the birds' happy song and their disdain for those who later take them captive. This symbolism is quickly overtaken by another, however, the birds' weeping, which is expressive of women's privation, as love object, of even the means to actively seek sexual satisfaction. "Canción de Florencia Pinar" begins and ends with a *cuarteta* (abab) and thus is somewhat different in form from the other two poems. Like these poems, however, the opening lines of the second stanza constitute a *redondilla*, with the rhyme scheme cddc. Again, the theme addressed is love and sexual passion, with a focus on sexual division and men's aggression against women. Love is a cancer, a worm that gains its object through trickery and something that must be guarded against. Once it enters the body, it cannot leave without ripping out the entrails. The decidedly phallic, but also clearly dangerous, image of the worm entering the body symbolically warns women against victimization, stressing the suffering that results from love's deceits.

All three of Pinar's poems suggest a link between women's more passive role as poetic theme and patron, their more active role as writers and readers, and the development of a peculiar "women's" language to give women's voices authority in the official world of writing. Distinguished by the use of terms that project a nonmaterial image of the world, the register (stylistic, tonal level) of the lament, and a peculiar articulation of passion and sexuality, the poems suggest a singular relationship between medieval women writers and the theme of love. Neither wholly love object nor wholly poetic subject, Florencia Pinar's poetic voice may have been crafted as a mode of resistance to domination in a culture where men routinely assume women's signifying and representing functions.

See also Borja, Tecla; Capellanus, Andreas; Catalan Women Poets, Anonymous; *Chanson de Femme* (Women's Song); *Novela Sentimental*/Sentimental Romance; Reyna de Mallorques, La

BIBLIOGRAPHY

Primary Source
Cancionero general recopilado por Hernando del Castillo [1511]. Edited by Antonio Rodríguez-Moñino. Madrid: Real Academia Española, 1958.

Secondary Sources
Broad, Peter. "Florencia Pinar y la poética del cancionero." In *La Escritora Hispánica*, edited by Nora Erro-Orthmann and Juan Cruz Mendizabal, 26–36. Miami: Ediciones Universal, 1990.
Deyermond, Alan. "The Worm and the Partridge: Reflections on the Poetry of Florencia Pinar." *Mester* 7 (1978): 3–8.

————. "Spain's First Women Writers." In *Women in Hispanic Literature: Icons and Fallen Idols*, edited by Beth Miller, 27–52. Berkeley: University of California Press, 1983.

Flores, Angel, and Kate Flores. *The Defiant Muse: Hispanic Feminist Poems from the Middle Ages to the Present*. New York: Feminist Press, 1986.

Fulks, Barbara. "The Poet Named Florencia Pinar." *La Corónica* 18.1 (1989–1990): 33–44.

Mirrer, Louise. *Women, Jews, & Muslims in the Texts of Reconquest Castile*. Ann Arbor: University of Michigan Press, 1996.

Recio, Roxana. "Otra dama que desaparece: La abstracción retórica en tres modelos de canción de Florencia Pinar." *Revista Canadiense de Estudios Hispánicos* 16.2 (1992): 329–39.

Snow, Joseph T. "The Spanish Love Poet: Florencia Pinar." In *Medieval Women Writers*, edited by Katharina M. Wilson, 320–32. Athens: University of Georgia Press, 1984.

Wilkins, Constance L. "Las voces de Florencia Pinar." In *Studia Hispanica Medievalia*, vol. 2, edited by Rosa E. Penna and María A. Rosarossa, 124–30. Buenos Aires: Universidad Católica Argentina, 1990.

LOUISE MIRRER

PINZOCHERE (13th–14th centuries). The *pinzochere* (sing.= *pinzochera*) were laywomen penitents in Italy, often compared to, and confused with, the beguines, or *bizzoche*, as they were called in Italian. The *pinzochere* seemingly emerged "from the dust," as some Churchmen noted with alarm (see Sensi, 72n.12), during the same movement that produced the Mendicant ("begging") Orders like the Franciscans, Dominicans in the early thirteenth century, and later, the Carmelites (c.1245) attracted aristocrats seeking spiritual fulfillment beyond what the existing Church offered. These women tended to be wealthy widows or unmarried virgins and other single women choosing a life of poverty, chastity, charitable and hospice work and contemplation. Unlike the *bizzoche*, who did not take vows and belonged to no monastic order, the *pinzochere* professed vows to the prior of the community of friars to which they attached themselves, and wore that order's habit, while living in their own homes. They were also called *mantellate*, because of the special mantel they wore, or *beatae* ("blessed women"). Professed *pinzochere* have existed from as early as 1309, as in the case of Lady Diana Buzzadelli in Florence (McMahon).

Because they evolved into one of the most independent strata of women in later medieval society, even by secular, aristocratic standards, their freedom and occasional abuse of it incurred increasing resentment and distrust. The Church thus attempted to regulate the *pinzochere*, along with the *bizzoche*, by transforming them into communities of nuns who would then be enclosed, especially after the papal decree called *Periculoso* (1298), throughout Italy and Spain. In 1452, the Carmelite prior in Florence, Bartolomeo Masi, obtained the bull from Pope Nicholas V known as *Cum nulla*, which authorized the Carmelites to accept *pinzochere* and mantellate as nuns, much to the order's advantage (McMahon). Other, larger orders—the Dominicans, Franciscans (whose nuns were called Poor Clares or *Clarisses*), and Augustinian nuns absorbed them as well in France, Italy, and Spain. The latter's most famous *pinzochere*-based Carmelite monastery, in Avila, would produce St. Teresa of Avila (1550–1582). In Italy, one of the nicer residential streets of Florence is named Via delle Pinzochere.

See also Beguines; *Bizzoche*; Catherine of Siena, St.; Clare of Assisi, St; Convents; *Periculoso*; Rules for Canonesses, Nuns, and Recluses

BIBLIOGRAPHY

Benvenuti Papi, Anna. "Mendicant Friars and Female *Pinzochere* in Tuscany: From Social Marginality to Models of Sanctity." In *Women and Religion in Medieval and Renaissance Italy*, edited by

Daniel Bornstein and Roberto Rusconi, 84–103. Translated by Margery J. Schneider. Chicago: University of Chicago Press, 1996. Original *Mistiche e devote nell'Italia tardomedievale*. Naples: Liguori, 1992.

Guarnieri, Romana. "Pinzochere." In *Dizionario degli Istituti della Perfezione*, edited by Guerrino Pelliccia and Giancarlo Rocca, 6: 1721–49. Rome: Edizione Paoline, 1980.

McMahon, Patrick. "*Cum nulla* and the Origin of the Nuns in the Family of Carmel." *Carmelite Review* 41 (2002). Online http://www.carmelite.org/cumnulla/pmcmahon.htm

Sensi, Mario. "Anchoresses and Penitents in Thirteenth- and Fourteenth-Century Umbria." In *Women and Religion*, 56–83. *See above under* Benvenuti Papi.

NADIA MARGOLIS

PLACE-NAMES, ENGLISH, WOMEN IN. The majority of surviving English place-names were coined during the Anglo-Saxon period and originated as a description of the settlement or of its topographical setting. The defining element in a number of instances is an Old English personal name, and where these names are of feminine gender, they testify to the importance of the role played by women within the community. Examples include Alford in Somerset "Ealdgyth's ford," Hilborough in Norfolk "Hildeburh's stream or enclosure," Sevington in Kent "Sægifu's farmstead," and Wollerton in Shropshire "Wulfrun's farmstead." Some of the personal names are unrecorded in documentary sources, as with Beaduburh in Babraham, Cambridgeshire, Heahgyth in Eythorne, Kent, and Heahthryth in the lost Nottinghamshire place-name Hartrey Bridge. These add to our knowledge of early personal nomenclature. Others can occasionally be identified with known historical figures. For instance, the first element of Tetbury in Gloucestershire is a feminine personal name Tette, plausibly associated with Abbess Tette, a sister of the seventh-century King Ine of Wessex. According to Bede, Bamburgh in Northumbria takes its name from a former queen called Bebbe, now generally identified with the wife of King Æthelfrith (593–617). Hilbre in Cheshire contains the personal name Hildeburh and may conceivably refer to St. Hild, Abbess of Streoneshealh. A certain instance is Bibury in Gloucestershire, named from a woman called Beage who inherited the lease of the estate from her father Leppa during the mid-eighth century. Similarly, Aughton in Wiltshire is named from Æffe, who inherited the estate from her husband Wulfgar during the tenth century. Wolverhampton in the West Midlands contains the name of the lady Wulfrun, to whom it was given in 985, and Tolpuddle in Dorset was bequeathed to Abbotsbury abbey between 1058 and 1066 by Tola, the widow of Urk. Edith Weston in Leicestershire bears the name of Queen Eadgyth, wife of Edward the Confessor.

Interpretation of the significance of personal names in place-names has undergone substantial revision in recent years. Early scholars such as Stenton believed such personal names to be those of the founders of the village in question, and it therefore appeared to follow that the women named had played a leading part in the establishment of new communities during the early Anglo-Saxon period. Some reassessment of this theory has proved necessary in the light of names now identified with those of people living in the tenth or eleventh centuries. It is currently thought that in a number of instances, the relationship between an individual and a settlement bearing that individual's name may have been manorial, and this in turn means that the women named are likely to have been later holders of the estate rather than the original settlers. So too, whereas Stenton took place-names in which a feminine personal name combines with Old English *burh* to refer to monasteries founded by those ladies, Gelling argues persuasively in favor of an alternative meaning "manor house" for place-names of this type, as Fladbury in Worcestershire and Bibury in Gloucestershire.

The names of Scandinavian women are less common in English place-names than those of Anglo-Saxon origin, but instances are found in the Danelaw and other areas of Scandinavian settlement. For example, Helperby and Helperthorpe in North Yorkshire contain the feminine personal name Hjalp, Gunby in Humberside and Gunthorpe in Nottinghamshire contain the feminine personal name Gunnhildr, and Raventhorpe in Lincolnshire is named after a woman called Ragnhildr. Overall, the proportion of feminine names of either nationality is small in comparison with masculine names, but they represent a significant minority.

Not all references to women in place-names take the form of personal names. Some comprise words such as Old English *mægden* in Maidenhead, Berkshire = "landing-place of the maidens," Old English *cwene* in Quendon, Essex = "valley of the women," and Old English *cwēn* in Queniborough, Leicestershire = "fortified manor of the queen." Queenborough in Kent became a borough in 1367 and was named after Queen Philippa, the wife of Edward III. In modern times, the affix of Royal Leamington Spa in Warwickshire was granted after a visit by Queen Victoria in 1838.

References to religious foundations are fairly common, sometimes as affixes to existing place-names. Old English *myncen* "nun" in Minchinhampton, Gloucestershire, alludes to ownership by the nunnery of Caen, in Normandy (France) in the eleventh century, and references to Benedictine nunneries occur in Nunburnholme, Humberside, and Nuneaton, Warwickshire. Maiden Bradley in Wiltshire is so named because the nuns of Amesbury had a cell there. Interpretation of Maiden Newton in Dorset is less certain, but the name may suggest that the manor was once owned by nuns. Abbess Roding in Essex alludes to its possession by the Abbess of Barking, and White Ladies Aston in Herefordshire and Worcestershire to its possession by the Cistercian nuns of Whitstones. Elsewhere, however, instances of Old English *hlǣfdige* or Middle English *levedi* = "lady" in place-names usually refer to land dedicated to the Virgin Mary. Field-names such as Lady Close, Lady Field, and Lady Meadow designate land whose profits were used for the maintenance of a chapel or shrine. Other references to women in field-names include numerous occurrences of Widow Pingle, Widow's Allotment, Grandmother Meadow, Grammers Croft, and the like, representing dower land that would provide an income for the late owner's widow. Old English *wīf* = "woman" may occur in place-names like Winestead in Humberside and Westoe in Tyne and Wear, but is difficult to differentiate from a personal name Wifa. Also problematic is the interpretation of place-names like Bridford in Devon and Birdforth in North Yorkshire, where the traditional derivation from Old English *brȳd* = "bride" has recently been challenged by Hough. Occurrences of Old English *morgengifu* = "morning-gift" in place-names such as Moor Farm in Essex and Black Morray in Shropshire reflect the custom whereby land was settled by a husband on his bride; and Coates has raised the possibility of a similar interpretation for some place-names from Old English *mund*, as Badmonden and Delmonden in Kent. Old Norse *deigja* "dairy maid" may occur in Dalestorth, Nottinghamshire. Finally, Old English *port-cwēn* = "prostitute" in Portinscale, Cumbria, testifies to the pursuit of an old profession, although an alternative interpretation, "townswoman," has recently been suggested.

The most reliable source of information on English place-names are the county volumes of the English Place-Name Society, published annually since 1924 and each presenting detailed coverage of a county or part of a county. In addition to a systematic study of both major and minor place-names, each county survey includes an analysis of place-name elements, including personal names. This material is being entered into a database at the Institute for Name Studies, University of Nottingham, so that it will soon be possible to use computerized searching techniques to identify and to analyze the occurrence of different groups of material in place-names, such as feminine personal names, occupational terms, and references to marriage customs, prostitution, dower land, or nunneries. The standard place-name dictionary to date is by Ekwall, but this will be superseded by a new dictionary by Watts.

See also Boniface, St., Mission and Circle of; Dower; Dowry; Hild (Hilda), St.; Norse Women

BIBLIOGRAPHY

Cameron, Kenneth. "Stenton and Place-Names." In *Stenton's Anglo-Saxon England Fifty Years On*, edited by Donald Matthew, 31–48. Reading, U.K.: University of Reading, 1994.

Coates, Richard. "Towards an Explanation of the Kentish–*mondens.*" *Journal of the English Place-Name Society* 18 (1985–1986): 40–47.

Ekwall, Eilert. *The Concise Oxford Dictionary of English Place-Names.* 4th ed. Oxford: Clarendon, 1960.

Fellows Jensen, Gillian. *Scandinavian Personal-Names in Lincolnshire and Yorkshire.* Copenhagen: Akademisk Forlag, 1968.

Field, John. *English Field-Names: A Dictionary.* 2nd ed. Gloucester, U. K.: Alan Sutton, 1989.

———. *A History of English Field-Names.* London: Longman, 1993.

Gelling, Margaret. *Signposts to the Past: Place-Names and the History of England.* 2nd ed. 162–90. Chichester: Phillimore, 1988.

Hough, Carole. "English Place-Names: The Leverhulme Project." *Journal of the English Place-Name Society* 26 (1993–1994): 15–26.

———. "The Ladies of Portinscale." *Journal of the English Place-Name Society* 29 (1997): 71–78.

———. "Place-Name Evidence Relating to the Interpretation of Old English Legal Terminology." *Leeds Studies in English* 27 (1996): 19–48.

———. "The Place-Names Bridford, Britford and Birdforth." *Nottingham Medieval Studies* 39 (1995): 12–18.

———. "Women in English Place-Names." In *"Lastworda Betst": Essays in Memory of Christine E. Fell with Her Unpublished Writings*, edited by Carole Hough and Kathryn A. Lowe, 41–106. Donington, U.K.: Shaun Tyas, 2002.

Insley, John. *Scandinavian Personal Names in Norfolk: A Survey Based on Medieval Records and Place-Names.* Acta Academiae Regiae Gustavi Adolphi, 62. Uppsala, Sweden: Almqvist & Wiksell, 1994.

Mills, A. D. *A Dictionary of English Place-Names.* Oxford: Oxford University Press, 1991.

Smith, A. H. *English Place-Name Elements.* 2 vols. EPNS, 25, 26. Cambridge: English Place-Name Society, 1956.

Stenton, Frank Merry. "The Historical Bearing of Place-Name Studies: The Place of Women in Anglo-Saxon England." *Transactions of the Royal Historical Society.* 4th ser. 25 (1943): 1–13. Reprint in *Preparatory to Anglo-Saxon England: Being the Collected Papers of Frank Merry Stenton*, edited by Doris Mary Stenton, 314–24. Oxford: Clarendon, 1970.

The Survey of English Place-Names. Cambridge and Nottingham: English Place-Name Society, 1924–.

———. "Personal Names in Place Names." In *Introduction to the Survey of English Place-Names*, 165–89. EPNS, 1. Cambridge: English Place-Name Society, 1924.

Watts, Victor. *The Cambridge Dictionary of English Place-Names*. Cambridge: Cambridge University Press, 2003.

CAROLE HOUGH

POOR CLARES. *See* **Clare of Assisi, St.**

POPE JOAN. *See* **Joan, Pope**

PORETE, MARGUERITE (d. 1310). Marguerite Porete (or Porette) was a charismatic beguine mystic whose heretical but widely circulated book, *Le Mirouer des simples ames* (*The Mirror of Simple Souls*), led to her being burned as part of the Inquisition. Her book is considered the oldest surviving mystical work in French (Orcibal) and one of the few book-length writings composed by a woman before 1300 (Larrington).

Because most of what we know about her life comes from Inquisition records and from passages in her *Mirouer*, not much is known of her early life, other than that she was a beguine (woman leading a religious life in a community without taking vows) and, since she is also referred to as Margarita de Hannonia, scholars assume that she came from the Hainaut, a region south of Flanders and Brabant, today part of France and Belgium. Moreover, because the *Mirouer* was burned in front of her at Valenciennes in that region, Porete may have belonged to the beguinage there; Valenciennes may even have been her birthplace. As Ellen Babinsky suggests, she may also have been a solitary itinerant, preaching to any and all who would listen. She also must have been well educated, given the content, or even the existence, of her book. Porete lived and died a victim of the growing hostility on the part of the Church toward various nonorthodox spiritual groups that were regarded as rivals or heretics because of their teachings on sin and the state of the soul, and were ardently pursued during the reign of Philip the Fair (Philippe le Bel, 1285–1314). The sparse known chronology of key events in her life is as follows: between 1296 and 1306, she wrote her *Mirouer*; her text was approved by three orthodox Church leaders, among them Godefroi (Godfrey) of Fontaines (fl. Paris 1285–1306), who cautioned her on her language and ideas in certain passages; c.1306, when, because others strongly disapproved, it was condemned as heretical by Guy de Colmieu, bishop of Cambrai, who ordered it to be publicly burned in its author's presence; in 1306/1307, during the episcopate (bishop's reign) of Philip of Marigny, successor of Guy, she was again accused of heresy and of leading people astray; late in 1308, because of her persistence in her beliefs, Porete was arrested and imprisoned for eighteen months, and then, because she refused to give testimony and the Dominican Inquisitor prejudicially misquoted a list of offending articles from the *Mirouer* to the regents at the University of Paris, she was burned as a relapsed heretic in the Place de Grève, Paris, June 1, 1310. According to witnesses, she was courageous in meeting her death. In contrast, her supporter, Guiard de Cressonessart, a Beghard (male Beguine), was tried along with her, but he recanted and thus was spared.

The full title of her book is *Le Mirouer des Simples Ames Anienties et qui Seulement Demourent en Vouloir et Desir d'Amour* (*The Mirror of Simple Annihilated Souls Who Remain*

Only in the Will and Desire for Love). We have no other evidence of her activity apart from accounts of the proceedings of her trial and a few allusions to it in fourteenth-century chronicles (see Verdeyen; Lerner). Romana Guarnieri, the first to identify Porete conclusively as its author, suggests that its author must have been highly educated, especially in theological matters (notes to Guarnieri ed. of *Mirouer*). Of the *Mirouer*, three Old French manuscripts survive; with twelve manuscripts in translation, of which five are Latin translations from the Old French; three are Middle English translated from the Old French; a Latin translation from the Middle English; and two different Italian versions done from a Latin translation; one of the Italian versions exists in three copies (Guarnieri 1965). This unusually high number of manuscripts signals the *Mirouer*'s continued popularity in the fourteenth and fifteenth centuries.

The form of her 60,000-word work is that of a dialogue between *Amour* (Love) and *Raison* (Reason) concerning the conduct of *l'Ame* (the soul). It consistently addresses women, yet without excluding men (Petroff; Lerner). Like many medieval edifying treatises, its self-identification as a "mirror" invites contemplation and emulation. It is thus a theological treatise whose abstract concepts, often Neo-Platonic (as when she shows herself dwelling on *le plain de Verité* (Plain of Truth), are given—to render them more understandable and appealing—courtly love (*fin'amors*) allegories such as one finds in lyric poetry and in the more scholastic-philosophical *Roman de la Rose* (*Romance of the Rose*, thirteenth century)—a popular book, authored by Guillaume de Lorris and Jean de Meun, containing an encyclopedic quest for love at that time—especially in Porete's insertion of debating allegorical figures (Love et al.), speeches and exempla. This merging of profane courtly constructs with sacred mystical theology, though unthinkable at the outset, actually enables each highly refined mode to profit from the other in expressing and attaining the ideal union with the beloved object (see Newman). This complementarity of style and message between the courtly and mystical modes also manifests itself in what Dronke analyzes as Porete's "lyrical moments" and "quasi-dramatic passages" punctuating her narrative. This tendency is most noticeable in her use of fixed poetic forms: in her structuring of her prologue as a *canzone*, and, toward the end, her insertion of a *rondeau* to help crystallize her final thoughts. Her *Mirouer* thus hovers generically between poetry and prosimetrum—prose and poetry mixed for effect, as in Boethius's *De consolatione Philosophiae* (*Consolation of Philosophy*, c.524).

Porete writes of her quest for union with God, thus exemplifying the prevailing mystical themes of *unio mystica* and *Brautmystik* (the soul as Bride of Christ). She advocates the complete and perfect passivity of will in attaining the divine experience, thus rendering the sacramental ministry of the Church unnecessary (this infuriated her Inquisitorial readers, since it bypassed the Church hierarchy and also equated a person in this stage with the angels) in the final few of the seven stages of grace encountered during the soul's ascent to perfection. Annihilation, as heralded by *anienties* in the title, is a key theme. The idea that the soul annihilated in the love of Gods needs neither to pursue virtue nor to perform exterior practices of devotion (a controversial "antinomian" aspect) is often repeated throughout the *Mirouer*. Porete's "Greater Church," the Church of the Spirit (analogous to what orthodoxy calls the Church Triumphant), is the ideal assembly of free souls, an invisible community to which she aspires to belong and which she is certain should guide and judge the "Little Church," which is the empirical Christian assembly on earth (what orthodoxy calls the Church Militant). It is difficult to say whether she regarded herself as one of the free souls, though her doctrinal heresy was regarded to be of the "Free Spirit" variety. As a Free Spirit she was accused of pantheism (seeing God in all things) and antinomianism (belief that Christians are free by grace from the need to conform to moral law; faith alone leads to salvation).

Porete boldly laid claim to new perceptions of the divine Realm and of the Church. Like Hildegard, she severely criticized those in all ranks of the clergy who failed to welcome her unique insights, but unlike her, Porete spoke only in the name of the "free souls." Also unlike the cloistered Hildegard and others, Porete, a public speaker, was much more visible—and thus more vulnerable to the constant persecution she suffered in a politically perilous time. In terms of Inquisitorial history, articles in the *Mirouer* express ideas similar to those denounced by the Council of Vienne, France (1311–1312), soon after Porete's martyrdom. These beliefs were attributed to the Brethren of the Free Spirit, an antinomian movement first targeted by St. Albert the Great near Augsburg, Germany (1270s), for contending that a person's union with God freed him or her from obeying moral law and conventional social norms. Much of what they preached consisted merely in Bible excerpts uttered in a fresh context; as with the early Franciscans, among the people and away from the standard trappings of the Church, and so these Brethren were still viewed as a threat in such intolerant times. Porete has thus been called "the first apostle of France of the German sect of the Brethren of the Free Spirit." The *Mirouer* was the only significant document before the Council of Vienne to embody this heretical doctrine, but since it cannot be proved that an identifiable sect existed, it is difficult to prove that she was its spokeswoman.

A virtual unknown for too long (the first translation of her *Mirouer*, in 1927, leaves it anonymous), Marguerite Porete has benefited from a recent surge of scholarly appreciation, a movement arguably ushered in first by Peter Dronke's highly influential *Medieval Women Writers* (1984), lamenting her neglect despite her literary worth as substantiated by his discussion of her, and second, by the Guarnieri and Verdeyen edition (1986), itself heralded by Guarnieri's previous extensive research, which led to modern-language translations into French, German, Italian, and Spanish, as well as English.

See also Angela of Foligno, Blessed; Beatrijs van Nazareth/van Tienen; Beguines; Bride of Christ/*Brautmystik*; Christina Mirabilis; Hadewijch; Hildegard of Bingen, St.; Ivetta of Huy; Joan of Arc, St.; Juliana of Mont-Cornillon; Mechthild of Magdeburg; *Mulieres Sanctae*; Witches

BIBLIOGRAPHY

Primary Sources

Porete, Marguerite. *Le Mirouer des simples ames/Margeretae Porete Speculum simplicium animarum.* Edited by Romana Guarnieri and Paul Verdeyen. Corpus Christianorum Continuatio Medievalis, 69. Turnhout, Belgium: Brepols, 1986. [Authoritative ed. contains surviving late fifteenth-century French text with facing-page Latin text; commentary in Modern French; see Guarnieri's preliminary studies and texts in next section below].

———. *Margaret Porette. The Mirror of Simple Souls.* Translated and introduced by Edmund Colledge, J. C. Marler, and Judith Grant. Foreword by Kent Emery Jr. Notre Dame Texts in Medieval Culture, 6. Notre Dame, Ind.: University of Notre Dame Press, 1999. [Authoritative English trans.].

———. *The Mirror of Simple Souls.* Translated with commentary by Ellen Babinsky. Foreword by Robert Lerner. Classics of Western Spirituality. New York: Paulist Press, 1993.

————. *The Mirror of Simple Souls, by an Unknown French Mystic of the Thirteenth Century, Translated by M. N.* Translated by Clara Kirchberger. London: Burns, Oates & Washbourne, 1927. Abridged by Charles Crawford. Dublin: Gill & Macmillan; New York: Crossroad, 1981. [For reception-historical interest only; not even the recent abridged version knew of Porete; identity of "M. N." still a mystery].

————. *The Mirror of Simple Souls*, ch. 118. Translated with commentary by Don E. Levine. In Petroff, 294–98. See below under Secondary Sources.

————. "Lyrical moments from *Le Mirouer*." In Dronke, 275–78. *See below under* Secondary Sources. [Original French text].

————. "The Mirror of Simple Souls. As Middle English Translation." Edited by M. Doiron. *Archivio Italiano per la Storia della Pieta*, 5 (1968): 242–382.

Trial Documents

Corpus Documentorum Inquisitionis Haereticae Pravitatis Neerlandicae, edited by P. Frédéricq, 1: 159–161; 2: 63–64. Ghent: J. Vuylsteke, 1889–1903.

Verdeyen, Paul. "Le Procès d'Inquisition contre Marguerite Porete et Guiard de Cressonessart (1309–1310)." *Revue d'Histoire ecclésiastique* 81 (1986): 47–94.

Secondary Sources

Arsenault, John A. "Authority, Autonomy, and Antinomianism: The Mystical and Ethical Piety of Marguerite Porete in *The Mirror of Simple Souls*." *Studia Mystica*, n.s. 21 (2000): 65–94.

Bothe, Catherine M. "Writing as Mirror in the work of Marguerite Porete." *Mystics Quarterly* 20.3 (1994): 105–12.

Bynum, Caroline W. *Fragmentation and Redemption: Essays on Gender and the Human Body in Medieval Religion*. New York: Zone Books, 1992.

Dronke, Peter. *Women Writers of the Middle Ages: A Critical Study of Texts from Perpetua (†203) to Marguerite Porete (†1310)*. Cambridge: Cambridge University Press, 1984.

Guarnieri, Romana. "Il Movimento del Libero Spirito, Testi e Documenti." *Archivio Italiano per la Storia della Pieta* 4 (1965): 350–708.

Heimerl, Theresia. *Frauenmystik—Männermystik? Gemeinsamkeiten und Unterschiede in der Darstellung von Gottes- und Menschenbild bei Meister Eckhart, Heinrich Seuse, Marguerite Porete und Mechthild von Magdeburg*. Mystik und Mediävistik, 1. Münster: Lit, 2001.

Hollywood, Amy M. *The Soul as Virgin Wife: Mechthild of Magdeburg, Marguerite Porete, and Meister Eckhart*. Studies in Spirituality and Theology, 1. Notre Dame, Ind.: University of Notre Dame Press, 1995.

Lacassagne, Miren. "Marguerite Porete." In *Dictionary of Literary Biography: Vol. 208: Literature of the French and Occitan Middle Ages: Eleventh to* [sic] *Fifteenth Centuries*, edited by Deborah Sinnreich-Levi and Ian S. Laurie, 241–45. Detroit: Gale/Bruccoli Clark Layman, 1999.

Larrington, Carolyne. *Women and Writing in Medieval Europe: A Sourcebook*. New York and London: Routledge, 1995.

Leicht, Irene. *Marguerite Porete: Eine fromme Intellektuelle und die Inquisition*. Freiburger Theologische Studien, 163. Freiburg, Germany: Herder, 1999.

Lerner, Robert. *The Heresy of the Free Spirit in the Later Middle Ages*. Berkeley: University of California Press, 1972.

Lichtman, Maria. "Negative Theology in Marguerite Porete and Derrida." *Christianity & Literature* 47.2 (1998): 213–27.

McGinn, Bernard, ed. *Meister Eckhart and the Beguine Mystics: Hadewijch of Brabant, Mechthild of Magdeburg, and Marguerite Porete*. New York: Continuum, 1994. [Important collection of essays].

McLaughlin, Eleanor. "The Heresy of the Free Spirit and Late Medieval Mysticism." *Medievalia et Humanistica* n.s. 4 (1973): 37–54.

Müller, Catherine M. *Marguerite Porete et Marguerite d'Oingt: de l'autre côté du miroir*. Currents in Comparative Romance Languages and Literatures, 72. New York: Peter Lang, 1999.

Newman, Barbara. "*La mystique courtoise*: Thirteenth-Century Beguines and the Art of Love." In Newman, *From Virile Woman to WomanChrist: Studies in Medieval Religion and Literature*, 137–81. Middle Ages. Philadelphia: University of Pennsylvania Press, 1995.

Orcibal, Jean. "Le *Miroir des simples ames* et la 'secte' du Libre Esprit." *Revue d'Histoire des religions* 176 (1969): 35–60.

Petroff, Elizabeth A., ed. *Medieval Women's Visionary Literature*. New York: Oxford University Press, 1986. [See esp. 280–83, 294–98].

Robinson, Joanne M. *Nobility and Annihilation in Marguerite Porete's* Mirror of Simple Souls. SUNY Western Esoteric Traditions. Albany: State University of New York Press, 2001.

Sargent, Michael. "The Annihilation of Marguerite Porete." *Viator* 28 (1997): 253–79.

ARISTOULA GEORGIADOU

POWER OF WOMEN (12th–15th centuries). The power of women constitutes a thematic cluster, or *topos*, in medieval European art and literature emerging with the growth of vernacular (non-Latin) language and literature in the twelfth and thirteenth centuries and developing throughout the fourteenth and fifteenth centuries. It is characterized by a select mix of biblical, ancient historical, or medieval-romance literary figures within the same narrative, whether pictorially or verbally, whose general message suggests or strongly advocates that women are more powerful than men. However, it is rarely feminist in the modern sense, since this power derives mainly from female sexuality and man's vulnerability to it, whether in sincere, virtuous romantic love and marriage or malevolent amorous deceit. Rather than eliciting or conveying a profound or revolutionary message therefore, this topos availed the artist or author of the opportunity to evoke heroes and heroines creatively from varied literary traditions and historical epochs for the aesthetically pleasing, or humorously entertaining, edification of the audience. The demonstration of women's seductive superiority over parades of the greatest of men—ranging from Aristotle, Alexander, or Arthur, to Virgil and Zeus—challenged artists and writers while it captivated audiences.

Not surprisingly, Church officials found this topos morally threatening, especially because of its erotic component, and sought to control it by adapting it to their agenda. Their polemicists and preachers invoked Power of Women as a strictly negative concept, descended from Eve's role as perpetrator of the Fall and Expulsion from Eden, in the abundant misogynistic (antiwoman) and antimarriage literature and art sponsored by the clergy. Later, as literate audiences became more secular and sophisticated, and as women came to play a greater role as literary producers (authors, illustrators, patrons, readers) rather than as stereotyped malicious seducers in the stories, the Power of Women assumed a more positive orientation. Deceit by love (Venus) and lust (Luxuria), so long as both the man and woman adhere to the same rules, could be delightfully painful, as opposed to the misogynistic image of the "evil" female's cruel sexual deceit of an "innocent" man. The power convention continued to evolve, allowing insertion of both misogynistic and feminist viewpoints within the same work in the form of a debate, one of the most famous cases being Chaucer's prologue to his "Wife of Bath's Tale," combining the misogynistic litany illustrating the power as a source of male suffering delivered by Jankyn, the Wife's fifth husband, which the Wife spiritedly counters with positive examples.

A principal vehicle for representing the Power of Women was the genre of tale known as the *exemplum*, a morally edifying story, developed by the clerics in their writing and

Aristotle and Phyllis. A German woodcut from 1515 depicting a woman literally riding a man, with bit and bridle in his teeth. Courtesy of the Dover Pictorial Archive.

preaching. Such exempla evoked not merely Eve but also Delilah and similar Old Testament temptresses, mixing them with those from Classical Antiquity. Because of the wide audience reached by sermons, manuals of good conduct, and illustrations and sculpture, these popular-cultural exempla also transmitted a medieval reinvention of pagan Greco-Roman culture more successfully than scholars could ever disseminate the authentic material. One such tale is "Aristotle and Phyllis," recounting Aristotle's seduction into humiliation: he allows Phyllis to ride him like a horse in exchange for sexual favors (never granted, in the end) by a beautiful mistress of Alexander. It is completely absent from Antique sources, yet it enthralled unsuspecting medieval readers and spectators as the "Mounted Aristotle" icon, depicting with wicked humor the triumph of feminine guile over male intellect in a multitude of representations, such as the carved wooden detail to a misericord (the kneeling part of a church bench seat) in the church of St. Catherine in Belgium. An important literary instance is the thirteenth-century romance, *Amadas et Ydoine* (c.1190–1220), interweaving Tristan, Paris, Achilles, Ulysses, Samson, and others. Within the visual arts, a similar scene, titled *The Triumph of Love*, painted on a salver (type of serving tray), now in London, depicts Virgil in a basket, Mounted Aristotle, and Samson and Delilah.

See also *Belle Dame sans Merci*; Capellanus, Andreas; Chaucer, Geoffrey, Women in the Work of; Criseyde; Griselda; *Miroir de Mariage* (*Mirror of Marriage*); Nine Worthy Women; *Roman de la Rose*, Debate of the; Valkyries

BIBLIOGRAPHY

Primary Sources

Amadas and Ydoine. Roman du XIIIᵉ siècle. Edited by John R. Reinhard. Classiques français du Moyen âge, 51. Paris: Champion, 1926. Reprint Paris: Honoré Champion, 1986.

"Aristotles und Phyllis." In *Codex Karlsruhe 408. Edition einer spätmittelalterlichen Sammelhandschrift*, edited by Ursula Schmid, 348–62. Bibliotheca Germanica, 16. Bern and Munich: Francke Verlag, 1974.

Chaucer, Geoffrey. "The Wife of Bath's Prologue;" "The Wife of Bath's Tale." In *The Riverside Chaucer*, edited by Larry D. Benson. 3rd ed. Boston: Houghton Mifflin, 1988.

Mounted Aristotle. Misericord detail (wood). Church of St. Catherine, Hoogstraeten, Belgium.

Triumph of Love. Painted salver. Victoria and Albert Museum, London.

Secondary Sources

Davis, Natalie Zemon. "Women on Top." In Davis, *Society and Culture in Early Modern France*, 124–51. Stanford, Calif.: Stanford University Press, 1975.

Gourlay, Kristina E. "A Positive Representation of the Power of Young Women: The Malterer Embroidery Re-Examined." In *Young Medieval Women*, edited by Katherine J. Lewis, Noel James Menuge, and Kim M. Phillips, 69–102. New York: St. Martin's Press, 1999.

Smith, Susan L. *The Power of Women: A Topos in Medieval Art and Literature*. Philadelphia: University of Pennsylvania Press, 1995.

NADIA MARGOLIS

PREFECTION. *See* Dower

PROBA, FALTONIA BETITIA (c.322–c.370).

A late-Antique Latin poet, Faltonia Betitia Proba is also variously identified as Faltonia (in some manuscripts: Falconia), Betitia Proba, Anicia Faltonia Proba, and Petronia Proba. Little is known about Proba aside from her sole surviving poem, a nonetheless important Virgilian cento in 694 hexameter verses paraphrasing several stories from Genesis and the life of Christ. She is also thought to have composed, as her first effort, an epic poem on a civil war in Rome during her time, but this work has been lost.

A cento (plural *centones*) is a poem or sequence (Byzantine Greek: κεντρων) with very ancient roots; the earliest evidence of cento techniques may be those in the Old Attic (Greek) comedies of Aristophanes (late fifth century B.C.E.). A cento is comprised of shorter sections from one or more existing poems well known to the public, hence the Latin *cento* = "patchwork" often susceptible to parodic and satirical uses, but also as serious works in which the allusive segments increase the new cento's aura of authority. Since she was a Roman aristocrat, Proba wrote specifically in the Latin cento tradition, based on the poems of Rome's greatest classical poet, Virgil (70–19 B.C.E.) and present in the works of such better-known Latin authors as Petronius's *Satyrica* (first century C.E.) and Ausonius's risqué *Cento nuptialis* (*Wedding Cento*, c.374). Of the extant Christian Latin *centones*, hers is the longest and the most carefully written: an exceptional example that apparently influenced what few remain by other authors over the fourth through sixth centuries. As for her other works, now lost, the only information we have on them is her own reference in her cento (vv. 1–8) to a historical epic she had written, probably about the struggle between Constantius and Magnentius (under whom her husband served as prefect), occurring 351–353. This may establish a *terminus post quem* (earliest time-frame) for her biblical poem. The oldest surviving manuscript is that referred to by Martin von Schanz as Parisinus 13048, from the eighth or ninth century, a later one (thirteenth century) is at Cambridge University, Trinity College 1335. The first complete printed edition was published in Venice in 1472.

Although she calls herself simply Proba (v. 12), she most likely was the aristocratic matron Faltonia Betitia Proba, wife of Clodius Celsinus Adelphius, who was *praefectus urbi* (prefect of the city) in 351. If so, her approximate dates are 322–370. She is certainly not to be confused with Anicia Faltonia Proba, Faltonia Betitia's granddaughter (Schenkl). Well connected by birth as well as through marriage, she belonged to the prominent family of the Anicii, and several of her close relatives were consuls. Her sons Olybrius and Alipius also held high rank, that of consul and *praefectus urbi*, respectively. The final lines of the cento (vv. 692–94) indicate that her husband may have been a recent convert to Christianity, or that she was hoping to influence him in this direction. An epitaph Clodius eventually put up (preserved in the *Corpus Inscriptionum Latinarum*, 6. 1712) indicates that she predeceased him.

The original title of her poem is as uncertain as its date. Different manuscripts give it different headings: *Cento Probae* (*Proba's Cento*), *Versus Probae* (*Proba's Verses*), *Opus Probae matronae* (*Works of Proba the Matron*), and the like. A dedicatory preface addressed to the Emperor Honorius (384–423) was obviously added by a later transcriber of the poem. Within Proba's poem itself, the ensuing selection of biblical incidents is not entirely predictable; their treatment even less so. Proba weaves in Old Testament episodes: the Creation, the Fall, Cain killing Abel, and the Flood; and from the New Testament, some main events in the life of Christ, from Nativity to Ascension. It is a mark of her originality— a quality potentially present even in so derivative a form as the cento—that she chooses to deal with the creation of Eve much more fully than that of Adam, that she invents a death by fire for the Holy Innocents, and that she makes Christ irate rather than meek during the Crucifixion. An orthodox reader of her poem may well react to the latter instance as bizarre, although one will probably not find it difficult to admire her very skillful treatment of the Creation, with its adroit adaptation of lines from Virgil's *Georgics* and powerful scenes such as the slaughter of the Innocents or the storm on the Lake of Galilee. The changes she introduces into the biblical account are to a large extent by-products of the cento technique, for she is entirely limited in her phraseology and vocabulary to lines and half-lines culled from the works of Virgil, her only source in this regard. The most obvious instance of such limitation is her inability to fit biblical proper names into her verse. Hence, as well as for other reasons, her mode of presentation is allusive rather than direct (Pavlovskis).

As a learned woman, Proba must have known all of Virgil's poetry virtually by heart and written for an audience whom she also expected to be constantly mindful of the original setting of her borrowings as well as the new use to which she put these. The result is more sophisticated in its aesthetic and semiotic assumptions than may readily appear at first. In her own time, Proba's poem seems to have been well received. The Emperor Arcadius (383–408) admired this cento enough to commission a manuscript copy of it. However, under the influence of St. Jerome's (c.347–420) severity toward cento writing in his *Epistles* (53.7), the Church officially disapproved the cento. The so-called *Decretum Gelasianum*, although probably not authentic itself, declared her poem "apocryphal," to be tolerated if read privately but not included in a list of works definitely approved by the Church. Nevertheless, Proba's popularity continued throughout the Middle Ages. Her cento appears in the catalogues of numerous monastic libraries, very often as a school text bound together with such then-familiar schoolbooks as Symphosius's riddles (fourth to fifth centuries?). As late as the mid-fourteenth century, the Italian humanist Boccaccio does homage to her in his *De Claris Mulieribus* (*Famous Women*, ch. 97). In more recent times, undoubtedly under the influence of the more restrictive modern concept of originality, Proba has suffered not only neglect but derision. Schanz's description of her work as "an absurd product" is typical but by no means the most severe. In the last few years, scholarship influenced by feminist attitudes has once more found Proba an interesting, if not outstanding, figure. Certainly superficial dismissal of the cento tends to be oblivious of the typically derivative nature of all of classical literature, of which phenomenon the cento is but an extreme example.

See also Boccaccio, Women in, *De Claris Mulieribus*; Eudocia; Teachers, Women as

BIBLIOGRAPHY

Primary Sources

Boccaccio, Giovanni. "De Proba Adelphi coniuge/Proba, wife of Adelphus." In *Famous Women* [*De claris mulieribus*], edited and translated by Virginia Brown, 410–17. I Tatti Renaissance Library, 1. Cambridge, Mass. and London: Harvard University Press, 2001.

Corpus Inscriptionum Latinarum. Vol. 6: *Inscriptiones urbis Romae latinae*, edited by G. Henzen et al. 1: 1712. Berlin: G. Reimer, 1862–.

Jerome, St. (Eusebius Hieronymus). *Epistulae*. Edited by Isidor Hilberg. Vol. 1. Corpus scriptorum ecclesiasticorum latinorum, 54. Vienna: Österreichischen Akademie der Wissenschaften, 1996. [Latin critical ed.].

Proba. [Cento] Venice: Bartholomaeus Girardinus, 1472.

———. In *Poetae christiani minores*, edited by Karl Schenkl, part 1. Corpus Scriptorum Ecclesiasticorum Latinorum, 16. Vienna: F. Tempsky, 1888. [Latin text with introduction and notes, replacing defective one in the *Patrologia Latina*].

———. In *The Golden Bough, the Oaken Cross: The Virgilian Cento of Faltonia Betitia Proba*, translated by Elizabeth A. Clark and Diane F. Hatch. American Academy of Religions, Texts and Translations, 5. Chico, Calif.: Scholars Press, 1981.

———. Translated by Jeremiah Reedy. In *A Lost Tradition, Women Writers of the Early Church*, edited by Patricia Wilson-Kastner et al., 45–68. Washington, D.C.: University Press of America, 1981.

Secondary Sources

Clark, Elizabeth A., and Diane F. Hatch. *See under* Primary Sources *above*. [Detailed study of Proba's cento].

Consolino, F. E. "Da Osidio Geta ad Ausonio e Proba, le molte possibilità del centone," *Atene e Roma* n.s. 28 (1983): 133–51.

Ermini, Filippo. *Il centone di Proba e la poesia centonaria Latina*. Rome: Loescher, 1909.

Harrison, Steven J. "Cento." In *The Oxford Classical Dictionary*, edited by Simon Hornblower and Antony Spawforth, 309a. 3rd ed. Oxford and New York: Oxford University Press, 1996.

Herzog, Reinhart. *Die Bibelepik der lateinischen Spätantike, Formgeschichte einer erbaulichen Gattung*. Munich: Fink, 1975.

Kastner, George R., and Ann Millin. "Proba: Introduction." In *A Lost Tradition* (*See under* Primary Sources *above*), 33–44.

Matthews, John F. "Proba." In *The Oxford Classical Dictionary*, edited by Simon Hornblower and Antony Spawforth, 1249a. 3rd ed. Oxford and New York: Oxford University Press, 1996.

Pavlovskis, Zoja. "Proba, or the Semiotics of the Narrative Virgilian Cento." *Vergilius* 35 (1989): 70–84.

Schanz, Martin von. *Geschichte der römischen Literatur bis zum Gesetzgebungswerk des Kaisers Justinian*. 4th revised ed. by Carl Hosius. Munich: Beck, 1966.

Schenkl, Carl. "Introduction." See under Primary Sources, above.

ZOJA PAVLOVSKIS-PETIT

PROSTITUTION. Few medieval writers who discussed prostitution were concerned with defining it. Towns attempting to clear their streets of prostitutes did not find it necessary to specify exactly who fell into that category. The terms *meretrix* (Latin), *putain* or *folle femme* (French), common woman or whore (English), and others, could be used for any woman considered promiscuous, indeed any who had sex outside of marriage. When we find them in the sources we cannot assume they mean someone engaged in commercial sex, although they often do. Canon lawyers, who theorized about sexual behavior more systematically than most medieval thinkers, did not consider financial exchange the determining factor. For them, the essential feature of a prostitute was her promiscuity; some canonists also stressed her notoriety and deception.

There was no single medieval attitude toward prostitution either as a cultural or as a commercial phenomenon. We know the most about it from the fourteenth century on. In the Middle Ages, as today, it was primarily an urban occupation, although there were some rural prostitutes and some who traveled with court or army. Towns took one of three general approaches to prostitution: they outlawed it (with more or less success), tolerated and regulated it (either de jure or de facto, by means of fines that were not intended to suppress but rather to tax the trade), or institutionalized it.

Many towns in England, France, Germany, and Italy had municipal brothels, founded mainly in the late fourteenth and early fifteenth centuries (the claim of the stews [brothels] of Southwark in England to have been established in 1162 is false; Post, 420). The town or seigneurial authority either hired brothelkeepers or farmed out the brothel to them. In some areas these brothelkeepers were men, in others women. Where a brothel was merely municipally licensed rather than owned, leading citizens in the town often had a financial interest in it. These officially established or licensed brothels had sets of regulations covering such issues as restrictions on the prostitutes' movement, times and days when the brothels must close, relations between the prostitute and the brothelkeeper (financial and otherwise), relations between the brothelkeeper—who in some cases owned the brothel and in others managed it for the town—and the local authorities, who was allowed to be a prostitute and who a customer, rates of pay, conditions under which women were allowed to leave, and other controls on the women's lives, such as restrictions on their having lovers. Many of the laws attempted to protect the prostitutes from the brothelkeepers in various ways, such as prohibiting beatings or setting fixed prices for victuals. In practice, however, the brothelkeepers exerted a great deal of control over the women and, of course, profited from the enterprise.

The justification for the establishment of the municipal brothels was the "lesser evil" argument. The greater evils that prostitution sought to prevent were several. There was the offense to public decency: if prostitutes walked the streets the scandal would be open, whereas when confined to a house they would be less obtrusive. There was fear of contamination: if prostitutes were allowed to walk about they might associate with respectable women and somehow harm their respectability. There was homosexuality: the city fathers of Florence hoped that by staffing a brothel with attractive women they might convince the young men to discontinue their practice of sodomy (which concerned the authorities not because it was sinful but because they believed it was a major cause of the low birth rate). Finally, there was the corruption of honest women. The male sex drive, like a dammed-up river, would build up until it burst its bounds, leading the men to seduce or rape the respectable wives and daughters of the city. If prostitutes were available, they would serve as a safety valve. Despite medieval medical theories, which held that the feminine sex drive was as strong as or stronger than the masculine, it was only men for whom brothels were thought necessary.

Most towns shut down their institutionalized brothels in the mid-sixteenth century. Protestant reformers certainly succeeded in closing brothels in many German towns, but the public brothels of France and Italy closed at about the same time. Scholars tend to agree that shifts in morality were primarily responsible, shifts that took place in both Protestant and Catholic countries at this period (Otis, 41–45; Trexler, 1003–05; Roper).

Many towns not having official brothels (owned or licensed by the local municipal or seigneurial authority) nevertheless sanctioned prostitution, either restricted to one street or district within their borders, or just outside their walls. Many had concentrations of brothels in the immediately adjacent suburbs. While towns with official brothels usually sought to suppress independent prostitution on grounds of public order or because it competed with the official brothels, other towns allowed brothelkeepers or prostitutes to operate independently as long as they followed regulations on such issues as opening times and clothing. In Paris, for example, an active prostitution trade was regulated though not administered by both the city and the royal government (Geremek, 211–41.)

Sumptuary legislation, prohibiting prostitutes from wearing certain types of clothing, requiring them to wear special identifying garments, or occasionally prohibiting all women but prostitutes from wearing particular styles, was one of the most common types of regulation (Brundage 1987; P. Schuster, 147–50). The ostensible purpose of this legislation varied: to demarcate the prostitutes so respectable women would not be taken for them and harassed in the streets, to cut down on the expense for husbands by preventing their wives from competing with prostitutes' finery, to prevent women from wishing to become prostitutes to be able to wear fancy clothing.

In other towns, though prostitution was illegal, the fines levied on practitioners and facilitators may have been in the nature of de facto licensing fees. These towns recognized the continuing existence of prostitution and attempted to benefit fiscally. Since those practicing other occupations were fined in similar ways, prostitution in these towns can best be studied in the context of other sorts of earning opportunities open to women. In many cases neither prostitution nor brothelkeeping was a full-time, long-term occupation; women who engaged in these trades combined or alternated them with petty retailing and victualling (supplying food and drink for payment). Women's earning opportunities, of course, varied with economic and demographic change, and more work remains to be done in connecting these changes with the prevalence and treatment of prostitution.

While women entered prostitution for economic reasons, the way society treated them, and hence the circumstances of their lives as prostitutes, was affected by cultural notions about sex, gender, and sin. Chastity was the most prized virtue for women in the Middle Ages. The prostitute, who so directly countered that virtue, could represent the epitome of feminine sinfulness. At the same time, however, because of the depth of sin she embodied, the prostitute could represent in a very powerful manner the message of repentance. The prostitute could be used as a metaphor for all sinners, or as an example: if she could repent and be saved, then surely so could everyone. The legends of saints who were former prostitutes—including most prominently Mary Magdalene—demonstrate the two ways in which medieval society used the image of the prostitute.

The prostitute played a much greater role in medieval culture than simply that of a hagiographical topos. Despite the fact that money was not seen as the defining feature of prostitution, the connection of feminine sexuality and money was prominent in literature, and the prostitute embodied this connection (Lorcin, 65). One reason for the various municipalities' desire to regulate the prostitute's life may have been some distrust of independent women who controlled their own money.

A key concept in discussions of prostitution in medieval culture is marginalization. The individual prostitute was in some ways a marginal character, excluded from the community in the same way anyone not a member of a family or of a religious order was excluded. However, she was also integrated into the community in some ways: as part of local gossip networks, as a witness in court, and so forth. In some places, public prostitutes played a formal role in civic rituals and celebrations. Prostitutes were physically marginalized by restriction to certain streets or areas of a town. They were also conceptually marginalized. Yet, though prostitutes, as a group, were identified, circumscribed, and controlled, in some ways they were central parts of society.

Medieval society regarded prostitution as necessary, and was not attempting to abolish it. The efforts to control it were part of a specifically medieval scheme of regulation of all sexuality that differed from the norm. Yet, at the same time prostitutes were cast as "other," not belonging *in* the society, they were also considered to belong *to* the society, that is, to be in a sense the common property of all men. This, and not only a wish to keep pimps out of the trade, may be behind the prohibition on their having particular lovers. In some towns forcible sex with prostitutes was not legally rape, because they did not have the power to withhold consent. The term "common woman" implied not only openness to all but in a sense possession by the community of men.

Only extremely rarely do we have the words of prostitutes themselves about their own experiences, and even then generally in court testimony, which someone other than the prostitutes recorded in Latin. (Ironically, the only account from a prostitute in medieval England that fully describes her life and mode of operation turns out to come from a male transvestite; Karras and Boyd.)

Prostitutes were often foreigners or at least strangers to the towns in which they worked, although in some cases they came from immediately surrounding areas. In some towns, no daughter of a citizen was allowed to work in the official brothel; the towns thus enforced the prostitutes' outsider status. Age and life-cycle information, like that on place of origin, is hard to come by because the records only rarely give the ages of prostitutes. It is very difficult to trace them in other sorts of records to find out what happened to them once they left the trade. In some cases, prostitutes seem to have been in their early teens or younger, perhaps a reflection of job opportunities (or lack thereof), since quite young girls were expected to leave home and look for positions in domestic service. It may also be, however, that the courts emphasized the youth of prostitutes and called them "young girls" as a means of casting blame on procuresses (female pimps) or brothelkeepers, mainly women, for leading the young girls into sin; the customers were less blamed (Karras 1992; Roper). In fact, many former prostitutes became procuresses and continued their careers in the sex trade.

Some women became prostitutes because they could not get the jobs they were seeking in domestic service. Others were deceived into becoming prostitutes, thinking they were being offered some other kind of work. We know from the early modern period that it was often women who were known to have lost their virginity (by rape or by choice), especially servants who became pregnant (often by their masters), who had to become prostitutes: they had neither job nor marriage prospects. This was probably common in the Middle Ages as well. Some women may have become prostitutes for family reasons, sending money home to their kin; indeed, some women were pawned as prostitutes by their parents specifically to pay off debts, although this practice was prohibited in many jurisdictions. Some husbands pimped for their wives and kept the money. Often, however, prostitution provided one means for women to obtain access to cash, albeit a small amount after the brothelkeeper or procurer took a cut. Very few of the prostitutes, however, grew rich from the trade. A minute number left wills indicating that they had acquired property, but in the main, prostitutes remained among the poorest women in the towns.

Women in a municipally established house were often at the bottom of the stratification within the profession, then streetwalkers, then women who worked with a procuress and had a steady clientele. Some prostitutes worked in their own homes, some in taverns, some in bathhouses, some in houses of assignation that made rooms available. Many were not professionals in the sense of engaging in the trade on a regular basis, rather they used it to supplement meager wages, for example from domestic service. While women in the regulated houses were not supposed to have particular lovers, many clandestine prostitutes did have male friends or husbands whom they supported and who may have pimped for them as well. The notion that prostitutes had their own guild in some towns, which is found in some older scholarship, is not based on reliable evidence (Bullough 1982), and although they were grouped together in official brothels or Magdalene houses, the degree of solidarity they felt with one another is unknown.

There are few descriptions of the exact sexual practices of the prostitutes, although the fact that male transvestites were able to pass themselves off as women indicates that oral, anal, manual, or interfemoral sex may have been common. Prostitutes may have preferred such acts for contraceptive reasons, although obviously they did not practice them to the exclusion of vaginal intercourse, since they did bear children. The evidence for these children, however, is less than one might expect—there are few records of them in foundling homes, for example—and legal and moral writers do not seem to concern themselves with the birth, abandonment, or infanticide of illegitimate children as one of the harms of prostitution. Medieval medical theory held that prostitutes were less fertile than other women (Jacquart and Thomasset, 25, 63–64, 80–81). This may indicate that contraception or nonprocreative intercourse was common.

Brothels were intended to cater to the sexual needs of young unmarried men, and their regulations often prohibited married men, priests, and Jews from patronizing them. Nevertheless, court records and literature reveal that priests and other religious were frequent customers. The socioeconomic level of customers is difficult to determine, and of course varied depending on the type of prostitute; rich men could have women brought to their homes, poorer men might visit a brothel or pick up a streetwalker.

Often, efforts were made to convert prostitutes to a more virtuous way of life. Sometimes these efforts were merely lip service: requiring prostitutes to attend church at certain times, or having special sermons preached to them. In other instances, however, practical action was taken: making dowry money available so that young women could marry instead of entering prostitution, or providing houses of refuge (Magdalene houses), organized like convents, so that women who sought to leave the trade would have somewhere to go (Cohen). The fact that many women not registered as prostitutes claimed to be such to gain entry into these refuges indicates the tremendous need for a means of support for these women. We do not know how many prostitutes eventually left the profession—not for a Magdalene house—but for marriage, which would be a good indication of how marginal the individual prostitute actually was in the society.

We do not know whether the prostitutes internalized the degradation that law, literature, and other contemporary writing associated with them. Did they see what they did as depraved and sinful? Did they see it as just another job? Were there social class differences in attitudes toward promiscuity, so that what the Church and the temporal authorities might label as prostitution the participants might see simply as a typical casual liaison? These questions remain open for further research and discussion.

See also China, Women in; *Frauenfrage*; Guilds, Women in; Hagiography (Female Saints); Law, Canon, Women in; Marriage; Medicine and Medieval Women; Norse Women; Shore, Elizabeth (Jane); Transvestism; Virginity

BIBLIOGRAPHY

Primary Sources
[See notes and appendixes to works listed below].

Secondary Sources
Brundage, James A. "Sumptuary Laws and Prostitution in Late Medieval Italy." *Journal of Medieval History* 13 (1987): 343–55.
———. *Law, Sex and Christian Society in Medieval Europe*. Chicago: University of Chicago Press, 1987.
———. *Sex, Law and Marriage in the Middle Ages*. Variorum Collected Studies, 397. Aldershot, U.K. and Brookfield, Vt.: Variorum, 1993. [Collection of articles from the career of a major authority].
Bullough, Vern L. "The Prostitute in the Later Middle Ages." In *Sexual Practices and the Medieval Church*, edited by Vern L. Bullough and James A. Brundage, 176–86. Buffalo: Prometheus, 1982.
Cohen, Sherrill. *The Evolution of Women's Asylums Since 1500: From Refuges for Ex-Prostitutes to Shelters for Battered Women*. New York: Oxford University Press, 1992.
Geremek, Bronislaw. *The Margins of Society in Late Medieval Paris*. Translated by Jean Birrell. Cambridge: Cambridge University Press, 1987.
Irsigler, Franz, and Arnold Lassotta. *Bettler und Gaukler, Dirnen und Henker: Randgruppen und Außenseiter in Köln 1300–1600*. Cologne, Germany: Greven Verlag, 1984.
Jacquart, Danielle, and Claude Thomasset. *Sexuality and Medicine in the Middle Ages*. Translated by Matthew Adamson. Princeton, N.J.: Princeton University Press, 1988. Original *Sexualité et savoir medical au Moyen âge*. Paris: Presses Universitaires de France, 1985.
Karras, Ruth Mazo. "The Latin Vocabulary of Illicit Sex in English Ecclesiastical Court Records." *Journal of Medieval Latin* 2 (1992): 1–17.
———. *Common Women: Prostitution and Sexuality in Medieval England*. New York: Oxford University Press, 1996.
———, and David Lorenzo Boyd. "*Ut Cum Muliere*: A Male Transvestite Prostitute in Fourteenth-Century London." In *Premodern Sexualities*, edited by Louise Fradenburg and Carla Freccero, 101–16. London: Routledge, 1996.
Kettle, Anne J. "Ruined Maids: Prostitutes and Servant Girls in Later Medieval England." In *Matrons and Marginal Women in Medieval Society*, edited by Robert R. Edwards and Vickie L. Ziegler, 19–32. Woodbridge, U.K.: Boydell Press, 1995.
Lorcin, Marie-Thérèse. *Façons de sentir et de penser: les fabliaux français*. Paris: Honoré Champion, 1979.

Otis, Leah Lydia. *Prostitution in Medieval Society: The History of an Urban Institution in Languedoc.* Chicago: University of Chicago Press, 1985.

Perry, Mary Elizabeth. *Gender and Disorder in Early Modern Seville.* Princeton, N.J.: Princeton University Press, 1992.

Post, J. B. "A Fifteenth-Century Customary of the Southwark Stews." *Journal of the Society of Archivists* (1978): 418–28.

Roper, Lyndal. "Discipline and Respectability: Prostitution and the Reformation in Augsburg." *History Workshop* (1987): 3–28.

Rossiaud, Jacques. *Medieval Prostitution.* Translated by Lydia G. Cochrane. Oxford: Blackwell, 1988. Original *La Prostituzione nel medioevo.* Rome: Laterza, 1984.

Schuster, Beate. *Die Freien Frauen: Dirnen und Frauenhäuser im 15. Und 16. Jahrhundert.* Frankfurt: Campus, 1995.

Schuster, Peter. *Das Frauenhaus. Städtische Bordelle in Deutschland (1350–1600).* Paderborn, Germany: Ferdinand Schöningh, 1992.

Trexler, Richard. "La prostitution florentine au XVe siècle: patronages et clientèles." *Annales: Economies, Sociétés, Civilisations* 36 (1981): 983–1015.

RUTH MAZO KARRAS

PROUS BONETA, NA (c.1290–1325). Na Prous Boneta (or Naprous Boneta, Prous Boneta, or Bonet; the *Na* prefix is a shortened form of Latin and southern-French *domina*, "lady"), a visionary preacher, Spiritual Franciscan and follower of Peter John Olivi, was martyred during the Inquisition. The only account we have of her life is her statement to the Inquisition in Carcassonne made on August 6, 1325.

She was born somewhere in the region of Provence, southern France, the daughter of Durand Bonet, and lived in Montpellier, a major southern-French university town, from the time she was about seven. Never married, she and her sister Alisseta lived independently in Montpellier. That she was called *Na* Prous Boneta indicates she may have been of some social standing, or at least the head of a household (Müller). While still quite young she became involved as a layperson with the Spiritual Franciscans in her region, and was first arrested by the Inquisition in 1315 because of her association with the now-heretical group. She identified herself as a visionary as a result of her experiences in 1320 and 1321. She had visions in which she was given revelations about the spiritual mission of the remaining Spirituals (members of her group), depicting the current pope, Pope John XXII, as the Antichrist, and herself as the new vessel of the Holy Spirit. She died in nearby Carcassonne, a few days after August 6, 1325, burned at the stake for her ideas.

In probing more deeply into the events that both shaped her life and that she affected in her turn, we note that during her youth such historical occurrences became a part of the visionary myth she preached. The Spiritual Franciscans in southern France had been led by the zealous Franciscan, Petrus Joannis (Peter John) Olivi (b. c.1248–1298), whose apocalyptic theology and radical social message advocating poverty caused him to be seen by some as a second Christ by the time he died. Although he died quietly, at peace with the Church, and was immediately acclaimed a saint, there were those who said his bones were dug up and burned a few months after interment. Soon after becoming pope, John XXII declared the Spirituals' teaching on apostolic poverty to be a formal heresy (1317), and intensive prosecutions of recalcitrant Spirituals and affiliated beguines quickly followed. But the persecution of the Spirituals had been going on since the 1280s, and as early as 1315 Na Prous had been connected with them, for in that year she was caught and imprisoned by the Inquisition at Montpellier but released. In 1317, she may have seen some beguines burned at Narbonne, and in 1318 four friars were burned at Marseilles. After their death they were publicly venerated as martyrs by those sympathetic to the cause of the Spirituals. Na Prous and her sister Alisseta, by their own later confession, made their home in Montpellier a center for radical religious ideas and activities, giving refuge to many fugitives. At the time of their arrest, two others were taken into custody with them: another woman, Alaraxis, and an apostate Franciscan named Raymond John, both related to Olivi (see Newman). Alisseta Boneta was also interrogated by the Inquisition at the same time, remained obdurate for three years in prison, and finally recanted in 1328 (see trans. Burr).

Na Prous has been viewed as an unoriginal follower of Olivi, but in actuality she seems to have been a leader of a heretical group of laypeople. She was still a child when Olivi died, if the accepted date of her birth (c.1290) is correct, and it is unlikely she learned his teachings directly from him. In her visions commencing 1320, and on Holy Thursday 1321, Christ gave her the Holy Spirit "as completely as it had been given to the Virgin." It seemed to her that the promises of the Everlasting Gospel were about to be fulfilled, and that the Third Age, prophesied by Olivi and the Italian mystic Joachim da Fiore (c.1135–1202), among others, was about to begin. In this new age, she preached, the sacraments of the altar and of confession were not valid, for the pope had betrayed the promises made by Christ to St. Peter. The papacy too ceases to exist; the only sacraments remaining were those of matrimony and penitence, the latter now a purely internal sacrament, for priestly intercession was no longer needed for the forgiveness of sins. Because of the failure of the Church, "more souls could be saved until the Holy Ghost underwent passion and death. This second Crucifixion has been accomplished, according to Prous, by the condemnation of Olivi's works and by the rejection of her own message" (ed. May, 5). By this time she had come to believe in herself as in some way the Holy Spirit, and that others would be saved if they had faith in her.

Everything else in which she had believed earlier had been taken away from her by the papal pronouncements of the last few years. Like other Franciscans, and doubtless many medieval Christians, she believed that Christ's poverty in the Gospels was the only true model for humankind; she could not accept a papacy that declared such a belief to be heretical. She knew that Peter John Olivi had died in hiding after years of struggle over his ideas, and the other leaders either had died, recanted, or disappeared into hiding. As she tells us, even the laws of ordinary decency seemed suspended by the Church, which approved of the mass burning of lepers in France in 1321 and 1322. This manifestation of hysteria, which only the Spirituals seem to have opposed, she saw as the equal of Herod's massacre of the Holy Innocents (Matthew 2: 16–18). Since the persecution of the Spirituals and the burning of the books written by Olivi, she tells us in her statement, the sacraments have no more validity for her, and she asserts that the pope who has caused this is the Antichrist. Some of her beliefs are borrowed from the apocalyptic ideas of Joachim da Fiore, as well as from Olivi, but she has made them her own and is ready to die for them. She tells the notary who took down her words for the Inquisition that he is damned, as were all her accusers, but she knows that she will soon be in heaven, "a glorious martyr in Paradise."

In examining her written sources as evidenced in her testimony, we find that, despite her references to three kinds of written texts—the Gospels, the burned books of the

Spirituals, and the hated decrees of the popes—there is no indication in her statement that she is literate herself. The fact that she says thirty Paternosters ("Our Father" prayers) for each of the canonical hours suggests that she could not read Latin, and she makes no reference to personal knowledge of the many banned spiritual books and prophecies written in the vernacular and circulating in southern France. (Raymond John, who was arrested with her, did possess condemned writings by Peter John Olivi.) Her testimony was dictated in Provençal (southern-French language), but taken down in Latin, with occasional phrases in Provençal either paraphrased or left untranslated. As was typical of Inquisition proceedings, the text was read back to her as the interrogation proceeded, and she was asked to confirm what it said. The questions she was asked would have followed a standard protocol designed to elicit a confession along particular lines; in her case, the questioners wanted a confession that she shared the beliefs of the *begghini combusti* ("burned beguines") of earlier years. In spite of these formalities, Na Prous manages to make her vision of the world dominate the proceedings, and her courage in knowingly condemning herself after ten years of resistance to the Inquisition is very moving.

The text of her confession, because it contains her personal history and responses to the Inquisition in southern France in 1325, also provides the spiritual autobiography of Na Prous Boneta, visionary and teacher. Even though this confession was probably drawn from her under torture, we are given a vivid portrait of an unlettered but gifted woman who saw with great clarity what was wrong with her world, and who attempted in her visions and her talks, to create a mythology that would offer the hope of a new age of Christianity, a reliving of the story of Genesis and the Gospels in a new form (see Newman). She remained a layperson, and gathered a community around her in the home she shared with her sister Alisette.

See also Beguines; Clare of Assisi, St.; Guglielmites; Joan of Arc, St.; Porete, Marguerite

BIBLIOGRAPHY

Primary Sources
Prous Boneta. "The Confession of Prous Boneta, Heretic and Heresiarch." Edited and introduced by William Harold May. In *Essays in Medieval Life and Thought, Presented in Honor of Austin P. Evans*, edited John H. Mundy et al., 3–30. New York: Columbia University Press, 1955.
———— and Alisseta. [Confession]. Translated by David Burr. Online www.majbill.vt.edu/history/burr/heresy/beguins/Prous.html [With useful links and Latin text from the Paris B.n.F., Collection Doat].
————. "The Confession of Na Prous Boneta, Heretic and Heresiarch, Carcassonne, France, 6 August 1325." Translated by Elizabeth Petroff. In *Medieval Women's Visionary Literature*, edited by E. Petroff, 284–90. New York: Oxford University Press, 1986. [Abridged trans., English text only, and commentary].
————. In *Tradition and Diversity: Christianity in a World Context to 1500*, edited by Karen Louise Jolly, ch. 18. Sources and Studies in World History. Armonk, N.Y.: M. E. Sharpe, 1997.

Secondary Sources
Burnham, Louisa. "So Great a Light, So Great a Smoke: The Heresy and Resistance of the Beguins of Languedoc (1314–1330)." Ph.D. diss., Northwestern University, 2002.
Burr, David. "Na Prous Boneta and Olivi," *Collectanea Franciscana* 67 (1997): 477–500.
————. *The Spiritual Franciscans: From Protest to Persecution in the Century after Saint Francis*. University Park: Pennsylvania State University Press, 2001.

Müller, Daniela. "Der Prozess gegen Prous Boneta: Begine, Ketzerin, Häresiarchin (1325)." In *Ius et historia: Festgabe für Rudolf Weigand*, edited by Norbert Höhl, 199–221. Würzburg, Germany: Echter, 1989.

Newman, Barbara. "WomanSpirit, Woman Pope." In Newman, *From Virile Woman to WomanChrist: Studies in Medieval Religion and Literature*, 182–223. Middle Ages. Philadelphia: University of Pennsylvania Press, 1995.

ELIZABETH A. PETROFF

PULCHERIA. *See* **Eudocia**

R

RĀBI'A AL-'ADAWIYYA (d. 801). Little real information survives about this Islamic woman saint and mystical (Sufi) writer; hence we must rely primarily on hagiography and legends. Rābi'a was born in Basra, in what is now southeastern Iraq, at the fertile confluence of the famous Tigris and Euphrates rivers, and thus a major center for military strategy, commerce, and Arabic cultural development. It was eventually overtaken by Baghdad as supreme center of Arabic learning, not long after Rābi'a's death. Her birthplace, like her Sufi religion—a mystical, ascetic Muslim sect—and gender, only heightened her allure for hagiographers, historians, and novelists, both contemporary and modern.

Rābi'a has been credited with no prose works, but the Arabic verses on earthly and divine love attributed to her—though her authorship of these, too, is considered highly suspect, and even a hoax (Gelder)—are among the earliest examples of mystical verse.

See also Hagiography (Female Saints)

BIBLIOGRAPHY

De Jong, Frederick and Berndt Radtke, eds. *Islamic Mysticism Contested: Thirteen Centuries of Controversies and Polemics.* Leiden: Brill, 1999.

El Sakkakini, Widad. *First among Sufis: The Life and Thought of Rabia al-Adawiyya, the Woman Saint of Basra.* Translated by Nabil Safwat. Introduction by Doris Lessing. London: Octagon Press, 1982 [Original Arabic title: *Ashiqah al-mutasawwifah.*].

Gelder, Geert van. "Rābi'a's poem on the two kinds of love: A Mystification?" In *Verse and the Fair Sex: Studies in Arabic poetry and in the Representation of Women in Arabic Literature,* edited by Frederick de Jong, 66–76. Utrecht: M.Th. Houtsma Stichting, 1993.

Hifni, Abd al-Munim. *al-Abidah al-khashiah Rabiah al-Adawiyah: imamat al-ashiqin wa-al-mahzunin.* Cairo: Dar al-Rashad, 1991.

Smith, Margaret. *Rābi'a the Mystic and Her Fellow Saints . . . in Islam.* Cambridge: Cambridge University Press, 1928. Reprints Amsterdam: Philo Press, 1974; Oxford: Oneworld, 1994.

NADIA MARGOLIS

RADEGUND, ST. (c.518–587). The Merovingian queen and abbess Radegund (or Radegunde, Radegunda) was one of the most beloved and widely celebrated holy women of her time. She founded the St. Croix (Holy Cross) monastery in Poitiers (west-central France) and fostered a new kind of cult worship during the Christianization of barbarian Europe. Radegund's cult represents the merging of ideals for Frankish aristocratic women

Radegund seated at Clothar's table. Folio 24r of *Life of Saint Radegund*, Poitiers BM MS 250, tenth- to eleventh-century manuscript. © The Art Archive/ Bibliothèque Municipale de Poitiers/Dagli Orti.

with those of Catholic monasticism. While other Frankish queens, such as Fredegund (d. 597) and Brunhild (d. 613), also achieved notoriety, it was for negative reasons: their ruthless, even bloodthirsty, ambition won them no favor with contemporary chroniclers. Radegund, however, was lauded by her contemporaries as exemplary among medieval queens.

Even before delving into the multiple perspectives of Radegund's biographers, we find the events of her life quite revealing for this period in history. Born the daughter of a prince of Thuringia, a province in central Germany, at about age twelve she was captured by the invading Franks under King Clothar (or Clotaire) I, as a prize (531). By the terms of a judicial decision arbitrated by Merovingian bishops, Radegund lived and worked at Clothar's Gallo-Roman estate near Athies, Picardy (northern France), where she learned to read, write, and study the Catholic religion, which encouraged her pious nature. Clothar was the son of Clovis (d. 511), king of the Franks, and Clothild (d. 544)—the future saint who converted her husband and the Franks to Christianity (c.496). But Clothar himself was anything but saintly, having murdered his half-brothers to claim the throne, among other brutal deeds. Since the widowed and maternally bereaved Clothild had retired farther south to Tours by the time of Radegund's arrival, one wonders whether the two holy women ever chanced to meet before Clothild's death. Even though Radegund's extreme piety deterred her from wishing to marry, she nonetheless consented to be the evil Clothar's bride, evidently as an act of charity (c.540). The couple had no children. Clothar took various concubines, leaving Radegund free to pursue her ascetic interests: caring for the sick and needy, particularly women, for whom she built a kind of luxurious shelter, with beds and baths, in which she could bathe them and tend to their ailments. The queen chose thus to be a servant to the poor.

After six years, when Clothar murdered Radegund's brother because he posed a threat to Clothar as ruler of Thuringia (c.550), Radegund now felt justified in fleeing Clothar's court and concubines, to the shrine of St. Martin at Tours. At the altar, she exchanged her jewels and fine clothing for her consecration, and convinced Médard, bishop of Noyon, to ordain her a deaconess. She then traveled to another royal villa, in Poitou, to care for lepers among other unfortunates, with whom she was as unstintingly kind as ever, even kissing them, as her chronicler tells us. Soon thereafter, Clothar tried to force her to return to him as his wife, but instead of aiding him in this cause, the bishops of Tours and Paris negotiated with Clothar toward a better cause: helping Radegund to establish a nunnery (c.560), by allowing revenues from estates that were previously part of her marriage gift to fund her independent royal community in Poitiers.

More than two hundred women lived immured in the Holy Cross monastery, for which she adopted the rule (constitution) written by Bishop Caesarius of Arles (c.470–542), originally for his sister Caesaria. Radegund obtained a copy via correspondence from Abbess Caesaria the Younger, the bishop and his sister's female successor. One of the rule's salient tenets was enclosure, or claustration, which must have appealed especially to Radegund in that it protected her from her husband (McNamara) in addition to its original intent of preserving the ideal, serene conditions for spiritual perfection. Some historians believe her monastery was a double monastery: one housing both a male and a female convent, separately but contiguously, and governed by a common superior. The male section was St. Mary's; the women's, Holy Cross (Ranft). In any case, Holy Cross became an important spiritual, intellectual, and political center, so much so that, despite the political struggles in Poitiers after Clothar's death in 561, Radegund managed excellent relations with Lord Sigebert and was eventually able to obtain a most precious relic for her monastery from Emperor Justin II: a sizable piece of the True Cross (569).

During her lifetime, Radegund upheld the independence and stability of the monastery from the local bishops as provided by Caesarius's rule, but after her death, matters changed. The Holy Cross nuns revolted in protest against their mistreatment (starvation, workmen in their bathroom, beatings) by the Abbess Leubevera, whom they also accused of playing backgammon and entertaining lay visitors, among other faults. The approximately forty nuns, led by royal cousins (one, a known troublemaker named Basina, the other, Clothild, natural daughter of King Charibert), broke Holy Cross's rule—strict enclosure—by exiting their cloister. The rebellious nuns then roamed through the Merovingian kingdoms seeking sanctuary and help for the community; others plotted to reenter Holy Cross by force and kidnap Leubevera. Influenced by letters from bishops, the kings' response to the nuns was to appoint a council of bishops to pass judgment; they acquitted the abbess. Bishop Gregory of Tours's record of the nunnery revolt and the testimony heard by the kings and bishops suggests that Bishop Maroveus of Poitiers was at fault. In the end, however, even the Merovingian bishops who had been loyal to Radegund decided to place the nunnery under the control of the local bishop. The rebels were excommunicated, although their uprising may well have been one of the first memorable women's rebellions in history. The Holy Cross community survived for centuries but not as the independent institution for women envisioned by Radegund.

Queen Radegund has been more written about than she was a writer. However, from her own pen we do have a record of her correspondence with the bishops of Merovingian Gaul as well as evidence of her letters sent to make peace among the warring factions within her kingdom. Perhaps the most documented woman of her age (McNamara), Radegund's place in history has been assured by the three narratives composed between the time of her death in 587 and 600, all by authors who knew her well, yet who came from vastly disparate backgrounds informing their differing perspectives. Two of these are complementary hagiographies: the first by the Italian poet-priest who became her confessor, Venantius Fortunatus (c.530–610); the second, a sort of supplement to Fortunatus, by the Frankish nun Baudonivia, who was raised at Holy Cross. Fortunatus, who knew Radegund both as a queen at court and as an abbess, emphasizes her heroic activities as a royal ascetic, an ideal Christian queen; while Baudonivia portrays her more as a model nun. Both biographers virtually omit recounting the violent circumstances preceding her marriage (though Fortunatus dramatizes her flight from Clothar afterward) and later, the political upheavals following Clothar's death. They also downplay the nun's revolt, then recently resolved, as if to do their part as historians in returning Holy Cross to its halcyon days under Radegund (McNamara; Graus). The third account of Radegund is by St. Gregory of Tours (538/9–594) in his *Historia Francorum* (*History of the Franks*). Gregory acted as advocate for Radegund's interests during confrontations with the bishop of Poitiers about important relics for the nunnery and a revolt of the nuns, in his *Epistle* written before the Council of Tours (567). Although he tends to depict the "darker side of women's monasticism" as Patricia Ranft observes—since it is he who provides the details of the nun's revolt—he is favorable toward Radegund. Her feast day is August 13.

See also Baudonivia; Brunhild; Caesaria, St.; Double Monasteries; Hagiography (Female Saints); Nunneries, Merovingian; Rules for Canonesses, Nuns, and Recluses

BIBLIOGRAPHY

Primary Sources
Baudonivia [supplement to Fortunatus]. *De Vita Sanctae Radegundis Liber II*. Edited by Bruno Krusch. *Monumenta Germaniae Historica, Scriptores rerum merovingicarum* [=*MGH, SRM*], 2: 358–64, 377–95. Hannover: Hahn, 1888. [Intervening pages contain the work of Venantius Fortunatus].
———. *Life of Radegunde*. In *Handmaids of the Lord: Contemporary Descriptions of Feminine Asceticism in the First Six Christian Centuries*, translated and edited by Joan M. Petersen, ch. 10. Kalamazoo, Mich.: Cistercian Publications, 1996.
———. *Life of Radegund*. In *Sainted Women of the Dark Ages*, edited and translated by Jo Ann McNamara, John E. Halborg et al., 87–105. Durham, N.C.: Duke University Press, 1992.
Fortunatus, Venantius. *De Vita Sanctae Radegundis, I. MGH, SRM*, 2: 364–77.
———. *La Vie de sainte Radegonde par Fortunat: Poitiers, Bibliothèque municipale, manuscrit 250 (136)*. Edited by Robert Favreau. Preface by Jean Favier. Paris: Seuil, 1995. [Latin and French texts].
———. *Life of St. Radegunde*. In *Handmaids of the Lord*, ch. 10. *See above under* Baudonivia.
———. *Life of St. Radegund*. In *Sainted Women*, 60–87. *See above under* Baudonivia.
Gregory of Tours. *Epistula ad episcopus*. In *Historia Francorum*, bk. 9. Edited by Bruno Krusch and Wilhelm Levison. *MGH, SRM*, 1–450. [Internal evidence in primary sources for other correspondence, but manuscripts not identified by scholarship to date].
———. "The Death and Funeral of Radegunde." In *Handmaids of the Lord*, ch. 9. *See above under* Baudonivia.
———. In *The History of the Franks*. Translated by Lewis Thorpe. Harmondsworth, U.K.: Penguin, 1974.

Secondary Sources
[See also notes to above eds., esp. *Handmaids of the Lord, La Vie*, and *Sainted Women*].
Friese, Michael. *Die heilige Radegunde von Thüringen*. With English translation by John Gledhill. Erfurt, Grüne Reihe Thüringen, 12. Erfurt, Germany: Verlagshaus Thüringen, 2001.

Graus, Frantisek. *Volk, Herrscher und Heiliger im Reich der Merowinger*. Prague: Nakladatelství Ceskoslovenské akademie ved, 1965.

Kleinmann, Dorothée. *Radegunde: Eine europäische Heilige: Verehrung un Verehrungstätten im deutschsprachingen Raum*. Graz, Austria: Styria, 1998.

Moreira, Isabel. *Dreams, Visions, and Spiritual Authority in Merovingian Gaul*. Ithaca, N.Y.: Cornell University Press, 2001.

Pischel, Barbara. *Radegunde: Zür europäischen Volkskunde*. Europäische Hochschulschriften, 19. Volkskunde, Ethnologie, A: 41. Frankfurt and New York: Peter Lang, 1997.

Ranft, Patricia. *Women and the Religious Life in Premodern Europe*. New York: St. Martin's, 1996.

Schulenburg, Jane Tibbetts. "Sexism and the Celestial Gynaeceum from 500–1200." *Journal of Medieval History* 4 (1978): 117–33.

Duey White

RAPE. The complexity and contradictions surrounding medieval rape laws—both Church and secular—seem to begin on the linguistic level, for the original Latin term *raptus* signifies either abduction or forcible sexual intercourse or both, as echoed in English usage through the early modern era (e.g., Alexander Pope's eighteenth-century mock-heroic poem, "The Rape of the Lock"). During the Middle Ages, rape was viewed as another prerogative of male power over a vanquished foe, part of a feudal manhood rite, often rendered heroic or comical-satirical in hagiography (saints' lives) and other medieval literature, as examined by several scholars, and in the visual arts (see Wolfthal), even in societies claiming to consider it a crime. As perspectives on rape evolved—and not always in a consistently positive progression over time—prime emphasis also alternated between the concept of a woman's body as (parental or spousal) property and that of her own consent.

Although rape is a topic treated in legal systems worldwide, and on which much information survives since Classical Antiquity (see Tomaselli and Porter), the following discussion deals primarily with medieval English and French law, with reference to other European cultures. Plentiful firsthand evidence from these cultures exists in canon law, in regional secular legal records, and in literary texts, of which a representative sampling is provided in the bibliography. As recent scholars such as Kim Phillips, Corinne Saunders, and Kathryn Gravdal demonstrate through separate methodologies and focal points, it is essential to balance the separate notions of truth in literary representations of rape against that of historical documents, and in the language of the records themselves, since, when properly used, each complements the other in providing a truer picture of evolving medieval attitudes toward rape and women as reflected in laws, practices, penalties, and their enforcement.

Canon law (laws governing Church and clergy) was unified and standardized by Gratian (c.1140) in his *Decretum* or *Corpus Iuris Canonici* (*Body of Canon Law*), which enabled it to separate from civil law, whose own principles had been established by the Roman emperor Justinian as the *Corpus Juris Civilis* in the sixth century. Before Justinian, *raptus* simply meant the seizure or theft of a woman as property, which the emperor's code then enlarged under the heading *De raptu virginum* to encompass the sexual assault dimension, but only criminalized the rape of virgins, nuns, and widows (Justinian, *Corpus Iuris Civilis*, 2: IX. xiii. i). Canon law's definition was even narrower and more lenient, despite Gratian's explicit recognition of *raptus* as "illicit coitus": the victim had to be unmarried and the abduction had to be from the paternal home for it to be deemed a crime. The element of consent was also complex, since the parents' wishes counted as much as the victim's and could even override their daughter's in either direction, but it was certainly a factor (Gratian, *Corpus*, ed. Friedberg, vol. 1: II. xxxvi. 1. 2). Medieval theologians, armed with the scholastic preoccupation with formulating definitions and categories, devised various categories of rape. Simple rape, a sin of lechery, meant violation without abduction. Distinctions were made between rape as the deflowering of a virgin (the gravest form) and that of a married woman or prostitute. The clerics also paid attention to the perpetrator's intent and absence or presence of the victim's consent, as with other sins. Gratian's infusion of the principles of Christian love eased matters—not for the woman victim but for the *raptor* (rapist)—given that the Church should not shed blood as in capital punishment. He therefore determined the fitting penalty for raptus to be excommunication, although he also realized that this would be difficult to enforce (Gratian, *Corpus*, vol. 1: II. xxvii. 2. 48; see Brundage 1978, 1982, 1987), not exactly stiffened by the provision granting sanctuary from secular prosecution to a rapist taking refuge in a church. A rapist belonging to the clergy, at least as recorded in the northern-French abbey of Cerisy's *Registre de l'Officialité de Cerisy* (1314–1457), was even more difficult to convict.

Secular legal systems dealt with rape in different ways depending on geography and century. Whatever regulations that were on the books were not always implemented in real life for various reasons.

In England, two major systems intertwined: the Anglo-Saxon and the above-described Roman; the Anglo-Saxons also knew the fourth-century Theodosian code, which condemned rape without stipulating chastity (Saunders). Anglo-Saxon laws clearly condemned rape, and women's rights were actually better off under this code, conceived by Alfred the Great (d. c.900), than after the Norman invasion (1066) when definitions of raptus became obfuscated by continental influences (Saunders). The collection of laws known as *Glanvill* (after its supposed compiler, Ranulf de Glanville, late twelfth to early thirteenth centuries) declared rape a felony, punishable by death. But as in many cases where punishment is severe, convictions occurred infrequently. By the thirteenth century, a variety of penalties were suggested in search of the most equitable justice. By the code of laws attributed to Henry de Bracton (thirteenth century), the rape of a virgin incurred dismemberment or blinding for the perpetrator. The Statute of Westminster I (1275), despite broadening the definition to include married women, also remelded violation with abduction. This statute diminished the gravity of rape as a crime and thus its punishment to imprisonment, though ten years later, the Statute of Westminster II, reflecting King Edward I's alarm over the increased number of rapes (signifying both forced coitus and abduction), recategorized it as a felony punishable by death or dismemberment (Post; Carter). However, it took over fifty years for the penalty actually to be applied; in the meantime, offenders could simply pay a fine (Post; Hanawalt). Recently, Kim Phillips has analyzed medieval English legal records of rape—rape narratives as found in legal compendia like those in Bracton, *Glanvill*, and another collection known as *Fleta*, then to the *Year Books of Henry VI* (1422)—to chart the extent to which rape was described as an assault on a woman's body, ranging from vivid details of bleeding virgins to minimal physical symptoms, rather than on her will, and also how each legal compendium's language in this regard reflects the moral and political concerns of the royal regime that nurtured it.

In Italy, specifically Venice (thirteenth to fourteenth centuries), laws categorized rape as an offense against women. Yet at the same time, such victimization was not severely criminalized but rather tacitly accepted as a fact of life and thus not heavily penalized either. However, the rapes of minors, old women, or family members (incestuous rape) were condemned more vigorously; while that inflicted on nubile women, married women, and widows—or lower-class women—received more lenient treatment (Ruggiero).

German custom, as preserved in Eike von Repgow's *Sachsenspiegel* (early thirteenth century) and its High-German counterpart the *Schwabenspiegel* (c.1275), allowed a woman to initiate court proceedings against her attacker by herself, though she was required to have a guardian as the trial progressed. A key factor in her case was her ability to provide witnesses who at least heard her scream and resist, if not eyewitnesses the assault. German law throughout the medieval period mandated the death penalty (decapitation or live burial) for rape, and in some instances even destruction of the rape-scene building and decapitation of animals present at the scene, although in actual practice, as recorded in specific cases, the penalties were often lightened and the crime could be redeemed by marriage to the victim (Rieger; Buschinger). Women may also have been deterred from filing charges, beyond the usual social pressures, because any children born of rape received no legal protection (Eike von Repgow, ed. Dobozy, notes).

Northern France adhered to the Justinian principle concerning rape: sexual intercourse without the woman's consent—the precise Old French term was *fame esforcier* (literally to force a woman)—and punishable by death (see Gravdal for further definitions). Philippe de Beaumanoir, in his *Coutumes de Beauvaisis* (*Customs of the County of Beauvaisis*, 1283) notes that, because rape was considered a crime as serious as murder and treason, the convicted rapist was to be "traînés et pendus" (dragged through the streets and hanged; Philippe de Beaumanoir, 1: 129. 824). On the other hand, the Cerisy Abbey *Registre* reports few cases of rape, since even back then, "only virgins or high-status rape victims actually had their day in court" (Gravdal); the situation was similar in England at that same time (fourteenth centrury; see Hanawalt). The Cerisy court records also contain more disheartening facts, for example, that women were punished more harshly than men for illegal sexual behavior, and that a woman—specifically a widow—raped in her own home after her attackers had broken in, had to pay a fine for "allowing" her rapists to have their way (Cerisy *Registre*, no. 3631; cited in Gravdal). The notion of a woman's partial cul-pability in her own rape was neither new nor would it disappear with the passage of time, though outwardly less-civilized societies, like that of medieval Russia (see below), did not manifest this prejudice. The Saint-Martin *Registre Criminel* (fourteenth century), if more systematic, reveals that this court treated women just as unfairly, if not more so. Despite stringent penalties on parchment for rapists, a woman victim bore all the burden of proof and risked harsh retribution should she not prevail. Apparently, as in England too, only virgin rape victims stood a chance of winning justice, which was still rather minimal. A man who raped a virgin could make amends by marrying her, provided she were not of higher social rank, or by paying a sum to her parents. If a rapist could not pay reparations, he risked castration. However, during the later Middle Ages in France, growing judicial indifference to the plight of women facilitated monetary restitution in lieu of imprison-ment or dismemberment.

The oldest (c.1175) and most esteemed "branch" (*Branche VIIa*) of the satirical beast epic titled the *Roman de Renart* (*Reynard the Fox*), celebrates rape within the larger context of a satire of both medieval law and courtly romance. The *Renart* borrows from its Latin prototype, the *Ysengrimus* (early to mid-twelfth century) and develops the episode in which the hero, Reynard the Fox, violates the queen figure, a she-wolf with whom he has already committed adultery, in front of her cubs, and thereby cuckolding his enemy, the king. Much of humor derives from the humiliation of a typically (since she was an empowered female, according to the *Renart* public's belief system) concupiscent queen and from the extended, detailed parody of solemn legal discourse and procedure in bringing Reynard to justice in the ensuing branches (see Gravdal).

Christine de Pizan's observations in her *Cité des dames* (*City of Ladies*, 1404–1405) are quite unique as a late-medieval French woman moral-political thinker's assessment of rape. In an oft-cited passage lambasting men for speciously arguing that women wish to be raped (*efforciees*) and emphasizing that, on the contrary, rape is their "douleur sur toutes autres" ("their greatest sorrow above all others"), Christine, invoking the legend of the Roman rape victim Lucretia who stabbed herself to death out of shame, advocates the death penalty for rapists (*Cité*, 2.44.1). Earlier (1401–1402), in her letter to Pierre Col, one of her adversaries in the Debate of the *Roman de la Rose* (*Romance of the Rose*) she inveighs against men who, as wrongheaded admirers of Ovid's *Ars Amatoria* (*Art of Love*), deploy what should be fine sentiments as a pretext for taking women by force (Christine, *Débat*, Hicks ed., 139. 779).

But not all women authors were appalled by rape. Moving back to the tenth century, the extraordinary German canoness Hrotsvitha, traditionally credited as the first medieval playwright of either gender and renowned for her Latin poetry and dramas, bases her *Calimachus* on rape as a means of converting the virgin victim's attacker to Christianity. The learned dramatist merged the sophisticated comedy of the pagan Roman Terence (d. 159 B.C.E.) with the intense early Christian drama of the women's saints lives in which she was steeped as much as in Classical Latin literature—an unlikely combination at which she nonetheless succeeds artistically and ideologically in deftly transferring sinfulness away from the conventional target of female sexuality and toward the heathen male perpetrator (see Gravdal).

In his *Confessio Amantis* (*The Lover's Confession*), John Gower (d. 1408) has attracted much attention from feminist medievalists for his depictions of rape and the woman victim's psychology and social situation (Dinshaw; Mast), despite his classification of rape along the old lines of raptus: seizure as a sin of robbery (of a man's property) rather than of lechery. Like Christine de Pizan, although independently, Gower too rethinks Ovid on rape in several instances (e.g., *Confessio*, 5: 6746–51) and re-creates the story of Lucretia (7: 5000–5023). As Isabelle Mast affirms, Gower is one of the rare male authors who realize that "it is not the victim who is dehumanized [...] but the victimizer [...] that women are victimized not just by their rapists but by their social environment."

In Orthodox Slavic countries, rape was a serious crime according to Rus's church Law, but is noticeably absent in secular law. Punishment for abducting or violating the wife or daughter of a *boyar* (nobleman) was the same as that exacted for calling her a whore: approximately sixty ounces of gold (=$21,000), which the woman shared with the local metropolitan (bishop). Donald Ostrowski notes the positive significance of the wronged woman's compensation, in comparison with other societies (like some described above), that would have the victim do penance for her dishonor: the Muscovite (Russian) woman "was not considered dishonorable even though she had been dishonored." Old Russian views on rape as defined by the woman's nonconsent, in contrast to seduction, may be traceable to the ancient Greek view, which made this same distinction (Ostrowski; Lefkowitz).

In general, medieval notions of rape command increasing attention from feminist literary and legal historians since, when tempered with convincing admonitions against "presentist" reading of medieval texts from scholars including Evelyn Vitz, they have much to tell us about how our current perceptions and conflicts on this matter came to be (see Roberts; Robertson and Rose).

See also Christine de Pizan; Concubines; Grazida (Grazida Lizier); Guinevere; Hagiography (Female Saints); Hrotsvitha of Gandersheim; *Jus Primae Noctis*; Law, Canon, Women in; Law, Women in, Anglo-Saxon England; Muscovy, Women in; Prostitution; *Sachsenspiegel* and *Schwabenspiegel*; Slaves, Female; Virginity

BIBLIOGRAPHY

Primary Sources

Bracton, Henry de. [*De legibus*]. *Bracton on the Laws and Customs of England.* Translated with commentary by Samuel E. Thorne. 4 vols. Buffalo, N.Y.: W. S. Hein, 1997. [Latin and English; see esp. vol. 2: 403–18, ff. 122, 146–48].

Britton [Jean le Breton]. *Britton: The French Text.* Edited, translated, and introduced by Francis M. Nichols. 2 vols. Oxford: Clarendon Press, 1865. Reprint Holmes Beach, Fla.: W. W. Gaunt, 1983. [Old French original plus English trans.; see esp. 1: 17, 55].

[Cerisy, abbaye de]. *Registre de l'Officialité de Cerisy 1314–1457.* Edited by M. G. Dupont. *Mémoires de la Société des antiquaires de Normandie,* 3rd ser. 10 (1880): 271–662.

Christine de Pizan. [*Cité des dames*]. *La Città delle dame.* Edited by E. J. Richards. Translated (Italian) with introduction by Patrizia Caraffi. Biblioteca medievale, 2. Milan: Luni, 1998. [Original Middle-French text with commentary in Italian].

———. *Book of the City of Ladies.* Translated by E. J. Richards. Foreword by Natalie Zemon Davis. Revised ed. New York: Persea, 1998.

———. *Le Débat sur le Roman de la Rose.* Critical ed. by Eric Hicks. Bibliothèque du XVᵉ siècle, 43. Paris: Honoré Champion, 1977. Reprint 1997.

Eike von Repgow. *The Saxon Mirror: A Sachsenspiegel of the Fourteenth Century.* Translated with an introduction and notes by Maria Dobozy. The Middle Ages. Philadelphia: University of Pennsylvania Press, 1999.

Fleta. Edited by Henry G. Richardson and George O. Sayles. Selden Society, 72, 89, 99. London: B. Quaritch, 1953–1955. [Latin original with English trans.; see esp. 1: 88–89].

Glanville, Ranulf de. [*Tractatus de legibus*] *The Treatise on the Laws and Customs of the Realm Commonly Called Glanvill.* Edited, translated, introduced, and annotated by George D. G. Hall with Michael T. Clanchy. Oxford Medieval Texts. Oxford: Clarendon Press; New York: Oxford University Press, 1993.

Gower, John. *Confessio Amantis.* In *The English Works of John Gower,* edited by George C. Macaulay, 1–2. Early English Text Society, e.s., 81–82. 2 vols. London: Kegan Paul, Trench, Trübner, 1900–1901.

[Gratian]. *Corpus iuris canonici.* Edited by Emil Friedberg. 2 vols. Leipzig, Germany: Tauschnitz, 1879. Reprint Graz, Austria: Akademische Druck, 1955.

Hrotsvitha. *Hrosvit: Opera Omnia.* Edited by Walter Berschin. Bibliotheca Scriptorum Graecorum et Romanorum Teubneriana. Munich and Leipzig, Germany: W. G. Saur, 2001.

[Justinian]. *Corpus iuris civilis. 2. Codex Justinianus.* Edited by Paul Krüger Hildesheim: Weidmann, 1989. Original 1877 [Greek and Latin texts only; see esp. p. 378].

Philippe de Beaumanoir. *Coutumes de Beauvaisis.* Critical ed. by Amédée Salmon. Textes pour servir à l'enseignement de l'histoire, 24, 30. 2 vols. Paris: A. Picard, 1899–1900. Reprint with 3rd vol.: *Commentaire historique et juridique,* by G. Hubrecht. Paris: Picard, 1970–1974.

—. *The Coutumes de Beauvaisis.* Translated by F. R. P. Akehurst. The Middle Ages. Philadelphia: University of Pennsylvania Press, 1992.

Pleas before the King or His Justices, 1198–1212. Edited by Doris Mary Stenton. Selden Society, 67–68, 83–84. 4 vols. London: Quaritch, 1952–1967. [See esp. 2: 74. 337; 2: 76. 342; 2: 92. 395; 4: 114. 3491].

Roman de Renart (Branches I–XVII). Critical ed. by Mario Roques, vol. 3: 1–17. Classiques Français du Moyen âge, 81. Paris: Honoré Champion, 1955.

[Saint-Martin]. *Registre criminel de saint-Martin-des-Champs au XIVe siècle.* Edited by Célestin Louis Tanon. Paris: Léon Willem, 1877.

Select Cases in the Court of King's Bench under Edward I–Henry V. Edited by George O. Sayles. Selden Society 55, 57–58, 74, 76, 82, 88. 7 vols. London: B. Quaritch, 1936–1966. [See esp. 4: 59. 20; 6: 159–60. 108].

[Theodosian Code]. *Codex Theodosianus.* Edited by Theodor Mommsen. 2 vols. in 3. Berlin, 1905. Reprint Hildesheim, Germany: Weidmann, 2000–2002. [See esp. Book 9: *tituli* 24–25].

—. *The Theodosian Code and Novels.* Translated, with commentary by Clyde Pharr et al. Corpus of Roman Law, 1. Princeton, N.J.: Princeton University Press, 1952.

Year Books of Henry VI, A.D. 1422. Edited by Charles H. Williams. Selden Society, 50. London: Quaritch, 1933. [See esp. p. 1.1].

Secondary Sources

Brundage, James A. *Law, Sex and Christian Society in Medieval Europe.* Chicago: University of Chicago Press, 1987.

—. "Rape and Marriage in the Medieval Canon Law." *Revue de droit canonique* 28 (1978): 62–75.

—. "Rape and Seduction in the Medieval Canon Law." In *Sexual Practices and the Medieval Church,* edited by Vern L. Bullough and J. Brundage, 141–48. Buffalo, N.Y.: Prometheus Books, 1982.

Buschinger, Danielle. "Le Viol dans la littérature allemande au moyen âge." In *Amour, mariage et transgressions au moyen âge,* edited by D. Buschnger and André Crépin, 369–81. Göppingen, Germany: Kümmerle, 1984. [Summarizes medieval German laws on rape, 369–73].

Carter, John M. *Rape in Medieval England: An Historical and Sociological Study.* Lanham, Md.: University Press of America, 1985.

Dinshaw, Carolyn. "Rivalry, Rape, and Manhood: Gower and Chaucer." In *Violence Against Women in Medieval Texts,* ch. 8. *See below under* Roberts.

Gravdal, Kathryn. *Ravishing Maidens: Writing Rape in Medieval French Literature and Law.* New Cultural Studies. Philadelphia: University of Pennsylvania Press, 1991. [Legal/literary-historical summaries in 1–20, 122–40].

Hanawalt, Barbara A. *Crime and Conflict in English Communities, 1300–1348.* Cambridge, Mass.: Harvard University Press, 1979.

—. *Of Good and Ill Repute: Gender and Social Control in Medieval England.* New York: Oxford University Press, 1998.

Kittel, Ruth. "Rape in Thirteenth-Century England: A Study of the Common-Law Courts." In *Women and the Law: A Social-Historical Perspective,* edited by D. Kelly Weisburg, vol. 1. Cambridge, Mass.: Schenkman, 1982.

Laiou, Angeliki E., ed. *Consent and Coercion to Sex and Marriage in Ancient and Medieval Societies.* Washington, D.C.: Dumbarton Oaks Research Library, 1993.

Lefkowitz, Mary R. "Seduction and Rape in Greek Myth." In *Consent and Coercion,* 17–37. *See above under* Laiou.

Mast, Isabelle. "Rape in John Gower's *Confessio Amantis* and Other Related Works." In *Young Medieval Women,* edited by Katherine J. Lewis, Noel J. Menuge, and Kim M. Phillips, 103–32. New York: St. Martin's, 1999.

McCracken, Peggy. "The Body Politic and the Queen's Adulterous Body in French Romance." In *Feminist Approaches to the Body in Medieval Literature,* edited by Linda Lomperis and Sarah Stanbury, 38–64. New Cultural Studies. Philadelphia: University of Pennsylvania Press, 1993.

Ostrowski, Donald. *Muscovy and the Mongols: Cross-Cultural Influences on the Steppe Frontier, 1304–1589*. Cambridge: Cambridge University Press, 1998.

Phillips, Kim M. "Written on the Body: Reading Rape from the Twelfth to Fifteenth Centuries." In *Medieval Women and the Law*, edited by Noël James Menuge, 125–44. Woodbridge, U.K.: Boydell Press, 2000.

Post, J. B. "Ravishment of Women and the Statutes of Westminster." In *Legal Records and the Historian*, edited by John H. Baker, 150–64. R. H. S. Studies in History, 7. London: Royal Historical Society, 1978.

Rieger, Dietmar. "Le Motif du viol dans la littérature de la France médiévale: entre norme courtoise et réalité courtoise." *Cahiers de Civilisation médiévale* 31 (1988): 241–67. [See 242–46 for a legal-historical overview].

Roberts, Anna, ed. *Violence Against Women in Medieval Texts*. Gainesville: University Press of Florida, 1998. [Essays by major scholars on English and continental literature, tenth to sixteenth centuries].

Robertson, Elizabeth, and Christine M. Rose, eds. *Representing Rape in Medieval and Early Modern Literature*. The New Middle Ages. New York: Palgrave, 2001. [Extensive collection of essays by leading scholars on European texts from twelfth to sixteenth centuries].

Ruggiero, Guido. *The Boundaries of Eros: Sex Crime and Sexuality in Renaissance Venice*. Studies in the History of Sexuality. Oxford: Oxford University Press, 1985.

Saunders, Corinne. "A Matter of Consent: Middle English Romance and the Law of *Raptus*." In *Medieval Women and the Law*, 105–24. *See above under* Phillips.

———. *Rape and Ravishment in the Literature of Medieval England*. Cambridge and Rochester, N.Y.: D. S. Brewer, 2001.

Subrenat, Jean. "Rape and Adultery: Reflected Facets of Feudal Justice in the *Roman de Renart*." In *Reynard the Fox: Social Engagement and Cultural Metamorphoses in the Beast Epic from the Middle Ages to the Present*, edited by Kenneth Varty, ch. 2. Polygons, 1. New York: Berghahn Books, 2000.

Tomaselli, Sylvana, and Roy Porter, eds. *Rape: An Historical and Social Enquiry*. Oxford and New York: Basil Blackwell, 1986.

Vitz, Evelyn Birge. "Rereading Rape in Medieval Literature: Literary, Historical, and Theoretical Reflections." *Romanic Review* 88 (1997): 1–29.

Walker, Sue Sheridan. "Punishing Convicted Ravishers: Statutory Strictures and Actual Practice in Thirteenth- and Fourteenth-Century England." *Journal of Medieval History* 13 (1987): 237–50.

Wolfthal, Diane. *Images of Rape: The "Heroic" Tradition and Its Alternatives*. New York: Cambridge University Press, 1999. [Major art-historical study of rape in medieval and Renaissance art].

NADIA MARGOLIS

RELICS AND MEDIEVAL WOMEN. Relics were material objects associated with the saints that served to incorporate the sacred power of those holy people. The words commonly used in Latin for relics provide some sense of their significance: they were *reliquiae*, that which the saint had "left behind" as an inheritance, or *pignora*, "pledges," of the saint's intercessory power. Saints had such power because at death they were judged worthy of immediate entrance into the kingdom of God, in whose court they now resided. Their relics most obviously included their own corpses, as well as (and certainly more commonly) smaller parts of their bodies that had been specifically separated for the purpose of veneration. Relics also included items that had belonged to or been used by the saint, such as clothing, official insignia, or books. Moreover, items brought into contact with relics—pieces of cloth touched to a shrine, vials of water that had washed a corpse, or blood miraculously exuded from a long-defunct corpse—themselves became relics. These categories have since been defined respectively by the Roman Catholic Church as first-, second-, and third-class relics.

Reliquary bust of St. Clare (1268-1308 Italian), containing her heart, where a fragment of the True Cross was found. © The Art Archive/Chiesa di Santa Clara Montefalco/Dagli Orti.

The veneration of relics to gain the intercession of the saints before God was one of the cornerstones of medieval Christian piety. It is important to realize that for medieval Christians the dead body was essential to the personal identity of the saint. The body remained in this world to be reunited with the soul at the time of the last judgment. Prayers said in front of a tomb or reliquary were not addressed to a dead bone, but to a vibrant inhabitant of the court of heaven. Relics provided a direct physical link between the kingdom of heaven and the mundane world. The public honor or *cultus* offered to the saints through their relics took many forms. Large shrines were erected over the tombs of saints or in those places to which the saintly bodies had been moved (that is "translated"). Shrines— such as those of Iago or Jacques (James) at Compostella, Foy (Faith) at Conques, and Thomas à Becket at Canterbury— attracted pilgrims from near and far. More fragmentary corporal relics were placed into altars as part of the process of consecration or set into elaborately jeweled cases called reliquaries. These later decorated churches and ecclesiastical institutions; they could be also obtained by wealthy laypeople for private devotion. Relics not only served pious Christians during their lifetimes, but in death as well. Burial near the shrines of the saints (*ad sanctos*) was highly prized, for on the Day of Judgment one would be near the body of a saint called to eternal glory.

Images of the saints or of incidents taken from their lives were an important adjunct to the cult of relics. The walls of churches in Western Christendom were often decorated in frescoes that could serve a didactic purpose for the laity. Reliquaries often bore images describing the deeds of the saint whose bone(s) rested inside or sometimes took on the very form of the saint in a kind of sculptured bust. Painted images of saints, commonly called icons, were a particular staple of Byzantine devotion. Indeed, icons took on many of the characteristics and functions of relics, which by the eleventh century they had virtually surpassed in importance throughout eastern Christendom. The veneration of relics was also inseparable from the liturgical (prescribed public ritual) cult of the saints. Every region of Christendom celebrated its own calendar of feasts dedicated to saints. Those feasts served to create a sacred time in much the same way shrines of the saints served to create a sacred space.

The term "relic" was also used to describe sacred objects connected to those most holy of all humans, Jesus and Mary. Their corporal relics were few, as it was commonly believed that the body of each had been transported into heaven at the time of their death. Rather, it was pieces of the true cross, of the kerchief worn by Christ during his agony, and of the Virgin's veil, that were scattered in reliquaries throughout Christendom. Images also served as the centerpieces of important shrines: numerous miracle-working statues of the Virgin, for example that at Rocamadour, France, or Christ's *Volto Santo* (Holy Face) at Lucca, Italy. Despite some theological objections, certain corporal relics existed in great numbers: vials containing body fluids such as Christ's blood or Mary's milk, or pieces of the body shed over the natural course of life, such as the milktooth and the foreskin of Christ.

Gender and misogyny structured the veneration of relics in medieval Christianity in many ways. Women always constituted a minority of the people celebrated as saints by Christian communities and an even smaller minority of those saints whose relics gained widespread veneration. Living women were largely excluded from positions of clerical and political authority over the cult of saints. Women were even at times prohibited from access to the relics of the saints. At the same time, clerics considered women to be more susceptible than men to those superstitious delusions leading to the improper use of the relics of the saints.

Martyrs were those whom Christian communities first recognized as saints and whose relics those communities first venerated. The earliest surviving piece of Christian hagiography, the *Martyrium Polycarpi* (*The Martyrdom of Polycarp*, c.167), records both the preservation of the body of St. Polycarp—the leading Christian figure in Roman Asia (second century)—as a relic and the celebration of the day of his death as a feast. Thus it is clear that both the cult of relics and the liturgical cult of the saints find their origins among the earliest Christian communities. Christians celebrated the memory of martyrs with feasts held at their tombs in suburban cemeteries. Small shrines were also erected over some tombs, for example that of Peter on the Vatican hill near Rome. But it was only in the wake of the Edict of Milan (313) and other official recognitions of Christianity that the public cult of the saints attained full acceptance and began its true growth. A council of bishops meeting in Gangra (c.340), in ancient Paphlagonia (now northern Turkey, on the Black Sea) went so far as to decree excommunication for any Christian who despised relics. Over the course of the fourth century, large churches were built at the shrines of many martyrs. Here, as in other aspects of Christianity, the newly converted Emperor Constantine (d. 337) took the lead, building an influential shrine church over the tomb of Peter at Rome. These shrines, largely outside the city walls, became a key part of the urban topography of the late Roman Empire. Some of these early martyria were dedicated to women, among them the shrine of Eulalia at Merida in modern Spain, that of Crispina at Tebessa in modern Tunisia, and that of Thecla at Seleucia (Silifke) in modern Turkey. Perhaps the most important of these was the shrine of Euphemia at Chalcedon near Constantinople (now Istanbul, Turkey), a massive affair consisting of three separate churches. According to Evagrius of Ponticus (d. 399), a mechanical device allowed sponges to be inserted into the tomb where they were covered with miraculous effusions of blood, thus becoming new relics that pilgrims carried away. The great council of Chalcedon (451) was held in the main basilica of the shrine.

It was not only as saints, however, that women could become involved in the cult of saintly relics. Women had traditionally born significant responsibilities for the burial and care of the dead in Mediterranean societies. Christian women of the Roman aristocracy thus became early and deeply involved in the process of providing shrines for the relics of the martyrs. While this activity was diminished by growing episcopal (Church officials') control over the cult of relics, women of the imperial—and later other royal—families would long continue to exercise significant authority over the initiation of new shrines. Indeed, two of the most significant discoveries of relics in the late Roman world were attributed to women, for by at least the time of Ambrose (d. 397), Constantine's mother Helen (d. c.330) was credited with the discovery of the remains of Christ's cross on Golgotha, while the Empress Pulcheria oversaw the discovery of the relics of the Forty Martyrs of Sebaste in 451. Women also significantly numbered among the devout Christians who attended the feasts and flocked to the shrines of the saints. Their presence can particularly be detected in the shrill warnings of churchmen who fretted about the "unregulated sociability" of such times and places, suggesting, in Antioch for example, that women only attend the feasts held in honor of the martyrs if they could go on muleback.

Over the course of the fourth and early fifth centuries, people other than martyrs, in particular ascetics, came to be recognized as saints. The shrines of saints such as Martin of Tours (d. 397) in Gaul and Simeon the Stylite (d. 459) in Syria were very popular, and their relics and feast days were widely disseminated. Although women were important in the ascetic movement throughout the Roman Empire, relatively few female ascetics came to be included in the liturgical calendar or to have their tombs honored as shrines.

The fifth and sixth centuries saw the migration of various Germanic tribes into the Western empire. It was the Franks, who settled in the province of Gaul and converted to Catholic rather than Arian Christianity, who most quickly adopted the veneration of relics. Two elites—the native Gallo-Roman clergy and the Frankish nobility—clashed over control of the cult of saints. The results demonstrate the complexity of the cultural conflict. The Frankish queen Chlotild (or Clotilde) (d. 544) established a shrine for Genovefa (or Genevieve), a native Christian killed opposing the Frankish conquest (c.502) and thereafter revered as the patron saint of Paris. Another Frankish queen, Radegund (d. 587), used her political connections to obtain relics of the True Cross from the eastern Roman emperor for a convent that she founded in Poitiers (in western France), a cult that challenged the authority of the local bishop and the cult of the local patron saint. A number of Frankish female ascetics, including Radegund herself, came to be recognized as saints. Gregory of Tours (d. 594) knew of miracles associated with relics of Radegund, as well as with the tombs of other female ascetics, such as Papula (c.early sixth century) and Monegunde (d. 570). Texts such as the *Translation of St. Balthild* (d. c.680) and the *Miracles of St. Austreberta* (d. 703) testified to the real, if local, appeal of their cults in the Frankish kingdom. Even in the Catholic minority of the Visigothic kingdom in the Iberian Peninsula, the cult of the ancient martyr Eulalia continued to hold extraordinary importance. In the shrinking Roman Empire, now limited to the eastern Mediterranean where it came to be known as Byzantium, the cult of the relics and icons of the Virgin Mary began to outstrip those of all other saints in importance. She was recognized as the chief patron of the imperial capital of Constantinople by the late fifth century.

The development of the Carolingian empire in the West during the eighth and ninth centuries brought with it a reorganization of the cult of saints under strict episcopal supervision. Many cults, including those of most female saints, waned in importance or were even suppressed. The shrines that emerged with renewed importance came increasingly under the control of monks and canons. Their patron saints were generally men: martyrs, early bishops, founding abbots. A telling exception was the acquisition of the relics of the female martyr Faith in 865 by the monks of Conques, relics that became the focus of a great pilgrimage shrine. As communities of celibate men came to control the great shrines, access to relics was sometimes denied to women. A monk of Fleury, for example, explained how "women were prohibited by ancient authority from going within the exterior gates of the monastery" and thus prevented from venerating the shrine of St. Benedict of Nursia contained within its church. The same strict enforcement of the cloister meant that few important shrines existed in female convents, although that of St. Potentianus at Jouarre (where the relics were translated in 847 by Abbess Hermentruda) was an exception. When Hrotsvitha of Gandersheim related how important the acquisition of the relics of a martyr had been to the foundation of her convent (c.845), it was clear they were not venerated by pilgrims.

In the kingdoms of Celtic Ireland and Anglo-Saxon England, on the other hand, cults of some female saints—such as Brig (or Brigid, d. c.523) who came to be buried near Patrick and Aethelthryth (or Etheldreda [= Audrey], d. c.630) whose shrine at Ely was an important pilgrimage center—enjoyed wide popularity. In contrast to continental practices, churches could be found throughout the western islands dedicated to these and other female saints.

In the Byzantine east these centuries witnessed profound changes in the devotion to relics. The Islamic conquests of the seventh century removed the shrines of the Holy Land and other provinces from Christian control. During the iconoclastic controversy lasting from 726 until 843, a party of monks and theologians mounted a concerted attack on the veneration of religious images. Many icons were destroyed and churches stripped of their decoration; even the status of relics was called into question. Women of the imperial family played an important role in these struggles, and the public veneration of icons was restored briefly under the patronage of the Empress Irene (d. 803). The end of the controversy, generally called the "restoration of orthodoxy," seems to have provided the cult of icons with renewed status and impetus for growth.

During the tenth and eleventh centuries, the cults of female saints, in particular martyrs, began to reemerge in Western Christendom. This was the period of great growth at Conques, where construction of a new church "in which the body of the holy virgin was to be placed in a tomb so that it could be approached more easily for those who assiduously streamed in to see it," began. The iconography of the cult was striking: the tympanum of the church depicts her as a young woman kneeling in prayer to intercede for her pilgrims before an enthroned Christ, while a statue that held her relics shows a woman with a crown seated on a royal throne. New shrines of ancient female martyrs were also founded. Simeon of Trier (d. 1035) imported relics of Catherine of Alexandria into Germany, while Abbot Geoffrey (d. 1052) "rediscovered" the relics of Mary Magdalene at Vézelay, France. The legends of these women—as well as of such other female martyrs as Margaret of Antioch and Ursula of Cologne—were rewritten and widely circulated, sometimes in the vernacular (i.e., French, German, English) as well as Latin, giving impetus to the celebration of their feasts and the collection of their relics. This vogue reached its apex in 1155 when graves unearthed outside the walls of Cologne were identified as those of Ursula and her eleven thousand companions in martyrdom, an identification that provided the churches of Europe with an enormous number of reliquaries in the following years. At one point, a living holy woman, Hildegard of Bingen (d. 1179), was asked to determine the authenticity of some of these relics through her prophetic powers. Over these centuries women also gained virtually untrammeled access to shrines, as monastic reformers dropped their objections to female pilgrims entering male cloisters.

During the twelfth and thirteenth centuries the importance of the traditional shrines of long-dead patrons was somewhat displaced by shrines dedicated to such recently deceased saints as Thomas Becket (d. 1170) at Canterbury and Francis (d. 1226) at Assisi. Only a few of these new saints were female, such as St. Frideswide (d. 727/735) in Oxford, whose patron saint she became; even she represented a special case as an Anglo-Saxon hermit whose relics were discovered at this time. But if female saints were not well represented among the roster of the great shrines of Western Europe, the continuing popularity of female martyrs made them staples of the liturgical calendar, relic collections, iconography, church dedications, vernacular hagiography, drama, and other manifestations of the cult of saints. The devout laity of the Later Middle Ages would have regularly called on the powers of female saints.

It was also in these centuries that relics associated with Christ and the Virgin Mary gained greatly in popularity. Important Marian shrines developed in virtually every region of Western Christendom: Chartres, Rocamodour, Einsiedeln, Montserrat, and Walsingham provide only a partial list. Marian piety, although theologically and historically a separate topic in its own right, should be considered as a powerful adjunct to the cults of female saints. The progress of the crusades, the development of trading links to the east, and above all the conquest of Constantinople by Western armies in 1204 opened a large market in relics. Innumerable pieces of the True Cross, vials of Christ's blood and Mary's milk, and bones of martyrs enriched the relic treasuries of the West.

The "feminization" of sanctity during the thirteenth and fourteenth centuries in the West made numerous new female intercessors available to the prayers of Christians. Over a quarter of the saints who were confirmed by official processes of canonization undertaken by diocesan or papal courts in the years between 1184 and 1417 were women. These inquests explicitly investigated posthumous miracles performed by the candidates for sainthood. They provide clear evidence that shrines for new saints, including a number of women, developed over the course of this period, but they also suggest a decline in the perception of a need for physical proximity to a saint's relics to receive such miracles. While Elizabeth of Thuringia (d. 1231), Margaret of Hungary (d. 1270), Birgitta (Bridget) of Sweden (d. 1373), Catherine of Siena (d. 1380), and others thus became important patrons for late medieval Christians, their relics did not carry the same significance that would have been attached to them in earlier times. The bodies of these saints were nevertheless carefully preserved, because the lack of putrefaction was regarded as a decisive sign of sanctity. As a result, the "uncorrupted" bodies of such saints as Clare of Assisi (d. 1253) and Catherine of Bologna (d. 1453) can be viewed today enshrined in glass coffins. In contrast, the late medieval saints of the Byzantine east were almost exclusively male, although the relics and icons of early female saints, and above all the Virgin Mary, continued to be popular.

There was a slow but profound transformation of the piety of the cult of saints in the late medieval West, one that increased the importance of private devotion to the saints in local churches and chapels, a devotion based on images, reliquaries, and liturgical prayer. Women, as saints and as devotees, played an important role in this more domestic piety. Lay reading of vernacular hagiography grew in scope. A devotional manual addressed to women that appeared in several editions around 1600 charged its reader to "read the stories and consider the constancy of the female martyrs and saints," explicitly mentioning among others, Elizabeth of Hungary and the martyrs Barbara and Cecilia. Paintings of the Annunciation frequently showed the Virgin in the pose of an idealized pious lay-woman, in her chamber reading and surrounded by woodcuts or other reminders of female saints.

Ever so slowly the importance of the great shrines—with the exception of those dedicated to Mary and Christ—waned. The new pilgrimage shrines of the fifteenth century such as Wilsnack (near Wittenberg, Germany) were similarly almost all dedicated not to the saints, but to Christ or the Virgin. During the sixteenth century, the age of the Protestant Reformation, the criticisms of the reformers ended the veneration of relics, pilgrimage, and indeed most of the trappings of the cult of saints in Protestant regions, yet the cults continued unabated in Catholic areas. In Spain, Italy, and elsewhere, relics of female saints and of the Virgin Mary seem to have grown in relative importance to those of male saints during the early modern period. In eastern Christendom, almost completely under Islamic domination after 1453, the great shrines were abandoned or converted to mosques, yet relics and icons continued to nourish what was becoming, in many regions, a minority faith.

See also Aldegund, St.; Birgitta of Sweden, St.; Catherine of Bologna, St.; Catherine of Siena, St.; Chelles, Nun of; Clare of Assisi, St.; Elizabeth of Hungary/Thuringia, St.; Hagiography (Female Saints); Hildegard of Bingen, St.; Mary, Blessed Virgin, in the Middle Ages; Radegund, St.; Thecla, St.; Virginity

BIBLIOGRAPHY

Aigrain, René. *L'Hagiographie: Ses sources—Ses méthodes—Son histoire*. 2nd ed., with a bibliography by Robert Godding. Subsidia hagiographica, 80. Brussels: Société des Bollandistes, 2000.

Angenendt, Arnold. *Heilige und Reliquien: die Geschichte ihres Kultes vom frühen Christentum bis zur Gegenwart*. Munich: C. H. Beck, 1994.

Brown, Peter. *The Cult of the Saints: Its Rise and Function in Latin Christianity*. Chicago: University of Chicago Press, 1981.

Bynum, Caroline Walker. *Fragmentation and Redemption: Essays on Gender and the Human Body in Medieval Religion*. New York: Zone Books; Cambridge, Mass.: MIT Press, 1991.

———; and Paula Gerson, eds. *Body-Part Reliquaries and Body Parts in the Middle Ages*. Published as a special issue of *Gesta*, 37/1 (1997).

Caviness, Madeleine H. *Visualizing Women in the Middle Ages: Sight, Spectacle, and Scopic Economy*. Philadelphia: University of Pennsylvania Press, 2001.

Davidson, Linda Kay, and Maryjane Dunn-Wood. *Pilgrimage in the Middle Ages: A Research Guide*. New York: Garland, 1993.

Davis, Stephen. *The Cult of St. Thecla: A Tradition of Women's Piety in Late Antiquity*. Oxford: Oxford University Press, 2001.

Dubois, Jacques, and Jean-Loup Lemaître. *L'hagiographie médiévale*. Paris: Editions du Cerf, 1993. [Bibliography on relics, predominantly in French, 247–319].

Gauthier, Marie-Madeleine. *Highways of the Faith: Relics and Reliquaries from Jerusalem to Compostela*. Translated by J. A. Underwood. London: Alpine Fine Arts, 1983. Originally *Les Routes de la foi: Reliques et reliquaires de Jérusalem à Compostelle*. Paris: Bibliothèque des Arts, 1983.

Geary, Patrick. *Furta Sacra: Thefts of Relics in the Central Middle Ages*. Revised ed. Princeton, N.J.: Princeton University Press, 1900.

Hamburger, Jeffrey. *The Visual and the Visionary: Art and Female Spirituality in Late Medieval Germany*. New York: Zone Books; Cambridge, Mass.: MIT Press, 1998.

Head, Thomas. *Hagiography and the Cult of the Saints: The Diocese of Orléans, 800–1200*. Cambridge: Cambridge University Press, 1990.

Holladay, Joan. "Relics, Reliquaries and Religious Women: Visualizing the Holy Virgins of Cologne." *Studies in Iconography* 18 (1996): 67–118.

Jansen, Katherine. *Making of the Magdalen: Preaching and Popular Devotion in the Later Middle Ages*. Princeton, N.J.: Princeton University Press, 2000.

Maraval, Pierre. *Lieux saints et pèlerinages d'Orient, histoire et géographie. Des origines à la conquête arabe*. Paris: CERF, 1985.

Morrison, Susan. *Women Pilgrims in Late Medieval England: Private Piety as Public Performance*. London: Routledge, 2000.

Reber, Ortrud. *Die Gestaltung des Kultes weiblicher Heiliger im Spätmittelalter: Die Verehrung der Heiligen Elisabeth, Klara, Hedwig und Birgitta*. Hersbruck: K. Pfeiffer Verlag, 1963.

Schulenburg, Jane Tibbetts. "Gender, Celibacy, and Proscriptions of Sacred Space: Symbol and Practice." In *Medieval Purity and Piety: Essays on Medieval Clerical Celibacy and Religious Reform*, edited by Michael Frassetto, 353–76. New York: Garland, 1998.

Sheingorn, Pamela. *Writing Faith: Text, Sign and History in the Miracles of Sainte Foy*. Chicago: University of Chicago Press, 1999.

Smith, Julia. "Women at the Tomb: Access to Relic Shrines in the Early Middle Ages." In *The World of Gregory of Tours*, edited by Kathleen Mitchell and Ian Wood, 165–80. Leiden: Brill, 2002.

Sumption, Jonathan. *Pilgrimage: An Image of Mediaeval Religion*. Totowa, N.J.: Rowman & Littlefield, 1975.

Wilson, Steven, ed. *Saints and Their Cults*. Cambridge: Cambridge University Press, 1983. [Bibliography on relics, predominantly in English, 309–417].

THOMAS HEAD

RESPONSE DU BESTIAIRE (mid-13th century). The *Response du Bestiaire* was a supposedly woman-authored rebuttal to a popular work with strongly misogynistic overtones, *Li Bestiaires d'amours* (*The Bestiary of Love*), by the northern-French canon, chaplain, and chancellor Richard de Fournival (1201–c.1260). Richard, a respected theologian of encyclopedic knowledge in letters and sciences, produced his hybrid parody first in prose, then later in verse, of two medieval didactic genres—the bestiary (a descriptive catalogue of animals often relating their traits to those of humans) and the arts of love, whose tradition can be traced back at least as far as the Roman poet Ovid (43? B.C.E–17 C.E.)—in a highly learned, yet mocking exposé of love's stratagems. More than in conventional bestiaries, however, Richard selected only those animal traits useful to illustrating love psychology in both genders, representing women's love by such beasts as the weasel, viper, and especially, the "three natures" of the wolf. In addition, Richard composed this iconoclastic "love bestiary" with the perfectly executed solemnity of a sermon, which heightened its effectiveness and eventual popularity. In the four manuscripts containing both Richard de Fournival's *Bestiaire d'amour* (modern spelling) and the *Response du Bestiaire*, the *Response* author is termed merely "sa dame" in one manuscript (Paris, BnF MS fr. 412) and "la dame" in another (Vienna, ÖNB MS 2609). Since the date of the *Bestiaire d'amour* is at best approximate, but no earlier than 1252, the date of the *Response* is even more so. The extant manuscripts that first contained it date from between 1280 and 1300.

The authorship of the *Response* is mysterious. It would be rash to rely on biographical details provided in Richard's bestiary, which was visibly influenced by the charming, though often misleading, courtly conventions of its time. The *Bestiaire d'amour* contains nevertheless idiosyncratic elements that depart from the *topoi* (commonplaces) of love literature, for example, a paternal teacher-figure occasionally irritated by the young Anonymous pupil-figure. In addition, Richard mentions some specific details of their relationship (the circumstances of their meeting, and her attitudes then and now) that the *Response* subsequently debates. It is possible, therefore, that an actual relationship existed, perhaps one between a teacher/confessor (the "chier maistre" ["dear Master"] addressed in the *Response*) and a pupil/novice (the "bele, tredouce amie" ["fair, most gentle friend"] addressed in the *Bestiaire d'amour*).

If biographical details about the *Response*'s author are vague, her literary persona is clearly defined. She begins confidently with the dictum that a man of intelligence should not use that intelligence to corrupt either man or woman. While rendering superficial homage to her "biaus maistres" ("fair Master") by citing him as her inspiration, she consistently challenges him and his authority. For example, she agrees with the statement in his prologue that no one can know everything and that there is an accumulated stock of human knowledge; but where he uses this to acknowledge humanity's debt to the ancients, she uses it to claim to know something, as a woman, that he, a man, does not.

Her prologue, unique in its womanly independence and audacity, challenges all conventional interpretations of the Creation story. She describes God's simultaneous creation of man and woman out of dust. When Adam was dissatisfied with God's first efforts to create a woman for him, he murdered that woman, justifying his act by citing the woman's insignificance and his lack of love for her: "She was nothing to me, and I could not love her." God, he goes on to explain, then "in his courtesy" created Eve, who was superior to Adam both in workmanship and in substance. The dignity of woman and God's good will toward her is thus affirmed before the bestiary imagery begins, and, moreover, Adam is judged "according to certain authorities" to have been responsible for original sin. That phrase "according to certain authorities" should not be dismissed as a truism. The author's Creation narrative has real affinities with various Jewish legends of mankind's Creation and almost certainly reflects other than orthodox sources.

Having reprimanded Richard for neglect of his responsibilities toward the "non-sachanz" ("non knowing") while extolling "savoir" ("knowledge") in his prologue, the woman now constructs a womanly bestiary using Richard's model, countering each of his symbolic interpretations with her own. Her dominant theme—self-preservation—replaces his pleas for protection in love. Her most valuable defense becomes her pride, which he had criticized as a flaw and an impediment. "Death" is now interpreted as loss of honor and as that very love that would bring life to him. Moral, social, and psychological attitudes reflect female rather than male preoccupations. The author of the *Response* ends with a bitter castigation of clerics and, after her "multiple refusals," begs for mercy and good understanding.

The emotional range of the *Response* is wide: from pathos to satire, from objective exposition to irony. The literary baggage of the author is lighter than Richard's. The popular *clerc-chevalier* (cleric-knight) debates, pitting learned, clerical ideals against chivalric-warrior ideals (and, perhaps, the strongly anticlerical mood in Amiens in her time) may have inspired her castigation of any cleric who is willing to ruin himself and the woman he courts. In a scathing attack on his cajoling requests for love, Richard is abusively termed "Renart" (the sly fox of the well-known Old-French *Roman de Renart* series, 1150–1250) as the author exclaims "Ah, Renart, how far out your tongue is hanging!" Punning references to clerics as *oiseaux de proie* (birds of prey) may derive from similar metaphors in lyric poetry.

Her omissions of Richard's material, especially her consistent neglect of Richard's naturalistic digressions (which he culled directly from his bestiary source, Pierre de Beauvais' *Bestiaire* [early thirteenth century]) are significant. The *Response* is thematically economical and single-minded in its logic, because ultimately its best argument against Richard's criticism of woman's unreason was a pragmatic demonstration of her power to reason. As for her astonishing rewrite of Genesis 2: 23 and her insistence on the importance of the woman's voice, they made the *Response* unique in its time. A similarly effective combination of cogent argumentation and impassioned indignation would be seen again when Christine de Pizan injected herself into the Débat du *Roman de la Rose* (Debate of the *Romance of the Rose*, 1402–1404).

See also Belle Dame sans Merci; Capellanus, Andreas; Christine de Pizan; Power of Women; *Roman de la Rose*, Debate of the

BIBLIOGRAPHY

Primary Sources
Richard de Fournival. *Le Bestiaire d'amour suivi de la Réponse de la dame*. Edited by Célestin Hippeau. Paris: Aubry, 1860. Reprint Geneva: Slatkine, 1969, 1978. [Inferior, outdated ed.].
———. *Li Bestiaires d'amours di Maistre Richart de Fornival e li Response du Bestiaire*. Edited by Cesare Segre. Milan and Naples: Riccardo Ricciardi, 1957. [Authoritative ed.].
———. *Master Richard's Bestiary of Love and Response*. Translated by Jeanette Beer. Illustrated by Barry Moser. West Hatfield, Mass.: Penny Royal Press, 1985. [Numbered art ed.].
———. *Master Richard's Bestiary of Love and Response*. Translated with preface by Jeanette Beer. Illustrated by Barry Moser. Berkeley and Los Angeles: University of California Press, 1986. Reprint West Lafayette, Ind.: Purdue University Press, 2000. [Attractive ed. with useful notes and bibliography.]

Secondary Sources
Beer, Jeanette. *Beasts of Love: Richard de Fournival's* Bestiaire d'amour *and a Woman's Response*. Toronto: University of Toronto Press, 2003.
———. "*Le Bestiaire d'amour en vers*." In *Medieval Translators and Their Craft*, edited by Jeanette Beer. Kalamazoo, Mich.: Medieval Institute Publications, 1989.
———. "Duel of Bestiaries." In *Beasts and Birds of the Middle Ages: The Bestiary and its Legacy*, edited by Willene B. Clark and Meradith T. McMunn, 96–105. Philadelphia: University of Pennsylvania Press, 1989.
———. "Gendered Discourse in Two Thirteenth-Century Texts." *Journal of the Institute of Romance Studies* 3 (1994–1995): 27–32.
———. "Woman, Authority and the Book in the Middle Ages." In *Women, the Book and the Worldly*, edited by Lesley Smith and Jane H. M. Taylor, 61–69. Cambridge: Cambridge University Press, 1995.
Krueger, Roberta L. *Woman Readers and the Ideology of Gender in Old French Verse Romances*. Cambridge: Cambridge University Press, 1993.
Solterer, Helen. *The Master and Minerva*. Berkeley: University of California Press, 1995.

JEANETTE BEER

REYNA DE MALLORQUES, LA (early 14th century). Sharing time, space, and tradition with philosopher Ramon Llull (Raymond Lull, c.1232–c.1315) was a poet identified simply as "La Reyna de Mallorques" ("The Queen of Majorca/Mallorca"). She was probably Constança d'Aragó (1313–1346), sister of Pere el Cerimoniós of Aragon, or perhaps Violant de Vilaragut, both of whom were wives of Jaume III of Majorca. Her only extant poem, found in the collection of lyric poems known as the "Cançoner Vega Aguiló" in the Biblioteca de Catalunya in Barcelona, belongs to the *descort* (a love-debate genre) of the troubadour tradition. The first half of the poem also appeared in the Catalan translation of the Italian Giovanni Boccaccio's *Decameron* (1351–1353) in 1429. The poem, a lament on the absence of her husband gone to France, ends with the following *tornada* (a type of troubadour-lyric closing):

> Merce, mairitz, que sufren pas
> los mals que.m dats, e donchs tornats,
> que nulh tresor/no val un cor
> que per vos mor,/ab amorosa pença.
> (ed. Cluzel 371–73)

(Mercy, my husband, I'm suffering so/from the pain you cause, so come back,/no treasure/can be worth a heart/that's dying for you/with thoughts of love).

See also Borja, Tecla; Catalan Woman Poets, Anonymous; Isabel de Villena; *Malmojades, Les*; *Trobairitz*

BIBLIOGRAPHY

Primary Sources
Reyna de Mallorques. "Ez yeu am tal qu'es bo e bel." Miscellaneous Medieval Poetical Manuscript 8. Biblioteca de Catalunya, Barcelona.
———. "Ez yeu am tal qu'es bo e bel." In Irénée Cluzel, "Princes et troubadours de la maison royale de Barcelone-Aragon." *Boletín de la Real Academia de Buenas Letras de Barcelona* 27 (1957–1958): 371–73.
———. "I love one who is good and lovely" ["Ez yeu am tal qu'es bo e bel"]. Translated by Kathleen McNerney. *Catalan Review* 5.2 (1991): 163–67.

Secondary Sources
Badia, Lola. "Reina de Mallorca." In *Double Minorities of Spain: A Bio-Bibliographical Guide to Women Writers of the Catalan, Galician, and Basque Countries*, edited by Kathleen McNerney and Cristina Enríquez de Salamanca, 211–12. New York: Modern Language Association, 1994.
Massó i Torrents, Jaume. "Poetesses i dames intel.lectuals." In *Homenatge a Antoni Rubió i Lluch*, 1: 405–17. 3 vols. Barcelona: n.p., 1936.
Pagès, Amédée. "Les poésies lyriques de la traduction catalane du *Décameron*." *Annales du Midi* 46 (1934): 201–17.
Riquer, Martí de, Antoni Comas, and Joaquim Molas. *Història de la literatura catalana*, 1: 519–20. 11 vols. Barcelona: Ariel, 1964–1988.

KATHLEEN McNERNEY

RHETORIC, WOMEN AND. Rhetoric was the art or *techne* (in Greek) that sought to teach, to move, or to persuade. It was institutionalized and codified by the likes of the great fourth-century B.C.E. Greek philosophers Plato and Aristotle, the renowned Roman orator, Cicero (first century, B.C.E.), and his anonymous contemporary imitator (some call

Logic and Rhetoric, fresco of the Liberal Arts, late fifteenth century, Chapel of Relics, Cathedrale Notre Dame, Le Puy, Haute Loire, France (*detail*). © The Art Archive/Dagli Orti.

him Cornificius) who penned the *Rhetorica ad Herennium* (*Four Books on Rhetoric, Addressed to Gaius Herennius*), and then by Quintilian, in his *Institutio oratoria* (*Training of Orators*, first century, C.E.). According to the dictum of Cato, it was practiced by "the good man [*vir bonus*] skilled in speaking." The influence of this doctrine of rhetoric—as not only an art but also as a moral force—spanned an impressive interdisciplinary scope extending far beyond law and politics into theology, philosophy, literature, pedagogy, and, perhaps of greatest interest in the context of this volume, the cultural construction of gender.

As early as the first century, rhetorical theorists had elaborated a complex hermeneutic, or interpretive, framework by which to conceptualize the gender of the speaking rhetorical voice, including such features as intonation, musicality, and what we might call the "testicular" (because of its male-centeredness) language of the body. In a fascinating and, until relatively recently, egregiously neglected aspect of the rhetorical corpus, we find theorists discussing the various sexual identities of the oratorical voice as "masculine," "feminine," or "effeminate." First and foremost, Cato's "good men" were to serve the State in its political bodies and law courts with a virile (note presence of Latin *vir* [man] again) eloquence devoid of any traces of femininity or effeminacy. For example, in that pillar of the medieval educational system the *Rhetorica ad Herennium*, the Pseudo-Cicero claimed that "sharp exclamations" in oratory were "suited rather to feminine outcry than to manly dignity [*ad virilem dignitatem*] in speaking" (*Ad Herennium*, 3: 22). That also held true for other manifestations of rhetoric such as philosophy, music, epic, and theater, into which dastardly traces effeminacy and prostitution had infiltrated. Quintilian rued the day when those once ennobled and manly genres were "emasculated by the lascivious melodies of our effeminate stage, destroying such manly vigor as we still possessed" (*Institutio oratoria* 1: 10.31–32). The second-century satirist, Lucian of Samosata, found that the penis was a necessary tool for the philosopher: "I may well pray that my son (who is still quite young) may be suitably endowed for the practice of philosophy with other tools than brain or tongue ("The Eunuch," 12–13). And, even though the late-fifth-century Martianus Capella's Lady Rhetoric was an armor-clad maiden with the power to "lead men where she would and to hold them back when she would, to bring them to tears or to rouse them to frenzy, and to bring about a change in attitudes and convictions in governments as well as in armies at war" (*De Nuptiis Philologiae et Mercurii* [*On the Marriage of Philology and Mercury*], ed. Miller et al., 3), the history of rhetoric clearly shows that male theorists also found it convenient to masculinize her—actually, to castrate her. So it was that Quintilian complained that declaimers who bore a "false resemblance to the female sex [were] guilty of exactly the same offense as slave-dealers who castrate boys to increase the attractions of their beauty" (*Inst. Or.*, 5: 12.17–20).

Thus, the questions that have increasingly preoccupied both historians of rhetoric and feminist critics are as follows: Faced with centuries of expulsion, marginalization, and denigration, could medieval women indeed become rhetoricians? If the hegemonic male rhetorical script did not allow for female discourse and performance, how could a woman espouse her opinions, ideology, or politics when any educational model to which she might have been fortunate enough to be exposed was necessarily grounded in institutional referents that were masculine? Could she benefit from and reinvent a rhetorical tradition that actually constituted one of the most effective weapons used against her?

Not surprisingly, it is far easier to study the rhetoric of medieval female characters than it is to reconstruct the history of women as actual rhetoricians. Learned medieval authors frequently depict women manipulating rhetoric: Eve is the first temptress and, in a play such as the anonymous *Jeu d'Adam* (*Play of Adam*, thirteenth century), the first persuasive rhetor whose only possible trainer is the Devil; Chaucer's Prioress in his *Canterbury Tales* (c.1400) and Jean de Meun's Duenna in his *Roman de la Rose* (c.1278) are endowed with elocutionary skills rivaling those of any scholastic philosopher; the martyred saints of hagiography effectively exploit the rhetorical proofs of pathos in the speeches that accompany their tortures; in countless morality plays, a male psyche is depicted as the interior struggle between feminine voices; the Four Daughters of God appear in Passion plays to litigate the redemption of humankind in a celestial law court; and, in *L'Advocacie Nostre-Dame* (fourteenth century), the Virgin Mary is "a good and wise lawyer who often delivers us through litigation" (93–101) and whose forensic litigation is composed of crying, flailing, and showing her bare breasts as part of her right "to intercede in certain particular cases before all courts; and in such cases, they have priority: small, under-aged children, piteous widows: such persons—confounding all the devils in the world—may women rightfully defend and the judge must accept them" (890–900).

However, any inquiry into women and rhetoric in the Middle Ages must also recognize that such examples, abundant though they may be, constitute a feminine rhetoric rhetorically constructed by men. Equally important to this topic are the more rarefied instances of an art of rhetoric conceived and/or practiced by medieval women. In the larger pursuit of that topic, scholars might find it fruitful to focus their discussions on individual rhetorical canons and genres. That is to say, while there are no bona fide rhetorical manuals written by medieval women, nevertheless, their writings contain many formulations and reformulations of specific components of that discipline. Rhetoric was composed of five parts or canons: *inventio*, which dealt with the discovery of the subject matter for a speech; *dispositio*, or the structuring of those materials; *elocutio* for embellishing them with stylistic tropes and figures; *memoria* to think them through and store them; and *actio*, which offered detailed advice about how to perform the materials so invented, ordered, stylized, and memorized with the full gamut of vocal intonation and gesture. Classical rhetoricians and their medieval successors also divide rhetoric into three genres: the forensic rhetoric of the law courts, the deliberative oratory of the political body, and the epideictic (declamatory) discourses of praise or blame. Medieval theorists make further refinements by categorizing several *artes* of grammar (*grammatica*), poetry (*poetria*), letter-writing (*artes dictaminis*), and preaching (*artes praedicandi*).

Specifically, then, as early as the twelfth century, the importance of the rhetorical tradition is apparent enough to Marie de France, who invokes it along with grammar in the prologue to her *Lais*: "Whoever has received knowledge/and eloquence in speech from God/should not be silent or secretive/but demonstrate it willingly" (1–4). Her near contemporary, Heloise, who had the "privilege" of receiving an education dominated by the rule of the rod from her Master/Lover Abelard is so familiar with the rhetorical conventions of the ars dictaminis that she is able to apply its precepts in her Letter 3: "I am surprised, my only love, that contrary to custom in letter-writing and, indeed, to the natural order, you have thought fit to put my name before yours in the greeting which heads your letter [...]. Surely the right and proper order is for those who write to their superiors or equals to put their names before their own, but in letters to inferiors, precedence in order of address follows precedence in rank" (127). Margery Kempe comprehends that a proem (brief introduction) should preface her book: "Here begins a short treatise and a comforting one for sinful wretches, in which they may have great solace and comfort for themselves, and understand the high and unspeakable mercy of our sovereign Saviour Jesus Christ" (35). Herself "moved and stirred" by the rhetoric of Christ's Passion, she exploits the juridical, clerical, and curative powers of rhetoric (as described by such authors as Augustine [354–430] and Alan of Lille [twelfth century]) to move and stir an audience with a rhetoric of her own—one that includes the nonverbal but pathetic efficacy of tears that, in other literary contexts, characterize the Virgin Mary. Saint Gertrude the Great is eminently familiar with such classic imagery of mnemotechnics as the wax block or treasure house: "I beheld my soul, under the similitude of wax softened by the fire, impressed like a seal upon the bosom of the Lord; and immediately I beheld it surrounding and partly drawn into this treasure house, where the ever-peaceful Trinity abides corporeally in the plenitude of the Divinity" (in Petroff, 228). In her *Livre de la Cité des dames* (*Book of the City of Ladies*, 1404–1405), Christine de Pizan offers a female exemplar in the tale of Hortensia, who had been encouraged by her father to "learn letters and study the science of rhetoric, which she mastered so thoroughly that she resembled her father Hortensius not only in wit and lively memory but also in her excellent delivery and order of speech—in fact, he surpassed her in nothing" (2: 36.2). And, particularly noteworthy in the medieval rhetorical arena, are the participation of Christine herself in one of the most interesting debates of her day, as she matched wits with powerful contemporaries Jean Gerson and Pierre Col about the rhetoric of *Roman de la Rose* (*Romance of the Rose*); and the trial of Joan of Arc, who steadfastly faced her accusers and responded calmly and intelligently to their manipulations of forensic rhetoric (see Sullivan) with the same ability as Jesus before the Doctors in so many Passion Plays. Finally, Hrotsvitha of Gandersheim (tenth century) prefaces her plays by entering an entire forensic continuum as she responds to the charges against women launched by theologians and literary theorists. In a revitalized and regendered vision of the long-denounced lasciviousness of theatre, she endeavors to create a model for female performance: "Many Catholics one may find, and we are also guilty of charges of this kind, who for the beauty of their eloquent style, prefer uselessness of pagan guile to the usefulness of Sacred Scripture" (3). Well-versed in topoi (commonplaces, motifs) of both imitation and false modesty, she proposes to repair the status of women and drama alike in her own *imitatio Christi*: "I have not refused to imitate Him in writing whom others laud in reading, so that in that selfsame form of composition in which the shameless acts of lascivious women were phrased the laudable chastity of sacred virgins may be praised within the limits of my little talent" (3).

Imbricated, then, in the history of women and rhetoric in the Middle Ages are crucial issues of power, marginalization, and social praxis issuing from language. On the one hand, the persistent association articulated by male rhetoricians between theatrics, bad rhetoric, and effeminacy had three particularly effective consequences inflicted in one diabolically well-conceived blow: it marginalized women, bad oratory, and theatre by casting each as perverse, disempowered speech. According to that rationalization, oratory was bad because flowery, feminine, or histrionic affectations rendered it "effeminate"; theatre was bad because such effeminate histrionics were its hallmark; and women and homosexuals were bad because of the encroachment of their histrionics into the once ennobled discourses of law, politics, and liturgy. In a triumph of counterintuition, male rhetors regularly attempt to regain the power of seductive, rhetorical display that they simultaneously deny having lost. They assimilate and purify the theatrical, feminine, and effeminate qualities they most despised and rationalize that assimilation. What renders those strategies particularly relevant to such critical approaches as feminism or queer theory is that the one apparent target, women's speech, is never really feminine at all but male—even if effeminate; and the other apparent target, effeminate speech, is never really queer at all but heterosexual.

On the other hand, the medieval female responses to that assimilation are not always the sociocultural victories modern feminism has frequently sought to make them. Even in the learned rhetoric of Christine de Pizan's *Cité des dames*, her "future ladies" remain curiously silent, immobile, and even victimized at the end of the didactic tale, as when those who have been so unlucky as to receive brutish husbands strive to endure them in patient silence (3: 19.2). Even the burgeoning interest in issues of female subjectivity cannot retrofit the rhetoric of medieval women to make the transition from epistemology to agency if that agency is undocumented. In any event, one assertion can be made with certainty: The critical restoration of the ubiquitous rhetorical tradition to our readings of the discourse of medieval women demonstrates that medieval authors were just as interested as we are in exploring the notion that the gendered self is a rhetorical construct.

See also Belle Dame sans Merci; Boccacio, Women in, *De Claris Mulieribus*; Bokenham, Osbern; Chaucer, Geoffrey, Women in the Work of; Christine de Pizan; Epistolary Authors, Women as; Gertrude the Great, of Helfta, St.; Hagiography (Female Saints); Heloise; Hrotsvitha of Gandersheim; Humanists, Italian Women, Issues and Theory;

Humility Topos; Joan of Arc, St.; Kempe, Margery; *Kharja*; Marie de France; *Roman de la Rose*, Debate of the; Umiltà of Faenza, St.

BIBLIOGRAPHY

Primary Sources

L'Advocacie Nostre-Dame et la Chapelerie Nostre-Dame de Baiex: Poème normand du XIVe siècle. Edited by Gaston Raynaud. Paris: Académie des Bibliophiles, 1869.

Christine de Pizan et al. *Le Débat sur le Roman de la Rose.* Edited by Eric Hicks. Bibliothèque du XVe siècle, 43. Paris: Honoré Champion, 1977. Reprint 1997.

———. *La Querelle de la Rose: Letters and Documents.* Edited and translated by Joseph L. Baird and John R. Kane. Chapel Hill: University of North Carolina Press, 1978. [English trans. only].

———. [*Le Livre de la Cité des dames*]. *Città delle dame.* Edited by E. J. Richards. Introduction and translation by Patrizia Caraffi. Revised ed. Milan: Luni, 1998. [Bilingual Middle-French and Italian ed. with notes].

———. *The Book of the City of Ladies.* Translation with commentary by E. J. Richards. Foreword by Natalie Zemon Davis. New ed. New York: Persea, 1998.

Cicero, Marcus Tullius. *Rhetorica ad Herennium. See under* Pseudo-Cicero *below.*

Cornificius. *Rhetorica ad Herennium.* See under "Pseudo-Cicero" below.

Heloise. [Letter 3]. In *Letters of Abelard and Heloise,* translated with introduction by Betty Radice. New York: Penguin, 1974.

———. [Letter 3 = Letter 4]. In *Abélard. Historia Calamitatum.* Critical ed. by Jacques Monfrin. Bibliothèque des textes philosophiques. Paris: J. Vrin, 1959. Revised ed. 1978. [Latin text].

———. *Hrosvit: Opera Omnia,* Edited by Walter Berschin. Bibliotheca Scriptorum *Graecorum et Romanorum Teubneriana.* Munich and Leipzig, Germany: W. G. Saur, 2001.

———. *The Plays of Hrotsvit of Gandersheim* Translated by Katharina Wilson. Garland Library of Medieval Literature, 62. New York: Garland, 1989.

Jean de Meun. In *Guillaume de Lorris et Jean de Meun. Le Roman de la Rose,* critical ed. by Félix Lecoy, vols. 1: 125ff., 2–3. Classiques Français du Moyen Âge, 92, 95, 98. Paris: Honoré Champion, 1966–1976.

———. In *The Romance of the Rose,* translated with introduction and notes by Frances Horgan. World's Classics. Oxford and New York: Oxford University Press, 1994.

Kempe, Margery. *The Book of Margery Kempe.* Edited by Sanford B. Meech and Hope Emily Allen. Early English Text Society, o.s. 212. London: Humphrey Milford, 1940.

———. *The Book of Margery Kempe.* Translated by Barry A. Windeatt. Harmondsworth, U.K. and New York: Viking Penguin, 1985. New ed. Longman Annotated Texts. New York: Longman, 2000.

Marie de France. *Lais.* Edited by K. Warnke. Translated (Modern French) with commentary by Laurence Harf-Lancner. Lettres gothiques. Paris: Livre de Poche, 1990. [Bilingual Old-French and Modern French ed.].

———. *The Lais of Marie de France.* Translated by Robert Hanning and Joan Ferrante. 1978. Reprint Durham: Labyrinth, 1982.

Martianus Capella. *De Nuptiis Philologiae et Mercurii.* Critical ed. by James Willis. Bibliotheca Scriptores Graecorum et Romanorum Teubneriana. Leipzig, Germany: B. G. Teubner, 1983.

———. [Extracts in translation]. In *Readings in Medieval Rhetoric,* edited by Joseph M. Miller, Michael H. Prosser, and Thomas W. Benson. Bloomington: Indiana University Press, 1973.

Murphy, James J., ed. *Three Medieval Rhetorical Arts.* 1971. Reprint Berkeley: University of California Press, 1985.

Petroff, Elizabeth Alvilda, ed. *Medieval Women's Visionary Literature.* New York: Oxford University Press, 1986.

Pseudo-Cicero. *Rhetorica ad Herennium.* Latin text with an English trans. by Harry Caplan. Loeb Classical Library, 403. Cambridge, Mass.: Harvard University Press, 1999. Originally 1954.

Quintilian. *Institutio oratoria.* Edited and translated by H. E. Butler. 4 vols. Loeb Classical Library. 1920. Reprint Cambridge, Mass.: Harvard University Press, 1980.

Secondary Sources

Biesecker, Barbara A. "Coming to Terms with Recent Attempts to Write Women into the History of Rhetoric." In *Rethinking the History of Rhetoric: Essays on the Rhetorical Tradition*, edited by Takis Poulakos. Boulder, Colo.: Westview, 1993.

Burns, E. Jane. *Bodytalk: When Women Speak in Medieval French Literature*. Philadelphia: University of Pennsylvania Press, 1992.

Butler, Judith. *Gender Trouble: Feminism and the Subversion of Identity*. New York: Routledge, 1990.

Bynum, Caroline Walker. *Jesus as Mother: Studies in the Spirituality of the High Middle Ages*. Berkeley: University of California Press, 1982.

Cherewatuk, Karen, and Ulrike Wiethaus, eds. *Dear Sister—Medieval Women and the Epistolary Genre*. Middle Ages. Philadelphia: University of Pennsylvania Press, 1993.

Ede, Lisa, Cheryl Glenn, and Andrea Lunsford. "Border Crossings: Intersections of Rhetoric and Feminism." *Rhetorica* 13 (1995): 401–04.

Enders, Jody. "The Feminist Mnemonics of Christine de Pizan." *Modern Language Quarterly* 55 (1994): 231–49.

———. *The Medieval Theater of Cruelty: Rhetoric, Memory, Violence*. Ithaca, N.Y.: Cornell University Press, 1999.

———. *Rhetoric and the Origins of Medieval Drama*. Ithaca, N.Y.: Cornell University Press, 1992.

Erler, Mary C., and Maryanne Kowaleski, eds. *Gendering the Master Narrative: Women and Power in the Middle Ages*. Ithaca, N.Y.: Cornell University Press, 2003.

Fenster, Thelma, and Daniel L. Smail, eds. Fama: *The Politics of Talk & Reputation in Medieval Europe*. Ithaca, N.Y. and London: Cornell University Press, 2003.

Halperin, David M., John J. Winkler, and Froma I. Zeitlin, eds. *Before Sexuality: The Construction of Erotic Experience in the Ancient Greek World*. Princeton, N.J.: Princeton University Press, 1990.

Irvine, Martin. "Heloise and the Gendering of the Literate Subject." In *Criticism and Dissent in the Middle Ages*, edited by Rita Copeland, 87–114. Cambridge: Cambridge University Press, 1996.

Kelly, Douglas. *Medieval Imagination: Rhetoric and the Poetry of Courtly Love*. Madison: University of Wisconsin Press, 1978.

Kennedy, George A. *Classical Rhetoric and its Christian and Secular Tradition from Ancient to Modern Times*. Chapel Hill: University of North Carolina Press, 1980.

Lees, Clare A., and Gillian R. Overing. *Women and Clerical Culture in Anglo-Saxon England*. Middle Ages. Philadelphia: University of Pennnsylvania Press, 2001.

Lunsford, Andrea, ed. *Reclaiming Rhetorica: Women in the Rhetorical Tradition*. Pittsburgh: University of Pittsburgh Press, 1995.

The Medieval Epistle. Edited by Richard Utz and Carol Poster. *Disputatio*, 1 (1996).

Murphy, James J. *Rhetoric in the Middle Ages: A History of Rhetorical Theory from Saint Augustine to the Renaissance*. 1974. Reprint Berkeley: University of California Press, 1981.

Patterson, Lee. " 'For the Wyves love of Bathe': Feminine Rhetoric and Poetic Resolution in the *Roman de la rose* and the *Canterbury Tales*." *Speculum* 58 (1983).

Roberts, Anna, ed. *Violence against Women in Medieval Texts*. Gainesville: University Press of Florida, 1998.

Sullivan, Karen. *The Interrogation of Joan of Arc*. Medieval Cultures, 20. Minneapolis & London: University of Minnesota Press, 1999.

Woods, Marjorie Curry. "Rape and the Pedagogical Rhetoric of Sexual Violence." In *Criticism and Dissent in the Middle Ages*, edited by Rita Copeland, 56–86. Cambridge: Cambridge University Press, 1996.

JODY ENDERS

ROMAN DE LA ROSE, DEBATE OF THE (1401–1404). The *Debat sur Le Roman de la Rose* (*The Romance of the Rose*)—also called the "Querelle (Quarrel) de la *Rose*"—occurring through a series of letters exchanged among the elite Parisian intellectual and

Que ia mille exes my ferose.
ffore sa voulente et la mope.

se la mant iouplist de la rose.

The Lover embraces the Rose. From the *Romance of the Rose*, illustrated by Robert Testard, fifteenth century. Douce 195 folio 155v. © The Art Archive/Bodleian Library Oxford/The Bodleian Library.

literary milieu, was one of the first debates about the status of women in literary history. The issues and aspects debated also furnished a milestone in the development of gender theory and its discourse.

It addresses exclusively Jean de Meun's continuation of the *Roman de la Rose*: the 17,000 lines added during 1269 and 1278 to Guillaume de Lorris's original 4,000 lines, composed c.1236. Lorris inaugurates and describes a very conventional allegorical dream vision of a love quest: the Lover, a naïve narrator, alternatingly hindered and helped by various allegorical figures representing psychological and social facets of all love affairs, hopes to win the rose ensconced in the garden. The rose symbolizes the lovely maiden he ardently desires. Lorris's Lover's quest is typical of that informing many love quests in the so-called *fin'amors* (courtly love) tradition most famously discussed by Andreas Capellanus (twelfth century), to denote a sort of idealized, yet intensely erotic type of love, usually outside of marriage. The fulfillment of the Lover's desire presents a quandary inherent in courtly love values: How can the Narrator-Lover consummate his sensual love for the rose without defiling his idealized image of her? Lorris leaves his part unfinished, whether due to premature death or inability to resolve his quandary about love. More recent critics argue that Lorris left his romance unfinished on purpose, as a maneuver to guarantee his immortality by forcing continuation of his work (Hult 1986). Jean de Meun changes Lorris's very conventional allegorical dream vision into a more humanistic, encyclopedic reflection—often irreverently incisive about the very work he claims to be continuing—on various topics. Lorris's original main plot, the conquest of the rose, resurfaces only from time to time, returning to the forefront of the narration when the rose approaches its final destiny, its defenders' defeat and the plucking of its rosebud by the lover.

In response to an epistolary conversation about the merits of Jean de Meun's *Roman de la Rose* among the provost of Lille, Jean de Montreuil (1354–1418), Christine de Pizan (1365–1430?), another member of Parisian officialdom known only as the "notable clerc" (notable cleric), and himself, dating from the beginning of 1401, Jean de Montreuil composed the famous *Opusculum gallicum* (*A Little Work in French*). The main arguments of this laudatory treatise on Jean de Meun's *Rose*, unfortunately lost to us today, have been reconstructed from the ensuing letters by modern scholars like Eric Hicks in his edition of the Debate. The correspondence resulting from this very questionable piece of work in Christine de Pizan's eyes triggered the first epistolary debate in the French literary world. Christine, in response to her opponent, sent him a counter-treatise in which she primarily rebukes the obscene language used by various allegorical personages in the *Rose*, such as Reason, as well as the defamations of women expressed by the Old Woman, the Jealous Husband, and Genius. Jean de Montreuil, in turn, obtained the support of his colleague Gontier Col, who avidly attacked Christine in two epistles openly asking her to withdraw her statements that, in his mind, constitute an insult to the greatest literary work of contemporary times. Christine, however, did no such thing and, contrary to her adversaries' demands, elevated the Debate to a more public sphere by publishing the correspondence exchanged up to that point (beginning of 1402). She then sent this compilation to Isabeau of Bavaria, queen of France, accompanied by a letter asking for her support. To mark her point, Christine then took advantage of the tradition of St. Valentine's Day to found the "Order of the Rose" with the publication of her *Dit de la Rose* (*Tale of the Rose*) where, this time in verse form, she again asserts her position against the *Rose*. Christine's most powerful supporter in the matter was Jean Gerson (1363–1429), chancellor of Notre Dame and of the University of Paris, who, even though not exactly echoing Christine's criticism, also severely refuted certain aspects of the *Rose* in a treatise written in May 1402 and then in a series of public sermons given in December of 1402. One of the anti-*Rose* criticisms Christine contributed to the Debate concerns one of her pervasive preoccupations, expressed for the first time in the *Epistre au Dieu d'Amours* (*Epistle of the God of Love*) (1399) two years earlier: the fragility of female honor that is incessantly endangered by masculine behavior associated with courtly love or even in learned works by male clerics. Her outrage is aimed at the most effective tool any writer or poet possesses: language, which Christine considers in the *Roman de la Rose* to be searingly offensive (*mots actisans et enflammans*: "provocative and inflaming words") to women (see especially Solterer).

After two years of epistolary exchange, rather than abandoning her pursuit of protecting and defending female virtue and honor, she veered away from this genre to express her views in a possibly more effective manner. In the two years following the Debate, Christine composed *Le Livre de la Cité des dames* (*The Book of the City of Ladies*, 1404–1405), probably her best-known text today thanks to the emergence of feminist studies. She followed it with a more practical-manual sequel, *Le Livre des Trois Vertus* (*The Book of the Three Virtues*, 1405–1406) a *summa* of advice on how to acquire virtue. This text is addressed to women of all social strata: the young noble woman, the married woman, the widow, the prostitute, and so forth.

By engaging herself as she did in the Debate about the *Roman de la Rose*, Christine de Pizan fundamentally changed her literary orientation and moved away from her lyric-poetic creation of ballads, rondeaux, and virelays to a more pragmatic expression that also extends to her works following the Debate. As a female reader of masculine texts, of which *Roman de la Rose* is but one example, and as a female writer who succeeded in penetrating the close, male-centered circle of clerics at the end of the Middle Ages, she changed the way women should look at the process of reading. Female reading of misogynist texts should not lead to a loss of faith in the female sex and all the characteristics attached to it by the literary canon. Rather, women should reread: that is, they should revise what they read as Christine herself rewrites masculine historiography in the *Cité des Dames* to read with a restored female dignity.

Her later diptych, the *Cité des dames*, and its sequel, the *Trois Vertus*, conveyed that very message to Christine's contemporary and future female readership. Contrary to Jean de Meun's *Roman de la Rose*, her *Trois Vertus* can be read publicly in front of women without any danger of offending anyone, as she says in the conclusion to her work. As Susan Schibanoff has pointed out, Christine's own "instruction in the art of reading as a woman serves her well." On the other hand, readers like David Hult observe in her mandates a propensity for censorship (1997). Christine probably had a similar goal in mind when she focused her attention on rewriting Boccaccio's *De claris mulieribus* (*Famous Women*, c.1350–1360?) in the *Cité des dames* or on providing women with a manual on how to acquire virtue in the *Trois Vertus*. On a more global level, Christine's involvement in the Debate presages the *querelle des femmes* (quarrel about women) tradition of the Renaissance through seventeenth centuries—not only in France, but throughout Europe.

See also *Belle Dame sans Merci*; Boccaccio, Women in, *De Claris Mulieribus*; Capellanus, Andreas; Christine de Pizan; Epistolary Authors, Women as

BIBLIOGRAPHY

Primary Sources

Christine de Pisan, Jean Gerson, et al. *Le Débat sur* Le Roman de la Rose. Critical ed. by Eric Hicks. Bibliothèque du XVe siècle, 43. Paris: Honoré Champion, 1977. Reprint Geneva: Slatkine, 1997. [Authoritative ed. of all related original Middle-French and Latin texts, with Modern French translations and commentary].

———. *La Querelle de la Rose: Letters and Documents*. Edited and translated by Joseph L. Baird and John R. Kane. Chapel Hill: University of North Carolina Press, 1978. [English trans. only].

Lorris, Guillaume de, and Jean de Meun. *Le Roman de la Rose*. Critical ed. by Félix Lecoy. 3 vols. Classiques Français du Moyen âge, 92, 95, 98. Paris: Honoré Champion, 1965–1970. Reprinted 1970–1976, 1982. [Old-French texts with Modern French commentary].

———. *The Romance of the Rose*. Translated by Frances Horgan. The World's Classics. Oxford: Oxford University Press, 1994.

Secondary Sources

Badel, Pierre-Yves. Le Roman de la rose *au XIVe siècle. Étude de la réception de l'oeuvre*. Geneva: Droz, 1980.

Brownlee, Kevin. "Discourses of the Self. Christine de Pizan and the *Romance of the Rose*." In *Rethinking the* Romance of the Rose. *Text, Image, Reception*, edited by Kevin Brownlee and Sylvia Huot, 234–61. Philadelphia: University of Pennsylvania Press, 1992.

Fenster, Thelma S., and Clare A. Lees, eds. *Gender in Debate from the Early Middle Ages to the Renaissance*. New York: PalgraveMacmillan, 2003.

Hicks, Eric. "Situation du débat sur le *Roman de la rose*." In *Une femme de lettres au moyen âge. Études autour de Christine de Pizan*, edited by Liliane Dulac and Bernard Ribémont, 51–68. Orléans: Paradigme, 1995.

Hult, David. *Self-fulfilling Prophecies: Readership and Authority in the First Roman de la Rose*. Cambridge: Cambridge University Press, 1986.

———. "The *Roman de la Rose*, Christine de Pizan, and the *querelle des femmes*." In *The Cambridge Companion to Medieval Women's Writing*, edited by Carolyn Dinshaw and David Wallace, 184–94. Cambridge: Cambridge University Press, 2003.

———. "Words and Deeds: Jean de Meun's *Romance of the Rose* and the Hermeneutics of Censorship." *New Literary History* 28 (1997): 345–66.

Huot, Sylvia. *The* Romance of the Rose *and its Medieval Readers: Interpretation, Reception, Manuscript Transmission*. Cambridge: Cambridge University Press, 1993.

McMunn, Meradith. "Programs of Illustration in *Roman de la rose* Manuscripts Owned by Patrons and Friends of Christine de Pizan." In *Au champ des escriptures. IIIe Colloque international sur*

Christine de Pizan, edited by Eric Hicks et al., 737–58. Études christiniennes, 6. Paris: Honoré Champion, 2000.

McWebb, Christine. "The *Roman de la rose* and the *Livre des trois vertus*: The Never-Ending Debate." In *Au champ des escriptures* [see above entry], 309–24.

Potansky, Peter. *Der Streit um den Rosenroman*. Munich: Fink, 1972.

Richards, Earl Jeffrey. "Rejecting Essentialism and Gendered Writing: The Case of Christine de Pizan." In *Gender and Text in the Later Middle Ages*, edited by Jane Chance, 96–131. Gainesville: University Press of Florida, 1996.

Schibanoff, Susan. "Taking the Gold out of Egypt: The Art of Reading as a Woman." In *Gender and Reading: Essays on Readers, Texts and Contexts*, edited by Elizabeth A. Flynn and Patrocinio P. Schweickart, 83–106. Baltimore and London: Johns Hopkins University Press, 1986.

Solterer, Helen. "Flaming Words: Verbal Violence and Gender in Premodern Paris." *Romanic Review* 86 (1995): 355–78.

CHRISTINE McWEBB

ROSAMOND, FAIR (c.1133–c.1176). Most probably identifiable as Rosamond Clifford, Rosamond was the beautiful mistress of King Henry II of England (1133–1189), thus arousing the jealousy of Henry's wife, Eleanor of Aquitaine (1122?–1204), and becoming one of the most frequently rewritten medieval women figures in later literature, surpassing even Jane Shore (d. 1527) in popularity as an "unfortunate concubine" personage. Her basic history is this: Rosamond was born one of six children to Walter de Clifford (d. 1190?) and Margaret de Toeni, either at Fretherne Lodge in Gloucestershire (western England) or in nearby Clifford in Herefordshire (near the Welsh border). Walter, a Norman who had fought for Henry in Wales, seems to have been a prosperous knight, owning several manors and endowing several monasteries, notably Godstow, where his daughter was educated. Rosamond and the king met (perhaps during the Welsh campaign) and fell in love in c.1165, some thirteen years after his marriage to Eleanor. To protect her from prying eyes in general and his wife's wrath in particular, Henry had a maze constructed at Woodstock Park, a splendid royal refuge and palace built by Henry I (1068–1135). No one but Henry (and perhaps a keeper) knew the clue to the labyrinth during their decade-long affair, but somehow Queen Eleanor finally found her way through it, confronted Rosamond, and forced her to die either by drinking a cup of poison or by a dagger. Rosamond chose to die by poisoning, and was buried by the nuns at Godstow. King Henry supposedly imprisoned Eleanor for her vindictiveness (though historians now say that the queen was already imprisoned by him for having led her sons in rebellion against him, and thus could not have murdered Rosamond [see Kelly]). An epilogue appended to some versions relates how, fifteen years after Rosamond's death, Hugh, Bishop of Lincoln, shocked at how the Godstow nuns treated her tomb so reverently in special rituals, ordered them to remove the sinner's body from the church. This the nuns did, but they also secretly gave it a proper burial. An epitaph is also often mentioned and cited, but it is the addition of a comic or befuddled later author, since the tribute obviously refers to Rosamunda, queen of the Lombards (sixth century).

Her status as mistress to Henry II is recorded by contemporary commentators: the chronicle of Henry II's and Richard I's reigns (1169–1192) commonly attributed to Abbot Benedict of Peterborough, the treatise on the education of princes by Giraldus Cambrensis

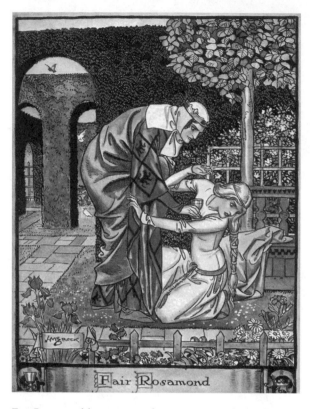

Fair Rosamond being given the poison cup of "deadlye draught" by the Queen. From H. M. Brock's illustrations to *A Book of Old Ballads*, 1934. © 2003 Charles Walker/Topfoto/The Image Works.

(Gerald of Wales, 1146?–1223), and in chronicles by Roger de Hoveden (d. 1201?). Ever thereafter, English chroniclers such as Ranulf Higden (Trevisa's version, 1357) and Robert Fabyan (1516) added their own touches, quickly assimilated by their colleagues and successors, who copied and propagated these fabrications. Then came the poets, prose writers, and dramatists who have enriched her story with additional characters, plot twists, and shifts in time and place, as Virgil Heltzel has carefully documented, from the sixteenth (beginning with Samuel Daniel's *Complaint of Rosamond*, 1592) through the twenty-first centuries (Richard C. Low's *Tigress and the Rose: Eleanor and Rosamond*, 2003). Nor is this tradition confined to England. In Spain, for example, no less an author than Cervantes significantly restyled her in his verse romance, *Los trabajos de Persiles y Sigismunda* (*The Adventures of Persiles and Sigismunda*, 1617), in which she is a sixteenth-century "lustful courtesan," a "telling embodiment of lust and its powers of exploitation" (Lucas), rather than the tragic victim of lust and jealousy more typical of the Rosamond tradition.

See also Eleanor of Aquitaine; Godiva, Lady; Shore, Elizabeth (Jane)

BIBLIOGRAPHY

Primary Sources

Benedict of Peterborough. *Gesta Regis Henrici Secundi*. Edited by William Stubbs, 2: 231–32. Rolls Series, 49. London: Longmans, Green, 1867.

Giraldus Cambrensis. *De principis instructione*. Edited by George F. Warner. In *Giraldi Cambrensis Opera*, Rolls Series, 21, vol. 8: 232. London: H. M. Stationery/Eyre & Spottiswoode, 1891. Reprint Nendeln, Germany: Kraus, 1966.

———. *Concerning the Instruction of Princes*. Translated by Joseph Stevenson. Felinfach, Dyfed, Wales: J. M. F. Books, 1991.

Roger de Hoveden. *Chronica*. Edited by William Stubbs, 3: 167–68. Rolls Series, 51. London: Longman, 1870. Reprint Wiesbaden, Germany: Kraus, 1964.

———. *Annals of Roger de Hoveden [. . .] 732–1201*. Translated, with notes, by Henry T. Riley. London: Bohn, 1853. Reprint New York: AMS, 1968. Reprint Felinfach, Dyfed: Llanerch, 1997.

Secondary Sources

Heltzel, Virgil B. *Fair Rosamond: A Study of the Development of a Literary Theme*. Northwestern University Studies in the Humanities, 16. Evanston, Ill.: Northwestern University Presss, 1947. Reprint New York: AMS, 1970.

Kelly, Amy. *Eleanor of Aquitaine and the Four Kings.* Cambridge, Mass.: Harvard University Press, 1950.

Lucas, Karen. "Rosamunda: A Cervantine Mingling of History and Fiction in *Persiles.*" *Cervantes: Bulletin of the Cervantes Society of America* 10 (1990): 87–92.

NADIA MARGOLIS

RULE FOR ANCHORESSES. *See Ancrene Riwle*

RULES FOR CANONESSES, NUNS, AND RECLUSES. With the proliferation of monasteries in the early Middle Ages, each with its different ideal, a need arose for practical guidelines to maintain order and harmony while also honoring the collective identity of the convent as its members pursued their spiritual goals, or, in the case of recluses, to help them in their solitary path of spiritual perfection. These guidelines, or "rules," as they were called, evolved over time, deriving their ideals from the writings of the Church Fathers (early founders of Church doctrine, such as Jerome and Augustine) and earlier, Eastern theological sources, then, as various rules were devised, later ones built upon their precursors. The more complete rules governed all aspects of life in the cloister or cell, not only day by day, but even by hours, scheduling proper times for prayer, meals, work, and contemplation—including thought progressions—depending on the monastery's individual purpose and ambience. Although, as the names of the rules imply (Rule of Basil, Rule of Augustine, etc.), it was the male clerics who usually wrote the rules, even those intended for female communities, this was often done in consultation with the abbess and other leading members of a monastery. It is no coincidence that the men who wrote these rules tended to have resourceful monastic "sisters" (whether biological or spiritual) who often made names for themselves and doubtless inspired their brothers to consider the role of women as serious members of the Church, both Eastern and Western.

The principal categories of female religious for whom rules were written also require some preliminary definition: "canonesses" (a term not used before the eighth century), female counterparts to "canons," were usually noblewomen living as a religious community but without renouncing their property; "nuns," in correct Church usage, belonged to orders of women living in strict enclosure, a cloister; "recluses" were those who vowed to live in isolation from the world, in meditation and prayer. Female recluses, like the males, existed according to different subcategories: anchoresses led solitary, silent lives of prayer and self-mortification within cells or "anchorholds." "Hermits" are solitary but not necessarily confined. "Coenobites," like many anchoresses, confined themselves to separate dwellings, but these would be grouped together. Canonesses therefore enjoyed the most worldly contact while recluses chose the least; for recluses, solitude was their community. There was also a fair amount of variety among the different orders of nuns. These rules were also adapted for double monasteries: those housing both a male and a female convent, separately but contiguously, and governed by a common superior.

The three major Western Church-approved rules, originally meant for male monasteries but that would later be used for women, include one attributed to St. Augustine (354–430), one devised by St. Benedict for his monks (c.540), and the *Regula prima* of St. Francis (1223). The more recent of these derived to some extent from the earlier ones and other sources while also contributing to later ones. Certain favored aspects, such as enclosure for monastic men as well as women, existed before these rules were formulated. Generally speaking, as these rules were taking shape, originality was less important than the rule's viability for its specific community.

Earlier, the Rule, or Rules, of St. Basil, written by Basil the Great of Caesarea (c.330–379) during 358–360s, became and remains the chief rule guiding the Eastern Church, based on, among other sources, the Coptic rule of St. Pachomius (d. 346), founder of coenobitic Christian monasticism (later translated into Latin by St. Jerome [d. 420]). Basil's sister was Macrina the Younger (c.327–380), who probably helped him shape his rule, since she was the family's spiritual mother. It would also influence St. Benedict's and other later rules adopted by the Western Church. Basil's rule actually underwent a metamorphosis, beginning with the eighty so-called "moral rules" and then culminating in his *Asceticon*, based on his experiences debating questions on the monastic life. In fact, the *Asceticon* is presented as a series of questions and answers. The *Asceticon* too went through several versions: one translated from Greek into Latin by Rufinus (397), some parts in Syriac as well as in Greek, revised by Basil's followers, and finally, the most widespread version—called the "Vulgate" *Asceticon* (sixth century), containing moral rules, the *Epitamia*, prescribing punishment for offenders, fifty-five questions and answers on practical details of monastic life, and 315 "short rules" for how to implement the other sections. As its title indicates, the *Asceticon* advocated an austere way of life, but not so strict as to attract the more radical element like the desert hermits. Instead, asceticism is seen a means of service to God, practiced communally; prayer is scheduled according to specific hours, along with manual labor and charitable works, especially ministering to the poor. Basil's rule also prescribed chastity as well as poverty—two important aspects of most monastic rules in the West. Children were educated in schools attached to the monasteries. Overall, Basil's rule conceived of the monastery as a spiritual family living under one roof (Ranft).

The so-called Rule of St. Augustine is more elusive because of its origins. It consists of various monastic texts (whose interrelationship has been disputed)—principally, the *Ordo monasterii* (*System for the Monastery*), the *Praeceptum* (*Precept*), and Augustine's *Epistula* (*Epistle*) 211, paras. 5–16—which were later made by others into a rule and (in the case of the first two texts) attributed to the famed bishop of Hippo, in North Africa (354–430), whose interest in monastic ideals is evident in his *Confessions*. Among the significant women in Augustine's life was not only his mother, St. Monica, but also others more directly associated with monasticism, like the Roman matron-turned-ascetic Marcella (d. c.410), St. Melania the Younger (d. c.438), and Augustine's sister, for whose monastery at Hippo he wrote part of what became known as his rule. This part of Augustine's rule, his 211th *Epistula*, written in 423, was definitely intended for women and, though largely ignored at first, would eventually become adapted for monks as well and widely accepted in the twelfth century (after the eleventh-century formation of the Augustinian Canons Regular—so-called because of their adherence to his rule [*regula*]), by such major orders as the Dominicans, the Augustinian Friars, and the Ursuline nuns. Austere but not extreme, Augustine rule's main contribution to monastic regulation was the primacy assigned to the community's quest for perfection over the individual's, despite Augustine's early admiration for the solitary ideal of the coenobitic ascetics. He therefore stressed, for his nuns, authority and obedience to the mother superior, since it was these qualities that guaranteed the monastery's stability against the menace of rebellious and fractious nuns, or parties of nuns. In Augustine's scheme, no single member could attain perfection apart from the whole community.

The first monastic rule known to have been written exclusively and completely for women was composed by Caesarius of Arles (470–542), for his sister, Caesaria, who was equally committed to the monastic life. Upon rising to become bishop of Arles, Caesarius designated his sister to lead her own monastery, St. John's, at Arles (512). She proved to be an excellent abbess, under whom her community prospered by the tenets of her brother's rule for nuns, which was continued by their successor, Caesaria the Younger. More precisely, Caesarius wrote two rules: one for monks and the longer one for nuns. In constructing his rule, Caesarius, nurtured by the flourishing abbey at Lérins (founded c.410)—a small island (now: Saint-Honorat) off Cannes, southern France—fused its scholarly tradition with Augustine's rule and the *Institutes* of the Scythian monk John Cassian (c.360–c.430), the latter influenced by Pachomius. Caesarius emphasized strict enclosure and offered many details for living the ideal female monastic life in Merovingian times; the nuns renounced all worldly possessions on entering the convent to live in virtuous, egalitarian poverty with frequent fasting and prayer. All the nuns, except for the abbess and prioress, shared in cooking, sewing, and cleaning, and bedrooms were communal. Yet they were also expected to pursue some kind of literate, intellectual activity for at least two hours per day; even when at manual labor, a nun read to them. They built a school for the younger members and a library. Though historians used to downplay the impact of Caesarius's rule on monastic history, they have since surmised that this rule may have helped to foster increased numbers of enclosed monasteries in France by the mid-sixth century. Furthermore, Donatus of Besançon would borrow from it to compose his own a century later, as would St. Radegund (c.518–587) in founding her monastery of the Holy Cross.

The Rule of St. Benedict, written around 535–545, by Benedict of Nursia (c.480–550), would become the best known and most influential of all monastic rules because of its common-sense equilibrium between moderate ascetic spirituality and administrative practicality, with an aura of prudence and humanity. Like Caesarius and Augustine, Benedict too had a sister, St. Scholastica (c.480–c.543), who established a convent at Plombariola, near Benedict's renowned monastery at Monte Cassino (between Rome and Naples). Scholastica, who regularly discussed spiritual matters with her brother, would become the patron saint of female Benedictine monasteries around the world. Benedict's rule functions as a decisive point in the constitutional history of Western monasticism. Under this rule, his monks elected the patriarchal abbot for life. The abbot appointed his council members with whom he consulted on routine affairs, but all the brethren gathered to advise the abbot on matters of grave common interest. Each monk took the vow of stability, binding him to lifelong residence in the monastery of his profession. The central duty of the monastery was the Divine Office (*Opus Dei*), accomplished through private prayer, spiritual reading, and manual labor. Benedict also prescribed the correct amounts and types of food and drink (for example, each monk's daily ration: one-quarter liter of wine; one pound of bread, made more of coarse flour than fine; no meat from quadrupeds, etc.) with special provisions for the sick. He outlined disciplinary measures for offenders, and other similar details, allowing for special situations when necessary. Promoted by Pope Gregory the Great as of 600, this rule gradually spread throughout Europe so that, by the time of Charlemagne (c.742–814), the Rule of St. Benedict was the common code of most of the monasteries of his Empire, though often altered, extended, and in some cases, obscured by liturgical and other customs. Women's communities also adopted this rule, in which cases the chapters on the priesthood were eliminated and the canonesses did not take the vow but remained in the religious community.

Meanwhile, St. Columbanus (d. 615), a learned, charismatic abbot and missionary from Ireland, sailed to Gaul (now France and Belgium) and founded several monasteries, including Luxeuil, in the Vosges mountains, in 590, before moving on to convert barbarian tribes like the Alamanii and finally to settle in Bobbio, Italy. Columbanus's severe Monk's Rule and Communal Rule, infused with Irish tradition (which would later cause him difficulties with the Gallic bishops), revolutionized monastic living by emphasizing confession, private penance, and constant reading, which revitalized Christianity's presence in Gaul. Merovingian Frankish aristocrats took an interest in his precepts, but later, Luxeuil, for example, after its destruction by the Saracens (732) and restoration under Charlemagne, adopted the Benedictine rule.

Both Abbot Waldebert, a successor to Columbanus at Luxeuil, and Bishop Donatus of Besançon (fl. 627–658) composed rules expressly for nuns that relied heavily on Caesarius's rule, adding their own modifications and aspects of other rules to suit their needs. Waldebert, having previously spread Columbanus's rule, on finding it too severe, tempered it with details from Benedict's rule. Donatus's rule (c.620) eased the requirement of strict enclosure for rural monasteries. He concerns himself with the quality of the abbess and the instruments of good works, with how the old and infirm are to be governed, with women who come late—whether to the work of God or to meals—with fostering reverence in prayer, and the observance of various holy days. It also dictates how the sisters should strive for silence, daily confession, and avoid gossip, criticism, and contention. Waldebert urged abbesses to review their nuns' faults systematically three times a day.

During burgeoning Renaissance of the twelfth century in France, two religious luminaries, Heloise (d. 1164) and the renowned, controversial philosopher Abelard (1097–1142/3), are usually remembered for their tragic love affair (1116–1117) and the eloquent letters recollecting it. But it is also essential to note that, for a greater portion of their lives, as also revealed in their letters (referred to as the "Letters of Direction," distinct from the abovementioned "Personal Letters"), both were serious intellectuals and very capable monastic administrators, with Heloise devoting herself to the house of nuns called the Paraclete since her arrival there in 1129 (near Troyes, north-central France). The Paraclete's original base, an oratory (chapel), had been founded by Abelard. In her third letter, Heloise asks Abelard to explain the origin of nuns as an institution and also to provide her with a rule for her convent: the first to enable her to understand how nuns came to be, according to theological doctrine, and the second request, for the rule to enable her to serve the Paraclete more completely and with a deeper understanding of the goals of the monastic life (a life, after all, not originally chosen by her, but rather imposed on her). As she also avers in her letter, she had grown discontented with the Benedictine rule, under which she had lived until then (about fourteen years), and on which she offers a critique of its sections unsuitable for women. Abelard obliges with a long letter, its outline laced with Classical and religious citations and commentary, conveying a rule that borrowed from Benedict while emending it according to Heloise's expressed points of the older rule's inadequacy or her disagreement with it. Abelard's and Heloise's changes sought to accommodate women's different (from the men's) physical capabilities (affecting diet, fasting, and dress; hours of prayer as well as manual labor), their desire for more spiritual training (thus a longer novitiate), and so forth. Abelard's rule thus mandates more comfortable and practical habit for the nuns, he adjusts the standards of cleanliness and sanitary protection to women, he forbids self-imposed fasting and unnecessary mortification of the flesh, allows the nuns more sleep than did the Benedictines' demanding schedule of canonical hours, and so on. Moreover, since he and Heloise keenly advocated education, literacy should be afforded all capable nuns, while the less capable ones could be consigned to manual tasks. As in Abelard's own theology (much to the dismay of mystics like Bernard of Clairvaux, his chief adversary), rational understanding was essential to worshipping God, although he also invokes the Bride of Christ (*Brautmystik*) concept, in depicting the nun's relationship to Christ (the Bridegroom).

By the twelfth century also, rules for recluses appear to have grown quite lax, if we are to believe the Saxon-born Cistercian abbot of Rievaulx (in Yorkshire), St. Aelred (or Ailred, 1109–1167). Composed for his anchorite sister, Aelred's rule, *De institutione inclusarum* (*On the Education of Recluses*, c.1160) purports to guide her toward living as a true recluse, instead of the current trend he deplores, in which anchoresses could be found gossiping through their windows with outside visitors and even prostitutes. Aelred's motive here lies not in stereotypical male protectivism but in the deeper principles behind anchoritism: enclosure enables the anchorite to resemble Christ more closely, since, as Aelred says, Christ first assumed human form within a virgin's womb. Aelred's anchoritic vision also engages the *Brautmystik* when characterizing Christ as the anchorite's Bridegroom (Cannon).

Far better known was the English Rule for Anchoresses, the *Ancrene Riwle* or *Ancrene Wisse* (thirteenth century), for which Aelred's rule served as the primary source. In distinguishing between recluses and canonesses, it states that "the true recluses are indeed birds of heaven, that fly aloft and sit on the green boughs singing merrily; that is, they meditate, enraptured, upon the blessedness of heaven that never fadeth, but is ever green, singing right merrily." Yet this fails to represent the anchoress's true condition, also clearly represented in *Ancrene Wisse*, as one of "confinedness and bitterness" (ed. White, 173), since this is the true way to Christ.

St. Francis (1181/2–1226) and St. Clare (1193/4–1253), founders of the Franciscan Order (for men) and Poor Ladies, later called Poor Clares (for women), respectively, represent another important monastic regulatory movement. Profoundly inspired by Francis's teachings, the aristocratic Clare renounced her worldly possessions and followed him. Frances first placed her at Benedictine houses in Bastia and Panzo, which she left to pursue and promote her own, Franciscan, ideal at San Damiano, near Assisi, central Italy. Clare was made abbess of San Damiano (1215), a position she held for the rest of her life. Predicated on Francis's *Formula vitae* (*Rule for Life*, 1215), Clare's rule, which she, too, titled the *Formula vitae*, was the first rule composed by a woman; it also won papal approbation (Innocent III). Stressing complete poverty (indeed, poverty was a rare, papally granted "privilege" to Clare, meaning all members must renounce all possessions) and the imitation of Christ, her rule was the most austere of any women's religious community. Unlike most other monastic orders, however, the Franciscans and Poor Clares entered the cities to perform charitable works by day, returning to their cells for solitary contemplation at night. How both the Franciscans and Poor Clares managed to elude the usual pressure for new orders to accept an existing rule, such as the Benedictine, attests to the aptness of their spiritual doctrine and their diplomatic skills with Innocent III (d. 1216). This changed in 1218 under the new pope, Honorius III, whose cardinal protector, Ugolino Segni, appropriated all Poor Clare houses for the papacy, imposing on them a rule similar to the Benedictine and thus strict enclosure. This new rule for the Franciscan women denied them their chief identifying traits: complete poverty and the imitation of Christ. The formidable Clare's continued, relentless resistance to these changes caused Segni, now Pope Gregory IX (as of 1226), to allow her house at San Damiano the original privilege of poverty while deleting it for the other Poor Clare houses. Interestingly enough, Clare viewed absolute poverty as more essential to imitating Christ than freedom of movement, asserting that one could manage to imitate Him within monastery walls. As she lay dying, the papacy made the gesture of finally approving her original rule, only to overturn this decree after her death. From 1219 to 1263 she had provided her own and sister communities with at least six rules in all (Petroff).

In the fourteenth and early fifteenth centuries, recluses were given a rule by the Parisian theologian, preacher, and reformer, Jean Gerson (1363–1429), who sensed the same sort of spiritual decline among them as Aelred had earlier. Gerson, orator and chancellor of Notre Dame and of the University of Paris, was exceptionally conversant in Classical Latin literature as well as scripture. His rule for recluses draws upon the older rules, glossed by him with a mosaic of scriptural texts to fashion an ascetic and religious lifestyle. He enjoined the recluse to exercise an ardent zeal for the observance of the laws of God, to abstain moderately from food and drink, to strive for solitude of mind; to read spiritual books; to obey the superior and to hold all uncommon visions suspect, unless they clearly lead to humility contempt for the vices.

These rules, whose texts were usually housed within the monastery's library, were most commonly disseminated within their communities via the saints' lives, customarily read at mealtimes or during work periods as inspirational models. These *vitae* often contained details of the rules to highlight the subject's holiness and obedience. In a manner analogous to the rule of enclosure itself, the rules for women religious responded to a need for protection and self-understanding as well as discipline, with the abbesses governing out of a sense of maternal responsibility, during a dangerous and uncertain era (McNamara et al.; Ranft).

See also *Ancrene Riwle*; Beguines; Birgitta of Sweden, St.; Bride of Christ/*Brautmystik*; Caesaria, St.; Clare of Assisi, St.; Convents; Double Monasteries; Dress, Religious Women's (Western, Christian); Heloise; Julian of Norwich; Katherine of Sutton; Law, Canon, Women in; Maria of Venice (Maria Sturion); Melania the Younger, St.; Merici, Angela, St.; Music in Medieval Nunneries; Nunneries, Merovingian; *Periculoso*; Radegund, St.; Sister-Books (*Schwesternbücher*); Syrian-Christian Women; Virginity

BIBLIOGRAPHY

Primary Sources
Abelard and Heloise. *Letters* [Heloise's 3rd, Abelard's first response (On the Origins of Nuns)]. Edited by James T. Muckle. *Medieval Studies* 15 (1953): 240–81.
———. [Letter containing Abelard's Rule (Latin Text)]. In the most complete collection of his works, *Patrologia Latina*, 178, edited by J.-P. Migne.
———. [Letters here numbered 5 (Heloise's request, and critique of Benedictine Rule) and 7 (Abelard's Rule)]. In *The Letters of Abelard and Heloise*, edited and translated by Betty Radice, 159–79, 183–269. London: Penguin, 1974. [English texts with commentary].
Aelred/Ailred of Rievaulx. *De institutione inclusarum*. In *"Quand Jésus eut douze ans,"* edited and translated (French) by Joseph Dubois. Sources chrétiennes, 60. Paris: Éditions du Cerf, 1958. [Latin and French texts with commentary].

————. *Aelred of Rievaulx's De institutione inclusarum: Two English Versions*. Edited by John Ayto and Alexandra Barratt. Early English Text Society, 287. London and New York: Oxford University Press, 1984. [Old English Texts].

————. *Rule of Life for a Recluse*. In *The Works of Aelred of Rievaulx*, vol. 1: *Treatises: The Pastoral Prayer*, translated by Mary P. Macpherson. Introduction by David Knowles. Cistercian Fathers, 2. Spencer, Mass.: Cistercian Publications, 1971. Reprint Kalamazoo, Mich.: Medieval Institute, 1982.

Ancrene Wisse: Guide for Anchoresses. Edited and translated by Hugh White. Harmondsworth, U.K.: Penguin, 1993.

Augustine. *Augustine of Hippo and His Monastic Rule*. Edited and translated by George Lawless. Oxford and New York: Oxford University Press, 1987. [Latin and English].

Basil the Great. *Regulae* [All 3 forms]. In *Patrologia Graeca*, edited by J.-P. Migne, 31: 653–870, 881–1428.

————. [Rule]. *The Ascetic Works of St. Basil*. Translated with introduction and notes by William K. L. Clarke. Translations of Christian Literature: Greek Texts. London: Christian Knowledge; New York: Macmillan, 1925.

Benedict of Nursia. *RB 1980: The Rule of St. Benedict in Latin and English*, edited and translated by Timothy Fry, Imogene Baker, et al. Collegeville, Minn.: Liturgical Press, 1981.

Caesarius of Arles. [*Regula sanctarum virginum*]. In *Œuvres monastiques*, introduced, edited and translated (French) by Adalbert de Vogüé and Joël Courreau. 2 vols. Paris: Éditions du Cerf, 1988.

————. *Rule for Nuns*. Translated with introduction by Mary McCarthy. Studies in Medieval History, n.s. 16. Washington, D.C.: Catholic University of America Press, 1960.

Cassian, John. *Institutions cénobitiques*. Edited and translated (French) by J. C. Guy. Sources chrétiennes, 109. Paris: Éditions du Cerf, 1971. [Latin and French texts, with French commentary].

Columbanus. *Regula S. Columbani*. In *Patrologia Latina*, edited by J.-P. Migne, 80.

Donatus of Besançon. *Regula ad virginis*. In *Patrologia Latina*, edited by J.-P. Migne, 87: 273–98.

————. *Rule*. Translated by Jo Ann McNamara and John Halborg. In *The Ordeal of Community* by Jo Ann McNamara. Peregrina Translations, 5. Toronto: Peregrina, 1990.

Clare of Assisi. *Regulae monialium Ordinis Sanctae Clarae*. In *Escritos de Santa Clara y documentos contemporaneos*, introduced, edited, and translated (Spanish) by Ignacio Omaechevarría et al. Biblioteca de autores cristianos, 314. Madrid: Editorial Católica, 1970. [Latin and Spanish texts].

————. *Rule and Testament of St. Clare: Constitutions for Poor Clare Nuns*. Translated by Mother Mary Francis. Chicago: Franciscan Herald Press, 1987.

————. In *Francis and Clare. The Complete Works*, translated by Regis J. Armstrong and Ignatius C. Brady, 189–234. Classics of Western Spirituality. New York: Paulist Press, 1982.

Gerson, Jean. *Opera Omnia*, 2. Edited by Louis Ellies Du Pin. Hildesheim, Germany and New York: Olms, 1987.

Morton, Vera, ed. and trans. *Guidance for Women in Twelfth-Century Convents*. Essay by Jocelyn Wogan-Browne. Library of Medival Women. Woodbridge, U.K. and Rochester, N.Y.: Boydell & Brewer, 2003. [Select source texts on convent life].

Pachomius. *Regula*. In *Pachomiana Latina*, critical ed. by Amand Boon. Bibliothèque de la Revue d'Histoire Ecclésiastique, 7. Louvain, Belgium: RHE, 1932.

Waldebert of Luxueil. *Regula cuiusdam patris ad virgines*. In *Patrologia Latina*, edited by J.-P. Migne, 88: 1053–70.

————, Donatus, Columbanus, et al. *Regulae*. In *Règles monastiques au féminin*, introduced and translated by Lazare de Seilhac, Bernard Said et al. Vie monastique, 33. Begrolles-en-Mauges, France: Abbaye de Bellefontaine, 1996. [French trans. and commentary on all rules in the Benedictine-Columban tradition].

Secondary Sources

Beckwith, Sarah. "Passionate Regulation: Enclosure, Ascesis, and the Feminist Imaginary." *South Atlantic Quarterly* 93 (1994): 803–24.

Cannon, Christopher. "Enclosure." In *The Cambridge Companion to Medieval Women's Writing*, edited by Carolyn Dinshaw and David Wallace, 109–23. Cambridge: Cambridge University Press, 2003.

Holmes, Augustine. *A Life Pleasing to God: The Spirituality of the Rules of St. Basil*. Kalamazoo, Mich.: Cistercian Publications, 2000.

Knowles, David. *From Pachomius to Ignatius: A Study in the Constitutional History of the Religious Orders*. Sarum Lectures. Oxford: Clarendon Press, 1966.

Lehmijoki–Gardner, Maiju. "Writing Religious Rules as an Interactive Process; Dominican Penitent Women and the Making of Their *Regula*." *Speculum* 79 (2004): 660–87.

McNamara, Jo Ann, John E. Halborg, with E. Gordon Whatley, eds. and transs. *Sainted Women of the Dark Ages*. Durham, N.C.: Duke University Press, 1992. [Excellent anthology of women saints' lives and commentary].

Mulder-Bakker, Anneke B. "The Prime of their Lives; Women and Age, Wisdom and Religious Careers in Northern Europe." In *New Trends in Female Spirituality: The Holy Women of Liège and Their Impact*, edited by Jocelyn Wogan-Browne and Juliette Dor. Turnhout, Belgium: Brepols, 1999.

Oxford Dictionary of the Christian Church. Edited by F. L. Cross. Revised by E. A. Livingstone. 3rd ed. Oxford and New York: Oxford University Press, 1997.

Petroff Elizabeth. "A Medieval Woman's Utopian Vision: The Rule of St. Clare of Assisi." In E. Petroff, *Body and Soul: Essays on Medieval Women and Mysticism*, 66–79. New York: Oxford University Press, 1994.

Ranft, Patricia. *Women and the Religious Life in Premodern Europe*. New York: St. Martin's, 1996.

Smith, Julie Ann. *Ordering Women's Lives: Penitentials and Nunnery Rules in the Early Medieval West*. Aldershot, U.K.: Ashgate, 2001.

Warren, Ann K. *Anchorites and Their Patrons in Medieval England*. Berkeley: University of California Press, 1985.

Wogan-Browne, Jocelyn. "Chaste Bodies: Frames and Experiences." In *Framing Medieval Bodies*, edited by Sarah Kay and Miri Rubin, 24–42. Manchester, U.K.: Manchester University Press, 1994.

EDITH BRIGITTE ARCHIBALD

RUSSIA, WOMEN IN. *See* **Muscovy, Women in**

S

SACHSENSPIEGEL AND SCHWABENSPIEGEL. The Middle-Low German *Sachsenspiegel* (*Saxon Mirror*) and its later High-German counterpart, the *Schwabenspiegel* (*Swabian Mirror*) are among the earliest custumals, or written collections of legal customs, in the German language and constitute important sources for the study of medieval women and gender, drawing as they do from both legal ideals and lived traditions. As literary forms, these works belong to the *speculum* (Latin = mirror) tradition: a genre of didactic, or instructional, literature, usually aimed at future princes and other ranks of the ruling classes, on which these young men could model or mirror themselves, according to the ideal presented often via both practical prescription and exemplary anecdotes from history.

Eike von Repgow composed the *Sachsenspiegel* between about 1220 and 1235, dividing it into two parts: the rural law (*Landrecht*), concerning "personal rights and obligations, family relations, real and movable property, criminal acts, and judicial procedure;" and the feudal law, delineating "the legal customs governing feudal land tenure among the nobility in Saxony" as Maria Dobozy characterizes it in her translation's introduction (*Saxon Mirror* [henceforth = Dobozy], 6). Eike states that he was translating a Latin source, but none has been found. He also had few vernacular models at his disposal. The mirror metaphor in the title indicates that the text was intended as a reflection of an ideal law, emanating from God Himself. Though a written text, the *Sachsenspiegel* arose from living oral tradition. Its style, grammar, syntax, and associative linking of topics preserve traces of oral delivery (Schmidt-Wiegand 1980). Eike may well have been a *Gerechtssprecher*, or traditional (oral) legal practitioner. His name appears in documents between 1209 and 1233 linking him to powerful and influential men such as Count Heinrich von Anhalt, himself a poet, and a margrave (a count and judge ruling a German march, or border province) named Dietrich von Meissen, a noted literary patron. Eike wrote the *Sachsenspiegel* for his patron, Hoyer von Falkenstein, also known as a benefactor of the influential convent of nuns at Quedlinburg.

As a territorial law, the *Sachsenspiegel* applied to a large geographical area in Germany, roughly centered on the city of Magdeburg, encompassing the duchy and Palatine county of Saxony, the Landgravate (another German territorial unit) of Thuringia, and newly settled areas to the east. People of different ethnic origins mixed in this region, and the *Sachsenspiegel* recognized and accommodated many legal customs that apply only on the basis of ethnicity. For example, Swabian women settled in Saxon territory were subject to the more limited inheritance rights of ethnic-Swabian custom, according to the *Sachsenspiegel* (Dobozy, 1.17). Society in these territories was also stratified: the *Sachsenspiegel* applies to the free peasantry, mainly villagers, and to the knightly classes, touching only briefly on matters pertaining to unfree persons. But even though its application was limited in its original context, the *Sachsenspiegel* circulated widely over time and territory and came to be regarded as nearly universal in its force.

With a staggering total of 465 known manuscripts, the *Sachsenspiegel* was one of the most appreciated and widely owned books of the later Middle Ages (Hüpper). No manuscript is clearly linked to the author himself. Given the considerable editorial difficulties spawned by its tangled manuscript tradition, the standard edition of the *Sachsenspiegel* remains Eckhardt's normalized text of which Dobozy translates a single manuscript, that found at Wolfenbüttel, Germany, at the Herzog August Bibliothek, the Codex Guelf. 3.1 Aug. 2, dated 1358–1362.

The text "proliferated and metamorphosed in several ways: through translation into several dialects and languages, through copying and adaptation for use in several territories, and through innovative glossing and commentary" (Dobozy, 29). Sixty years after its composition, the *Sachsenspiegel* acquired a remarkable set of colored illustrations that "make visible, augment, and elucidate the text continuously throughout the entire codex" (Dobozy, 32). Although reception research is still rudimentary, families, both noble and urban, owned manuscripts of the *Sachsenspiegel*; copies were present in cathedral and monastic libraries; other copies owned by the council and citizens of various municipalities were intended for semi-public use (Hüpper). The present state of knowledge does not permit generalizations about women's knowledge or ownership of the *Sachsenspiegel*, although some women surely had access to it, especially in family contexts.

Articles regulating gender relations appear throughout the *Sachsenspiegel*, integrated into the most diverse thematic contexts. Three topics of importance to women crystallize from this nonsystematic text: guardianship, women's property and inheritance rights, and to a lesser extent, women in criminal law.

The articles on guardianship in the *Sachsenspiegel* arise from the fact that women were almost entirely excluded from any direct participation in the legal process. They could not bring suit on their own behalf, nor appear in court as witnesses, nor carry out certain kinds of transactions required by the law such as giving or receiving security. Nevertheless, women were protected by the law and subject to its prescriptions, unlike people who were beyond the law's reach—persons born out of wedlock, for example, or persons who had forfeited their rights through criminal acts ("outlaws"). Unchaste conduct could not damage a woman's rights (Dobozy, 1.5). Women's mediated relationship to the community of law was accomplished by means of guardianship. Every woman was entitled and required to have a guardian who was her legal representative. This requirement is justified with reference to the story of Calefurnia who "misbehaved before the emperor in a fit of rage because her demands could not proceed without a spokesman" (2.63). Her story is briefly retold in the *Sachsenspiegel*, with variations from manuscript to manuscript, and illustrated in the illuminated manuscripts. The social identity of the guardian was carefully prescribed to ensure that he have the same standing as his ward and so be able to realize all of her rights. A married woman's guardian was her husband, even if he had a different social status, since a wife assumed her husband's standing "once she enter[ed] his bed" (1.45). In this way, the *Sachsenspiegel* protected marriage between unequal partners, but also defended both marital and social hierarchy. A widow's guardian was a close agnatic relation, that is, someone who could represent her according to her birth standing to which she returned in widowhood. The wardship of girls and unmarried women is covered less extensively, probably because the family context—the presence of fathers and brothers—made it more straightforward. Although the guardian's powers were extensive, the *Sachsenspiegel* took a narrower view of guardianship than had the earlier Germanic law codes, limiting it to matters of property management and legal representation (Ketsch). If a guardian misappropriated a woman's land or her right to the profits of land, she herself could go to court to complain against him (Dobozy, 1.41, 1.44). How often women made use of this option is not clearly known.

The *Sachsenspiegel* is rich in information about how women's property was defined and inherited. In the course of her lifetime, a woman might have the rights to: "allodial" land (which she owned outright, exempt from rent or duties), a fief, a dowry, a *Morgengabe* (morning gift, a gift given by a knight to his wife the morning after consummation of their marriage), *Gerade* (personal belongings), and a *Leibgedinge* (loan of land and its income) for support in her widowhood, often guaranteed in a marriage contract. Widows also received a portion of the food stocks. In marriage, these types of property were merged under the husband's guardianship and control, although legal historians debate the exact form of the merger. On death, however, property reverted to these various pieces for purposes of inheritance.

Gender determines the course of inheritance in that a woman's *Gerade* was set aside for her undowered daughters or closest female relative on her mother's side, called her niece (1.20). The *Sachsenspiegel* enumerates the items in a typical *Gerade*: women's clothing, rings and bracelets, chests, household linens and textiles such as wall hangings, wash basins and iron lamps, sheep and geese, and devotional books (1.24). This inventory offers a rich insight into the material world of women and the scope of their domestic activities (as viewed from the standpoint of Eike, his sources, and those who continued his work). It is also a rare, early confirmation of women's book ownership. Evidently, devotional books were seen to have such significance in women's lives that they could be bequeathed through the female line (rather than the male line governing most inheritances), although they were not necessarily the only books a woman owned. In a passage concerned to protect the material well-being of the widower, the *Sachsenspiegel* prescribes the actions a niece (sister's daughter) should perform when she came to claim her *Gerade* (3.38). The remainder of the woman's estate went to her next of kin, presumed to be male (husband, sons, etc.).

Husbands inherited from wives, but wives did not inherit from husbands. For this reason, the *Sachsenspiegel* provides detailed protections for widows, especially guaranteeing their right to the Leibgedinge, which often consisted of income from land they did not own outright. These protections suggest that in actual experience, widows had to fend off the heirs to property. The morning gift, because it exceptionally did come under the widow's sole possession on the death of her husband, or by divorce, had to be disentangled from the rest of the estate, and a definition of a standard morning gift like the one in the *Sachsenspiegel* could have proved both helpful and, in the case of larger gifts, limiting. There are further protections for pregnant widows, who could not be expelled from their husband's property by his heirs (who would also have been her sons in most cases), and for widows who chose to remain with their children (3.38; 3.75–76). One series of articles outlines the duties of a woman in the immediate aftermath of her husband's death (1.22–24). The instructions are prescriptive in a manner that foreshadows conduct literature and are especially detailed about her handling of her husband's military equipment that followed a special path of inheritance.

Women do not receive separate mention in the articles on criminal law, which suggests equal treatment with men, although a woman's *wergeld* (compensation for homicide or other criminal damages) was only half that of a male of her status (3.46). An exception is lighter punishment for pregnant women (3.3). A woman could initiate a rape trial personally, but needed a guardian to continue (1.43, 2.64). If her own guardian were not available, the judge would appoint one. She had to provide witnesses, persons hearing her "hue and cry" at the time of the assault (2.64). This legally mandated distress call assumes certain circumstances during an assault, for example, that the victim is not risking her life by resisting or calling out and that witnesses are within earshot. The punishment for a convicted rapist was beheading (2.14). One provision calls for the beheading of all living creatures such as farm animals present at the scene of the rape, as well as for the razing of the building in which the rape occurred or to which the victim was taken (3.1). Children born of rape were without legal protection (1.37). These onerous procedures and punishments, while seeming to take rape as a horrendous crime, may well have deterred women from prosecuting (Dobozy).

The *Schwabenspiegel*, or *The Swabian Mirror*, composed about 1275/76 in Augsburg Franciscan circles, was the most significant High-German reworking of the *Sachsenspiegel*. There are some differences in the treatment of women and gender relations, such as a slightly more advantageous definition of property in marriage. These differences are conveniently summarized by Peter Ketsch in his study. Like its model, the *Schwabenspiegel* was vastly popular with 311 known manuscripts still extant. One woman is known to have played a key role in its dissemination: in 1356, Countess Agnes von Helfenstein commissioned translation of the *Schwabenspiegel* into Latin by Oswald von Anhausen (Johanek).

See also Dowry; Law, Canon, Women in; Law, Women in, Anglo-Saxon England; *Miroir de Mariage* (*Mirror of Marriage*); Rape; *Vertu du Sacrement de Mariage, Livre de la*

BIBLIOGRAPHY

Primary Sources
Eike von Repgow. *Sachsenspiegel: Die Wolfenbütteler Bilderhandschrift Cod. Guelf. 3.1 Aug. 2*. Edited and translated by Ruth Schmidt-Wiegand. 3 vols. Berlin: Akademie Verlag, 1993.
———. *The Saxon Mirror: A Sachsenspiegel of the Fourteenth Century*. Translated with an introduction and notes by Maria Dobozy. Middle Ages. Philadelphia: University of Pennsylvania Press, 1999.
Sachsenspiegel, Land- und Lehnrecht. Critical ed. by Karl August Eckhardt. *Monumenta Germaniae Historica*. 3rd ed. *Fontes iuris Germanici antiqui*. n.s., 1: 1-2. Göttingen, Germany: Musterschmidt, 1973.
Der Schwabenspiegel oder Schwäbisches Land- und Lehen-Rechtbuch nach einer Handschrift von J. 1287. Edited by Friedrich L. A. von Lassberg. Tübingen, Germany: L. F. Fues, 1840. 3rd ed. by K. A. Eckhardt. Bibliotheca Rerum Historicarum, Neudrucke, 2. Aalen, Germany: Scientia Verlag, 1972.

Secondary Sources
Altenkirch, Christel, and Horst Kuntschke. "Rechte der Frau und Vormundschaftsrecht im 'Sachsenspiegel.'" In *Deutsches Recht zwischen Sachsenspiegel und Aufklärung: Rolf Lieberwirth zum*

70. *Geburtstag*, edited by Gerhard Lingelbach and Heiner Lück, 27–36. New York and Bern: Peter Lang, 1991.

Fricke, Friedrich–Wilhelm. *Das Eherecht des Sachsenspiegels: Systematische Darstellung*. Frankfurt, Germany: Haag and Herchen, 1978.

Hüpper, Dagmar. "Auftraggeber, Schreiber und Besitzer von Sachsenspiegel-Handschriften." In *Der Sachsenspiegel als Buch*, edited by Ruth Schmidt-Wiegand and Dagmar Hüpper, 57–104. Frankfurt, Germany: Peter Lang, 1991.

Huebner, Rudolf. *A History of Germanic Private Law*. Translated by Francis S. Philbrick. Continental Legal History Series, 4. New York: Augustus M. Kelly, 1968.

Johanek, Peter. "Rechtsschriftum." In *Geschichte der deutschen Literatur*, edited by Ingeborg Glier, 3.2, 396–431. Munich: C. H. Beck, 1987.

———. "Schwabenspiegel." In *Die deutsche Literatur des Mittelalters, Verfasserlexicon*, edited by Kurt Ruh and Gundolf Keil, vol. 8, cols. 896–907. 2nd ed. Berlin and New York: Walter de Gruyter, 1992.

Ketsch, Peter. *Frauen im Mittelalter. 2: Frauenbild und Frauenrechte in Kirche und Gesellschaft: Quellen und Materialien*. Studien Materialien, 19: Geschichtsdidaktik. Edited by Annette Kuhn. Düsseldorf, Germany: Schwann, 1984.

Oppitz, Ulrich-Dieter. *Deutsche Rechtsbücher des Mittelalters*. 3 vols. Cologne, Germany: Böhlau, 1990.

Rummel, Mariella. *Die rechtliche Stellung der Frau im Sachsenspiegel-Landrecht*. Germanistische Arbeiten zu Sprache und Kulturgeschichte, 10. New York and Bern: Peter Lang, 1987.

Schmidt-Wiegand, Ruth. "Die Bilder Handschriften des Sachsenspiegels als Quelle der Kulturgeschichte." In *Der Sachsenspiegel als Buch*, edited by Ruth Schmidt-Wiegand and Dagmar Hüpper, 219–260. Frankfurt, Germany: Peter Lang, 1991.

———. "Eike von Repgow." In *Die deutsche Literatur des Mittelalters, Verfasserlexicon*, edited by Kurt Ruh and Gundolf Keil, vol. 2, cols. 400–409. 2nd ed. New York and Berlin: Walter de Gruyter, 1980.

———. "Hochzeit, Vertragsehe und Ehevertrag in Mitteleuropa." In *Die Braut: Geliebt, verkauft, getauscht, geraubt; Zur Rolle der Frau in Kulturvergleich*. Edited by Gisela Völger and Karin von Welck, 1: 31–47. Cologne: Rautenstrauch-Joest-Museum, 1985.

Text–Bild–Interpretation: Untersuchungen zu den Bilderhandschriften des Sachsenspiegels. Edited by Ruth Schmidt-Wiegand. Munich: Fink Verlag, 1986.

Sarah Westphal-Wihl

SALIC LAW (1350s–1550s). Allegedly a founding law of the French kingdom, the ancient *Loi Salique*, or Salic Law, text purportedly resuscitated around 1406 was a forgery designed to exclude women from monarchic rule. (Its name derives from the early [fifth to ninth centuries] Salian Franks of the Ijsel on the Lower Rhine [*les Francs saliens*], as distinct from Franks in other areas.) The Carolingian redaction of the Franco-Germanic Salic Law Code, dated 802–803, contained an ordinance titled "On allodial lands" (*De allodio*), which read: "Indeed, concerning Salic land no part of the inheritance may pass to a woman, but all the inheritance of land goes to the virile sex." Taken out of context, that ordinance is misleading, because it was mediated by other titles in the ancient code that permitted women to inherit allodial lands (essentially family farms), sometimes favored transmission through female lines, and allowed other lands, even if held in grant from rulers, to pass (in the absence of men) to women. In around 1000, when Salic laws and Roman laws had meshed through common usage, the Salic Code disappeared for some time. In northern France from the 1100s–1300s, regional customary laws (*coutumiers*) were developed, and ordinary allodial lands were distinguished from the royal domain of the kingdom. In French customary law, compiled by kings (1454, 1494, 1509) and redacted in the *Coutume de Paris* (*Custom of Paris*, 1510, 1580), women succeeded to lands, and some who did not inherit directly passed inheritance rights to successors as practiced in the Paris region. Although there was no French public law that excluded women from rule in these centuries, some zealous exclusionists searched for one. Richard Lescot, *Genealogia aliquorum regum Francie* (*Genealogy of the Kings of France*, 1358), actually spoke of a "Salic law" by name and insinuated (by reference to the male genealogy) that it had secured the male right to rule. But he provided no text of the Salic ordinance and kindled no official interest. Kings soon promulgated French ordinances regulating royal succession—father to eldest son (1375, 1392, 1407)—but none of the ordinances specifically excluded a daughter, or her son (if no royal sons survived), and none cited a Salic law forbidding rule to women. In the wake of challenges to female exclusion at home and abroad, the attempt in the early 1400s to transform the Salic ordinance from a civil law of the Salian Franks (regulating inheritance of allodial lands, 500s–800s) into a public law of the French kingdom (regulating succession to the royal domain and monarchic rule, 1400s) triggered a long political debate over the exclusionary precept.

That debate was provoked by Christine de Pizan, whose political treatise, *Le Livre de la Cité des dames* (*Book of the City of Ladies*, 1404–1405), validated rule by women (actually and potentially), negated what can be labeled as the "female-defamation litany" of moral precepts dictating female inferiority (in body, hence mind), and exposed the efforts under way to legitimize female political exclusion by resort to defamation. Christine also reinterpreted an important tenet of medieval political thought—the analogy between two concepts, the body politic and the body mystical—likening kings to bishops as heads of those bodies respectively, hence denying to queens the sacred anointment given to kings in the French coronation, just as with bishops in ordination. Providing a unique female route for queens called to coronation, she did not mention an exclusionary Salic law because it had not yet been invented. In the *Cité des dames*, written while Isabeau of Bavaria, queen of France, was regent for her incapacitated husband, King Charles VI, Christine reiterated several points she had made earlier during an epistolary quarrel waged with Jean de Montreuil and cohorts over defamatory practices (1399–1404), called the *Debat du Roman de la Rose* (Debate of the *Romance of the Rose*. Here again she criticized Jean de Meun, *Le Roman de la Rose* (*The Romance of the Rose*, 1269–1280), who had defamed woman, the entire sex, and also, by association, Montreuil, who had praised Meun and defamed Christine, denying her, as a woman, full intellectual capacity and labeling her a courtesan for taking writings to the public. Between 1406 and 1409, as the *Cité des dames* circulated in political quarters, Montreuil decided to refute its major argument: that women may rule, have ruled in the world over time, and if called to monarchic office, can rule in France or elsewhere.

In his treatise *A toute la Chevalerie de France* (*To All of French Knighthood*, c.1409–1413), Montreuil produced a fragment of the ancient Salic Law text attended by an interpolation (here, in italics) which effected a forgery: "Indeed no part *in the realm* may pass to a woman." Then, in his *Traité contre les Anglais* (*Treatise Against the English*, 1413, 1416), he provided a fuller, corrected text: "No part of the inheritance may pass to a woman, but all the inheritance of land goes to the virile sex," to which Montreuil attached his own unsupported claims holding that this Salic Law absolutely "excludes women from succession to the crown of France" and also excludes "their sons." In attempting to negate several of Christine's specific arguments, Montreuil also resorted to the female defamation litany; but defamation, increasingly linked with libel, had just been publicly exposed in the rancorous epistolary quarrel he had lost. In these works, therefore, he fabricated a French Salic Law fixed in perpetuity (unlike French custom subject to change over time) that would juridically exclude women from rule. Although a royal official apparently read a copy of the problematic Salic ordinance around 1418, it was again ignored in those circles. Another writer took a different exclusionary route coupling French custom with defamatory Aristotelian notions (those claiming a basis in Aristotle's moral-political philosophy, fourth century B.C.E.) in vogue.

In yet another approach, that rooting French custom in the prevailing concept of nature, Jean de Terre Rouge, in *Contra rebelles suorum regum* (*Against the Rebels of the Kingdom*, c.1420), did not mention a Salic Law in his treatise. Admittedly beholden to Aristotelian biological concepts of propagation, which contrasted inferior female incapacity (lack of seed) with the superior male capacity to generate and transmit formative male seed, Terre Rouge politicized that biogenetic view. Moving from nature, male reproductive replication (father–son "filiation") to shape a political parallel, male monarchic replication (king–dauphin "simple succession"), he posited the metaphysical notion of an immortal body politic incorporated (through male seed) in a construct labeled "The King's One Body," regenerated through a series of kings over time. The metaphysical view and the juridical one vied for place. While several royal officials and scholars who saw the correct Salic ordinance, 1430s–1440s, continued to bypass it; another writer revived the spurious juridical claim for its current legitimacy.

Ignorance of the written Salic Law reached its most menacing level when the succession of Charles VII found his claim to the throne threatened by English domination and attendant propaganda concerning his legitimacy. To a certain extent, Joan of Arc—whose own legitimacy Christine de Pizan was the first vernacular author to extol in her *Ditié de Jehanne d'Arc* (*Tale of Joan of Arc*, 1429)—saved French male succession by saving Charles, bereft of a text of the Salic Law (Beaune; Hanley 1997).

Confirming arguments made by Montreuil and Terre Rouge, while disputing Christine, Jean Juvénal des Ursins's *Audite celi que loquor* (*Listen to Heaven of Which I Speak*, 1435) and *Tres crestien, tres hault, tres puissant roy* (*Most Christian, Most Great, Most Powerful King*, 1446) reproduced correctly the whole text of the ancient Salic ordinance. To rationalize the conspicuous textual lacunae (no mention of the royal domain, or the French kingdom), Juvénal drew on both the forged and the fabricated versions of Salic Law produced earlier by Montreuil. Advancing his own unsupported claim that the "Salic land" in the ordinance actually referred to the "royal domain" of the French kingdom, Juvénal deemed Salic Law a French public law. Dispelling legal doubt with moral certainty, he also invoked the female defamation litany now girded with the biogenetic link between the male body and the body politic and held that "virility" in the ordinance signaled a unique male generative trait. By the 1450s, a writer, troubled by the inadequate Salic Law text—requiring overt manipulation to exclude women—and the tautological reasoning applied to legitimize it, offered a compromise along extended metaphysical lines reminiscent of Terre Rouge.

Turning to nature and French custom, Noël de Fribois, in *Abrégé des chroniques de France* (*Abridged Chronicles of France*, 1459), rooted a political model of male command in a structural homology of immortal corresponding spheres: nature and polity. Following nature, French custom justly grounded rulership in the regenerative capacity of a series of kings who embodied the immortal polity (actually and potentially) in the King's one body. Dictated by nature and imprinted in the male body, impressed on French custom and finally transformed into public law, the male right to rule, as set forth by Fribois, was mirrored in all law—natural, Roman, Canon, and French—including the Salic ordinance, which meant, he noted, to identify the virile sex as male: "No part of the inheritance may pass to a woman but all the inheritance of land goes to the virile sex"—"*which means man*" [his added comment in italics]. Although salvaged by Fribois, Salic Law was dislodged from its primary position as a founding law of the kingdom to an ancillary one, as an ordinance reflecting a more ancient French custom of male biogenetic affiliation writ in nature.

As this debate continued into the 1460s, Salic Law proponents, bested in the argument, opted for blatant forgery. The anonymous *Grand traité de la loy salique* (*Great Treatise on the Salic Law*, c.1464), produced a flagrantly forged text through an extended interpolation (here, in italics): "No part of Salic land may pass as an inheritance to a woman, *because [Salic land] is interpreted as the royal domain [of France] which is not dependent or subject to anyone in contrast to the precept that covers other allodial land which is divisible*, but all the inheritance [of Salic land = royal domain] goes to the virile sex." Pronouncing Salic law a French public law that excluded women from rule and held the royal domain inalienable, this gross forgery, aided by the usual defamatory injunctions, was circulated into the 1480s, printed in 1488, reprinted five times from 1522 to 1557, and finally retitled, *Loy salique, premiere loy des françois* (*Salic Law, First Law of the French*). Yet the times were out of joint. From the 1460s through the 1500s, Europe witnessed rule by women, as predicted by Christine de Pizan—queens in Spain, England, and Scotland; queen-regents in France—further challenging female defamation and exclusion. Between the 1540s and 1550s, French jurists, renowned for their philological and historical expertise, discovered in the archives uncorrupted copies of the ancient Salic ordinance, realized the full extent of the forgery perpetrated in the 1400s, and discarded the fraudulent Salic Law. Lacking a juridical base for excluding women from rule, they formulated an early modern political theory of male right grounded in the law of nature (male generation), exemplified in the King's one body, and juridically institutionalized in the French civil and public law tenet—the king is the husband of the kingdom, the domain the dowry of his crown—which underwrote a new system of marital regime government upholding the male right to rule, husband and king, in parallel entities, household and state, from the 1550s through the 1700s.

See also Christine de Pizan; Dowry; Le Fèvre de Ressons, Jean; Le Franc, Martin; Natura; *Roman de la Rose*, Debate of the

BIBLIOGRAPHY

Primary Sources
Anonymous. *Grand traité de la loy salique*. In Claude de Seyssel, *La Grand monarchie de France*. Paris, 1557.
Monumenta Germaniae Historica, Leges Nationum Germanicarum: Pactus legis salicae. Edited by Karl August Eckhardt, 4: 1 [Merovingian redaction c.507–511]; and 4: 2, *Lex salica* [Carolingian, 802–803]. Hannover: Historisches Institut des Werralandes, Göttingen, 1962, 1969. [See art. 6, tit. 34, Systematic version; tit. 62, Standard version].
Christine de Pizan. [*Livre de la Cité des dames*] *La Città delle dame*. Middle-French critical ed. by Earl Jeffrey Richards and Italian trans. by Patrizia Caraffi. Revised ed. Milan: Luni, 1998.

―――. *The Book of the City of Ladies*. Translated by Earl Jeffrey Richards. New York: Persea Books, 1982. Reprint with a Foreword by Natalie Zemon Davis, 1998.

Jean de Montreuil. *Traité contre les Anglais*; *A toute la Chevalerie de France*. In *Opera. 2: L'Œuvre historique et polémique*. Edited by Ezio Ornato, Nicole Grévy, and Gilbert Ouy. Torino, Italy: G. Giappichelli, 1975.

Jean de Terre Rouge. *Contra rebelles suorum regum*. Edited by J. Bonaud de Sauset. Lyon, 1526.

Jean Juvénal des Ursins. *Écrits politiques de Jean Juvénal des Ursins*. Edited by Peter S. Lewis. 2 vols. Paris: Klincksieck, 1978, 1985.

Lescot, Richard. *Chronique de Richard Lescot, religieux de Saint-Denis (1328–1344) suivi de la Continuation de cette chronique (1344–1364)*. Edited by Jean Lemoine. Paris: Laurens, 1896.

Noël de Fribois. *Abrégé des chroniques de France*. In "Noël de Fribois et la loi salique," edited by Kathleen Daly and Ralph E. Giesey, Appendix. *Bibliothèque de l'École des Chartes* 151 (1993): 5–36.

Secondary Sources

Beaune, Colette. *Naissance de la nation France*. Paris: NRF/Gallimard, 1985.

―――. *The Birth of an Ideology: Myths and Symbols of Nation in Late-Medieval France*. Edited by Fredric L. Cheyette. Translated by Susan Ross Huston. Berkeley: University of California Press, 1991. [Trans. of a clearer rendering of above entry].

Drew, Katherine. *The Laws of the Salian Franks*. Philadelphia: University of Pennsylvania Press, 1991.

Giesey, Ralph E. "The Juristic Basis of Dynastic Right to the French Throne." *Transactions of the American Philosophical Society* n.s. 5.5 (1961): 3–42.

Hanley, Sarah. "La loi salique." In *Encyclopédie politique et historique des femmes*, edited by Christine Fauré, vol. 1. Paris: Presses Universitaires de France, 1996. 2nd ed. 1997. American ed. New York: Fitzroy Dearborn Press, 2000.

―――. "Identity, Politics and Rulership in France: Female Political Place and the Fraudulent Salic Law in Christine de Pizan and Jean de Montreuil." In *Changing Identities in Early Modern France*, edited by Michael Wolfe, 78–94. Foreword by Natalie Zemon Davis. Durham, N.C.: Duke University Press, 1997.

―――. "Mapping Rulership in the French Body Politic: Political Identity, Public Law and the King's One Body." *Historical Reflections/Réflexions Historiques* 23 (1997).

―――. "The Monarchic State in Early Modern France: Marital Regime Government and Male Right, 1500–1800." In *Politics, Ideology and the Law in Early Modern Europe*, edited by Adrianna E. Bakos. Rochester, N.Y.: University of Rochester Press, 1994.

Solterer, Helen. *The Master and Minerva: Disputing Women in French Medieval Culture*. Berkeley: University of California Press, 1995.

Wood, Charles T. *Joan of Arc and Richard III: Sex, Saints & Government in the Middle Ages*. New York: Oxford University Press, 1988.

SARAH HANLEY

SCALA, ALESSANDRA (1475–1506). A Florentine humanist particularly known as a Hellenistic scholar as well as Latinist, Alessandra Scala was the daughter of Bartolomeo Scala (1430–1497), an eminent Florentine official in the orbit of Lorenzo de' Medici (1469–1499). She frequented lofty social and intellectual circles, studying Latin with Angelo Poliziano (Politian, 1454–1494) and Greek with Constantine Lascaris and Demetrius Chalcondylas. Alessandra Scala was also admired for her Greek intonation and authentic pitch accent when interpreting the role of Sophocles's Electra in a salon performance (Brown). Her two extant writings are a Greek epigram and a 1492 letter in Latin to Cassandra Fedele (1465–1558).

These letters are nothing if not relevant to the conflicts learned women faced in their pursuit of learning. Scala compliments Fedele on her "intellect, learning, and manners," which "have made illustrious not only our sex but also this age." Fedele's letter refers to Scala's dilemma: "And so, my Alessandra, you are of two minds, whether you should give yourself to the Muses or to a man. In this matter I think you must choose that to which nature more inclines you." For King and Rabil this question and its answer encapsulate "the conflict learned women felt between learning and marriage—a conflict no learned man had to face." Alessandra's choice was to marry Michele Marullo (called "Firenze"), after which she apparently abandoned her studies. On his death in 1500 she entered a convent.

See also Fedele, Cassandra; Humanists, Italian Women, Issues and Theory

BIBLIOGRAPHY

Primary Sources
Poliziano, Angelo. [Letters between Poliziano and Scala]. "Lettere inedite del Poliziano." Edited by G. Pesenti. *Athenaeum* 3 (1915): 299–301.
Scala, Alessandra. [Letters between Scala and Fedele]. In *Clarissimae feminae Cassandrae Fidelis venetae epistolae et orationes posthumae* [...], edited by Jacopo Filippo Tomasini, 163–64. Padua: Franciscus Bolzetta, 1636.
———. [Letters between Scala and Fedele]. In *Her Immaculate Hand: Selected Works by and about the Women Humanists of Quattrocento Italy*, edited by Margaret King and Albert Rabil Jr., 87–88. Medieval & Renaissance Texts & Studies, 20. Binghamton, N.Y.: Center for Medieval & Early Renaissance Studies, 1983. [Excellent introduction and notes].
———. Latin and Eng. trans. excerpts in Parker, 267–69, see below under Secondary Sources.
Scala, Bartolomeo. *Humanistic and Political Writings*. Edited by Alison Brown. MRTS, 159. Tempe, Ariz.: MRTS, 1997.

Secondary Sources
Brown, Alison. *Bartolomeo Scala (1430–1497), Chancellor of Florence. The Humanist as Bureaucrat*. Princeton, N.J.: Princeton University Press, 1979.
Pesenti, G. "Alessandra Scala, una figurina della Rinascenza fiorentina," *Giornale Storico della Letteratura Italiana* 85 (1925): 241–67.
Parker, Holt. "Latin and Greek Poetry by Five Renaissance Italian Women Humanists." In *Sex and Gender in Medieval and Renaissance Texts: The Latin Tradition*, edited by Barbara K. Gold, Paul Allen Miller, and Charles Platter, 247–85, esp. 267–69. SUNY Medieval Studies. Albany: State University of New York Press, 1997.

REGINA PSAKI

SCHOLASTICA, ST. *See* Rules for Canonesses, Nuns, and Recluses

SCHWESTERNBÜCHER. *See* Sister-Books (*Schwesternbücher*)

SCRIBES AND SCRIPTORIA (c.400–1500).

Women played an important role in medieval book production and the transmission of learning by transcribing or copying manuscripts as scribes working within a manuscript-producing workshop known as a scriptorium (plural: scriptoria). Since women's scriptoria were often affiliated with monastic movements, as were their male counterparts', surviving manuscripts and studies of monasticism provide the most substantial information on them. In addition, we can sometimes make reasonable suppositions from the historical record, provided we do not hastily expand particular-case evidence into more generalized significance. Manuscripts can thus either indicate the existence of a full scriptorium or can simply be a series of isolated documents produced by diverse scribes for private use. We must therefore interpret with particular caution and considerable examination of pertinent sociohistorical facts whatever relatively sparse information, compared to that for male scribes, is available for women scribes.

The earliest monastic rules for women—St. Augustine's in the fifth century, Cæsarius of Arles's (513, adopted in 570 by St. Radegund for her nuns in Poitiers, France), Donatus of Besançon's in the seventh—include provisions for a library presided over by one of the sisters. Some of the codices or manuscripts contained in these libraries were possibly copied on the premises; for example, the abbess of St. Cæsarius in Arles (southern France), Liliola, is reputed to have written the copy of the community's rule that was transmitted to Radegund. However,

Minnesinger, or poet musician, Remman von Zwet dictating his poems to a female scribe. From facsimile of the Manesse Codex, 1305–1340 German manuscript. © The Art Archive/University Library Heidelberg/Dagli Orti.

given the lack of manuscript evidence and the fact that reading and writing were very distinct skills in the Middle Ages, one cannot conclude from the language of the first monastic rules for women that early women religious routinely copied manuscripts.

That Anglo-Saxon nuns were skilled scribes is, however, undisputed. St. Aldhelm of Malmesbury (c.639–c.709)—often called "the first English man of letters"—wrote a treatise praising virginity (*De virginitate*) that also appealed to the learnedness of the nuns at the double monastery of Barking (founded 666). In addition, Aldhelm thanks them for manuscripts copied on his behalf. E. A. Lowe traced an eighth-century manuscript of the little-known commentator Apponius's *In Canticum canticorum expositionem* (*Commentary on the Song of Songs*; Boulogne-sur-Mer, France, Bibliothèque Municipale, 74), executed by a certain Burginda, to the south of England. The correspondence of the great Anglo-Saxon missionary to Germany, St. Boniface (c.674–754), provides further evidence of female scribal activity in England, a tradition carried to the continent through his apostolate and through the example of his women followers. Boniface requested women religious friends at home to send him copies of manuscripts, for example, when he asks Eadburga, abbess of the Isle of Thanet (in Kent), to copy St. Peter's *Epistulae* (*Epistles*) in letters of gold to help him be more effective in his preaching (letter 35) c.735; in another missive (letter 30), Boniface thanks Eadburga for a number of manuscripts already received. A possible scriptorium is connected with Lioba (or Leoba), a relative of Boniface's, and abbess of Bischofsheim, who founded a number of other convents and was a frequent guest at Charlemagne's court. Lioba, having studied poetic composition with Eadburga, sent at least one of her works to Boniface for commentary and correction (letter 29), c.732. Excavations of the double Benedictine abbey of Whitby, founded in the seventh century and first directed by St. Hilda, show that it had a scriptorium (Mate).

Würzburg, Germany, likely harbored another nuns' scriptorium, according to Bernhard Bischoff's findings (1952) on the basis of two surviving manuscripts: one containing Gregory the Great's sixth-century *In evangelia homiliæ* (*Homilies on the Gospels*) copied by Abirhilt (Würzburg: Universitätsbibliothek, M. p. th. f. 45), and a second, titled the *Liber scintillarum* (*Book of Sparks*; Universitätsbibliothek M. p. th. f. 13), signed by a certain Gunza, both copies dating from the second half of the eighth century. Bischoff (1981) also deciphered the name "Hugeburc" in an authorial cryptogram in a manuscript of the *Vitæ Sancti Willibaldi et Wynnebaldi* (*Lives of Sts. Willibald and Wynnebald*; Munich, Bayerische Staatsbibliothek, Clm 1086), which suggests the possible activity of female scribes in the double monastery of Heidenheim, Germany, where the English-born Hugeburc, who died sometime after 786, resided during her mission to convert the Germanic peoples north of the Danube.

Evidence of early female scribal activity in France is provided by an eighth-century manuscript of the famous first-century B.C. Latin poet Lucretius's *De Natura rerum* (*The Nature of Things*; Laon, France, Bibliothèque Municipale 423) signed by a certain "Dulcia," who most likely lived at the monastery of Notre-Dame-la-Profonde founded in Laon by St. Salaberga (or Sadalberga) (d. c.670). This monastery, renamed St. Jean in the twelfth century, was associated with Luxeuil in the ninth and tenth centuries, as evidenced by their closely related minuscule scripts. A joint scriptorium in northern France, near Meaux, probably at Faremoutiers or Jouarre, is suggested by an eighth-century copy of St. Augustine's *De Trinitate* (*On the Trinity*; 399–419) belonging to the Municipal Library of Cambrai (MS 300), whose script bears similarities with that of the primary authority for the early Roman liturgy known as the *Sacramentary of Gellone* (Paris, Bibliothèque nationale de France, latin 12048) from the Benedectine abbey of Gellone in southern France, dating from the eighth century as well (Lowe). These manuscripts also contain similar decorated initials: the Cambrai manuscript shows the name "Madalberta" inscribed within an initial "I," and the name "David" is written in two initials in the Gellone *Sacramentary*. In addition, T. A. M. Bishop attributed the design and execution of the first late-eighth-century copies of the *Liber glossarum* (*Book of Glosses*), a dictionary-encyclopedia considered a milestone in the Carolingian renaissance, to nuns of Corbie, the celebrated northern-French monastery, also related to Luxeuil. On the other hand, the reformer St. Benedict of Aniane's *Institutio sanctimonialium* (*Instruction of Monastics*, 816), a monastic rule systematizing for nuns the sixth-century rule of his predecessor, St. Benedict of Nursia, provided neither for a scriptorium nor a library. Despite Benedict of

Aniane's disinterest in the intellectual activity of women religious, Frankish female communities continued to copy manuscripts. The monastery of Chelles, east of Paris, provides an outstanding example in which Charlemagne's sister Gisla and his daughter Rotrude, both abbesses, exchanged learned correspondence with Alcuin, a prime mover of the Carolingian renaissance (eighth to ninth centuries). Bischoff (1966) identified ten nuns responsible for works transcribed at Chelles for Archbishop Hildebald of Cologne, Germany between 783 and 819, and connected a number of other manuscripts with this prolific scriptorium. One more convent from this period perhaps housing a scriptorium is represented by an exemplar of Priscian's fifth- to sixth-century *Institutiones grammaticæ* (*Instruction of* [*Latin*] *Grammar*) signed in Greek letters by a nun named Eugenia in the late ninth century (Paris, BnF lat. 7560). In an age when Greek had ceased to be formally taught, was this display of erudition mere ostentation or an act of homage to this Latin monument? Evidence exists of women scribes at Remiremont, founded in 620, the oldest monastic community in the Vosges mountains of eastern France. Nuns at the abbey apparently kept their own necrology, or *Liber memorialis*, and letters of abbesses survive from both the ninth and fifteenth centuries. However, recent studies of the Remiremont account books reveal that in the latter part of the Middle Ages, the abbey's records and correspondence were handled by clerics living nearby, and that new manuscripts were commissioned both from monks, in the neighboring communities of Hérival and Saint-Mont, and from numerous artisans working in the area (Gasse-Grandjean). In Brescia, Italy, the wealthy Benedictine monastery of San Salvatore, founded c.755 by Desiderius, king of the Lombards, and his wife Ansa for their daughter Anselberga, is mentioned as having a scriptorium in an early tenth-century inventory.

During the later medieval period, female scribal evidence varies greatly according to region. For England, modern scholars lament the paucity of written sources left by nuns, which is not surprising given that manuscript copying was largely commercialized from the thirteenth century on, and that even male monasteries had ceased to be major centers of production (Taylor, A.). A rare exception is a manuscript containing moral treatises and sermons copied around 1100 in Winchester and attributed to a nun who signs herself simply as *scriptrix* (female scribe; Oxford, Bodleian Library, Bodley 451). Anthony Doyle concludes that not a single manuscript can be definitely attributed to a woman scribe in England between the years 1375 and 1530. David Bell, after mentioning five manuscripts that might have been wholly or partially copied by women religious for private use at Shaftesbury, Barking, Ickleton, and Chester between the twelfth and sixteenth centuries, provides as the only proof of women's work a number of amateurish personal breviaries by the Bridgettines in Syon (Middlesex), who, like the nuns at Barking and Nunnaminster, did have a librarian. Recent scholarship on the *Revelations* of the great mystic Julian of Norwich (1342–c.1416) points to the likelihood that Julian physically wrote her own texts, then revised them over a number of decades. Julia Boffey brings to light the comparable example of Dame Eleanor, a fifteenth-century translator of a number of French devotional works, who almost certainly copied an exemplar for her own use, although such a text has apparently not survived.

The documentation for France is more promising than that for England, despite the unavailability of surviving inventories of women's monastic libraries before the end of the fifteenth century, and, as Geneviève Hasenohr points out, relatively few manuscript colophons (inscriptions giving information on the manuscripts containing them) identifying

French women religious copyists. Anne Bondeelle-Souchier's study of Cistercian convents reveals that while the number of books owned by each convent varied, scarcity was the rule; moreover, the few books Cistercian nunneries possessed were provided by either aristocratic families or Cistercian monks. No French Cistercian women scribes are recorded before the sixteenth century. For the south of France, a lone woman scribe named Jacobina has been identified by François Avril and Patricia Stirnemann as having copied the first part of Gratian's *Decretum* (c.1140) in the late thirteenth century (Paris, BnF lat. 3896). The *Decretum*—a huge compilation of papal decretals, conciliar canons, patristic writings, biblical quotations, and Roman law—became the basic text of canon law as taught throughout Europe, including the papal court. Two notable instances of women's scriptoria can be cited for France in the twelfth and fifteenth centuries, the first of these albeit speculatively, and they provide for France the first examples of women copying and even disseminating works by women. Heloise, twelfth-century abbess of the Paraclete, corresponded with her husband Peter Abelard and Peter the Venerable. (We accept the now mainstream belief that Heloise did indeed author the letters to her spouse, even if surviving manuscripts may not convey her exact words.) She also wrote the introduction and scriptural questions addressed to Abelard in the *Problemata* (*Problems*), which incorporate Abelard's answers. Since, in addition to the replies in the *Problemata*, Abelard wrote a number of works, including hymns and sermons, for the exclusive use of the nuns at the Paraclete, it can be assumed that the monastery had a material interest in preserving these texts. This theory is supported by the content of Abelard's rule for the house that, unlike those written for other women's orders in that period, encouraged nuns to engage in both reading and writing toward the intense cultivation of the intellectual life. In contrast to this monastic scriptorium, Christine de Pizan offers a unique example of late medieval lay manuscript production; more than fifty manuscripts of her works copied by three principal scribes—one of them widely believed to be Christine herself—survive from the years 1399 and c.1420. These scribes quite often collaborated on the same manuscript, suggesting that they worked together in the same physical space; they are responsible for all but a couple of the copies of Christine's works surviving from this period (Ouy and Reno). A principal correcting hand, surely the author's, can be seen at work in every one of these manuscripts, many of which were richly decorated by artists including the Epistre Master and the *Cité des dames* master, who take their names from works of hers they illustrated, as well as one Anastasia, whom Christine immortalized in the *Cité des dames* (*City of Ladies*, 1I: 41). Christine had lavishly illustrated presentation copies prepared for patrons such as Charles VI and his queen, Isabeau of Bavaria, as well as the Dukes of Orléans, Berry, and Burgundy (Meiss).

Italy's female scribes were also active, as attested by numerous colophons. The *Sermones* (*Sermons*) of St. Umiltà of Faenza (1226–1310), foundress of the Vallombrosan Sisters, were written for the most part by her secretary Donnina. A fourteenth-century Florentine painting, now in the Uffizi, depicts Umiltà dictating to a group of women religious. From the convent of San Giovanni Evangelista at Lecce, founded in 1133, twenty-one archival documents dating from the twelfth through the sixteenth centuries have survived and were quite probably written by the nuns there. In Tuscany in the second half of the fifteenth and into the early sixteenth century, as Kate Lowe has found, liturgical books were copied by nuns but illuminated by laymen; however, at the convent of Santa Maria Maddalena in Siena, nuns both copied and illuminated religious manuscripts between the 1440s and the 1470s.

For the area encompassed by present-day Belgium, the biography of Ida of Nivelles (*Acta Sanctorum*, 29 Oct.) testifies to the prolific activity of this thirteenth-century Cistercian at the community of La Ramée; another Cistercian nun, Beatrijs of Nazareth, was sent to La Ramée in 1221 to learn the art of copying from Ida and wrote choir books for her convent in Maagdendval, none of which have survived. An antiphonary (liturgical choir book for singing alternating parts of the Choir, Mass, and Office) copied in the convent of Nazareth identifies the scribe as a nun named Agnes and its musical notator as Christina, who was most likely Beatrijs's sister. The beguines from this area also play an important role in the history of women's writing. Between 1249 and 1263, the Dominican order supervising them forbade the beguines along with Dominican nuns to engage in the copying of books, specifically psalters. In 1274, on the eve of the Council of Lyons, the Franciscan Guibert de Tournai castigated the beguines for having dared to translate the Bible into French. Judith Oliver attributes a number of extant psalters of "less than professional quality" to the beguines; these include the Lambert-le-Bègue Psalter (London, British Library Additional 21114) and the Lardanchet Psalter, probably produced by Beguines in Liège (Geneva, Bibliothèque Publique et Universitaire, Comites Latentes Coll. 239, privately owned).

A number of women's scriptoria have been identified for the areas corresponding to modern-day Germany, Austria, Alsace, and Switzerland. At the wealthy imperial abbey of Gandersheim, the canoness Hrotsvitha (tenth century) wrote several plays, poetic legends, and two epic poems; at least one of her manuscripts, now in Munich, is believed to be the product of her community (Bayerische Staatsbibliothek, Clm 14485). In the second half of the eleventh century, Diemudis of Wessobrunn listed in a missal the vast number of liturgical and religious works she had copied; this list was brought to light in the biography written in 1513 by an anonymous monk of Wessobrunn and is recorded in the *Acta Sanctorum* (Oct., vol. 13, p. 128). Lesley Smith observes how the nun Guda most strikingly exemplifies the self-effacing attitude of women scribes in comparison to male scribes, for although Guda dared to depict herself in a manuscript initial written around 1180 (Frankfurt, Stadt- und Universitätsbibliothek, Barth. 42, f. 110v), it is not explicitly as scribe and illustrator; she is not actually writing but merely clutching the scroll on which she signs herself "Guda peccatrix mulier scripsit et pinxit hunc librum" ("Guda, a sinful woman, wrote and decorated this book"). Jacques Stiennon reproduces letters written by a mid-twelfth-century nun in Lippoldsberg, simply signed "H," and her "elder brother in Christ," a certain Sindold. The latter provided H with all the supplies necessary to produce a liturgical manuscript: twenty-four quires of parchment, paints, leather, and silk, thus acknowledging H's professional status if not her full name. The reasons underlying such self-effacement derive from more concrete factors than simple humility: Jeffrey Hamburger (1998) describes the extent to which later medieval German monasteries cultivated female pious literacy only to control it rigidly, whether in Dominican, Franciscan, or Benedictine convents. Nevertheless, as Smith and others demonstrate, German nuns have left more evidence of their scribal activity than those from other countries.

One of the few luminaries among women authors and scribes for this region, Herrad of Hohenberg wrote over a period of several years (1159–1175) the encyclopedic *Hortus Deliciarum* (*Garden of Delights*) at the abbey she directed in Alsace. It is quite likely that she enlisted the collaboration of the members of her community for both the transcribing of that monumental work, with its Latin text and German glosses, and the execution of its elaborate program of illustrations. Unfortunately, this medieval treasure and a complete seventeenth-century copy were destroyed during the Franco-Prussian War (1870–1871). While nineteenth-century tracings of the original illuminations and copies of most of the text still survive, these are not helpful, Thérèse McGuire cautions, for studying the circumstances of the original manuscript's production. The nuns from the double Benedictine monastery at Admont in Steiermark were celebrated for their literary and scribal activity, producing numerous liturgical and nonliturgical books and numerous letters, some of which survive in Admont, Stiftsarchiv Ii/i (see Beach 2002). As Jeffrey Hamburger (1992) notes, the fragmentary life of the twelfth-century magistra Gertrude records that this learned woman continued dictating in the silence imposed after compline (end-of-day prayer), but was scrupulous enough to use Latin, which she considered "less sinful" than the vernacular. In the generation after Gertrude, two nuns named Irmingard and Regilinda transcribed the biblical commentaries of the abbot Irimbert (1172–1176); however, the miniature in Admont, Stiftsbibliothek 34, f. 17 pictures Irimbert dictating said commentaries to a monk. Although the most famous German author of the twelfth century, Hildegard of Bingen, dictated her works to a succession of male scribes, the convent she founded at Rupertsberg did have a scriptorium at which members of her community reproduced and preserved her writings. While the original Rupertsberg codex of one of her major works, the *Scivias* (*Know the Ways* [*of the Lord*]) disappeared in World War II, a microfilm copy had fortunately been made, yielding a modern facsimile (Führkötter). The thirteenth-century Beguine mystic Mechthild of Magdeburg recorded her visions, spiritual reflections, and prayers in her own hand, and Heinrich of Halle, pupil of the illustrious Albertus Magnus, compiled these in book form. This book, *Das fliessende Licht der Gottheit* (*The Flowing Light of the Godhead*), was completed by dictation to a nun at Helfta, where Mechthild, now blind, spent the last dozen years of her life. Helfta, a hub of women's intellectual and spiritual activity, housed at the time two other famous mystics, Gertrude the Great (1256–c.1301) and Mechthild of Hackeborn (1241–1299). Gertrude recorded in elegant Latin, with a nun collaborator, Mechthild of Hackeborn's revelations, the *Liber specialis gratiae* (*Book of Special Grace*) and authored two works of her own in Latin, plus a number of vernacular works that have not survived; her *Legatus divinae pietatis* (*Herald of God's Loving-Kindness*), apparently dictated to her sister companions, contains several references to writing tablets that she and other nuns at Helfta carried around with them so that they could write even outdoors. History has preserved the names of other nuns who worked on manuscripts at Helfta: a certain "Sophia Senior" who worked as a copyist and her sister Elisabeth who was an illuminator (Finnegan).

Again in Germany, the beautifully executed antiphonary surviving as Stockholm, Kungliga Biblioteket A 172 was both copied and illuminated by a fourteenth-century Poor Clare (Franciscan nun) from Cologne, Sister Loppa de Speculo. Gertrude Jaron Lewis has brought to light nine "Sister Books" (chronicles of female monastic communities with passages on lives of individual nuns) written in Latin and Middle-High German in fourteenth-century Dominican convents; most surviving manuscripts thereof were copied in those same communities in the fifteenth century. From the convent of Gnadenthal, established at the end of the thirteenth century outside the walls at Basel, Switzerland, emerge in 1483 the names of the abbess Anna Flötzerin, "*scriptrix superior*" of a work on St. Alban, and the nun Brigida Liespergin as "*subscriptrix*" (subscribe). The nearby Dominican convent of St. Marie Madeleine, established within the city walls, also had a scriptorium in the late Middle Ages. Although two other Basel convents, St. Clare and the Dominican house in Klingenthal, have not left us any writings, we know from other sources that by the thirteenth century they had reputed women copyists. Albert Bruckner has identified a breviary in Bern, Switzerland (Bibliothèque Publique 524 and 524B) as being both written and illuminated in an Augustinian convent in Interlaken in 1440. In 1461, Lene Masserine copied a collection of German psalms and prayers at the convent of St. Clare in Villingen. Between 1469 and 1472, the nuns of Ebstorf copied and illustrated a whole new set of choir books under the direction of their prioress, who had ordered the old ones destroyed as part of a liturgical reform (Hamburger 1992). Carla Bozzolo determines a Latin manuscript in Hamburg (Staats- und Universitäts Bibliothek theol. 1045) to have been copied in 1476 by two nuns from the Augustinian convent of St. Agnes in Trier, as well as a German manuscript (Cologne, Stadtarchiv G.B. 8 130) copied by a Benedictine nun at Rolandswerth in 1497. From the late Middle Ages survive twenty-two collections of rather rustic prayerbooks produced in convents in Lower Saxony whose simple decorative styles reflect a lack of artistic models (Hamburger 1992). The manuscripts illuminated by the Poor Clares in Cologne and the Cistercians in Lichtenthal during this same period were no doubt of better quality; Bischoff (1966) identified these two convents as having had true workshops for manuscript illumination. Research on the library of the Katherinenkloster (St. Catherine's Convent) in Nuremberg in the fifteenth century has brought to light the names of thirty-two nun scribes for that period, the most prolific being Kunigunde Niklasen, connected with thirty-one manuscripts, as well as that of Margareta Karthäuserin, who specialized in books for the Divine Office. Lewis estimates that a half of the convent's extensive library, now located in the Nuremberg Municipal Library, was produced by the nuns there. She also states that St. Catherine's served as a lending library for the entire province of Teutonia.

With the progressive secularization of intellectual culture in the thirteenth century and the parallel development of universities, much scribal activity moved out of religious houses and into cities where manuscripts were produced commercially in separate stages by artisans who specialized in copying, decoration, illumination, or binding. In Bologna, Italy, two women are mentioned among the 139 professional scribes on record between 1265 and 1268; seven women illuminators have been identified as working in that city in the thirteenth and fourteenth centuries. In Germany, where manuscript production remained largely the province of religious houses, we know nonetheless of a widow named Tula who worked as a rubricator (one who letters rubrics) in thirteenth-century Cologne, and another named either Hilda or Illa who painted miniatures alongside her husband in Cologne a century later. A professional scribe named Clara Hätzlerin, whose case has attracted such modern feminist historians as Germaine Greer, worked in Augsburg in the latter half of the fifteenth century; seven of her manuscripts survive. The commercial manuscript trade has perhaps been most thoroughly studied as it relates to France. Richard Rouse and Mary Rouse, and Kouky Fianu have uncovered archival records documenting the activity of numerous Parisian women stationers, copyists, and illuminators who worked with their husbands and who, for the most part, make the historical record only because they continued to work after their husband's death. Rouse and Rouse describe women's role in the Paris book trade as "probably pervasive, but for the most part invisible (2000, 1: 237). For Rouen, Marie-Thérèse Gousset has found evidence of women illuminators working in family businesses during the late fourteenth and early fifteenth centuries. Finally, women of the middle class had multiple reasons to learn how to write; however, even fully literate women (as well as men) frequently dictated personal correspondence to scribes. Nonetheless, as Frances Gies and Joseph Gies point out, numerous handwritten letters from Margherita Datini, a late-fourteenth-century merchant's wife residing in Prato just outside of Florence, came about from her desire to carry on a correspondence with her traveling husband in private. From late medieval England have come down autograph letters from various women in the Paston, Cely, Stonor, and Plumpton families (Boffey).

Such surviving remnants scattered throughout Europe across the medieval centuries do not permit a comprehensive, definitive estimate of women's role in the production of medieval manuscripts, leaving us only to theorize that women's activity was more extensive than extant documents permit us to verify. In this regard, the verbal-visual self-portrait of the aforementioned Guda can perhaps be seen as emblematic of many women scribes whose identity remains confined, if known at all.

See also Artists, Medieval Women; Beatrijs van Nazareth/van Tienen; Beguines; Birgitta of Sweden, St.; Boniface, St., Mission and Circle of; Burginda; Chelles, Nun of; Christine de Pizan; Double Monasteries; Gertrude the Great, of Helfta, St.; Heloise; Herrad of Hohenberg/Landsberg; Hild (Hilda), St.; Hildegard of Bingen, St.; Hrotsvitha of Gandersheim; Hugeburc of Heidenheim; Julian of Norwich; Mechthild of Hackeborn; Mechthild of Magdeburg; Paston, Margaret; Radegund, St.; Rules for Canonesses, Nuns, and Recluses; Sister-Books (*Schwesternbücher*); Theuthild; Umiltà of Faenza, St.

BIBLIOGRAPHY

Primary Sources
[See also bibliographies to articles on individual figures as cross-referenced above].
Acta Sanctorum, Octobris, vol. 13. Paris: Victor Palme, 1866–1883.
Aldhelm. *The Prose Works*. Translated by Michael Lapidge and Michael Herren. Cambridge: D. S. Brewer, 1989.
Apponius. [*In Canticum canticorum expositio*. Latin and Modern French]. *Commentaire sur le Cantique des cantiques*. Text, translation, and notes by Bernard de Vrégille and Louis Neyrand. 3 vols. Sources chrétiennes, 420, 421, 430. Paris: Éditions du Cerf, 1997–1998.
Bénédictins du Bouveret. *Colophons de manuscrits occidentaux des origines au XVIᵉ siècle*. 6 vols. Freiburg, Switzerland: Éditions Universitaires, 1965–1982.
[Boniface, St.] *S. Bonifatii et Lulli Epistolae*. Edited by Michael Tangl, 1: 215–433. *Monumenta Germaniae Historica* (= MGH), *Epistolae Selectae*, I. Berlin: Weidmann, 1916; 2nd ed. 1955.
———. *Epistolae merowingici et Karolini aevi*. Edited by Ernst Ludwig Dümmler. MGH, 3. Berlin: Weidmann, 1891. Reprint 1957, 1978.
———. *The Letters of St. Boniface*. Translated by Ephraim Emerton. New York: Columbia University Press, 1940. Reprint New York: Octagon, 1973. Reprint, with a new introduction and bibliography by Thomas F. X. Noble. New York: Columbia University Press, 2000.
Christine de Pizan. [*Cité des dames*] *La Città delle Dame*. Original text edited by E. J. Richards. Italian translation and introduction by Patrizia Caraffi. Milan, Italy: Luni Editrice, 1997. Revised ed. 1998.
———. *The Book of the City of Ladies*. Translated with notes by E. J. Richards. New York: Persea, 1982. 2nd revised ed., with a foreword by Natalie Z. Davis, 1998.
Herrad of Hohenburg. *Hortus deliciarum*. Edited by Rosalie Green et al. 2 vols. London, and Leiden: Warburg Institute, 1979.